THE HISTORY OF LUDLOW

MASSACHUSETTS

WITH BIOGRAPHICAL SKETCHES OF LEADING CITIZENS, REMINISCENCES, GENEALOGIES, FARM HISTORIES, AND AN ACCOUNT OF THE CENTENNIAL CELEBRATION, JUNE 17, 1874

FIRST EDITION
COMPILED BY

Alfred Noon, A.M.

A FORMER PASTOR OF THE TOWN

—SECOND EDITION—
Revised and Enlarged

Originally Printed by Vote of the Town

HERITAGE BOOKS
2010

HERITAGE BOOKS
AN IMPRINT OF HERITAGE BOOKS, INC.

Books, CDs, and more—Worldwide

For our listing of thousands of titles see our website
at
www.HeritageBooks.com

A Facsimile Reprint
Published 2010 by
HERITAGE BOOKS, INC.
Publishing Division
100 Railroad Ave. #104
Westminster, Maryland 21157

Copyright © 1912 Springfield Printing and Binding Company

— Publisher's Notice —
In reprints such as this, it is often not possible to remove blemishes from the original. We feel the contents of this book warrant its reissue despite these blemishes and hope you will agree and read it with pleasure.

International Standard Book Numbers
Paperbound: 978-0-7884-1215-8
Clothbound: 978-0-7884-8396-7

PREFACE

The day of appreciation of a work like this is never at the time when it is issued. The labor of research and compilation must be in a measure a labor of love.

The apparent unimportance of our contribution to the public may, after all, exist only in appearance. Few prominent public men claim Ludlow as their birthplace, nor does the town seek, like seven cities of old, to rest her fame on the reputation of some ungrateful son. This is but a quiet little neighborhood, occupying a humble position in the grand old Commonwealth.

But while the town has been unsung by bard, or unwritten by annalist, or unknown to the greater events of busy humanity, she may, from these very reasons, argue an individuality which is worthy of note. Her life is not merely memoir or public history, but is unique in possessing few of those features which so largely enter into the picture of towns farther famed.

If New England has done aught for humanity, her accomplishments have had their inception in her homes, among her own sons and daughters. Her power found its origin at her firesides. The world must know that New England has had a life by itself. The student of that life, in all its characteristics, discovers an individuality and seeks to trace its causes. In such towns as Ludlow, they may be discovered easily. The glare of popular feats and popular men removed, we are permitted to look upon a specimen of pure, unadulterated New England life.

As the reader examines our folk-lore, then, we take pleasure in introducing him to the true New England home. These hardy yeomen, these toiling matrons, who have quarried and polished the hearthstones of a century, have been good fathers and mothers, and have been permitted to see successive generations of noble sons and daughters grow up around them, to call them and their institutions blessed. The forefathers sleep their last long slumber, but if you would see their handiwork, look not only at the broad acres and spacious barns, but also peer into the faces of their descendants, and read of the excellences and wisdom of their sires.

We lift the veil of a century. If the fresco behind show in places the marks of age, need we wonder? If here and there a tint is so faded as to be indistinct, a stripe once distinct and beautiful may seem to have lost the uniformity at first given to its breadth, or the beauty of its curvature, charge the defacement to the account of Old Time itself. A magnificent work by one of the old masters has been lost by an attempt to renovate it; we give you our little picture as nature hands it to us.

The materials composing this volume have been, in the main, rescued from memories which soon must fade away. In the absence of fulsome annals, the incidents have been obtained by conversation with octogenarians, and even nonagenarians, at their firesides and those of their neighbors. Grandsires hastening to the grave have been arrested in their faltering steps, and grandams disturbed in their meditations, that they might tune afresh the harps of early days for the eager ears of generations come and coming. Yellowed old deeds, lichen-painted tombstones, silent cellar holes and well-nigh forgotten boundary lines have been tributary to the work.

To all who have so kindly aided in giving desired information, we would extend hearty thanks. To the assiduous and painstaking chairman of the Committee of Publication and his colaborers, in gathering the materials so profusely furnished the compiler, the town is under particular obligation. The beauty of these pages, and tasty appearance of the volume, themselves speak for the publishers. The thanks of the town is more than due to them who have so cheerfully furnished those portraits of themselves or their friends, with which the volume is embellished. The Centennial Exercises will be read again with delight, and reread by successive audiences, who shall by their interest give the meed of praise to those who rendered that eventful celebration a feast of reason as well as a glad reunion.

More than a word is due to the historian of that day. Other towns may glory over the prowess of their corporate ancestors, but it will be discovered that our historian regaled his appreciative auditors with choicest tidbits from the town's own life. The pens of other ready writers may have improved such occasions in tracing excellent homilies on grand themes; the gentleman, to whom reference is made here, found in the word "Ludlow" an inspiration all-sufficient for his task.

The compiler of the history, as sensible of his own incapacity, perhaps, as the sharpest critic, asks the indulgence of those most interested, wishing to them and their successors on the domain of Ludlow the fondest blessings which can come from enterprise and thrift, and good homes, and good hearts.

Ludlow Center, 1875.

PREFACE TO THE SECOND EDITION

To RETAIN intact this former preface with its beauty of sentiment and expression, and to retain intact with additions and corrections to date the entire history of the town of Ludlow as published in 1875, has been the desire and aim of the Ludlow Town History Committee of 1911.

The passage of the thirty-six intervening years has brought to Ludlow the many changes which only time can bring Many families prominent in the town in 1875 are with us now only in name. Old homes full of historic lore and interest are abandoned and fast falling into decay. New homes and new people are making their impress upon the history of the town from day to day. Any effort to make our history more authentic, must come at this time while we still have access to the experiences and memories of those who have known and lived in the earlier days, and of those, whose present day experiences are still fresh in mind.

While this work probably cannot be absolute, the committee have appreciated the ready response to all inquiries, and the personal interest manifested by many of the townspeople, former and present, and desire to express their thanks to all. Especially do the committee appreciate the untiring efforts and work of their honorary member, whose years of close association with town affairs and experience as a member of the History Committee of 1875, have made invaluable his services rendered.

For themselves the committee would quote the words of the former compiler and "ask the indulgence of those most interested, wishing to them and their successors on the domain of Ludlow, the fondest blessings which can come from enterprise and thrift, and good homes, and good hearts."

> BENJAMIN F. BURR, *Honorary member*,
> MISS EVANORE O. BEEBE, *Honorary member*,
> HENRY I. CARVER,
> GILLEN D. ATCHINSON,*
> DANFORTH W. SIKES,
> MRS. AMELIA J. CLARK,
> MRS. ALEXANDER C. BIRNIE,
> GEORGE H. SPRAGUE.

Ludlow, 1911.

* Deceased. George H. Sprague chosen to fill the vacancy.

TABLE OF CONTENTS

PART I

		PAGE
I.	ANTE-LUDLOW	19
II.	TOPOGRAPHY	43
III.	TOWN ANNALS	47
IV.	TOWN DEVELOPMENT	93
V.	FIRST OR TOWN CHURCH	127
VI.	OTHER CHURCH ORGANIZATIONS	177
VII.	INDUSTRIAL HISTORY	207
VIII.	EDUCATIONAL INTERESTS	235

PART II

I.	BIOGRAPHIES	265
II.	HISTORIC REMINISCENCES	319
III.	GENEALOGIES	337
IV.	FARMS OF LUDLOW	475

PART III

| THE CENTENNIAL | 506 |

LIST OF ILLUSTRATIONS

Chester W. Chapin	Frontispiece
Town History Committee	ix
An Old-fashioned Fireplace	18
Interior of F. L. Burr's Bungalow	29
Bungalow of F. L. Burr on Facing Hill Rock	30
On Stepstone of one of the First Houses Built in Ludlow	34
Arthur D. King's House	35
The Dorman House	37
Farm Buildings of James M. White	40
Joshua Clark Place	54
A Tax Bill of 1815	56
Tax Bill	57
Hartford Banknote of 1826	60
Boston Banknote of 1828	61
Town Officers, 1911	65
Revenue Receipt	72
Grand Army Veterans, Sons of Veterans, Cadets, and School Girls, Memorial Day, 1911	80
Cadets in Front of Soldiers' Monument, Memorial Day, 1911	81
Headstone of Hannah Olds	84
Footstone of Hannah Olds	85
Old Ludlow Bridge Across Chicopee River	94
Ludlow Reservoir with Gate-house and Dwelling	101
Home of George N. Hubbard	104
The Ely Fuller Tavern	105
The Dan Hubbard House	106
Interior Ludlow Savings Bank	110
Ludlow Court Room	113
Hubbard Memorial Library	115
Saddlebags Formerly Belonging to Ashbel Burr	116
Sword, Sash, and Belt Presented to Captain H. A. Hubbard by the Town of Ludlow	117
Ludlow Hospital Building	119
Edward Earle Chapman	122
First Meeting-house	126
Pew in First Church Building	132
First Congregational Church, Ludlow Center	133
Parsonage of First Congregational Church, Ludlow Center	136
Rev. Elijah Hedding, D.D.	149
Rev. E. B. Wright	153
James Osmyn Kendall	169
First Communion Service	171
Old Methodist Church at Ludlow Center	176
Interior of Methodist Church	183
New Methodist Church, Ludlow Village	185
Union Church, 1845	187
Methodist Church, Jenksville	191
Home of Col. John Miller	191
Union Church, 1905	196
St. Andrew's Episcopal Church	200
St. Andrew's Episcopal Church—Interior	201
St. Jean Baptiste Church	205
A Ludlow Farmer	207
Calkins' Chairs, and Bottles from Ludlow Glass Works	208

LIST OF ILLUSTRTIONS

The Harris Mill	209
Arch below H. I. Carver's Mill	210
Henry Ingalls Carver	214
Henry I. Carver's Mill, Ludlow City	215
An Old-time Picture of Jenksville	218
One of the First Houses Built at Jenksville by the Springfield Manufacturing Company	219
One of the Notes Issued by the Company	221
Officers of the Ludlow Manufacturing Associates	224
Office Building of Ludlow Manufacturing Associates	226
No. 6 Mill	227
Red Bridge Dam	229
Business Block, Showing Post Office	230
Athletic Field	231
Stevens Memorial Building	232
Grammar School, Chestnut Street	234
Mrs. Julia (Miller) Smith	240
Dr. J. W. Hannum's Residence	242
Ludlow High School	245
School Committee and Assessors	252
"Winding Wave"	261
Lemuel Hawley Brigham	268
Benjamin Franklin Burr	271
Dr. James Wilson Hannum	278
"Chums"—Alice Hannum and Her Dog	280
Nathan Alonzo Harris	282
James Henderson	285
Captain Henry A. Hubbard	289
The Miller Brothers	293
Dr. Aaron J. Miller	297
Wilbur Fisk Miller	301
Deacon Elisha Taylor Parsons	304
Charles Dexter Rood	307
C. D. Rood and Little Friends	309
J. Dexter Rood	310
Mrs. J. Dexter Rood	310
Deacon and Mrs. Alva Sikes	312
A Family Gathering at W. F. Miller's	336
Colonel John Miller and Family	427
Sons of Asahel Rood	453
Charles A. White	471
Marvin King	476
Home of Mrs. Warren D. Fuller	480
Elisha Fuller House	481
The B. F. Burr Homestead	483
Home of Henry A. Munsing	484
Farm Buildings of C. D. Rood	486
The Moses Rood Place	488
The Franklin Nash House	489
Home of Charles S. Bennett	490
Home of Edward Earle Chapman	492
Henry Damon House at Ludlow City	493
Home of Rutherford H. Ferry	494
Home of Henry I. Carver	495
Home of Arthur T. Warner	496
Centennial Committee	510
Rev. J. Webster Tuck	537

PART I

An Old-fashioned Fireplace

THE HISTORY

I

ANTE-LUDLOW

Who constitute a town—The red man—Indian names—Relics of a departed race—An ancient armory—Legend of camp fires—Of the Leap—Of the alleged Facing Hills murder—The tenure of soil—Springfield of old—Charles II.—A Yankee trick—The commons—Sections of commons—Line of commons—Allotments—The river—Early settlers—The tar business—Joseph Miller—Others—A wooing—Glimpse at the region—Church service—Proposition for district—Will they get an organization?

A COUNTRY, a state, a town, consists of the inhabitants thereof. Whatever the place is, or fails to be, depends not upon the conditions of its soil or weather, so much as on the people enjoying or braving the same. Spain, in the most favored of latitudes, may fail to influence its nearest neighbors, while a band of hardy colonists among the frozen seas, singing their sagas while reefing the sails of rude smacks, may make the name of Iceland famous. Our first acquaintance, then, will be with the earlier inhabitants of the territory now known as Ludlow.

The history of the region before the paleface had appropriated these lands is preserved only in tradition. Some portions of these broad acres were, evidently, favorite haunts of the red man. The names Mineachogue and Wallamanumps preserve the flavor of the aboriginal. The former name seems to have been applicable to the whole eastern region of Wilbraham and Ludlow, and signifies "Berry land." The latter word seems to have been applied to falls of the "Chicuepe," now at Ludlow Mills and Indian Orchard. Places are pointed out in the town which the red man made his favorite resorts. At one spot the discoloration of the rocks is alleged to have come from the frequent camp fires of the Indians. At other places, both in the extreme north and all the plain region, the frequency with which arrowheads are found, and chippings of flint and stone, indicate that another nation than our own once used this region as the seat of an extensive armory.

Of the legendary lore of the territory, there seem to have been some specimens. After the destruction of Springfield by fire, October 4, 1675, the warriors retreated eastward six miles, as we are informed by the annalists. The place of their encampment is said to have been on the peninsula, in the south part of the town, known as the Indian Leap, where twenty-four smoldering camp fires and some abandoned plunder were all the vestiges remaining the next morning.

Of course, the story of all stories concerning the Indians, within the limits of the present town, is the familiar one respecting the leap of Roaring Thunder and his men, in the time of King Philip's war. Although the account is wholly legendary, there is therewith so fine a flavor of the aboriginal, that it has ever been popular among those fond of folklore. It is reported that the band of warriors was camping on the sequestered peninsula, lulled into quiet by the sound of the roaring fall of water, precipitously tumbling scores of feet over the rocks, within a half mile of the stream bed. Some aver, that upon this point there were spread the wigwams of the Indians, and quite a company of them made the place their home; that at the time these tragic events occurred, the red men had captured one of the women from Masacksick (Longmeadow), and were pursued by the intrepid settlers, and finally discovered in their rude home on the banks of the river. In the midst of their quiet and solitude, came the alarm that the white men were closely following up their trail into the thicket. There was no retreat. They had taught the paleface the meaning of "no quarter," and could expect naught but retaliation. Only one way of escape presented itself, and that was into the jaws of death. To the brink of the fearful precipice, then, before the backwaters of the corporation pond had reduced the distance a hundred feet, did the painted braves dash on, and over into the wild waters and upon the ragged rocks they leaped, directly into the arms of hungry death. Roaring Thunder is said to have watched while each of his company leaped into the frightful chasm, and then, taking his child high in his arms, casting one glance back upon the wigwam homes, he followed the rest into the rushing waters. The pursuers looked, wonderingly, over the jutting sandstone walls; but one living redskin met their eyes, and he was disappearing among the inaccessible forest trees which skirted the other shore.

There have been received two accounts of the Indian Leap affair; one from Hon. G. M. Fisk of Palmer, the other from Hon. Edwin Booth of Philadelphia, both connoisseurs in local traditions. We give the points of divergence from the narration of the text. Mr. Fisk says:

The story purported to have come from a Spirit. The little island near the Leap was said to be the place where the Indians sat around their council fires and judged their captives. There used to be a cave in the rocks where, it was said, the chief had his headquarters, and I believe to this day there is a sort of hole in the ledge where the Indians pounded their corn.

The story was that a party of Indians had assembled on the island to judge a captive, when they were surprised by the whites, fled to the shore, leaving in their haste their weapons behind them, and betook themselves to the little peninsula forming the Indian Leap. Here they were trapped, as there was no alternative but surrender or plunge down the precipice. They hesitated a moment, when the old chief took his little son in his arms, gave the war-whoop and plunged down the precipice. The rest followed, and all were killed except a squaw, who caught on an overhanging limb, but a shot from the pursuing party put an end to her.

The following poem by Mr. Fisk was published in pamphlet form in 1844.

> The Autumn frosts had sear'd the leaf,
> And weary peasant stored his sheaf;
> And cold December bent his bow
> To shoot the wintry storms of snow.
>
> 'Twas night, the curfew chime had past,
> And footsteps traced the sidewalk fast;
> The Moon rode victor of the night
> And bathed the village in her light.
>
> I wander'd forth in thoughtful mood,
> To muse on Earth's unequal brood;
> When sad imagination's guide
> Led me along the river side.
>
> One special path I chose to trace
> And in its windings kept my pace,
> Which led o'er mounds from tree to tree
> And overlooked the Chick-o-pee.
>
> A little isle that breaks the stream
> Pale Luna showed me by her gleam.
> I paused awhile, the spot I viewed,
> And then again my course pursued.

But suddenly beneath my feet
A precipice my gaze did meet;
And far down in the rocky shade
The river with the ledges played.

And from its wild and bold career
A voice ascended to my ear,
That seemed to speak in verbal tones
Of tragic days long past and gone.

Long, long I gazed far down the steep,
Where foaming waters never sleep;
Until my brain reeled from its base,
And caused me to my steps retrace.

Another path my feet betook,
That bound a grove by lengthy crook,
Which I pursued o'er mound and ledge
Until I reached the river's edge.

And there beside an ancient tree
I sat myself in reverie;
Watching the ripples of the stream,
That glisten'd in the moon's pale beam.

The Autumn breeze went sadly by,
With notes of grief and plaintive sigh;
And through the branches o'er my head,
It softly whispered of the dead.

My thoughts were turned to days of yore,
When red men trod that very shore;
And while the truth upon me broke,
I raised my head and thus I spoke:—

"O! tell me now, thou moaning breeze,
Ye gray old rocks and ancient trees,
Tell me, sad river, in thy flow,
Where is that race of red men now?"

Scarce had I spoke, when all around
The cliffs gave echo to the sound,
And whispering spirits flitted by,
And climb'd the ledges wild and high.

Then on the lucent stream I gazed,
Where meteors fell and faintly blazed,
When I beheld with wonder, too,
An Indian in his bark canoe.

ANTE-LUDLOW

My heart beat quick, then sank with fear,
As he to me his course did steer.
And soon the wielding of his oar
Brought safe his bark unto the shore.

Scarce had he reached the river's side
Ere to its rocks he made a stride,
And with a strong, intrepid hand
He drew his skiff upon the land.

Then, turning with an air so bold
It made my very blood run cold,
Towards my seat his steps he bent,
As if on some revenge intent.

An instant more and at my feet
The warrior stood in form complete;
His plumes and dress in tatters hung,
His knife was gone and bow unstrung.

He upward gazed upon the sky,
While lightning darted from his eye.
And at the sight fear from me fled,
And unto him I spake and said:—

"O! tell me, red man, whence thou came,
What is thy errand, what thy name,
Where is the race that claims thy bow,
And where are all thy kindred now?"

He turned his eyes, they fell on me.
He spoke and said, "Paleface, 'tis thee
That brought me to this rocky shore,
Which often I have traced before.

"I am not mortal, but my name
Was Wa-ha-waugh, 'tis still the same,
And from the land of spirits fair
I've come with dress I once did wear."

Here then he paus'd, and dropp'd his head.
I spoke again to him, and said,
"Immortal red man, if thou art,
A tale I wish thee to impart.

"I've heard of one about yon cove,
Where I this very night did rove;
And since this land is known to you
I ween you'll tell me if 'tis true.

"O! tell me of the tawny race
That once this shore were wont to trace,
And tell me why thy bow's unstrung,
And why thy quiver is unslung?

"'Tis wondrous strange to see thee here,
At first thou fill'd my soul with fear,
But now I trust thou mean'st no ill,
Then answer me if 'tis thy will."

He turned to me, as was my choice,
And thus began with hollow voice,
While his wild eye flash'd deathly fire,
As if in rage of kindred ire:

"Paleface, thou need'st not harbor fear,
The Great High Spirit sent me here;
He heard thee long for truth invoke
And thus to me the Spirit spoke:

"'Go, red man, go, thou chieftain brave,
Go tell the paleface of thy grave;
Go tell him one sad tale of yore,
And of the wrongs thy kindred bore.'

"At his command I quickly came.
You know my errand and my name.
And now a tragic tale I'll tell,
Of what unto my kin befell.

"When o'er these fields in gone-by days,
The wild red deer were wont to graze
And oft while sporting free apace,
Fell bleeding by the hunter's chase.

"A mighty race my kindred were
That roamed the forest wild and fair,
They built their wigwams thickly round
And happiness their firesides crown'd.

"These pleasant lands were all our own
And where we chose we made our home.
No prowling foe our track besought
Nor cruel wrongs our vengeance taught.

"This eddying river in its flow
Has often borne the light canoe,
And here the wild duck sporting came,
But floated bleeding by our aim.

"But fleeting years produced a change,
O'er winding vale and mountain range.
Our scenes of comfort turned to war,
Which ended life and mark'd a scar.

"The pale men o'er the ocean came,
And left a land of wealth and fame.
We spread our blankets for their bed,
And for their food our venison spread.

"At first they were a little band,
Weak and defenseless in our land;
But soon they strengthen'd in our view,
And to a mighty nation grew.

"They cleared our forests, kill'd our game,
And built their hamlets on the plain.
They robb'd our streams, and spoil'd our chase
And dealt ungrateful with our race.

"We saw their wrongs and their intent
And on revenge our hearts were bent.
We bared our knives, our bows we strung,
And on our shoulders quivers hung.

"We burned their dwellings in the night
And scalp'd their young men in the fight.
We bound our captives to the tree
And seal'd with death their destiny.

"Our council fires that nightly burned
Were fed with blood when squads returned.
The victim's cry and dying groan
Could only for our wrongs atone.

"But ah! the white men were too strong,
They bravely fought my brothers long;
They slew our bravest in the field,
And we at length were forc'd to yield.

"And on the lands that skirt this stream
Was witnessed once a tragic scene.
Here died the remnant of my tribe
The end of which I will describe.

"On yonder island which you saw
My little band once sat in awe.
Two captives there in terror stood
To wait their doom, be what it should.

"I scarce had gave the dread command,
 Ere we beheld a paleface band,
 Displaying pomp and martial skill,
 Come rushing down yon rising hill.

"Fear filled our hearts, we seized the oar
 And darted swiftly to the shore,
 Leaving our captives at the stake,
 Determined our escape to make.

"But ah! our fate we soon did know
 For we could not evade the foe.
 With deathly shots my band they drove
 Until we reached yon fearful cove.

"And there our doom, our death was sure
 For no escape could we procure.
 Our fate ill fortune strong did bind
 With cliff before and foe behind.

"Our choice was given, though seal'd with woe,
 To yield to them, or leap below,
 Whiche'er we did was certain death,
 But soon we chose to plunge beneath.

"Within my arms I took my son
 And to the awful brink I run,
 Then one wild, deathly whoop I gave,
 And cried, 'Come on, my warriors brave.'

"O! then what pain my bosom felt,
 I drew the hatchet from my belt
 And hurled it down beneath my feet,
 Then headlong plunged my death to meet.

"A moment and the scene was o'er,
 My brothers breathed in life no more.
 Each of my tribe, unflinch'd and brave,
 Had sought with me a watery grave,

"Save one old squaw by accident
 Escaped the death of her intent,
 But soon a bullet from the foe
 Laid her within the river's flow.

"Thus, paleface, we red men died,
 By cruel hands that sought for pride.
 And by yon cove where whirlpools play
 Our fractured bones in silence lay.

"You ask me why my bow's unstrung,
And why my quiver is unslung.
Alas, the tale too true I've told,
We died defenseless, but were bold.

"Long years have passed since that dread day.
My kin are gone, and where are they?
Ah! paleface, 'twas thy cruel race
That drove them from their native place.

"And now where yonder dwellings rise
And towering steeple stares the skies,
The red man's hut once quiet stood
Well lined with furs and stored with food.

"But all have gone, go thou, pale son,
Go, tell thy kin of wrongs they've done.
But now the Spirit calls me home,
Farewell, farewell, my tale is done."

One moment more and he was gone.
I gazed around, I was alone.
A gloomy aspect nature wore,
But that red chief I saw no more.

I homeward turn'd my strolling feet,
And soon they trac'd the village street.
And when I reached my dwelling door,
The bell pealed forth the midnight hour.

I paused and sadly gazed around
But deathly silence reigned profound,
Save the low wind that sighing came
With piercing breath that chill'd my frame.

Gladly I sought my couch to rest,
While sadness settled in my breast.
But soon my thoughts were hush'd in sleep
And I forgot the Indian Leap.

NOTE.—The story of the Great Cove, I believe no history contains, but it has been handed down from generation to generation and bears the character of truth. In the fields around this spot are often found Indian arrows, knives, etc., which give evidence that the aboriginal tribes formerly occupied the spot. The serious wanderer who visits this place finds himself doubly repaid for his pains. As the spectator stands upon the dizzy brink, gazing down upon the foaming waters dashing from rock to rock, the scene awakens in the mind the sublimest thoughts that imagination can produce. A beautiful grove borders its edge, affording a pleasant walk to those that desire it, and it is often enjoyed by the residents of the neighboring villages.

The account by Mr. Booth will probably be more pleasing to young lady readers, from the different standpoint it assumes. We regret the necessity upon us to cut out any of the interesting narration. His story is abridged as follows:

On this narrow tract of land tradition says there lived in all their native simplicity a small tribe of the red men. They had for a long succession of years there erected their rude wigwams, their wives and children had there rested amid the most retired and happy security, whilst he who was master of the lodge was chasing the frightened fawn or with eager eyes watched the stealthy fox, or, reclining upon some favorite rock, barbed the darting fish. They lived in peace with all their Indian neighbors and spent their time in hunting or in fishing. The squaw or little one greeted the return of the red man to his wigwam with the smile of affection, and listened with interest to the tale of his hair-breadth escapes. The chieftain, called by the English, Roaring Thunder, cultivated a spirit of love and peace among his band.

Philip of Pokanoket had been roused from that state of peace and harmony which so long had existed between his father and the English. He had put out the pipe of peace, and the tomahawk and scalping-knife were ready for their bloody use. By the most artful means he had aroused nearly all the Indians of Massachusetts and Connecticut to take arms with him against the paleface. Cries of the helpless, sounding terror and distress, were heard far and wide through the colonies. The bloody tales of Springfield and Deerfield massacres had been recited, and the inhabitants assembled at their places of worship with arms in their hands, and when they rested at night it was with one arm encircling the child trembling with fear and with the other grasping the firelock, expecting to hear the dread footsteps of the Indian ere the sun arose. Years rolled around, and the mighty chief and many of the tribes were conquered.

In all this struggle the little band of Caughmanyputs were the true friends of both red and white man. They harmed no one. On their isolated peninsula they lived harmoniously. The land they occupied was barren, and the white men were justified in forcing the Indian from the fruitful soil in other parts. This, we could readily suppose, would offer no temptation for a war of extermination against Roaring Thunder and his little band. But this could not be so. The Christian paleface was envious of the happiness of the Caughmanyputs, and was more disposed to believe their happiness arose from some hidden treasure in the earth rather than from contentment or domestic enjoyment. Preparations for an extermination were commenced and soon complete.

It was the habit of Roaring Thunder to take his little son of twelve with him each morning in the pleasant season to the extremity of the neck, and tell him of the land where dwelt the Great Spirit, and to which they must soon go. He would there pay devout homage to that Spirit whose voice he had heard in mighty thunder or roaring wind. After returning one morning from his service to the wigwams, where his people were amusing themselves in innocent pastimes, the startling intelligence came that a band of soldiers was seen approaching. Roaring Thunder at once commanded his men to arms to defend their soil and loved ones, gathering them into the narrow passage which led to their houses, and there waited to defend dearest rights. The soldiers, led on by their captain, advanced with slow and cautious step, and the first intimation of the presence of the Indians was a shower of arrows among them. Falling back for a moment, they fixed bayonets and charged. The Indians retreated to their wigwams, where they again attempted a defense, but were soon driven from their shelter by the merciless palefaces, who, still advancing, heeded not the cries of children or lamentations of squaws. They drove the band of Caughmanyputs to the consecrated rock. Obeying the command of their chief, in an instant a score of red forms were seen leaping into the air, then sinking amid the foaming surge below. All but Roaring Thunder and his boy had gone. The old man clasped to his breast the black-eyed boy, as with uplifted eyes he committed him to the care of the red man's God. Then turning slowly around, as though he would even from his enemies conceal the dreadful deed, he dashed him on the rocks below, and gazing saw the waters hurry off his mangled form. Raising himself to his utmost height, conscious of his majesty of form, he takes a survey of his once happy home. The objects of his affection are not there. He gazes far upon his hunting grounds, his fishing-places and his target-sports, and to them he waves a deep farewell, then with an eye of vengeance sharp he looked upon his deadly foes,—throwing up his keen dark eyes into the blue arch of Heaven, he gave a terrific spring and a savage yell, and fell upon the rocks below, a mangled corpse,—the last of the Caughmanyputs.

> His spirit went
> To safer world in depths of woods embraced,
> Some happier Island in the watery waste
> Where slaves once more their native land behold,
> No fiends torment,—no Christians thirst for gold.

One other account, perhaps quite as probable as those already related, bears a later date. On a prominent part of Facing Hills rocks there rises an abrupt precipice, from which eminence a surpassingly grand outlook upon the region is to be obtained. This rock is supposed to have been the theater of one of those tragic events, too common in the days of early settlers. (In 1907 Frederick L. Burr built a bungalow and barn upon this rock.) Away down the valley of the Chicuepe was a little

INTERIOR OF F. L. BURR'S BUNGALOW

hamlet of hardy adventurers—so runs the story. Among the company was a family in which were two women. Surprised by the bloodthirsty savages one day, when the men were out in the fields at work, one of the two found an opportunity to escape to the cellar and hide

BUNGALOW OF F. L. BURR ON FACING HILL ROCK

under a tub. The other was so unfortunate as to become a prisoner, and accompanied the captors as they speeded away up the valley. Soon as possible the settlers were aroused, and started in pursuit. It was a fearful chase, and a fruitless one; for the Indians, hurrying their booty along with them, reached this point on Facing Rocks, and, close pursued, put the victim out of misery by a tragic death. This event probably happened July 26, 1708. It bears a strong resemblance to the account of the massacre of the Wrights at Skipmuck. (See Holland's Western Mass., vol. 1, 158.)

But the day of the red man is drawing to a close, and other claimants to the soil have appeared. The record of the purchase of the lands hereabouts from the Indians is very clear, and shows that the settlers had all the rights of tenure which could flow from such transfers of property as gave the white man his possessions. That a connected account of the settlement of the region may be before the reader, it will be necessary to go back a little.

The original boundaries of Springfield circumscribed a region twenty-five miles square, including, west of the river, the land now comprising the towns of West Springfield and Agawam, the city of Holyoke, and part of Southwick and Westfield in Massachusetts, and Suffield in Connecticut; on the east side of the river, besides Springfield, Longmeadow, Wilbraham, Chicopee, and Ludlow in this State, and Enfield in Connecticut. So Ludlow comprises the northeasterly section of the Springfield of long ago.

The grant of land to William Pynchon, in 1636, included all this region, but no one had laid claim to the easternmost and westernmost limits. In the latter part of the century the oppressive policy and evident hostility of the English king, Charles II., gave color to the fear lest he should take measures to cause these out-regions to revert to the crown.

Massachusetts had grown and prospered greatly and at the Restoration had become a powerful commonwealth. Soon Charles II., jealous of her increasing importance, proceeded to hinder it. He accused the people of transcending their charter and violating the Navigation Acts and finally succeeded in 1684 in having the charter annulled by the high court of chancery. However, the Springfield colonists did not propose to be cheated out of their wood-lots by the crown, and so, with Yankee ingenuity, devised a plan to ward off the danger impending. In town meeting, February 3, 1685, they voted that, after reserving three hundred acres for the ministry, and one hundred and fifty acres for schools, on the east side of the river, and due proportions for like purposes, on the west side, the remainder should be divided among the one hundred and twenty-three heads of families, or legal citizens. With the ministry and school lots, there were thus one hundred and twenty-five proprietors, among whom the land was to be divided. Not that there were, good reader, that number of actual citizens, for it seemed no harm to add to the list the names of all male persons under age.

The "commons"[1] east of the "Great River" seem to have included two sections, bounded by a line extending north and south; the line on the east side commenced at Newbury Ditch, so called, on the eastern boundary of the land formerly owned by William Clark, now by Rutherford H. Ferry, and extended from the hill west of the Norman Lyon home-

---
[1] For more complete account, see "Mill Privilege of H. I. Carver."

stead, now owned by Lucien N. Lyon. The Lyon house and barn, now burned, stood a little south of the present home of George Gates and on the same side of the road. This boundary line passed southward near the Ezekiel Fuller place (where Hiram Davenport now lives) behind the rear of the Haviland house (John O'Neil's) and near the crossing of the Springfield, Athol and Northeastern railroad with the Three Rivers road, across the river, and near the Stony Hill road, in Wilbraham. The land divided, as above described, was the outward commons, eastward of this line. Each of the one hundred and twenty-five took a share in each of the three sections east, and the two west of the Great River. None of this outer common land was considered very valuable, but the method of division indicated was certainly fair.

Proprietors of the Outward Commons, East of the River, North Division, called in records "First or Upper Division":

No. of Lot.	Name.	Rodds.	Foots.	In.	No. of Lot.	Name.	Rodds.	Foots.	In.
*1	Jonathan Burt, Jr.,	5	13	7	27	John Keep's estate,	6	5	0
*2	Eliakim Cooley,	11	1	6	*28	Joseph Ely,	1	5	0
*3	John Warner,	11	1	7	*29	Increase Sikes, Sr.,	10	8	0
4	James Warriner, Sr.,	20	0	8	30	James Osborn,	2	5	2
5	Jonathan Ball,	11	13	0	*31	Obadiah Miller, Sr.,	0	8	9
6	Jonathan Morgan,	5	10	1	32	Benjamin Stebbins, Sr.,	5	4	10
*7	Qr. Mast. Geo. Colton,	25	7	3	33	Obadiah Cooley, Sr.,	20	5	8
8	Mr. John Holyoke,	26	4	0	34	Widow Beamon,	8	12	0
9	Widow Parsons,	10	6	8	35	Joseph Leonard,	10	10	7
10	Japhet Chapin,	23	2	1	36	James Dorchester,	12	11	0
*11	Samuel Stebbins,	9	11	9	37	Thomas Taylor, Sr.,	6	7	3
12	Dea. Benj'n Parsons,	12	6	7	38	Thomas Swetman,	2	10	0
13	Samuel Osborn,	1	15	6	39	Lt. John Hitchcock,	22	2	4
14	Thomas Merrick, Sr.,	18	15	7	*40	Widow Sikes, Sr.,	9	6	6
15	William Brooks,	0	8	9	41	Nathaniel Bliss, Sr.,	9	8	10
*16	Samuel Marshfield,	18	2	6	42	Nathaniel Sikes, Sr.,	4	0	9
*17	Ebenezer Jones,	6	7	10	43	Capt. Thomas Colton,	10	13	8
*18	Benjamin Knowlton,	5	11	0	44	Samuel Miller,	5	7	6
19	Samuel Jones,	3	13	0	45	Peter Swink,	3	13	3
20	Victory Sikes,	1	11	1	46	John Colton,	1	5	0
21	Obadiah Miller, Jr.,	2	15	3	47	Luke Hitchcock, Sr.,	10	7	6
*22	James Petty,	4	6	3	*48	James Munn,	1	12	0
23	Joseph Marks,	1	5	9	49	Jonathan Ashley,	14	11	4
24	Samuel Ball,	12	4	0	50	Thomas Jones,	1	12	0
25	Daniel Cooley,	13	9	5	51	Thomas Taylor,	1	10	0
26	Ephraim Colton, Sr.,	15	10	8	52	John Dumbleton,	11	4	3

ANTE-LUDLOW

No. of Lot.	Name.	Rodds.	Foots.	In.
53	Jonathan Taylor's est.,	5	11	0
*54	David Throw,	1	5	6
55	Nathaniel Burt, Sr.,	23	0	4
56	Samuel Ely, Sr.,	11	7	9
57	Thomas Stebbins,	5	10	6
58	Samuel Bliss, Jr.,	10	14	6
59	John Hannon,	9	13	0
60	Lt. Abel Wright,	16	14	4
61	John Dorchester,	22	2	9
62	Thomas Cooper,	18	7	3
*63	Widow Bedortha,	4	3	4
64	John Clarke,	2	3	11
65	John Stewart,	7	7	10
66	Rowland Thomas,	12	6	7
67	Daniel Beamon,	1	5	0
68	Samuel Bedortha,	4	14	3
69	Joseph Ashley,	14	11	4
70	Widow Munn,	2	10	0
71	Edward Foster,	9	7	4
72	Richard Wait,	1	5	0
73	John Bliss,	18	9	0
74	Isaac Morgan,	0	13	1
75	John Scott,	7	9	7
76	Ensign Joseph Stebbins,	15	12	0
77	Henry Gilbert,	4	2	10
78	Widow Riley,	4	13	10
*79	John Burt, Sr.,	5	4	10
80	John Norton,	8	3	8
81	School Lot,	18	9	0
82	Goodwife Foster's est.,	9	7	4
83	Lazarus Miller,	2	6	6
*84	James Stephenson,	1	4	1
85	John Clark's estate,	6	11	2
86	Phillip Mattoon,	5	11	0
87	Edward Stebbins,	5	4	5
88	Joseph Thomas,	9	5	2
89	Samuel Bliss, Sr.,	18	3	8
90	Joseph Cooley,	5	14	6
91	John Withers,	1	5	0
92	Samuel Owen,	9	6	11
93	Miles Morgan,	10	1	10
94	Benjamin Cooley,	7	3	6
*95	Col. Pynchon,	133	15	9
96	Nathaniel Munn,	3	8	10
97	John Baggs, children of	6	2	5
98	John Crowfoot,	3	8	0
99	John Miller,	6	5	0
100	Thomas Day, Sr.,	16	5	3
101	Joseph Leonard,	14	8	9
102	Widow Horton,	19	2	9
103	Henry Rogers,	9	8	8
104	Dea'n Jonathan Burt,	12	6	7
105	Rev. Mr. Glover,	21	8	9
106	Nicholas Rust,	7	0	0
107	James Barker,	5	4	0
108	Henry Chapin,	19	4	0
109	Lott for the Ministry,	37	4	0
110	John Lamb,	17	10	2
111	Thomas Miller,	8	4	6
112	Thomas Gilbert,	5	8	4
113	David Morgan,	9	13	6
114	Samuel Bliss, 3d,	2	14	4
115	Joseph Bedortha,	9	6	0
116	Joseph Crowfoot's est.,	7	14	0
117	Ensign Cooley's estate,	6	9	10
118	David Lombard,	8	1	11
119	Samuel Terry, Sr.,	9	6	11
120	Abel Leonard,	6	3	9
121	Nathaniel Pritchard,	8	1	11
122	Isaac Colton,	13	3	3
123	Charles Ferry,	14	10	11
124	Benjamin Leonard,	10	13	13
125	John Barber,	0	11	4

Second, or Middle Division, north of the Chicopee River:

No. of Lot.	Name.	Rodds.	Foots.	In.
1	Samuel Marshfield,	18	2	6
2	Coll. Pynchon,	133	15	9
3	David Throw,	1	5	0
4	John Warner,	11	1	7
5	Samuel Stebbins,	9	11	9
6	James Stephenson,	1	4	1
7	Benjamin Knowlton,	5	11	0
8	Joseph Stebbins,	15	12	0

No. of Lot.	Name.	Rodds.	Foots.	In.	No. of Lot.	Name.	Rodds.	Foots.	In.
9	Obadiah Miller, Jr.,	0	8	9	15	John Burt, Sr.,	5	4	10
10	Ebenezer Jones,	6	7	10	16	James Petty,	4	6	0
11	Eliakim Cooley,	11	1	6	17	Quartermaster Colton,	25	7	3
12	Jonathan Burt, Jr.,	5	13	7	18	James Munn,	1	12	5
13	Widow Bedortha,	4	3	4	19	Joseph Ely,	1	5	0
14	Increase Sikes, Jr.,	10	8	0	20	Widow Sikes, Sr.,	9	6	6

The list of the first division is from the records kindly furnished by Clerk Folsom of Springfield; those of the second from Stebbins' Wilbraham, page 196. A glance at ancient deeds will identify many of these lots. Those drawing lots in Ludlow in both divisions are starred in the first. The discrepancy in names and amounts may occur from a variation in the draft, first placed in good shape for preservation a hundred years after the allotment, or from an error on the part of copyists, or from former misprints. Lots Nos. 33 to 39 were not far from Gilbert Atchinson's house; the school lot, No. 81, was in the range of the present Center schoolhouse; No. 66 was near S. P. Parsons', and No. 104 passed through D. K. Paine's farm. Others can be readily traced. For a long period the commons were free plunder, so far as pasturage, wood, or herbage were concerned.

On Stepstone of one of the First Houses Built in Ludlow

The committee to run the outward and inward common line was Capt. Natha. Downing, Henry Burt, and Pelatiah Glover, the latter to arrange for a meeting of the committee. The allotment was made March 13, 1698-9. The commons are said to have extended four miles and forty rods to the Chicopee River.

A glance at the map will show that the northern section of the east outward commons, and a small portion of the middle section, lie to-day in the town of Ludlow. The shares were not equal, but according

ARTHUR D. KING'S HOUSE
Formerly a tavern kept by Aaron Colton

to valuation of course varying much. It is said that the narrowest were eight feet wide, measured at sixteen feet to the rod, much to the perplexity of proprietors in following generations. These original territorial divisions may be seen to-day on Wilbraham mountain, indicated by the parallel lines of wall running east and west.

In the north section, east, the school and minister lots ran through Cedar Swamp and over the north end of Mineachogue mountain. The south boundary of the section must have passed not far from the south shore of Wood pond, and past the Miller Corner school lot to the river. The Chicopee river seems generally to have been considered the dividing line between Ludlow and Wilbraham, but it is not entirely. There is a point at the southeast corner of Ludlow where Belchertown, Palmer, Wilbraham, and Ludlow join; the monument marking the beginning of these towns stands on the sidehill between the East Cemetery and the river. By a singular oversight, the hither shore of the stream seems in the case of both Ludlow and Wilbraham to have been fixed as the limit of the respective towns, leaving the Chicopee to flow uninterruptedly downward through the limits of Springfield, disowned by both towns on the borders.

This little section of the middle portion of the outward commons, east, has the honor of being the first settled in the territory since bearing the name of Ludlow. Who was the first settler is as yet a question undecided. Tradition gives the post of honor to one Aaron Colton, who must have settled prior to 1751. His home, once a tavern, where Arthur King now lives, was situated on the bluff just above the Chicopee river. James Sheldon, Shem Chapin, and Benjamin Sikes are said to have been living in the town at the same period. James Sheldon is supposed to have lived on the site occupied by Elijah Plumley's red house, where the late Alexander Whitney lived; Benjamin Sikes, on his allotment of commons, at the place just north of the Mann farm, now E. J. Streeter's; and Shem Chapin near the Samuel White farm, where James M. White now lives. Thus of the first four homes known in the town, three were in the outward commons. It is rumored that a man named Antisel occupied a log house on the edge of Facing Hills, subsisting on game, and that he antedates all these settlers. One Perez Antisel was deer-reeve in 1777.

We read, also, that "about 1748, Mr. Abel Bliss, of Wilbraham, and his son, Oliver, collected in the town of Ludlow, and west and south part of Belchertown, then called Broad Brook, a sufficient quantity of pine, to make two hundred barrels of tar, and sold it for five dollars per barrel." With the proceeds, Bliss built a fine dwelling house in Wilbraham, the envy of all the region.

In 1751, came the family of Joseph Miller, braving the terrors and real dangers of a journey fourteen miles into the forest, away up the Chicopee river, to the Elihu J. Sikes place, later the home of Frank Sikes, now owned by the Collins Manufacturing Company. The friends in their former home, West Springfield, mourned them as dead, and tradition has even stated that a funeral sermon was preached over their departure. Under their careful management, a pleasant home, charmed by the music of the running stream, was soon secured. As the wild forest trees succumbed to the prowess of the chopper, tender plants grew up in the home, and made the desert region glad by the echoes of childish prattle. They brought with them a female slave, who afterwards married. A little later, in 1756, Ebenezer Barber's eyes turned toward "Stony Hill," and, beholding acres of attractive land, sought out for

THE DORMAN HOUSE

himself a home near Shem Chapin's, in the inward commons. Mr. Barber's home was later the Dea. Elisha T. Parsons place. It adjoins the farm of the late Gillen D. Atchinson on the north. The advent of others was, after this, quite frequent; so much so that when the town was incorporated, in 1774, there were from two to three hundred inhabitants. In 1757 Jonathan Lumbard commenced to clear a farm in the upper part of Cherry Valley. In 1767, Joshua Fuller, probably bringing his father, Young Fuller, with him, came and cleared a spot just south of the old Methodist Church at the Center and made a home. This was later the Dorman place and is now owned by Charles M. Foster. No doubt this was the one built at that time as it was an old house seventy years ago, and has been lived in until a recent date. It was one of the houses where town meetings were held. Joshua Fuller was chosen one of two wardens and, in 1778, chosen one of three to hire a minister; one of the privileges of such a committee was to entertain candidates when preaching on trial. Stephen Burroughs, afterwards notorious, preached his first sermon here, under the assumed name of Davis, was entertained in this house and informed by Mr. Fuller that the people did not agree to hire him longer. This was also one of the places to post notices of town meetings. James Kendall seems to have made the common line his eastern boundary, when he came into town, May 2, 1769. In 1770, Jonathan Burr, great-grandfather of Benjamin F. Burr, moved in ox carts, from Connecticut, and settled south from Mary Lyon's (now Mrs. Solon Lyon's) toward the mountain. Formerly there was a road leading to the house. In 1772, came Joel Willey to Miller Corner; while a young man from Wilbraham, Isaac Brewer, Sr., who had cast furtive glances toward the developing charms of Captain Joseph Miller's daughter, and had braved the terrors of ford and ferry and wilderness, that he might visit there, became more and more enamored, until her graces, and her father's lands, won him from the home of his boyhood, for life. The happy young couple found a home near the banks of the Chicuepe, where the same musical ripple delighted them as had charmed the girlhood of the bride. They settled south of the present highway leading from Edward E. Fuller's to Arthur D. King's, on land later known as the Lawrence place, and now owned by the Ludlow Manufacturing Associates. There is a road leading from the main highway to the cellar hole.

Of the other families who came to town and settled about this time, we have but room to give the names. Northward of Colton and Miller, and towards the present Center, lived Benajah Willey, afterwards the first district "clark." Just south of him was a Mr. Aynesworth, whom fame has left without a memoir. Benjamin Sikes, the father of Benjamin, Abner, and John, occupied the ancestral farm north of the Center, later the John Mann place, now owned by Elbridge J. Streeter, while his son, Lieutenant John Sikes, remained with his father. The son Abner went away to the eastward, three miles, to settle, near the present

Farm Buildings of James M. White

Alden district schoolhouse. Near the line of the commons, and westward thereof, was, in 1774, quite a settlement. The Hitchcock home, occupied by Josiah and his son Abner, with families, was later the Lucius Simonds place and is now owned by Lucy Simonds; while another son, Joseph Hitchcock, lived next west, and probably Ezra Parsons and John Hubbard, not far away. Beriah Jennings was near the present site of the Ezekiel Fuller house, now Hiram Davenport's. Shem Chapin's neighbors were: Jacob Cooley and Aaron Ferry at the Torrey place, on the opposite side of the highway from where the late Gillen D. Atchinson lived; Noah Barker, on the Samuel White farm, now owned by James M. White; Israel Warriner, a little below; and farther to the south, at the mill privilege, was Ezekiel Squires, who built the first gristmill, and hard by were Oliver Chapin and the Zechariah Warners, father and son.

The region thus peopled must have been wild indeed. The roads were, in this period, hardly laid out, much less prepared for travel. No dams obstructed the onward flowing of the Chicuepe, no bridges spanned its stream for the convenience of the townspeople, and others. The grand highways of travel then, as now, were without the confines of the town, the northeasterly route from Springfield crossed the plains within the inward commons, the southeasterly trail of the red man went through the South Wilbraham gap, as that of the white man must sooner or later, while the "Grate Bay Rode" wound its way over plains and through passes just across the river to the south, as far from Joshua Fuller and his neighbors as the more pretentious successor of the "Rode" is to-day from his descendants, occupying the old acres.

The surface of the land was in no desirable condition. What are now blooming fields spreading to the sun their luxuriant herbage, were then malarious bogs and sunken quagmires. The ponds caught the blue of heaven then as now, it is true, but their approaches were swamps, and their shores were diversified with decayed logs and decaying underbrush. The region was infested with wolves and bears, while fleet-footed deer browsed confidently upon the foliage of Mineachogue mountain, sipped the waters of Mineachogue pond, and reposed in slumber sweet under Shelter rock, in Cherry Valley. Into such a region as this came the hardy adventurers, from Springfield, from West Springfield, from Ashfield, from Wilbraham, from Shutesbury, from Ellington, from Glastonbury, from Somers, from Brookfield, from Bridgewater, until a goodly settlement was made in all parts of the present territory.

Where these people attended church is left to conjecture, but conjecture is not difficult. The Miller Corner people would naturally go southward, to listen to the excellent sermons of the Reverend Noah Mirick, and, doubtless, it was while there the furtive glances of young Isaac Brewer met, in spite of vigilant tithing-men, those of Captain Miller's daughter, until their blushes would display the ripening admiration. The other people, from the northwest part, most likely sought the blind trail across the wooded plain, following the blazed trees, until the center of the town of Springfield was reached.

There could have been no unity between the various parts of the town, for a while. After a time, however, neighborhoods were formed for mutual defense, the people stopping at night at some convenient headquarters, safe from an attack by savage wolf or bear, or no less savage Indian, to disperse in the morning, each family to its own rude cabin, for the day's duties in the field, and home again at night, to heed the horn in lieu of curfew bell, and hie them to their lodging-house.

But as time rolled on the people began to tire of this condition. The waters of the Chicabee were, at times, so swollen they could not cross them; the rude paths so wet or rough they could not with convenience traverse them. Why not form a community of their own? Could they not have a church, and a minister? Could they not gather at some nearer center, and enjoy the immunities of other towns and districts?

Would that the records of these preliminary meetings could be spread before us to-day! But we may almost read of their doings. Captain Miller and his son-in-law, from the bank of the stream, Joshua Fuller, from the present Center, the Hitchcocks, and Jenningses, and Kendalls, from the common line, the Chapins, and Bowkers, and Cooleys, from over the hill westward, the Lombards, and Sikeses, with their neighbors, would meet at Abner Hitchcock's, or Jacob Kendall's, or Joshua Fuller's, and talk the matter over, until in their minds the town was already in existence, and then the work was easy. A petition was drawn up, very likely by Benajah Willey, praying "His Excellency, the Honorable Governor, Thomas Hutchinson," representative of His Royal Majesty, the King, "Dei Gratia," to grant to the people the rights and privileges of a district. The petition was duly signed and sealed, and either carried by special messenger, or sent by some traveler, by way of the Grate Bay Rode, to the headquarters of the Massachusetts Bay Colony, in the far-off town of Boston. And with what result?

II

TOPOGRAPHY

Location — Boundaries — Dimensions—Elevations—Ponds—Streams—Swamps—Villages and hamlets—Water power.

LUDLOW is situated in the northeastern corner of the original town of Springfield. Granby and Belchertown, in Hampshire County, bound it on the north; Wilbraham and Springfield on the south; Belchertown on the east; and Chicopee on the west.

The northern, eastern, and western boundaries of the town are straight lines, excepting a break of about a fourth of a mile between it and the town of Chicopee. The southern boundary very nearly follows the tortuous course of the Chicopee River. The dimensions of Ludlow are about four and a half by six miles, with an area of 27 square miles, or 17,280 acres, of which there is much forest or unimproved land.

NATURAL FEATURES

The surface of the town is, in general, comparatively level, excepting a few important elevations. The most prominent of these are the "Facing Hills," in the northern part of the town. They attain a considerable altitude and their summits afford an excellent view of the surrounding country. Mineachogue Mountain, southeast of the center of the town, is an interesting landmark. A detached elevation south of Facing Hills bears the name of Jefferson's Peak. Turkey Hill, in the northeastern part of the town, partly in Belchertown, is the highest elevation.

Many small ponds of water give variety to the landscape. The most important in the northern part of the town are Pickerel and Second; in the southern part, Chapin, Wood, Miller, and Bliss.

The principal branches of the Chicopee River are Broad Brook, draining the larger part of the town lying east of the highlands; Chapin Brook in the south, and Higher Brook, which drains the central and southwestern parts, passing through Harris and Eaton Ponds, and flowing into Chicopee River about a mile west of the town line. Stony Brook drains the northwestern part and flows into the Connecticut in the town of South Hadley.

Swamps

Several huckleberry swamps are found about the town, the largest being Torrey Swamp, in the western part of the town, and Fuller Swamp in the eastern part. Buck Swamp lies in the northern part of the town.

Cedar Swamp at the Center, just west of the First Church, is famous for its treacherous bottom. When it was decided to construct a road through the swamp to connect with the western part of the town, trees and stumps without number were used for filling. Some years later Reuben Sikes contracted for the repair of the road and after inspection left his cart and tools in the swamp ready for the next day's work. On arriving the following morning he found that they had almost completely disappeared from sight. Every few years the roadbed has to be refilled.

Villages and Hamlets

The principal village of the town is Ludlow Village, situated in the southwestern part of the town on the Chicopee River. It was formerly called "Put's Bridge," after the bridge erected at that point by Eli Putnam. Later it was called Jenksville, in honor of Benjamin Jenks, who established the first cotton factory there. The village is modern in every particular and grew up around the prosperous industrial enterprises which were attracted there by the excellent water power. The Ludlow Manufacturing Associates have now ten large mills and 79 warehouses, giving a total space of 30 acres. There are 350 dwelling houses, several shops, four churches, four school buildings, a handsome library, a clubhouse, and a hospital.

The oldest village of the town is Ludlow Center. It was here that the first meeting house was built and the first measures for the organization of the town were adopted. Around it are clustered the most historic landmarks. There are 20 dwelling houses, a Congregational Church and chapel, and a schoolhouse.

In the northwestern part of the town is a small collection of houses called Ludlow City. Most of the people are farmers. Henry I. Carver's sawmill and butter mold factory are the only manufacturing industries.

Moody Corners is a small collection of houses at the crossing of two roads near the western edge of the town. There are a sawmill, a gristmill and a cider mill here.

Miller Corner, in the southeastern part of the town, is so named because it was first settled by the Miller family. A considerable collection of houses has been built on the Ludlow side of the river opposite North Wilbraham, or Collins Depot, as it was formerly called. Some of the most thrifty people of the town reside here.

Water Power

The Chicopee River, during its course of three or four miles along the border, furnishes excellent water power, the best being at Red Bridge, Collins, Ludlow Village, and Indian Orchard. At Red Bridge the water falls 50 feet over a dam of solid masonry, generating over 5,000 horse power. At Collins the water descends a distance of 13 feet, generating about 600 horse power. At Ludlow Village, at the Falls of Wallamanumps, the water passes through a narrow rocky channel with a descent of 42 feet in a distance of 100 rods, generating about 1,500 horse power; at Indian Orchard, less than a mile distant, it descends 33 feet from the top of the dam to the still water below. The river just below the Falls of Wallamanumps forms a peninsula containing a few acres of land, elevated about 80 feet above the water, and formerly densely wooded, the extremity of which has long been known by the name of Indian Leap. This extremity is composed of red sandstone.

III

TOWN ANNALS

Governor Hutchinson—Troublous times—Incorporation of district—The Charter—First district meeting—Original office holders—Origin of the name—Ludlow's code—The new name—Dwellings—Provincial Congress—Taxes—Relics—General act—Ministry and school lands—County of Hampden—First post office—Value of commodities—Incidents—Town meetings—Town officers—Representative districts—Representatives—Military history: Revolutionary War, Shays Rebellion, War of 1812, the Ludlow Militia, Mexican War, Civil War—Soldiers' Monument—Memorial Day—Cemeteries: Sikes, Fuller, East, Center, Island Pond—Gifts and bequests—Epitaphs—An old deed.

THOMAS HUTCHINSON was Governor of Massachusetts Bay Colony when the inhabitants of Stony Hill, in Springfield, applied for a town charter. He had fallen upon troublous times. There were mutterings frequent and painfully apparent against the ruling power. Men had even dared to question the right of the King to control their actions or their revenues. Three thousand miles of ocean waves, and no steam navigation, or telegraphic cable, to connect the shores, did not strengthen the weakening bonds. Each winged messenger over the seas brought from the old country tidings of the adoption of rigorous measures against the colonists; returning, the same vessels bore to the perverse government news of increasing disaffection on part of the Americans. Some had even averred that the people of the New World could take care of themselves and spend their own revenues, while the more sagacious of English leaders foresaw the impending events, but in vain pointed out the true remedies. The more disaffected the colonists became, the more arbitrary were the measures of the crown.

One of the measures adopted by England for the control of the American subjects was the reduction of the representative power. As the inhabitants increased in numbers, they formed themselves into town organizations, having as one privilege that of sending a representative to the general assembly. As these towns increased, of course the number of representatives became larger, until an unwieldy body was assembling at the headquarters of the colony each year, rapidly assuming power, and endangering the tenure of the crown. As a measure of safety, it was at length decided to give further applicants for town charter all rights save that of representation, calling the organizations *districts* instead of towns.

At precisely this juncture in affairs did the Stony Hill settlers send in their petition for incorporation. There seems to have been no good reason why the application of the people should not be granted, and it was evidently passed with no particular trouble. We append the answer received, in the language of the State records:

AN Act for erecting that part of the Township of Springfield, called Stony Hill, into a separate District by the name of Ludlow.

Whereas, by reason of the remote situation of the inhabitants of that part of Springfield, called Stony Hill, from the center of the town and parishes of which they are now parts, and their incapacity thereby of receiving any advantages from a longer union and connection therewith; and they have represented to this court that they are of a sufficient number and estates to support the charges of a district, and have prayed that they may be accordingly erected into a district:

Be it enacted by the Governor, Council and House of Representatives, that that part of the Township of Springfield called and known by the name of Stony Hill, and the inhabitants thereof, included and contained within the following lines and boundaries, namely, bounding southerly on Chicabee River, east on the east line of said Springfield and west line of Belchertown, northerly on the north line of said Springfield, or partly on Belchertown and partly on Granby, and extending westward so far as to include all that part of the outward commons, so called, that lies in the north-east corner of the Township of Springfield, and extending also in a line parallel with the west line of said outward commons, one mile and three-quarters farther west into the inward commons, so called, in said Springfield, north of Chicabee River, be erected into a separate District, by the name of Ludlow, and be invested with all the powers and privileges which towns in this Province enjoy by law; that of choosing and sending a Representative to the General Assembly only excepted.

And that the said District shall have full right and liberty from time to time to join with the town of Springfield in the choice of Representatives to represent them in the General Assembly, and that the said District of Ludlow shall, from time to time, be chargeable with, and pay their proportion and part of the charge and expense of such Representatives, and the free-holders and other inhabitants of the said District of Ludlow, shall be notified of the time and place of such election in like manner as the inhabitants of said Springfield, by a Warrant from the Selectmen of Springfield, directed to the Constable of said District, requiring him to warn the inhabitants thereof to meet and assemble in the meeting for that purpose, at the time and place therein appointed, and that the pay of such representatives be borne by the said District, and the towns of Springfield and Wilbraham, in such proportion as they respectively pay to the province tax.

And be it further enacted that the said District of Ludlow and the inhabitants thereof shall stand charged with the payment of their share, part and proportion of all debts and sums of money due and owing from said town of Springfield, and all grants, rates and assessments already made, and that this Act shall not extend to abridge or affect the rights of the inhabitants of the town of Springfield to the timber, herbage, or stone on any lands in said District.

And be it further enacted that the Honorable John Worthington, Esq., be empowered and directed to issue his warrant, directed to some principal inhabitant of said District, requiring him to warn the inhabitants of said District qualified by law to vote in town meetings, to assemble at some convenient place in said District, some time in March next, to choose all such officers as may be necessary to manage the affairs of said District, and which by law ought to be chosen, which at such meeting they are hereby required to choose.

And be it further enacted that if the said west line of the before described tract of land, now erected into a District, should not extend so far as to include and contain the farms of Zachariah Warner, Zachariah Warner, Jun., Oliver Chapin, and Ezekiel Squires, that their said farms and lands, situate in said place called Stony Hill, be made part of, and annexed to, said District, to all intents and purposes, and that the same, with the inhabitants thereof, have and receive all the privileges, duties and burthens of the said District, in as full manner as though the same were contained within the limits and boundaries first described.

And be it further enacted, that the said District of Ludlow and the inhabitants thereof, be, and hereby are at all times hereafter, freed, discharged and exempted from all future duties, taxes and assessments in the several parishes and precincts to which they before this Act belonged and appertained; and that they be forever after disunited and separated from all other parishes and precincts, and no longer be, continue or remain, part or parcel thereof, or in any wise connected therewith: provided, nevertheless, that they remain charged with the payment of their part and proportion of all grants, taxes, and assessments, heretofore made by the respective parishes to which they before appertained.

And be it further enacted, that the said District of Ludlow shall have and hold their share and proportion of all ministry and school lands lying in the outward commons, so called, on both sides of Connecticut River, in said Springfield, and of all the stock of ammunition, and of all sums of money in the treasury of said town, and of all debts due and owing to said town (excepting the sum of two hundred pounds heretofore granted and appropriated for building a bridge over Chicabee River), there to be divided, appointed and set off to them in such share and proportion as the inhabitants there paid and were assessed to the last Province tax in said town, and that the said District shall at all times be chargeable with the maintenance and support of the present poor of the town of Springfield, in the same proportion, and with their proportion of the maintenance and support of any person or persons heretofore belonging to said town, but now removed from thence, who shall be returned thither and become the public charge thereof.

February 23, 1774. This Bill, having been Read three Several Times in the House of Representatives, Passed to be Enacted.

Thomas Cushing, Speaker.

February 23, 1774. This Bill, having been Read three Several Times in Counsel, Passed to be Enacted.

Thomas Flucker, Sec'y.

February 28th, 1774. By the Governor.
I consent to the Enacting of this Bill.

T. Hutchinson.

A true copy. Attest, John Cotton, D. Secr'y.

"The Honorable John Worthington" issued his "Warrant," according to direction, and then probably sent out a Springfield citizen to see that the "inhabitants of said District" conducted themselves with due legal propriety at their first district meeting. The warrants were posted, attracting such attention as never since have like documents, and the Ides of March were eagerly awaited. At an early hour came the proud yeomen. From both sides of Mineachogue, from the margin of Higher Brook and its tributaries, from the edge of Shingle Swamp northward, and Bear Swamp eastward, on foot and on horseback, came the men and their boys, until the kitchen of Abner Hitchcock was well filled. The hand of Benajah Willey traced out for the curious of later days the following record, in chirography that would bear favorable comparison with later specimens:

"The first district meeting was held at the house of Abner Hitchcock, March 16th, 1774. Moses Bliss, Esq., of Springfield, was chosen moderator, Benajah Willey, clerk, Aaron Ferry, Abner Sikes, and Joseph Miller were chosen selectmen, Joshua Fuller and Jacob Kendall, wardens,

Joseph Jones, John Hubbard, Jr., and Joseph Hitchcock, assessors, John Sikes and Jacob Cooley, constables, Joseph Miller became the treasurer, Beriah Jennings, Joel Willey and Noah Bowker were elected surveyors, James Kendall and Oliver Chapin, tithing-men, Israel Warriner and Isaac Brewer, fence viewers, Isaac Warriner and Ezra Parsons, hog-reeves, Ezekiel Squires, Aaron Colton, and Jonathan Lombard, deer-reeves"—surely a distribution of spoils.

It is a singular fact that the origin of the name of Ludlow has never been satisfactorily settled. If the result of repeated investigations had been to clear up this matter, we might be satisfied; the fact is, however, such examination has only resulted in throwing doubts upon theories previously advanced. The titles of towns were derived from the most trivial circumstances, oftentimes. It is rumored that a provincial governor crossed the sea in a vessel named the Blandford. One of the earlier events of his official life was the incorporation of a new town west of the Great River. Assuming the prerogative of naming the town, he thought well of the ship which brought him safely over, and the town was *yclept* Blandford. This fact illustrates the difficulty encountered by inquirers of a later day in tracing the naming of town titles. We find no assistance in the earlier archives. Prior to 1774, the region is called Mineachogue, Outward Commons, the "Cow Pasture," Stony Hill. The act of incorporation passes, and the new district is Ludlow. We are unable to trace any connection with the geographical name as elsewhere employed, and find ourselves forced into the annals of biography for the more likely theories.

The other places bearing the name are as follows: Ludlow, County Salop or Shropshire, England. A considerable town near the borders of England and Wales, of ancient origin, sending two members to parliament. Governed by a mayor and aldermen. Known widely because of its famous castle just without the town, now in ruins, but for many years playing an important part in the affairs of the kingdom, forming as it did, one of the frontier outposts of England. Ludlow, Windsor Co., Vt., a large manufacturing village on the Black River, just at the base of the Green Mountains, on the Cheshire railroad. Ludlow, Northumberland Co., New Brunswick, on one of the branches of the Miramichi. Ludlow, Miami Co., Ohio; Ludlow, Dubois Co., Ind.; Ludlow, Scott Co., Miss.; Ludlowville, Lansing, Tompkins Co., N. Y.; Ludlow, Champaign Co., Ill.; Ludlow, Allamakee Co., Iowa; Ludlow, Kenton Co., Ky.; Ludlow, McKean Co., Pa.

The first biographical theory, presented by the able speaker at the Centennial Celebration[1], points to Sir Edmund Ludlow, an ardent republican living in England at the time of the protectorate, who was one of the king's judges. Always opposed to the idea of the protectorate, he won a warm place in the esteem of all true patriots by twice standing firmly against the ruling power in the interests of republicanism. He flourished in the middle of the fifteenth century. The theory suggested relative to the association of Ludlow and Hampden, persons and names, seems hardly probable, as there was an interval of thirty-eight years between the christenings. Would a tory like Hutchinson have honored the memory of Ludlow?

A second suggested origin of name is from one Roger Ludlow, a prominent citizen in early New England colonial history. He came to Roxbury about a dozen years after the Mayflower arrived, and was ever a prominent character. Presented to the people as a candidate for the governorship of the Massachusetts Bay Colony in 1634, he failed of an election. Deeply chagrined at his defeat, and stung by charges against his management as deputy, he left the colony, removing to Windsor, Conn. Here he became a leading man, at one time being employed to draw up for the people a code of laws, long known as Ludlow's code. This code bears the date 1694. Among its provisions were a fine of five shillings for non-attendance at church, and one of 10 shillings for swearing. Tobacco was not to be used by any under twenty, except on recommendation of a physician. A fine of 6d. was to be levied for the use of the weed in public. Roger Ludlow removed after some years to Fairfield, whence, after an altercation with the officials of New Haven colony, he departed to Virginia, and disappeared from public sight at once and forever.

A third theory is that it is from one Rodger Ludlow, who was prominent in the colonial history at the time Ludlow was settled, and owned lands in that vicinity.[2]

An objection against the two former suggested sources is the remoteness of the characters, a full century intervening between them and their supposed namesake.

In response to a note of inquiry sent to the mayor of Ludlow in England, the following very pleasant and hearty letter was received:

---

[1] See Historical Address, Part III.
[2] See Vol. II, "The Connecticut Towns in Colonial History."

Ludlow, Shropshire, England, December 21, 1874.

Sir:—I have received your letter of the 5th instant, and I have made enquiries upon the subject about which you write. I am afraid there is no record of the origin of the name of your town here;—those with whom I have conversed think that it may either have been taken from some *person* of the name of Ludlow, who accompanied the first settlers, or from a noted republican of that name, or from the fact that Milton, the poet, whose republican opinions were well known, was connected more or less with our town. But this is all conjecture.

I am sending you by book-post a small sketch of our town. The real history of Ludlow, which is an 8vo volume of 500 pages, and written by Thomas Wright, the antiquary, is very interesting, but too large to send.

Ludlow is said to be a Saxon word—Low or "Hlaw," signifying a hill or tumulus, and "Lud" or "Lude" may be the name of a person: —London is said to be the Luds' town;—or it may be a name signifying a number of people: the word "lewd" having been originally applied to "common people" not necessarily wicked, or lawless.—In Wiclif's New Testament, Acts ix., verse 13, the apostles are called "unlettered, and lewed."

The word Ludlow may thus mean "the grave, or burial hill of the people." A tumulus formerly existing in the present church-yard was lowered in A. D. 1199, and bones of three men were discovered, who were made out to be Irish saints. They are now supposed rather to have been Roman or Celtic remains. There is a place called Ludford just below the hill on which Ludlow is built;—on the other side of the river Teme.

If I can afford you any further information I shall be happy to do so.
   I am, sir, yours faithfully,
       John Adney, Mayor of Ludlow.
Alfred Noon, Esq.

In speaking of names, it is worthy of remark that while the name of Stony Hill, formerly given to Ludlow, has been appropriated by a section of Wilbraham, our town preserves in its most prominent landmark, Mt. Mineachogue, the title once given by the aborigines to all outward commons.

The provision made in the charter for the incorporation of certain farms within the limits of the district, probably accounts for the angles in the western line of the town, evidently made so as to include those lands belonging to the proprietors named. The original boundary was evidently very similar to the present.

The world may smile at the earlier annals of New England history, but while smiling, may still read and ponder. There was little in the rugged commons which foretold a town. There was little in the appearance of these husbandmen that prophesied the Ludlow yeomen of to-day. If you would learn of the principle that gave to these seemingly inchoate elements their unity and combined strength, read of their religious longings. When will the lesson be remembered, that our nobler institutions had their bases planted on the stone once rejected, but now "the Head of the Corner"?

Many a family lived in a log cabin, the older inhabitants remembering such establishments in various parts of the town. One stood near the

JOSHUA CLARK PLACE, FORMERLY OWNED BY ZACHARIAH DAY

Norman Lyon house, one on "Stallion Hill," near Miss Mary Lyon's (now Mrs. Solon Lyon's), another opposite the Loren Wood place, and another in the extreme southeastern part of Ludlow. Frame dwellings followed in due time, indicating the progress of their owners.

At the second meeting, held April 22, 1774, it was voted to hire a minister and a committee was chosen "for to agree" with him. With an eye to order, as well as sanctuary privileges, they "voted that Swine Should run at large yok[d] and with a Ring in their Nose as the law Directs."

At an adjourned meeting held "June 1th," a committee was chosen to locate the center of the town in order to build a meeting-house thereon.

In October, 1774, the district in meeting assembled ratified the action of the ministerial committee, and authorized it to continue its services, but nothing having been accomplished by the second committee, it was dismissed and another chosen. It was at this meeting that there occurred the first official measure bearing upon the coming struggle with the mother country. The call to a meeting of all the province had gone out to every town and district, asking for the appointment of one or more delegates from each corporate body, to a Provincial Congress to be held at Concord. Joseph Miller was appointed to go, and went, not only to this but to the succeeding session at Salem, held a little later, and also to still another like gathering at Cambridge, and another at Watertown the next May. A little idea of the expense of these journeys may be obtained from the item recorded later:

Voted that Joseph Miller be allowed his bill for attending the Several Congresses, which is £11 13s 2d, likewise voted that the said Capt. Joseph Miller have Two Shillings pr. Day for Thirty Two Days Service attending the Several Congresses.

It was a trying time for a new town, when its revenues were diverted to pay the costs of war, and its young men sent off to bear the musket. Yet the people persist in living, in supporting the institutions of religion among themselves, and, moreover, in planning for the interests and development of the town as well.

A pound was erected near Elisha Hubbard's in 1776, thirty feet square, which, sixteen years later, had fallen into decay. A little later a new one was erected of white oak, near Oliver Dutton's house (now Mrs. E. Newton Fisher's), and the timber of the old sold at vendue.

As occasion required, delegates were appointed to the conventions relating to troubles culminating in the Shays rebellion; the first representation to the State legislature was in 1785, when Joseph Miller bore the honors. A committee of seven was intrusted to instruct him, though in what branch of education we have no intimation. A similar honor was borne by John Jennings in 1787, his tutors being five in number. John Jennings attended the constitutional convention of 1788.

We find but little in the records about warning people out of town, though in 1790 certain citizens were instructed to take the matter into consideration and three years later they made public the names of twelve persons who had signified their intention to locate without the town's consent, and who must leave within fifteen days. This course was very likely taken in order that paupers thus once warned out could be thrown upon the State for support.

The town appropriated £6 for a singing school in 1791. With potatoes ten cents per bushel and lumber two dollars per thousand, our

---

JOHN SIKES

Your Taxes for 1815 are,

	D.	C.	M.
STATE TAX,	2	13	
TOWN, do.	3	60	
PARISH, do.	2	18	
SCHOOL, do.	4	92	
COUNTY, do.	2	32	
	$15	15	

CALVIN SIKES, *Collector.*

Rec'd Payment, pr WILLIAM PEASE.

A TAX BILL OF 1815

---

ancestors gave liberally to the arts. They also had special lessons in penmanship by an expert teacher who taught a very good style of vertical writing. In 1804, the town magnanimously appropriated twenty-five dollars "to the present singers, on condition they sing well and still continue to sing to the Edification of the Inhabitants of s[d] Town," and two years after a committee was empowered to hire a singing master.

In municipal affairs, the people seem to have proceeded much as others did at the same period. At first, the clerk and treasurer were separate officers, but the positions were finally vested in one person in 1796, John Jennings then wearing the double honor. Tax-collecting for the year seems at one time to have been intrusted to several constables, but after a while this mode was unsuccessful. The next method was by two collectors, one for the outward and one for the inward commons. For a single year, one man undertook the Herculean task of collecting for the whole district. It was probably the custom at the warning of some of the earlier town meetings for the constables to notify the voters individually, but this method became too troublesome, and after a while the town resolved to post notices in several stipulated places: "the meeting-house and the houses of Joshua Fuller, Capt. Joseph Miller, Gideon Beebe, Benjamin Sikes, and Joel Nash's mill."

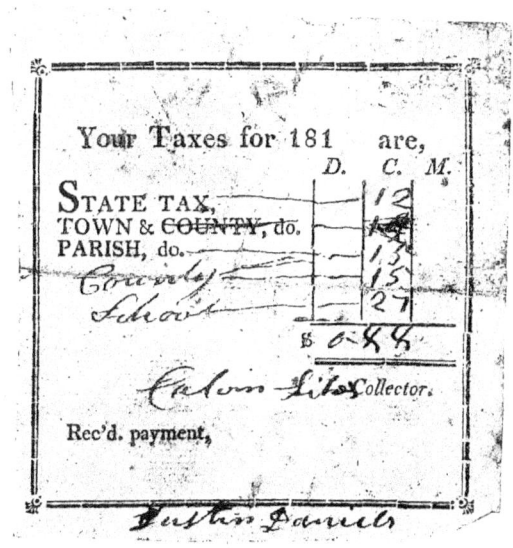

TAX BILL

At the close of the eighteenth century the deer and wolves and bears must have been mostly driven away, but for a while they were doubtless frequently seen. It is said that when the first Lumbard was one day in the neighborhood of where Lyman Graves now lives, he found a large bear and two cubs. Having killed one of the cubs, the old bear pursued him, driving him to a well-known precipitous rock near by, on which he took refuge. Foiled in her attempt to avenge the death of her young, she kept guard nearly a whole night, springing frequently from the ground up the sides of the rock. Wolves were seen near the former home of Ambrose Clough and near where Warren G. Fuller now lives. But such days passed away, and with them the beasts which infested the region.

As relics of these days are shown at the present time a shoe worn by Captain Miller's grandchildren, and a shell used for calling together the "men-folks," whose resonant sounds (those of the shell, not of the men-folks) are said to have been heard three full miles when blown at the brink of the Chicopee.

At the very beginning of the Revolutionary War, August 23, 1775, the General Court of Massachusetts admitted the districts to the full privileges of towns, by a general act, as follows:

And be it further Enacted and Declared by the authority aforesaid, That every Corporate Body in this Colony, which in the act for the Incorporation thereof, is said and declared to be made a District and has by such act granted to it, or is declared to be vested with the Rights. Powers, Privileges or Immunities of a Town, with the Exception above mentioned, of chusing and sending a representative to the Great and General Court of Assembly, shall hereafter be holden, taken, and intended to be a Town to all Intents and Purposes whatsoever.

We have seen by the charter and various references that the town once held certain lands in trust for the maintenance of the ministry. From the time of its organization there had been committees chosen by the town to arrange a settlement with the town of Springfield concerning certain ministerial and school lands lying in the north division of the outward commons, which was included within the territory of Ludlow. A settlement was finally effected in 1802, and the town of Ludlow was to pay the town of Springfield $100, the First Parish of Springfield $250, and to Bezaleel Howard $250, or $600 in all, in consideration of which all rights in said lands were forfeited and they were deeded to the town of Ludlow to be held in trust for the support of the gospel ministry and schools forever. These lands were sold mainly in three years, 1803, 1804, 1805, and the report made by the committee of sale, November 13, 1806, acknowledged the amount received to be $2,265.80. This fund, we shall find, became later the source of considerable contention. The official report of this committee is as follows:

The Committee appointed to sell the Ministry and school land the property of the town of Ludlow have attended that service—and have sold the whole of the said Ministry lott lying within the said town from the inward Commons eastward to Chicopee River Also have sold some part of said school lott (viz) beginning two rods east of the inward Commons and extending eastward the whole width of said lott to the road leading Northerly from Titus Hubbards dwelling House also all that part of s^d lott which lieth east of the town Pound and north of the town road leading from thence to the Meeting house and west of the Cedar-swamp so called also beginning at or near the foot of the Hill east a few rods from the Meeting house and easterly the whole width of said lott to Belchertown line. Also one other piece of s^d lott lying west of the pound & North of the road leading westerly from s^d pound, leaving unsold all that part of said school lott which lieth west of the foot of the Hill east of the said Meeting house the whole width of said lott so far as the west side of the Cedar swamp afores^d, also all that of said lott which lieth west of said Cedar swamp and south of the town road leading west from said Meeting House so far as the Country road leading Northerly from Titus Hubbard's. And having agreeably to directions and orders from said town Made and excuted Warrantie deeds for and in behalf of the Inhabitants of said town—And have also received for and in Consideration of said sales and for the use and benefit of said Inhabitants Notes and Obligations of the following descriptions (viz) one signed Elisha Hubbard & Job Pease for the sum of 45 doll 9 cents dated Augt 24th, 1804—one signed Timothy Clough & Titus Hubbard for the sum of 37 doll 50 cents dated June 16 1805—one signed James Kendal for the sum of 67 doll 50 cents dated Augt 24th 1804—one signed John Jennings for the sum of 23 doll 25 cents dated Sep^t 28 1804—one signed Timothy Clough & Jon^a Clough for the sum of 600 doll dated June 16 1803—one signed Abel Wright & Abel Wright Junr for the sum of 116 doll dated June 27th 1803—one signed Elisha Fuller for the sum of 336 doll 31 cents dated Augt 24th 1805—one signed Aaron Colton, J^r, and Moses Wood for the sum of 185 doll dated June 26th 1803—one signed Timothy Wright & Aaron Colton for the sum of 100 doll dated June 16 1803—one signed Saml Olds for the sum 47 doll 60 cents dated March 8th 1805—one signed Stephen Wright & George Miller for the sum 85 doll 25 cents dated June 17th 1803—one signed Elisha Fuller for the sum of 324 doll 73 cents dated Augt 24 1805—one signed Benjn Sikes for the sum of 26 doll 51 cents dated March 8 1805—one signed Ruben Burt & George Miller for the sum of 150 doll dated June 17th 1803 Containing in the whole the sum of 2145 doll 34 cents all on Interest from their dates—The Committee have rec^d in Cash over and above the aforementioned Notes to and for use and benefit of the s^d Inhabitants the sum of 26 doll 5 cents—which sum added to the sum of the Obligations afores^d makes in the whole the sum of 2171 doll 39 cents—The Committee further submit to the town the expediency of any further sale of all or any part of the remainder of said land conceiving it necessary at least to reserve some ground Cotiguous to the said Meeting House for the use ease and bennefit of the Inhabitants of said town.

And the Committee further report that they hold themselves accountable and in readiness to deliver to any Person or Persons authorised to receive the foregoing Obligations and effects or other Obligations and effects of equal Value.

        Jon^a Burr
        Aaron Colton
        John Jennings   Committee.
        Benj^a Sikes

After having proceeded as above stated the Committee have proceeded further and sold all that part of the school lott which lieth west of the Cedar-swamp and south of the town road leading westerly from the Meeting house so far west as Mr Titus Hubbard's dwelling-house and have received to and for the use and bennefit of the Inhabitants of said town of Ludlow one Obligation or Note for the sum of Ninety three dollars sixty nine cents which being added to the sum in the foregoing report makes in the whole for the bennefit of said town the sum of two thousand two hundred and Sixty five dollars and 8 cents and the Committee further state that agreeably to their orders and directions from the said town they have made and executed a warrantee deeds of the last mentioned piece of land as well as that mentioned in the foregoing report and that this last mentioned Note of 93 dollars and 69 cents is dated June 16, 1803, signed by Titus Hubbard and Gad Lyon.

        Aaron Colton }
        John Jennings } Committee.
        Benj^a Sikes }

The bounds of the town were changed in 1805 so as to include a large slice of Springfield, from the mouth of Higher Brook northward to the

HARTFORD BANK NOTE OF 1826

South Hadley line. In 1813 this had evidently been returned to its former association.

Our annals become more and more mere recitals of detached facts, because the various interests of the town, considered in town meetings, are treated in special articles by themselves.

The voters seem to have indulged in all the privileges of American citizenship. At one time they solemnly and with full assurance "voted that James Bowdoin, Esq., be governor."

There was a genuine smallpox scare in 1810, a committee being appointed to introduce the inoculation of the cowpox.

In 1812, the County of Hampden was formed, a great convenience to the Ludlow people, whose distance to the county seat, Northampton, was lessened one half. Another convenience was the post office at Put's Bridge, established not far from 1815.

As illustrations of the value of commodities and wages paid, we cite the following: Ezekiel Fuller cut his logs, paid two dollars a thousand for sawing at the mill, drew the stuff to Willimansett, and sold it, nice

Boston Bank Note of 1828

yellow pine, for two dollars and a half per thousand. As late as 1820, good potatoes brought ten cents a bushel. A curious idea of the extent of the earlier crops of this esculent may be gained from the fact that one man who had half a hogshead and another showing a crop of four barrels were the wonder of the town. In 1841, allowances for labor on the highways were sixty-seven cents a day in the spring and fifty cents in the fall.

A few incidents may perhaps be noted. The citizens at town meeting adjourned on May-day of 1837 to attend in procession the funeral of their aged neighbor, Lewis Barber.

There were two hundred and fifty-seven votes cast in 1840. The anti-masonic vote in the Morgan days was thirty-two in a hundred and sixty-one.

The town clerk was so much impressed with a twelve-hours thunderstorm, March 25, 1842, that he made note of the fact—the only attention paid to meteorology in all the town books, unless we infer that the earlier fathers adjourned from the meeting-house stake to the house of Joshua Fuller because of the cold.

Town Meeting

In the early days of the town, the old First Church building was used for a place of divine worship and for the transaction of town business. Until 1835, when the church was incorporated, all matters relating to it were voted upon in town meeting. In 1841, after a new house of worship had been built, religious services were discontinued in the old building and it was purchased by the town. The town house was changed little by little from time to time, though the most marked alterations, in the partition and fitting up of a town office, and the removal of some of the old seats were of more recent date; the latter, in fact, having been made necessary by the centennial celebration. All town meetings were still held there. But March 14, 1881, at the annual town meeting, the selectmen were instructed to procure a suitable place in the village of Ludlow for the next annual State election, and Joy's Hall was secured. This was only the beginning of an effort to have all the meetings of the town held at the village; and at the annual meeting, March 13, 1893, the town voted that future annual town meetings be held in the village, and a committee of five was appointed to secure suitable accommodations. Joy's Hall was engaged for all meetings and a room in the basement of the building for use of the town officers. At a later meeting, the voters in the uptown section made a strong effort to return to the Center for the annual meetings, but the village people outvoted them and all meetings have since been held at the village. In November, 1906, Joy's building was destroyed by fire. A new building was soon erected and larger quarters were secured for the town officers in the basement of the building. The town records are kept here in a fireproof safe and vault. A room for a lock-up was also secured in the basement of this building.

There has been agitation occasionally for the erection of a new town house, and at a meeting of the town in April, 1872, it was voted to raise $3,500 for the erection of a new town house and that a schoolroom be connected therewith. A committee was chosen to look for a location and report at a future meeting. At a later meeting the vote was reconsidered and there has been no further action taken.

In 1873 the woodchucks were so plentiful and troublesome to the farmers, that a bounty of ten cents for each one killed was offered by the town. To prove one's right to the money, at first the heads were taken to the treasurer, later only the ears were required. Nearly $150 was paid for this purpose during two or three years.

At the annual meeting, March 8, 1880, the first woman voter of the town, Miss Asenath Jones, appeared at the polls, escorted by Major John P. Hubbard, and deposited her ballot for school committee.

It is noticeable that the town, since the temperance agitation has been under way, never has licensed the sale of intoxicating liquors.

The voters of Ludlow in 1888 will always remember the great blizzard of March 12, of that year. It was the day of the annual town-meeting held in Ludlow Center. Little attention was given by the voters to the storm, which commenced in the morning. At noon two or three of the men started for home but returned. When the meeting closed, and the voters prepared to go home, the roads had in some cases become impassable and others nearly so. Seventeen of the men were obliged to remain all night in the hall, while others were obliged to stop on the way, few reaching their own homes. One of the selectmen was forced to stay three or four days with a friend. Some of the roads were impassable for a week.

At a meeting of the town held March 9, 1896, the town paid tribute to Governor Greenhalge, who died in office, by the adoption of the following resolutions:—

Resolved by the citizens of Ludlow in annual town meeting assembled: That in the death of Governor Frederic T. Greenhalge, every town in the Commonwealth, however small, has lost a true friend, an able champion for its petitions, an honorable, just, and wise chief magistrate, who took pride in serving the whole people, even unto death. And with sincere feelings of sorrow we extend to the afflicted family our most heartfelt sympathy.

Resolved: That these resolutions be placed upon the records of the town and that a copy be sent to the family of the deceased Governor.

MODERATORS OF TOWN MEETINGS

The number appended to each name denotes the number of times that person has served.

Moses Bliss, 1; John Hubbard, 3; Joseph Miller, 24; Jonathan Bartlett, 8; Joseph Hitchcock, 10; Jeremiah Dutton, 3; Abner Hitchcock, 1; Joshua Fuller, 3; James Kendall, 28; Joel Nash, 22; Gideon Beebe, 1; Israel Warriner, 14; John Jennings, 18; Jonathan Burr, 13; Eli Putnam, 7; Dr. Francis Percival, 1; John Miller, 1; Dr. A. J. Miller, 4; Elisha Fuller, 1; Oliver Dutton, 27; Benjamin Sikes, 1; Jonathan Clough, 2; Sherwood Beebe, 4; William Pease, 28; Ezekiel Fuller, 2; Increase Sikes, 1; Gad Lyon, 3; Dr. Simpson Ellis, 2; Joshua Fuller, 2; Noah Clark, 6; Timothy Nash, 13; Ashbel Burr, 3; Theodore Sikes, 4; Alva Sikes, 3; Alexander McLean, 2; Paoli Lathrop, 1; Dr. Elijah Caswell, 1; E. T. Parsons, 30; John Gates, 2; Nathaniel Chapin, 3; Henry Fuller, 1; Col. John Miller, 9; Dennis Knowlton, 1; Eli M. Smith, 15; John B. Alden, 1; Jerre Miller, 2; Dr. W. B. Alden, 2; George Booth, 3; William Ray, 1; Alanson Pool, 1; Dr. T. W. Lyman, 1; Artemas H. Whitney, 1; Henry Charles, 1; Edmund Bliss, 1; John P. Hubbard, 3; Chauncey L. Buell, 13; Francis F. McLean, 9; Gillen D. Atchinson, 3; Jackson Cady, 1; Adin Whitney, 1; Benjamin F. Burr, 4; Charles F. Grosvenor, 3; George A. Birnie, 12; James B. Knowlton, 2; Austin C. Gove, 1; Charles Greenhalgh, 1.

Town Clerks

The following have acted as town clerks:

Benajah Willey, 1774, 1775; Jeremiah Dutton, 1776–1779; Dr. Aaron J. Miller, 1780–1782; Samuel Arnold, 1783–1785, 1788; Elisha Fuller, 1786; Solomon L. Fuller, 1787; John Jennings, 1789–1792, 1794–1796, 1798–1799; Pliny Sikes, 1793, 1797; Increase Sikes, 1800–1808; Ely Fuller, 1809–1829, 1831; Theodore Sikes, 1830, 1833–1835, 1839–1841; Dr. Washington B. Alden, 1832, 1836–1838; Samuel S. Bucklin, 1842; Dennis Knowlton, 1843–1845; Maj. John P. Hubbard, 1845–1853, 1856–1861, 1864; George Booth, 1855; Albert Fuller, 1862–1863; George E. Root, 1865; Benjamin F. Burr, 1866–1879; Warren D. Fuller, 1879–1888; Alfred H. Bartlett, 1889–

Selectmen

The following have been chosen to serve as the town fathers. To the names is appended the number of years of service, so far as ascertained.

Aaron Ferry, 2; Abner Sikes, 12; Joseph Miller, 6; Joseph Hitchcock, 2; Joshua Fuller, 1; John Hubbard, Jr., 2; Benajah Willey, 1;

Alexander C. Birnie

Frank A. Towne

Michael T. Kane
Chairman Selectmen

ʀLES S. Browning, Treasurer

Alfred H. Bartlett, Clerk

TOWN OFFICERS, 1911

Jonathan Bartlett, 2; John Sikes, 3; Moses Wilder, 1; Timothy Keyes, 2; Jeremiah Dutton, 1; Joel Nash, 6; Israel Warriner, 7; James Kendall, 2; Samuel Arnold, 1; Isaac Brewer, 1; Jonathan Burr, 9; Samuel Frost, 6; Dr. Francis Percival, 4; Aaron Colton, 3; Ephraim Chapin, 2; Benjamin Sikes, Jr., 9; Pliny Sikes, 1; Eli Putnam, 1; Lt. Joseph Munger, 2; Sherwood Beebe, 6; Job Pease, 1; Timothy Nash, 14; Jonathan Sikes, 4; Gad Lyon, 2; Ezekiel Fuller, 1; Gates Willey, 7; Joseph Miller, 1; Joshua Fuller, 5; Daniel Sprague, 2; Nathaniel Lyon, 1; Titus Hubbard, 1; Nathaniel Lyon, 1; James Sheldon, 1; Ashbel Burr, 13; John Dorman, 10; Elias Frost, 5; Asahel Rood, 5; Gordon B. Miller, 3; Theodore Sikes, 4; Elam Wright, 1; Chester Sikes, 8; Elijah Fuller, 1; John Town, Jr., 1; John Gates, 7; William Ray, 11; Waterman Fuller, 3; Dan Hubbard, 5; Daniel King, 1; Artemas H. Whitney, 12; Edmund W. Fuller, 2; John Miller, 6; Elijah Plumley, 3; David Lyon, 2; Alva Sikes, 2; Elisha T. Parsons, 2; Jerre Miller, 5; Henry Fuller, 3; Willis Keyes, 1; Homer Lyon, 1; Aaron Davis, 2; Seth J. Bennett, 1; Simeon Jones, 2; Elijah G. Fuller, 1; Benjamin Sikes, 7; Gilbert E. Fuller, 6; Roderick Collins, 4; Jacob S. Eaton, 3; F. F. McLean, 3; Henry Charles, 1; John P. Hubbard, 2; Samuel White, 9; Eli M. Smith, 3; Reuben Sikes, 3; John Ray, 5; Chauncey L. Buell, 1; David C. Jones, 5; Ambrose Clough, 4; George D. Greene, 1; Edward E. Fuller, 9; Jackson Cady, 2; George R. Clark, 3; David Joy, 1; Benjamin F. Burr, 7; Charles F. Grosvenor, 4; Franklin Bramble, 4; James M. White, 3; Austin F. Nash, 3; Frank A. Towne, 19; John W. Hubbard, 13; Frederick L. Burr, 3; Albert E. Fuller, 6; Michael T. Kane, 6; Alexander C. Birnie, 3.

Assessors

The following have served the town in the capacity of assessors, each the number of years indicated:

Joseph Jones, 1; John Hubbard, Jr., 5; Joseph Hitchcock, 5; Isaac Brewer, Jr., 2; Benajah Willey, 2; Joshua Fuller, 1; Jonathan Bartlett, 1; Jonathan Lombard, 1; John Sikes, 5; Samuel Arnold, 6; Jeremiah Dutton, 2; Oliver Chapin, 1; Ezekiel Fuller, 2; James Kendall, 2; Joel Nash, 3; Solomon L. Fuller, 1; John Jennings, 2; Samuel Scranton, 1; Ephraim Chapin, 2; Pliny Sikes, 7; Gideon Beebe, 1; David Lyon, 2; Aaron Colton, 1; Jonathan Burr, 2; Dr. Francis Percival, 2; Gad Lyon, 8; Increase Sikes, 6; Timothy Nash, 3; Peter Damon, 1; Joseph Miller,

Jr., 1; Dr. Aaron J. Miller, 1; Samuel Frost, 1; Benjamin Sikes, 2; Eli Putnam, 1; Sherwood Beebe, 4; Stephen Jones, 2; Jonathan Sikes, 4; Oliver Dutton, 2; Ezekiel Fuller, 2; Asa Pease, 1; Gates Willey, 14; Lemuel Keyes, 3; Joshua Fuller, 3; Calvin Sikes, 1; Daniel Sprague, 1; Dr. Simpson Ellis, 1; Elias Frost, 4; James Sheldon, Jr., 6; Dr. Elijah Caswell, 1; William Brainerd, 6; Ely Fuller, 7; Theodore Sikes, 9; Elijah Fuller, 5; Alva Sikes, 10; John Moody, 2; Ira Stacy, 1; Nathaniel Chapin, 6; Sumner Chapin, 1; Joseph Miller, 1; Charles Alden, 7; Elihu Collins, 1; Elisha T. Parsons, 4; Henry Fuller, 3; Dr. Washington B. Alden, 3; John Miller, 3; Alva Sikes, 6; George Booth, 7; Simeon Jones, 3; Dennis Knowlton, 3; Jerre Miller, 6; John P. Hubbard, 6; Eli M. Smith, 1; Charles Bennett, 2; Dr. William B. Miller, 1; Aaron Davis, 3; Seth J. Bennett, 1; William Ray, 2; Elijah C. Eaton, 4; Albert Fuller, 22; Jeremiah Dutton, 1; Lucien Cooley, 1; Adin Whitney, 7; James W. Kendall, 1; Jacob S. Eaton, 2; Reuben Sikes, 4; Francis F. McLean, 4; David K. Paine, 3; David C. Jones, 2; Henry S. Jones, 11; Jere Dutton, 1; Jackson Cady, 2; Charles S. Bennett, 4; Davenport L. Fuller, 2; Norman Lyon, 2; Charles W. Alden, 2; Edward E. Fuller, 11; Lucien N. Lyon, 1; Austin F. Nash, 12; Arthur D. King, 20; Charles F. Howard, 1; F. S. King, 1; George D. Greene, 11; Charles P. Jones, 9; Frank G. Bennett, 3; Charles B. Bennett, 4.

Representative Districts

In 1876, in conformity to the law of the State, the county commissioners of Hampden County divided the county into districts for choosing representatives to the General Court at Boston. The towns of Palmer, Wilbraham, and Ludlow formed District No. 2 and were entitled to one representative.

In 1886 the county was again divided into districts, and Ludlow was placed with Palmer, Brimfield, and Holland, forming District No. 10, with one representative. In 1896 the towns of Ludlow, Wilbraham, Hampden, East Longmeadow, Agawam, Southwick, Granville, and Tolland were made one district called District No. 2, with one representative.

In 1906 the county was redistricted a third time and Agawam, Blandford, East Longmeadow, Granville, Hampden, Longmeadow, Ludlow, Montgomery, Russell, Southwick, Tolland, West Springfield,

TOWN ANNALS 69

and Wilbraham, were made District No. 2, with two representatives. This is often spoken of as the "Shoe-string" district.

REPRESENTATIVES TO THE GENERAL COURT

1784, 1785, Captain Joseph Miller; 1787, John Jennings; 1800, Elisha Fuller; 1801, 1802, Dr. Aaron J. Miller; 1806, Gad Lyon; 1807, Increase Sikes; 1808, Gad Lyon; 1809, John Jennings; 1810, Gad Lyon; 1811, Sherwood Beebe; 1812–1815, 1827, Ely Fuller; 1829, Rev. Alexander McLean; 1830, Dr. A. J. Miller; 1831–1836, Theodore Sikes; 1837, 1838, Joseph Bucklin; 1840, 1842–1844, Dennis Knowlton; 1845–1847, Artemas H. Whitney; 1848, Eli M. Smith; 1849, Alva Sikes; 1854, John P. Hubbard; 1855, Jerre Miller; 1856, 1857, Elisha T. Parsons; 1859, Albert Fuller; 1862, Hezekiah Root; 1865, Jacob S. Eaton; 1872, Reuben Sikes; 1879, Benjamin F. Burr; 1883, Warren D. Fuller; 1888, Charles F. Grosvenor; 1893, Edward E. Fuller; 1898, Arthur D. King; 1907, George D. Green.

MILITARY HISTORY

The Revolutionary War.—Ludlow has no occasion to be ashamed of her history in this struggle. One in seven of her inhabitants left for a longer or briefer time their homes and loved ones to engage in the fray. In the defenses at home, in the conflicts at the capital (it is reported that Dr. Aaron J. Miller was in the "tea party" at Boston), in the battles on the frontier, at the carnage of Trenton, were found the representatives of the little district in the Province of Massachusetts Bay. A glance at the names of the men who went from the district will make it evident to any one familiar with the earlier history of the place, that the best blood was represented in the Revolution. (See Historical Address, Part III.) The records make evident the fact that every burden imposed was borne, every tax paid. The people seem to have taken "joyfully the spoiling of their goods." In one of the provincial congresses, held February 1, 1775, Ludlow was assigned the care of ten of the inhabitants of Boston, and March 20th the people vote "that the Constables pay into the hand of Henry Gardner, Esqr, of Stow, all the moneys Due from this District Respectively to supply the said pressing Exigencies of the Colony, according to a resolve of the late Provincial Congress." In the apportionment of coats for soldiers in the service in 1775, Ludlow is to find twenty-three, and no doubt the district complied. An annual bounty of £12 for two years was offered to volunteers in 1777, while a bounty of £30 was necessary, or deemed so, two years after. As money degenerated later in the year, it became necessary to raise £160 for war purposes. Other instances of patriotism have been cited by another pen. (See Historical Address, Part III.) The noblest monument of the loyalty of Ludlow in her infancy, however, is in that noble list of thirty strong men who went forth at their country's call.

But the darkest nights end in gleamings of dawn, and after all this self-denial and inconvenience and manifold peril, we turn over but few pages of the records before we discover references to "the late war."

The Shays Rebellion.—In 1787, came the events of the Shays Rebellion, in which Ludlow had her share, furnishing, it is claimed, recruits to both sides, though the general impression seems to be that the town rather sympathized with the rebellent hosts. The track of the Shays part of the malcontents is supposed to have passed through the town on their way to the Springfield fight, and also in their retreat. On their passage through South Hadley a Ludlow man, Isaiah Call by name, was killed by a chance shot from a house. The others in the Shays forces whose names are preserved, going from this town, were Tyrus Pratt, John Jennings, and Samuel Olds. From local traditions it may be presumed the latter did not win many laurels, nor allow the grass to grow much under his feet when he returned homeward. Shays came into town from Ludlow City and down the road, quartering his troops at Fuller's tavern, in the West Middle. (Now it is the home of Hiram Davenport.) On Shays's inglorious defeat he retreated to Ludlow and thence northward, at a high rate of speed. It is said that Ezekiel Fuller joined the forces at the tavern and marched as far as Wallamanumps, where his friends persuaded him to desert. The pursuant troops sought out John Jennings in vain, for on their arrival at his home he had found it convenient to make an engagement elsewhere.

War of 1812.—It is singular that the war of 1812 should have passed with no occasion for record on the town books. Let no one, however, question the loyalty of Ludlow. Military organizations had existed in town for a long time, probably for most of the period of organization. In 1808 a goodly number went to a general muster at Old Hadley, occurring September 28, but were unsuccessful in getting their expenses paid by the town. The famous Horse Company was formed in 1802 from recruits of four towns, Springfield, Longmeadow, and Wilbraham joining Ludlow. The place of drill and muster was usually the Five Mile House, east of Springfield village. The captain was a Longmeadow man, Colton or Flint, perhaps both, at different times. The Ludlow names were as follows: Adin Parsons (lieutenant), Gaius Clough, Mordecai Clough, Warren Hubbard, Erastus Munger, Daniel Miller, Sylvester Miller, Francis Nash, Julius Nash, Asahel Rood, and Martin Smith. The full number on the company was about forty. When the War of 1812 broke out, this company was in fine order. It is related that while at drill on their mustering grounds one day, when the captain had formed them into line, he requested all who would volunteer as minutemen for the national service to march forward so many paces. Not a man started in obedience to the sudden request, until the captain himself advanced to the assigned place. Then a large number of the company followed his example, among whom were all the Ludlow men but two, and of those one furnished a substitute. The names of those from the town actually participating in the service during the war were as follows:

Henry Acres,
Gideon Cotton,
Samuel Gates, substitute
    for Selah Kendall, drafted.
Chester Kendall,
Amos Root,
Charles F. Wood,

Benjamin Ainsworth,
Lemuel Gardiner,
John Howard,
Reuben Parsons,
Veranus Shattuck,
Gordon B. Wood,
Harvey Wood.

Facts are facts, and it must be recorded that two of these men deserted from the ranks and concealed themselves at their homes. One narrowly escaped capture by concealment for days inside a large stone chimney then standing in the southwest part of the town, and by a kindly warning from a female friend who knew officers were on his trail. The other was not so fortunate. Taken prisoner, he was court-martialed and sentenced to be shot. The coffin was produced and he was bound and made to kneel upon it. The soldiers drawn up to execute the rigorous military law included his own brother-in-law. But just as the fatal shot was about to send him to eternity a reprieve was granted and a pardon eventually obtained, through the instrumentality of a Lieutenant Clary of Springfield.

HISTORY OF LUDLOW

Among the souvenirs of these days of war is a revenue receipt for payment by Benjamin Sikes of a tax of one dollar "for and upon a 4 wheel carriage called a waggon and the harness used therefor owned by him."

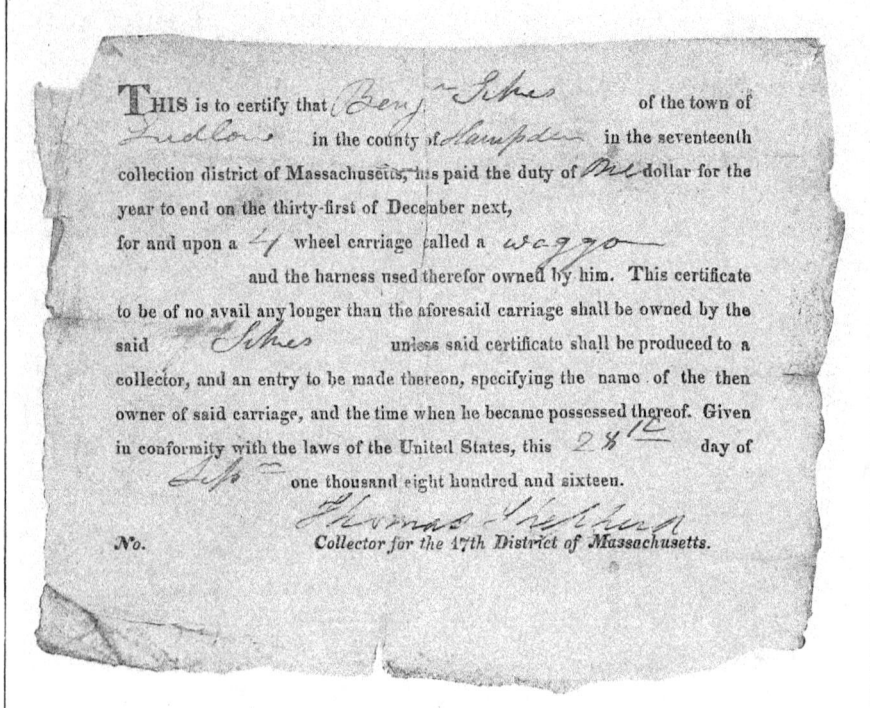

The Ludlow Militia.—The time in which the once famous Ludlow militia figured was mainly from 1820 onward to 1843. In the earlier days of this period the training was under the State militia law, compelling all within a certain age to bear arms at stated times. The company was then called by the graphic title of "Flood-wood." On one occasion somewhere about 1830, a notable occurrence took place. The captain having tendered his resignation, the duties of command rested on the highest lieutenant, who happened to be John Miller. Orders having been sent from the headquarters in Springfield for general muster, Miller warned his company, trained them at the usual place, Ely Fuller's tavern at Ludlow Center, and proceeded to the place of rendezvous. By the rank of the captain the company had a certain position in the regiment, but as Ludlow was then, as now, out in the woods, the colonel proposed to put Miller's men in an inferior position. Having first tested the spirit of his men, Miller informed the colonel that he must have his rightful position or none, and the position was that belonging to the captain whose command he represented. His demands not being allowed, he gave a signal to his men and their musicians (the best in the regiment) and led them away from the place of muster to the sound of fife and drum. Unfortunately, and wholly without intention on the part of Lieutenant Miller, the signal was given and obeyed during the service of prayer. As a result the officer was court-martialed and deprived of commission for a year. It was in this interim that Veranus Shattuck ("Dr. Foggus"), a veteran of the war of 1812, was elected captain, Miller's sentence having prevented the first choice of the men from consummation. When the time was up, however, Miller was triumphantly elected captain, from which position he rose to be eventually lieutenant-colonel, commanding a regiment. Later he was chosen captain of a picked company of militia, called light infantry, which consisted of something like sixty men.

The Mexican War.—The Mexican war fever reached Ludlow, but only took effect in one case, Joseph Rood, who is supposed to have been wounded in one of the frays in the land of the Aztecs.

The Civil War.—There was but one sentiment manifest in Ludlow during the fearful days of the great Civil War,—allegiance to the Union. There were few towns more active, none more loyal.

Ere the echoes of Sumter's guns had fairly died away, the citizens met (April 27, 1861) and appropriated $2,000 for those who would enlist in the service of the United States; $15 per month to be paid each volunteer engaged in actual drill service, $5 per month when in actual service, and $5 per month to each family of volunteers engaged in drill or actual service. In August, 1862, the town voted to pay $100 to each of seventeen men who would enlist to fill the quota required of the town in the call of the president for 300,000 men. Samuel King (son of Marvin King and brother of Arthur D. King) drew up before the grateful people fifteen strong yeomen who had responded. Meeting after meeting was held, keeping the interest at white heat. In March, 1863, the town voted to give $3,000 for the use of families of those who had volunteered into the service of the United States, and in November of the same year, $2,400 was voted as bounty for volunteers to fill the quota for a second call of the president for 300,000 men, each enlisted man to receive $150. In March, 1864, the town appropriated $3,000 for aid to families of volunteers, and in April of the same year $1,275 was raised to pay the volunteers and $500 to pay the bounty promised to those mustered into the service under the call of October 17, 1863. In April, 1865, the town appropriated $2,500 for the aid of the families of the volunteers.

We need not cite the events which so frequently repeat the story of those terrible days. Another hand has traced the account, and from his narration we will draw our sketch in the main. (See Mr. Banister's address following, also Mr. Tuck's, Part III.) Suffice it to say, that of the men who went and suffered, some of them even unto death, nearly all were of the best blood in the town. They did not act in vain.

The war being ended, Ludlow welcomed home those remaining of her gallant sons, with thanksgivings mingled with tears for those who had fallen during the strife. Measures were taken in 1866 to erect a monument to the memory of the fallen. The committee was appointed (Hezekiah Root, chairman; F. F. McLean, J. P. Hubbard, S. White, and C. L. Buell), money raised, and a contract made with W. N. Flynt & Co. of Monson, resulting at last in the completion of the beautiful structure standing near the old town-house. (See Mr. Tuck's address, Part III.) The memorial with the iron fence around it cost about $1,300. At its dedication, in the summer of 1867, a goodly company assembled and listened to an appropriate address from Rev. D. K. Banister, part of which we are permitted to place before the reader:

A worthy and patriotic object has called us together this morning. We have met to embalm the memories of those who, like the leader in the great conflict, fell, martyrs, in their country's cause. In this great struggle and successful contest, not merely a Lincoln, a Grant, a Sherman and others high in command have borne a noble and important part, but the lower grades of officers and the rank and file of the loyal hosts were all essential and are worthy of heroes' fame. The privileges our institutions bring, and the civilization they uphold, proclaim their excellence. The masses are lifted up, the avenues to eminence are open to the sons of the lowly and the poor, as well as the rich and honorable. How does the humble but meritorious backwoodsman find his way to the chief magistracy of a great nation, and this by his wisdom and goodness, and become the admiration of the world and of ages yet unborn? Whence the men whose discoveries have so marked the age in which we live? . . .

This principle not only opens the way for aspiring genius and fosters it, but invests every loyal citizen with privileges beyond price. The value of our government is measured by the sum aggregate of its value to each of the loyal millions.

Whatever was thought at first, it soon became apparent that we had on our hands no mere holiday work, but a contest of fearful proportions. The frequent calls for men, for three hundred thousand men, to fill the fearful gaps in the loyal ranks, gave warning that to enlist was to meet a storm of great fury and power. These men most of them saw the danger and faced it. . . . Our war-meetings sometimes presented scenes well worthy the painter's pencil and the poet's pen. I recollect attending one not far away, well worthy of remembrance. Volunteers were called to come forward and give their names. A young man [Lyon] of noble spirit and form erect came forward and said in substance: "I love my country, and, if need be, I am willing to die for it, but I have aged parents that need my care; if I can be assured they will be cared for, I am willing to go;" while tears told the earnestness of his heart. The desired pledge was given, and he enlisted. Another [Pratt], of stalwart form and generous impulses, said, "I am willing to go if my family, my wife and children, can be cared for, if I return no more." The promise desired was given, and he also enlisted. Another [Pott], English by birth, said he felt the cause to be worthy, and he was willing to stake his life for his adopted country, and gave his name. Of low stature, he expressed much concern lest he should be rejected on that account by the examining officer. They all went, and fell or died in their country's service.

The first one that enlisted in the town [Brooks] is a case worthy of note. He lived in the village. He was a young man of intelligence, and in a good financial position. But hearing the call, his patriotic impulses were moved as though by inspiration. His room was embellished with mottoes like these: "Our country calls and we must go;" "Boys, our country needs us." He, like other noble spirits, without the pressure and incidental inducements of after years, enlisted, and fell a hero on the battle-field. . . . By such sacrifices the area of liberty has been extended and greatly promoted. The four millions of bondmen became free, the slavery remaining in the civilized world is doomed. . . .

Free institutions, under the influence of an open Bible and general intelligence, are strong and reliable, as well as most benign; none stronger or so secure. This republican nation stands erect and purified, rebuking oppression everywhere, feared by its foes and respected by all, the world over. She bears the banner of freedom for the world. . . When the prophetic day of seven suns lighting up the world with millennial splendor shall be ushered in, it will be seen that this great contest and triumph had a marked and mighty influence in hastening the glorious consummation.

We append the names of those who went from and for the town as soldiers in the Civil War, referring the reader for incidents to a following page. (See also Historical Address, Part III.) We give the names in alphabetical order, as the records show them, starring those who fell:

Philo W. B. Alden,
Preston Alden,
Hiram W. Aldrich,*
Wilson Allen,
Dennis Anderson,
George Ashton,
James Bagley,
Leonard Baker,
Lemuel Bennett,
Lyman Bennett,*
Warren D. Bennett,
Sumner Bodfish,
Lyman Brewer,
John H. Brines,
Edward F. Brooks,*
James Buckley,
Joseph A. Bugbee,
Amaziah E. Burcham,
Francis A. Burcham,
Henry Bushey,
Andrew Carpenter,
Darwin Caswell,
James Chapin,
Augustus Chapman,*
William F. Christian,
Benjamin F. Clark,
William Clements,
John Coash,*
Charles B. Comstock,
Caspar Converse,
Calvin Cooley,
Thomas Cowan,
Daniel D. Currier,*
Caleb Crowninshield,*
John B. Dunn,
Benjamin C. Davis,
John B. Davis,
Wilber Davis,
Cornelius Dugan,
Elisha Dutton,
Charles B. Fay,
George Feathers,
Edward E. Fuller,
J. R. Fuller,
Horace Gates,
Marvin Giboney,
Austin C. Gove,
Thomas Higgins,
Isaac T. Hines,
Henry Hobson,
John Hobson, Jr.,
Henry A. Hubbard,*
James B. Kellams,
Andrew Kenney,
James D. Kenney,
Henry Keyes,
Arthur King,
Homer K. King,
Samuel King,
Francis R. Lemon,
Dexter Lombard,
Isaac Loury,
Thomas I. Lyndes,
Ebenezer Lyon,*
John Mack,
Julius M. Marshall,

Harry Martin,
John McCutcheon,
John McDonald,
Charles McFarland,*
Charles McFeathers,
Charles McKenney,
Charles McSheney,
Wilbur F. Miller,
Thomas Mockler,
Edward Morrill,
Michael Munsing,
Charles W. Nash,
James L. Nash,
Stephen O'Holloran,
David M. Olds,
Robert Parsons,*
Henry M. Pease,*
Levi L. Pease,
Lyman Pease,
James E. Perry,
Anthony O. Pott,*
Daniel Pratt,*
Edwin Price,
Flavius J. Putnam,*

Michael Reinhart,
Andrew Renny,
Wilson Rogers,
Joseph Rood,
William Sanderson,
Daniel R. Sanger,
Peter Scott,
John Shangnesey,
Alexander Shaw,
Charles Sikes,
Charles Simonds,
Francis F. Simonds,
Franklin R. Simonds,
Josiah Stephens,
Edward H. Stewart,
George L. Streeter,
Addison Waide,
George Wallace,
Charles S. Washburn,
William E. Washburn,*
Abram W. Watson,
Lovinski White,
Loren Wood.

Henry Hobson was on board the *Kearsarge*, which sank the *Alabama* off Cherbourg, France, in the Civil War.

From detailed accounts of the life and incidents of the stay in Andersonville, sent by surviving comrades who were there, we are permitted to cull brief selections:

From Jasper Harris of Holyoke:

The brigade including my regiment (16th Connecticut Volunteers) was captured April 23, 1864, at Plymouth, N. C., and taken en route for Andersonville, where our rebel guard told us was a splendid, shady camp, with plenty of new barracks for shelter. We arrived at the Andersonville station at dark on the evening of May 9. The next morning we were marched towards the stockade, a quarter of a mile away. Just before arriving at the main gate we came to a rise of ground from which could be seen the whole stockade, and most of the inside of it. I shall never forget the gloomy and depressed feeling with which I looked on the horrible sight. The high log stockade was composed of straight young pines, cut sixteen feet long, hewn on two sides, the bark peeled off, and then the log sunk on end in a trench six feet deep, close together, leaving ten feet at least above ground on the inside. Cross-pieces were spiked to each timber horizontally, making a fence strong enough to hold cattle instead of men.

Rations were issued daily, being drawn into the stockade by a mule team, and when divided and subdivided furnished each man a pint and a half of cob-meal and from two to four ounces of bacon. For a few days we received two common-sized sticks of cord wood to be divided among ninety men.

Grant's campaign had now commenced and soon more prisoners began to come in. After a while came the Ludlow boys. The first man I met was Sergeant Perry, looking every inch a soldier, and in excellent health. The next was Flavius Putnam, a new recruit, captured in his first battle. I always knew him as being a thoroughly good man when I lived in Ludlow, and exceedingly strong and quick in farm work, and always cheerful.

If I should attempt to write a complete description of Andersonville and its horrors, of Wirtz, his guards and his bloodhounds, and all the sights and incidents which came under my own eye there and at other prisons during my eight months' stay, of the murders and robberies amongst our own men, of the hanging of six of them by a court of our own men,—it would fill the pages of a large book, while a part would be descriptive of such monstrous cruelty and so striking to sensitive minds that I am afraid it would not be believed if written.

From an account by James E. Perry of Adrian, Mich.:

Just two weeks from the time we were captured found us marching into the renowned Andersonville prison pen. When introduced into that foul den of crime, wretchedness, and sorrow, our hearts failed us, and we made up our minds for the worst, and we would rather have risked our chance with the regiment even in those bloody battles of the campaign of 1864. One third of the men who occupied that vast charnel pen lie buried there to-day.

Willie Washburn died August 21, Daniel Pratt, August 22, Ebenezer Lyon, September 11, Caleb Crowninshield, September 15, Hiram Aldrich, the latter part of September, John Coash, during the fall, Flavius Putnam, some time in September, Joseph Miller (not from Ludlow) and Albert Collins of Collins Depot, during the summer. Putnam and Coash were admitted to the hospital and died there. I think it can be truly said that these men died of starvation, for we received nothing that a sick man could relish or eat.

Grand Army Veterans, Sons of Veterans, Cadets, and School Girls, Memorial Day, 1911

Cadets in Front of Soldiers' Monument, Memorial Day, 1911
George Chamberlain, Captain.

Memorial Day

Memorial Day is observed every year by the veterans of the Civil War and citizens of the town. An appropriation is made each year by the town for the use of the Grand Army in the observance of the day. The children from the schools, the boy cadets, under command of Captain George Chamberlain, the veterans, and citizens form in line at the village and march to the different cemeteries, to decorate the graves of the soldiers therein, then return to the soldiers' monument at the Center, where exercises are held. Later they proceed to the church, where the annual address is given. Afterwards the boy cadets give an exhibition drill near the monument. Dinner is served for all who wish by the ladies of the church.

Cemeteries

From the house of God to the resting-place of the dead is a frequented path. There are sufficient references to the places of burial to assure us that these busy scenes were often interrupted by the service funereal.

The first cemetery of Ludlow was given by Benjamin Sikes, the earliest in town of that name, and is known as the Sikes Cemetery. It is situated about a mile northwest of the Center, near Truman Hubbard's. Mrs. Anna Sikes, wife of Lieut. John Sikes, was buried here in 1772. Benjamin Sikes was great great-grandfather of Otis Sikes, Mrs. Jackson Cady, and Danforth Sikes. There is something touching in the record of the transaction.

Receiv^d a deed of Gift from Mr Benjamin Sikes of a Certain piece of land in order to or as a place to bury our Dead—voted also that the Thanks of the Town be return^d for the same to the said Mr Sikes for his Benevolence.

A board fence around it was ordered in 1782. In 1865, Edward Sikes of Wisconsin, a descendant of the Ludlow Sikeses, and whose ancestors are here buried, left a sum of money to help build a wall around it, which was erected in the following year. This cemetery is still in use and in good condition. Many of the earliest settlers of the town are buried within it.

In 1792, the selectmen were instructed to procure a bier and keep it in the meeting-house. There are a few (1911) living who remember this bier. It was made of four-inch square white pine timber, the handles being rounded. It was entirely painted black.

In 1794, a committee was appointed to obtain a deed of another burying ground, and, seven years later, although a little late in the courtesy, the town thanks Elisha Fuller for the cemetery adjoining the church on the south. (Elisha Fuller was the grandfather of Edward E. and Henry S. Fuller.) This is known as the Fuller Cemetery. The first person buried in it was a grandchild of Captain Joseph Miller, who was crushed to death beneath a cart wheel. Some of the stones indicate that it must have been in use as a place of burial some time before the formal ceding of the ground. It was probably laid out in 1786, the first burial taking place that year.

HEADSTONE OF HANNAH OLDS

It became necessary in 1805 to fence this yard with posts and rails and half wall. A dozen years later the people met to "spell" in repairing the fence.

In 1823 the town appropriated thirty dollars for a hearse. Before this time the dead were borne on biers to the grave, a journey of miles on foot being often required.

In 1825 the fences of both yards needed repairs. Simeon Pease, the wit of the town, bid off the repairs of the center yard at the sum of five cents, evidently to postpone the work until the town would do it with thoroughness. In a few weeks he became one of a committee to build a thorough half-wall fence, with sawed posts and rails above. Great excitement was caused about this time by a proposition to move all the bodies previously interred in this yard, the proposition being scornfully rejected—how wisely is not evident.

A hearse-house was erected in 1827. It stood near the southwest corner of the present First Church and was painted red.

The East Cemetery, familiarly called the "Ould Burying Ground," lying partly in Ludlow and partly in Belchertown, is inclosed by one fence, each town caring for its own portion. It was laid out in 1801. The oldest stone in this cemetery is that of Hannah Jones Olds, who is buried in the Belchertown portion of the yard. She was born in 1728 and died in 1802. Here also lie "Nick" and "Tarzy," though on opposite sides of the dividing line. A bequest from Ludlow has been left for a lot in that yard.

The Center Cemetery, containing three acres, was purchased from Increase Sikes, and opened in 1842. Mr. Sikes found three cemeteries upon his farm at that time. The first person buried was John Q. Day, son of Zachariah Day; the second, a son of Henry or Harry Fuller, and brother of Edward E. Fuller; third, Harriet E. Burr, daughter of Lyman Burr, and sister of Benjamin F. Burr. All were buried in September, 1843.

The lots in this cemetery were given to the residents of the town without cost, when a lot was needed, but not before. The remains of three of the Ludlow pastors lie in this yard, Rev. Ebenezer B. Wright and Rev. Jeremy Webster Tuck, who were pastors of the First Church for long terms, and Rev. Daniel K. Banister, who was pastor of the Methodist Church and was here when the Civil War broke out, and whom the whole town loved. He attended the funerals of many of the people of the First Church and Society, as they had no pastor at that time. These beloved pastors are buried near each other on the east side of the cemetery and north of the hearse-house. A minister from an adjoining town said as he stood by their graves, "What a pleasant spot for the burial of ministers, where they lie facing the East!" There are many handsome monuments in this cemetery.

FOOTSTONE OF HANNAH OLDS

The first mention of the cemetery at the village, which was later removed to Island Pond Cemetery, was on May 30, 1842, the year the town was asked to enlarge it. The tomb was constructed in 1846, at a cost of $100.

The Island Pond Cemetery is the latest laid out. In 1891, the town elected three cemetery commissioners, Benjamin F. Burr for three years, Charles F. Grosvenor for two years, and Edward E. Fuller for one year, also Jackson Cady and Danforth W. Sikes in addition, together with the selectmen, to choose a site for a new cemetery. They purchased eighteen acres of land of Michael H. Lyons near Chapin Pond, about a mile north of the village. Charles F. Grosvenor took charge of laying out and getting it ready for use.

A year or two later the bodies from the old cemetery in the village were removed to the new cemetery and the old site was deeded to the Ludlow Manufacturing Associates.

In 1893, Robert Kyle was elected to succeed Mr. Grosvenor; in 1907, Elbridge J. Streeter succeeded Mr. Fuller, and Arthur M. Jones succeeded Mr. Burr, who resigned; in 1908, H. Berton Payne succeeded Mr. Kyle; in 1911, the commissioners are Minor M. Wilder, Arthur M. Jones, Charles Graham.

Many have left bequests, and others have given sums of money that the income may be used by the town for perpetual care of their lots. The town, however, takes good care of all of them, besides giving special care to those for which a fund has been left.

Bequests and gifts have been made by the following persons: Rufus Kimball, Mrs. Sarah Swart, Mrs. Joanna Fuller, Mrs. Martha Billings, Mrs. Martha B. Kendall, Mrs. Delia E. Talmadge, Austin F. Nash, Mrs. Susan A. Green, Mrs. Amnie Hubbard, John B. Alden; Mrs. Olivet B. F. Bridge, Mrs. Theodosia P. Clough, Isaac H. Plumley, Alexander Whitney, Mrs. Charles Beebe, Mrs. Lucy A. Perry, children of Daniel Brewer and Ela Walker, Mrs. Harriett A. Baggs, Mrs. Mary Tuck Vinal (daughter of Rev. J. W. Tuck), D. M. Collins, Benjamin F. Burr, and Chauncey Davis.

EPITAPHS

The following quaint epitaphs are found in the three oldest cemeteries in Ludlow: the first six in the old Center or Sikes Cemetery, the next ten in the North yard or Fuller Cemetery, and the last four in the East yard or "Ould Burying Ground."

This stone is erected
to the memory of a son
and a Daughter of Capt
Joseph and M$^{rs.}$ Mary
Miller (viz) Wilder, who
died Oct 13 1786 in the 5
year of his age.
And Joanna who died Dec
10, 1787, in the 3 year of her age.

When death receives the dire command
None can elude or ftay his hand
Nor can a hope or beauty fave
From the dire conquest of the grave.

In memory of Mr.
Cyprian and Mrs.
Lucy Wright
who died as follows
viz. She died
August 22nd 1794
in the 37th year
of her age
he died Jan 7th
1779 in the 45th
year of his age.

Kind reader, when these lines you see
Think how uncertain life may be:
We once had life & health like you
But now have bid the world adieu.

In Memory of Chester
the Son of Mr Asa & M^{rs}
Sarah Dodge who Died
Sept^m 11th 1805, aged 3
years 4 Months & 18 days

With disentery & with worms
God did Death licence give
To take my precious Soul away
And fay I fhould not live.

In memory of
Doc^r Philip Lyon
who died July 25
1802 aged 40 years
Who after having
experienced the
sweets of connubial
bliss died leaving no
family. his amiable
consort died at Randolph Oc^t 1801.

Sacred to the
memory of Capt
Joseph Miller,
who departed this
life at West Spring
field April 3 1803
Aged 79 years.

Praifes on tombs are
titles vainly spent.
A mans good name is
his beft monument.

In memory of
Mr Gad Lyon
who died
Dec 26, 1815
aged 47 years.

Depart my friends
dry up your tears
Here I must lie
till Christ appears.

SACRED TO THE MEMO
RY of Mr^s Mary wife of
Mr Leonard Miller who died
in Childbed June 6th 1790
in the 38th year of her age
Befides a birth and fhe left 8 fmall
te
Children to mourn her untimely fa

In Memory of
Mr^s Cyrena Sikes
the Consort of
Mr Jonathan Sikes
who died
Dec. 11, 1808.
Æt, 28.

Lie here dear Wife
& take thy reft
GOD cols the hum
For he tninks it beft

In memory
of Mrs Sarah
wife of M^r
Timothy Root
who died
Mar 3
1785 in
her 44 year
Also
an infant bury
-ed by her
side

In memory of Lieu^t
JOHN SIKES who died
July 27, 1807 in the
60 year of his age

Friends nor phyficians
could not fave
This mortal body from the grave
Nor can the grave confine it here
When Chrift commands it to appear.

In memory of
M^RS HANNAH SIKES
the wife of
Mr Benjamin Sikes
who died Apr 17 : 1790
Aged 84 years

Life is uncertain
Death is fure
Sin is the wound
& Chrift the cure

In memory of
Mr ABNER SIKES
who died
Jun 24th 1800
in the 70 year
of his age

Our age to Sevnty
years are set
& not but few who
to them get

Submit dau^tr of M^r
Reuben & Mrs Mary
Chapin was born
July 3^d 1774 & died
Oct 16th 1776

Merick Son of
above Nam^d Chapin
died at Fifhkill a e
16 22 Jan 1778 aged
16 Years

In memory of
M^RS Anna ye wife
of Mr John Sikes
who died June 9
1772 in ye 23rd Year
of her Age

Boaft not thyself
of tomorrow for
thou knoweft not
what a day may
bring forth.

In Memory of
M^RS MARY SIKES
wife of
Mr Abner Sikes
who died
March 10th 1818
85 years
Æt

by faith in Christ
I left this Stage

In Memory of
MISS SARAH SIKES
daughter of
Lieu^t John Sikes &
Mrs Sarah his 2d
wife who died Sep^t
19th 1806 aged 20
years———.

The longest life must have
an end
Therefore beware how
time you spend

In Memory of
MR BENJAMIN SIKES
who died
Auguft 2^d 1781
Aged 77 years

Death is a debt
To nature due
Which I have paid
& fo muft you.

IN MEMORY OF
THE WIDOW HANN^{ah}
OLDS WIFE OF MR
JONATHAN OLDS
DECEAST WHO DIED
FEB 3^d 1802 IN
74 YEAR OF

(illegible)

Mortals we are none can deny
Farewell my friends prepare to die

In
memory of
NICHOLAS DANIELS
who died
April 26, 1827
Æt. 65

In memory of
MR BERIAH JENNINGS
who died May 12th 1776
in the 45 year of his Age.

BERIAH JENNINGS JU^R
fon of
Beriah & Eunice Jennings
who died Decr 8th 1775
in the 22 year of his age.

Blessed are the dead
which die in the Lord.

Mr. David Paine
Departed this
Life July 2nd
1807 (by a cart
wheel runing acrofs
his breast: he expired
instantly) Æt. 70
He was a friend
to Religion &
Piety

Return my friends without a tear
Devote your lives unto God's fear:
That you with him may always live
This is the last advice I give.

Mrs
Mahitable
wife of
Rev Ephraim Scott
died
May 25 1831
Æ 34

There is rest in heaven.

COPY OF AN OLD DEED
(The original is in the Historical Room in the Library)

To All People to whom these Prefents Shall come, GREETING:
KNOW YE, That I Chauncy Brewer of Springfield in the County of Hampshire & State of the Mafsachusetts Bay Esqr For and in confideration of the Sum of Fifteen Pounds Current Money of the State aforesaid, to me in Hand paid before the Enfealing hereof by Elisha Fuller of Ludlow in the aforesaid County Yeoman the Receipt whereof I do hereby acknowledge and am fully fatisfied, contented and paid, HAVE given, granted, bargained, fold, aliened, released, conveyed and confirmed, and by thefe Prefents, do freely, clearly and abfolutely give, grant, bargain, fell, aliene, releafe, convey and confirm unto him the faid Elisha Fuller his heirs and Affigns for ever, A certain Lot of Land lying & being in the Town of Ludlow; being Lot No. 99: Originally laid out to John Miller; said Lot being Six Rods & five feet in width & four Miles in Length & Containing fifty Acres be the same more or lefs.—

TO HAVE AND TO HOLD the before granted Premifes, with the Appurtenances and Privileges thereto belonging, to him the faid Elisha Fuller his Heirs and Affigns: To his and their own proper Ufe, Benefit and Behoof forevermore. And I the faid Chauncy Brewer for myself my Heirs, Executors and Administrators, do Covenant, promise and Grant unto and with the faid Elisha Fuller his Heirs and Affigns, for ever, That before and until the Enfealing hereof, I am the true, fole, proper and lawful Owner and Poffeffor of the before-granted Premifes, with the Appurtenances. And have in myself good Right, full Power and lawful Authority to give, grant, bargain, fell, aliene, releafe convey and confirm the fame as aforefaid; and that free and clear, and freely and clearly executed, acquitted and difcharged of and from all former and other Gifts, Grants, Bargains, Sales, Leafes, Mortgages, Wills, Intails, Joyntures, Dowries, Thirds, Executions and Incumbrances Whatfoever.

AND FURTHERMORE, I the faid Chauncy Brewer for myself my Heirs, Executors, and Adminiftrators, do hereby Covenant, Promife and Engage the before-granted Premifes with the Appurtenances unto him the said Elisha Fuller his Heirs and Affigns, for ever to Warrant,

Secure and Defend againſt the lawful Claims or Demands of any Perſon or Perſons whatſoever.

And I Amy Brewer wife of the ſaid Chauncy, do hereby relinquish all my Right of Dower or Thirds in or unto the afore bargain[d] Lot of Land.

In Witneſs Whereof We have hereunto ſet our Hands & Seals this Twenty third Day of June Dom: 1780.

Sign[d] Seal[d] &   CHAUNCY BREWER (seal)
Delivered in   AMY BREWER (seal)
Preſence of
    NATH[L] BREWER
    EUNICE BREWER

                Chauncy Brewer & Wife
                  Deed to Josh[a] Fuller
                  Rei[d] June 24th 1780
                            Wſees

Hampshire ſs. June 24th 1780

              Then the within named Chauncy Brewer acknowledged written Instrument to be his free Act & Deed—

                    before W[m] Pynchon Jun[r] Just Pacis

Hampſhire ſs Springfield June 24th 1780

Received & Registered in Lib. 15. fol. 715 and Examined
                  P[r] W[m] Pynchon Jun Reg[r]

IV

TOWN DEVELOPMENT

Population—Longevity—Highways and bridges: Early roads; First bridges: Put's bridge; Cooley bridge; First bridge at Collins Station; Red bridge; Iron bridge—Care of highways, Wages, Commissioner, State highway—Railroads: Boston and Albany; Springfield and Athol; Hampden—The street railway—The Ludlow reservoir—Fire department—Fire alarm system—Lighting: Gas, Electric lights—Telephones—Post office: At Jenksville, Postmasters; At Ludlow Center—Rural free delivery—Taverns—Stores: Center, Village—Savings bank—Court—Library—Antiques and relics—Hospital—Fraternal organizations: Brigham Lodge of Masons; Ludlow Farmers Club; Patrons of Husbandry, Ludlow Grange, No. 179; Women's Club; The Ludlow Social and Debating Club—Physicians—Lawyers.

POPULATION

IN 1774, the settlement at Stony Hill numbered two or three hundred. No further statistics are available till 1835, when the number given is 1,329; in 1840 it was 1,268; in 1850, 1,186; in 1860, 1,174; in 1870, 1,136; in 1880, 1,526; in 1890, 1,939; in 1900, 3,536; and in 1910, only a few less than 5,000.

Ludlow has long been noted for the longevity of its inhabitants. Of twenty deaths in 1874 (the year of its centennial) nine were of persons over sixty years of age, and one had borne the weight of a hundred winters less three.

HIGHWAYS AND BRIDGES

Taking in survey the period from the incorporation of Ludlow to the end of the eighteenth century we find that it was a time ot establishment. At its close, across the trackless wilds of 1774 were marked the lines of travel. The embryo neighborhoods of the earlier date had developed into considerable communities, while clusters of houses had been formed elsewhere. The fertile slopes of the eastern base of Mineachogue had been improved by the Danielses, Oldses, and Wrights; the dense woods along Broad Brook above had been invaded and appropriated by the Aldens, then nearer than now kindred of John Alden and "Priscilla, the

Puritan maiden"; and there are not wanting those who trace the fairness of many a Ludlow maiden back

"To the damsel Priscilla, the loveliest maiden of Plymouth."

The Lyons also had commenced a settlement where their descendants now live and thrive, while the falls of Wallamanumps already had constant admirers in those dwelling near by.

OLD LUDLOW BRIDGE ACROSS CHICOPEE RIVER
Taken from Springfield side

The early annals of the highways are very defective, so much so that they can with the greatest difficulty be traced at all. The first roads in the town were merely bridle paths which were marked by blazed trees. After the incorporation of the district, the roads from the present west schoolhouse to Ludlow City, and from L. Simonds's to Jenksville, are the first mentioned. The old Cherry Valley road through to John Wilson Hubbard's, but not entirely as now, was laid out in 1782, and that from the Mann place (now E. J. Streeter's) to W. G. Fuller's in the same year. A highway from the East Cemetery to Miller Corner was projected in 1784, and the same year one across Cedar Swamp. The road from the Congregational Church northward was laid out in 1800, and the land damages were one shilling per square rod. In 1793, a petition was sent the county officers to lay out a road corresponding to the route from Collins Station to Granby, as part of a line which shall "commode the travil from the eastern part of Connecticut to Dartmouth Colledge in New Hampshire."

The first reference to guideboards is in 1795, when it needed a committee of nine to erect "way-posts."

Nearly every highway east of the mountain was either laid out or relaid before 1811; a different course was marked out and worked from John Wilson Hubbard's and between Lovinski White's and the mountain south, where Jonathan Burr lived, to the Center post office, in 1803, involving the first construction of the terrible Cedar Swamp causeway, so long an eyesore to exasperated townspeople and bewildered selectmen. In 1817 was established the highway from Joy's store to Plumley's, to accommodate, it is said, travel from the Jenksville to the Three Rivers factories. A year later somebody called down the wrath of the county commissioners on the principal north and south roads through the town, resulting in general repairs and relocation of the Put's bridge and Belchertown and Collins and Granby routes. In 1826 we find one of the earlier movements toward a money system of repairing the highways.

The road from the present Danforth W. Sikes place southward was laid out in 1834, and one or two smaller ways of travel established, while of course Cedar Swamp continued to perplex the citizens.

Before the opening of the eighteenth century only the most inexpensive modes of crossing the Chicopee were employed. It can hardly be presumed that the bridge for which provision is made in the charter was on the Ludlow line. A memorandum of highway survey bearing the date of 1776 speaks of the north end of a bridge which was probably at Wallamanumps. There were "riding places" or fords at Wallamanumps and where now Collins bridge spans the stream. As early as 1781, a committee from Ludlow was to meet another from Springfield to see about the construction of a bridge at Wallamanumps. In 1788 £50 was granted for a like purpose in April, and in November a committee on subscriptions was appointed, possibly to secure a better bridge than the town felt able to construct unassisted. In 1792 the bridge, which must have made pretensions to respectability, had probably become a river craft, for the town petitions the county authorities for another.

In 1794 plans more or less elaborate were consummated for a structure, which was inspected by a solemn committee in the later autumn. The conditions of building are worthy of preservation.

Voted that any Person or Persons that will undertake and build with good materials a good substantial Bridge over Chicopee River, so called, at Wallamanumps Falls, and shall keep the same in good repair, shall receive sixty pounds from the town of Ludlow—Provided that the Person or Persons being so entitled to the said sum of sixty pounds for building the said Bridge shall procure sufficient bonds to the Town Treas^r in the sum of one hundred and twenty pounds for the return of the same money into the Treas^r of said Town if the same bridge so built shall not stand the rapidity of the Floods and the Breaking up of the winter, for four years—And also that the same Person or Persons that shall build the same shall be entitled to all the fare or toll allowed by Law from all Persons not being inhabitants of the Town of Ludlow forever.

Eli Putnam, moderator of the meeting at which this action was taken, evidently considered the vote as a challenge, and proceeded to the erection of the first Putnam's or Put's bridge, also, probably, the first toll bridge at that point. Whether it was worthy of the capitals in the town record cannot be determined at this date. It seems, however, to have answered the requirement, for all is quiet until 1801, when the town again finds itself bridgeless. After an unsuccessful attempt to saddle the burden upon the county and an attempt equally unsuccessful to build from town funds, a committee for soliciting subscriptions was appointed, who, it may be presumed, built a bridge, for nothing was said for eleven years. This brings us to the time of the construction of the famous Cooley bridge, which started from a point near the north abutment of the present structure, then ran to a pier in the mid-stream, then at a different angle to an abutment considerably west of the present south abutment. It was a covered bridge, and one through which no one could see. Its height must have been good, for some camels once passed through. The boys of the village were apprised of the coming wonder. The beasts passed through in the night, but Yankee ingenuity could not be baffled by darkness, and so a section was illuminated. It became convenient

TOWN DEVELOPMENT 97

to arrest the camels at the toll house, on the south end, inasmuch as astute legislators had failed to place these animals on the toll list. The delay accomplished at least its intended result, in giving the boys a good glimpse at the rare beasts of burden. So says Hezekiah Root, then one of the "boys." Capt. Ariel Cooley received five hundred dollars for his work, he guaranteeing a free and safe passage across the stream so long as the life of the charter continued.

This bridge having been worn out or carried away, measures were taken to build another, resulting in 1822 in the completion of a substantial structure at a cost of $3,347.30, which stood until 1897, when it was replaced by the present bridge. Abner Putnam, Benjamin Jenks, and Simeon Pease were the committee of construction. References to a bridge where now stands the "red bridge" begin in 1836, while in the following year the present structure was erected. Before reaching it, there was once a dry bridge near the river. The practice of lighting the Jenksville bridge is mentioned first in 1842 as the duty of the town. The road from Eaton's mills to Indian Orchard, including the iron bridge spanning the Chicopee River at that village, was built by order of the county commissioners in 1866. The first bridge at Collins Depot, a pier bridge, dates before 1850, but was carried away by a flood. The present structure was erected in 1851. In 1873 the "red bridge" was thoroughly overhauled and made serviceable for many years; it was a wooden covered bridge. In 1900 an iron bridge was built at Red Bridge.

On October 5, 1869, there was a great flood which carried away bridges and caused heavy damage to highways and railroads.

The condition of the old covered bridge across Chicopee River at the village known as "Put's Bridge" had led the citizens of the town to consider the question of a new one, and in 1896, a committee consisting of J. E. Stevens, E. E. Fuller, and Benjamin F. Burr, was appointed to consider the matter of a new bridge and report at a future meeting of the voters. A careful study of the questions involved and conferences with the authorities of the City of Springfield, the County Commissioner, and the Ludlow Manufacturing Company were held. After an expert examination of the old bridge, the committee reported that the bridge was of doubtful stability, that it could not be left in its existing condition with safety, and recommended a new one.

The town then voted to build, in accordance with the recommendations of the committee, a substantial iron or steel bridge, near the site of the old one. In 1897 an agreement was made among the parties concerned, whereby the City of Springfield and the Town of Ludlow were to contribute equally to the construction and maintenance thereafter. The City of Springfield and the Ludlow Manufacturing Company were each to pay one half the expense of the approaches on the Springfield side, and the Company and the Town of Ludlow were to arrange mutually for those on the Ludlow side. The town appropriated $8,000 for its share of the cost. A fine and substantial iron structure was erected, greatly improving the entrance to the town.

The care of highways in former years was assigned to men in each district and taxpayers were given the opportunity to work out their taxes on the highway if they desired. The compensation has varied at different periods. In 1864 one shilling per hour was allowed. In 1871 twenty cents an hour before July 1, and one shilling per hour after that time, was allowed. In 1877 three dollars and fifty cents a day was allowed for a man with team, and one dollar and twenty-five cents for a man alone, at ten hours' labor. In more recent years the compensation has been increased, and only pay for actual labor performed on the highway allowed, the time spent in going to and from the work not being counted.

In 1879 the town voted that the care of the highways and bridges, except those over the Chicopee River and Higher Brook below Harris's sawmill, and at Ludlow City near Carver's sawmill, be contracted to one man for the term of five years. At the expiration of this term the highways were contracted to one man for one year. In 1899 the highway surveyor was instructed to divide the town into districts and appoint a man in each district to go over the roads at least once in four weeks to remove small stones, repair water courses, and fill up ruts. A highway commissioner who has charge of all the highways in the town is now elected by the voters at the annual town meeting.

In 1896 the town voted to instruct the selectmen to make application for a State highway, and that this road should be located between the village and Ludlow Center. Three hundred dollars was appropriated to defray the expenses of making the application. The efforts of the selectmen were not successful and no State road has yet been located in town.

Railroads

The opening of the Western (now the Boston and Albany) Railroad of course was a matter of interest and indirect value to the town.

There is one railroad extending through the town, the Springfield and Athol, now a part of the New York Central Railroad. When the road was under contemplation, the promoters endeavored to secure town aid in consideration of passing through Ludlow Center. The town voted 89 yeas against 68 nays to take stock in the road, the amount not to exceed three per cent of the valuation of the town, provided the road came within one fourth of a mile of Ashbel P. Chapin's, or what is called the "old Tavern Stand," at Ludlow Center. These terms were not accepted by the railroad, which was built through the village of Ludlow, and passed through the outskirts of the town, stopping its trains at Collins Station and Red Bridge. The construction of this railroad demanded another bridge across the Chicopee, spanning the stream at the Indian Leap, where also the aqueduct for the City of Springfield connects the proximate cliffs on either side of the stream.

A new railroad through the town, called the Hampden Railroad, is now under construction (1911). The entire route covered lies between Athol Junction in the city of Springfield, and Hastings Crossing in the town of Palmer, crossing the town of Ludlow, west to east, from the land of Jackson Cady to the Red Bridge district.

Street Railway

In the winter of 1907 and 1908, the proposition for a street railway in the town was first discussed at a conference of the selectmen with representative officials from the Springfield Street Railway Company and the Ludlow Manufacturing Associates. The first proposition was that the Ludlow Associates should furnish the power, and in addition to the regular traffic, that the Springfield Street Railway should run extra cars, at reduced fares morning and evening, for the accommodation of the mill employees. Lacking agreement, the proposition was abandoned, to be revived later with another, that the Springfield Street Railway furnish all the power and equipment.

The route of the road was mapped out and a franchise about to be granted when a question of fares and transfers once more delayed the work. In the summer of 1910, all the interested parties having finally come to an agreement, a franchise was granted by the selectmen to the Springfield Street Railway to lay rails from the end of the Indian Orchard line across the bridge, along East Street to Sewall, and from Sewall along Winsor to the terminus at Franklin, a distance of nearly one mile.

The work of construction was awarded by contract to the Birnie, Adams & Ruxton Construction Company, who began their work in September, 1911, all the work overhead being done by the Springfield Street Railway Company. Cars were first sent over the tracks December 21, 1911, and the townspeople are looking forward to the increased accommodation with keen pleasure. It is hoped there may be a belt line of the town eventually.

The Ludlow Reservoir

The Ludlow Reservoir, built in 1873 and 1874, is in the eastern part of the town, in the portion familiarly called Cherry Valley. Three natural streams, Broad Brook, Jabish Brook, and Higher Brook, have been diverted to feed this body of water in addition to the large natural watershed. This tract contained some of the best farming land in the town. The reservoir furnishes water to the Town of Ludlow and was until 1910 the principal supply for the City of Springfield, by whom it was built.

It was remarked by one of the reporters of our centennial celebration that "the genius of change has conquered even this stronghold of old New England conservatism at last; as Ludlow was recalling her most treasured associations around the church, Springfield was laying her obnoxious water-pipes at the very door of the old house of worship." When the region known as Cherry Valley was added to the proposed locations of the reservoir for the Springfield water supply, there were few, in town or out, who supposed the place would be selected. The year 1873, however, had hardly begun before the announcement was made that Ludlow brooks would be diverted into an aqueduct leading to the city. The last month of the year found a large number of employees at work upon the basin and the eastern dam. By the first of April the basin and its slopes had been cleared of wood, enough having been cut off to make a solid fence a considerable portion of the way around. On the 6th of April the trenching for the pipes was begun and work resumed upon the dam. On the 9th of October the gangs going towards and from Springfield met, thus practically finishing the work of laying the "big main." Of this largest piping about a half mile of cast iron tube was laid from the southern dam to Higher Brook, while cement-lined sheet iron tubes extend from that point to the city. The number of acres in the bed of the reservoir is four hundred and forty-five, to which must be added a marginal area of three hundred and sixty acres. Of this entire territory two hundred and eighty acres were woodland. Six and three eighths acres of swamp were covered with 13,924 cubic yards of sand, and a little over one half as much was sanded between the south dam and the filter. The land was purchased of Benjamin Sikes and Sons, Reuben

LUDLOW RESERVOIR WITH GATE-HOUSE AND DWELLING

Sikes, Silas Billings, Adelbert L. Bennett, Charles S. Bennett, John L. Banister, Mrs. Margaret Sikes, Marvin King, and Charles W. Alden. A ditch of a mile in length turns Higher Brook into the reservoir, and one, longer and larger, taps Broad Brook just north of the town line. No pains was spared to put the bed of the reservoir into proper condition, as the report of the Water Commissioners for 1875 shows:

In excavating for the trench to take the water from the general level of the flats above the Cherry Valley dam, the material thrown out, which consisted for the most part of coarse gravel, was used to cover the peaty bottom. The area thus trenched and covered was about ten acres. That portion between the Ludlow dam and the filter, an area of three and three fourths acres, has been covered with about two feet in depth of good clean sand. From the Ludlow dam, extending in the valley northeasterly on the low ground for about fifteen acres, a mass of decaying pine stumps has been pulled out and burned. Much pains has been taken to char large stumps while burning the ground over, and burn them up as far as practicable. For this purpose a considerable quantity of kerosene oil has been used with which to ignite them. In this manner, although the stumps would not be entirely consumed, they are so far charred or consumed by the operation as to be rendered much less harmful than they would otherwise be. Of the peaty and swampy portions of the bed of the reservoir, none are covered with less than twelve feet of water with a full pond, the most of which will not be less than sixteen feet.

The commissioners under whose direction the enterprise was carried out, were C. O. Chapin, D. L. Harris, A. D. Briggs, S. W. Porter, G. C. Fisk, and Horace Smith, while Hon. Phinehas Ball of Worcester was chief engineer. A large number of Ludlow men were employed as overseers or workmen.

Ludlow Fire Department

In the month of June, 1910, the Board of Selectmen decided that the town should have a regularly organized fire department. Previous to this date fire protection was dependent upon the fire department belonging to the Ludlow Manufacturing Associates. At the regular town-meeting in April, 1910, there was appropriated the sum of $2,000 to buy land and erect a fire station in the district known as "Little Canada." The necessity of organizing a fire company for this station was very apparent to the selectmen.

The Fire Department was then organized with a chief engineer and twelve men to respond to calls for fires in their respective districts during the night. The chief engineer was appointed the executive officer of the department to take charge of all fires occurring in the town.

When the fire station at the corner of Holyoke Road and Mero Street was completed, it was placed in the care of the newly organized Fire Department. All the fire apparatus which had been previously stored in a shed on Stebbins Street was removed to the new building.

This company since its installation, has given complete satisfaction, especially to the immediate vicinity, where a feeling of security was not possible previously when fire protection was dependent upon the village department.

The village, since the introduction of the waterworks, has been cared for in this respect by the mill fire department, which was reorganized in 1907. It responds to all fires, both day and night, that may occur in the town. There are six small hose houses located at convenient points in the village. Twenty-one Gamewell fire alarm boxes connected with the mill steam whistle are conveniently placed, besides modern hydrants for fire service specially.

The town has also in its service a hose wagon equipped with four hundred feet of first class cotton rubber-lined 2⅝ inch hose, with other necessary equipment, which is kept in the rear of A. H. Bartlett's house on North Street. The first company responding to an alarm of fire in the immediate vicinity uses this wagon.

A fire alarm system was installed in the village in 1907, and in the same year the town voted to establish not fewer than twelve watchmen's stations inside the limits, the same to be placed so as to give the most efficient supervision possible for the entire village. The chief of police was instructed to carry a watchman's clock and visit each station at least once in every two hours between 6 P.M. and 4 A.M., the last round to be finished not later than 3.30 A.M. The clock was to be in charge of the town treasurer, who was to keep paper dials on file for inspection.

Lighting

The village is lighted by electricity, an appropriation being made by the town each year for that purpose and a contract made with the Ludlow Manufacturing Associates to light the streets with all-night service.

The earliest lighting was by means of gas. In 1906 the town granted the Springfield Gas Light Company the right to lay pipes in the village and thus supply the families and business firms with gas.

Telephones

The New England Telephone and Telegraph Company extended its lines into Ludlow in 1903 and many of the farmers as well as the residents of the village installed telephones. Day service only was at first granted, but both day and night service is now in operation. There are in 1911 about 75 telephones in use in the town.

The Post Office

The first post office was established in 1815 at Ludlow Village, supposedly in the store of Benjamin Jenks. The mail route for a while was through the town from north to south, a cavalier with drawn pistols carrying the precious bag.

Home of George N. Hubbard
Formerly a Tavern kept by Elam Wright

The first postmaster, Benjamin Jenks, was appointed February 15, 1821. His successors were Joseph Bucklin, appointed April 23, 1839; E. C. Jenks, February 20, 1843; William B. Miller, August 10, 1848; S. B. Stebbins, May 30, 1849; Jerre Miller, June 18, 1850; W. S. Miller, August 28, 1857; Lewis Harrington, April 26, 1859; E. M. Smith, June 17, 1868; David Joy, January 17, 1873; D. N. Beckwith, June 6, 1878; James Haviland, April 4, 1888; George A. Birnie, December 23, 1889; James Haviland, July 31, 1893; George A. Birnie, August 2, 1897.

The Ludlow Center post office was established June 15, 1874, and opened early in July. Mrs. Susan A. Chapin was appointed first to the headship, and was succeeded November 12, 1891, by Leavitt Perham.

There are two rural free delivery routes in Ludlow. Number one was established February 1, 1902, and number two, May 1, 1902. The carrier for Route No. 1, William C. Walker, was unable to cover his course one day and but half of it on another, during the nine years. Carrier No. 2, Adelbert Corwin, lost one day and covered all but one

THE ELY FULLER TAVERN
Louis Chapin

fourth of his on another in the same time. These are remarkable records.

TAVERNS

On the old Dorman place to the south of the center, it is said, stood the oldest tavern in Ludlow. Another called "The Ark" was kept by Ezekiel Fuller, and stood at the "west middle" part of the town in 1787. It was afterwards the home of Amos Kendall. John Jennings was proprietor of a third tavern at an early date at the Jennings place. About the same time another was kept by Elam Wright near Ezekiel Fuller's.

The first tavern at the center was kept by Ely Fuller for a number of years. It was known as the "old Fuller tavern stand," and was a favorite place of resort. In tavern days this house had piazzas two stories high extending the full length of the house, with an annex

THE DAN HUBBARD HOUSE
Formerly a Tavern. Headquarters of the "Know Nothing Club"

built towards the east with a driveway under the second story. It was a much more pretentious building then, and had a tall sign in front. The green at the front was used as a muster ground for the Ludlow militia between 1820 and 1843. An occasional sham fight made a day to be remembered by the boys and girls who were chaperoned thereto by a trusty neighbor. The town clerk's office was in this house for many years, as Mr. Fuller was the town clerk.' After his death his family

TOWN DEVELOPMENT

lived there for some time. Isaac Plumley succeeded them and was proprietor for a few years.

Calvin Eaton kept the first tavern at Jenksville. He was followed in turn by a Mr. Sawin, Ashley Haydon, and Jerre Miller. There is no tavern or hotel in Ludlow at the present time.

A hundred years or more ago, Ezekiel Barton built what is known as the Dan Hubbard house (south of the one where Charles Fairbanks lives) for a hotel, which was kept by him. Later one of the rooms was used as place of meeting by a political body known as the "Know Nothing Club."

STORES

Elisha Fuller had one of the first stores in Ludlow. It was on the corner opposite the Fuller tavern in Ludlow Center. The date of its opening is not known, but his account book shows charges against Rev. Antipas Steward, who was ordained in 1793 as the first pastor of the town. Mr. Fuller kept this store as late as 1840. About 1850 Lucien Cooley had a store in the Fuller shop. Another was kept at one time in the L of the hotel building. Homer and Arthur King, Chester Graves, F. O. Taylor, E. E. Pease, and Jasper Knight have also been merchants at Ludlow Center.

As early as 1814 Benjamin Jenks and his partners had a store in Jenksville. After the failure of his company in 1846, Ephraim Jenks & Son traded there for a time. Jerre Miller in 1855, and later his son Austin, also had stores there. Harrington & Root, Walter S. Miller, Daniel Beckwith, Eli M. Smith, and David Joy were also storekeepers in the same building. Another store was opened by Howard & Beckwith in 1878. Other merchants in Ludlow Village have been Harmon Booth, Henry P. Jenks, James Jenks, M. DeL. Towne, Frank A. Towne, and Edmund Bliss.

LUDLOW SAVINGS BANK

The Ludlow Savings Bank, situated at the corner of East and Sewall Streets, in the business block owned by the Ludlow Manufacturing Associates, was incorporated February 21, 1888. The incorporators were George A. Birnie, Dr. James W. Hannum, Marquis DeL. Towne, James Henderson, Franklin W. Sturgis, John Edward Stevens, and Charles W. Hubbard. The bank opened for business August 1, 1888, since which time it has paid a four per cent rate of interest. During its twenty-three years' existence, the investments and business ventures of the bank have been unusually successful. In this time there have been but two foreclosures. These were not forced, but deemed advisable by the investment committee. An actual loss of $32.85 represents the only amount lost during the twenty-three years. Ludlow people are justly proud of an institution whose record it would be difficult to excel. Taking into consideration the relative size of the town and the bank with that of larger places, the showing of Ludlow ranks with the best.

The following is taken from the report made to the savings bank commissioners, and shows deposits for the end of each fiscal year:

October 31, 1889, $13,114; 1890, $21,221; 1891, $32,819; 1892, $41,279; 1893, $49,151; 1894, $53,569; 1895, $61,093; 1896, $67,083; 1897, $84,689; 1898, $86,009; 1899, $102,337; 1900, $118,060; 1901, $138,673; 1902, $177,020; 1903, $215,103; 1904, $263,207; 1905, $333,828; 1906, $408,009; 1907, $503,204; 1908, $486,983; 1909, $525,535; 1910, $518,122. These statistics emphasize better than words the size of the bank and its rapid growth. Every application for a loan is referred to the investment committee, which considers the security carefully, and passes judgment accordingly. This method has thus afforded an opportunity for the bank to establish a reputation of being too hard a nut for the grafter or man with a bogus deal to crack.

The investment committee consists of the president, James Henderson (1911), George D. Green, Michael H. Lyons, Walter S. Colwell, and Edward E. Fuller. The personal business sense of each member of the committee has led them to make sound and conservative judgments, that have oftentimes rendered it easier to secure more on loan from larger institutions. Trustees are elected each year from the members of the corporation. At present there are twenty-three. Since its incorporation the bank has had five presidents. The first was Charles F. Grosvenor, now of Springfield, Vt.; the second, George D. Green, now of Springfield, Mass.; the third, Alfred S. Packard, now of Springfield, Mass.; the fourth, Dr. J. W. Hannum, of Ludlow, Mass.; the fifth, James Henderson, of Ludlow, Mass. At no time during its incorporation has the bank been in a better financial condition than at present (1911); it has the confidence of the townspeople of all nationalities.

Treasurer George A. Birnie is the active head of the bank, through whom all financial dealings are made. Ludlow is doubly fortunate in

TOWN DEVELOPMENT

possessing men with the executive ability to establish and to carry an institution so successfully.

To safeguard further the interests of its investors, the accounts are audited thoroughly twice a year by four of the bank trustees appointed for the purpose. Every account is carefully followed up and rechecked. This gives the auditors a thorough knowledge of the bank's doings. The present auditors are Charles W. Gowan, James Henderson, Harley W. Morrill, and Frank N. Moore (1911).

Court History

In spite of all the influences that make for good in a community, there are sure to be disturbing elements. For this reason laws must be made and offenders must be punished. Ludlow was not exempt from this necessity and accordingly a court was established and a trial justice appointed.

The first trial justice of the town was John Padelford Hubbard. He was appointed in the year 1875 and continued in office until his death in 1881. He was succeeded by Charles F. Grosvenor, who was appointed by Gov. John D. Long in 1881, reappointed in 1884 by Gov. George D. Robinson, in 1887 by Gov. Oliver Ames, and resigned in 1888. At the solicitation of the selectmen and others, he was again appointed trial justice in 1891 by Gov. William E. Russell and held the office until he moved to Palmer in 1892. The most exciting of all events connected with his administration was at the time of a strike at the mills of the Ludlow Manufacturing Company, when upon the complaint of Mr. L. H. Brigham, who was agent of the mills at that period, Mr. Grosvenor was routed out of bed to issue warrants. These trials were held in the rear of the store occupied by Druggist C. S. Browning, in the old Joy building, North Street, and later at Mr. Grosvenor's place of business on Hubbard Street. During his term of office the criminal and civil business gradually lessened, until there was practically nothing to do. From 1892 until 1905 the court proceedings were held in Springfield and sometimes in Palmer.

For the convenience of the people Gov. Eben S. Draper appointed George A. Birnie trial justice in 1905. The town had made a large gain in population and it became necessary to have a resident trial justice. When Justice Birnie assumed the duties of the office, there was much lawlessness, which through his efforts has been reduced to a minimum.

He had a number of severe cases to deal with and was not long in impressing upon the minds of the offenders that he would insist on good behavior in the town. During his term of office he has had a number of cases of illegal liquor selling, which is always likely to exist in a no-license town. It was during his term of office that George Freeman Cook shot and killed Herbert E. White and was committed to the grand jury.

The Library

In 1881, for the benefit of the employees of the Ludlow Manufacturing Company, a small library with reading room and social room in connection was opened, under the direction of Mr. Hubbard. This room was in the "Old Tavern house," which formerly stood a short distance from the present library building. At its beginning this little library contained four hundred volumes, while the reading room boasted half a dozen magazines. After a time it was moved to a building standing where the present office of the Ludlow Manufacturing Associates' office is located. In 1890 the collection of 1,500 volumes was removed to the new library building.

This building was presented to the town by the family of the late Charles T. Hubbard, formerly of the Ludlow Manufacturing Company, with the following conditions:

(1) The building is to be forever maintained in proper repair at the expense of the town as a public library and reading room; (2) the library to be open for the delivery of books at least two evenings in a week for two hours each evening; (3) the lower rooms to be used for educational and social purposes, but not for town or political meetings; (4) the inscription "Hubbard Memorial" to be maintained over the entrance, together with a bronze tablet in the porch bearing the inscription, "Erected to the memory of Charles Townsend Hubbard by his wife and children, 1888."

At a special meeting of the town in May, 1888, it was unanimously voted to accept this proposed gift and also a proposed gift of about fifteen hundred volumes from the Ludlow Manufacturing Company to be placed and maintained in the library building to be erected.

At this meeting the following resolution was passed: Whereas the family of the late Charles T. Hubbard has proffered to the town of Ludlow for its acceptance, under merely nominal conditions, a building

LUDLOW COURT ROOM, NORTH STREET

TOWN DEVELOPMENT 115

for library purposes as well as a social home for the townspeople; a building which promises to be a source of pleasure and pride, "a thing of beauty and a joy forever," therefore be it resolved, that we, the voters of the town of Ludlow in town meeting assembled, appreciate heartily the interest expressed in our welfare and the sympathy felt for our aspirations, as well as the liberality and generosity illustrated by the gift, and we desire further to pay our tribute of respect to him whose memory this hall perpetuates. And be it further resolved, that we also

HUBBARD MEMORIAL LIBRARY

wish to give expression to our pleasure and gratitude in receiving the gift of their library at the hands of the Ludlow Manufacturing Company.

The new building was erected in 1889 and the following spring was presented to the town by Governor Robinson in the presence of a large audience of townspeople assembled in Mill No. 6 of the Ludlow Manufacturing Company. The gift was accepted for the town by Mr. Benjamin F. Burr.

More volumes have been added to the collection from year to year by the family of Mr. Hubbard and the Ludlow Manufacturing Associates. There are at present between four and five thousand volumes. The reading room is supplied with a large number of newspapers and magazines from an annual appropriation made by the town.

Antiques and Relics

At the regular annual town meeting held in March, 1907, a committee on antiques and relics was appointed as follows: Gillen D. Atchinson, E. T. Potter, Wilbur F. Miller, Irene T. Jones, and Mrs. A. C. Birnie.

The purpose in appointing this committee was to preserve the antiques, relics, and curios of the town. The use of the west room on the first floor of the Hubbard Memorial Library building was secured through the courtesy of the library trustees. An effort has been made to secure the photographs of all the clergy of the five churches from the date of their organization to the present. These photographs are hung on the south wall of the room in groups according to the church. There are three cases containing many valuable articles. An old cradle, spinning wheels, saddlebags, several old guns, andirons, etc., are arranged on the floor.

SADDLEBAGS FORMELY BELONGING TO ASHBEL BURR

Among the specially notable articles in the collection are: a pewter communion service given to the Congregational Church in Ludlow Center by the First Church of Springfield, and used from 1789 until 1846, when a silver service was presented to the church by Abner Cady; the first pewter communion service used by the Methodist Church in 1835; the sword, sash, and belt given to Captain H. A. Hubbard by the people of Ludlow; a list of the company he raised and his picture, given by his nieces; an old cartridge box carried through the Revolutionary War by Deacon Oliver Dutton; a collection of bottles, one blown in the glass factory once located north of Ludlow Center; a machine to pare apples, made by a Ludlow boy when only sixteen years old; a Testament used by the Rev. Alexander McLean; a very rare Masonic jewel; and a britannia teapot, loaned by Mrs. Frances (Chandler) Sikes.

THE LUDLOW HOSPITAL

On April 28, 1908, a meeting of the citizens of the town was called for the purpose of organizing a society to accept, maintain, and carry on a hospital for the benefit of this and adjoining towns, on the provisions offered by the Ludlow Manufacturing Associates.

This meeting was largely attended, among those present being Charles W. Hubbard, treasurer of the Ludlow Manufacturing Associates, who made the following offer: The Associates would give to the society, if formed, the use of the hospital rooms as arranged, fully equipped with all necessary furnishings, lighted and heated, free of rent, and for every dollar received by said society, either in contributions or membership fees, they would contribute a dollar; that the society be known as the Ludlow Hospital Society, should be composed of a president, vice-president, secretary and treasurer, membership committee, aids and charities committee, and visiting committee; the president, vice-president, treasurer, and the chairman of the above three committees should be the executive committee to take charge and manage the affairs of the hospital.

This offer was accepted by the meeting and an organization was immediately formed by the election of Dr. J. W. Hannum, president; George D. Green, vice-president; George A. Birnie, secretary and treasurer; James B. Irwin, chairman of membership committee; Robert Kyle, chairman of aids and charities; Miss Emma A. Warner, chairman of visiting committee.

By-laws were adopted, and after an address by Dr. Palmer of South

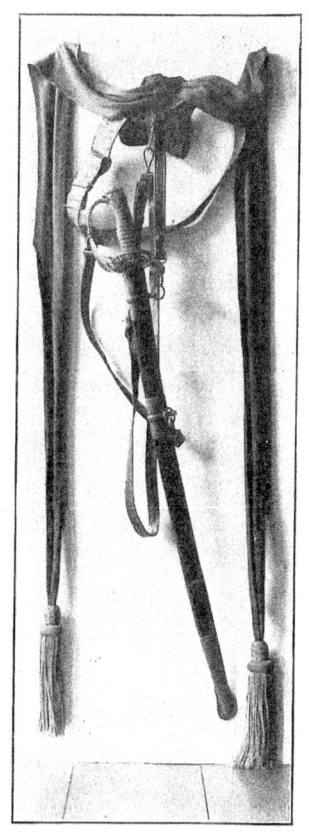

SWORD, SASH, AND BELT PRESENTED TO CAPT. H. A. HUBBARD BY THE TOWN OF LUDLOW

Framingham, Mass., on hospitals in general, and the beginning and development of the South Framingham Hospital, the meeting adjourned.

The hospital was opened for business July 3, 1908. Only the top floor of the two rear sections of the building was used for hospital purposes. Not having been able to secure the services of a superintendent, two nurses were engaged from Springfield, who, under the direction of the president, managed the hospital until July 20, 1908, when Miss Emma M. Glover, assistant matron and superintendent of nurses at Waltham, became superintendent.

The Misses Annie and M. Louise Stebbins and Mrs. Thornton Parker, as a testimonial to their father, a former president of the Ludlow Manufacturing Company, furnished the operating room and also an X-ray machine, which, with the furnishings supplied by the Ludlow Manufacturing Associates, make the Ludlow Hospital one of the best equipped small hospitals in this section of the state.

Rev. Father Power of Indian Orchard donated to the society a communion set, which has been used upon all occasions when the rites of the Roman Catholic Church have been observed in the hospital, and the gift has been appreciated by society and patients.

The hospital has been in successful operation three years. The first year (1908–1909) 41 patients were admitted, the second (1909–1910), 85, and the third (1910–1911), 170.

As a charitable and educational institution the Ludlow Hospital should remain a permanent interest among the activities of the town.

Fraternal Organizations

Brigham Lodge of Masons.—Until 1891 the Masons of Ludlow belonged to lodges in Chicopee, Wilbraham, and Springfield. On account of the distance from their homes and the inconveniences of travel, it was suggested that efforts be made to establish a lodge in Ludlow. Acting on this suggestion a meeting was called and finally 33 Masons petitioned the Grand Lodge in Boston to grant a dispensation for a new branch. This was allowed, and the lodge was instituted. The meetings were held in a room on the top floor of the grammar school building. The lodge was called Brigham Lodge in honor of Lemuel H. Brigham, a retired agent of the Ludlow Manufacturing Company, who had given valuable assistance in its establishment. Through the efforts of John E. Stevens, then agent of the company, the said company erected a Masonic Hall in

Ludlow Hospital Building

Winsor Street, and rented it to the lodge on a five-year lease, this lease to be renewed every five years thereafter. The first three officers were Charles F. Grosvenor, W. M.; Albert H. Halford, S. W.; Frank King, J. W. Worshipful Albert H. Halford in 1903 became district deputy grand master of the sixteenth Masonic District, to which district Brigham Lodge belonged. Worshipful Hugh M. Cramond was appointed grand marshal. Brigham Lodge now (1911) has 145 members. Regular communications are held on the first Tuesday in each month; the annual communication occurs on the first Tuesday in November. Indian Orchard Lodge, recently instituted (1911), is the child of Brigham Lodge, as Brigham Lodge was the offspring of Newton Lodge of Wilbraham.

Charter Members.—Charles F. Grosvenor, Frank S. King, Frank A. Towne, Emerson F. Lovett, George L. Streeter, Henry Burke, Alfred J. Hobson, Alfred H. Bartlett, Oscar J. Hunt, Charles Sikes, Benjamin F. Burr, John L. Mason, Austin E. Morse, William O'Neill, Charles A. Smith, David L. Fuller, David C. Jones, Albert H. Halford, Frederick L. Burr, Charles F. Howard, Walter B. Atchinson, George W. Miller, John Hobson, Austin F. Nash, George F. Greenhalgh, Marquis DeL. Towne, James Lowe, Gilbert S. Atchinson, George Elphinstone, Henry W. Keyes, Edward E. Fuller, Jean B. Bergeron, George D. Green.

Past Masters.—*Charles F. Grosvenor, †Albert H. Halford, George W. Miller, Walter B. Atchinson, †James Henderson, *William H. Tipping, Alexander H. Fobare, Hugh M. Cramond, †Richard Tipping, James W. Simes, Alexander F. Winton, Simpson McPhail, Walter Bennett, George Elphinstone, Jr., William T. Eaton, Walter Winton.

Ludlow Farmers Club.—About fifty years ago a farmers' club was started by a few middle-aged men and women for social pleasure and farm profit. The idea became very popular and soon the club numbered twenty couples. Meetings were held every two weeks during the winter, with a summer outing to Mount Holyoke, the Shaker Settlement at Enfield, and other places of interest. Guests were invited from outside making usually a party of 100 persons. At the regular meetings guests were frequently present. The members were very punctual in attendance, meeting in the afternoon at two o'clock. Supper was served at six, and in the evening the men and women assembled in separate rooms until nine o'clock, when they came together for an hour of social intercourse, closing at ten. These meetings continued for twenty years

*Demitted. †Deceased.

with no break; no serious illness and no deaths came to interrupt this friendly and helpful gathering. Within two years' time seven strong men died. This affliction was more than the members could endure and no meetings were held after this time. The young people, the sons and daughters of the old members, took up the work and organized the Young People's Farmers Club of Ludlow. Their meetings were conducted along similar lines with much success, but the club was finally absorbed by the Ludlow Grange.

EDWARD EARLE CHAPMAN

Ludlow Grange, Patrons of Husbandry, No. 179, was organized by George R. Chase, assisted by Francis E. Clark of Wilbraham, October 21, 1889, with 26 charter members. Mr. C. L. Buell was the first master. Until 1894 the meetings were held in the Congregational chapel or Methodist vestry, but during that year the Grange voted to petition the town "to see if they will give the Grange, free of rent, the use of the lower floor of the Town Hall, with the privilege of making such repairs and alterations as they may see fit." This was done, and the present Grange Hall was fitted up at the expense of the Grange, which has since occupied and controlled it. No. 179 is included in the jurisdiction of Springfield Pomona Grange, which is entertained here once a year. This grange has supplied many officers for Pomona, among them three masters—Frank G. Bennett, Edward E. Chapman, and Charles B. Bennett; also two State deputies—Frank G. Bennett for two years, Edward E. Chapman for ten years; also one State officer—Edward E.

Chapman, who has been overseer of the Massachusetts State Grange for 1910 and 1911. Meetings are held twice a month, at which business is transacted and a literary program given, consisting of music, readings, papers, etc., and questions of interest are discussed.

List of Worthy Masters.—1889, Chauncey L. Buell; 1890, 1891, Gilbert S. Atchinson; 1892, 1893, Frank G. Bennett; 1894, Fred O. Taylor; 1895, 1896, Frank E. Sikes; 1897, Gillen D. Atchinson; 1898, 1899, 1900, Edward E. Chapman; 1901, 1902, Charles B. Bennett; 1903, E. Newton Fisher; 1904, 1905, Elbridge J. Streeter; 1906, Caleb B. Estey; 1907, 1908, Edward E. Chapman; 1909, 1910, George Davis; 1911, William Ashwell.

Ludlow Women's Club.—This club was organized February 26, 1908, with seven members. During that year the number was increased to twenty-six. The purpose of the club is to consider topics of vital interest,—social, literary, scientific, artistic, historical, ethical,—and other fields of importance; to promote culture, and cordial personal relations among women, and to contribute to the welfare of the community.

The Ludlow Social and Debating Club.—In 1892, the Scotchmen of Ludlow formed the Ludlow Burns Social Club for the purpose of conducting the entertainments on New Year's Eve and Robert Burns's birthday, and to lend a helping hand to those in need. The charter members were: William P. McFarlane, president; George Elphinstone, secretary; George Mackintosh, treasurer; and Charles Mitchell, guard; William Palmer, Walter Duncan, Hugh M. Cramond, Charles Graham, David Ogilvie, Richard Proctor, James Wilson, John Duffy, John Craige, and George Ogilvie. In 1897, many others having become interested in the work of the Club, expressed a desire to join it and enlarge its activities. They were admitted and the name was then changed to the Ludlow Social and Debating Club. Much pleasure and benefit have been derived by this change.

Physicians

Dr. Aaron John Miller was the first physician to practice in Ludlow. He was a surgeon in the Revolutionary War, and is reliably reported to have been a member of the original Boston Tea Party. The next in order are: Francis Percival; Benjamin Trask, who practiced here in 1777; a Dr. Wood, who lived at "Miller Corner" about the same time; Simpson Ellis; David Lyon; Sylvester Nash, who married a daughter of the Rev.

Antipas Steward; Philip Lyon, in 1802; Drs. Taintor, Sutton, Munger, and Hamilton; Estes Howe, from Belchertown, a commissioned officer in the Continental Army, June 17, 1775; Elijah Caswell, who practiced many years and lived on the "Caswell place," west of the Center; Washington B. Alden, at Ludlow Center; Dr. Bassett, about 1840; R. G. English; William B. Miller, at Jenksville, but later removed to Springfield; Henry M. T. Smith, C. B. Smith, Robert Wood at Jenksville; Dr. King, Benjamin K. Johnson, Horace B. Miller, J. W. Lyman (died about 1880), C. J. Ray, M. B. Landers, A. J. Treichler, C. H. Lortie, J. W. Hannum (died Dec. 9, 1911), G. H. Aldrich, and P. A. Hoyt.

Lawyers

John Jennings practiced in Ludlow at a very early date and is said to have been the only one who ever did so. His office was in his house near the Ezekiel Fuller residence. That he was a regular licensed attorney is not known. That he served his clients well is fully attested. His main usefulness seems to have been in drawing up legal papers and in giving wholesome advice.

First Meeting-House, Ludlow Center

V

THE FIRST OR TOWN CHURCH

THE MEETING-HOUSE—Places of meeting—Location of center of district—Site chosen—Erection of building—Improvements—New building—Fire—Third building—Dedication—Additions.

THE MINISTERS—The first minister, Rev. Pelatiah Chapin—Other early ministers—Stephen Burroughs—First ordination and installation—Rev. Antipas Steward—Mr. Steward and his chorister—Selection from one of his sermons—Dissatisfaction—Dismissal of Mr. Steward—Union efforts—Elder Elijah Hedding—Rev. Alexander McLean—Difficulty—Rev. E. B. Wright—Rev. D. R. Austin—Rev. Alonzo Sanderson—Rev. Jeremy Webster Tuck—Succeeding ministers—Pastors.

CHURCH ORGANIZATION — Early membership — First great revival—Additional members—Succeeding revivals—Deacons—Organization of parish—Ministry fund—Parish membership rule—Adoption of church creed and covenant—Church regulations—Incorporation of church and parish—Church harmony—Benevolences—Children's Sunday—Prayer meetings—Old Home Sunday—Choristers—Musical instruments—Organists—Gifts and bequests—Deacons—Clerks of parish—Church societies—Sabbath school.

THE MEETING-HOUSE

IT seems to have been the universal practice of our New England fathers to provide themselves with the ordinances of religion as early as possible after a settlement was made. The first meeting had been held, the new district named, and all preparations made for a corporate existence, but nothing had been done to establish a church. They desired a place for convenient worship, and so those worshiping westward turned from their ecclesiastical home to find another eastward; those whose heartstrings had entwined about the Wilbraham sanctuary loosened the tendrils and trained them about the remoter center northward.

We are not left wholly to conjecture respecting the places used for transacting town business and for public worship previous to the erection of a building devoted especially to these purposes. The first district meeting was held at the home of Abner Hitchcock, March 16, 1774. The second meeting was also held at Abner Hitchcock's a few weeks later

(April 22). A third (adjourned) meeting was held on June 1st, probably at the same place, though the record does not state. We find that the three favorite places for the early district meetings were the homes of Abner Hitchcock, Joshua Fuller, and Jacob Kendall. In 1777 the houses of James Kendall and Samuel Scranton were prescribed as places for assembly in worship and for town business. Barns also seem to have been brought into requisition. One formerly standing opposite the home of James Leroy Simonds, and torn down within the memory of many now living, was thus used. Public worship was also held in a barn in the vicinity of the Dorman place and near the old Methodist Church. It was here that the notorious Stephen Burroughs is said to have preached. A barn in front of the residence of Simeon Pease was likewise utilized.

June 1, 1774, in the first year of the incorporation of the district of Ludlow, it was voted to choose a committee to find the center of the district as the location for a meeting-house. Abner Sikes, Edmond Damon, and Jonathan Bartlett were chosen. What this committee did or did not do in the matter of finding the center of the town as a location for a meeting-house is not recorded. If they came to any conclusion, it was not satisfactory. Another committee, Abner Sikes, Edmond Damon, Samuel Ackley, and Oliver Chapin, appointed for the same purpose, seems to have accomplished no more. It is rumored that the original finding of the center was in the midst of Cedar Swamp—a somewhat shaky foundation for town ecclesiastics! It has since been ascertained that the actual center of the district is just west of the present First Church and the town has erected a stone marker there.

The first public act with reference to building a meeting-house was on December 17, 1778, but it was subsequently reconsidered. The causes to which Mr. Tuck refers in his Historical Address (see Part III)—the scarcity of money and the absorption of interest in the Revolutionary War—were doubtless instrumental in the delay experienced in erecting the desired place of worship.

In the town meeting of March 25, 1780 (*vide* records), Dea. Nathan Smith of Granby, Dea. David Nash of South Hadley, and Dea. John Hitchcock of Wilbraham were asked to serve as a committee to set a stake where the meeting-house should be built. These worthy deacons performed their task acceptably and set the stake just in front of where the present house stands. The next year (November, 1781) there is a record of a town meeting called at the stake. But evidently the people

THE FIRST OR TOWN CHURCH

did not find the stake sufficient shelter for the transaction of business, for after organizing they adjourned to the house of Joshua Fuller (near the post office).

February 26, 1782, it was voted that a meeting-house be erected on the place designated by the honorable committee above-mentioned. It was further voted that £200 be raised for the purpose. On January 28, 1783—the year of the close of the Revolutionary War—John Sikes, Moses Wilder, Timothy Keyes, James Kendall, and Isaac Brewer were chosen a committee to erect said house. On the following April 7, it was voted to raise £30 to procure shingles and nails to be used in the erection of said house. June 9 it was voted that the building should be underpinned with hewn stone. A Mr. Loomis of Monson received the contract for framing the building. The work of hewing the timbers and nearly all that of construction seems to have been performed gratuitously by the people of the community. Probably the building was done by odd jobs between planting and hoeing and after haying. The summer had passed and it was late autumn before the frame was ready to be raised, for it was the 23d of October that the building committee was authorized by a town meeting held at the stake to procure "a sufficient quantity of rum for raising the meeting-house frame." (See Historical Address, Part III.) On December 22 of the same year an additional £200 was voted to be used to finish said house. The building seems to have proceeded slowly, for not until August 3, 1784, was it sufficiently completed to be used for a town meeting. For several years it remained unfinished, with neither clapboards nor plaster, and if there was a floor it was of the roughest kind. Alfred Putnam was told by Stillman Alden that the audience stood throughout the service in the early days of its occupancy, before the pews were built. The pulpit at first was a carpenter's bench, and the seats rough planks supported by blocks. Later a high pulpit was built. (See Historical Address, Part III.) During the winter people used to go a mile or more at noon for live coals to heat their foot stoves for the afternoon meeting.

In June, 1788, some of the people evinced a desire to have the building improved, but failed to secure the approbation of the town. The agitation evidently was beneficial, for four months later (October 13), Varriner, Miller, and Burr were made a committee to repair the house. Very likely there were needed the chats of a winter to discuss the matter. On March 2, 1789, specific instructions followed. They were to lay a floor, make doors, and clapboard the building. On the following October 27, £30 was allowed for the work. Surely the temple was now goodly indeed; what more could man desire?

O the pride of humanity! June 11, 1791, it was voted to pay sundry charges for building the meeting-house, and on the following November 11, a committee was chosen to paint said house and £18 was appropriated for that purpose. One might go around the world half a dozen times while they were doing the work, but the bill finally appeared in July, 1793. One extravagance breeds another, and in 1795 the town voted its third £200 for making "said house more elegant and commodious." It may not be amiss to state that federal money was now fast displacing English currency, and the above sum appeared on the last day of November, 1796, as $666.66. On November 2, 1797, in rather ambiguous language, it was "voted a committee to seat the meeting-house." In two years and a half the indignant citizens vote to bring their slothful contractor, one "Lomis," to terms by law if need be, and appoint a committee to put glass in the windows.

The church edifice seems to have been serving its day and generation, gradually succumbing to wind and weather, and occasionally pressing a claim for repairs, with infrequent success. Used as meeting-house in a municipal as well as religious sense, it had every opportunity for a display of its excellences or its defects. In 1805 there is record of a loud call for glass in the windows and for wooden steps up which the worthies might climb on their entrance to the sanctuary, nor was the cry disregarded. The people could not have been over-nice in their architectural demands, for they abide in patience a brace of decades. Then the pent-up longings of years burst forth wildly as demands began to be made. The honest sashes again demanded glass, the wooden steps, probably never painted, had rotted away, while some who had found necessity for an umbrella in church averred to the astonished managers that the roof needed patching; whereat there were orders at solemn conclave that measures should be taken to stop the "leaks in the roof, if there be any." On July 1, 1825, it was voted that individuals have liberty to paint the meeting-house and place stone steps at the door.

Dea. Stephen Jones passed a paper around for the purpose, and obtained $146.32, of which sum $25 was given by the "Springfield Manufacturing Company." One year later, these improvements having been consummated, the town had the daring to allow a committee of

THE FIRST OR TOWN CHURCH

three (who must be immortalized—they were Benjamin Jenks, John Moody, Eliphal Booth) to put in a stove, at the expense of individuals. It was purchased of the Jenks Company and is still in use. Wilbur F. Miller's mother, a member of the choir, was in church on the Sunday after its installation. She remembered that a lady fainted away, though not because the church was overheated, for there had never been a fire in the stove. Possibly the thought of the supposed heat was overpowering.

As years glided by the old church had been falling into decay, until a new edifice seemed a necessity. At least so thought a majority of the people after holding several meetings in regard to the advisability of making extensive repairs or of building anew. In 1839 a committee to solicit subscriptions was appointed, which soon obtained over $3,000.

After services were discontinued, the old building was purchased by Increase Sikes for about $50, and removed to its present site, where it has stood ever since, a shield for those noble oaks which link the days of successive generations. Mr. Sikes planned using it for sheep and began taking out the pews, but, instead, sold it to the town, and until 1893, with few exceptions, it was used for town meetings, and more or less for political and religious purposes. It has been in a way made over, and is now known as Grange Hall, the upper story being used for a hall and the lower story by the Ludlow Grange.

A tablet containing the following inscription, written by Benjamin F. Burr, has been placed in the ancient building:

THE FIRST CHURCH BUILDING OF LUDLOW

This building was the first church erected in Ludlow, in 1783 and 1784, and stood on the ground where the Soldiers' Monument now stands. It was moved to its present location between 1841 and 1845, and used as a town house. It was turned one quarter way round. The present entrance faced the east. The west side faced the south and was the main entrance, and had large double doors. The north end faced the west and was the west entrance.

One of the original pews is in the southwest corner of the building.

The second church building was begun in 1840 and was completed in April, 1841. Asa Wright, Theodore Sikes, and Noah Clark were the builders, and John Moody, Simeon Pease, Chester Sikes, Theodore Sikes, and Noah Clark were the building committee. As usual the plan was enlarged somewhat during the construction. A portico and a bell weighing about 300 pounds were added, making the total cost, $4,127.09. The total subscriptions were about $3,800, leaving a debt of a little more than $300.

PEW IN FIRST CHURCH BUILDING

It seems to have been the custom to give to the lowest bidder the care of the meeting-house, the ringing of the bell, and other necessary work, the sums ranging from $16.50 to $24.00 per annum. The slips were rented in January, and the house was dedicated January 20, 1841. The following order of exercises was observed:

1. Singing; 2. Invocation, by Rev. Mr. Rogers of Chicopee Falls; 3. Reading Scriptures; 4. Singing; 5. Prayer, by Rev. Mr. Rogers; 6. Singing; 7. Sermon, by Rev. Mr. Clapp of Cabotville; 8. Prayer of dedication, by the pastor; 9. Singing; 10. Benediction; 11. Singing.

This building, after undergoing some changes and repairs, was burned in the early hours of Saturday morning, January 15, 1859. The cause of the fire is unknown. The loss was about $4,000. It was insured for $2,000 in the old Springfield Fire Assurance Company.

At first pastor and people were disheartened, but soon courage was renewed. This event, which so saddened the last days of his ministry, Mr. Tuck has described in his Historical Address (see Part III). There was no delay in services after the fire. A courteous invitation from the Methodists to the privileges of their sanctuary for the time being was declined. An informal meeting of the church and society was held on the next Monday, and it was voted to continue the services in the venerable town house. At a meeting later in the month it was

First Congregational Church, Ludlow Center

THE FIRST OR TOWN CHURCH

unanimously voted to build on the same site a suitable house of worship, and to circulate papers out of the parish for the purpose of securing subscriptions, and that the parish by a tax on the polls and estates of its members should raise the balance of such sum as might be needed in the erection of said house.

By the aid of generous subscriptions and the insurance on the burned building, it was possible to begin the erection of a new church at once. Mr. Chauncey Shepard of Springfield was the architect, and Messrs. Mayo and Hallett, also of Springfield, the contractors.

There were busy days throughout that year, but they were days of profit and success, for their labors resulted in the present symmetrical and commodious structure. The total cost of the building was $6,021.88; of the church furnishings about $500, provided by the Social Circle; of the organ $215, raised by subscription.

The dedication occurred December 7, 1859, and was of course a notable event. Mr. Tuck, that very day dismissed from the church, preached the sermon from Zech. 4:7, "He shall bring forth the headstone thereof with shoutings, crying, Grace, grace unto it," and Revelation 22:21, "The grace of our Lord Jesus Christ be with you all. Amen." Besides the singing, the other exercises consisted of the invocation by Rev. L. H. Cone, prayer by Rev. S. Miller, and dedicatory prayer by Rev. J. Vaill, D.D. An original dedication hymn by Hon. G. M. Fisk, a native of the town, was sung. We cannot refrain from giving a portion:

> O'er the ashes of the Past,
>   We this holy temple rear;
> And of thee, O Lord, we ask
>   To reveal thy presence here;
> Make this house thy dwelling place,
>   Make this roof thy sheltering hand,
> Fill these courts with heavenly grace—
>   Fill them with thy chosen band.
>
> May thy servant who shall toil
>   In this vineyard of the Lord,
> Find that here is Christian soil
>   Which shall yield a rich reward;
> Strengthen him to guide aright
>   Those who heavenly wisdom seek,
> Leading them from gloom to light,
>   By the truths that he shall speak.

A chapel was erected at the cost of $1,514.94 during the pastorate of Mr. Bridgman.

At a meeting held December 30, 1874, it was voted to build a parsonage at a cost not to exceed $2,500, and to raise this sum, first, by subscriptions, and the remainder to cover the amount by assessing a tax upon the polls and estates of the members of the parish. The parsonage was erected in 1875, at an expenditure of $2,451.77. May 1, 1877, fruit and ornamental trees were set out around the parsonage.

PARSONAGE OF FIRST CONGREGATIONAL CHURCH, LUDLOW CENTER.

July 1, 1877, the church was struck by lightning, slight damage being done to the ceiling and carpets. In May, 1880, fourteen persons set out fourteen trees upon the grounds about the church. A new Clough & Warren organ was presented to the church in 1883 by Mrs. Samuel White. In 1897 the pulpit, which was a monument of Mr. Pierce's workmanship, was removed, the platform lowered, and new furniture built, consisting of six pieces, the work being done chiefly by the pastor, Rev. Mr. Francis; the expense for all, including new carpet, being $69.75.

THE FIRST OR TOWN CHURCH

The money was raised by subscription in part and given otherwise so as to include all portions of the church and congregation, as follows: From the men, for the platform, $28.25; from the ladies, for the carpet, $23.00; from the King's Daughters, for a desk, $5.00; from the young people, for chairs, $3.00; from children under 8 years, for a large chair, $4.50. The new pulpit was dedicated in June, on Children's Sunday,

In 1903, four of the front pews in the church were removed, the platform enlarged, and the pulpit moved forward to make room for the choir to be seated behind the pastor, and on July 19 of the same year, they occupied their new place.

THE MINISTERS

We learn from the records that on April 22, 1774, about two months after the incorporation of the district of Ludlow, the people gathered at the house of Abner Hitchcock and voted "to hire Mr. Pelatiah Chapin," whom they desired to have preach. John Hubbard, Abner Sikes, and Joseph Jones were chosen "for to agree with Mr Chapin."

In October, the committee chosen "for to agree with Mr Chapin," having harvested a crop, planted since their appointment, reported that they had seen Mr. Chapin, and secured his services. The district ratified their action, and authorized them to continue in their official relation.

At a meeting held March 20, 1775, a committee was chosen to hire Rev. Pelatiah Chapin to preach for six months. In 1776, another committee was appointed to apply to the neighboring ministers "to request that they or any of them will give us a day's preaching," and they were also to advise with these neighboring ministers with regard to hiring a minister. In 1777, the selectmen were instructed to "provide a place for a candidate to board at while preaching among us." In December of that year, it was voted "to hire the Rev. Mr. Davenport for one month and longer, if the committee see fitt." He seems to have made little impression, for in 1778, Jonathan Bartlett, Joshua Fuller, and Joseph Hitchcock were selected "to hire a Candidate." Who supplied from 1777 to 1783 the records do not show. It may be inferred that Rev. Mr. Hutchinson preached at some time during those years, for in 1783 it was voted "to hire Mr. Hutchinson to preach with us again." Stephen Burroughs in 1783 or 1784 preached his first sermon in this town under the assumed name of Davis. He played an important part in an episode of which he gives the account following. The Fuller named must have been Joshua, and the place of entertainment, the old Dorman house.

After mentioning the chain of circumstances leading to his determination to preach, and describing his clothing, "which consisted of a light gray coat, with silver-plated buttons, green vest, and red velvet breeches," Mr. Burroughs goes on thus:

> Hearing of a place called Ludlow, not far distant, where they were destitute of a clergyman, I bent my course that way, it being Saturday, and intended to preach the next day, if I proved successful. I arrived about noon, and put up at the house of one Fuller, whom I found to be a leading man in their religious society. I introduced myself to him as a clergyman, and he gave me an invitation to spend the Sabbath with them and preach. You will readily conclude that I did not refuse this invitation. . . . I retired to rest at the usual time, and after I had composed my mind sufficiently for reflection, I began to consider under what situation my affairs now stood, and what was to be done under present circumstances. I had engaged to preach on the morrow. . . . People had been notified that a sermon would be delivered. This business I never had attempted. . . . What, said I, would be my feelings, should I make some egregious blunder in traveling this unbeaten road? . . . These considerations made so dismal an appearance, that I at once concluded to get up, take my horse privately out of the stable and depart, rather than run the risk of the dangers which were before me. But upon more mature reflection, I found the hard hand of necessity compelled me to stay. When I awoke the next morning, my heart beat with anxious palpitation for the issue of the day. . . . The time for assembling approached! I saw people began to come together. My feelings were all in arms against me, my heart would almost leap into my mouth. . . . Why, said I, am I thus perturbated with these whimsical feelings? I know my dress is against me, and will cause some speculation; but I cannot help it, and why need I afflict myself with disagreeables before they arrive? I endeavored to calm my feelings by those reflections, fortified my countenance with all resolution, and set out with my Bible and psalm-book under my arm, those being the only insignia of a clergyman about me. When I made my appearance, I found a stare of universal surprise at my gay dress, which suited better the character of a beau than a clergyman. My eyes I could not persuade myself to raise from the ground till I had ascended the pulpit. I was doubtful whether I had the command of my voice, or even whether I had any voice. I sat a few moments, collecting my resolution for the effort of beginning. I made the attempt—I found my voice at command—my anxiety was hushed in a moment, my perturbation subsided, and I felt all

the serenity of a calm summer's morning. I went through the exercises of the forenoon without any difficulty. . . .

During the intermission, I heard the whisper in swift circulation among the people, concerning my appearance in such a dress. The question was often asked with great emphasis, "Who is he?" but no one was able to give those answers which were satisfactory. A consultation took place among some leading members of the society, relative to hiring me to continue among them as a preacher, as I had intimated to Mr. Fuller that I should be willing to continue among them in that capacity should such a matter meet with their approbation. I attended on the afternoon's exercises without any singular occurrence. The meeting being dismissed, and the people retired, I was informed by my landlord, that they did not agree to hire me any longer; accordingly, I found my business here at an end.

I was advised by Mr. Fuller to make application to Mr. Baldwin, minister of Palmer, for information where were vacancies. I accordingly set out for Palmer on Monday morning.

Again taking up the account from the records of the hiring of ministers we find in 1784, the next year after the hiring of Mr. Hutchinson to preach, that the committee was instructed "to hire Mr Haschal to preach 2 months." This reverend gentleman enjoys the distinction of being the first to receive a call from the townspeople, a vote "to give Mr. Haschal a call to settle in the gospel ministry among us," bearing record "thursday the 19 Day of october," the same year. A committee of three was to apply to neighboring ministers for advice. Thirty-one days later it was voted "to give Mr. David Haschal one hundred and Fifty Pounds Settlement & Sixty Pounds Sallery yearly, So Long as he Supplies the Town in the gospel ministry." For some reason, it is certain he was not settled, for the next year the committee was instructed to apply to him again for a supply.

The records show that there were persons in the town at this time of the Baptist faith, for on August 8, 1786, it was voted "to excuse David Daniels, David Paine, and John Scranton from paying the ministry and meeting-house taxes in the town, since they produce certificates of their being of the Baptist principles." These certificates are duly signed by "Elder Seth Clark, minister of the Baptist church, Wilbraham."

In January, 1788, the town voted "that the committee apply to the Rev. Stephen Fuller to preach the gospel in this town," and in April of the same year it was "voted £20 for preaching." In June of the same year it was voted "to hire Rev. Allen Pratt two Sabbaths."

In July, 1789, it was voted to give a call to the Rev. William Stone to settle in the gospel ministry, with the same settlement as was offered Mr. Haschal and a "Sallery of £50 yearly, and also that the sum to Increase forty shillings per year after the first, until it shall amount to £65 per annum." Some days later it was voted to reconsider the settlement of Mr. Stone, and we do not find that any further attempt was made to retain him.

In November, 1790, it was voted "to hire the Rev. Mr. Woodward for a longer time." In March, 1791, it was voted "to hire the Rev. Mr. Snell four Sabbaths, to give $3 per Sabbath and pay in grain." It appears that his services were not required for a longer time, for in May it was voted "to hire the Rev. Mr. Woodward to preach the gospel," and in June it was voted to hire him two months longer. It is likely that Mr. Woodward continued with the people of the town longer than the two months for which he was hired in 1791, as it was proposed at a meeting on July 5, 1792, to call him with a settlement of £150 to be paid in two years from ordination, and a salary of £40 per year to be increased £5 each year until it amounts to £60, the said sum to be paid in grain or stock. Again were the efforts to settle a pastor unsuccessful; his name at this point drops forever from the records.

In 1793, another effort was made to secure a settled pastor, and on July 1, it was voted "to give Rev. Antipas Steward a call to preach the gospel in this town." A committee, consisting of Timothy Keyes, John Sikes, David Lyon, John Jennings, Elisha Hubbard, Israel Warriner, and James Kendall was appointed to estimate the amount needed for his support and to report in four weeks. Whether they had difficulty in agreeing is not known, but it is certain that the next town meeting did not occur until August 26, when it was voted, "to give Rev. Antipas Steward £60 and 30 cords of wood annually so long as he shall be able to officiate in the gospel ministry." A long delay follows, but the people are not further doomed to disappointment, for on November 14, the citizens transacted the following business:

1st, Voted, Esq[r] James Kendall Moderator of said meeting.

2[d], Voted that the ordination of M[r] Steward be on wen[d]sday the Twenty seventh of Nov[m] Instant.

Voted to grant £20 to be asessed on the Polls and Estates of said Town to defray the Charges of M[r] Steward ordination.

Voted that a Committee of three be appointed to See how the Said money is Expended and make preparation for the Council on said day and that John Sikes Esqr, James Kendall & Elisha Hubbard be Said Committee.

Voted that Mr Joshua Fuller be appointed to keep good order and Regulations on ordination day.

It was a proud day for Ludlow, that November 27, 1793. Every citizen stepped firmly, every matron put on her best gown, every damsel smiled sweetly, for was it not ordination day, and was not Ludlow to have a parson of her own? Bezaleel Howard came from Springfield, and probably Joseph Willard from Wilbraham, Joseph Lathrop from West Springfield, Nehemiah Williams from Brimfield, Richard Salter Storrs from Longmeadow, and, if his health allowed, John McKinstry from the present Chicopee, as council, with perhaps others. The session could not have been tedious, for Mr. Steward was then an old preacher. From that £20 there must have come something good for the inner man, and very likely the Washingtonians of a half century later would have held up their hands in holy horror could they have been permitted to catch the telltale odors.

Antipas Steward

The above is a facsimile of the autograph of the Rev. Antipas Steward. He was born in Marlboro, Mass., in 1734, and was graduated at Harvard University in 1760, eminently qualified by scholastic attainments. For a time he was a tutor in the University. It seems that when he was assigned a room as tutor, in his absence, he having solicited single apartments, he and one Mr. Fyler were placed together, that gentleman and he having been the only ones presenting such a request, and hence deemed suitable associates.

It has been generally assumed that he had been settled over other pastorates before coming here, but his induction here was ordination; this would imply that this was his first settlement. Nothing has been found to show that he had ever been settled as pastor anywhere, though he had preached in many places widely apart. A sermon from I Peter 4:18, "If the righteous scarcely be saved, where shall the ungodly and the sinner appear?" is marked as having been preached at Ludlow, August, 1793, and previously at Guilford, Conn., Marlboro, Framingham, Holliston workhouse, Sandy Bay, and Gloucester, Mass., and Brattleboro, Vt.; the first date is July 1, 1776, at Mr. Diman's. From the fact that this is marked so many times we conclude it was regarded by Mr. Steward as one of his standard sermons.

Mr. Steward was a small man, but slightly built and short of stature, carrying with him a small cane, which, preserved to-day, cannot be more than thirty inches in length. He was near-sighted; his chirography was good, as the specimen indicates, but so close and fine that much of it is to-day read with difficulty. Greek, Latin and Hebrew quotations are freely and legibly interlined. He was obliged to hold the manuscript close to his eyes while reading. Mr. Steward possessed a stentorian voice, and was withal very fond of exercising the same in psalmody. Gad Lyon, who at that time led the singing, was similarly blessed. He used to stand in front of the minister, and line out the psalms of easy meter. Irreverent auditors used to say the parson and chorister vied with each other to see who could make "the most noise." Forming his opinions under the shadow of Harvard long before the Revolution, Mr. Steward was probably a tory, nor is it likely he ever changed his views very much in this regard. He was remembered as a fine specimen of the ancient province-man, who, in powdered locks and a three-cornered hat, was accustomed to visit the homes and schools, encouraging the children by a pat upon the head and an exhortation to be good, or warning them with a statement that if they lied he would find it out, though miles away.

From an old sermon of Mr. Steward's the following specimen selection is taken, illustrating not only the quaintness of style and peculiarity of thought, but also the real strength of the man, who, despite all caricature, was no unworthy representative of his profession at that day. The selection may be of use to those who, by reason of a storm, may some day be prevented from attending— town-meeting:

First, I am to Show what we are to understand by ye Injunction in ye Text "work out y^r Salvation," &c., but before we enter upon a Discussion of the Command, it may be pertinent to premise a few Things; and obviate some objections w^{ch}, if allowed, it would follow that the Proposition is of no Manner of Importance; being either wholy void of Meaning, or else requiring an utter Impossibility: but granting

THE FIRST OR TOWN CHURCH 143

These, one or the other, it will appear of no great Weight, and not, as in Truth it is, "worthy of all Acceptation"; and demanding our highest Concern:

Some may alledge, and say, that inasmuch as God sees and determines all ye Actions, wch are done by any of his Creatures thro' the Universe, they & their Ways being entirely under his Inspection, and at his Disposal. None of them can do anything voluntarily, but altogether by Necessity; not being able to perform any Operation spontaneously, and according to the Dictates of Reason. . . . .

To such suggestions as these we reply, and 'say: that Altho' we allow that God is infinite in Knowledge and Power; sees and determines all events in the Kingdom of Nature and Providence; yet we suppose this doth by no means hinder the Liberty of Will in the Creature; but they may act as freely, this notwithstanding, as tho' they were absolute, and independent Beings; and had the entire Disposal of their Wills.

The drift of thought very plainly indicates that Mr. Steward was Arminian in view.

He lived on the Adelbert L. Bennett place, now owned by the City of Springfield, near the Springfield Waterworks. The house is torn down but the cellar hole is still visible. He had two daughters, one of whom married Dr. Sylvester Nash, and the other, a Bardwell of Belchertown, and was mother of the late Oramel Bardwell, well known to our townspeople, and to whom we are indebted for most of these facts.

The ministry of Mr. Steward did not prove acceptable to all the people, for in 1799 a committee was chosen "to signify to Revd Mr Steward that the town are willing that he should be disconnected from the people in this place, if he should be willing himself." On March 10, 1800, a committee is instructed "to confer with the Rev. Mr. Steward, to agree with him to relinquish his claim of salary after the first day of June, and the town shall demand no further services of Mr. Steward, and all arrearages shall be paid by the 27th of November next, and at the same time there shall be paid from the treasury of the town the sum of $80, as a gratuity or free gift from said town as a token or mark of the sincerity of the inhabitants of the town in their peaceable directions to their committee and as a pledge of their Benevolent conduct toward their minister in future." Said agreement was approved and signed by the committee and Mr. Steward. The committee also assured Mr. Steward "that it is the invariable disposition of the inhabitants of this town to cultivate peace, love, concord and good agreement among themselves and a good understanding towards their minister." Mr. Steward still continued with the people.

The next movement appears to have been made by the friends of the pastor, asking in 1801 for a reconsideration of the action just before taken, but the movement failed in securing approval of the town, at least openly. Some sort of a truce must have been made, however, for the incumbent is still here in October, and foils by his influence, evidently, a movement of the opposition "to hire a candidate to preach the gospel." The "ins" are almost always better than the "outs," and possession gave tenure another year, when again the warrant bristled with the notes of war. The presence of even an errant presiding elder would have been welcome, doubtless, for things had come to such a pass that the town fathers felt constrained to try a desperate alternative, even "to see what the town will do relative to the Continuance of the Rev^n Antipas Steward among us in the manner in which he stays at present, and to take such measures as shall be thought proper to Cause Mr Steward to be Dismissed from any further care of the Church and People in said town." They had stripped from him his revenues, but an insatiate crowd demanded also his miter, and in December, 1802, went so far as "to choose a Committee of five members to join a Committee of the Church or any part thereof, to take the most effectual measures to remove Mr Antipas Steward from the Church and People in this town." Two days later the troubled minister received a suggestive note which has been preserved:

To the Revnd Antipas Steward, Pastor of the Chh in Ludlow.
Rev. Sir

Whereas the Situation of the Pastor and Church in this place is such as we Suppose need advice and counsel this is to Request you to call a meeting of the Church to see if the pastor chh and town can agree upon a mutuall council to advise and direct us what is expedient to be done in our present circumstances

Ludlow, Dec^m ye 8, 1802.

        Timothy Keyes
        Tyras Pratt
        James Kendall
        Elisha Hubbard
        Stephen Jones
        Moses Wilder
        Leonard Miller

THE FIRST OR TOWN CHURCH

The town committee was thus reinforced by Messrs. Keyes, Pratt, Jones, Wilder, and Miller, probably from the church, while John Jennings, Aaron Colton, and Timothy Nash, also appointed by the town, for some reason withheld their signatures. Of course there was little use to resist such an appeal, and the council met in due time and dismissed Mr. Steward in 1803, a little less than ten years from the date of his installation. (See Mr. Tuck's account of proposed texts, Part III.)

RESULT OF COUNCIL AT LUDLOW TO DISMISS REV. ANTIPAS STEWARD

At an Ecclesiastical Council convened at Ludlow, by letters missive, at the home of Mr. Stephen Jones, April 19, 1803.

The council was called by the Rev. Antipas Steward and the Brethren of the Church in that place, and was composed of the following Pastors and Delegates, viz.:

Pastors	Delegates
Rev. Justus Forward,	Jonas Walker, Belchertown,
Joseph Lathrop, D.D.,	Moses A. Chapin, West Springfield,
David Parsons, D.D.,	Dea. Seth Coleman, Amherst,
Rev. Joel Hayes,	Dea. Silas Smith, South Hadley,
Rev. Bezaleel Howard,	William T. Pynchon, Springfield,
Rev. Moses Warner,	Dea. Enoch Burt, Wilbraham,
Rev. Elijah Gridley,	Samuel Clark, Granby.

The Council made choice of the Rev. Justus Forward as moderator, and the Rev. David Parsons as scribe, and the Rev. Mr. Gridley as assistant scribe.

The Council was opened with prayer by the moderator. Upon this a paper was laid before the Council purporting to be an Agreement between the Rev. Mr. Steward and a committee of the town and signed by the parties of the following towns, viz.:

"We, the subscribers, being appointed a Committee to confer with the Rev. Mr. Antipas Steward, and to agree with him upon reasonable terms, to relinquish his claims upon the town for annual salary, have attended that service, and, after having maturely considered the circumstances of Mr. Steward and the society, have unanimously agreed to propositions made us by Mr. Steward, which are: that, from and after the first day of June next, the town and society shall demand no further services of Mr. Steward, and that Mr. Steward after that time shall demand or receive no further salary, but that the arrearages which shall be due or unpaid shall be wholly paid and discharged by the twenty-seventh day of November next ensuing, and that by the twenty-seventh day of November aforesaid Mr. Steward shall have received out of the treasury of said town the sum of eighty dollars as a gratuity or free gift from said town as a token of worth and of the sincerity of the inhabitants of the town in their peaceable directions to their Committee, and as a pledge of their benevolent conduct toward their minister in future.

> Timothy Keyes,
> John Jennings,
> Aaron Colton, } Committee."
> Moses Wilder,
> Pliny Sikes,

    We, therefore, as a Council, being invested to assist and direct what is expedient to be done upon the present circumstances of this church and people and to endeavor to heal their divisions, and to persuade them to live peaceably together, or to separate in peace, as we, in our wisdom, may judge most consistent with the honor of the Deity and the welfare of the church, having fully considered the agreement made between the Rev. Mr. Steward and the town of Ludlow,—the divided state of the church and people,—and the improbability of Mr. Steward being further useful in the work of the ministry in this place, are unitedly of the opinion that the ministerial relation subsisting between the Pastor, the Church, and the People in Ludlow ought to be dissolved and hereby declare that it is dissolved.

    While the Council feel themselves in duty bound to make that declaration, they are happy to find no allegations have been exhibited to the Council against the moral or ministerial character of Mr. Steward, and therefore, in justice to him, do recommend him to improvement in the Church wherever God in His Providence may open a door for it.

    Still, they are of the opinion that the present state of this church and people is such that it will prove detrimental to the cause and interest of religion for Mr. Steward to minister to them, or to any part of them.

    The Council are seriously impressed with the unhappy divided state of this church and people, fully believing that unless a change of temper takes place, there will soon be an end, in this place, of all ecclesiastical order, Christian fellowship, and religion. We do, therefore, at this time, earnestly recommend to all those who, for certain reasons, have been for some time opposed in sentiment, to coalesce, to lay aside their party prejudices, to embrace each other in the arms of friendship, and to unite in building up the church and cause of Christ here. You will be reminded, friends and brethren, of the observation of the Apostle, that "where contention and strife are, there is confusion and every evil work." The infinitely important interest of religion, of every other consideration, ought to arrest your attention, and prompt you to reach after unanimity, and a settlement of the gospel ministry as speedily as may be.

    We wish grace, mercy, and peace may be multiplied unto you and commend you to God and to the word of His grace, who is able to build you up and give you an inheritance among all them that are sanctified.

Voted unanimously by the Council.

Justus Forward, Moderator.

A true copy attest.
David Parsons, Scribe.

At the close of his pastorate here in 1803, Mr. Steward retired from the active ministry and made his home for the remainder of his days with his daughter, the mother of the late Oramel Bardwell, in Belchertown, where he died in 1814, at the age of 80 years, and where his dust is buried.

The Ludlow Israel seems to have tired of a king for a season, for we hear of no attempts at settlement or propositions for protracted service for half a score of years. After the dismissal of Rev. Mr. Steward, the church again resorted to supplies, disregarding the advice of the council, and the condition of things became no better, but rather grew worse.

Money was raised each year to hire preaching, and from the records we learn that Rev. Laban Thurber, said to be a Baptist, supplied a while in 1805 and 1806. In 1808 Rev. Abner Phelps was hired to "preach out" the money granted by the town, which was $100. The amount allowed about this time was not to exceed five dollars per Sabbath—not a severe restriction either, as money was valued then. A reluctance to grant money for the support of the gospel is evident very soon, no doubt largely influenced by the primal sounds of the cry for the dissolution of church and state. We shall see that the influence of the teachings of New England dissenters was beginning to be felt, even in Ludlow, as early as 1810.

In May, 1810, it was voted "to choose a Ministerial Committee, two from each denomination, to supply the pulpit with preaching and make the town no expense." The committee comprised Samuel Frost and Uriah Clough, representing the Methodists, Dea. Stephen Jones and Ezekiel Fuller, the Congregationalists, and Abel Wright and William Pease, the Baptists.

Elder Elijah Hedding, having been appointed presiding elder of the Methodist Church in the New London district, came to Ludlow to live that he might be more conveniently located near the center of his district. Finding the ecclesiastical affairs in so lamentable a condition in the town of his adoption, he set himself to remedy the same. Paying no attention to the unsuccessful designs of some to oust him from the town by proposing to have him warned out as having "no visible means of support," the good minister accepted an invitation to preach in the meeting-house on a Sabbath when he was at home. Gaining the good-will of the people, he supplied another Sabbath when at liberty, as his district work occupied his time but eight Sabbaths in a quarter. A very satisfactory arrangement was finally made whereby Mr. Hedding supplied the desk every Sabbath at his command, filling some of the others with the services of a talented local preacher, Joshua Crowell of Ware. Under this administration prejudices were disarmed very speedily, and all brought into sympathy with the minister who thus uniquely combined the duties of presiding elder in the Methodist church and stated supply in the Congregational. This arrangement lasted as long as Mr. Hedding lived in town—a year.

On November 2, 1812, the town voted to ask Elder Elijah Hedding to come and preach to them and voted to give him $300 a year, to be paid annually so long as he should supply the desk, and his performances were satisfactory. It was also voted that the above $300 should be raised as follows: first, the interest arising from the town fund should be applied as far as it would go, then the balance made up by a tax on the polls and estates in town. The conference session drew near, and with it the limitation of Mr. Hedding's agreement. The people were suited, desired him to stay, asked him to stay. It was a trial to him. On the one hand were home and ample support, a satisfied and loving people—on the other, a life of wandering, with all the uncertainties and privations of the earlier itinerancy. Yet he did not waver, but took his next charge without murmuring.

In 1813 war was being waged against Great Britain, and the people were in a state of excitement. All on the seacoast became nervous, and flocked to the inland regions in troops. Among these refugees from the dangers of the war with England was a small, bright-eyed man from Provincetown, on Cape Cod, who strayed into Ludlow in the fall. After severe defeats in the northwest, President Madison issued a proclamation for a day of fasting. It so happened that the Provincetown stranger arrived here at just about the day appointed for the fast service. He inquired for a meeting, and was told that there was no minister in the town and no service had been appointed. He replied that he was a clergyman, and would be pleased to conduct worship if the people so

REV. ELIJAH HEDDING, D.D.
Bishop of the Methodist Episcopal Church

desired. They gladly accepted the proposition, assembled, and listened to a flaming sermon from a Methodist local preacher on the fitting text: "The people of Nineveh believed God and proclaimed a fast." Among other good things he hoped that in the company there were "no immoderate eaters and drinkers, no gluttons or wine-bibbers." Such was the advent of Alexander McLean into Ludlow.

So much pleased were the people with the sermon and the man, that arrangements were at once made for a trial service of four weeks as minister. The townsfolk then insisted that Mr. McLean should be hired for a year, and he was engaged on the same terms as had been made with Mr. Hedding. Ludlow was henceforth his home. He lived in the long red house that once stood south of the highway, on the place now owned by Eugene Clark. The late James Kirke McLean was his great grandson. Mr. McLean's facsimile is here presented:

Alexander McLean

Under his administration, which continued until 1816, matters went on quite smoothly, at least for a while. True, there were some who objected to the idea of a settled Methodist preacher, but as the town managed the ecclesiastical affairs, there was little room for objection. The causes of disquiet are easily surmised.

In 1814 there was a great mortality in the town, numbers of homes being made desolate. Under the ministrations of evangelists and Mr. McLean a powerful awakening followed, "more extensive," says our informant, "than ever was known in the town before." Large numbers professed a hope in God. Of course a question of church relationship arose. Intimately associated with this was another. Mr. McLean was not, according to existent church rules, competent to administer the ordinances of baptism and the Lord's supper. Wordy altercations between the parties followed, which resulted in alienation of feeling. The Congregationalists signed a declaration of church relationship, and would no longer affiliate with the town's minister. In 1817 his official services seem to have terminated. Later in the year the town again authorized the three denominations to furnish the pulpit supply, but with the proviso that the money should be expended within the meeting-house. An unsuccessful attempt to press a call to Mr. Eli Moody indicates the presence of that gentleman a little after, while veterans spoke with animation of frequent supply from Rev. Mr. Johns of South Hadley.

In September, 1819, a call was extended to Rev. Ebenezer Burt Wright to settle in the gospel ministry. He was to have an annual salary of $350, in addition to the annual interest arising from the ministerial fund. The records state that "he shall give six months' notice at any time that he wishes to leave his charge, and that he shall have a right to leave on giving said notice. Also the legal voters in his society can dismiss him whenever two thirds of said society desire his dismission." Mr. Wright's reply is as follows:

My Christian Friends:

I have seriously considered the invitation which you gave me to settle among you in the gospel ministry. I regret the disappointment that I may have occasioned by delaying my decision so long, but in case of so great consequence I could not presume, and am persuaded you would not wish me, to decide hastily.

I am happy to state that my doubts are at length chiefly removed. There is a God who reigns. I have endeavored to ascertain His will, and I dare not proceed contrary to what His will appears to me to be. I hope I do not mistake the path of duty in concluding to accept your call, from events that have taken place since I have been attempting to preach the gospel among you. I hope God designs to make me (unworthy as I am) an instrument in building up the Kingdom of His Son in this place. Most cheerfully do I devote myself to a people in whose welfare I feel much interest. For you I trust I shall heartily labor, and permit me to expect that my labors will be constantly assisted by your prayers.

Yours in the bonds of Christian affection,
E. B. Wright.

Mr. Wright was born in Westhampton, and graduated at Williams College in 1814. He pursued theological studies at Andover, was licensed by the Salem Association at Danvers, April, 1817. He was a young man, full of fire and zeal, having a profound conviction of duty and a lofty reverence for his exalted office, when he came as a candidate to Ludlow. He was ordained and installed pastor, December 8, 1819.

The influence of such a man in the town could not fail to be salutary in the highest degree. The little band of church members, reduced to about half a dozen when Mr. Steward left, had been, to be sure, increased by revival influences and accessions from other towns. Yet, with no

Minister of the Town for Sixteen Years.

organizer and leader, healthy growth was almost impossible. Mr. Wright's ministry was well qualified to induce confidence in the society— not only mutual confidence among his own people, but a feeling of respect on the part of the scattering numbers of Baptists and slowly increasing company of Methodists, as well as outsiders. When the town had at length commenced the process of divorcement from the church, we see from year to year the records of the clerk referring, probably in accordance with the verbiage of the day, and yet with real or fancied fondness, to "Řev. E. B. Wright's society." No one ever questioned his sincerity or purity. The Wilbraham historian appreciatingly speaks of "that saintly man, Ebenezer B. Wright." (Stebbins' History, p. 150.) On two occasions (1823 and 1827), having been made acquainted with the real or imaginary weakened financial ability of the town, he relinquished a hundred dollars of his salary. His honesty was proverbial—at times almost leaning to credulity. On account of ill health he found himself obliged to ask in 1830 a release from his labors for one year, relinquishing his salary.

In May, 1833, on account of Mr. Wright's health, a colleague was settled, Rev. David R. Austin of Norwich, Conn., a graduate of Union College, New York, of the class of 1827. He continued with the church until July, 1837, winning friends by his earnestness and geniality. He was the last minister hired by the town, the First Parish having been formed in 1835.

Although Mr. Wright remained in office until 1835, he was unable to preach for about three years. He was afterwards settled in Chicopee and Norwich. We learn from the records that he was given a call to become pastor of this church again in 1837. He replied that he could not consistently accept the kind invitation of the church and society. He died at Huntington, August 17, 1871, aged 76, and his remains are interred in the Ludlow Center Cemetery.

Mr. Wright lived in the house later owned by Albert Fuller, and now (1911) owned by Mr. Hatch. It was known as the "Parson Wright place."

The parish continued without a settled minister for nearly two years. At a parish meeting held June 18, 1838, it was "voted unanimously to give the Rev. Alonzo Sanderson a call to settle with us in the gospel ministry, at an annual salary of $550." Mr. Sanderson's reply was accepted at a meeting December 10, and is as follows:

To the First Church and Congregation in Ludlow,
  Dear Brethren and Friends:
  The call you have given me to become your pastor and minister I have made a subject of much reflection and prayer, and have endeavored to examine it in its various bearings, both as it regards the good of the parties concerned and the general interest of the cause of Christ. In examining the subject I have tried to look at it as a matter of duty, endeavoring not to be influenced by worldly considerations any further than warranted by the word of God, and now though it is with trembling that I reply to your call, knowing the responsibility that rests upon me, yet feeling it to be my duty, I answer in the affirmative. The remuneration you have offered for my services, I regard as generous and with ordinary prosperity as sufficient for my support. Upon this point, however, I feel no anxiety, believing that I am among those who will not suffer me to want while I labor among them in the ministry. In giving my answer I have thought it proper to make the following requests: (1) that my salary be paid semiannually; (2) that should I think it necessary, I may be released from supplying the desk four Sabbaths a year, but with the understanding that should my circumstances be such as to enable me to supply every Sabbath, I am to do it without further remuneration.
  Praying that the Lord may be our guide, and bless us in the contemplated union, I am, dear brethren and friends,
                Affect. yours in Christian bonds,
                              Alonzo Sanderson.

Mr. Sanderson was ordained and installed January 2, 1839. By vote of the parish his yearly salary was to begin the first of March. He was born in Whately and graduated at Amherst in 1834. He afterwards studied theology at Andover, and, like Wright and Austin, came to Ludlow with the flush of youth upon his brow. He is remembered as an earnest, pious, and devoted minister, with broad Christian views.

In 1843, on account of some difficulties between the church and Mr. Sanderson, it was agreed to call an ecclesiastical council, and their report is as follows:

At an Ecclesiastical Council convened at the Congregational Meetinghouse in Ludlow, March 30, 1843, by letters missive from the Congregational Church and its Pastor, for the purpose of investigating difficulties, and the dismission of Rev. A. Sanderson, if deemed practicable. Present from the First Church in Springfield, Rev. Samuel Osgood, D.D., pastor, and Brother John B. Kirkham, delegate; from the Church in

Monson, Rev. Alford Ely, D.D., pastor, and Dea. Andrew Porter, delegate; from the Church in Westfield, Rev. Emerson Davis, pastor, and Dea. J. W. Atkins, delegate; from the Church in North Wilbraham, Rev. John Bowers; from the Fourth Church in Springfield, Rev. E. Russell, pastor, and Dea. Joseph Whipple, delegate.

The Council was organized by the choice of Rev. Samuel Osgood, D.D., moderator, Rev. E. Russell, secretary. Prayer was then offered by the moderator, after which the Council appointed a committee to confer with Rev. A. Sanderson and the Committee of the Church and Society in reference to the mode in which the investigation of the difficulties should be prosecuted, when it was mutually agreed to omit an inquiry into specific charges and base the doings of the Council on general reasons or grounds. The Council, after hearing statements from Rev. A. Sanderson and the Committee of the Church and Society and giving these statements long, careful, and patient attention, voted:

In view of all the circumstances, it is expedient that the Pastoral relation between Rev. A. Sanderson and the Church and Society in Ludlow be dissolved, the dissolution to take place after the lapse of six weeks from this date, unless the parish shall terminate the same by paying him his salary for that term of time or he shall wish to terminate it sooner.

In view of the circumstances which have led to the separation the Council moves and earnestly beseeches the Church to regard their present condition as of the frown of their Redeemer and to return to Him by penitence and prayer. They earnestly beseech the members of this Church and Society mutually to forget and forgive and study for things which make not collision and strife, but for harmony and love.

Voted, also, to recommend the Rev. A. Sanderson as an able and devoted minister of our Lord and Saviour and worthy of the confidence of the churches of Christ wherever God in His Providence may call him to labor.

Mr. Sanderson was dismissed in March, 1843. He was afterwards settled in Tolland and from there removed to Ohio.

Very soon after Mr. Sanderson was dismissed, a unanimous call was given to Rev. J. W. Tuck at a salary of $550. Mr. Tuck's reply is as follows:

To the Congregational Church and Society in Ludlow:

On Monday, the 31st day of July, I was met by your respective Committee acting in your behalf and presented with a call to become your pastor and religious teacher. In that call you thought fit to offer me $550 per annum as a support, while laboring among you. Before you had taken any decisive action in reference to my remaining with you as pastor, I had preached with you eight Sabbaths and passed my time in the place. It is now two weeks since your call was placed in my hands. Therefore each of us has the satisfaction to know that we have not acted prematurely in reference to the anticipated relation. After prayerful consideration and seeking the advice of older and more experienced persons, I have concluded to accept your call. This has been done with much diffidence and trembling, and with painful solicitude in respect to the future, lest I may not be all that you desire and need in your spiritual adviser and guide. I now cast myself on your leniency, begging a constant remembrance in all your prayers and a place among the affections of your hearts.

Dear brethren, may the Lord ever be with and smile upon you by conferring abundantly both spiritual and temporal blessings, and may each and all of us in all our relations in life and especially in the important and solemn one we soon hope to enter on, seek and receive divine wisdom from on high, that in our ways we may please the Lord. The above may be considered as an answer in general to the very respectful call you have been pleased to give me, and is now submitted to you at your disposal.

Very respectfully yours,

J. W. Tuck.

Ludlow, Aug. 14, 1843.

Mr. Tuck was ordained and installed September 5, 1843.

Jeremy Webster Tuck was born in Kensington, N. H., graduated at Amherst in 1840, and passed through the theological instruction of Andover and East Windsor. Two days before his ordination he was married to Irene M. Moody of South Hadley, who died after a year or so of married life. The Mrs. Tuck so well known here bore from infancy the name of Mowry.

In October, 1852, the pastor requested permission to suspend preaching through the winter on account of ill health. Permission was granted, and it was voted that his salary be continued as usual, and he should supply the pulpit at his discretion. A committee was chosen to advise with him and render him such assistance as might be deemed advisable. Mr. Tuck's salary was increased in 1855 to $600, and again in 1857 to $700. In January, 1859, Mr. Tuck sent in his resignation as pastor. He was asked to withdraw this but decided not to do so. It was not till November that a vote was passed to call a council to dissolve the relations between the pastor and people. He was dismissed December 7, 1859.

At a parish meeting held February 13, 1860, it was "voted to give Rev.

Warren Mayo a call to settle in the gospel ministry and labor among this people at a salary of $700." It does not appear that Mr. Mayo was settled, but the report of expenses found in the records show that he was paid a salary as late as the year 1862.

In 1863 we find Rev. F. Alvord was paid $480, and the year ending March 1, 1864, the report shows he was paid $100 for ten Sabbaths. The same year several other ministers supplied the pulpit.

Rev. Chester Bridgman was given a call to become the pastor and was settled May 18, 1864. He remained until July 24, 1866. During his ministry here the chapel was built.

October 1, 1866, the parish voted to unite with the church in giving a call to Rev. C. L. Cushman to settle among them at a salary of $1,000, and he was settled in November. In 1871 Mr. Cushman received a call from the Second Church in Amherst and resigned the pastorate of the Ludlow Church, but as the Church would not accept his resignation he remained until September 1, 1874.

Rev. S. V. McDuffee became the pastor in 1875 and remained with the church until March 1, 1882. On March 6, 1882, it was "voted to have but one preaching service every Sunday during the ensuing year."

In February, 1883, a unanimous call was given to Rev. Myron P. Dickey to become the pastor at a salary of $700 and the parsonage. A council convened the 14th of June to install Mr. Dickey. In 1887 his salary was increased $100.

June 23, 1889, was observed as the one hundredth anniversary of the organization of the Church. At this time Rev. Mr. Dickey delivered a historical sermon in the afternoon. Others who took part were: Rev. J. W. Tuck, a former pastor; Rev. Mr. Buckingham and Rev. Mr. Cone of Springfield, Rev. Mr. Howard of Wilbraham, Rev. Simeon Miller of Ludlow, and Dea. Elisha T. Parsons.

Mr. Dickey resigned in 1893 to accept the pastorate of a church in Milton, N. H.

In June, 1893, Rev. E. P. Allen of Sanford, Me., was given a call to this pastorate. He commenced his labors June 25, remaining but one year.

Rev. Everett D. Francis of the Theological Seminary at Hartford, Conn., was secured to supply the pulpit for one year, beginning in March, 1895. In November of that year, he was invited to become the pastor and on the twentieth of the month he was ordained and installed. A few months after he married Miss Alice M. Clark, a member of the parish. Mr. Francis resigned April 16, 1905. A council was convened to dismiss him May 16, and he closed his labors the first of July, when he moved to Springfield.

Rev. W. Stanley Post of Northampton was next called and accepted the pastorate, commencing his labors here December 1, 1905. He remained until April, 1910, when he accepted a call from a church in Boothbay Harbor, Me.

August 11, 1910, Rev. John S. Curtis of Indian Orchard was called, and commenced his work October 1, and is the pastor at the present time (1911).

List of Pastors

		Commenced	Left
Rev. Pelatiah Chapin,		1774	1775
" David Haschal,		1784	1786
" Aaron Woodward,		1789	1793
" Antipas Steward,	Installed,	1793	1803
" Elijah Hedding,		1810	1811
" Alexander McLean,		1813	1816
" Ebenezer B. Wright,	Installed,	1819	1835
" David R. Austin,	"	1833	1837
" Alonzo Sanderson,	"	1839	1843
" J. W. Tuck,	"	1843	1859
" Warren Mayo,		1859	1862
" Chester Bridgman,	"	1864	1866
" C. L. Cushman,	"	1866	1874
" S. V. McDuffee,	"	1875	1882
" M. P. Dickey,	"	1883	1893
" E. P. Allen,		1893	1894
" E. D. Francis,	"	1895	1905
" W. Stanley Post,		1905	1910
" John S. Curtis,		1910	(the present Pastor)

CHURCH ORGANIZATION

The church was organized in 1789, so tradition says, but nothing in regard to the event can be found, either in the town archives or in the

THE FIRST OR TOWN CHURCH

ecclesiastical records of the neighboring churches. No certain statement of facts can be affixed as to the number of members at first nor who they were. There must have been some formal proceedings, something that served the purpose of a council, to render the organization regular so as to be received into the fellowship of the neighboring churches.

But whatever formal proceedings there may have been, they were probably such as did not call for any action of the town and were participated in by only the small number actually interested in religion. The number of members at first was small, not over fifteen, according to the more trustworthy traditions, this number very likely including not more than five to eight men. The committees to hire ministers and transact church business at that time doubtless included men who were original members of the church. The population of the town then was about two hundred inhabitants.

The first committee to hire a minister comprised John Hubbard, Abner Sikes, and Joseph Jones. Others chosen for various purposes included Abner Hitchcock, Oliver Chapin, Joshua Fuller, John Sikes, Moses Wilder, Isaac Brewer, Timothy Keyes, and James Kendall. More would not necessarily be church members, but if there were any men of business talent in the church membership they would be likely to be put on such committees. One man on the building committee, Timothy Sikes, is known to have been a deacon of the church when Rev. Antipas Steward was pastor, so he may have been one of the original members. Dea. Jonathan Clough, of whom we have the record of dismissal with his wife to the church in Wilbraham in 1808, must have been a member.

James Kendall was the first sexton, having been chosen in 1782; his house has been mentioned as one of those used for public worship, and since there is no record of his admission to the church later and there is a record of his death as a member of this church in 1820, the presumption is that he may have been another of the original members. From such facts we conclude that the membership probably included Timothy Keyes, Jonathan Clough, James Kendall, and after these perhaps Abner Hitchcock, Oliver Chapin, and Joshua Fuller.

Therefore, we may conclude a considerable portion of the original membership must have been from the families of these men. A further addition of fifteen members is said to have been made in 1793, when the first pastor, Rev. Antipas Steward, was ordained; but the losses during the first quarter of a century more than equaled the gains, and at the time Mr. Steward left (1803) there were only some half dozen members; and in 1813 there were but five more members, yet the church never became extinct.

The following is a copy of a letter of recommendation to the Church of Ludlow, during the ministry of Mr. Steward, with his endorsement:

To the Church of Christ in Ludlow

Rev'd & Beloved:—These may certify that Sabrina Wilson, the Wife of John Wilson has been admitted as a Member in full Communion with the 2^d Church of Christ in Chatham. While with us, she walked, so far as appears agreeably to her Christian profession. She is therefore with the consent of the Brethren recommended to your christian watch communion and fellowship in all gospel Ordinances as a meet member of the Church of Christ.—Wishing that grace mercy and peace from the glorious head of the Church may be multiplied to you & the Church universal & asking your prayers for us We subscribe ourselves yours in the faith of the gospel.

David Selden
"Pastor of the 2^d Church in Chatham."

Chatham, 22 February, 1798.

Endorsement:—"Read and voted Admission, according to the Design of the Contents April 29th 98, and $M^{rs.}$ Wilson *received* to our *Watch* and *Fellowship*.

A. Steward.

The records previous to the year 1814 have not been preserved, but about that time occurred what is supposed to be the first large religious awakening enjoyed by the church. There had been much sickness. A fatal fever had swept through the community carrying death to many homes. This fact is noted as producing a serious feeling. Rev. Nathan Perkins of East Amherst, assisted by other ministers in the neighboring churches, labored with so much success that 38 were added to the church, all of them being leading citizens of the town with their wives.

In 1819 a further addition of 31 members was made, the fruits of labor by Rev. Mr. Curtis of Hadley. In these baptisms of the Holy Ghost the church really began its spiritual life.

The condition of the church at the time of Rev. Mr. Wright's coming was very much improved. There were 95 members, of whom 35 were

THE FIRST OR TOWN CHURCH

male. Stephen Jones, Oliver Dutton, and Benjamin Sikes were deacons. There was no other church organization in the town at this time. In the first years of Mr. Wright's ministry there were large additions by letter from neighboring churches. The natural inference regarding this unusual number of additions by letter at this time is, that owing to the previous disorganized condition of things, many who had come here to live had neglected to change their church relations and others were unwilling to do so as long as the divided state of feeling existed. The union of the church membership of the community was the first step to the ingathering of those outside.

In 1827 and 1831 large accessions on confession of faith were received, 20 uniting in 1827 and 42 in 1831. The church had grown in the fourteen years, 1819 to 1833, from 95 to 151, of whom 51 were males and 100 females. Rev. Almon Underwood, the most successful evangelist that has ever labored for this church, then in the beginning of his career, was present for a time during Rev. Mr. Austin's pastorate. As many as 60 additions were made to the church membership during his term of four years. The membership must have reached nearly or quite 200 and exceeded that of any other time. Since that time there have been several periods of especial religious interest when large numbers were added to the church. The years of largest additions were 1843, 1849, 1858, 1866, and 1873. A continuing spiritual interest is shown in the marked increase of other years. The present membership is about 170.

In the year 1824, during Mr. Wright's pastorate, a vote was passed by the church to choose a standing committee of three members of the church whose duty it should be to converse with such members as may be guilty of public misdemeanors, with a view to reclaiming them. The three names that head the list of those who have served on this permanent committee were Joseph Miller, 2d, Noah Clark, and Joshua Fuller. The same year, September 2, this same Joseph Miller and Ashbel Burr were elected deacons of the church, the special vacancy being the retirement from active duties of the office by Dea. Oliver Dutton. Deacons Miller and Burr accepted the office and served with fidelity; Deacon Burr until 1839, when, on account of advancing years, he wished to be released from the active duties, and Alva Sikes was chosen in his stead. Deacon Burr died November, 1861, aged 84 years. "Strong in the Lord and in the power of His might" is the record concerning him. Deacon Miller resigned in 1848, being about to remove from town, but he afterwards returned and died here in 1871, aged 84 years.

It is said that Dea. Oliver Dutton and Dea. Benjamin Sikes, who were hard of hearing, used to stand in the pulpit beside the minister while he was preaching.

The first meeting of the parish to organize according to the Statutes of the Commonwealth was held at the meeting-house on the 9th of December, 1835. Officers were chosen and a committee of three "to seat the meeting-house." Daniel Miller, one of the petitioners, executed the warrant for the first meeting, Elisha T. Parsons was the moderator, Elisha A. Fuller the treasurer, and Theodore Sikes the clerk. This organization probably grew out of the controversy concerning the ministry fund. This fund became the source of much contention as the religious societies developed. According to the charter, the town held certain lands in trust for the maintenance of the ministry. Early in the century these lands were sold and the money put into the care of a committee of trustees appointed by the town from year to year. For a number of years its revenues were equally divided among the various denominations, all of whom were represented in the pulpit as the years passed on. After the existence of the "Methodist Legal Society," the agitation respecting the fund was carried on with increasing force until some parties petitioned for its disuse in the support of the ministry, and its appropriation to the purposes of education. A suit followed, which was afterwards carried to the Supreme Court and the case was decided in favor of the defendants. The money has since been used by the Congregational Society for the support of its ministry.

At a meeting of the parish, January 2, 1836, the following rule was voted by which any persons may become members of said parish, viz.: "They shall present to the committee, if there be one, and, if there be not one, to the assessors of said parish, a declaration signed by them in substance as follows: The subscribers, being desirous to attend public worship with the members of the First Parish in Ludlow and to bear their part of the burdens of supporting the same, request that they may be received as members of said parish. And when a majority of said committee or assessors shall endorse their approval of said declaration, the applicant shall become a member by filing the same with the clerk."

During Rev. Mr. Sanderson's pastorate several events are noted, among which were the adoption in 1839 of the church creed and covenant

THE FIRST OR TOWN CHURCH 165

and regulations for the discipline of members and the government of the church. Perhaps it is not understood by all that there were no formulated creeds in the early Congregational churches of New England. Not till 1821 did the First Church in Springfield have any formal confession of faith. The Bible was the creed and every man was free to interpret its rule of duty for himself in the light of conscience and the Holy Ghost, responsible unto God to give his revelation an honest interpretation, and impelled thereto by the momentous concerns of his own personal salvation. The adoption of a formal creed, which is now general and has been for more than three quarters of a century, grew out of the necessity of defining distinctly and precisely what one regarded as the essential doctrines of Scripture.

As far back as 1892, a committee had been appointed by the parish to investigate the advantage of having the church and parish incorporated as one legal body. No decision seems to have been reached until, in 1897, at a parish meeting held March 1, it was voted to transfer all its property, both real and personal, with its debts, to the First Church in Ludlow, and a committee was appointed, consisting of Charles P. Jones, Elbridge J. Streeter, and Warren G. Fuller, to make the transfer. At an adjourned meeting, March 29, the committee reported, that they had a quit-claim deed made by R. W. Ellis and dated March 20, 1897, conveying the property to the church. It was then voted to dissolve the parish.

The relations of this church with other churches in the town are very pleasant and friendly. There have been in the past closer relations with the Methodist Church than others from the fact of said church having been located at the Center not far from the Congregational Church, until a few years ago, when they built a church at the Village and discontinued services at the Center. The pastors of the two churches worked together very harmoniously, and for some years union services were held every month. The social gatherings of each church were attended by members of both churches, and unity and kindly feelings prevailed in the community. We learn from the church records that in years past, a half century or so ago, there were often differences between some of the members which called for the deliberations of the church to settle and in some cases it was necessary to call a council from other churches for advice and their decision as to a just settlement of the difficulties. In more recent years the relations of the members toward each other have been of a pleasant and amicable nature.

The benevolences of the church in late years have been well sustained and we suppose the earlier periods would bear the same record. Though there has never been the peculiar interest which comes from having one of our own members engaged in the missionary work abroad, there is a good and intelligent interest in mission work, both home and foreign.

The first observance of Children's Sunday by the church was in June, 1884. At that time was established the custom of giving a Bible to children baptized in infancy and having reached the age of seven years. This custom is still continued.

Prayer meetings in the early days of the church were seldom known. When they were first established as a weekly meeting the records do not show. They are considered a necessary part of religious worship at the present day.

During the ministry of Rev. Mr. Francis the observance of "Old Home Sunday" was established, the first being in July, 1900, and since then the day has been observed several times in the month of August. Members and friends from other parts of the town and from other towns have come and united with the resident members in the worship of God, as was done in earlier years, by holding morning and afternoon services and singing the hymns of "ye olden time." Sermons and addresses are usually given by former pastors and friends of the church. After the morning service an old-fashioned box lunch is enjoyed under the beautiful oak trees near the church, and old acquaintances are renewed. Usually a large number are present. In 1911 the following invitation was issued:

OLD HOME SUNDAY, JULY 30, 1911

You are most cordially invited to participate with us in the observance of Old Home Sunday, July 30, 1911, at the First Church, Ludlow Center, Mass. Services at 10.45 A.M. and 2.30 P.M. It is expected that the people will bring an old-fashioned box lunch to enjoy at noon. Carriages will meet the cars arriving from Springfield and Palmer at Ludlow Bridge at 9.45 to convey people to the church and return after the afternoon service, at an expense of 25 cents for the round trip. Please send acceptance card to the Committee on Invitations. We trust there will be a large reunion of former members and friends of church and place.

John Springer Curtis,	Mrs. Charles P. Jones,
Elmer H. Carver,	Mrs. William M. Ashwell,
George H. Sprague,	Alfred T. Jones,
John F. Perham,	Committee on Invitations.

July 16, 1911.

THE FIRST OR TOWN CHURCH

In accordance with this the sixth Old Home Sunday service was held in the First Congregational Church. In spite of the threatening skies there was a large attendance. A long time before the service commenced teams filled every place provided for their accommodation. The church was well filled.

The exercises opened with singing, "Praise God from Whom All Blessings Flow." The choir, consisting of many of the people who years ago assisted in the music, was seated in the high gallery in the rear of the audience room. Miss Marion Jones presided at the organ. The congregation joined in repeating the Lord's Prayer. The choir sang "Jerusalem, My Glorious Home." Rev. John S. Curtis offered prayer and read from the Scriptures. The choir and congregation sang, "Come Thou Almighty King." The morning offering was received. Willis S. Fisher sang "Grass and Roses."

Rev. John S. Curtis gave an interesting address, taking his text from Mark 16:15, "Go ye into all the world and preach the Gospel to every creature." He spoke on "The Message of the Country Church," saying that the Gospel message was the same under all conditions, but the emphasis should be different to fit the people to whom it was presented. He said, in part:

"The especial message of the country church should be to say to every one, 'This is the way, walk ye in it.' What a condition it would be if the church did not present the message that would convict of sin!"

At the noon hour the 200 guests enjoyed the luncheon which they had brought, in the grove of massive oaks in the yard. Families and acquaintances gathered in groups, renewing old friendships and making new ones. Afterwards many visited the two cemeteries near, where so many of the former church members rest.

The afternoon's service opened at 2.30 with "Sherburne" sung by the choir. Rev. Mr. Curtis offered prayer and E. E. Chapman sang "Light of Our Way."

The speaker of the afternoon was Rev. C. B. McDuffie of Three Rivers, taking for his text, "I am come that ye might have life and that ye might have it more abundantly." He dwelt particularly on the hopeful side of life as presented by the Gospel and earnestly advised the members of the Ludlow country church to be earnest and faithful.

Many former residents made it a point to come to Ludlow to visit again the scenes of their childhood and attended this service. Guests were present from New York City, Lancaster, Pa., Worcester, and the surrounding towns.

Leaders of the Singing in the First Church

To the worthy line of choristers and singers, who without compensation have contributed so much to the public worship of God, great gratitude is due. The history shows that the changes in choristers have been less frequent than in the ministers, and there are more than one of these leaders of the singing whose term of service has outlasted by several years the longest pastorate of the church.

Probably Gad Lyon was one of the first leaders of the choir in Ludlow. He was the great-grandfather of David L. Fuller and Mrs. Frederick L. Burr. David L. Fuller has a pitchpipe which Gad Lyon used.

One of the early leaders was Gates Willey. He was grandfather of Mrs. Harriet Baggs.

David Lyon, son of Gad Lyon and grandfather of Mrs. Frederick L. Burr, was also a leader.

The next leader that we can get any trace of was Hubbard Dutton, son of Dea. Oliver Dutton and father of Caroline Sikes, wife of Charles Sikes. Deacon Dutton was a leader for many years and also taught singing school several times in town.

It is thought that Lyman Fuller was a leader. He was grandfather of Mrs. Charles P. Jones.

Dr. Washington B. Alden is believed to have been a leader.

Davenport L. Fuller was a leader of the First Church choir for about twenty-five years. He also led the choir in the Methodist Church in Ludlow and taught singing school in town.

Jeremiah Dutton, nephew of Hubbard Dutton, is believed to have been a leader.

James S. Sikes, son of Chester Sikes, led for a time.

Benjamin F. Burr was leader of the choir for thirty years almost continuously. The church desiring to recognize his faithful services, adopted the following testimonial at their annual meeting, held January 3, 1889: "Whereas Brother Benjamin F. Burr has decided, much to the regret of the people, to retire from the office of chorister, it has seemed fitting that some recognition of his long service in the public worship of this church be expressed. Therefore it is

THE FIRST OR TOWN CHURCH

resolved: that this church extends to Brother Benjamin F. Burr its warm appreciation of his more than twenty years' leading of the singing in our public worship; for his conscientious fidelity in attendance, his fine sense of fitness in suiting the music to the various occasions of sorrow and joy; for maintaining such continuous harmony not only among the members of his choir, but with the congregation and the pastor. And also we would gratefully remember the many years that he served under other leaders before his services as chorister. For these manifold services we express our thankful appreciation and commend him to the great Rewarder, who suffers not that a cup of cold water rendered in his name shall be without recompense of reward."

JAMES OSMYN KENDALL

Other leaders have been: Mrs. Maude Fuller Rhodes, Edward E. Chapman, Willis Fisher, Mrs. Lillian Jones Blish, and Miss Marion Jones, who is the present leader. The last two are daughters of Charles P. Jones.

MUSICAL INSTRUMENTS

The first musical instruments known to be used in the first church (which is now the town house) were a bass viol and violins. The bass viol was played by Miss Caroline Fuller, daughter of Ely Fuller. Violins were played by Edmund and William Sikes, and Lyman Burr, father of B. F. Burr.

After leaving the first church building and going into the new church more instruments were added. A flute was played by Nathaniel Stebbins, uncle of B. F. Burr, also one double bass viol and one single bass viol. Later, at times, more violins and flutes were used. Austin Dutton, nephew of Hubbard Dutton, and Dr. W. B. Alden and Chauncey L.

Buell played the bass viols. Violins were played by Edmund Sikes, William Sikes, Albert Fuller, and Lyman Burr; Albert Fuller, also a Mr. Wilcox, and B. F. Burr, played flutes. There was then quite an orchestra.

In May, 1836, a flute was bought "for the use of the choir of singers in the first parish in Ludlow, to be parish property." In accordance with a vote passed April 16, 1838, a violin was purchased "for which was paid fourteen dollars and fifty cents, to be parish property."

In 1867 there was a change of musical instruments in church. Dea. Joseph Miller presented the church with a fine Excelsior organ that was used for some time and then the church placed it in the chapel and bought a seraphine. In 1885 Mrs. Angeline White, widow of Samuel White, presented the church with a Clough & Warren organ, which is now in use.

The organists, as remembered, have been: Mrs. Eliza Dutton Alden, daughter of Hubbard Dutton; Mrs. Julia Parsons Bodfish, daughter of Dea. Elisha T. Parsons; Miss Harriet Fuller, daughter of Gilbert E. Fuller; Mrs. Angelia Fairbanks Wait, widow of L. C. Wait; Miss Carrie Sikes, daughter of James Sikes; Mrs. Emma Lyman Charles, widow of Edmund Charles; Mrs. Sarah E. Fisher, wife of E. N. Fisher; Mrs Lillian Jones Blish and the present organist, Miss Marion Jones.

The church has received several bequests and gifts during its existence as follows:

Bequests

In 1869 from the Pamelia Sikes estate, $300; an income tax of $18 was paid, leaving the net amount,	$282.00
In 1874 from the Chester Sikes estate,	225.00
In 1892 from the Parma Grout estate,	984.41
In 1892 from the James O. Kendall estate,	1,000.00
In 1898 from the Samuel C. Ray estate, $100. The per cent in his estate paid, reduced the sum for the church to	32.00
In 1903 from the Susan A. Green estate,	500.00
In 1907 from the Theodocia P. Clough estate,	200.00
In 1909 from the Angeline White estate,	300.00
In 1911 from the Miss Mary C. Atchinson estate,	500.00
	$4,023.41

Gifts

In 1789, from the First Church in Springfield a communion service, used by the Ludlow Church until 1846. On this service was inscribed the date 1742. It is probably the most ancient service used in that town, and is made of pewter. Now in the Historical Room in Ludlow Village.

In 1837 a bass viol was given by individuals. It was burned in 1894, when C. L. Buell's house was burned.

In 1841, from Edwin Booth of Philadelphia, a Bible for the desk of the church. It was burned in 1859 with the church.

In 1846, from Abner Cady, a prominent member of the church and citizen of the town, a silver communion service at a cost of $75. It was used by the church until January, 1908. Now in the Historical Room of the Hubbard Memorial building at the Village.

In 1867, from Dea. Joseph Miller, a fine Excelsior organ.

In 1870, from William Graves, $20. He did not assist in parish support twenty years ago.

In 1885, from Mrs. Angeline White, a Clough & Warren organ—the price paid by the committee chosen to purchase it was $175. It is still in use.

First Communion Service

This pewter communion service bearing the inscription, "Springfield First Church, 1742," was presented to the First Church in Ludlow in 1789.

In 1887, from Mrs. Harriet Burr (widow of Lyman Burr), 8 dozen silver-plated spoons of the value of $18, and by subscription enough was raised to purchase 7 dozen silver-plated knives and forks, costing $51.90.

In 1907 and 1908, Charles D. Rood of Springfield, Mass., a native of Ludlow, who has always manifested a deep interest in the town, gave to the Church the munificent sum of $10,000, the interest of which is to be used perpetually and annually, to be divided as follows: the sum of $1,000 for the Sabbath school; $1,000 to add to the pastor's salary; $1,000 for repairs to the church; $2,000 for the worthy poor of Ludlow Center; $1,000 for prizes to the best scholars in the different schools; $4,000, known as the Centennial Fund, to be used for the centennials of the town in 1974, 2074, 2174, and 2274.

The church passed the following resolutions at their annual meeting, after a vote was taken "to accept the bountiful and generous gift of Charles D. Rood with its various provisions":

Resolved: That the First Church of Ludlow wish to extend to Charles D. Rood of Springfield their hearty thanks for his generous Christmas gift and for the heartfelt interest he manifested in making such a donation to the old Church in the town which was the home of his father and grandfather and also the place of his birth, and in which he has always manifested a deep interest.

Resolved: That whereas these gifts are to be perpetuated through future generations, the giver has endeared himself not only to us but to our children and children's children.

Resolved: That his thoughtfulness to provide for the poor, the Sunday School, and the encouragement to young men to grow up to clean, pure, and noble manhood is the beautiful side of such a gift, and we feel that as the years go by the gift will be more and more appreciated.

In 1908 a group of pictures of the former and present deacons of the church was presented by Benjamin F. Burr and hung at the right of the pulpit.

In the same year Charles D. Rood gave to the church an individual communion service, to the value of $55. He also gave $20 towards repairs on the parsonage and later gave a new carpet at a cost of $281.48.

Other gifts are $25 from Mrs. James Talcott of New York City to the young people to help procure an organ for the chapel, and from A. W. Lincoln and J. C. Bridgman of Springfield, who gave in 1859 a Bible for the pulpit, and after the erection of the chapel a Bible for use in the chapel.

Mr. and Mrs. Moses Clark of Newton, Mass., gave to the church a baptismal ewer about 1908.

Deacons of the Church

Jonathan Bartlett (?)	Benjamin Sikes
Timothy Keyes	Oliver Dutton
Jonathan Clough (?)	Joseph Miller chosen in 1824
David Lyon	Ashbel Burr " " 1824
Job Pease	Alva Sikes " " 1839
Stephen Jones	Elisha T. Parsons " " 1848

THE FIRST OR TOWN CHURCH

George Booth	chosen in 1853		Alfred T. Jones	chosen in 1900		
Oshea Walker	"	" 1854	Elbridge J. Streeter	"	" 1904	
Henry S. Jones	"	" 1866	George H. Sprague	"	" 1904	
George R. Clark	"	" 1866	Elmer H. Carver	"	" 1907	
Herbert E. Miller	"	" 1893				
Gillen D. Atchinson	"	" 1897				

The last three named persons are the present deacons.

Clerks of the Parish to 1897

Theodore Sikes
Simeon Jones
Chauncey L. Buell
George Booth
Benjamin F. Burr
Edwin Booth
Gillen D. Atchinson
J. O. Kendall
Benjamin F. Burr

Lucien N. Lyon
George R. Clark
Herbert E. Miller
Charles P. Jones
Rev. M. P. Dickey
George H. Sprague
Mrs. Amnie Hubbard
Alfred T. Jones
Rev. Everett D. Francis

We find that the records of the church business were made by the pastors previous to the year 1867. In that year, Rev. C. L. Cushman was elected clerk; he signed the records as scribe.

Church Clerks after Incorporation in 1897

Rev. Everett D. Francis, 1897–1905
George H. Sprague, 1905
A. Lincoln Johnson, 1905–1906
Leavitt Perham, 1906–

The last named person is the present clerk.

In January, 1900, a Young People's Christian Endeavor Society was organized, which was well supported by the young people of the church. Meetings were held in the chapel every week and much interest manifested. In 1909 the society was given up and for several months no young people's meetings were held. In the winter of 1910 and 1911, meetings were again held under the auspices of the young people of the church, and in May, 1911, a new Christian Endeavor Society was formed.

Other organizations in the church are the Ladies' Missionary Societies, auxiliaries of the American Foreign Missionary Society and the Home Missionary Society, to which they contribute annually.

There is a Ladies' Society which looks after the social interests of the church. It contributes to the home expenses of the church and for other worthy objects in the community.

The Sabbath School of the First Church

The first Sabbath school was established in the spring of 1820, during the pastorate of the Rev. Mr. Wright. He was chosen president and Messrs. Jonathan Sikes and Eliphal Booth, directors. Their work was like that of the superintendent of the present day. There were about 50 members at that time.

The order of exercises consisted of recitations of portions of the Scriptures and hymns, and the Ten Commandments. (Perhaps portions of the Catechism were committed to memory, but there is no record to that effect.)

No records of the school were kept in the first twenty-seven years and they are very imperfect for the most part since that time. But it is safe to say that the history of the Sunday school of this church, though unwritten, is one of its brightest pages. In few churches have the members so generally attended the school and by example, as well as diligent interest in the study of the Word, commended Bible study to the youth. This is true now and was as true a half century ago, when the Sunday school was regarded more of a children's institution than it is to-day.

In 1847, the year when the records were begun, Elisha T. Parsons was chosen superintendent and continued until 1850 in that capacity. There are no records from 1850 to 1857, when the election of Henry S. Jones is noted; he was re-elected in 1858.

Following are the names of the superintendent from 1850 to 1911: James W. Kendall, 1859, 1860; Franklin P. Tilley, 1861; no record for 1862; David C. Jones, 1863, 1864; Chauncey L. Buell, 1865, 1866, 1867; Franklin P. Tilley, 1869; Davenport L. Fuller, 1870, 1871; Lucien N. Lyon, 1872, 1873; Gillen D. Atchinson, 1874, 1875; E. E. Charles, 1876; James O. Kendall, 1877, 1878; George R. Clark, 1879 to 1884; Rev. M. P. Dickey, 1885 to 1889; Robert H. Jones, 1890; Gillen D. Atchinson, 1891, 1892; George H. Sprague, 1893, 1894; Frank E. Sikes, 1895 to 1897; Gillen D. Atchinson, 1898 to 1901; Edwin A. Davenport, 1902; A. Lincoln Johnson, 1903 to 1905; Charles W. Streeter, 1906 to 1908; Charles E. Chapman, 1909 to 1911.

Old Methodist Church at Ludlow Center

VI

OTHER CHURCH ORGANIZATIONS

THE METHODIST CHURCH—The beginnings—The first itinerants—"Master Frost"—Evangels—The first class—The quarterly meeting—Elder Elijah Hedding—Alexander McLean—"Methodist Legal Society"—Rev. Wilbur Fisk—Building the church—"Parson Jennison"—Difficulty—McLean's appeal—Aid—A great revival—Other revivals—Millerism—Remodeling—"Father Banister"—War record—Rev. Alfred Noon—Wesleyan Praying Band—New edifice—List of preachers.

THE UNION CHURCH—Beginnings—Pioneer—A revival—Meeting places—Erection of church—Question of privileges—Division—Congregational organization—Original members—Financial disaster—Reorganization—Union Church—Rev. Austin Gardner—Renovation of church interior—Rev. John Coyle—Improvements—Other pastors—Rededication—Present pastor—List of pastors—List of deacons.

ST. ANDREW'S CHURCH—Early efforts—A mission—First services—First confirmation—Building the church—Dedication—Officers—Memorial gifts—Boy choir.

ST. JOHN THE BAPTIST CHURCH AND PARISH—Parish formation—Rev. M. A. Desrochers—First meeting place—Gift of church site—Erection of church—Dedication—Size of parish—Increase—Value of buildings—Present pastor.

THE METHODIST CHURCH

THE beginnings of Methodism in Ludlow occurred in the last decade of the eighteenth century. The first itinerant to visit the town was probably George Pickering, and the second was George Roberts. The efforts of both antedate 1793. The first prominent layman was Samuel Frost, familiarly known as "Master Frost," who lived in the southwestern part of the town. This same Samuel Frost was a very liberal man, and gave freely of his means to support the itinerant preachers. To those remonstrating at his prodigality, he retorted that he could raise "Methodist ears of corn" as long as his arm. In 1793, Mr. Frost invited the itinerants to visit the town and to preach at his house. Nathaniel Chapin, Uriah Clough, and Joel Farnum responded and services were held. The experiment was successful in awakening an interest, and in 1795 the Tolland circuit itinerants supplied statedly for a time. The names of the evangelists have been preserved; the most prominent being Menzies Rayner, Lemuel Smith, Zadoc Priest, Daniel Ostrander, and Laban Clark.

These flying evangels left their pointed message and sped away, leaving no organization and no apparent lasting results, save the good seed sown, which, to all appearances, was buried deeply.

But these old itinerants knew no such word as fail. In 1801, probably on invitation of "Master Frost," the preachers again visited the town and were successful. Meanwhile the new cause had received accessions. In the autumn of 1801, David Orcutt removed hither. The first Methodist class was organized March 22, 1802, by Henry Eames, a circuit preacher. There were about a dozen members and David Orcutt became the first class leader. For seven years at least meetings were held at the house of Samuel Frost. Augustus Jocelyn, the next circuit preacher, established a Sabbath appointment in Ludlow and spent a considerable portion of his time here.

In August, 1802, occurred a notable event in the history of the movement—what is now remembered as an "old-fashioned quarterly meeting." The place appointed, of course the house of Samuel Frost (on what is now the Kellogg place, near Eaton's mills), being too small, was enlarged for the occasion by the addition of a rude shed covered with brush and tree branches. Preparations complete, an audience was not wanting, for crowds assembled. A large delegation from the towns around, even as far as East Hartford, Granville, and Pomfret, came to the place of rendezvous. The townspeople, of course, were out in force to see the first real demonstration here of what some have been pleased to term "Christianity in earnest." A sermon by the presiding elder, Daniel Ostrander, perhaps his grandest effort, made the occasion memorable to all. From this time to 1808 there were maintained services, private and public, without much omission. For a while there were preaching services in two places in town. Among the preachers were Gove, Tucker, Sampson, Norris, and Lambord. There was rather decrease than otherwise in the latter part of the time mentioned, until finally the class was discontinued by Lambord. Uriah Clough, however, gathered the remnants of the organization into another class after a little delay. This class seems to have lasted during half a score of years at least.

In 1810, or in the succeeding year, came Elder Elijah Hedding to Ludlow. Appointed to the New London district as presiding elder, he

OTHER CHURCH ORGANIZATIONS 179

found it desirable to move from his itinerant's home at Winchester, N. H., to some convenient point in the central part of the field assigned. The feebleness of the denomination in New England at the time is evident from the fact that Mr. Hedding selected Ludlow as his home. His oversight reached from New Hampshire line to Long Island Sound, from Needham to the ridge of the Green Mountains.

Here he uniquely combined the duties of presiding elder in the Methodist church and pastor in the Congregational for a year, both with complete satisfaction.

The Rev. Alexander McLean has already been introduced as the acting pastor of the Town church from 1813 to 1817, when he terminated his official services.

Of course no demonstrations towards a pulpit supply were made during the labors of Hedding and McLean. Yet during the ministry of the latter he seems to have encouraged the visits of Methodist preachers, who often, we are told, spoke in the old meeting-house. Quarterly meetings were held in the edifice, and a local preachers' conference once occurred there. He also reorganized the West Middle class on a more permanent basis.

After 1816 there was little done by the Methodists for a number of years. Occasional preaching services occurred throughout the town, and the social meetings were more or less faithfully attended. Yet there was little accomplished save by the agitation of the Arminian tenets and preparation for future successes. About 1820 the opponents of the parish tax law formed an organization under the name of the "Methodist Legal Society," with McLean as nominal pastor. The class was almost defunct in 1825, when aid came from an unexpected quarter.

The earlier itinerants were not men of eminent scholastic attainments, and hence found themselves at a disadvantage when before many of the New England people. And yet their natural qualifications were not to be despised, while the experience gained in their peculiar work was better for them than a collegiate education. Still, advantage would frequently be taken of their lack of specific education by pedantic clergymen of the standing order. Not always did the itinerant come out second best, even in these encounters. The anecdote of Jesse Lee is illustrative of this. An Orthodox minister addressing him in Greek, he replied in Low Dutch, much to the discomfiture of his antagonist, who supposed the response was in Hebrew.

But when Rev. Wilbur Fisk, a graduate of Brown University, went into the Methodist itinerancy, the new movement received a dignity not before obtained this side of the sea. As he took the school recently established in the northern wilds of Newmarket, N. H., and transplanted it to the town of Wilbraham, scarcely less undeveloped, the people of the standing order looked on at least with respect. And when this same Wilbur Fisk, as pious as learned, as earnest in mission work as in founding schools, of rare eloquence and rarer earnestness, left his classes behind and rode into Ludlow to preach the gospel to handfuls of people, it began to be understood that Methodism had come to town to make its abode here.

Dr. Fisk was not long in winning the confidence and attention of those who were willing to convene at the residence of Rev. Alexander McLean (the present home of Eugene Clark) to listen to his earnest proclamation of the gospel truth. Soon there was a harvest of souls and a demand for organization into a church. In a few months Mr. Fisk, through Mr. McLean, caused letters missive to be sent through the town, inviting the Methodists and all favorable to the enterprise, to meet at the house of Zera Fuller (where Mrs. A. J. Chapin now lives), on the afternoon of February 5, 1827, to consult with reference to "erecting a house for the Public Worship of God, to be located as near the center of the M. E. Society in this town as possible." Soon everything was under way. Captain Joseph Miller furnished the timber. Rev. Isaac Jennison, preacher, architect, and boss-carpenter, went with the old gentleman and his little grandson (the late Dr. William B. Miller of Springfield) to select the tall straight pines for the sills, posts, and plates. They were gathered from the forest near Wood's pond, where Sylvester Miller, (brother of Col. John Miller and uncle to Wilbur F. Miller) cut down the first tree marked.

McLean was a valuable and persistent worker in the enterprise, soliciting funds and labor and material the whole town over. Few, if any, were slighted in those invitations. The axe and adze were made to fly (by none more dexterously than by Parson Jennison), the patient oxen and sturdy drivers conducted the logs to the mill, and soon the hand of Jennison had framed the massive timbers. The crowd who came to that raising saw every stick take its place in order, every mortise receiving its tenon to the very shoulder, every trunnion going home tightly, and no rum to help either, thanks to the advance in temperance principles in half a century. The building was 40 by 50 feet. At last the work was done and the place ready for the dedication, which occurred, probably, July 5, 1828.

Methodism was now fairly established in the town. Parson Jennison and Noah Perrin supplied the charge that year, while a new minister was appointed to preach after the dedication.

A lamentable difficulty with Mr. McLean occurred just at this time, creating hard feelings, and much discussion, oral and printed, and resulted in the withdrawal of that gentleman from the denomination and the closing up of the affairs of the so-called "Methodist Legal Society" of Ludlow.

Following are extracts from "An Appeal to the Public" sent out by Rev. Alexander McLean in 1828.

The town of Ludlow, Hampden Co., Mass., being the place in which I, Alexander McLean, reside. . . . it may not be . . . uninteresting to give a short account of my introduction into said town in the character of a minister of the gospel, with a sketch of the rise and progress of Methodism in the place, from that time to the present.

In the month of October, 1813, the inhabitants of Ludlow, in town meeting, legally assembled, passed a vote inviting me to supply the desk for one year, making ample provision for my support. I accepted their invitation, and on the first Sabbath of November following commenced my ministerial services with flattering prospects. In the course of the year, much attention was paid to the subject of religion and many professed to experience it, and appeared to rejoice in its divine consolation. Everything moved pleasantly and agreeably between myself and the inhabitants of the town. . . . Methodist traveling preachers introduced themselves into the place . . . made an attempt to form a society. About twelve persons were formed into a class; the class placed under the care of the traveling connexion, and the town taken into the Tolland circuit.

. . . I continued to preach, as the town's minister for six years; at the expiration of which time, the Congregationalists by a majority of votes obtained the meeting-house and ministerial fund, and soon after settled the Rev. Mr. Wright, a respectable clergyman, who still continues with them in much harmony and love.

A portion of the inhabitants formed themselves into a Religious Society by the name of the Methodist Episcopal Society, and chose me for their minister, which relation continued until the first of March, 1828. Since the settlement of Rev. Mr. Wright, and my establishment over the Methodist Legal Society, few towns, it is presumed, have enjoyed more tranquillity than Ludlow.

In the autumn of 1827, a revival of religion commenced in the town; the Methodist traveling preachers were active in it; they added a considerable number to the church, and took charge of them. In the month of February, 1827, a meeting was called, to see if the members of the Methodist Church, and their friends, thought it expedient to unite in erecting a chapel. The conclusion was to draft subscription papers. This was done without delay; I was active in their circulation; obtained generous subscriptions; subscribed liberally myself, and it was believed the sums subscribed, with considerable assistance, would warrant the undertaking. At the opening of the spring the business was commenced with much spirit and energy; on the tenth of May, the chapel was raised; and on the first Sabbath in August made comfortable to meet in. . . . The views of the Committee and subscribers extended no further in our first engagement respecting the chapel than to finish the outside, and lay the lower floor. . . . I paid, in money and subscribers' notes, $189.25; balance due on book, $75.67.

Whenever I preached on the Sabbath, at the Springfield Manufacturing Establishment (called "the river") my uniform practice has been to spend the time from the close of the afternoon service to the setting of the sun, with some family in the village; and after that time to return home, a distance of about three miles.

A considerable debt remained upon the people after closing up the affairs of the Methodist Legal Society. This was partially relieved by contributions from the churches of the denomination elsewhere. All was in readiness for the revival efforts under the ministry of Samuel Davis, in 1831, which resulted in a very demonstrative work of grace. A large number from the place attended a camp-meeting in Haddam, Conn., and brought back with them some who had there professed conversion. At meetings following in the church, lasting eight days, about two hundred made a profession of religion, of whom more than one hundred and fifty claimed to find peace at the church altar. The news spread about in all the towns around. A large load of wild young men came from Northampton to have a "good time" at the service, but it is averred that every one was brought under conviction and went home with a different purpose and a changed life. A man addicted to profanity, named Kendall, left his work in the field under profound convictions, went to the church, cried for mercy, and passed out a better man. Was this enthusiasm? Surely it could not be baneful to arrest the plan of rioters and displace cursing by praises.

We find incidental allusions to another work of grace in 1837, under

INTERIOR OF METHODIST CHURCH

Philo Hawkes, while there are still living witnesses to the revival scenes in Dadmun's ministry in 1842. The Millerite excitement of 1841-1843 made little impression in Ludlow, although so near the home of the leader in those scenes. Miller came repeatedly into town to hold meetings, but with little lasting success. Ludlow takes slowly to new and startling ideas, but grasps firmly whatever it accepts as truth. Clapp, minister in 1843, was the first careful annalist of the church, while Fleming (1844) will be remembered as the preacher in charge when the parsonage was erected. Of them all C. D. Rogers (1834) bears the palm for quaintness.

The Methodist Society has moved along very quietly and with a degree of efficiency. Its pulpit has never failed of a supply; its ministers never left without a support. In 1858 the chapel was repaired and enlarged, and a bell hung in the tower. The best of all was, God was with them, and under the labors of the pastor, Rev. Franklin Fisk, and his co-operators, some persons were wonderfully transformed. One, well-known, an innholder, took his liquors to the street and poured them away, and then renounced his life of sin, to manifest ever afterward a determination to stand approved before his Maker.

This church suffered severely in loss of membership during the Civil War, two of its class leaders (Putnam and Crowninshield) and one local preacher (Potts), besides others of its most devoted members (laymen), going away to return no more. Rev. D. K. Banister, or "Father Banister," as he was affectionately called, was virtually the pastor of the town, and very active during the earlier days of the trying conflict. Under his ministry, as well as the two following, there were special revival scenes. During Rev. Alfred Noon's pastorate the well-known Wesleyan Praying Band of Springfield rendered efficient service in special religious work.

NEW METHODIST CHURCH, LUDLOW VILLAGE

The relations between the two societies at the Center have ever been harmonious. Each has recognized the other, each has welcomed the other's pastor to its own pulpit. While the Methodist church was in process of reconstruction the doors of the Congregationalist edifice were thrown open to them, and we have seen how the compliment was returned in the following year. (See page 132.) In every good work the churches are ready to co-operate. Here surely may be found an exemplification, in the true spiritual sense, of the words of inspiration, "Behold how good and how pleasant it is for brethren to dwell together in unity."

In 1904, on account of the increasing number of the congregation residing in the village, it was deemed advisable to transfer the place of worship from the Center. Accordingly a new edifice was erected in the village at a cost of $12,218, and dedicated January 4, 1905. The land on which it stands was given by the Ludlow Manufacturing Associates.

The old church and parsonage were sold by the Methodist Society to Arthur D. King. The latter was moved across the street and remodeled. The church still occupies its old site, but is no longer used for religious purposes.

Methodist Preachers
Itinerants

George Pickering	—— Goodhue
George Roberts	—— Jocelyn
Nathaniel Chapin	—— Nichols
Uriah Clough	—— Batchelder
Joel Farnum	—— Willard
Menzies Rayner	—— Thomas
Lemuel Smith	—— Hill
Christopher Spry	—— Tinkham
Nicholas Snethen	—— Smith
Zadoc Priest	—— Gove
—— Martin	—— Tucker
—— Rogers	—— Sampson
Sylvester Hutchinson	—— Norris
Joshua Taylor	—— Lambert
—— Chickerton	—— Streeter
Daniel Ostrander	Elijah Hedding
Laban Clark	Alexander McLean
—— Ames	

Union Church, 1845

OTHER CHURCH ORGANIZATIONS

SINCE ORGANIZING THE CHURCH

1826	Wilbur Fisk	1861	William G. Leonard
1827, 1828	Isaac Jennison	1862, 1863	Daniel K. Banister
	Noah Perrin	1864–1866	William J. Pomfret
1829	Aaron Waite	1867, 1868	Levin A. Bosworth
1830, 1831	Samuel Davis	1869	Jonas M. Clark
1832	Salmon Hull	1870	John W. Lee
1833	Paul Townsend	1871, 1872	John W. Merrill, D.D.
1834	Charles D. Rogers	1873, 1874	Alfred Noon
1835	Amasa Taylor	1875–1877	Nathaniel H. Martin
1836, 1837	Philo Hawkes	1878, 1879	Charles H. Vinton
1838	Charles Virgin	1880	Alfred C. Godfrey
1839, 1840	James Nichols	1881–1883	William H. Adams
1841	William Campbell	1884–1886	Daniel Atkins
1841, 1842	John W. Dadmun	1887, 1888	William Ferguson
1843	William A. Clapp	1889, 1890	William H. Adams
1844	William Fleming	1891, 1892	George F. Durgin
1845	Asa Barnes	1893, 1894	G. Whitefield Simonson
1846	Ephraim Scott	1895, 1896	George W. Clark
1847	Luther B. Clark	1897, 1898	Newton M. Caton
1848, 1849	John Caldwell	1899, 1900	Francis M. Wheeler
1850, 1851	Moses Stoddard	1901–1903	Eaton B. Marshall
1852, 1853	James W. Mowry	1904, 1905	Putnam Webber
1854, 1855	Kinsman Atkinson	1906, 1907	Francis W. McConel
1856	Nathan A. Soule		Miss Ina L. Morgan
1857, 1858	Franklin Fisk	1908–1911	Levin P. Causey
1859, 1860	George Prentice		

THE UNION CHURCH

Any history of the early years of the Union Church of Christ in Ludlow must of necessity be more or less incomplete, because of the lack of connected records concerning the events of that period. The old-time community in the section of the town near the "falls of Wallamanumps" and known as Jenksville, seems to have received visits from Methodist itinerant ministers during the year 1828 and continuously after that time.

Rev. Mr. Foster, principal of the Wilbraham Academy, was probably the pioneer, and made his first visit on invitation of John Miller, compliant with the request of Benjamin Jenks. The events intimated occurred as early as 1831, the place being then a not unfamiliar one to Methodist ministers. Samuel Davis was the preacher in charge of Ludlow, and visited Jenksville in August with others of his profession. His own simple account is as follows:

About six weeks since, the work broke out at another factory village, [than Chicopee] on the circuit, called Put's Bridge, in Ludlow. The revival here took place while we were trying to hold forth the Saviour as the sinner's friend, and the necessity of each and all becoming reconciled to God. Much feeling was manifest in the congregation. At the close of the sermon an invitation was given to all that had resolved on seeking the Lord, to come forward, and fall on their knees, while the people of God should address the throne of grace in their behalf. At this instant, to our astonishment, more than one third of the congregation came forward, and fell on their knees, with groans and sobs enough to melt the hardest heart; but soon the mourning of some was turned into rejoicing. Our meetings from that time to the present have been very interesting. It has not been uncommon for six or seven to find peace and pardon at a meeting. The glorious work is still going on here. (From *New England Christian Herald*, October 26, 1831.)

Granted, if desired, that every one of these did not maintain a good profession through the days to come; granted, if it were the case, that the days of excitement soon passed away; yet there must have been a beneficial result flowing from such services, and we claim, in the absence of any other well-grounded reason to account for the conceded change for the better in the morals of the people, that there was an intimate relation between the revival and the reformation.

Religious services were held and special revival interest manifested at different periods. No church building was erected for some years, but meetings were held in the homes of the people and later in a room furnished for the purpose in the factory. Mr. W. F. Miller remembers attending Sunday services in the east end of the upper story of the old cotton mill, at which ministers from out of town and others supplied as preachers or leaders. Colonel Robb, commandant at the United States Armory, conducted the last service held there. Mr. Miller also remembers hearing Dexter Rood, father of Charles D. Rood, play a flute in the choir during the services at the mill.

Rev. B. F. Lambord (Meth.) served the community as minister in 1841 and 1842. During 1845 and 1846 Daniel E. Chapin (Meth.) was

OTHER CHURCH ORGANIZATIONS

preacher in charge, and during his successful ministry a church was erected by the property-owners in the community and the building dedicated as a union house of worship December 25, 1845. Rev. Dr. Holdich, of the American Bible Society, preached the dedicatory sermon from the sublime text, "Great is the mystery of godliness," and immediately afterward consecrated the place to the worship of God.

During the first year the church was occupied by both Methodists and Congregationalists, but was controlled by the Methodists. A

METHODIST CHURCH, JENKSVILLE
Built in 1847. Removed in 1863 to Warren

HOME OF COL. JOHN MILLER
Now owned by Wilbur F. Miller

question of privileges arising between the two, the former withdrew and built for themselves a church opposite Col. John Miller's which they occupied only a few years. On account of the financial disaster of 1848, the members were scattered and the society was left with an eighteen hundred dollar debt, which it was unable to lift, Colonel Miller, father of Wilbur F. Miller, being the only parishioner with means remaining in the place. For a time, Mr. Lee, a local preacher from Wilbraham, held occasional services, but later the church was closed, although the debt had become considerably reduced. The building was finally sold and removed to Warren.

From the original minutes of the scribe of the council of churches we find that on June 24, 1847, an ecclesiastical council was convened "at the meeting-house in Jenksville, Ludlow, for the purpose of organizing a Congregational Church." The following churches were represented: First Church in Springfield, Rev. S. Osgood, D.D., pastor; Fourth Church in Springfield, Rev. E. Russell, pastor, Bro. Thos. Shepherd, delegate; Sixth Church in Springfield, Rev. S. G. Clapp, pastor, Dea. J. K. Fletcher, delegate; Church in Ludlow Center, Rev. J. W. Tuck, pastor, Dea. Alva Sikes, delegate; Church in Wilbraham, Rev. J. Bowers, pastor.

After the organization of the council, statements were made by the committee respecting the preliminary steps for the formation of a church and the prospects for supporting the institutions of the gospel; the articles of faith and the covenant were read and approved; and the following members were then received:

John M. Spooner	Charles B. Pomeroy
Phoebe Spooner	Mary A. Pomeroy
Solomon Marsh	Harriet Willard
Jerusha Wilder	Lathrop Merrick
Martha Bugbee	Sally Merrick
Hannah Atwood	Sarah Sheldon
Esther King	Susannah Sheldon
Elmira C. Jenks	Abiathar Sheldon
Susan Lemon	Orlando Smith
Susan Putnam	Jonathan H. Andrus
Jerre Miller	Lucina Andrus
Mary B. Fiske	Mary Newell
Harriet Miller	Benjamin Sikes

A call was extended by the new church to Rev. William Hall, who was ordained January 20, 1848. But in the same year the Springfield Manufacturing Company, forerunner of the Ludlow Manufacturing Company, failed and suspended business; and in consequence the members of the church were scattered to other communities and Mr. Hall, feeling compelled to resign, was dismissed.

OTHER CHURCH ORGANIZATIONS

For several years, during much of the time from 1849 to 1866, no regular form of organized church work was carried on, with the exception of a Sunday school, though Methodist preachers were supplied by the conference for various years during that period. W. H. Daniels (Meth.), a student from Wilbraham Academy, was present during the revival interest of 1857 and was instrumental in carrying on an extensive religious work here.

The following spring brought a conference preacher again, Rev. David K. Merrill (Meth.), with annual successors: in 1859, L. R. S. Brewster (Meth.); 1860, Geo. E. Chapman (Meth.); 1862, John Noon (Meth.), father of the Rev. Alfred Noon, the author of "Ludlow: a Century and a Centennial"; 1863, J. A. Kibbe (Meth.).

In the year 1867, on June 6, a council was called to reorganize the church, under a creed which would be broad enough to include Christians of all denominations, and bearing the name, "Union Church."

That the result desired was attained may be seen from the fact that of the fifteen members, ten were from the Methodist denomination, one a Presbyterian, one a Congregationalist, and three without former church connection. A unanimous call to the pastorate had been extended to the Rev. Austin Gardner of Granville, Mass. A confession of faith and a church covenant were adopted, and the council, after examination of the candidate for the pastorate, proceeded with the exercises of installation and of recognition of the new church, the sermon being preached by the Rev. Richard G. Green, pastor of the First Congregational Church of Springfield. Rev. Mr. Gardner occupied the pastorate for about two years.

The following is from a letter written by the Rev. Austin H. Gardner:

I was called to Jenksville to be the first pastor of the Union Church. Rev. William C. Foster had been a missionary of the Congregational churches of Hampden County and it was thought that something could be done to build up a church at Jenksville. Business was flourishing. They made bags. But in 1868 the bottom fell out of the market, and the village was sold over our heads. It was estimated at $200,000, and sold under the hammer at $100,000. Many of the people moved away. We lived in the house south of the church. Mr. Root, formerly overseer of the mills, lived directly opposite. The family, I think, are all dead.

I went over the country in December to Canton, Conn., to bury a man from Ludlow. The result was I was called to the pastorate of the Canton Center Church in 1869 The church at Jenksville was small and there was no prospect of its growth. We buried a little boy in 1868, Frederick Robertson. His grave was in the cemetery a few rods northeast of the church. It has been subsequently removed somewhere up town.

The changes have been so great in following years that passing on the trolley from Palmer to Springfield a few years ago, I did not recognize Jenksville. It had outgrown itself. It gives me great pleasure to know that the little church of 1867–1869 is a strong and vigorous church. When I was installed over it in 1867, Dr. Vaille of Palmer and Dr. Buckingham of Springfield were on the Council, and at my dismissal in 1869, Martin S. Howard of Wilbraham was scribe of the Council, and I was scribe of the Council that settled him in 1868.

I would say that I am standing on the third round of the octogenarian ladder, and if I live to July 2, 1910, I shall be 84. God blessed me in Jenksville, and he has blessed me in all the days of my pilgrimage to the present, nor will He leave me when so near my journey's end. I expect to meet a great number in the better land, where the changes of time will be unknown.

Truly yours,
Austin Gardner, Pastor.

Willington, Conn., April 12, 1910.

After Mr. Gardner came two Methodist pastors,—in 1872, Rev. H. E. Crocker, and in 1873, Rev. J. A. DeForest. In 1874 a Congregationalist was called, the Rev. Timothy Lyman. During 1877 and 1878, the last years of his service, a general renovation of the interior of the church was made.

In 1878, the Rev. Chester L. Cushman (Cong.) of Phillipston, Mass., became acting pastor. Mr. Cushman was formerly pastor of the Congregational Church at Ludlow Center. He was a strong and effective speaker and an experienced pastoral worker. He remained here until his death, April 28, 1881.

In October, 1881, John P. Coyle became acting pastor of the church, having been licensed to preach by the Presbyterian denomination in Pennsylvania. He was ordained and installed as pastor May 3, 1882, by a council of which a majority of the members were Congregationalists, the others being Methodists. The interest and enthusiasm with which he carried on his work, the high type of Christian living he displayed, his sympathy and interest in the entire community, together with his ability as a student of religious and social problems, made his brief pastorate one of lasting benefit. He later occupied a prominent place

Union Church, 1905

in the Congregational denomination, filling important pastorates in North Adams, Mass., and Denver, Colo.

Following Mr. Coyle the church was faithfully served from 1884 to 1886 by the Rev. Preston Barr, of Pennsylvania, a man of exceptional ability along educational lines. His successor, the Rev. Edward Day, was ordained and installed as pastor September 15, 1886. He was dismissed in 1890, after a successful pastorate during which a substantial increase was made in the church membership.

The Rev. Abram J. Quick was called to the pastorate and installed October 15, 1891. After five years of service he was followed by the Rev. William Arthur Thomas, who acted as pastor from 1897 to 1900. He was a popular and successful pastor. Large additions were made to the church membership, and its social life received much inspiration from his labors.

The Rev. Thomas D. McLean served as acting pastor from 1900 till 1904; and the Rev. Claude A. Butterfield, from 1904 till 1907, each with a considerable degree of success. Mr. Butterfield was ordained by a council in June, 1904, and was actively identified with the extensive work done in remodeling and refurnishing the church building. A handsome new pipe organ was installed, together with complete new furnishings throughout the building. The re-dedication services were held March 22, 1905, the sermon being delivered by the Rev. O. S. Davis of New Britain, Conn.

In October, 1905, occurred the death of John E. Stevens, an honored and valued member of the church, who, though at the head of the large manufacturing interests of the town, yet found time to devote to the work of the church and was a regular attendant at its services. He served as deacon for several years, as superintendent of the Sunday school for two years, as member of the church standing committee at intervals, and in other capacities as a faithful, helpful, and most competent worker.

Rev. Henry F. Burdon, an experienced and successful pastor, was called to the position of acting pastor of this church, and assumed his duties February 1, 1908. He resigned February 1, 1912.

The rapidly changing conditions incident to life in this growing factory village have been such as to seriously affect the church,—the membership being constantly changing, and material interests in the community being prominent. But the church has gained much in influence as it has grown in membership and is filling an important

198 HISTORY OF LUDLOW

place in the moral and spiritual life of the town. At this writing (1911), the total membership is 266,—the parish comprising 180 families.

Ministers of Union Church

M.E.—Methodist Episcopal. Cong.—Congregational. Presb.—Presbyterian

1841, 1842 B. F. Lambord (M. E.)
1845, 1846 Daniel E. Chapin (M. E.)
1847 David Sherman (M. E.)
1848 Z. A. Mudge (M. E.)
1848 William Hall (Cong.)
1857 W. H. Daniels (M. E.)
1858 David K. Merrill (M. E.)
1859 L. R. S. Brewster (M. E.)
1860–1861 Geo. E. Chapman (M. E.)
1862 John Noon (M. E.)
1863 J. A. Kibbe (M. E.)
1867–1869 Austin Gardner (Cong.)
1872 Henry E. Crocker (M. E.)
1873 J. A. DeForest (M. E.)
1874–1878 Timothy Lyman (Cong.)

This list is defective, as there seem no records accessible.

1878–1881 Chester L. Cushman (Cong.)
1882–1884 John P. Coyle (Presb.)
1884–1886 Preston Barr (Presb.)
1886–1890 Edward Day (Cong.)
1891–1896 Abram J. Quick (Cong.)
1897–1900 William A. Thomas (Cong.)
1900–1904 Thomas D. McLean (Cong.)
1904–1907 Claude A. Butterfield (Cong.)
1908–1912 Henry F. Burdon (Cong.)

Deacons of Union Church

1892–1895 Albert Bly, Newton Wallace.
1895–1897 Albert Bly, Charles Mitchell, Sr.
1898 Albert Bly, John E. Stevens, A. H. Halford.
1899 Albert Bly, John E. Stevens, George Elphinstone, Sr., Alexander Cormack.

St. Andrew's Episcopal Church

St. Andrew's Episcopal Church—Interior

OTHER CHURCH ORGANIZATIONS

1900, 1901	Albert Bly, A. H. Halford, Robert Kyle.
1902	Albert Bly, Robert Kyle, Walter Bennett, Ransom M. Morse.
1903	Albert Bly, John E. Stevens, Robert Kyle, Ransom M. Morse, Walter Bennett.
1904, 1905	Albert Bly, Robert Kyle, John E. Stevens, A. A. Gove.
1906	Albert Bly, Robert Kyle, A. A. Gove, Dr. J. W. Hannum.
1907, 1908, 1909	Albert Bly, Robert Kyle, A. A. Gove, Dr. James W. Hannum, James Henderson.
1910, 1911	Albert Bly, Robert Kyle, A. A. Gove, Dr. J. W. Hannum, James Henderson, George Elphinstone, Sr.

Mr. Albert Bly has been Honorary Deacon since 1903.

ST. ANDREW'S CHURCH

One or two efforts prior to January, 1904, were made to hold services of the Episcopal Church in Ludlow, but nothing came of them.

In January, 1904, a report was circulated and appeared in the secular press stating that the Union Church of Ludlow had decided to disorganize. On hearing this a few faithful members of the Episcopal Church thought a favorable opportunity was presented to secure the services of their beloved church.

They applied to the bishop of the diocese, the Rt. Rev. Dr. Alexander H. Vinton in Springfield, and he promptly sent the Rev. W. T. Dakin, rector of St. Peter's Church in Springfield, to supply services. Soon after this a mission was loosely organized under the name of St. Andrew, and Mr. George A. Birnie appointed treasurer. The first services were held in the Masonic Building, January 17, 1904; Sunday school at 3 o'clock, evening prayer and sermon at 4 o'clock.

June 12, 1904, the Rev. Charles E. Hill (recently ordered deacon in All Saints' Church, Worcester) held his first service in St. Andrew's, having been appointed by the bishop to assist Mr. Dakin at St. Peter's and to have charge of the Ludlow work. June 26, Mr. Hill started what has since become the regular Sunday routine, morning prayer and sermon at 10.45, Sunday school at 12 o'clock. On St. Andrew's Day, November 30, 1904, the first class of 18 candidates was presented to the bishop for confirmation. The service was noteworthy as being the first occasion in the history of Ludlow of an official visitation of a bishop.

Quinquagesima Sunday, March 5, 1905, the project of raising funds for the building of a suitable church was started. Mr. Frederic M. Jones generously contributed his efficient services as architect, and September 30, 1905, the corner stone was laid by Bishop Vinton on land given by the Ludlow Manufacturing Associates, on the corner of East and Hampden streets. The church was opened for use and dedicated by the bishop on St. Andrew's Day, which fell in 1905 on Thanksgiving Day; the Bishop celebrated the holy communion at 8 a. m. and confirmed and preached at evening prayer at 8 p. m.

Meanwhile Mr. Hill had been ordained priest on Trinity Sunday, June 18, and St. Andrew's had been regularly organized August 14; Mr. Hill became priest-in-charge. Mr. H. B. Payne was elected warden; Mr. G. A. Birnie, treasurer; Mr. A. E. Booth, clerk, and Messrs. J. Black and W. Rae, vestrymen. A constitution and by-laws were adopted.

A beautiful altar (memorial to John Bliss Stebbins) and a memorial font, with suitable furnishings, were installed and blessed by the bishop, January 10, 1906. The Lent of 1908 was utilized for the holding of a "Lent mission," the fruit of which was the largest communion of St. Andrew's. Easter Day at 8 a. m. 62 communicants received the Holy Mysteries.

In January, 1909, All Saints' Mission in Springfield, of which Mr. Hill had been in charge for a year, since severing his connection with St. Peter's Church, occupied its new church, and as it was necessary to hold morning services in All Saints', Mr. Hill held his last regular service in St. Andrew's, Septuagesima Sunday, February 7, 1909. He resigned his office as priest-in-charge, November 12, 1909, when the Rev. Hugh W. Smith, ordered deacon on that day in Trinity Church, Boston, became deacon-in-charge under the supervision (while he remained deacon) of Mr. Hill. Mr. Smith had acted as lay-reader at St. Andrew's since February 14.

A vested choir of boys sang for the first time in Holy Week, 1910.

ST. JEAN BAPTISTE CHURCH AND PARISH

When it was decided that the French people of Ludlow would separate from St. Aloysius parish of Indian Orchard and form a parish of their own, Rev. M. A. Desrochers was chosen for the task. He came here in January, 1904, to establish the said parish. His first care was to find a place of meeting for the people on Sunday. This was given him by the late John E. Stevens, and the first mass was celebrated January 17,1904, in a room on the top floor of No. 5 Mill.

Later the trustees of the Ludlow Manufacturing Associates presented the parish with a site for the erection of a church. Rev. M. A. Desrochers began at once to raise a fund for the said church, and June 24, 1906, on

St. Jean Baptiste Church   (French Catholic)

the Feast of St. John the Baptist, Rt. Rev. Thomas D. Beaven, bishop of the diocese, dedicated the beautiful church on Hubbard Street to the service of God.

At the time of its foundation, the parish counted but 1,303 souls, whereas, the census taken in the fall of 1910 shows a total of 1,560. Still, this increase over the first census is not so large as it was in 1908, when there were 1,712 people. The buildings, consisting of the church and parsonage, were erected at a cost of over $60,000, and the mortgage to-day is less than $20,000, which shows the generosity of the parishioners.

The present pastor is Rev. Louis F. Gobeil.

VII

INDUSTRIAL HISTORY

Farming—Initial manufactures—Ludlow Glass Works—Minor manufactures—The mill privilege of H. I. Carver—The Lyman Burr industry—The Jenksville Mills—The Springfield Manufacturing Company—Failure—First Ludlow Manufacturing Company—Ludlow Mills Company—Second Ludlow Manufacturing Company—The Ludlow Manufacturing Associates.

FARMING has been the principal occupation of Ludlow since its settlement. Although several important manufacturing industries are established in the town, the inhabitants mainly devote their time and energies to the cultivation of their excellent farms.

EARLY MANUFACTURING

At the close of the eighteenth century initial attempts at manufacturing had already been commenced. In the lay of a road we find reference to "the sawmill of Jonathan Burr and Company," afterwards long known as the McLean privilege, what is left of it being now occupied by Warren D. Fuller. A mill of some kind was also in operation in the extreme northern part of the town, or the "city." At the southwestern corner, also, there was a sawmill at this period.

Very early in the nineteenth century Rufus Calkins had a little chair shop a mile up Higher Brook from the Center post office. Here were made many of the old chairs now to be seen in the more ancient homes. At one time he also adjusted a spindle by means of which he could spin flax or wool. His was the first manufacturing of the kind in the town.

A LUDLOW FARMER

Farther down, below Warren Fuller's privilege, was in 1814 a little fulling mill, operated by Gustavus Pinney. Near its banks at two different places successively, Elisha Fuller carried on a potash establishment, the last location being upon a spot opposite the old Methodist church, on the lot now owned by Charles M. Foster. Harris's mill privilege was under improvement in 1805, under the name of the "Continental Mill," owned by proprietors.

On Broad Brook were two new privileges, now unused: Thornton's sawmill was just at the foot of Burying-Ground Hill, and Alden's sash and blind shop a few rods above. At Ludlow City, it must be recorded, was at one time a distillery. (See "Mill Privilege of H. I. Carver.") Tar kilns were set up here and there, traces being still discernible on Facing Hills and elsewhere.

CALKINS CHAIRS AND BOTTLES FROM LUDLOW GLASS WORKS

Near the old Sikes place, south of the brook, a mile north of the Center churches, on the place of Quartus E. Fisk, are still shown the ruins of the once famous Ludlow Glass Works, the wonder of the region. Here stood a small building, partly masonry and partly wood, in which were ponderous furnaces and sweating laborers. The article made was green glass, mostly in the form of bottles. The industry lasted only a few years, was mismanaged, its proprietors became reckless, and eventually lost all, and left to posterity only a ruin of business and a wreck of finances.

The falls of Wallamanumps had early attracted attention. Late in the eighteenth century there was but one man living in all the region. In 1788, however, reference is made to "Dea. Timothy Keyes's milldam," at this point. Not far from the dawn of the nineteenth century

Abner Putnam came from the east and improved the privilege by erecting a shop for the manufacture of scythes. This he developed into a considerable business. The tools which had passed under Putnam's trip hammer were considered among the best made.

Of the minor manufacturing interests during the first half of the nineteenth century there is little to be said. Plumley's sawmill at the mouth of Broad Brook was made to use the fine privilege there, while the Alden mills above, previously mentioned, next to those of Thornton, were made useful in turning out forks and rakes. The Indian Orchard

THE HARRIS MILL

mills spoiled the romance of the lower falls of Wallamanumps, even trespassing upon the sandstone riches of the Indian Leap cliff. Otherwise that grand manufacturing interest, it seems, had only a general influence upon Ludlow. Hezekiah Fisk's mill at Ludlow City stood on the opposite side of the stream from Henry I. Carver's mill. Water was carried to Fisk's mill in a penstock from a point beginning near the schoolhouse. The mill turned out a durable and beautiful woolen fabric, well-known in the region. Here, too, fleeces from the neighboring farms were brought to be carded. Jacob S. Eaton also had a share of this trade at his mill, which stood where Albert Banister now lives, near Indian Orchard.

Graves's and Alden's mills, on Broad Brook, and Edmund W. Fuller's (now Warren Fuller's) shingle mill, on Higher Brook, were established after the middle of the nineteenth century.

The Mill Privilege of H. I. Carver

This property is situated in what was called in the early history of Springfield, "The Inner Commons." The common lands (or undivided

Arch below H. I. Carver's Mill

lands) of the town were known as the Outer and the Inner Commons. The Outer were those adjoining the unoccupied territory; the Inner those adjoining the town already laid out, and in this vicinity lying toward the east.

This property when first laid out was in tier No. 1. The tiers began at the county road near the cranberry swamp (probably now called the Slobbery Ponds in Chicopee) and ran easterly. Each tier was eighty rods wide, and each individual's lot was determined by his proportion of the town's Province tax. Thus, if the tax on five pounds would draw one acre of land, a man who paid taxes on fifty pounds would be entitled to ten acres of land.

The choice was made by drawing the right of choosing in open town meeting, and the amount of property one might have played no part in this. Sometimes a first and second choice were given and the one who was last in the first choice was first in the second.

When the first gristmill or any mill was erected on this site is not known. October 24, 1783, Edmond Damon of Ludlow sold to Joseph Munger of South Brimfield for the sum of two hundred and eighty pounds (£280), land lying in Granby and Ludlow. This included the lot that he lived on with the buildings thereon, together with the gristmill and utensils thereunto belonging. How Damon became possessed of this land the Springfield records do not disclose. The next mention of any mill is when on December 22, 1794, Joseph Munger, in consideration of sixty pounds sold to David Carver of Hebron, Conn., a parcel of land with the buildings thereon "containing the gristmill and two acres of land." (See deed following.)

In 1794, Joseph Munger (Sr.) of Ludlow, for £60, sold to David Carver, of Hebron, in the county of Tolland, in the state of Connecticut, yeoman; a certain tract or parcel of land lying and being in Ludlow afore-said bounded as follows: beginning at the county road about ten feet East of the Grist-mill and running Westerly on the North line of the said County road, 18 rods 4 feet and ten links to a heap of stones then North twelve degrees E 12½ rods to Granby line, then East 3^d N. 23 rods 12½ feet to a stake and stones the corner of the Crank land so called then South to the first bound with the buildings thereon standing, containing the Grist-mill, and two acres of land more or less.

Joseph Munger. ⎰ ***S
⎱ ***E
⎱ ***A
⎱ ***L

Ludlow, Mass.
Dec. 22, 1794.

September 21, 1794, Joseph Munger executed a lease to David Carver of the right of flowage from September 1st to May 1st of each year, said lease to run 900 years from September 5, 1794. On July 13, 1795, Munger sold a small piece of land to Carver extending along his west bound, containing about 90 rods.

On December 23, 1799, Joseph Munger of Paris, Oneida Co., N. Y., sold to David Cook, a blacksmith, the land on the west side of the brook to the Granby line with the buildings thereon.

On March 5, 1801, Cook sold to Asa Munger, goldsmith, the same property, and on November 26, 1803, Munger transferred the same to James Kendall, Jr. (See deed following.)

26 Nov. 1803, Asa Munger sold land in Ludlow to James Kendall Jr., be the same more or less, bounded as follows: beginning at Granby line, thence running about 4 rods to the Brook on the West side of the Road leading from Pliny Chapin's to Joseph Munger's; Southerly on the West side of the road to North and opposite Joseph Munger's Shed thence from the west side of the Horse Shed to the south-west end of the Gold-smith's shop thence running about two rods from thence Westerly to East end of the Mill-dam from thence on the E. side of the Pond at high water mark to the first mentioned bound with the buildings thereon.

Signed: Asa Munger { S**** E****
           Polly Munger { A**** L****

Ludlow, Mass.
26 Nov., 1803.

Soon after this date Asa Munger and his family moved to Oneida Co., N. Y. Asa Munger was the son of Joseph Munger (Jr.) and Hannah Fisk.

On the east side of the brook a little to the southwest of the sawmill stood a clothier's shop or fulling mill. The first proprietor of this establishment we find was Solomon Tarbox. Some time between October 17, 1794, and December 17, 1801, Tarbox came into possession of this fulling mill, the gristmill, and one third part of the sawmill, for on that date he conveyed the same to John Filer in part. On October 28, 1803, he conveyed the other part to Eli Dickinson and John Filer. In this conveyance reserve is made of a still room situated under the shearing room at the south end of the mill, with water sufficient for use.

November 19, 1803, David Carver, Jonathan Carver, Aaron Carver, and John Filer gave a lease to Joel Eastman, the consideration being $150.

May 6, 1804, Dickinson and Filer conveyed the gristmill to Joel Eastman and on April 15, 1807, Joel Eastman conveyed the same property to Joseph Eastman. On October 4, 1804, Dickinson and Filer conveyed the fulling mill to Gustavus Pinney, and January 28, 1806, Pinney sold to James Kendall, Jr., the goldsmith's shop of Asa Munger.

November 1, 1824, Asa Damon sold to Aaron Carver all the land "I have in Springfield, Ludlow and Granby, together with all the buildings thereon: also a sort of Still and Cyder Mill with the privileges belonging thereunto." March 23, 1836, Amos Kendall transferred to Aaron Carver land and "also a Distillery a few rods easterly of Hezekiah Fisk's dwelling house, together with the buildings thereon and all privileges belonging: likewise a still and worms." Carver deeded the same to Simeon Pease, August 18, 1837.

On May 19, 1812, James Kendall, Jr., sold to William Pease his holding on the west side of the brook, and on April 1, 1825, Pease conveyed the property to Harry Witt and Eleazer Owen.

March 9, 1820, Joseph Eastman conveyed his interest in the property, being the mill privilege and part of the mills, to William Hezekiah Fisk of South Brimfield, and in 1826 Witt and Owen conveyed their right to the said Fisk. At this time there was a sawmill on the east side of the brook and a clothing mill and gristmill on the west side. Mr. Fisk used the privilege for fulling cloth and operating machinery for picking and dressing. He also had a carding machine, a turning machine for turning spokes, and a machine to cut out felloes.

The old dam went off in September, 1828. Mr. Fisk then built a canal and at this time put up another building on the west side of the brook (Stony Brook so called), and put in a carding machine. He then built a dam about fifty rods above the old dam and dug a ditch from the dam to the mill. About three years after this, Mr. Fisk secured the right to dig a ditch about twenty-five rods above the dam, through land of Stephen and Pliny Chapin, into which the water was turned without any flowing, by building a dam across the brook.

A year after the old dam went off the sawmill was sold to William Carver of Granby, who with other parties moved it to Turkey Hill, about one and a half miles almost due east. They canalled the water to a twenty-foot overshot wheel. Finding the natural stream would not run the wheel, they built a dam about forty rods above the mill and by pulling a wire could let the water into the canal. Only lumber enough for three dwelling houses was sawed. The mill remained there about ten years and then Mr. William Carver moved it to Granby, one half mile above where it originally stood in Ludlow.

In January, 1828, Fisk conveyed the property to Henry Barton and Lewis Marsh and entered into an agreement with them to erect a two-story building about thirty-five feet square for the manufacture of paper, in which he was to have water power sufficient to run a fulling mill, a clothier's shop, and a carding and picking machine. In September of the same year the dam went off, and all agreements between Barton and Marsh and Fisk seem to be ended, as the dam was not rebuilt while owned by the above parties. In 1829 Barton and Marsh conveyed a part of the property to Simeon Pease and the same year the remainder to Josiah Simms. In 1830 the said Barton and Marsh were arrested in Ludlow for passing counterfeit money. It seems the sheriff had some difficulty in arresting them as the house was partly in Hampden County and partly in Hampshire County. They were tried and convicted and imprisoned for one year. It is said that when the sheriff was taking them from the house to the road one of them threw his pocketbook back of him, and his wife picked it up, put it in the stove and burned it. In the pocketbook was five dollars of good money.

HENRY INGALLS CARVER

Going back to 1798 we find there were other owners to the different works at the Stony Brook privilege not mentioned in the above records, which are given in the following record of conveyances.

In 1798 Elijah Washburn sold a house and blacksmith shop near Joseph Munger's in Ludlow to David Bullard for £50. In November, 1799, Bullard transferred the same by deed to Jonathan Carver for the same price, and in February, 1804, Carver transferred the same to Thomas Washburn. In March of the same year Washburn sold to Timothy Root. There was some trouble over this conveyance, as the matter came before the Supreme Judicial Court of Norfolk County in March, 1805, when proof of the signing and delivering of the deed was produced. To whom Root sold the records do not show. In 1829 we find that all the property of this privilege came into the hands of Simeon Pease and Josiah Simms, each having a separate deed for his part. In 1836 Simeon Pease and Josiah Simms each deeded his part to Jefferson Alden. Mr. Alden soon after commenced the manufacture of weaving reeds at this place and continued the business there for about ten years, when he

HENRY I. CARVER'S MILL, LUDLOW CITY

moved to Chicopee and manufactured reeds for about six years. He returned to Ludlow in 1853, built a dam and installed a gristmill in the Barton and Marsh building. In 1857 Rufus Kimball came into possession of this property by foreclosure of mortgage. In 1860 he conveyed to Alden Damon the property, containing about twelve acres, which was all the land and privileges mentioned in the above deed.

Alden Damon conveyed the said property to H. I. Carver in 1866. In June of the same year the Barton and Marsh building was taken down and removed. The same month Mr. Carver built a stone and cement dam on the foundation of the old dam and erected a sawmill 46 feet long by 20⅓ feet wide, and during the same year a shingle mill. The sawmill was started January 2, 1867. In 1879 one story was added to the sawmill, for the manufacture of a patented butter worker and mold combined, under the name of H. I. Carver & Co., which was continued for fifteen years. From that time to the present patented butter molds and stamps combined have been manufactured. For the last four years the industry has been carried on by Elmer H. Carver, son of H. I. Carver, under the name of H. I. Carver & Co.

The Lyman Burr Industry

About 1845, Lyman Burr began the making of coffins. Previous to that time, John Moody, a carpenter and a resident of Ludlow, used to make them after the person's death, which was probably the custom in other places. Probably there were no undertaking rooms in Springfield at the time. Mr. Burr began by making different sizes and keeping a stock of them on hand, which was a convenience, as the stains and varnish were dry and the coffins ready to be trimmed when ordered. At that time, if there were handles they were black and made of iron; iron butts were used to hang the lid, and common screws to put on the top. In a little while Mr. Burr began to fasten the lid with a metal hook and eye; then he began using brass handles, and butts for the lid. Brass tacks were the first materials employed for putting the name and age upon the coffin, but very soon he used the round head or gimp tacks; the first were black, then they were galvanized, and from that Mr. Burr advanced to the name plates, and afterwards to plated handles and tacks for trimmings.

As the coffin shape was growing in disfavor, Mr. Burr began to make the casket shape, and then the covered ones, using black velvet and broadcloth for draping them. At first he made them of whitewood, then of butternut and black walnut. His wife soon made robes; and after a while they began to stuff and line the coffins, using at the head white cashmere. Later Mr. Burr secured what is called a cooler in which to use ice to help preserve the bodies. This was superseded by embalming. He sometimes used a board to put on the top of the coffin after it was lowered into the grave, but soon substituted boxes in place of the board.

About 1875 Mr. Burr ceased making caskets, but people did not want him to give up the business, and came to him for assistance; so he made arrangements with the undertakers in the city to give him a commission, with the agreement that they would do all the embalming. He bought caskets, delivered them and assisted at the funeral services for the price of caskets in the city. At first the prices for coffins varied from one to six or eight dollars, according to size, except those made of black walnut, which cost from ten to twelve dollars.

Mr. Burr died in 1880, and his son, Benjamin F. Burr, as the people continued to come to him, kept up the business until 1895. Mr. Lyman Burr's trade extended over a large territory for many years, into all the surrounding towns, Belchertown, Granby, Wilbraham, Palmer, Longmeadow, Chicopee, and also Springfield. Probably B. F. Burr has attended, assisted, and sung at more funerals than any other person in town. There are not many houses up town which he has not entered in times of bereavement and some of them three or four times. The record book which was kept, he considers valuable for reference.

The Jenksville Mills

An account of the transfer of the property of Capt. Abram Putnam to Benjamin Jencks (later Jenks) in 1812 is found in the Historical Address of Rev. Mr. Tuck. Mr. Jencks gave as his reason for not selecting Rochester as his place of business that it was located among the Mohawk Indians. A company was formed in 1814, consisting of Benjamin Jencks, Washington Jencks, Joseph Bucklin, and George Wilkinson of Ludlow, and Stephen H. Smith of Providence, R. I. Smith in a little while sold his shares to Samuel Slater, afterwards so famous as a manufacturer. The original capital is not stated, but provision was made for an increase to $32,000. The property has since been sold for five times that sum. The grantors of deeds were Sylvester Moody, Abner Putnam, and Levi Pease. At one time the company held twelve hundred acres of land.

Operations were first commenced in a wooden building on the site later occupied by the stone factories, and consisted in the preparation of warps and yarn, which were sent out into all the adjacent country, and the webs were woven in hand looms. Wilbur F. Miller's mother (then about 15 or 16 years of age) wove some of the earlier ones while living at what was known as the Noah Clark place.

The stone buildings were commenced in 1821. The first building was a little way from the bridge, 103 feet long and 36 feet wide. This was completed the following year. Having received a charter, the proprietors met December 31, 1821, and organized as the Springfield Manufacturing Company. An additional mill westward, forty feet from the first, was erected in 1826, and was 115 feet long and 40 feet wide. The machinery was manufactured in the buildings, the lower stories being used for the purpose. The first looms were set in motion in 1823. The fabric was sheeting, three fourths, seven eighths, and a yard wide. The mills were

An Old-time Picture of Jenksville

well constructed, and became the ideal buildings of the region. Stukely Smith was the mason, and Zebinus Pierce the carpenter.

The change in a town from the simplicity of rural pursuits to the noise and bustle of manufacturing is ever a marked one. The stream meandering along the limits of Ludlow, unobstructed by dam and crossed by a bridge of the rudest kind, only furnished a convenient channel for bearing away the waters flowing from marsh and spring; the same stream, no less rapid or picturesque, checked for an instant in its rapid coursings in order to do obeisance to human direction, to follow the bent of human inclination, not only bears away the gathered deposits of a highly fertile soil, but with showers of wealth returns more than it has taken, a thousandfold.

The history of the town cannot well ignore the fact that a large share of that prosperity which has made the town locally so well known had its beginnings within the first half of the nineteenth century. Moreover, those families best known to the marts of trade hereabouts will, upon consideration, find that while to some of them there was given prestige by reason of extensive acreage and hereditary wealth, to more the resources in their hands gained their largest increment during this period. And

One of the First Houses Built at Jenksville by the Springfield Manufacturing Company
Birthplace of C. D. Rood and W. F. Miller

further still, they who concede truth wherever found, will find that the chief factor in producing this state of prosperity was the manufacturing interest at Jenksville, as the village was then called.

It was a new life to Ludlow. Every farm increased in value as the factories developed. Every article of produce was worth money It no longer paid to team lumber to Willimansett for fifty cents on a thousand, for the logs were worth vastly more as wood. The cattle became too valuable to send roaming at large over the common lands, for it was worth while to feed them well and so get heavier beef for hungry mouths; while the soil was so much more salable that true economy called for strong fences. And, if we may digress a little, thus will it be as time rolls on. Every new mill, every new boarding-house necessarily consequent, added to the rapidly increasing cluster of villages and towns and cities on or near our limits, will add first to the intrinsic, then to the exchangeable, value of Ludlow farms. The true conditions for successful labor,—health, sobriety, industry, piety,—being held in firm tenure, the town or its territory must have a future.

In 1833 it became necessary to enlarge the factories again. This time an addition was built eastward, 66 feet long and 40 feet wide, completing the range of buildings, except the changes made after a fire and the gap between the first and second stone mills, which was filled about 1844. All these principal parts were dedicated by religious services. The tenements were erected from time to time, dating mainly from the erection of the factories. In 1844 Slater sold to a resident of the town. In 1837 Barber's History represents the concern as possessing two cotton mills, with ten thousand spindles, using five hundred thousand pounds of cotton in a year, manufacturing sixteen hundred thousand yards of cloth annually, whose value was one hundred and sixty thousand dollars. Eighty-eight males and two hundred females were employed at that time. The capital invested had then increased to one hundred thousand dollars.

In 1840 the first building at the upper privilege was erected and used by the Company for gun works. They forged barrels under contract with the United States government, continuing their business for about six years. At the close of this period the privilege was used in the manufacture of cotton machinery.

Some applications of science to the arts first used in these works have proved a boon to manufacturers. The friction roller, now well-nigh indispensable in certain parts of machinery, was originated at Jenksville and given to the public with no restrictions of patent laws. It is also claimed, with good reason, that here anthracite coal was first used successfully in working wrought-iron. The principle, first brought out at Jenksville, is still in practical use, giving to the immense coal fields of this country and the world a vastly increased value.

Respecting the class of people who were brought into the town by these interests, it may be feared that the record cannot truthfully give a glowing description. Of course they were at first from the native population, largely gathered from rural towns. But this does not necessarily speak volumes in favor of moral or intellectual worth. The average native of two or three generations ago was not very far in advance of the average foreigner of to-day in many respects. The records of former days, the condition to-day of those who have not enjoyed such advantages as have been so freely offered hereabouts in later years, or of those dwelling beyond the immediate neighborhood of churches, plainly set forth the truth of the assertion made.

We are not surprised, then, to learn that the condition of society at the mills in Ludlow about a century ago was not eminently praiseworthy.

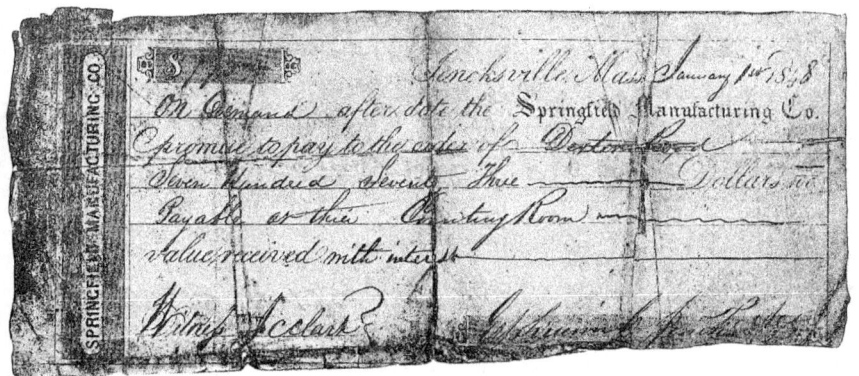

One of the Notes Issued by the Company

We need not be surprised to hear of very slight respect paid to the sacredness of the Sabbath or the rigid moral demands of the more deeply and intelligently pious people of to-day. Mr. Austin Chapman of Ellington, Conn., who resided in Jenksville about this time, gives the following doleful picture of these days: "As you pass the gun shops on Sunday some of the workmen would be busy, perhaps manufacturing articles for their own use. Near by would be a collection of boys playing ball. Soon we meet riflemen firing at a mark. A party of young people not far off are playing 'High-low-Jack.' A little further on are as happy a set as the brown jug could possibly make them, who in vain invited me to taste of the precious liquors inside the jug, which to my certain knowledge killed every one of the party inside of ten years. I have known a large field of rye to be harvested on the Sabbath day. The immoralities did not extend outside of the village."

The affairs of the Company had gone on meanwhile, apparently with prosperity. True, in lieu of cash the help and other creditors had been asked from time to time to accept Company notes, but these were even better than cash, in their estimation. A large business was in progress, with the fairest prospects. The treasury was a bank to the inhabitants. Scarcely was there a person in town who was not glad of an opportunity to lend money there.

But to a smaller circle of lookers-on there had been a growing anxiety in reference to the management of the affairs of the Company. No one distrusted the agent, who, with all his brusque manners, evidently had a kindly and honest heart and hand. But there was friction within the ranks of the proprietors. At last the crisis came. It was suddenly announced to the astonished creditors that the Springfield Manufacturing Company had failed! Surely 1848 was an ill-starred year for Ludlow. Mr. Hall was dismissed from the new church at Jenksville. The place fails to appear on the next Methodist minutes. The town appropriations for 1849 fell fourteen per cent. Many a poor girl lost all her savings, while cases of persons who had no money in the concern were cited as unusual. The affairs of the Company went into the hands of Wood & Merritt of New York City.

The firm of Wood & Merritt, managing from 1848 to 1856, was afterwards merged into the first Ludlow Manufacturing Company. The power was for a number of years leased to George H. Deane, who fitted up the stone mills for the manufacture of jute goods, and the upper mill for the manufacture of wadding. After the expiration of the lease, Mr. Deane purchased the property at auction, paying $102,000, and formed the Ludlow Mills Company. He manufactured seamless bags in which business he was a pioneer. A more recent sale was to the second Ludlow Manufacturing Company, of which Lemuel H. Brigham was agent. The goods made at the stone mills were: gunny bagging, various kinds of crashes, plain and figured (bleached and finished ready for market), all kinds of hardware twines, and linen warps; at the upper privilege, cotton warps and seamless grain-bags of the same material. About three hundred operatives were employed. The expenses of the corporation monthly, exclusive of the cost of stock, were $13,000. Charles T. Hubbard, of Boston, was the treasurer of the Company and

OFFICERS OF LUDLOW MANUFACTURING ASSOCIATES

its chief sales agent. There were connected with the establishment thirty houses, and a church, besides all the barns, sheds, etc. A fire so far injured a section of the stone mills that it was considered advisable to place an iron roof upon it.

It may be as well to say that at this time the Company owned seven hundred acres of land, a large portion of which was mapped out into streets and building lots. The extent of water power was estimated at over twenty-five hundred horse power, of which only a small portion was in use.

The Ludlow Manufacturing Associates

The beginning of the business now carried on by the Ludlow Manufacturing Associates dates back to 1848. In that year Charles T. Hubbard, then a junior partner in the old firm of Sewall, Day & Co., started the "Boston Flax Mills" at East Braintree, Mass., where there was a small water power. In 1852 the business was incorporated, the original subscription being $50,000. Of this Mr. Hubbard took $7,500, his father-in-law, Benjamin Sewall, took $11,000. These are the only original subscribers whose interest in the business has been continued to the present time. From 1848 till his death in 1887, Mr. Hubbard was the treasurer and managing head of the business.

In 1864 Cranmore N. Wallace, returning from service in the army, entered the mill as office clerk. He is now (1911) president and selling agent.

In 1868, Mr. Hubbard, acting for various creditors of the Ludlow Mills Company, bought their property in Ludlow, Springfield, and Wilbraham. The business was reorganized under the name of the Ludlow Manufacturing Company and Mr. Hubbard was chosen treasurer; Mr. Lemuel H. Brigham was retained as agent.

The property consisted of the old stone mills referred to elsewhere; also a small one and one-half story wooden cotton mill and a small machine shop. The cotton mill was run on seamless cotton bags until its destruction by fire, a few years later. The old stone mills were used for the manufacture of twines, and of bagging for covering cotton.

At this time the approach to the village was through an old-fashioned wooden bridge. The village consisted of very few old tenement houses, one church, and one single-room schoolhouse owned by the Company, situated on two country roads. The nearest railroad was the Boston and Albany, one mile distant. Later the Springfield and Athol Railroad was run through the village and a spur track laid into the mill yard.

In the meantime the Boston Flax Mills at Braintree had been growing by small additions here and there, until in 1878 there was such a conglomeration of small, detached mills with antique power equipment, that it was evident that the mills must be rebuilt entirely or moved to a new location.

OFFICE BUILDING OF LUDLOW MANUFACTURING ASSOCIATES

Mr. Hubbard then arranged to sell the good will and machinery of the Flax Mills to the Ludlow Manufacturing Company. To receive this machinery the latter company built a new mill (No. 4), and also the present lower canal (since enlarged).

About this time (1878) new streets were constructed, a number of new cottages and a six-room schoolhouse built.

In 1881, Mr. John E. Stevens was engaged as superintendent.

In 1887, Mr. Hubbard died and was succeeded by his son, Charles W.

Hubbard, the present treasurer, a graduate of Harvard College, class of 1878.

Since 1887 the managing officers of the Company have been: Charles W. Hubbard, treasurer; Cranmore N. Wallace, selling agent; John E. Stevens, manufacturing agent (died 1905); and Sidney Stevens, who succeeded his father in 1905.

Of the mills now standing, there existed in the spring of 1888 only No. 4; the old stone mills being condemned as unsafe, were temporarily

No. 6 Mill

strengthened; No. 5 mill was built to receive the machinery which was taken out of the old mills; and a canal was built on the upper dam, also a wheelhouse containing wheels of about 250 horse power to run this mill. The completion of this building was celebrated by a ball and supper given to the operatives and residents of the town.

The new gunny mill having been completed and running, in the spring of 1889 the directors voted to build a mill known as No. 6. Upon its completion this mill was used for the exercises dedicating the Hubbard Memorial Library.

The treasurer's annual report of 1889 says: "The village is steadily improving; the Company is extending its water pipes, and has made a start on a very complete system of drainage."

In the same year the Company secured an amendment of its charter (Chapter 200) authorizing it to establish an "effective and complete electrical plant," and to sell power to the inhabitants of Ludlow within a mile of the Chicopee River.

In January, 1891, finding it was necessary to make an immediate increase in the production of one of the departments, the management erected a temporary frame spinning mill, and the construction of No. 2 mill was authorized, together with the installation of 1,000 horse power water wheels. On December 15, 1891, an addition to the marline mill was voted.

After planning all the additions mentioned to mills and machinery, the managers found there was a shortage of power, and in view of future requirements, purchased in December, 1891, a mill site just above Red Bridge on the Chicopee River.

At a directors' meeting held on February 14, 1893, attention was called to the need of auxiliary steam power. In the treasurer's report, September, 1894, mention was made of a loss of sales from want of the power to run the machinery.

In 1894, the corporation acquired rights in Chapin pond, under Chap. 200, Acts of 1889.

September 20, 1894, the building of No. 1 mill and No. 3 mill was authorized, also a steam plant at No. 3 mill, and the construction of a machine shop. In accordance with this authorization there was installed at No. 3 mill a tandem Corliss engine of 1,500 horse power, also an electrical drive to the upper dam of 400 horse power.

In 1897 the Company urged upon the City of Springfield and the town of Ludlow the necessity of replacing the old covered wooden bridge across the river with a high level iron bridge; and by offering to pay half the cost of the approaches it succeeded in bringing about this improvement in the approach to the village.

The volume of their freight was growing at such a rate that direct connection with the railroad seemed to be an immediate necessity. In 1897 the Company bought the Moran farm lying between the Chicopee

River and the main line of the Boston and Albany Railroad, and surveyed for a branch line from their mill yard to connect with the main line, including a bridge across the river. This bridge was completed in 1905, and two or three miles of extra tracks and sidings were added to the Company's freight yard.

In the spring of 1898 the machine shop was doubled in size, and it was decided to build a plant not only sufficient to meet their immediate needs, but one that would last for several years to come. They bought

RED BRIDGE DAM

more land on the river above Red Bridge, and in 1900 commenced work on the present dam at that point.

At the same time No. 8 mill was started, and as it was expected that two years would be required before water power could be developed at Red Bridge, a steam plant of 1,000 horse power with electrical transmission was installed at the upper dam.

This power house was built twice as large as needed for this installation, as it was even then thought by the directors that the growth of the

Company's property would be so rapid as soon to absorb all the power at Red Bridge and the auxiliary steam power already installed at Ludlow. To provide for all this increased development of manufacture, six warehouses built in 1891 were torn down and State Street laid out and built, also a new mill office.

Upon the completion of No. 8 mill it was dedicated February 16, 1901, with a ball and supper given to the operatives and residents of the town, and a large number of invited guests from Boston and Springfield.

BUSINESS BLOCK, SHOWING POST OFFICE

The First Regiment Band of Springfield, consisting of thirty pieces, provided the music and about thirty-five hundred people were entertained.

In the same year (1901) a large block was built to provide stores and dwellings for the growing village.

In developing not only the manufacturing plant, but also the village itself, in laying out and building the village park and various streets, in constructing sewers, in providing club rooms, etc., the officials found they

were acting beyond the powers granted to them under the general laws.
This was one of the reasons for changing the form of organization to that
of the trust agreement, which went into effect January 1, 1902. This
new form of organization places the control of the business in the hands
of nine trustees, acting under a written agreement defining their powers.

In 1905, No. 8 mill having been outgrown, No. 9 mill was built; in
1906, No. 8 annex; and in 1907, No. 10 mill. In 1906 the Stevens
Memorial was built—a clubhouse for the use of the operatives, the

ATHLETIC FIELD

building of which had been under consideration for several years.
Later a large athletic and play field was laid out and fenced. It
provides a quarter-mile cinder track, fields for baseball and football,
a wading pool, a large platform and shelter for kindergarten plays,
besides various swings, teeters, and slides.

For about twenty years previous to the building of the Stevens
Memorial the Company had provided temporary quarters for the men's
and women's clubs.

The flow of water in the river during the fall of 1909 was unusually small, and even with steam power it was impossible to run all the machinery. The trustees, therefore, decided to enlarge the steam plant, and in the summer of 1910 installed at the upper power house three Babcock and Wilcox boilers and a General Electric turbine and generators, with a capacity of 2,500 horse power. The upper and lower steam plants were also connected by a 4-inch pipe, thus allowing one boiler plant, under usual conditions, to supply all the steam needed. Such has been the growth of the manufacturing plant at Ludlow.

STEVENS MEMORIAL BUILDING

Grammar School—Chestnut Street

VIII

EDUCATIONAL INTERESTS

Earliest appropriations—Districts—School meetings—Schoolhouses—Furnishings—Fuel—Pupils' equipment—Industrial work—The teacher—Teachers' wages—"Boarding around"—Mary Newell—Long service—Length of school year—Abolishment of districts—Village schools—New buildings—Grades—Course of study—Enrollment—High school—Manual training—Domestic science—Supervision district—First superintendent—High school graduates—Graduates from higher institutions—Evening schools—Extracts from school reports—Statistics—School committee—Open-air vacation school—Ludlow textile school—"Winding Wave."

OUR young people in school to-day, with their fine buildings, their abundant, free equipment, and their trained teachers, can hardly realize the privations, the hindrances, and difficulties which confronted parents, teachers, and pupils a century or more ago.

The earliest reference to education is in 1777, when, in troublous times and with an inflated currency, the town voted £400 for the support of schools. A little later came an appropriation of £20 ($67), which in 1794 had increased to £35 ($117). In 1800, the amount raised was $133. The appropriation of $150 in 1801 was lessened only one year, while it increased fifty dollars occasionally until in 1828 it had become $400, and in 1840, $500 was voted. Generally there were only prudential committees to manage the affairs, until in 1827 an examining committee was added. This seems to have been the period of the formation of school districts. To be sure, at its very beginning (1802) the south and southeast districts found it profitable to unite. It seems that there was an early district arrangement for all in that part of the town to attend at the house east of the present No. 9 district building. Afterward the Miller Corner people clamored for a change of location, and secured a district organization. The coalition of 1802 was another victory for Miller Corner. Leave was given in 1805 to move the Middle schoolhouse near to the pound, a location close by J. P. Hubbard's. The Alden district was set off in 1808, the Center in 1809, Wallamanumps in 1814, and the Lyon in 1822. The southeast people made another effort in 1818 and secured again a distinctive district existence. The first reference to West Middle is dated 1822.

The adjustment of school matters seems to have been given at first to the selectmen, but not always to the liking of the citizens, for in 1788 they vote to accept their arrangement of districts, "Except Eight Families East of Capt Joseph Miller's; and two Families North of Zephaniah Rood's."

Districts.—A committee for districting appointed the next year did their work successfully. District No. 1 included the present 1 and 2, very nearly; No. 2 was about the same as the present No. 3 ; No. 3 of that day was the Miller Corner of 1875 ; No. 4, Cherry Valley; and No. 5 the existing No. 9. The selectmen were to hire the schoolmasters and maintain six months' schooling in Nos. 1 and 3. In 1791, a committee to locate and build schoolhouses was intrusted with £90 for the purpose. Its recommendations for location were as follows: For the west district, a few rods south of Israel Warriner's house, probably at or near the present location; for the middle district, at the northeast corner of Elisha Hubbard's fence, on the meeting-house road, near the former residence of B. F. Burr, north of the road; for the south district, about twenty-six rods south of Capt. Joseph Miller's, at a stake, near the present home of Dwight Blackmer; for the southeast district, twenty rods west of David Daniels' barn, north of the highway, and a few rods north of the school lot of to-day; for the northeast district, near where the new reservoir road turns from the highway, south of the Reuben Sikes place. Mr. Peter Damon's land and money for school purposes were joined with the southeastern school in Granby, in 1794. Minor changes occurred in the location of schoolhouses from time to time, the principal one being in Miller Corner, where the lot now occupied was taken. In 1794, the school business passed into the hands of a committee from each district.

After years of contention we find in 1822, our town settled upon ten districts as the desired number. From the fact that they remained intact for sixty years, except Number 7, which was effaced by the Springfield Reservoir, the inference is that the plan was a satisfactory one. The people were loyal to their schools, working in every way for their good.

School Meetings.—In early spring each year the voters of the several districts, with the larger boys, gathered at the several schoolhouses to organize for the work of the year. A clerk was chosen, and, what was considered the main thing, a prudential committee, who was to hire the teachers and attend to the incidentals of school work. At those meetings more or less discussion arose, and it is likely that our elderly men of to-day who show so much oratory and parliamentary tactics in our town meeting took their first lessons in those district school meetings. There were many good things about the district system in those early days. The people felt that it was their school; they were responsible for the welfare of it. This feeling does not prevail to such an extent to-day.

Extracts from records kept by Elisha Fuller, clerk of District No. 10.—*Lucien Lyon Paper.*

At a regular meeting of the male inhabitants of School district No. 10 qualified to vote in town affairs the following votes were taken on the Articles in the warrant for said meeting viz

1^t Elisha A Fuller was chosen moderator,

2^d Elisha A Fuller was chosen Clerk and Treasurer,

3^d Voted to Buy the Shop and Land that s^d shop stands on together with Land north as far as corner of stone wall at the Price agreed upon with Mr Isaac Sheldon providing the district can have a good title and Elisha A Fuller is empowered to get such title for s^d district. Voted to adjourn to three weeks from this day at 6 O'clock P M

Ludlow, March 18th, 1833. Elisha A Fuller } Clerk

At the Adjourned meeting Voted to Adjourn to the first Monday in May at 6 o'clock P M

Paid Austin Carver for the Schoolhouse and land	17	00
David Lyon for bords	1	20
Philip Willcott for stove and pipe	10	96
November 4th, 1833.		
Noah Clark jr to two & half days work on the Schoolhouse	2	75
Stephen Lyon to plastering the Schoolhouse	0	83
to mortar bought of Jincks	1	50
to 11 pounds of nailes	0	77
to four days work of myself and truble	4	00
to 60 feet of Bords		45
Elisha A Fuller for 34 feet of Bords		50
	39	96
To four lights of Glafs	0	16

Schoolhouses.—When the ten districts had been fairly established, measures were taken to erect schoolhouses in each. These buildings were always oblong in shape, one story in height, and placed on the line of the highway with little or no room for playground except the street. They contained one room, usually with windows on three sides; at the entrance a narrow vestibule, called the "entry," where the pupils hung their wraps, and where fuel for the fire was kept in company with the ever desired water pail and dipper. At one side of the main room there was at first a fireplace, which could burn wood four feet in length. On the opposite side was a long desk fastened to the wall, in front of which was a long bench forming a seat for the older pupils. In front of this was another bench, lower and with no back, for the younger ones. When there was occasion for the older pupils to use the desk for writing or figuring, they were obliged to throw their feet over the bench and under the desk, thus facing the wall, with their backs to the teacher. The teacher's desk was a small stand or table. There were no other furnishings. No maps or pictures served their part in the education of this period. Visitors, who were few and far between, were obliged to sit on the benches or stand as they preferred.

Blackboards, commonly small, two by three feet in size, and made of boards painted black, were introduced about 1835, at which time stoves were also first furnished.

Fuel.—It was the custom for families to furnish the fuel for the school in proportion to the number of pupils sent, and this wood must be supplied by each family while the teacher was one of its members. Green wood was the common fuel, so the schools were provided with that brought in sled lengths to be "worked up" by the large boys. As this wood was often dumped into the snow, the fire which resulted was far from sufficient. In the coldest weather ink froze in the rear of the room during school hours. A half circle of children was allowed to stand before the fire, and when they were barely thawed out, another took its place.

Equipment.—The entire equipment for a pupil was furnished from the home. In cases where means were limited, books and supplies were often not secured until the term was nearly finished, and sometimes not at all. Pupils were obliged to borrow or "look over" as it was termed. Surely knowledge was pursued under difficulties,—such as we cannot adequately picture to-day. Slates were in constant use as paper was so rare and costly. Fortunate indeed was the family who possessed a reader, an arithmetic, a speller, and a geography, the full set of books, which was passed on from one to another in the family and sometimes through several generations. Writing books were made at home and of the coarsest paper. The copy was set each day by the teacher. All pens were made from goose quills, which were constantly in need of mending. Proud was the pupil who could make and mend his own pen. Papers written and signed by Bernis Hubbard, who taught in Ludlow previous to 1810, show penmanship which compares favorably with that of to-day.

Industrial training is by no means new, for the boys and girls of the early days in Ludlow combined this with their mastery of the three R's. The mothers carded, spun, and dyed the thread for their children's clothing at home. The teacher at school guided them in the use of these homemade dyes. The children cut their own stencils and made patterns upon bits of homespun for bibs, pockets, and stand covers. The boys whittled sticks and shuttles which the girls used in making yards of netting for trimming on valances and curtains. Each little miss wrought her own sampler, training her fingers so that the linen in her own chest was beautifully marked and numbered. Surely their training was wise and full of invention.

About 1830 the girls who were pupils in Miss Mary Newell's school were allowed to study fractions. This innovation was so radical that the fortunate girls made books in which every problem was recorded to be shown to doubting visitors.

The Teacher.—The most important factor of all, the teacher, was usually the daughter of a member of the district, frequently a recent member of the school in which she taught. In winter it was sometimes the custom to employ men, as the oldest boys of the district attended then. At the beginning of the school year in May, the prudential committee of ten were sometimes obliged to present themselves at the house of some member of the committee, with their ten new candidates to be examined and approved. It is related that not infrequently did the candidates turn about and question their examiners.

Teachers' wages were $1.50, sometimes $2.00 per week, in addition to their "keep," which was provided by "boarding around." This was often a severe hardship, on account of the distance from the school, the accommodations offered, and the variation in the fare. This system, however, had its advantages also; it gave the teachers and parents and pupils an opportunity to become mutually acquainted, in a manner otherwise impossible. Families provided board in proportion to the number of children they sent to school.

Many are the reminiscences, pleasant or otherwise, which seem strange in this day of special training, that can be recalled concerning

Mrs. Julia (Miller) Smith
Born in 1816

these early teachers. The following is interesting from its very wide contrast.

Mary Newell's pupils may have lacked resource and diplomacy, but not for want of object lessons.

Miss Newell kept a wonderful chest in the girl's wardroom, and when visitors were seen hitching their horses, Miss Newell left the recitation room to its own devices, soon appearing in wonderful finery with hair newly arranged and a fresh black silk apron, all due to the contents of that mysterious box. One curious committeeman entered

Dr. J. W. Hannum's Residence—North Street

The right wing directly on the street is the original "Old Brick Schoolhouse." An old grocery store is next.

the room too soon and began to search for the teacher. Guided doubtless by officious fingers pointing the way, he attempted to enter the girls' dressing room, but Miss Newell valiantly held the door until the proper time, then she came out resplendent in a new uniform and proceeded with her work calmly and without comment.

Perhaps it will not be amiss to mention the long terms of service as teachers of which one of the Ludlow families may well be proud; for it is doubtful whether there are any duplications in the school history elsewhere. John and Lucinda Miller's six daughters and son, William B. Miller, were principals and teachers for the total number of 89 years. The nephews and nieces, grandchildren of John and Lucinda, taught in the aggregate, 73 years, making a total of 162 years. Two are teachers at the present time (1911).

About 1872, there arose a laudable desire for more weeks of schooling. Six months was then the length of the school year, except in the village. Owing to the special needs of the manufacturing community in the village, the length of the school year was fixed at forty weeks there, the outlying schools being in session thirty-two weeks. In 1907, the school year for the districts was lengthened to 34 weeks, the following year to 38, and in the next year, 1909, it was made 40 weeks to correspond with those in the village.

In 1882, it was voted to abolish the district system. Ludlow was among the first few towns to pursue this course; later all districts were abolished by state law. It is a pleasant fact to relate that since that time to the present day no protest has ever been made against raising the amount of money asked for by the committee.

Village Schools.—The first village school began in the old red schoolhouse on North Street with 40 pupils, all there were at that time, taught very successfully for seventeen years by Miss Eliza Goodwill. This schoolhouse was later purchased by Dr. J. W. Hannum and remodeled as a dwelling. Owing to the changes in the business of this district, many families came here to live. At one time there were 70 pupils in this one room, with all grades from the child learning to speak English to the pupil doing high school work.

In 1883, when the Ludlow Manufacturing Company began to erect new mills and tenement houses, and to bring in many large families with children of school age, the need of more room was at once apparent. The company built a six-room building at a cost of $30,000, which was rented to the town for many years at a low sum. A grammar school was started in the new building, which has since (1910) been given to the town in addition to the land upon which it stands.

Until 1900 the schools at the village were all accommodated in the Ludlow Manufacturing Company's school building. This year there was an average membership at the village of about 250 pupils, and a school was opened in Masonic Hall to accommodate an overflow class.

In 1901 an eight-room brick building was erected on Chestnut Street. This was a period of unprecedented growth in the history of the town, the membership in the village schools doubling in the six years following the completion of this building, so that it was found necessary to provide more room, and in 1907 another eight-room building was erected. This is a duplicate of the one built in 1901 and is located on Park Place, so that the two buildings are back to back. The accommodations thus furnished proved adequate for a short time only.

A fine new high school building, costing $43,000, was added in 1910, completing the group of four buildings in which every grade of school work from the first through the high is conducted. They are located on an elevation surrounded by beautiful grounds. The borders of flowers, the groups of well-trimmed shrubbery, and the neatly-kept lawns make a delightful picture.

There is probably no town in the state where the schools are more centralized and, consequently, better organized. It has been possible to evolve a most satisfactory graded system.

Grades.—In the year 1890–1891 a course of study was adopted for the village schools. Prior to this time the five schools then existing were each made up of pupils of the same general attainment, but must necessarily have been brought together by a somewhat arbitrary classification. From this date, promotion from grade to grade is made to depend upon the completion of a definite amount of work each year, with satisfactory standing in the prescribed subjects. In 1894 the grading of the rural schools was begun.

It is the policy of the acting school committee of 1911 to transport all pupils in the rural districts above the fifth grade to the village schools. Thirty-one per cent of all the pupils enrolled in grades six to nine inclusive, at the village, are from the rural districts.

At the present writing (1911) the grades are distributed as follows: first and second grades in the primary building erected in 1907; the third, fourth, fifth, and seventh in the grammar building erected in 1901; the sixth and one division of the seventh occupying two rooms in the old high school building; and the eighth and ninth grades in the new high school building. The total enrollment for the month of November, 1911, is as follows: primary building, 295 pupils; grammar building, 248 pupils; old high school building, 78 pupils; new high school building, 101 pupils, 45 of whom are enrolled in the high school department. There are 58 pupils enrolled in the four district schools now

LUDLOW HIGH SCHOOL
Dedicated September 23, 1910

open, making a total enrollment in the public schools of the town of 793 pupils.

Our High School.—The high school was organized in 1895 with 17 pupils, and now (1911) numbers 45. In the early years of its history there were frequent changes of teachers, which did not tend to rapid advancement in school work. For the last six years Mrs. Helen M. Gushee has been principal of the school. The good feeling among the pupils, the harmony between pupils and teachers, and the industry shown in their work speak well for the future of the town. It is an interesting fact that fully one half the pupils come from outside the village, mostly from farmers' homes, some from five miles away, making ten miles to travel every day.

The opening of the new high school building in September, 1910, marked an important step in the development of the town's school system. This building is the fourth modern brick structure to be erected in the quadrangle of land bounded by Chestnut Street, Park Place, Winsor Street, and the Ludlow Manufacturing Associates' Park. The new building located on the slight elevation, commanding a view of the park, constitutes one of the most attractive features of the village, and with the others forms a group of which any town or even city might well be proud. There are four large and two small class rooms, a teacher's room and principal's office on the first floor, and a science laboratory, commercial room, typewriting room, assembly hall, and a small class room on the second floor. The basement, which is high and well lighted, is used for manual training and domestic science.

In the department of manual training, the work consists of wood-turning and bench-work carpentry, and is an elective course for high school boys, but is required for the pupils of the upper grammar grades. The shop is equipped with twelve individual benches, fully supplied with carpenters' tools, three turning lathes, with turning tools, a band saw, and a grindstone. The lathes, saw, and grindstone are operated by a 10 horse power electric motor.

The domestic science laboratory is equipped with special tables to accommodate 16 pupils in a division, each pupil having an individual set of cooking utensils, a gas plate, locker, and cupboard space. The room contains a large cabinet gas range, hot water boiler and gas heater, a refrigerator, and sinks with hot and cold water. This course with sewing is offered to all high school girls, as an elective, but is required in all the upper grammar grades.

Supervision District.—When the law was passed requiring towns receiving state aid to employ expert superintendents, Ludlow in 1893, united with the towns of Wilbraham, Hampden, Longmeadow, and East Longmeadow to form a supervision district, and secured Miss Mary Poland as the first superintendent. With a change in district, Miss Poland was assigned to other towns. The district was reorganized in 1903, Ludlow uniting with the town of Agawam and Mr. Walter E.

Gushee was chosen to be the next superintendent. He is still in office (1911).

The following is a list of the graduates of Ludlow High School since its establishment, showing in addition the connection of a part of them with higher institutions.

GRADUATES OF HIGH SCHOOL SINCE ORGANIZATION

1899

Bennett, Addie F.	Westfield Normal	Simmons College
Bennett, Archer		
Bennett, C. Ernest	Amherst College	Cornell University
Booth, Hattie M.		

1900

Dempsey, B. Francis	
Fuller, Henrietta E.	
Hubbard, Ida M.	Dickinson Hospital
Streeter, Charles	Mass. Agricultural College

1901

Bennett, Nina M.	Emerson College of Oratory
Burr, Julena E.	
Jones, Lillian M.	
Kyle, Grace Y.	Eastman College
Streeter, Cora E.	Westfield Normal
White, Clara V.	

1902

White, Josephine E.

1903

Jones, Arthur M.	Mass. Agricultural College
Roberts, Lula M.	Mt. Holyoke College

1904

Bartlett, Ruth M.	
Miller, Mary W.	Simmons College
Munsing, Carrie J.	
Munsing, Robert H.	Bliss Electrical School

1905

Jones, Wilfred	Worcester Polytechnic Institute
Miller, Oliver	
Nash, Elizabeth C.	

1906

Estey, Bertha M.	Westfield Normal
Fuller, Ada B.	Bay Path Institute
Patterson, Bertha	Westfield Normal
Potter, Carl H.	Lowell Textile School
White, Emily	Westfield Normal

1908

Bartlett, Katherine		
Henderson, Elizabeth		
Johnson, Mabel		
Jones, Pauline E.	Oberlin College	
Mackintosh, William	Clark College	University of Vermont
Munsing, Ruby L.		
Tourville, Bertram	Clark College	
White, Gladys		
Whitney, Ira E.	Bliss Electrical School	

1909

Adams, Carl	
Cochrane, Margaret	Westfield Normal
Gove, Eva L.	Westfield Normal
Griswold, Verena	
Howe, Francis	Bay Path Institute
Nelligan, Lillian A	
Paine, Blanche	
Paine, Ralph	Mass. Agricultural College
Perham, John	Mass. Agricultural College

1910

Chapman, Isabelle	
Irwin, Vivian	Mt. Holyoke College
Jones, Etta L.	Oberlin College
Jones, Marion E.	
Miller, Arthur L.	
Miller, Edith R.	Oberlin College
Miller, Leila A.	
Scannell, Ruth	Smith College

The following inhabitants of Ludlow (names of all that could be obtained) have received diplomas from higher institutions of learning:—

Jennie E. Banister (now Fuller), Wilbraham Academy, 1862.
Rev. Ephraim Chapin, Williams College, 1814.

EDUCATIONAL INTERESTS

Rev. Joel Chapin, Dartmouth College.
Sumner Bodfish, West Point Military Academy.
Lucinda Damon, Wilbraham Academy.
William A. Fuller, Wilbraham Academy, 1867.
Henry A. Hubbard, Union College, N. Y.
Rev. Dargo B. Jones, Miami University, Ohio.
Rev. Simeon Miller, Amherst College, 1840.
Dr. William B. Miller.
Matilda Munsing, Westfield Normal School, 1871.
Henrietta D. Parsons (now Howell), South Hadley Female Seminary.
Julia T. Parsons (now Bodfish), South Hadley Female Seminary.
Rev. Orrin Sikes, Union College, Maine.
John Stacy, Yale College.
Elizabeth Swan, Westfield Normal School.
Rev. Alvin E. Todd, Yale College.
George T. Greenhalgh, Wilbraham Academy, 1884.
Emma J. Fuller, Wilbraham Academy.
Ada M. Alden, Wilbraham Academy, 1888.
Alice M. (Clark) Francis, Westfield Normal, 1891.
Martha G. Clark, Bridgewater State Normal, 1894.
Alice Davenport, Wilbraham Academy.
Clifford P. Clark, Wesleyan University, 1895.
Gertrude M. Lombard, Wilbraham Academy, 1896.
Mari A. (Ruxton) Birnie, Chauncey Hall School, 1897.
Fred N. Milles, Wilbraham Academy, 1898.
A. Leroy Halford, Amherst College, 1900.
Mary J. Ogilvie, Wilbraham Academy, 1901.
Edward J. Ruxton, Mass. Institute of Technology, 1904.
Douglas D. Ruxton, Dartmouth College, 1908.
Mary E. Clark, Westfield Normal School.

Evening School

In the fall of 1905 the Ludlow Manufacturing Associates started a free evening school for the benefit of their non-English speaking employees, and, while this school was in the nature of an experiment, it proved so successful that it has been continued each year.

During the first year the school was held in the high school building, but this not being well suited for the purpose, the town school authorities gave the use of the grammar school building. The regular teachers in the town schools have been employed, and the grammar school principal has been in charge of the school since the beginning. Miss Cole and her associates have been very successful in arousing the ambition and keeping the interest of the pupils. The results obtained have been gratifying.

This school has differed from the public evening schools as conducted by cities and large towns, in that no one is compelled to attend, and, strange as it may seem, the attendance has averaged much higher than in the usual evening school. Probably this is due to the fact that those who enter do so voluntarily, having an earnest desire to learn. After once entering, satisfactory attendance is insisted upon, and pupils who do not attend regularly are not allowed to continue. In some years the attendance has averaged over 90%, and during the entire period it has ranged from 85% to 90%.

The total number of pupils enrolled during 1905–1906 was 52, divided into three classes, practically all non-English speaking, while in 1910–1911 there were 128 pupils enrolled, and six classes were conducted. In 1908–1909 advanced classes were formed, and have been continued, many pupils returning each year, being desirous of learning more than the mere rudiments of the English language.

The town school authorities have manifested great interest in the work of this school, and it seems to fulfill a definite need in the community.

The Open–Air Vacation School

Believing that something might be done to keep the children off the streets during the long summer vacation, the Recreation Association in 1909 instituted an open-air school on Recreation Park. They erected a large tent with permanent roof and open sides, furnished with seats and tables for drawing and other industrial work. For amusements, there are a merry-go-round, swings of various kinds, toboggan slides, teeter boards in abundance, and, the greatest joy of all, a concrete wading pool several square rods in area, supplied with running water a foot in depth.

In the morning the younger children assemble for kindergarten work and games. The more advanced pupils receive physical training in the afternoon. Marching, dancing, games, and swimming three times per week are included in the schedule. The largest boys have one side of the park reserved for their special use.

Children of school age are admitted to the school. It is the custom at the close of the term to give an exhibition of the work accomplished.

Albert A. Gove

SCHOOL COMMITTEE

Elmer H. Carver

Frank N. Moore

ASSESSORS

Charles P. Jones

Charles B. Bennett

Arthur D. King

EDUCATIONAL INTERESTS 253

School Committee

Rev. E. B. Wright,	1	Chauncey L. Buell,	27
E. T. Parsons,	13	Rev. George Prentice,	1
Charles Alden,	8	Warren D. Fuller,	3
Joseph Miller, 2d,	1	George R. Clark,	3
Rev. D. R. Austin,	2	Rev. W. J. Pomfret,	8
Rev. Salmon Hull,	1	J. Osmyn Kendall,	15
Harmon Booth,	2	Adin Whitney,	5
Dr. W. B. Alden,	7	Rev. A. Gardner,	1
Alva Sikes,	1	Rev. H. E. Crocker,	1
Nathaniel Chapin,	1	Rev. C. L. Cushman,	2
Abner Cady,	1	Rev. Alfred Noon,	1
George Booth,	18	Rev. N. H. Martin,	2
Rev. A. Sanderson,	2	Rev. Timothy Lyman,	4
Albert Clark,	1	Dr. J. W. Hannum,	3
Rev. J. W. Dadmun,	1	Rev. A. C. Godfrey,	1
Dr. William B. Miller,	5	James Haviland,	6
Rev. J. W. Tuck,	4	Charles B. Bennett,	14
Theodore Sikes,	1	George A. Birnie,	8
Dr. H. M. T. Smith,	1	Miss Irene T. Jones,	8
J. H. Wilcox,	1	Albert H. Halford,	5
Gilbert Pillsbury,	14	Edward E. Chapman,	10
E. C. Eaton,	1	Mrs. Alexander C. Birnie,	6
Rev. Franklin Fisk,	1	Albert A. Gove,	10
Elisha T. Parsons,	2	Frank N. Moore,	2
Dr. Robert Wood,	2	Elmer H. Carver,	1

Extracts from the school reports for the years 1879 to 1911 inclusive, showing the steady development and progress of the school system of Ludlow.

1879

The Ludlow Company fitted up a room in the church vestry, at their expense, for overflow, making two schools at the village.

1880

Enrollment at Jenksville, 100 pupils in two schools.
Outlying schools: Number 1, Number 2, Number 3, Number 5, Number 6, Number 7, Number 8, Number 9, Number 10.
Appropriation for schools, $2,200.
Length of school year:
    Outlying—33 weeks.
    Village—40 weeks.

1881

"Through the liberality of Ludlow Manufacturing Company, District Number 4 [Ludlow Village] has been furnished with a room for one of its schools in the church, a number of years, without cost."

The Ludlow Company contemplates building a schoolhouse.

1882

Assistant teacher employed in primary school, making three teachers employed at village.

First truant officers appointed.

1883

Abolition of district system.

The Ludlow Company begin building schoolhouse.

1884

First school census taken, children from 5 to 15 years—whole town, 394.

First tabular matter in school report.

In October of this year the Ludlow Company's new building used. Three rooms opened.

Number 7 school closed.

1885

Free text-books introduced.

Census shows 348 families.

1886

New schoolhouse built in District Number 8.

The Ludlow Company gave rent of building, teachers' salaries, and musical instruction, amounting to $1,145.

1887

The Ludlow Company paid a portion of the salary of the village teachers.

Have established a cooking school.

1888

The Ludlow Company paid one fourth of expense of teachers' salaries at the village, $269.25.

Differences existing between Ludlow Company and School Committee adjusted by "Memorandum of Agreement" (see page 22, 1888 Report). Agreement to be canceled by either party by giving a year's notice.

1889

The Ludlow Company paid one fourth teachers' salaries at village, amounting to $461.55.

Library building, nearly completed, presented to the town.

First mention in town report of necessity of high school.

1890

The Ludlow Company paid one fourth teachers' salaries at village, amounting to $540.50.

First evening school conducted; $300 contributed by the Ludlow Company.

High school subjects on recommendation of State Board introduced into grammar grades.

Failure to get good results in grammar grades reported by committee. The following is quoted from report: "It is an important question for our town to consider, whether a person living one hundred miles from the scene of operations, however competent he may be, knowing nothing of the needs of our schools, can direct the affairs of the same with as good results as would be if our town managed its own affairs." What person is meant?

Minority report submitted by one member of school committee, recommending the adoption of a course of study, systematizing financial matters, and the employment of a superintendent of schools. This is the first mention in reports of the employment of a superintendent.

Mr. Buell's last year as member of school committee.

1891

Value of schoolhouses and furniture, $5,000.

Value of schoolbooks and bookcase, $600.

First course of study adopted.

High school—two years' course adopted.

1892

Committee question the advisability of introducing, extensively, sewing, cooking, and manual training.

Consolidation and transportation recommended.

1893

First record of observance of Columbus Day in schools.

Agreed with the town of Granby, that for the next six years, beginning March 1, 1893, "That each town shall have charge of the school alternate years, Granby commencing." Formerly for five or six years Ludlow paid two fifths and Granby three fifths of the expense of maintaining

Number 6 school. By present arrangement each town is to pay per capita based on actual membership from both towns.

Article in the warrant for town meeting to see if the town would raise and appropriate money for employment of superintendent of schools.

1894

First superintendent of schools employed—Miss Mary L. Poland. Supervision District—Wilbraham, Hampden, Longmeadow, and Ludlow.

Grading of rural schools begun.

Rules for teachers and pupils adopted and printed.

1895

Number 7 school discontinued.

Number 10 closed for two terms.

"By vote of school board, pupils outside the village may enter the Union school when fitted for the eighth grade."

First graduation, class of eleven. As far as can be learned from school reports these had completed a two years' high school course.

Admission to high school determined by written examinations.

Law passed requiring display of flag.

Music teacher first employed, October 25, 1895—Miss Edith M. Clark. Not permanently established until later.

1896

Eighteen pupils from uptown attending village school, grades eight, nine, and ten.

Drawing teacher first employed—Miss Alice F. Willard.

Town voted to accept By-Laws in regard to truancy. (See 1895 Report, page 48.)

Voted at town meeting to "instruct school committee to make such arrangements with the Town of Granby as will place Number 6 school under the control of Towns of Ludlow and Granby for terms of four years each, and that Granby be granted control for first four years." (Above vote taken March, 1896.)

1897

First appropriation for high school, $1,000.

Ludlow high school established, two years' course with 9 pupils.

Vertical penmanship introduced.

1898

Number of grades in outlying schools reduced to six.

F. F. Smith engaged as principal of high school.

1899

No written or statistical report by School Committee or superintendent printed.

First class graduates from high school.

1900

Ludlow assumes charge of Number 6 school, spring term 1900, it having been under Granby's charge for last four years.

Overflow of pupils occupy Masonic Hall part of year.

New schoolhouse built in Number 2 district.

Cumulative record of pupils' standing and promotions established.

1901

Two schools maintained at Ludlow Center, a room in Mrs. Susan Chapin's house being used for the upper grades.

For a part of the year two teachers were employed at the Red Bridge school on account of its crowded condition. This was due to the influx of laborers with their families during the construction of the dam at Red Bridge by the Ludlow Manufacturing Associates.

Number 5 schoolhouse burned February, 1901. New one built in its place.

Eight-room brick building, erected at village, dedicated September 19, 1901.

1902

Grades five and six at the village opened to the uptown children.

Music under a supervisor permanently established, September, 1902.

1903

Evening school, self-supporting, for advanced pupils opened in high school building.

W. E. Gushee succeeds Miss Mary L. Poland as superintendent of schools July 1, 1903.

Supervision District reorganized, consisting, from this date, of the towns of Agawam and Ludlow.

1904

New eight-room building already overcrowded. Overflow of primary children placed in high school building. One half attend in forenoon, other half in afternoon.

Ward System of teaching reading adopted in September, 1903.

William K. Lane elected to succeed Mr. Smith as principal of the high school.

Mr. Lane resigned before the expiration of year. Succeeded by Frederick F. Williams.

1905

Most rapid growth in schools of any year thus far. Three new rooms opened in old high school building for primary grades.

High school occupies rooms on third floor of old building.

Number 8 school discontinued.

1906

Schools again overcrowded. Masonic Hall engaged again to accommodate overflow, and later the school parlor.

Special school for non-English speaking children opened.

Law raising compulsory school age for illiterates from 14 to 16 went into effect January 1, 1906. Special school opened for children who had to leave the mills on account of this law.

Number 10 school discontinued June 1, 1906.

Mr. Williams, principal of the high school, succeeded by Mrs. Helen M. Gushee, September, 1905.

Music introduced into the high school.

1907

New eight-room brick building, to be used by primary grades, completed and turned over to the school committee February 11, 1907. This building is similar to the one built in 1901 and fronts on Park Place.

Primary pupils in old high school building transferred from third floor to first floor of high school building.

State high school aid withdrawn.

First school gardens conducted.

Shrubbery planted extensively on school grounds.

During winter term about 25 children under compulsory school age refused admission on account of crowded conditions.

First transportation of uptown pupils to village at town's expense. All above fifth grade transported.

First medical inspector employed.

First eye and ear test given by teachers.

Opening of parochial school across the river removes nearly all our Polish children from the public schools.

Length of school year for district schools increased from 32 to 34 weeks.

1908

Commercial course introduced into high school with special teacher for department.

Drawing introduced into the high school.

New heating and ventilating system installed in grammar building. Hot air furnaces replaced by two steam boilers.

New primary building filled to its capacity.

Crowded conditions in grammar building necessitate transferring eighth and ninth grades to high school building.

Certificate privilege for admission to State normal schools granted by State Board of Education to graduates of high school. Certificate privilege also obtained from Simmons College.

Length of school year for district schools increased to 38 weeks.

1909

Fire extinguishers placed in all school buildings of the town.

Superintendent of schools changed residence from Agawam to Ludlow.

Length of school year for district schools increased to 40 to correspond with village.

1910

First award of prizes made from the Rood Fund.

Ludlow Manufacturing Associates deeded old high school building and site for new high school building to town.

1911

New high school building facing park completed and occupied September, 1910.

Manual training in the form of bench work and wood turning, and Domestic Science in the form of cooking and sewing established. These subjects required in grades above the sixth and elective in high school.

Bubbling fountains installed in all the buildings at the village.

Statistics of the progressive growth of the Ludlow schools by decades since 1881:

	1881	1891	1901	1911
Number of Grade schools				
Village	2	6	9	21
Town	9	9	8	6
Enrollment				
Village		211	250	663
Town		113	146	90
Expenditure	$2,415	$6,089	$9,888	$31,177
School year				
Village	40 wks.	40 wks.	40 wks.	40 wks.
Town	32 wks.	32 wks.	32 wks.	40 wks.
For new buildings		$750	$25,103	$29,300* $43,000†

High school

Enrollment	17	40
Expense	$1,300	$4,413*
Graduates	6	7†
Transportation	$112	$2,536

*1907.   †1910.

LUDLOW TEXTILE SCHOOL

The Ludlow Textile School is maintained by the Ludlow Manufacturing Associates for the purpose of training apprentices in those branches of the textile industry in which they are particularly interested. The varied activity of the Associates offers a very particular field of work for boys educated in the school. The school was started by the discovery that of the fifty or more overseers and second-hands employed, not one in forty years had been educated in the village schools. The majority received their technical training in the Scotch mills. This made it evident that the Associates must depend upon men trained abroad or else give boys an education which would fit them for positions in the various departments of the mills.

The instruction is divided into two kinds, practical or mill, and theoretical or school.

The boys of the school are divided into classes, so arranged that the work performed in the mill in the morning by one class is continued by the other class in the afternoon. The class attending the morning session of the school and working in the mill in the afternoon during one week reverses this arrangement the following week.

The boys must be between the ages of 14 and 16, in good physical condition, of good moral character, and must pass an examination which shows their possession of a fair knowledge of English and arithmetic. They do not sign a contract, but leaving the employ of the company means severing their connection with the school. The school work, conducted in a separate building devoted to school purposes, commences about the middle of August and continues for eleven months, with a short recess at Christmas. At the close of the eleven months the members attend a camp especially equipped for their purpose. This camp is located on a high elevation in the town of Becket. Here the boys under competent supervision, not only enjoy a delightful outing for practically five weeks, but are instructed in camp life and duties, each having his share of the work to do.

For his work in the mill and attendance at school each boy receives pay for an eight hour day for five days, and five hours' pay for one day, making a total of regular rate per hour for forty-five hours per week, instead of fifty-five hours, which constitute a full week's work.

The outline of the course of study at present is tentative, but includes four years' work. The school has a special shop arithmetic covering all

"Winding Wave," Ludlow, Massachusetts

the operations, calculations, and duplications performed in the mills, written by the former director and one of the overseers.

The janitor work of the school is all performed by the students.

The school aims to educate industrially its members, as well as develop desirable, healthy, and law-abiding citizens.

"Winding Wave"

In the early history of educational interests in Ludlow, "Winding Wave" school was of no little importance. It took its name from a winding or bend in the Chicopee River near by. It was established in 1854, in the house of Daniel Ray, whose daughter, Mrs. Gilbert Pillsbury, and her husband, were the founders. The chambers in this house were named for the stars. Both boys and girls were admitted to the school; there were fifteen or twenty boarding pupils, and thirty-five or forty day pupils in addition. Many of these came from surrounding towns. Latin, French, and the higher mathematics in addition to the common branches were taught. The school opened prosperously and continued with varying fortunes until the beginning of the war in 1861. Mr. and Mrs. Pillsbury then took up the work of the Freedmen's Bureau, which they continued throughout the war, and for some time later lived in the South. Mr. Pillsbury was mayor of Charleston, S. C. Upon returning to Ludlow, they reopened the school, which continued for two or three years and was then given up. There were many of the young people of that period who recall with pride and affection their training in "Winding Wave."

PART II

I

BIOGRAPHIES

THE history of every town, state, or nation is only the record of the deeds and lives of the men who have dwelt within its borders, and each notes with just pride those who have served it best. And so it is well that there be recorded in the history of Ludlow sketches of the lives of some of her sons who have contributed to her honor and welfare, both at home and abroad.

> "Fairer seems the ancient township,
> And the sunlight seems more fair,
> That they once have trod its pathways,
> That they once have breathed its air."

GEORGE ALEXANDER BIRNIE

George Alexander Birnie was born in Becket, Mass., May 28, 1842. His father was a son of George Birnie of Aberdeenshire, Scotland, who with his wife and a family of twelve children located in New Jersey in 1827. Alexander Birnie, father of George A., was a contractor. He built a large section of the Western Railroad, now the Boston and Albany division of the New York Central, and was engaged in other large public works. George A. Birnie attended the public schools in Hastings-on-the-Hudson, N. Y. Later he became a pupil of Sanford Lawton's select school in Longmeadow, Mass., and finished his education in the University School, New York City.

He then took a position with C. L. Covell of Springfield, and later was connected with J. R. Hixon in the boot and shoe business, leaving this to enter the grain business in partnership with his brother, William A. Birnie. After some years, this concern dissolved and Mr. Birnie became a traveling salesman. Failing health compelled him to retire, and about 1875 he came to live on a farm in this town. The city of Springfield was just commencing the construction of its waterworks in Ludlow and Mr. Birnie was appointed a foreman and had charge of the gang which dug the first section of the ditch for the mains.

After three years spent in Ludlow, Mr. Birnie returned to Brooklyn, N. Y., in the 70's, to become chief deputy United States marshal, under

Marshal Samuel R. Harlow of Brooklyn, where he served for six years. He returned to Ludlow and became private secretary to Agent John E. Stevens of the Ludlow Manufacturing Company. He was one of the incorporators of the Ludlow Savings Bank and has served as treasurer of the institution since it was chartered in 1888. As chief executive officer of the bank, Mr. Birnie takes a deep personal interest in its welfare and that of its depositors.

Mr. Birnie was first appointed postmaster by President Harrison in 1889, and with the exception of Cleveland's last term, when he was replaced by his brother-in-law, James Haviland, he has filled that office ever since.

Mr. Birnie served on the school committee for nine years and has been moderator at the annual town meeting for the past fourteen years. When the Ludlow Hospital Society was organized in 1908, he was chosen secretary and treasurer, and president in 1910.

Mr. Birnie was married in 1865 to Miss Julia W. Carroll of New York City, who died the following year. Five years later he married Miss Ellen Bowen of Weathersfield, Vt., who died in 1910. They had two children, Mary A., formerly librarian of Hubbard Memorial Library, and Alexander Cullen, a general contractor.

Outside of his business, Mr. Birnie has become identified with Ludlow affairs in many ways. He has won a place of honor and prominence in the business and social life, and has served the important interests confided to his charge with a high degree of sagacity and efficiency.

Edwin Booth

Edwin Booth, the youngest son of Eliphal Booth, was born in Enfield, Conn., May 12, 1814, and lived there until the family moved to Ludlow in April, 1818.

When he was fifteen, he went into the store of his brother Harmon, in Jenksville. Two years later he entered the employ of Montague & Hunt, in Springfield, where he remained until 1834, when he went to New York. He was a clerk there for J. & I. Clark & Hunt, on Pearl Street, Hanover Square. He was in New York during the great fire of December, 1835. He went to Philadelphia in 1837, where he lived for the greater part of his life.

On February 21, 1839, he married Mary, daughter of John Bryan and sister of Dr. James Bryan; she died March 25, 1848. He married second, November 29, 1849, Helen Elizabeth Rhodes, formerly of New York City and Newport, R. I.

He was an ardent advocate of the Whig party, and a great admirer of Henry Clay. In the latter's campaign for the presidency he took an active part. In 1853 and 1854, Edwin Booth was a member of the Board of Controllers of Public Schools, representing the fourth section or

Lemuel Hawley Brigham

district of Spring Garden. In 1857 he was a member of the Common Council, representing the fourteenth ward. Governor James Pollock in 1855 appointed him aide-de-camp on his staff, with the rank of lieutenant-colonel. He was appointed assistant postmaster at Philadelphia in 1861, and in the following year he was commissioned as special agent of the Post Office Department at Washington and added the duties of this position to those of the local office.

The later years of his life were passed in Philadelphia, with the exception of the last two in Jenkintown, Penn., where he died. His will was probated at Norristown, Penn., and he was buried in Central Laurel Hill Cemetery, Philadelphia.

Lemuel Hawley Brigham

Lemuel Hawley Brigham was born in St. Albans, Vt., August 17, 1816, the son of Dr. Luther Brigham, whose wife was Eunice Hawley of Arlington, Vt. Mr. Brigham was of good old Puritan stock, and justly proud of his ancestry, being a descendant of Thomas Brigham, one of the first of the Puritans to come to this country and who settled in Marlboro, Mass., about 1626. Mr. Brigham was educated in the public schools and Mount Pleasant Academy, Amherst, Mass.

In 1836 he went to Chicopee, where he was connected with the Dwight Manufacturing Company as superintendent for thirty-two years. He was actively interested in public affairs of the town, and as a member of the Lyceum Lecture Committee made the acquaintance of such men as Horace Mann, Horace Greeley, Emerson, and Beecher. He was an ardent abolitionist.

In 1868 he went to Ludlow as agent of the Ludlow Manufacturing Company, in which position he remained continuously till 1887, when he retired.

By virtue of his position and also because of his strong and benevolent qualities, Mr. Brigham was one of the most prominent men of Ludlow, and was very active in the history of the town during his nineteen years of residence, his influence being felt in many directions. He was a man of liberal spirit, carrying on large private charities in a quiet, modest way. In 1888 he moved to Springfield and bought a house on Dartmouth Street, where he lived until 1890, when he moved to Palmer.

He was a deep student and had traveled much in this country and Europe. He was a 32d degree Mason, a member of Chicopee Lodge and Unity Chapter. Brigham Lodge of Ludlow is named for him and much of its success is due to his efforts. He was also a member of Springfield Commandery, Knights Templars, and was for many years a director of The Masonic Mutual Insurance Company.

Mr. Brigham died in Palmer, May 6, 1896, and was buried in Maple Grove Cemetery, Chicopee.

Benjamin Franklin Burr

Few town officials in Western Massachusetts are more widely known or more respected than Benjamin F. Burr of this town, and only a very few have been fortunate enough to have had his varied experience in office.

From 1865 to 1909, he held office of one kind or another continuously. He began as tax collector, which office he held during 1865 and 1866, when the collection of taxes was auctioned to the lowest bidder. Mr. Burr secured the contract, bidding $69 the first year and a dollar more the following year. From 1867 to 1880, he was town clerk and treasurer and in 1879 was elected representative to the Legislature from this district. A year later he was chosen selectman and overseer of the poor, filling the latter office acceptably for nine years. He was a justice of the peace from 1876 to 1910, special county commissioner for a time and cemetery commissioner for nearly a generation. As administrator of estates Mr. Burr settled more than a hundred in Hampden and Hampshire counties. As a public official he has proved faithful and efficient, enjoying in the highest degree the confidence and esteem of his fellow citizens.

Mr. Burr is president of the Burr Company, Incorporated, dealers in grain, coal, and wood, his son being treasurer and general manager.

Aside from his business and official duties, Mr. Burr has devoted much time to music, being the possessor of a remarkably clear and sweet tenor voice. He has been a member of many male quartets, and has sung for years with Wilbur Miller, another noted Ludlow singer. He was chorister of the First Congregational Church for thirty years.

Benjamin Franklin Burr was born in Ludlow July 6, 1831, a son of Lyman and Harriet (Stebbins) Burr, and traces his ancestry back to Benjamin Burr, the progenitor of the Ludlow family, who came from England in 1630. He received his education in the public schools of his town and in Wilbraham and Monson academies. He married in 1854 Mary J. Brewer, a daughter of Daniel and Sarah K. (Miller) Brewer, a descendant of the Daniel Brewer who came to America about the same time. They have one son, Frederick L. Burr. They celebrated their golden wedding anniversary in 1904. For more than a half century they lived on a farm situated a short distance from Ludlow Center.

Hon. Chester W. Chapin

Chester Williams Chapin, an elegant portrait of whom appropriately opens our volume, is perhaps the best and most widely known to the world at large of any of the sons of this good old town. Mr. Chapin was born in the "Torrey house," in the west part of Ludlow, December 16, 1798. The cellar hole, where the house stood, is on the opposite

Benjamin F. Burr

side of the road from where the late Gillen D. Atchinson lived, and a little down the hill. Mr. Chapin was a direct lineal descendant, in the sixth generation, from Dea. Samuel Chapin, the founder of the family in this country. His grandfather, Ephraim Chapin, was one of the largest landowners of his day in this section, his estate covering lands in Chicopee, Ludlow, and Springfield. His father (also Ephraim by name) occupied a portion of the old Chapin estates, which at the time of his death had not been divided. Though rich in lands these early settlers were otherwise possessed of small means, and cultivated habits of the strictest economy. These were days of families inversely proportionate to the ready means of the householder, Chester being the youngest of a family of seven children.

Already, there had been instilled into the mind of the boy those lessons which served him so well, when at a tender age his father died and left the family, then at Chicopee Street, to manage for themselves. As his older brother, Ephraim, had been sent to college, the duty of remaining at home to care for the interests of his mother and her farm devolved upon Chester. While so doing he attended the district school at Chicopee, which ranked high as a school of its kind in those days, and was afterward sent to Westfield Academy, from which he entered upon the active pursuits of life. At twenty-one he went to Springfield, and first found employment at the bar of the old Williams Tavern, then kept by his brother Erastus. Not relishing the business, he next began keeping a store of his own at Chicopee Street.

Just across the way was another store kept by the late Stephen C. Bemis, and the two soon formed a copartnership which continued several months. At this time Mr. Chapin married Dorcas Chapin, daughter of Col. Abel Chapin of Chicopee. They had two sons and two daughters. Mr. Chapin then sold out his share of the store, and we next find him with his yoke of oxen engaged at Chicopee in preparing the foundation of the first mill where paper was made by machinery, built in the country. He took the contract for the foundation and masonry of this factory for the Ameses, and did the work so satisfactorily that when a few years later the mill was burned, they urged him to undertake a renewal of the job; but other engagements then intervened to prevent him from complying.

A change in business then occurred which turned the attention of the young man in the direction of his real life work. At the solicitation of Jacob W. Brewster of Hartford, he was induced to take an interest in the extensive stage lines of the Connecticut Valley. Here he first made the acquaintance of his lifelong friend, the late Major Morgan of Palmer, who was engaged in the stage line running east and west from Springfield. Occasionally holding the reins on the Hartford and Brattleboro line, Mr. Chapin was soon found to be more needed in developing the general interests of the route, which so prospered under his management as to yield him large returns on his investment.

Soon after the demonstration had been satisfactorily made by Thomas Blanchard that steamboats could journey from Hartford to Springfield, Mr. Chapin grasped the idea and utilized it. He bought out Blanchard in 1831 and until 1844 controlled the passenger traffic between the two places. Until his death he maintained his business relations with boating lines, finally controlling to a large extent the New York and New Haven lines of steamboats. Two of his vessels were in government employ during the Civil War.

A railroad had been talked of in the meantime, and Mr. Chapin with his accustomed sagacity saw its future and made arrangements to aid in its introduction. He became a director of the road between Hartford and Springfield in 1841, and later its agent, which office he held until 1844. When this road was completed to Northampton in 1846, Mr. Chapin discontinued his stage lines. He contracted to carry the mails between St. Louis and Terre Haute and sent his stages there. He then carried the mail by rail up and down the Connecticut Valley from Hartford to Stanstead, Canada, with branches on either side.

In 1850 Mr. Chapin became a director of the Western Railroad, but resigned the position to become president of the Connecticut River Railroad in the same year. In 1854, having attracted attention by successful management of that road he was elected president of the Western road, and accepted. In two years fifty miles of rails had been renewed, the bridge over the Connecticut River rebuilt, twelve first-class locomotives, one hundred and forty-five freight cars and six passenger coaches had been added to the rolling stock of the road.

He then began his life work, that of expanding and developing the Boston and Albany lines. In 1855 he went to England and negotiated a loan of half a million dollars to improve and complete the road. Very soon the road began to pay handsome dividends. The Albany bridges, the new iron bridge at Springfield, the continuous double track, with magnificent tidewater facilities, the huge elevator at Boston, and a large station at Worcester were some of his successful undertakings. His great desire was to consolidate the Western and Boston and Worcester Railroads as the Boston and Albany. This he accomplished December 1, 1867.

At various times during his presidency of the Western road, he was solicited to take the management of other large railroad interests, but always refused.

In business relations elsewhere, we find Mr. Chapin mentioned as a stockholder and director in the Hudson River and New York Central Railroads, as a prominent manager and owner of the Collins Paper Company's property and business at Wilbraham, and of the Agawam Canal Company at West Springfield.

In 1846 he started the Agawam Bank, was its president for a short time and a director till 1872, when the Chapin Banking and Trust Company, of which he became the first president, was formed.

He held a few minor offices in the town and city, and was a member of the Constitutional Convention of Massachusetts in 1853. He was elected a representative to the Forty-fourth Congress, serving from Dec. 6, 1875, to March 3, 1877, a fitting testimonial from an appreciative public—a testimonial, moreover, in which his little native town claims the privilege of giving a modest share.

On April 17, 1878, he resigned the presidency of the Boston and Albany Railroad. In 1879 he endowed Amherst College with $55,000.

Kind and obliging, of unblemished reputation, cool and decided but considerate, one whose "promise is as good as his bond," his native town rejoices to hold him up as an examplar for her young people. Mr. Chapin's presence at the Centennial was highly appreciated. The following tribute was paid him:

"While Mr. Chapin is naturally and by instinct a prudent and somewhat conservative man, a careful observer of his career will find that he has always been among the foremost to embrace every improvement in the onward march of civilization. At first a stage owner, he was quick to see and utilize the application of steam, first upon the waters of the Connecticut and then upon its banks. Instead of resisting the march of events as bringing into the field an element of rivalry and perhaps destruction to his interests in old methods, he was the foremost to contribute his capital and practical experience to the development of each new and improved project in the direction of cheap and rapid transportation."

Rev. Joel Chapin

Rev. Joel Chapin was born in Ludlow very early in the period of the settlement of the town. He was the son of Shem and Anna (Clark) Chapin. His marriage to Eunice Lucretia, daughter of Dea. Edward Chapin of Chicopee, was published November 10, 1789. They had three children. The following is quoted from the *New York Observer* of March 27, 1851: "Rev. Joel Chapin died in Bainbridge, N. Y., in 1845, aged 84. A soldier in the Revolution; then a graduate of Dartmouth College in 1791. He settled as a minister in the wilderness, on the Susquehanna, and was faithful as a minister of the gospel."

Ambrose Clough

Ambrose Clough, son of Mordecai Clough, was born in Franklin, N. Y., June 6, 1822, and though not a native of Ludlow, was one of its most useful and respected citizens. He came to Ludlow when eleven years of age and lived with Franklin Fuller on the place which he later owned. He married Theodocia Parsons, who also was a member of Mr. Fuller's family from an early age. Mr. and Mrs. Clough had a son and a daughter, whom they survived. He died April 2, 1889.

Mr. Clough was always keenly interested in town affairs, and served for some years as selectman and school committee. He was a leading spirit in the celebration of the town's centennial in 1874, and spent much time in the fall and winter of that year in collecting material for the town history, a labor of love.

Hon. Dexter Damon

Dexter Damon, the eldest of a family of ten children born to Henry and Ruby (Winchester) Damon, was born and brought up on the farm in Ludlow where Clarence Tilley now lives. When a young man he taught school for several winters in New Jersey.

About the year 1839, in company with his brother Austin, he went into business in Kirtland, Lake County, Ohio. This business was continued by the brothers for twenty years, when Dexter sold out and engaged in farming for several years. In 1851 he was elected to the legislature of Ohio, and served one term. In 1864 he sold his Kirtland property and moved to the adjoining town of Willoughby, where he lived until his death. In the fall of 1870, Dexter Damon established his two oldest sons in business in Winnebago, Minn., under the firm name of D. Damon & Sons, the sons being the company. This business has been conducted for forty-one years by the two sons, with no change in the name, and is still flourishing (1911). Mr. Damon married in Kirtland, Ohio, Harriet Matilda Frank. They had three sons and one daughter, all of whom are living. Mrs. Dexter Damon is still living (1911), in very good health, though nearly 92 years old. Her eyesight and hearing are good, and her mental faculties unimpaired.

Hon. Gordon M. Fisk

Gordon M. Fisk, editor and founder of the *Palmer Journal*, was born May 9, 1825, in the red house across the pond from Henry I. Carver's mill at Ludlow City. He was one of seven sons, his father being William H. Fisk. Gordon Fisk was named for a son of Dr. Aaron John Miller, who accompanied the name with a gift of *three sheep*. The family was large, the mother an invalid, the income small, so here was an opportunity for building up a strong man. The district school and family fireside afforded the only means for educating the children. A studious boy, Gordon early mastered all the books within reach, even to Dr. Johnson's dictionary and the Westminster catechism.

Dr. James Wilson Hannum

At the age of twenty-one he found an opportunity to gratify the longings of years, and purchased a printing press of one John Howe, of Enfield, who had used it in the publication of anti-orthodox pamphlets. It was a rude establishment, with ancient Ramage press, and ink balls instead of composition rollers. Having mastered the business by assiduous labor at night, he established the *Village Gazette* in Ware in June, 1847. He sold out in December, 1848, and moved to Palmer, where on the first of January he opened a printing office. In the fall he undertook, with another, to establish the *Holyoke Times* but abandoned the project, and issued the first number of the *Palmer Journal* April 6, 1850, which publication he continued until his death, also sending out the *Ware Standard* for nineteen years. A copy of the first issue of the *Palmer Journal* is in the Historical Room of the Hubbard Memorial Library.

His official record covers a period of over twenty years. In 1860–1861 he served as state senator, attending an extra session each year, and serving on a special commission to sit in the recess, for three years, for the purpose of surveying a ship canal from Barnstable Bay to Buzzard's Bay; was deputy United States collector 1862–1868, and inspector of the State almshouse and primary school at Monson 1857–1874, and from 1866–1879 (the year of his death) was connected with the visiting agency of the Board of State Charities.

Mr. Fisk possessed a local reputation as a poet, and several of his sketches are to be found in this volume.

Dr. James Wilson Hannum

Dr. Hannum was born in Williamsburg, Sept. 24, 1851, the son of John and Eunice (Squier) Hannum. His ancestors figured prominently among the first settlers of the Connecticut valley, the original Hannum coming from England and locating in the valley in 1630. His grandfather and father were the first manufacturers of woolen machinery in this section, having been engaged for years in manufacturing carding machines in Williamsburg.

Dr. Hannum received his early training in the schools of Williamsburg, working in the Westfield News Letter office during vacations. He began his training for the medical profession by taking a post-graduate course in Latin and Greek in the Westfield high school. When 20 years of age he went to study with Dr. James Dunlap in Northampton. A year later he removed to Hartford, where he continued his studies for the next year with Dr. Joseph Yale, and then took the medical course in the University of Michigan. He received his degree in 1877 from the College of Physicians and Surgeons, medical department of Columbia University. He began practicing in Whately, remaining until 1879, when he removed to Ludlow, where he continued till illness forced him to give up active work in 1911.

His ability as a physician cannot be spoken of too highly. He built up an extensive practice that was not confined to Ludlow, but extended throughout western Hampden county. He was town physician for a number of years and it was due to his efforts that the town escaped from the ravages of the smallpox epidemic which swept over this locality several years ago. For 25 years he was surgeon for the Ludlow Manufacturing Associates.

"CHUMS"
Alice Hannum and her Dog

Dr. Hannum was a member of the American Medical Association, the Massachusetts Medical Society, the Eastern Hampden Medical Association, the Hampden district branch of the State Association, and the Springfield Academy of Medicine. He served as censor and councilor of the State Association, and as president of the Eastern Hampden Association and the Hampden branch of the State Association. He frequently read papers before some of these societies, and during the early days of the germ theory he prepared an original paper on "Disease Germs" that was widely quoted. His paper on pneumonia was well received by the members of the state medical society.

Among the contributions that he made to medical science was the invention of a device that records the pulsations of the heart by means of a photographic film. This has proved valuable in detecting abnormal conditions of the heart. As examiner for a number of life insurance companies this device was used by him with great success. His inventive ability did not confine itself to medicine, for with his knowledge and love for applied mechanics he invented a number of mechanical devices, among which was one for regulating the supply of gasolene in gas engines. This was patented and manufactured by a Chicago company.

For a number of years he was president of the Ludlow Savings Bank and at the time of his death was a director. It was due to his efforts that the Ludlow hospital, one of the best equipped institutions of its kind in Western Massachusetts, was built. He served as staff physician in the hospital from the time of its foundation. He was interested in every movement that made for the betterment of the town and the residents, and although various offices within the gift of the town would have been his for the asking, the only town positions that he filled were those of town physician and member of the school board, an office he held for several years.

In 1886 he married Miss Maria Louise Miller, daughter of Mr. and Mrs. Wilbur F. Miller. He had two sons and one daughter.—Adapted from the *Springfield Union*, of Dec. 10, 1911.

николая Nathan Alonzo Harris

Nathan Alonzo Harris was born in Wilbraham, July 7, 1814, the son of Nathan and Mercy (Green) Harris. His grandfather, Eliphalet Green, served as a soldier in the Revolutionary army.

Mr. Harris's father died when he was three years of age, leaving to the widow the care of two small children, with only a small house and garden. Possessing the ability of a tailor, with needle and hand-forged shears (which shears are yet in the Harris family) the mother supported her children till Nathan was eight years old. Then he was placed with Willard Chaffee, who lived in that part of the town of Wilbraham which is now the town of Hampden. Here he had a home for two or three years. Later he worked for Oliver Dwight, farmer and tanner, who lived near the Baptist Church in East Longmeadow. When about seventeen years of age he commenced learning the carpenter's trade with a Mr. Burnham. Following the trade, business led him to Ludlow, Chicopee Falls, and to the Center (then called Cabotville). Returning to Ludlow on April 19, 1837, he married Marcia Ann Daniels, daughter of Asa and Sally (Blodgett) Daniels. In 1842 or 1843, he started a sash, door, and blind shop on Alden's Brook. This was among the earliest shops established for this purpose. He built the machinery and set it in operation, later selling his interest to Charles Alden.

In 1846, he moved his family to the western part of the town and started another factory on the water privilege, where formerly stood the "Continental Mill." Here Mr. Harris built all his machinery with the exception of a Daniels planer and a Fay tenoner. The water power was sufficient for him to employ at one time ten hands. His products were always considered the standard of merit.

Mr. Harris inherited an exceptionally fine voice with a great love for music and musical instruments. In the years of singing schools he taught music in Ludlow, Belchertown, Three Rivers, Granby, and East Longmeadow. Between 1835 and 1845 Ludlow had a brass band which was of no little repute. In this band Mr. Harris played the ophicleide and the slide trombone. The latter instrument still remains in the family, as well as his favorite instrument, the violin. The first melodeon and piano cases in the town of Ludlow were of his manufacture.

NATHAN ALONZO HARRIS

Mr. Harris led the singing in the Methodist church at the Center for thirty years. During a part of the time his violin was the only instrument used to accompany the singing.

JAMES HAVILAND

James Haviland, a former postmaster of Ludlow, who figured prominently in the early construction and development of the telegraph service in this country, was born at Pawling, Dutchess County, N. Y., August 13, 1825.

His father, John Ward Haviland, was a native of New York state, as was also his grandfather, and both were lifelong residents there. John Ward Haviland learned the clothier's trade in his younger days which he followed for some time, but later changed his occupation for that of a miller, settling in Elmira and continuing in that calling until his decease, which occurred at the age of sixty years.

His wife, whose maiden name was Anna Townsend, was a native of Kent, Putnam County, N. Y., and the daughter of Samuel and Keturah

Townsend. She was the mother of six children, and died at the age of eighty years.

James Haviland was very young when his father removed to Elmira, and he received his education at the public schools of that city. At the age of fifteen years he entered mercantile business as a clerk, and after remaining thus employed for two years, began the study of law with Judge E. P. Brooks of Elmira, and continued it later with Messrs. Thurston and Wisner. At this period the electro-magnetic telegraph had not only become an assured means of rapid communication, but was being extended to all parts of the country.

Mr. Haviland's interest in the new invention was aroused to such a degree that he relinquished his legal studies for the art of telegraphy, which he speedily acquired, and in 1847 was sent to Detroit, Mich., for the purpose of establishing a telegraph office in that city. From there he went to Chicago, where he made the necessary arrangements for opening an office. Upon its completion he proceeded to Milwaukee, Wis., in the same capacity, and there also opened the first telegraph office. The winter was an exceedingly severe one, and there being no railroads at that time running into Milwaukee, Mr. Haviland was weather-bound and forced to remain until the opening of the lake in April. He then returned to Detroit and when the line from Buffalo to Milwaukee was completed he was appointed secretary of the company and superintendent of the line, which position he most ably filled until 1855. After the consolidation of the Erie and Michigan with what was the Western and Union Company he continued in their employ for two years, after which he came East to enter the employ of the American Telegraph Company, and for the next year was engaged in constructing lines.

In 1858 Mr. Haviland was appointed to a clerkship in the Naval office at New York City, which he held for three years. In 1862 he was engaged by the United States Telegraph Company to construct the lines west of Toledo. He completed a double line from Buffalo to Milwaukee and another from Detroit to Bay City, Mich. After this he resided for a time at Evanston, Ill., and entered into the leather trade in Chicago. In 1871, Mr. Haviland purchased a farm in Ludlow, upon which he settled and from that time until 1888 followed the independent life of a farmer. In May of that year he received the appointment of postmaster at Ludlow, continuing as such for two years, and in 1893 was again appointed to office.

At the age of thirty years, Mr. Haviland was united in marriage to Miss Carrie Hall, a native of New York state. She lived but five years after the consummation of their union. In 1864 he wedded his second wife, Miss Annie Birnie, a native of Middlefield, Mass. Two children have blessed their union, Grace M. Haviland, now Mrs. George Taylor, and James Birnie Haviland.

Mr. Haviland was in every particular a most capable and popular official, and was a Democrat in politics. He died at the home of his daughter, Mrs. George Taylor, in Brookline, Mass., March 18, 1911, and is buried in Elmira, N. Y.—From *Hampden County Biographical Review*.

JAMES HENDERSON

James Henderson was born in Dunfermline, Fifeshire, Scotland, March 2, 1849, and died at Ludlow, December 22, 1911. He was the only son of Andrew and Jean Campbell (Buist) Henderson. His parents died while he was quite young, which made it necessary for him to become a wage-earner at an early age. While his education ceased in the school, his sturdy Scotch ancestry gave him that pertinacity and determination which successfully overcome all obstacles and he attended evening schools after his day's labor. He had very successful mill experiences in Lochee, Dundee, Scotland, Yorkshire, England, and Belfast, Ireland. He left Belfast in the spring of 1885 for Ludlow to assume charge of No. 4 Mill of the Ludlow Manufacturing Company. When the old stone mills were replaced by modern brick structures in 1895, he was given the oversight of these mills known as Nos. 1, 2, and 3 Mills.

In the fall of 1905 after the death of John E. Stevens, he was appointed general superintendent of all of the mills of the Ludlow Manufacturing Associates, which position he held at the time of his death. He was largely instrumental in forming the Ludlow Athletic and Recreation Association, beginning with rooms in one end of the present machine shop. These quarters were outgrown under his directorship and transferred to large and spacious quarters in the mill yards and now occupied by the present carpenter shop. In the fall of 1905 through his efforts and those of the late John E. Stevens, agent, who was also greatly interested in this work, and Charles W. Hubbard, treasurer of the Ludlow Manufacturing Associates, ground was broken for the new home of the Ludlow Athletic and Recreation Association. In the summer of 1906 this model building was dedicated to the memory of Mr. Stevens and given to the trustees of the Association. It was here that Mr. Henderson's work will be remembered. Through his energy and untiring efforts the membership was increased to 1000 members. Its social work through him was a large factor in making it enjoyable. He was also particularly interested in the children and was always on the lookout for the least detail with which to make them comfortable.

He was a member and deacon of Union Church, and a leader of the senior and junior choirs. He was a Past Master of Brigham Lodge of Masons in 1896 and 1897. At the annual meeting of the Ludlow Savings Bank in 1911 he was elected president, after serv-

James Henderson

ing on the board of trustees and as auditor. In town affairs he never held public office on account of his numerous duties. In politics he was a Republican. In 1874 he was married to Elizabeth Robertson, in Perth, Scotland, and by that union there were two children, James B. and Elizabeth C. Henderson. The following testimonial shows the high esteem in which he was held by his employers:

" It is with deep sorrow that the trustees of the Ludlow Manufacturing Associates announce the death of James Henderson, general superintendent of the mills. For 27 years Mr. Henderson has given to the Ludlow Company and to the village interests, the very best of his time, thought, and strength. In his death both the Company and the village have lost one whose life represented that honorable service which every man should render to his employer and to the community in which he lives.
"Ludlow Manufacturing Associates :
Cranmore N. Wallace,
Charles W. Hubbard,
Sidney Stevens.
Managing Trustees."

Charles Townsend Hubbard

Charles Townsend Hubbard, to whose memory the Hubbard Memorial Library is a fitting monument, was born in 1817, the son of Henry and Mary Hubbard. On account of his father's heavy losses in the cotton mills at Great Falls, New Hampshire, he was obliged to leave school at a very early age and enter business. For some years he was settled in New Orleans as a cotton broker.

In 1845 he married Louisa, daughter of Benjamin Sewall of the firm of Sewall, Day & Company, shipowners and manufacturers of cordage. He was soon taken into the firm as a junior partner.

Being dissatisfied with the work and responsibility given him, with Mr. Sewall's assistance, in 1848 he bought a small water-power at East Braintree, Mass., and began to manufacture flax. In 1852 this business was incorporated as the "Boston Flax Mills," and he was manager and treasurer of the mills until 1878 when they were abandoned, and the real estate disposed of. The machinery and good will of the firm were sold in 1868 to the company, which was reorganized under the name of the Ludlow Manufacturing Company, of which Mr. Hubbard was chosen treasurer, an office which he held until his death in 1887. Practically the whole of Mr. Hubbard's business career was devoted to these two companies, although he was interested in two or three similar concerns. None of these, however, received much of his attention and all were failures.

During all the period in which his interest was centered in Ludlow, Mr. Hubbard manifested deep regard for the development of the town and the betterment of its people. Whatever contributed to their comfort, pleasure, and progress was of heartfelt interest to him. This was most clearly shown by his efforts in establishing the first social and reading room for the benefit of the employees in the mills. To perpetuate his memory and keen interest in the people, the Hubbard Memorial Library was presented by his family to the town of Ludlow in 1888. (See page 112.)

By his first wife, Louisa Sewall, he had four daughters, one of whom died in childhood. He married second, in 1855, Elizabeth Blair Wells of Hartford, Connecticut, and they had two children, a son and a daughter. His early married life was spent in Boston and Newton. In 1855 he bought a farm in Weston where four of his children and three grandchildren are now (1911) living. He died very suddenly of heart disease January 18, 1887.

The following memorandum was inclosed in the call for a meeting of the stockholders of the Ludlow Manufacturing Company for Friday, January 28, 1887:

"Charles Townsend Hubbard, the founder and Treasurer of this Company and its predecessor, The Boston Flax Mills, died at his residence at Weston, Mass., Tuesday, January 18, 1887, in the seventieth year of his age, loved, respected, and lamented by all who knew him."

The following resolutions were adopted:

"The stockholders of the Ludlow Manufacturing Company desire to place on record their appreciation of the character and services of their late Treasurer, Charles T. Hubbard.

"Therefore voted; that in his sudden death the Company feels that it has lost a most efficient and upright Treasurer whose services for nearly twenty years have given success and character to the Company."

Captain Henry A. Hubbard

Henry A. Hubbard was born at Ludlow, Mass., August 25, 1836. His father was a citizen of official prominence in the town, and his mother a Brainard of Haddam, Conn., near of kin to the missionary, Rev. David Brainard. The early life of Captain Hubbard was passed upon a farm, in which time he not only studiously improved his opportunities at the public schools, but forced the hours when employed in manual labor to contribute to his store of knowledge. He fastened his book upon the plow and studied as he turned the soil, or left it at a convenient nook in the fence as he hoed the field, grasping some new advance upon each return. By teaching during the winter he secured means to pursue his studies at Wilbraham Academy, from which he was graduated with high honors. He continued his studies a year at Amherst College, and afterwards for a time at Union College, Schenectady, N. Y., but, deciding upon the legal profession, left the latter and entered the office of Beach & Bond, Springfield, Mass.

Poetry was his delight, Milton's "Lycidas" his favorite; and the hours after his daily toil were spent in close companionship with the choicest of American and English poets.

While engrossed with legal tomes, he united with the Union Guard of Springfield, and soon became adept in military tactics. Upon the opening of hostilities in 1861 he rallied his Ludlow neighbors and friends and drilled them in the "School of Soldiers," preparatory to the call he felt sure must come. When the raising of the Twenty-Seventh Regiment was authorized, Colonel Lee commissioned him to recruit for that organization, and the filling of the ranks of the Ludlow company so promptly was due mainly to his zeal and magnetism. He was mustered as captain, October 16, 1861, and continued with his command until their arrival with the Burnside Expedition at Hatteras Inlet, N. C. Here he contracted a serious and prolonged illness, from exposure. He remained upon the schooner "Recruit," and during the battle of Roanoke Island was on Croatan Sound just beyond the reach of the enemy's guns.

He heard our first cheer of victory, but died February 12, 1862, just after the return of the regiment to the vessel. Though prevented from participating in battle he died as really a martyr in his country's cause as though he had fallen amid the carnage of battle. His remains were buried with military honors at Ludlow, February 24, 1862, under the escort of his old comrades of the Union Guard. October 16, 1861,

CAPT. HENRY A. HUBBARD

two weeks previous to his departure for the seat of war, he married Amnie, daughter of Deacon Booth of Ludlow.

On the occasion of the death of Captain Hubbard the following lines were penned by Hon. G. M. Fisk of Palmer:—

>Comes there a mournful message,
> On wings of lightning sped,
>Thrilling the ear with sadness,
> Whispering, "He is dead!"
>
>Brief is the touching story,
> How at his country's call,
>Went he forth in his armor,
> To conquer or to fall.
>
>Bravely his comrades leading—
> On to the strife they go,
>Bearing the nation's standard
> To the soil of the foe.
>
>Over the trackless ocean,
> Rounding the stormy capes,
>Where the hurricane dashes
> The sea in mountain shapes.
>
>Hearing the distant thunder,
> Seeing the murky smoke,
>Knows he the strife of battle
> Rages at Roanoke?
>
>Turns on his fevered pillow,
> Starts with commanding word;
>Calls for his faithful comrades,
> Asks for his trusty sword.
>
>"Onward all! to the struggle!
> Charge! the foe is near!
>Mount to his frowning ramparts!
> Plant our standard there!"
>
>Wandering thus in fancy,
> He leads his comrades on;
>Crushing the foe before him,
> Until the field is won.

* * * *

Hushed is the din of battle,
  Hushed is the cannon's roar;
And sleeps the young commander—
  Sleeps to awake no more.

Homeward they gently bear him
  Over the foamy track—
Anxiously hearts are waiting,
  Waiting the welcome back.

Sad, oh, sad, is the welcome
  That greets the soldier's bier;
Voices are hushed in sorrow—
  Rapidly falls the tear.

Solemn the muffled drum-beat,
  Slow is the measured tread;
Bearing the youthful captain
  To his home with the dead.

Hark! 'tis the parting volley,
  Firing over his grave!—
The last sad act is finished,
  And rests the young and brave.

"Come to the bridal chamber,"
  Bind on the weeper's brow
Laurel wreaths of the soldier,
  Twined with the willow's bough.

"Green be the turf above him;"
  Peaceful his dreamless sleep;
Ever in fond remembrance
  His treasured mem'ry keep.

Ludlow, February 23, 1862.

John Jennings

John Jennings, one of the earliest settlers of Ludlow, was widely known in his day as the lawyer of the town. He lived at one time and had his office at the Ezekiel Fuller place, where Hiram Davenport now lives (1911). We first learn of him as surety for Wright and Paine in 1779, who were convicted of Sabbath breaking. He represented Ludlow in the Legislature in 1787, and again in 1809. He attended the Constitutional Convention in 1788. He was among the malcontents in Shays's forces in 1787. He served as town clerk from 1789 to 1792, 1794 to 1796, 1798 to 1799, and was the first man to hold the double office of town clerk and treasurer, in 1796. He was an assessor for two years, and acted as moderator eighteen times. It became his duty to make out many a deed of the lands of this region, and sign many important documents. His usefulness extended along many years, and found fields for display in larger circles than those of home.

The Miller Brothers

These four men whose portraits embellish this volume, Sylvester, Joseph, Daniel, and John, representative and worthy citizens of Ludlow, were the sons of Joseph and Mary (Wilder) Miller. Born in the latter part of the eighteenth century, their period of life extended well into the latter part of the nineteenth. Sylvester was 97, Joseph 90, Daniel 81, and John 88 years of age at death. All but Daniel attended the Centennial celebration in 1874, Sylvester being the oldest man present. Their attachment for each other was strongly marked. It is an interesting and remarkable fact that none of them used tobacco or spirituous liquors in any form. It is remembered of them that they were "such gentlemenly men."

Sylvester was of a very quiet nature, and took little part in public affairs. He retained unusual vigor to the end. Within two weeks of his death, he walked two and a half miles, a customary form of exercise.

Joseph went to Utica and Syracuse, living there a useful, but uneventful, life.

Daniel made his home in South Hadley, and was there during the establishment of Mount Holyoke Seminary. He was prominent in the early settlement of Holyoke. He was chosen a "minuteman" for the War of 1812

Colonel John Miller, the youngest of the quartet, filled all the town offices from first to last, and was also a "minuteman" with his brother. He was colonel of the 10th Regiment several years before the Civil War and was justly proud of his military career. All his commissions from sergeant in 1816 to colonel, during a period of twenty-four years' service, are in possession of one of his sons (1911).

For years Colonel Miller was an active member in the Methodist Church. Through his efforts the first Methodist preaching was begun and the Methodist Church established in Ludlow village.

DANIEL　　SYLVESTER　　JOHN　　JOSEPH

THE MILLER BROTHERS

Dr. Aaron John Miller

Aaron John Miller was well known in all the earlier history of the town as the family physician. He is said to have been one of the original Boston "tea-party," and went as surgeon to the Revolution. He was a member of the State Legislature. The following quotation from the *Palmer Journal* illustrates the man: "The first physician in Ludlow was Dr. Aaron John Miller. He was a very tidy sort of man, distinguished for wearing the highest-priced black broadcloth he could find, and always eating molasses instead of butter on his bread, drinking clear tea and a very little old New England, never any water. He was a rapid talker, made his fever powders of camphor gum and loaf sugar, and was never known to hurt his patients with his medicines. He usually walked on his visits to patients, always accompanied by his little yellow dog. He was intolerant of others' opinions, and emphasized his own with frequent thrusts of his cane."

The following acrostic, written by him, was found among the papers of his son, the late Gordon B. Miller:—

> Great chief, Columbia venerates thy name,
> Europe with awe proclaims thy deathless fame;
> On Asia's plains, where priests adore the sun,
> Rajahs and nabobs own great Washington;
> Grim Afric's sons, who war eternal wage,
> Earth's savage nations all revere our sage.
>
> Where Philadelphia graces yonder plains,
> Adorned with laurel our loved hero reigns;
> Serene he guides the helm of every State;
> His skill in war and politics complete.
> Illustrious statesman! thou in virtue's cause
> Now deign'st to sit, the guardian of our laws;
> Graced with the lovely olive branch of peace,
> Thy praise, O Washington, shall never cease!
> On thee this western world have turned their eyes,
> Ne'er to revert them till thou mount the skies.

From a poem of his entitled "Summer Evening Song of Connecticut River" are culled the following stanzas:—

> Flow on, loved Connecticut, majestic and slow,
> And mingle thy waters with ocean below;
> The god of the sea with his brine-dripping bride
> Exulting beholds thee still swelling his tide.

> The sun has gone down and the star of the west
> Is spreading delighted his beams on thy breast,
> While meek Luna, adorned with aspect serene,
> To grace with her graces the beautiful scene.
>
> I was born near thy marge in the year 'forty-nine,
> And love thee, still love thee and call thee divine;
> Not Ganges, nor Avon, nor Egypt's famed Nile,
> Could ever so sweetly my cares all beguile.

His "Epitaph on Little Bute," a favorite dog of his, is of a different character:—

> Hard was the fate of little Bute;
> With hungry wolves he did dispute;
> Amid the strife of battle din
> Received a grip beneath the chin.
>
> Adieu, my brother of the dust!
> Those savage whelps are doubly cursed;
> With horrid shriek and doleful yell
> I hear them howling now in *Hell*.[1]

Hon. Charles L. Miller

The following is quoted from an obituary notice:

Charles L. Miller, who dropped dead in the Capitol at Washington, on the 3d of January, 18—, was born in Boston in 1808, but moved to Ludlow when about four years of age. His father was Ithamar Miller, a native of Ludlow and brother of Dea. Joseph Miller of that town, and lived on the farm where Daniel Brewer now lives. Removing from Ludlow when Charles was fifteen years of age, the family settled in the State of New York, but subsequently moved to Constantine, St. Joseph County, Mich., where he became a merchant, town clerk, postmaster, and was afterwards elected clerk of the Senate. In 1844 he removed to Colon, and carried on successfully the business of general merchandise. He was elected representative to the legislature in 1853 and 1854, and in 1856 was elected judge of probate and served four years. In 1860, by invitation of Senator Chandler, he took the place of clerk of the United States Senate Committee on Commerce, and during every session since he has been at his post, drawing the text of all the important bills of that committee. With impaired health he returned to Washington at the

---

[1] A solitary and gloomy swamp, thus named, where the wolves used to gather and howl.

beginning of the session, and was at his duties daily. In fifteen minutes after entering the Capitol, on the morning of the 3d, he was found lifeless.

Senator Chandler says of him: "He was one of the purest and truest men I have ever met in my life. He was universally beloved, and the removal of such a man as Judge Miller seems to be a public calamity."

Rev. Simeon Miller

Simeon Miller was a son of Daniel and Parmela (Jones) Miller, and was born in Ludlow, March 20, 1815. He prepared for college at Hopkins Academy in Hadley; and graduated from Amherst College in 1840. He took the full course in Andover Theological Seminary (1841–1844), and was licensed to preach by the Andover Association, meeting with Prof. Ralph Emerson at Andover, April 13, 1844. He was acting pastor of Ireland Parish in West Springfield (now Holyoke), from 1844 to 1846, where he was ordained, May 7, 1846, and remained until 1870. He was installed pastor in South Deerfield, April 13, 1870, and continued there until 1872. He preached at Ludlow Mills, 1872–1873, at Andover, Conn., 1876–1882, and at Agawam in 1883, besides supplying other churches for shorter periods.

Mr. Miller was a member of the Holyoke school committee during his pastorate of twenty-five years there, for much of the time chairman of the board, and superintendent of schools from 1865 to 1866.

Mr. Miller married first, Charlotte Amelia Ewing, September 11, 1849; second, Lucretia White Lamb, Jan. 3, 1860. He had two daughters and four sons.

Rev. William B. Hammond (Class of 1843, Andover) of Andover, N. Y., wrote of Mr. Miller: "More than fifty years ago I was a classmate of Simeon Miller at Amherst College, and recall him as a model Christian man, who lived his religion every day, everywhere."

Rev. J. L. R. Trask, D.D., of Springfield (Class of 1867, Andover), who knew him well, both at Holyoke and Springfield, wrote: "Mr. Miller was an acute and vigorous sermonizer. A clear voice and dignified bearing added to the authority with which he spoke. The fineness of his feeling was evident in the tenderness and warmth of his pulpit manners. The appointments of his nature prevented him from being a stern preacher. But the face and form of his Lord were in all his utterances. What he was in the sanctuary, he was on the street, and in his home. If he had an enemy, it was never known. He had more tact than many ministers, and a quiet, sly humor served him well in difficult places. He was the soul of kindness. After he ceased to preach, he was a model parishioner. Appreciative, slow to criticise, his heart open to all good, ready to co-operate, he set a good example to all the congregation. He was loving and friendly to the last. Happy as were his years of pastoral service, he made no complaint when old age put its injunction upon him. He passed through grave domestic trials as one whose support was elsewhere, and this lowly faith was his unto the end. He used to say that his old teacher, Professor Stuart, admonished the students to preach once a year on Humility. Mr. Miller *lived* the doctrine his professor wanted him to preach, and because he was so sincerely humble, he was exalted amongst his parishioners and friends. And we believe he is exalted still."

WILBUR F. MILLER

When Wilbur Fisk Miller reached his seventieth birthday March 20, 1910, he had been singing in public for 60 years, and was still leading the choir of the Methodist Church in Ludlow, a record rivaled by very few people. He is the youngest of a family of 11 children, the son of Colonel John and Lucinda (Barton) Miller, and was born March 20, 1840. He is a farmer by occupation and lives in North street on the farm inherited from his father, from which he has sold lots for 125 houses in the village.

Mr. Miller is a musician of unusual ability, possessing a tenor of great power, range, and purity. He is one of the best-known singers in Western Massachusetts. He has never taken a lesson in music; he taught himself to sing, using a tuning fork to place the key. For a number of years after he began to sing, and even after he had charge of church singing, he could not read a note, though he mastered this art later by himself.

Mr. Miller began singing alto in the Ludlow Union Church when ten years of age, and when only eighteen was leader of the choir in Indian Orchard before he could read notes. This church was about to adopt modern hymn books in which were both the words and music. Fearing his deficiency in reading would be discovered, he refused to take the position if the new books were used. Two books were necessary by the old method, one containing words, the other music, and few possessed but one, the former. He led the singing in old Trinity Church, Springfield, for seven years, was at Grace Church two years, director in several others, including Highland Baptist, Springfield, one in Chicopee, and in Palmer. Since 1905, he has led the choir in the Methodist Church in Ludlow.

His singing has always been in great demand, and he has participated in many public performances. Among those recalled are the laying of the corner stone of the post office, Grace Church dedication, Grand Army fair, celebration at the re-election of President Lincoln, and numerous Masonic functions. He has sung in all parts of this country as well as in Europe, but he never made a profession of it; he has had many offers from opera companies and others to sing on the stage. Mr. Miller recalls many interesting reminiscences of his singing career.

Wilbur F. Miller

DEACON ELISHA TAYLOR PARSONS

On March 20, 1862, he was married to Miss Julia Maria Runnels, daughter of John and Almira (Butterfield) Runnels. They had one daughter and one son. Mr. Miller is a veteran of the Civil War, having been a member of the 46th Mass. Regiment, and is a member of E. K. Wilcox Post, a 32d degree Mason, a Knight Templar, a Shriner, belonging to Melha Temple, and a member of the Springfield Veteran Firemen's Association.

Elisha Taylor Parsons

Elisha Taylor Parsons was born in Enfield, Conn., April 1, 1805; the eldest son of Elisha and Lovisa (Gleason) Parsons. He was educated in the public schools of Hartford and vicinity, and afterwards became a district school teacher in the country towns. He taught in Ludlow in what is known as District No. 3, which extended from Ludlow City to the Chicopee River. In this school there were sixty pupils of various grades, many of his own age and older, all crowded into this little box of a schoolhouse. While thus engaged in Ludlow, he met Hannah D. Charles, who, in 1829, became his wife. He settled in the western part of the town, on the Lewis Barber farm, and identified himself heartily with the interests of the community. He filled many offices of trust and importance, and was captain of a local militia which flourished in the 30's, and for many years he served as moderator at town meeting, and twice represented his town in the state legislature (1855-1857).

For about seventy years he was connected with the First Congregational Church and for a large part of the time served as deacon. He was a man of sterling worth and was a type of the men whom New England produced during his generation.

He spent his last days in Washington, D. C., where he died March 12, 1895, nearly ninety years of age. He had endeared himself to a wide circle of friends in the National Capitol and was regarded as a wonderful man in many ways. He retained his mental vigor to the last and was deeply interested in all the great questions of the day.

His wife was born at Ballston Springs, N. Y., in 1807. She was the daughter of Danforth and Independence (Booth) Charles. She died in 1874, the worthy helpmate of a worthy man.

Charles Dexter Rood.

Charles Dexter Rood, the only child of J. Dexter and Clarissa (Walker) Rood, was born in Ludlow. His grandfather, Asahel Rood, removed to the town from Connecticut. When Charles D. Rood was eleven years old, his father was appointed station agent at Indian Orchard, and while the family lived there, the son attended the public schools at Dimmock Corner. Later he became a pupil in the famous "Winding Wave school," and finally a student at Williston Seminary. For a short period after leaving school, he was assistant paymaster and clerk at the Indian Orchard Mills. Then he engaged with Warren & Spadone, jewelers in New York City, at a salary of $500 per year. Within a year, one of the firm's traveling salesmen having given up his position, Mr. Rood was selected to finish his route and travel temporarily. After a three months' trip he returned and accepted an offer of a two years' engagement, his salary for the second year to be $2,500, more than double the amount ever before paid by the firm. At the expiration of this term, he became a partner in the firm, for five years. Within that time he was made an equal investor and partner under the firm name of Spadone, Rood & Co., manufacturers of fine jewelry and importers of watches and diamonds. They had the only United States agency for some of the most celebrated foreign watches, besides dealing extensively in those of American make. They used half the product of the noted Howard Watch Company, and altogether did a business of half a million dollars per annum. In 1876, Mr. Rood sold his interest in the manufacturing jewelry business, and early in 1877 was one of the organizers of the Hampden Watch Company which purchased the plant of the old New York Watch Company, and was appointed treasurer and manager, besides being a director. In 1884 he was made president in addition to his other offices. In 1888 the company removed to Canton, Ohio, building one of the finest plants in the country. The main building had a seating capacity of 2300 people. After selling his interests, except stock, in the Hampden Watch Company in 1890, he purchased a controlling interest in the Aurora Watch Company, located at Aurora, Illinois, where he operated for two years and then moved the tools, machinery, and materials to Lancaster, Pa., uniting with the Lancaster Watch Company. The two plants were finally merged under the name of the Hamilton Watch Company, the name retained in 1911 and 1912. The Hampden, the Aurora, and the Lancaster Watch companies each and all experienced very similar fortune. In turn changes were made to rehabilitate and make a success, but each proved a failure. Under Mr. Rood's management, the Hampden Company received orders for many times its product, and the stock increased from nothing to $400 or $500 per share. After the union of the Aurora and Lancaster companies the success was phenomenal; some years as many as thirteen 5 per cent cash dividends were paid besides a stock dividend of $500,000 and an increase of the assets nearly as much more. After the death of the superintendent, Mr. Rood gave his attention for several years to the details of the business, during which time the Hamilton Watch became the popular railroad watch of America. Having become interested in the telegraphone, Mr. Rood sold his interest in the Hamilton Watch Company and in 1911 was made president and manager of the American Telegraphone Company, capitalized for five million dollars, with factory and offices at Springfield, Mass. This

CHARLES DEXTER ROOD

instrument, one of the wonders of the twentieth century, can be used for dictating purposes as well as recording telephonic conversations. It registers the latter on a wire one-one hundredth of an inch in diameter—the finest piano wire—and retains it for years, or the record can be erased by using the wire for dictating again and again. The machine will be in the market in 1912, and the expectations for its success are very great.

Mr. Rood united with the Congregational Church at Indian Orchard when sixteen years old and still retains his membership. Mr. Rood married first, Anna S. Marble, daughter of Edwin S. Marble of New Haven, who died about a year later, leaving a little son, who lived to be nearly four years of age. Mr. Rood married second, Caroline Abbe, daughter of James T. Abbe, of Springfield. They have two daughters and one son. He is a member of both scientific and social clubs in New York, Philadelphia, and his own city of Springfield.

He has generously testified to his interest in, loyalty to, and affection for his native town Ludlow in donating, for various local purposes, a large sum of money to be disbursed by trustees appointed from the First Congregational Church at Ludlow Center. (See page 171.)

C. D. Rood and Little Friends
The sleigh is over 150 years old

J. Dexter Rood

J. Dexter Rood was born on the Newell place in Ludlow, February 22, 1815, the second son of Asahel and Asenath (Fuller) Rood. The family moved to the present Rood homestead in November, 1816.

At an early age Mr. Rood began working in the cotton mills owned by the Jenckses, in Jenksville. At the age of nineteen he was overseer in the weaving room. He continued with the company until just before their failure in 1848, when, according to the Hampden County records, the Springfield Manufacturing Company gave a mortgage to Dexter Rood and thirty others for $30,000.

J. Dexter Rood

Mrs. J. Dexter Rood

After the failure Mr. Rood moved to New York City and engaged in business with his brother Horace for a year or two. Returning to Ludlow, he engaged in farming on his father's farm. In 1853 he became station agent at Indian Orchard on the Boston & Albany main line. In 1867 he went to Illinois, remaining two years there in business with his brother Horace. In 1869 he became station agent on the Boston & Albany at West Warren, where he remained until his death, May 12, 1889, terminating a service of more than thirty-five years. He married Clarissa A. Walker. Charles D. Rood was their only child.

Deacon and Mrs. Alva Sikes

BIOGRAPHIES

Alva Sikes

Alva Sikes was born in Ludlow, March 19, 1796, the son of Jonathan and Mary (Montague) Sikes. He received his early education in the district schools of Ludlow and pursued an advanced course in a private school in Springfield. He taught school for the sum of ten dollars per month, boarding among the parents of his pupils. During the summer he assisted his father on the farm which he eventually inherited.

He served the town with credit in several offices, as selectman, assessor, and as representative to the General Court in 1840.

He married Emilia Walker, the daughter of Captain James Walker. They had two children, Reuben and Harriet.

Alva Sikes died August 6, 1856. He was a member of the Congregational Church and a deacon from 1839 to the close of his life. He was a man whose council was much sought.

Reuben Sikes

Reuben Sikes, a prosperous farmer and prominent citizen of Ludlow, was born April 25, 1824. In 1853 he lived on the Rood farm, in the western part of the town, and, in 1854, removed to Granby where he resided for one year. He then returned to Ludlow and settled upon the old homestead, where he lived until 1874, when the property was purchased by the City of Springfield for a reservoir. His next home was in North Brookfield, where he purchased the Dean farm and remained twelve years. Again he returned to Ludlow, bought land and built a house, living there until his death, July 22, 1901.

Mr. Sikes was a Republican from the time of its party formation. In 1871, he was elected to the state legislature. He was a selectman three years and an assessor four, in all of which capacities he served with distinction and honor. He was a deacon of Grace Union Church at North Wilbraham. He married first, Ann Eliza Keyes, a native of Ludlow, and second, Juliette Walker of Belchertown. He had five children, two sons and three daughters.

Theodore Sikes

Theodore Sikes was born in Ludlow in 1792, the oldest son of Benjamin and Catherine (Miller) Sikes. He was educated in the schools of the town, and was a teacher in them for a time. Later he became a farmer and carpenter, both of which trades he pursued for many years. He was keenly interested in the affairs of the town, and filled the various offices with success. His opinions and counsel were much sought. For years he was a justice of the peace, and in that period drew many wills, deeds, etc., as the records show. He represented the town five consecutive terms in the Legislature at the time when one representative was accorded each town annually. To him belongs the distinction of having represented the town oftenest in the political assemblies of the state.

In 1816, he married Anna Stebbins, and they had one son, Theodore, Junior. Mr. Sikes and his family resided in Ludlow until about 1850, when they removed to Cuba, N. Y., where he and his wife died, but they are buried in the cemetery at Ludlow Center. He died May 1, 1879.

Solomon Bliss Stebbins

(A memorial notice read at a meeting of the Board of Trustees of the Franklin Savings Bank, by Hon. James B. Richardson, member of the board, on October 31, 1910.)

Solomon Bliss Stebbins was born at Warren, Mass., on January 18, 1830. He was a lineal descendant of Rowland Stebbins who settled near Springfield in this state early in the seventeenth century. By the death of his father he became dependent upon his own efforts in his boyhood. He had limited advantages for school education; but Nature, more just than she often seems, as if anticipating such an unfavorable condition, compensated young Stebbins therefor, by a large endowment of practical good sense, which did not fail him during a long, busy life. He accomplished what he did, and became what he was, by his own work, energy, industry, and rare integrity. He appears to have very early secured the confidence of others, for we find him, according to our information, in charge of the post office in Ludlow at the age of eighteen years.

He came to Boston in 1850, and soon after that is found established in business as one of the proprietors of a public grain elevator at the North End, which is said to have been the first public grain elevator erected in that city. We find him soon taking an active part in public affairs, to which his taste and aptitude naturally led him. He became a member of the House of Representatives of the General Court in 1861; and he voted for the passage of the act, in March of that year, for the incorporation of the Franklin Savings Bank. In 1864 and 1865, he was a member of the common council of the city of Boston. He was a delegate to the convention in Chicago in 1864 which nominated Abraham Lincoln as a candidate for the presidency of the United States, and he was a member of the committee of the city council of Boston, to represent the city at the funeral of Lincoln in Washington on April 16, 1865. In 1866, he was a member of the Massachusetts senate. He became a member of the board of aldermen of the city of Boston in 1873, and held that office for the years 1873, 1874, 1875, 1876, 1878, and 1879, and also the year 1882, seven years. He was chairman of the board of aldermen in the years 1878 and 1882. He was a candidate for the office of mayor of Boston in 1879 and 1880. That he had the knowledge of and experience in the administration of the business of the city, the ability, integrity, and all other qualifications requisite for a successful performance of the duties of a mayor, no one then or since has ever questioned; but these qualifications both before and since then have sometimes failed of proper recognition in popular elections. He failed of election in 1880 by only 581 votes. He took his defeat for the mayoralty with great magnanimity, without animosity or bitterness; and at the request of many citizens he became the candidate, in 1882, for election to the board of aldermen, was elected, and was chairman of the board for that year; he continued in his loyalty, and best service and devotion to the city as before.

In 1885 he was appointed one of the three commissioners to take the land for and erect the new court house in Pemberton Square; and upon its completion was appointed custodian of the building, which position he filled acceptably for about twenty years, until his death June 8, 1910.

He was for forty-four years a member of the board of directors, and for twenty years president, of the Washingtonian Home. He was a trustee of the Mount Hope Cemetery, was one of the incorporators and founders of the Adams Nervine Asylum, and was an active member of the Boston Chamber of Commerce and its predecessors. He was elected trustee of this bank in 1861.

He was a useful member of many other organizations and societies, and gave a helping hand, to the extent of his ability, to many worthy causes. In all these various offices of honor and trust his character and record are clear. He never betrayed a trust, abused a confidence, violated his principles, or broke a promise. He was not a demagogue. To obtain office, he did not promise to do what he could not do, nor did he boast of things which he had or had not done. Opinions on subjects which many persons take by inheritance or accept on authority were with him the result of his own meditations. He could not accept for truth things which were contrary to facts, or what he thought to be so, or which did not harmonize with his sense of justice. This habitual self-reliance resulted in the formation of positive character, which when built up, as it was here, upon intelligence, honesty, integrity, and sincerity, is durable and abiding, not to be destroyed by popular breath or accident. And it is character after all, in the final analysis, which really impresses and interests us, for in it is to be found the man as he really was or is; other things are incidental. Mr. Stebbins lived an active, useful, unselfish, and honorable life, and we are the better for it.

Nature was also kind to him, in the bestowal of a uniformly benevolent, kindly, and companionable disposition, which continued beyond the allotted threescore years and ten. The frosts of eighty winters had not chilled the blood of a warm heart. Back of or beneath the public view of Mr. Stebbins and his work, existed a perfectly pure and spotless private life.

John Edward Stevens

John Edward Stevens, the third of a family of five children, was born in St. Petersburg, Russia, September 7, 1846. His father, Sidney Stevens, was the son of an English squire in the county of Hants, and his mother, Eliza Kennell, was of Scotch descent. His father went to Russia to engage in the manufacture of paper, in which he was very successful, and about 1850 he returned to England and leased a country estate near Croydon. Mr. Stevens was sent to a boys' school in Yorkshire, and there received his education. His father retained a large interest in the paper mill in Russia, and the failure of this resulted in the loss of his fortune, so that his son was obliged to leave school at the age of fourteen. He entered the machinery works of Fairbairn, Kennedy & Naylor, at Leeds, England. There he served an apprenticeship of seven years, upon the completion of which he went to Narva, Russia, as assistant superintendent of the large flax mills there. He remained one year, after which he returned to the Fairbairn works at Leeds. He traveled on the continent for them, and in 1871 first came to America as their agent. He traveled widely in this country in their interest. He married in 1873 Miss Harriet Louise Stevens of Dudley, Mass., and then went back to Russia to assume the position of superintendent of the Narva Flax Mills. After three years of life in Russia he once more returned to Leeds, remaining with the Fairbairn company until 1882 and represented them in Europe and America. He exhibited their machinery at Philadelphia Centennial in 1876.

In 1882 Mr. Stevens entered the service of the Ludlow Manufacturing Company as superintendent. Upon the death, in 1887, of the former treasurer and founder of the business, Charles T. Hubbard, and the election of his son as treasurer, Mr. Brigham, the agent, resigned, and the plant then came under the management of Mr. Stevens.

For eighteen years the business was conducted by Messrs. Hubbard, Wallace, and Stevens, and to their unity of administration is due the success of the business. This success may be measured by the statement that, of the twenty-five acres of mills and warehouses now standing, only three acres were in existence in 1887.

Mr. Stevens's success as a manufacturer was not only due to an acute and well-trained mind, but it was also due to the cordial relations which he maintained with his superintendents and overseers, and to the respect with which he was regarded by all the employees of the company.

John E. Stevens died suddenly in his office at the plant of the Ludlow Manufacturing Associates in Ludlow, Mass., October 5, 1905. He had been in unusually good spirits and health, having only recently returned from a vacation spent in Canada.

A doctor was summoned, but Mr. Stevens was dead before he arrived and the doctor pronounced his death as due to heart disease.

The village of Ludlow itself is a memorial to Mr. Stevens, and to associate more completely his name with his work for the people he so long served, the trustees passed the following vote:

"Voted: That the managing trustees be authorized to erect a building for club rooms and gymnasium, according to the plans prepared by the late John Edward Stevens, and approved by the officers of the Men's Club. That the building be located in the rear of the business block, the place selected by Mr. Stevens, and when completed, to be called the John Edward Stevens Memorial as a tribute to twenty-three years of loyal service to the people of Ludlow."

—Adapted from the *Cordage Trade Journal.*

II

HISTORIC REMINISCENCES

IN the last month of 1779, two young men, Jedediah Paine and Solomon Wright, living in the southeastern part of the town, went one Saturday to Springfield on business, driving an ox-team. Delayed in "town" until late, when they reached the fording-place at Wallamanumps, the shades of night had gathered about the stream, rendering the crossing dangerous. They tarried until morning light, and then availed themselves of its aid to accomplish the rest of their journey. But the Sabbath law was technically broken, and they had violated it. An eyewitness living near the ford complained of them, carrying the case to the county magistrates at Northampton. To this place the young men repaired upon summons, accompanied by some of their friends. Judgment was pronounced against them, and they were sentenced to pay fine and costs. John Jennings became surety for them, and they returned homeward. It was Christmas Day. While coming through South Hadley, over the fields, they undertook to cross a temporary pond on the new ice, but were so unfortunate as to lose their lives in the attempt. There was great lamentation in Ludlow over the melancholy event, some deeming it a judgment of God. Great indignation was felt against the informant, who received half the fees. An old lady used to exult at the recollection that two of the informant's children, born afterwards, were fools.

The following lines are attributed to a local bard, one Collins Hill, who was soon after warned out of town, though probably not because of the extent of his poetic talent. Indeed, while the committee were making inquiries respecting local traditions, a veteran lady informed them that she knew of no poetry on the matter, but "there was some *varses* writ about it."

>(Come all my friends and hear me tell
>Of two young men, what them befell)
>Two fmart young men who died of late
>'Twill make the hardeft heart to ache.
>Thefe two young men to Springfield went,
>To trade it was their full intent;
>We hope and truft they want to blame,
>But every thing did them detain.

The afternoon being almoft gone,
They left the town and fo went on,
Acrofs the river for to gain—
But dark commenced on Springfield plain.
For to go home they were debar'd,
Not having money to pay their charge:
A cart and oxen they both had—
To crofs the river made it bad.
This being the laft day of the week,
Which for their homes made them to feek,
They dropped their teams and ftayed that night,
And ftarted home by the morning light.
They both went home we well do know,
And to their bufinefs did go;
Not in the leaft were they afraid,
But foon went where they were betray'd.
He who complained was much to blame,
But we fhall not declare his name;
We hope repentance he will have,
Before he comes down to the grave.
But to declare what I intend,
A fpecial writ for them was fent;
December the 23d day,
They went to court, as many fay,
They were detained there that day,
Had both the fine and cofts to pay;
But foon appeared there a man,
Who gave his note for both of them;
Thefe two young men fat out for home,
Not thinking death would fo foon come.
They both were feen before 'twas night,
Just as the fun went out of fight:
Like two young roes run down a hill
And fteering right towards a mill,—
They left the bridge, we well may know
It was before determined fo.
The ice was thin, they both funk down,
Young people hear the folemn found;
Grim death did clafp them in his hand—
O, who is he can death withftand!
Thefe young men's hats next day were found,
Which foon alarmed all the town;
Ten in the morning they were found,
Laid their cold bodies in the ground.

Solomon Wright and *Jede. Paine,*
So this is true thefe were their names;
Thus in the heat of youthful blood,
They perifhed in the flowing flood.
Their fouls are gone to God the juft,
Who form'd them firft out of the duft.

In 1786, a grandchild of Capt. Joseph Miller was run over by a cart, this injury terminating fatally, and the body was the first laid in the old yard by the Congregational Church. In the following year Captain Miller's barn was burned, and in it a little two-year-old granddaughter.

A few months later a son of Isaac Brewer was taken away in the dawn of manhood, followed soon by his heartbroken father.

A singular accident occurred in 1794, an account of which we obtain from a notice penned soon after. On Friday, June 25, David Paine's son, who was riding on the top of a load of shingles, fell off, and the cart wheels, bound with cast iron, passed directly over the middle of his body. He was taken up for dead, but soon recovered, grew to a good old age, and was well known—the late Jonathan Paine.

The veteran David Paine was found, July 2, 1807, dead, in sight of his home, at the foot of Burying-Ground Hill, having fallen beneath his cart on returning from mill, and being crushed by the wheel.

But the most thrilling incident is that concerning the supposed Annibal murder. "In the year 1817, a man named John Annibal went from Belchertown to Connecticut to peddle wagons for Filer. On his return he was seen to enter Ludlow about sundown. Afterward his horse, with bridle cut, was seen in Granby, near Asa Pease's house. His portmanteau and saddle were found near Ezekiel Fuller's and blood was discovered in the road between these two points. Great excitement prevailed, as every one thought he had been robbed and murdered. An old woman who pretended to tell fortunes was consulted. She said he was murdered by a man with but one eye, living in a gambrel-roofed house, where three roads met. The house which answered the description was searched in the absence of the family, the doorsteps were removed and a large excavation made underneath them, but not the slightest trace of the missing man was found. The owner of the house was also searched as he was returning to his home, but no money was discovered about him. Then a pond was drained near the house of George Clark. In draining the pond it was necessary in one point to dig twenty-five feet deep. While the work of digging was going forward, camp fires were kept around the pond and sentinels with loaded muskets guarded the spot. When the ditch was completed, on Sabbath day, the water was drawn off, and a thousand people were supposed to be present; a line of men reaching from one side of the pond to the other held each other's hands, and waded through the soft mud. The pond covered nearly an acre of ground. No trace of the body was found. Search was then instituted in a smaller pond near by, the water being carried over the hill in pails. This effort also proved fruitless. Many then began to adopt another theory besides that of murder. His brother, who had been here and joined in the search for two days, said his business was such he could not possibly remain, and returned to his home. It was afterward learned that John Annibal had debts which he did not wish to pay, also that his marital relations were not the happiest. Some suggested that he might have spied a chance to kill two birds with one stone." (From Dea. George Clark's description of the affair.)

A possible sequel to this account was the finding of a skull years later at one of the points where suspicion had rested.

A serious affair is supposed to have occurred not far from the year 1830. One Wright, a deaf mute, residing over the mountain, disappeared quite suddenly. He was believed to have had an altercation with one of the citizens living in another part of the town, and some suspected foul play. A melancholy interest was added to the reminiscence by the finding of a skeleton in an out lot long afterwards, which bore unmistakable signs of identity with the frame of the missing man.

Chapman Kendall, while driving a yoke of oxen with a load of wood, on the road leading to Harris Mill from where Charles B. Bennett now lives, in some way fell beneath the wagon, which stopped with one of the wheels upon his neck. Gates Willey, noticing that the team had stood there for a long time, went to investigate and found Mr. Kendall dead. Beside the road is a stone monument, bearing the letters "C. K.," marking the spot where the accident happened.

Joshua Fuller lived on the Dorman farm. On a Sunday morning in June, 1796, while his father, Young Fuller, lay dead, the house caught fire and burned to the ground, necessitating the removal of the corpse to the orchard.

The following account of the death of Selectman Samuel White is taken from the *Springfield Republican* of May 17, 1875:

The quiet farming community of Ludlow, where so few unwonted events have marked the progress of a century, was saddened, Saturday, by the sudden, shocking death of one of her best citizens, Samuel White, chairman of the board of selectmen and nine years a town father. He was bitten by a boar so that he bled to death within a few minutes. Mr. White went out about 6 o'clock in the morning to feed the animal, and was attacked so suddenly that he could give no warning, but was able to crawl out of the pen, where he was discovered by one of his men when unable to speak. He was seized on the inner and upper part of the thigh, the brute's tushes tearing a hole in the flesh two inches long and severing the femoral artery. The men of the farm had complained of the ugly temper of the beast, but Mr. White, a man of markedly resolute character, had thorough belief in his own ability to manage him—indeed, had been laughing, only the day previous, at his "help" for their timidity. Mr. White was no doubt taken entirely off his guard, these creatures being very quick and crafty of attack.

The man thus cut off was 57 years old, perhaps the most thrifty farmer in town, and in every way a representative New Englander, held in high esteem. A Granby boy, he began life by "working out" for Henry Dickinson, where he saved $80, with which he bought a working team and began clearing off some woodland for Jefferson Alden, giving the latter one fourth of the profits realized from the sale of the lumber. His own share went into better teams until he had additionally earned enough to buy half of a farm at what was then Ludlow City. He became a drover, and since has made considerable money by the sale of stock. He came to his present farm twenty-three years ago, and has made it the finest place in the township. He was what Massachusetts people call a "good calculator," always rugged, a hard worker, frugal and honest beyond a cavil, and withal a neighborly, Christian man. For five years he has acted as chairman of the board of selectmen, and was conscientiously faithful always to the public service; he was also a prominent member of the Congregational Church. He leaves a wife and two children—James White, a farmer in Ludlow, and the wife of E. Harris.

INCIDENTS

Among the minor incidents related is one of Elisha Fuller, who early in the nineteenth century, while journeying westward with his young son Harry, met a personage so peculiar that it occurred to his mind the stranger was the incarnation of his satanic majesty, yet who proved to be the eccentric Lorenzo Dow, who the night before had preached at "Master" Frost's.

Among the unique characters in the town were two of special note. One, Veranus Shattuck, of Jenksville, known best under the sobriquet of "Doctor Foggus," we have met before as a soldier in 1812, in which strife he did valiant service, yet perhaps not always using the best of judgment. Later he figured as the little round-shouldered cobbler of Jenksville, almost as crooked as the sibilant, whose powers of oratory were seriously crippled by a strong nasal twang. Indeed, his only speech that has been handed down by indulgent fame was the one made on occasion of his election as captain of the military company of the town. At that time he is reported to have stepped forward to the astonished colonel (John Miller) and heralded through his facial protuberance the eloquent words, "Mr. Colonel, I excuse myself." Nor was he always the butt of ridicule, notwithstanding the wishes of malicious boys. It was his habit to sit near the entrance to the factory and see the people go in. The approving lads would signify their interest by patting him upon the head on passing his seat, sometimes with unpleasant emphasis. They did so once too often, for "Dr. Foggus" found an occasion when he did not "excuse himself," but sat down as usual, except as to the condition of his hat, as classic tyros would say. That useful covering, a tarpaulin by the way, he had adorned within with some bright sharp awls attached to a piece of sole leather, the leather resting upon his hair, the awl points aiming upwards. One by one the "boys" patted his head, as usual, and passed sadly along. We hardly need add that the "Doctor's" prescription was efficacious.

The hermit "Friday" was also well-known. His name is supposed to have been Timothy Haschall, and he became chargeable to the town in 1832, which relation was only broken by death about fifteen years later. He lived a while in a rude cabin near Red Bridge, subsisting on the vilest food, unless he was helped to better by neighbors or the town. Whence he came or who he was no one knew, nor could it be ascertained satisfactorily.

One Sunday morning, the minister of the First Church, in the midst of his sermon, asked the question, "How many Christians are there in town?" To make it more impressive, he repeated it a second and a third time. One of his hearers arose and replied, "Three, sir, yourself, Simeon Pease, and Asahel Rood."

Simeon Pease, with two or three others, was horseback riding one very windy, but clear, cold, moonshiny night. About twelve o'clock he rode up to a house in town, and rapped on the door with his riding whip. A man suddenly opened the door and said, "What is wanted?" Mr. Pease replied, "Hadn't you better take in your chimney? I think there is going to be a h—l of a storm." He hit his horse and sped away.

When Hubbard Dutton was leader of the singing in the First Church of Ludlow, he had a choir of thirty or forty singers. One Sunday during the singing, which did not suit him, Mr. Dutton, forgetting for the moment that it was not a rehearsal, suddenly brought down his foot with a noise that resounded throughout the church. He fully expected to be reprimanded by the minister. To his great surprise the minister met him at the foot of the gallery stairs and said, "Mr. Dutton, I was glad to hear your foot come down." Mr. Dutton taught singing schools, and for many years was leader of the choir in this church.

Elisha Fuller was a noted wag. He would perpetrate a joke at any expense. Every one has heard of his story about the pins, which he offered for sale from his store with the assurance that the pin-maker was dead and there was no further chance to buy. Taking up a pair of spectacles once at the Town house to try them, he averred he could see a hawk on Wilbraham Mountain. Nor would he listen to one word of disparagement of Ludlow. Some one remarking concerning the poverty of her soil, he declared that a traveler once lost his horse near the Center, and finding him in a field of corn, was obliged to clear a passage through the stalks with an axe. He once told the wondering auditors that he drove his horse at the time of a shower so fast that he himself kept ahead of the rain, while his dog swam just behind the wagon for a long distance. The ground extending lengthwise of his house is associated with him, as he might be seen, as long as he lived, after every snowstorm shoveling a good path around his house, always wearing a straw hat. He was a kindly man, familiarly known as "Uncle Elisha" in all the neighborhood, possessed of much energy and industry. He loved his land and believed in mowing the grass several times in one season. According to history he gave the land for the cemetery south of the church. He was not a believer in doctors or medicine. At one time when he had a fall, and lay in his long cradle, all he wanted was some porridge, and said he could set his own bones. Sitting in his armchair before a cheerful fire one evening, telling his grandson what was wanted at the village store, his words ceased; he had passed on as quietly as the snuffing out of a candle, at the age of 97 years, the eldest and last living child of Joshua Fuller, himself the father of thirteen children.

The following lines are attributed to Mr. Gad Lyon. He evidently courted the muses to some purpose.

Reflections

on the morning of Jan. 1ft 1804

WHEN the kind goddefs fleep all eyes did clofe,
And mortals all lay rapt in foft repofe;
No voice was heard to whifper thro' the gloom
But all was hufhed and filent as the tomb.
Then, then without a groan, the aged year,
Did tremble, totter, fall and difappear;
Compell'd by Fate to pafs that folemn bourn,
From which no period paft can e'er return.
Which proves this truth moft clear to reafon's eye,
That time itfelf, like mortal man, muft die.
How many millions of the human race,
Which hailed the morn when the paft year took place;
Whofe healthful days and profpects of delight,
Made them forget that it would e'er be night;
By death's deftroying fcythe have been cut down,
Whofe bodies now lie flumbering in the ground.
How many millions on this morn, appear
To wake and rife and wifh a happy year,
Before December's cold and freezing breath,
Shall haften to the fhades and tafte of death,

Who now like thoughtlefs fheep, no danger fear,
Nor dream the fatal meffenger fo near.
Since 'tis our fate for to refign our breath,
And pafs the folemn, lonely vale of death,
Let wifdom's choiceft dictates rule our heart,
And never from her facred rules depart.
Then fhould heaven's thunders fhake the ftarry roof,
And forked lightnings lick our fpirits up;
Should trembling earth her opening jaws extend,
And we into that fatal gulph defcend?
Should rapid whirlwinds fweep the foreft clean,
And we fall victims in that awful fcene?
Should inundations deluge all the plain,
And fhould we be among the thoufands flain!
Should peftilence walk dreadful o'er the land,
And with a ftern decree our lives demand!
Should blazing comets, in their raging ire,
Draw near and fet this trembling world on fire,
'Twould only waft us to the bleft abode,
And place us in the paradife of GOD.

The Oakley Ballad

The "Oakley ballad" tells its own story. It was written by G. M. Fisk, while a young man in his teens, in commemoration of the sad fate of Elizabeth Oakley, and was sung with a wail at many a Ludlow fireside.

Come old and young, list to my song,
While I its mournful strains prolong,
Of a young girl—come hear me tell—
Who did awhile in Jenskville dwell.

When young her mother did her give
Unto her friends a while to live,
And from her mother far she come
With stranger friends to make her home.

But soon these friends did falsely prove,
And showed to her no former love,
For she by them was cruel used,
And by her mistress was abused.

A toilsome task she had to do
Ere to the factory she did go;

And when into her room she went,
The cruel thong she often felt.

Her cheeks soon lost their rosy hue,
And she most melancholy grew;
And when these gloomy thoughts did rise,
The tears oft started from her eyes.

She told her mates within the mill
She did herself intend to kill,
And unto them these words did say,
Upon her last ill-fated day:

"I have a mother—lovely too—
O did she but my treatment know!
For me she'll weep when I am gone;
But all in vain—I can't return.

"Sorrow hath all my joy bereft
Since I my dear, dear mother left;
But me no more she'll ever see,
For with the dead I soon shall be."

The bell had tolled the hour for noon
When she, down-hearted, left her room,
And on the river bank she went
For to accomplish her intent.

The flowing deep soon o'er her closed,
And she in silent death reposed;
But none were there to view the scene
Of her while struggling in the stream.

The news soon spread that on that day
Elizabeth had gone away,
When search was made for her in vain,
No tidings of her could they gain.

A fortnight near had rolled its round,
Ere they her lifeless body found;
Then flocked the people to the shore,
To view the orphan girl once more.

Then in the coffin her they laid
And one short solemn prayer was said;

Then to the church-yard's lonely place
They carried her for earth's embrace.

Months passed by—her mother came
To view her darling child again;
Her heart within her breast beat high
As she unto the place came nigh.

And when the horrid news was told,
Her cheek turned pale, her blood ran cold;
Both night and day she did lament,
And she almost distracted went.

Elizabeth was fair and mild;
Her character was undefiled;
Her mind was free, her voice was sweet,
Her heart was void of all deceit.

Her age was scarcely four and ten,
And she by many loved had been;
And many mourned the shocking fate,
And oft this mournful tale relate.

No marble stone of sculptured name
Doth mark the spot where she is lain,
And her none evermore will see
Until they reach eternity.

The following letter, written at the close of the eighteenth century, will be appreciated as a sample of the style epistolary of those days. It is directed to "Dr. Sylvester Nash Ludlow."

Wilbraham Feby 4 1800

Sir it was with the greatift pleafure that I Received your letter dated November 2th Informing me of your health you gave me fome incouragement of comeing to fe me before long it is now 7 or 8 months fins I have feen you if I ant miftaken I expected to receive a vifit from you before now but it don t come. I hope that you have not forgot us I want to fe you very Mutch and fo do your acquaintance I hope to receive a vifit from you before long we are all well at prefent and I hope to hear of your good health and your family. I have nothing at prefent to wright only I want to fe you very mutch. I wrote this in a hurry you muft excufe my bad writing and fo I must wind off.

          I am your friend and well wifher,
                 Luke Brewer

If you can read it
I fhall be glad.

There can be little question as to the desire for a visit. What, however, was the occasion for the effusion on the third page is hardly so evident. It reads thus:

down	see	you	me
and	may	love	not
up	you	I	you
read	and	that	and

On a clear, cold, icy moonlight night, Seneca Wood, a quaint old gentleman, had been to the tavern at Ludlow Center kept by Jerusha Fuller (perhaps he had taken more than was good for him) and, while returning home, he slipped upon the ice. After repeated efforts to arise, a kneeling posture was all he could accomplish. One of his neighbors, returning from a prayer meeting with a team, stopped when he reached Mr. Wood, who was upon his knees, and said, "Seneca, what are you doing?" His reply was, "I am praying for you." Needless to say, he was taken home.

Paulina Rood, or "Aunt Polly Rood" as she was called, was a sister of Seneca Wood. She was noted for her skill in sickness or trouble of any kind, either as a nurse or physician. She often took the place of both. It was frequently said, "If we can get Aunt Polly Rood when we are sick, it does not make much difference about the doctor." She was always ready and willing to go wherever she could render service.

Nick and Tarzy

Melancholy was the story of "Nick and Tarzy" who were very worthy people.

Nicholas Daniels lived in the eastern part of the town on the farm of which the "Ould Burying Ground" was once a part. Thirza Olds lived over the line in Belchertown.

Nick was a fine specimen of the Yankee of the olden time with his "cue" tied with strips of eel-skin. He always wore a blue coat with shining buttons, regulation knee-breeches, his stockings being very smooth and fair. His shoe buckles, large and of shining silver, are treasured to this day by a descendant of his family.

For nearly two score years, he visited Tarzy every Sunday night, fondly anticipating the day which never came. It is said that on "general training day" he never failed to bring Tarzy a goodly cake of hard gingerbread when he came home.

Family legend claims that Nick had injured his hand with some sharp instrument. One cold, stormy Sunday evening in spring, he donned his best attire and despite the warnings of his family, wended his way to Tarzy's fireside, along the path which he had trodden for forty years. Exposure to the storm brought on lockjaw and he died in Tarzy's home.

Need we wonder that even the voluble McLean found his vocabulary straitened when he undertook to offer Thirza words of consolation?

Afterward poor Tarzy lived but to keep Nick's memory green. She observed training day, never failing to bake gingerbread of a most golden hue, which she distributed in her lover's name to the children who came to see her. She always turned her cow out to pasture on the anniversary of his death, and walked to Three Rivers, carrying her butter and eggs to exchange for tea and snuff. Going and returning, she never failed to pay a visit to his grave.

Anny Olds, a tiny tot, went with her one of the last times Tarzy made the journey. Anny carried a little basket with some eggs as a venture of her own. When the store was reached, she bartered the eggs for two dainty little salt cellars, one of which is still treasured in the family.

When the travelers reached Tarzy's home, Anny was offered some of the gingerbread, but, remembering the color of the snuff, she declined for the first and last time to accept it. Tarzy soon was laid to rest near Nicholas in the "Ould burying ground," just across the line on the Belchertown side. As in life they are divided. Her grave is marked with a fair stone, but, sad irony of fate! the most prominent word of Tarzy's epitaph is the word "Miss."

A local bard wrote the quaint ballad, "Nick and Tarzy, O!" containing the story of their love. When the centennial of Ludlow was celebrated in 1874, this ballad was printed, distributed among the people, and sung to the tune of "Benny Havens."

Into the conversation current of a generation has passed the expression "Courting as long as Nick and Tarzy."

(Verbatim copy)

"Nick and Tarzy"

Wilbur F. Miller, leader of the "Old Folks Concert," selected some music and it was sung at the Centennial.

Ye Original Ballad
concerning
Nick and Tarzy.

Founded upon fact   see Ludlow History for the account.
    Air.   Benny Havens.

O Nick and Tarzy, O! O, Nick and Tarzy, O!
    We sing to you a song that's true
        Of Nick and Tarzy, O!

There was a man in Ludlow town,
    Lo, many years ago,
As good a man as you might find—
    His neighbors tell you so.

He had one fault, and only one,
    Which time has handed down;
If folks would talk to him, forsooth,
    Of marriage, he would frown.

Chorus

O, Nick and Tarzy, O! O, Nick and Tarzy, O!
    We sing to you a song that's true,
        O, Nick and Tarzy, O!

You must not think our famous Nick
    Could never find a mate,
For never yet was lone young man
    Thus visited by fate;
Upon the hill whose eastern slope
    Reached Nick's mundane abode,
There lived a lass whose winsome smiles
    Illumined all the road.

Chorus

At least, so thought our hero, Nick,
    Whose foot-prints thither bent.
You might have found, most any night,
    If you for this were sent.
And Tarzy, she with blushing face
    Would greet him at the gate.
The neighbors said it was a match,
    And soon 'twould consummate.

Chorus

And thus the happy months sped on,
    Till lengthened into years,
With all the bliss of courting days
    Nor bane of wedded fears.
Years sped away, a score or two
    While some aver 'twas three
Before they called the parson in
    Their happiness to see.

Chorus

Alas for human hopes and joys,
    He came by far too late;
For Nick lay dead at Tarzy's home.
    Where he had met his fate.

A fell disease had laid him low,
  While calling there one day,
His time was come—he breathed his last,
  They carried him away.

        Chorus

The moral is to all young folks
  Who have such things in mind;
Be careful how you put it off
  Or you'll be found behind.
Remember how this worthy pair
  Were brought from weal to woe,
And take your warning while you think
  Of Nick and Tarzy, O!

        Chorus

O, Nick and Tarzy, O! O, Nick and Tarzy, O!
  The tale is true, we've sung to you
    Of Nick and Tarzy, O!

In the days when the country was rife with the preparations for maintaining the Revolutionary War, the recruiting agent was no uncommon sight even among the lonely farmhouses. Some of the companies formed were not so moral as was desirable to many of the families of the members.

It happened that a partly-formed company of the undesirable sort appeared one day to enforce the enlistment of Jonathan Olds. He and his wife, Hannah Jones, did not favor his joining this company. After a very brief consultation, Jonathan requested a few minutes respite for prayer with his family. The request was granted, the men waiting outside, jesting and laughing meanwhile.

Jonathan offered but a short prayer; the good wife Hannah took up the petition, while Jonathan quietly made his departure through the back door into the woods.

The lengthening shadows roused the officer to the fact that enough time had been used; he demanded Jonathan's immediate presence. As no one appeared he entered the house and asked for Jonathan. Thereupon Hannah replied, "I will not tell you; find him if you want him." Search was at once begun; so thorough was it that floors were torn up and feather beds ripped open, but all in vain and the men departed.

In the meantime Jonathan had swiftly made his way towards Springfield and in the morning was safely enlisted in one of the more orderly companies.

Again and again the call for troops was repeated, and so ready was the response that soon Hannah Olds found herself with but one son to help care for her family, and he a mere lad.

When the recruiting officer again appeared she dressed this son in his grandmother's gown and great frilled cap and seated him on a huge settle in the darkest corner of the room, by the fireplace. The officer inquired if she had a son at home old enough to enlist. She responded, "Yes," and was ordered to produce him; but she answered as before, "You must come and get him if you want him."

Again her home was invaded by a search party and ruthlessly torn up. Once more the search was fruitless, for none thought to peer under the cap frill for a soldier.

This woman is buried in the historic "Ould Burying Ground." Her grave is marked by a large slate tombstone, bearing the strange device of a great round face surrounded by clusters of fantastic stone curls. The entire stone is adorned with a conventional border of morning glories. The inscription may be found amond the epitaphs on page 90.

Samuel Olds, who was born in 1756, was probably the lad referred to in the preceding story. He was gifted in many ways with a phenomenal memory. It is said that after listening to a sermon he could repeat it word for word. He retained this faculty when an aged man. Frequently the young people read to him stories or poems, which he would later recite almost perfectly. Another of his gifts was that of rhyming. Many a local event is told to-day in his quaint jingles. Perhaps his greatest power lays in his "second sight." To that capacity is attributed the following story:

Having occasion to pass the "Ould Burial Place" very late one night, he saw a bright light in one corner of the yard. Upon looking at it steadily he also saw two figures, whom he recognized as his friends, Solomon Wright and Jedediah Paine, busily engaged in digging a grave.

His curiosity was aroused and he hastened to enter the yard to ascertain why they were doing this. The fastening of the gate proved obstinate and so fully occupied his attention that when he had succeeded in opening it, the light and men had disappeared. Careful search revealed nothing. He related the incident at home, but it was so uncanny that it was not talked about openly.

One can hardly picture the astonishment of Samuel and his family when the news of the tragic death of the two men was later announced. (See page 319.)

Samuel's prescience of things to come served to save property and sometimes life. As he was watching the coming of a thunder storm one summer afternoon, he several times expressed a fear that a certain neighbor's house would suffer damage. After the storm had begun, as the family were gathered within the house, he suddenly started up and shouted in terrified tones that the house in question had been smitten.

To pacify him his sons went to the house. They found a group of terror-stricken children, for their parents were away. A strange odor in the house made them hurry upstairs, where they discovered a great hole in the roof and a feather bed on fire. The flames were quickly extinguished. What a catastrophe his "second sight" had averted!

Lurana Olds Daniels, a sister of Samuel Olds and wife of Asa Daniels, was also noted for her wonderful memory. It is reliably asserted that she remembered accurately every birth, marriage, and death that had occurred in the part of the town where she lived, as well as the date of the erection or repair of all the buildings.

When William Hubbard Beebe and Rebekah Olds entered the room where they were to be married, the bride was on the wrong side of the groom. During the prayer, when every head was supposed to be bowed in reverent attention, one ancient dame arose, tiptoed her way across to the couple, changed them about and returned to her seat unobserved. When the prayer was over, the consternation of the assembled guests, to see the couple placed as conventionality demanded, may be imagined.

Feats of Strength

A company including Dexter Lyon, Homer Lyon, David Lyon, Selah Kendall, Isaac Sheldon and others had assembled at one time when a gentleman who was visiting at Dr. Alden's was introduced as a celebrated wrestler. A ring was quickly formed, and David Lyon, one of the smallest men, was appointed to try his hand with the champion, in order that the others might learn his methods. When they were ready to take hold, the stranger said to Dr. Alden, "You go the other side of the house and see where he strikes." But instead of sending David to the other side of the house the champion found himself lying upon his back. Picking himself up he wanted to take hold again. David said to him: "You acknowledge you were fairly thrown, don't you?" "O yes," said he. "Well," replied David, "it is no object for me to take hold of a man whom I can throw as easily as I can you."

Titus Pomeroy, a somewhat noted wrestler, claimed to be able to throw anybody in the vicinity of South Hadley Falls. Finally William Miller, son of Dr. A. J. Miller, was persuaded to go over and try his hand with him. When Miller was introduced, Pomeroy said: "Is that the man you have brought to wrestle with me? I could eat him up in a minute." They took hold. Pomeroy gave him a twitch and swung Miller around behind him. Miller, however, was all ready for his opponent, and tripped both feet from under him, so that Pomeroy came down in a very unexpected manner. Pomeroy said, as he shook off the dust, "I didn't think that little rascal could throw me."

Titus Hubbard once met a man who claimed a position in the road which was not fairly his; without ceremony Titus took up the offender bodily and set him aside.

Reuben Sikes is said to have repeatedly lifted one end of a very heavy sled-load of green hickory wood.

Benjamin Sikes, grandfather of Mrs. Jackson Cady, Otis and Danforth W. Sikes, was a very rugged man over six feet in height. He, with his hired man, was one day cutting wood for coal, which wood was not split. About four o'clock in the afternoon they ceased cutting, and began to pile it up. It was found that the hired man had cut four and one half cords, while Mr. Sikes had cut six and three fourths cords.

Benjamin Sikes had four sons who worked many days with their father. After one day of particularly hard work, one of the boys remarked, "Father will do more in a day than all of us combined," and these men were all in their prime at the time.

When Elijah Plumley was a young man he carried upon his shoulder fifty-two quarts, full measure, of the heaviest rock-salt, a mile and a half without resting, and then turned and proposed to those who had wonderingly accompanied him, to return with it before he rested.

Reminiscences of a Musical Life

While in Europe, a well-known musician told Mr. Wilbur F. Miller that he would be able to command fabulous prices for singing, if he would study for six months. Mr. Miller replied that he was satisfied to be a farmer.

While in London, he attended service in Rev. Charles H. Spurgeon's temple. The great building was crowded, and a precentor led the singing without accompaniment. Mr. Miller joined in the singing, and sang in time, while the rest of the audience were a half beat behind. He did this by watching the precentor's lips as he sang. People were attracted by his singing and looked about to see the person who sang so correctly and powerfully. He was urged to come again that they might hear him more. On the steamer returning from Europe a concert was given one evening by a troupe of colored singers, for whom Mr. Miller sang all the solos, being accompanied by Mlle. Rhea, the noted Belgian actress.

When he was engaged to sing in the Chicopee Church it was as a bass singer. On his arrival he found that a tenor was needed, so he offered to try to sing that part. The committee was somewhat skeptical as to his ability to do so as he had been engaged to sing bass. He was permitted to make the attempt and was promptly engaged to sing tenor.

Mr. Miller was the principal singer in a party of Knights Templars who went West a few years ago. He and two companions began to sing one night after midnight in front of the Palmer House in Chicago. So large a crowd gathered about their cab that police interference was necessary and in order to disperse the crowd the singers were asked to stop.

One Sunday in Rev. Henry Ward Beecher's church in Brooklyn, Mr. Miller attended service, and was obliged to stand. During the singing of the hymns, he sang with so much power that a pewholder promptly gave him his own seat.

When traveling in Canada at one time with Mrs. Miller, they attended a church service where Mr. Miller requested to be allowed to sit in the choir gallery at the rear. He took part in the singing, and greatly to the surprise of his wife, who was seated elsewhere, rendered a solo. In the afternoon he was visited by a delegation from three churches who invited him to sing at the evening service and at a music festival during the week.

A Family Gathering at Wilbur F. Miller's

III

GENEALOGIES

NOT all the genealogies desired have been obtained, which is due largely to the fact that representatives of many of the early families have long since left Ludlow. Those included may show inaccuracies and deficiencies, but they are careful compilations of the matter furnished.

THE ALDEN FAMILY.

The Aldens of Ludlow trace their ancestry from John[1] and Priscilla (Mullins) Alden, who came over in the "Mayflower," through Joseph,[2] Joseph,[3] Samuel,[4] and Josiah.[5]

Josiah Alden,[5] son of Samuel,[4] was born in 1738. He settled first in Bridgewater, then in Wales. His three sons, Azel,[6] Josiah,[6] and Benjamin,[6] came to Ludlow. Josiah[5] married in 1761, Bathsheba Jones. Children:

Elijah,[6] a Revolutionary soldier in 1775, married Rebecca Fuller.
Abiah,[6] married Benjamin Winchester.
Bathsheba.[6]
Charity,[6] married Peter Trask.
Azel,[6] born 1770; died 1854.
Josiah,[6] born 1773; died Sept. 3, 1833.
Lucy,[6] married Amos Fletcher.
Rebecca,[6] married Benjamin Snow.
Benjamin.[6]

Azel Alden,[6] son of Josiah,[5] was born in 1770 and died in 1854. He came with his wife and children and settled in the east part of Ludlow. He married in 1791, Bethany Wilbor, who died in 1804. Children:

Stillman,[7] born Aug. 22, 1791; died June 7, 1880.
Lovinia,[7] married Ira Barker.
Josiah,[7] born Aug. 16, 1796; died Jan. 11, 1881.

Azel Alden[6] married second, Cynthia Luell. Children:
Bethany,[7] married Henry Shumway.

Solomon,[7] married Loraine Claiborne.
Mary,[7] married William E. Smith.

Stillman Alden,[7] son of Azel,[6] was born Aug. 22, 1791, and died June 7, 1880; married Dec. 30, 1814, Amanda Beebe, born July 25, 1796, died Sept. 24, 1878, daughter of Sherwood and Bernis (Hubbard) Beebe. (See Beebe Gen.)

Lovinia Alden,[7] daughter of Azel,[6] married Ira Barker. Children: Addison Atwood,[8] Almon Alden,[8] Rebecca,[8] Paulina,[8] Sophia.[8]

Josiah Alden,[7] son of Azel,[6] was born Aug. 16, 1796, and died Jan. 11, 1881. He worked for the farmers of Ludlow until he was 21, then for two or three years in the Springfield Armory. Of a roving disposition, he set out to "see the world"; he traveled, mostly on foot, to New York and Pittsburgh over the Alleghany Mountains to Kentucky, down the Ohio and Mississippi rivers to New Orleans, working as he went. Yellow fever drove him north, but he was ill on the way to New York. He returned to Ludlow and married Nov. 27, 1827, Clarissa Willey, daughter of Gates and Jerusha (Parsons) Willey. (See Willey Gen.) He had a blacksmith shop at the fork of the roads, a little south of George Hubbard's. His principal business was making by hand printers' tools, especially composing sticks in which type was set. He received orders from New York, Boston, Albany, Hartford, and many other places. He made very excellent gunlocks, and invented a machine for making round collar boxes. During the last 15 years of his life he was a cripple, getting about in a wheel chair. He was the first one in town to vote the Abolition ticket. Children:

Madison,[8] died in infancy.
Harriet,[8] born April 2, 1832.
James,[8] born 1833; died 1900.
Caroline,[8] born 1835; died 1869; married Walter S. Miller. (See Miller Gen.)

Harriet Alden,[8] daughter of Josiah,[7] was born April 2, 1832; married William Baggs, who died in 1901. Children:

Ellen M.,[9] died at the age of 13.
William A.,[9] born 1855; died in Jan., 1903; married Mrs. Emma McClean.

Carrie J.,⁹ died in infancy.
Harriet J.,⁹ married in 1887, Edwin B. Taylor, who died in 1901.

James Alden,⁸ son of Josiah,⁷ was born in 1833 and died in 1900; married Ellen S. Atchinson, born 1839, died 1905, daughter of David and Abigail (Putnam) Atchinson. (See Atchinson Gen.) Child:
Frank A.,⁹ who lives in Waterbury; married Mary Mack. They have a son¹⁰ and daughter.¹⁰

Josiah Alden,⁶ son of Josiah,⁵ was born in 1773 and died Sept. 3, 1833; married first, Olive Brown of Wales. Children:
Azel,⁷ born Aug. 12, 1792; died Oct. 22, 1860.
Justus B.,⁷ born Sept. 15, 1793; died May 30, 1831.
Zenas,⁷ born Nov. 1, 1795; died in Jan., 1840.
Charity,⁷ born June 5, 1797; died Aug. 11, 1829.
Washington B.,⁷ born July 14, 1799; died Aug. 5, 1859.
Charles,⁷ born Dec. 6, 1803; died May 22, 1862.
John B.,⁷ married June 17, 1827.
Orsamus,⁷ born June 5, 1808; died June 29, 1878.
Mary Needham,⁷ born Sept. 13, 1810; married Henry Fuller. (See Fuller Gen.)
Eunice B.,⁷ born Dec. 23, 1813; died April 22, 1876; married Marvin King. (See King Gen.)
Josiah Alden⁶ married second, Mary Bates.

Azel Alden,⁷ son of Josiah,⁶ was born Aug. 12, 1792, and died Oct. 22, 1860; married May 20, 1821, Mary (Polly) Brainard, born Sept. 7, 1796, died May 25, 1880, daughter of Jesse Brainard of East Haddam, Conn. Children:
Sarah Sophia,⁸ born March 17, 1822.
John Brown,⁸ born Feb. 11, 1825.
Newell W.,⁸ born May 31, 1834.
Azel Brainard,⁸ born March 11, 1838; died Sept. 20, 1838.

Newell W. Alden,⁸ son of Azel,⁷ was born May 31, 1834; married in April, 1884, Susan Livonia Walker, born March 12, 1844.

Justus B. Alden,⁷ son of Josiah,⁶ was born Sept. 15, 1793, and died May 30, 1831; married Betsey Porter. Children: Josiah,⁸ George,⁸ Betsey,⁸ Olivet⁸ (married Austin Morse), Norman,⁸ Justus B.,⁸ Charity⁸ (married George Sherbrooke), Jemima⁸ (married George Lisherness), and a child⁸ who died in infancy.

Justus B. Alden,[8] son of Justus B.,[7] married April 25, 1852, Mary Madelia King, born Feb. 4, 1834, died Jan. 15, 1874, daughter of Marvin and Eunice (Alden) King. (See King Gen.) Children:

Edward C.,[9] born July 18, 1853.
Elmer E.,[9] born March 29, 1862.

Zenas Alden,[7] son of Josiah,[6] was born Nov. 1, 1795, and died in Jan., 1840; married Betsey Taylor. Children: George Washington,[8] Henry,[8] Charles,[8] Jane,[8] Caroline[8] (married a Mr. Taylor), and William.[8]

Washington Brown Alden,[7] son of Josiah,[6] was born July 14, 1799, and died Aug. 5, 1859. He was town clerk, treasurer, and school committee 15 out of 25 years he lived in Ludlow. He married Oct. 4, 1830, Hannah B. Bartlett, born Dec. 25, 1805. Children:

Helen C.,[8] born July 19, 1831; died 1898; married George W. Ray.
Mary S.,[8] born Aug. 7, 1834; died Sept. 24, 1864.
Philo W. B.,[8] born Oct. 30, 1835; married Eliza Dutton, born in 1837 or 1838, daughter of Hubbard and Adeline (Smith) Dutton. (See Dutton Gen.) They had one son and four daughters.

Charles Alden,[7] son of Josiah,[6] was born Dec. 6, 1803, and died May 22, 1862. He was a justice of the peace 18 years. He married first, Nov. 20, 1831, Lydia More, died July 1, 1841, daughter of George and Ruth More. He married second, Margaret More, died in Feb., 1852. He married third, Louisa Paine, born March 2, 1815, daughter of Jonathan and Sally (Hayden) Paine. (See Paine Gen.) Children:

Charles Wesley,[8] born Nov. 7, 1832; died March 19, 1901.
Elizabeth Jane,[8] born March 29, 1834.
Fletcher Clark,[8] born March 22, 1836; died in July, 1856.
Francis Washington,[8] born Feb. 23, 1845; died young.

Charles Wesley Alden,[8] son of Charles,[7] was born Nov. 7, 1832, and died March 19, 1901. "His family have in their possession a hammer brought over by John Alden." He married April 14, 1858, Lura Savilla Chapin, born May 23, 1837, daughter of Rev. Daniel Levi Chapin. Children:

Flora Delia,[9] born July 17, 1861.
Charles Ely,[9] born Oct. 2, 1863.
Ada E.,[9] born April 22, 1868; married June 20, 1900, Louis W. Chapin. (See Chapin Gen.)
Edith L.,[9] born Oct. 2, 1872; married Dec. 19, 1905, Clarence Pease.
Walter M.,[9] born Feb. 10, 1876.

Flora Delia Alden,[9] daughter of Charles Wesley,[8] was born July 17, 1861; married William A. Jones. Children:
Bessie M.,[10] born April 22, 1883.
Harold W.,[10] born Feb. 2, 1885.

Charles Ely Alden,[9] son of Charles Wesley,[8] was born Oct. 2, 1863; married Nov. 23, 1887, Affa Hunt. Children:
Ralph W.,[10] born Aug. 26, 1890.
Raymond W.,[10] born Aug. 26, 1890; died July 27, 1901.
Elton R.,[10] born Nov. 11, 1896.

John Brown Alden,[7] son of Josiah,[6] married June 17, 1827, Huldah Wright Clapp, daughter of Capt. John Clapp. Children:
Jane Olivet,[8] born March 12, 1828; married Pliny Robinson.
Eunice Brown,[8] born June 19, 1829; married Chester Canterbury.
John Brown,[8] born June 1, 1831.
Clarissa Ann,[8] born Aug. 25, 1833; died Sept. 29, 1833.
Arthur Rowley,[8] born Aug. 5, 1834; died Dec. 30, 1834.
Sarah Elizabeth,[8] born Aug. 26, 1835; married Richard L. Frost.
James Henry,[8] born Nov. 5, 1837; died Dec. 30, 1837.
Birdsey Brainard,[8] born Feb. 12, 1839; went to South Australia.
Preston Dwight,[8] born Feb. 25, 1841.
James Henry,[8] born Feb. 12, 1845; died Feb. 21, 1845.
Albert Leslie,[8] born May 16, 1846; died Aug. 25, 1849.
Edwin Herbert,[8] born June 27, 1848.
Frances Marion,[8] born Dec. 4, 1850; died May 22, 1852.

Orsamus Alden,[7] son of Josiah,[6] was born June 5, 1808, and died June 29, 1878; married June 24, 1842, Eliza Ann Lemmon, born May 18, 1818, died Dec. 2, 1877, daughter of Samuel Lemmon of Ware. Children:
Two died in infancy.[8]
Myraetta,[8] born Oct. 22, 1844; died Oct. 27, 1861.
Georgianna,[8] born July 7, 1846; died Sept. 25, 1862.

Elliot O.,[8] born Feb. 5, 1848.
Emma Francelia,[8] born Nov. 7, 1849.
Ida Alberta,[8] born Aug. 25, 1851; died Aug. 14, 1872; married a Mr. Brown.
Albert Prince,[8] born June 14, 1853; died Nov. 4, 1873.
Arthur Orvilla,[8] born Oct. 21, 1855.
Marcenia Melville,[8] born Dec. 5, 1857.
Isabella Emeretta,[8] born May 19, 1859; married Merrick H. Cooley. (See Cooley Gen.)
Clarence Elma,[8] born May 20, 1861.

Arthur Orvilla Alden,[8] son of Orsamus,[7] was born Oct. 21, 1855; married Nov. 14, 1888, Bessie Isabelle Sherman, born Feb. 5, 1865, died May 26, 1911, daughter of Edwin F. and Caroline M. Sherman. Children:
Dorothy Hazel,[9] born Sept. 6, 1890.
Roger Orvilla,[9] born Sept. 14, 1892.
Russell Drayton,[9] born Feb. 26, 1895.
Rexford Sherman,[9] born Jan. 17, 1898.
Florence Isabelle,[9] born Sept. 23, 1899.
Reginald John,[9] born June 15, 1901.
Richard Arthur,[9] born June 19, 1903.

Marcenia Melville Alden,[8] son of Orsamus,[7] was born Dec. 5, 1857; married April 19, 1885, Addie May Cooley, born Oct. 14, 1865, daughter of James and Angenette Cooley. Children:
Bessie May,[9] born Jan. 19, 1886.
Ethel Lillian,[9] born June 12, 1887.
Eleanor Jeannette,[9] born Nov. 26, 1888.
Marcenia Melville,[9] born Sept. 20, 1906; died Sept. 20, 1906.

Clarence Elma Alden,[8] son of Orsamus,[7] was born May 20, 1861; married Lillian Maud Wood, born June 19, 1873, died Sept. 30, 1900, daughter of Lorin and Angenette Wood. Children:
Florence Mildred,[9] born Sept. 14, 1889.
Harold Milo,[9] born March 14, 1892.

Benjamin Alden,[6] son of Josiah,[5] married Mary Hodges. Children:
Jefferson,[7] born Jan. 26, 1804; died in Aug., 1857.
Mary,[7] married Martin Richardson.
David,[7] born May 17, 1807; died Nov. 5, 1888.

Benjamin,[7] born March 12, 1811; died April 3, 1814.
Dexter,[7] born Oct. 13, 1812; died Oct. 8, 1885.
Caroline,[7] born June 26, 1815; died Sept. 8, 1885; married Dec. 27, 1861, Artemus Homan Whitney.
Lucinda,[7] born Dec. 4, 1817; died Jan. 19, 1899.
Eliza A.,[7] born July 8, 1822; died Jan. 19, 1876.
Sarah,[7] born Oct. 5, 1825; died Sept. 25, 1828.

Jefferson Alden,[7] son of Benjamin,[6] was born Jan. 26, 1804, and died in Aug., 1857; married Salome Kendall, daughter of Amos and Sila (Miller) Kendall. Children:
Malinda.[8]
George.[8]
Edward M.,[8] born Feb. 17, 1844; died Nov. 28, 1911.

Edward M. Alden,[8] son of Jefferson,[7] was born Feb. 17, 1844, and died Nov. 28, 1911; married Ida Smith. Children:
Edward S.,[9] born Aug. 18, 1875.
Ida Grace,[9] born Nov. 30, 1877; married in Nov., 1902, Amos T. Palmer.
Percy M.,[9] born Aug. 5, 1883.
Edith M.,[9] born Sept. 12, 1885.
John S.,[9] born April 11, 1889; married Aug. 17, 1911, Nina S. Rogers.

Edward S. Alden,[9] son of Edward M.,[8] was born Aug. 18, 1875; married Oct. 1, 1902, Mary J. Tate. Children: Alice,[10] Arnold.[10]

Mary Alden,[7] daughter of Benjamin,[6] married Martin Richardson. Child: Edwin.[8]

Edwin Richardson,[8] son of Mary Alden,[7] married Mattie Mills. Children: Edwina,[9] Alfred.[9]

Edwina Richardson,[9] daughter of Edwin,[8] married Joseph Stahl. Child: Lillian.[10]

Lillian Stahl,[10] daughter of Edwina Richardson,[9] married Frederick Duseberry. Child: Alvina.[11]

David Alden,[7] son of Benjamin,[6] was born May 17, 1807, and died Nov. 5, 1888; married Arethusa King, died July 25, 1894, daughter of Michael King. Children:
Sarah Elizabeth,[8] died June 10, 1860.
Lucius D.,[8] born Dec. 15, 1835; died May 16, 1898.
Mary Ellen,[8] died in infancy.

Emerette,[8] born Sept. 23, 1840.
Ellen,[8] born Nov. 21, 1846; married Charles Guy.

Sarah Elizabeth Alden,[8] daughter of David,[7] was born in 1834 and died June 10, 1860; married Elam Olcott Allen, died in Feb., 1889. Child:
Edgar Olcott,[9] born Oct. 10, 1859; married May Keefe.

Edgar Olcott Allen,[9] son of Sarah Elizabeth,[8] was born Oct. 10, 1859; married May Keefe. Child: Florence Emily,[10] born Aug. 5, 1908.

Lucius D. Alden,[8] son of David,[7] was born Dec. 15, 1835, and died May 16, 1898; married first, Feb. 17, 1859, Sarah Jane Holkiss. Children:
Jennie,[9] born Aug. 31, 1860.
George H.,[9] born Sept. 6, 1862.
Lucius D. Alden[8] married second, Lucy Chaffee, born Nov. 20, 1836.

Jennie Alden,[9] daughter of Lucius D.,[8] was born Aug. 31, 1860; married John Dunn. Children:
Delbert Alden,[10] born Nov. 10, 1884; married Gladys York.
Marion Abigail,[10] born Oct. 25, 1890.

George H. Alden,[9] son of Lucius D.,[8] was born Sept. 6, 1862; married Winifred McCormick. Children:
Winifred Mary,[10] born March 22, 1889.
Matthew David,[10] born Dec. 15, 1890.
Sarah Jane,[10] born Oct. 12, 1892.
John Dexter,[10] born May 16, 1894.
Ralph H.,[10] born Feb. 5, 1897.

Winifred Mary Alden,[10] daughter of George H.,[9] was born March 22, 1889; married Walter Reavey. Child: Catherine.[11]

Ellen Alden,[8] daughter of David,[7] was born Nov. 21, 1846; married Charles Guy. Child:
Maud Leanna,[9] born Dec. 31, 1872; married David Newell.

Dexter Alden,[7] son of Benjamin,[6] was born Oct. 13, 1812, and died Oct. 8, 1885; married first, Eliza Griswold, born Nov. 2, 1816. Child:
Anna Griswold,[8] born June 17, 1851; married Dec. 7, 1881, William T. Fields.
Dexter Alden[7] married second, Margaret Elizabeth Feeter, born June 13, 1832. Children:

Mary Elizabeth,[8] born April 16, 1861; died May 17, 1905.
Louise Gertrude,[8] born Sept. 9, 1863.

Mary Elizabeth Alden,[8] daughter of Dexter,[7] was born April 16, 1861, and died May 17, 1905; married March 27, 1884, Charles Kingsbury Billings. Children:
Charles Kingsbury,[9] born Nov. 21, 1885; married Oct. 12, 1910, Katherine Louise Murlless, born May 24, 1886.
Margaret Louise,[9] born Nov. 10, 1886.
Mabel Frances,[9] born May 3, 1888.
Julia Holmes,[9] born Jan. 17, 1890.
Mary Elizabeth,[9] born Feb. 7, 1892.
John Alden,[9] born Oct. 11, 1898.

Louise Gertrude Alden,[8] daughter of Dexter,[7] was born Sept. 9, 1863; married Nov. 23, 1886, William L. Howard, U.S.N. Child:
Helen,[9] born Dec. 19, 1888; married April 25, 1911, Charles Clifford Gill, U.S.N., born April 25, 1885.

Lucinda Alden,[7] daughter of Benjamin,[6] was born Dec. 4, 1817, and died Jan. 19, 1899; married Dec. 12, 1841, Josiah Amos Gardner, born June 17, 1818, died Feb. 26, 1885. Children:
Charles Alden,[8] born April 3, 1843.
Caroline Alden,[8] born July 25, 1845; married Aug. 9, 1893, Lyman Hewitt.
Ida May,[8] born Aug. 3, 1854; married Oct. 28, 1880, Luther Oliver Pomeroy.

Charles Alden Gardner,[8] son of Lucinda Alden,[7] was born April 3, 1843; married in 1884, Etta Rice. Child:
Ida May,[9] born Nov. 8, 1885.

Eliza Ann Alden,[7] daughter of Benjamin,[6] was born July 8, 1822, and died Jan. 19, 1876; married Samuel O. Gay. Children: Eliza,[8] Ellen F.[8]

The Atchinson Family

David Ladd Atchinson,[2] son of Gillen[1] and Arethusa (Ladd) Atchinson, was born in Wilbraham, Dec. 16, 1809, and died in Ludlow, Sept. 25, 1875; married Oct. 18, 1832, Abigail Waters Putnam, born in Springfield, May 16, 1811, died in Ludlow, June 6, 1886, daughter of Amos and Susan (Miller) Putnam. (See Putnam Gen.) They moved to Ludlow in 1835 to a farm in the western part of the town, known as the Ebenezer Barber farm, which remained in the Atchinson family for three quarters of a century. Children:

Abigail Elizabeth,[3] born March 13, 1835; married March 6, 1855, William Leach of South Wilbraham, now Hampden. They had four children.

Mary Celeste,[3] born Jan. 7, 1837; died Feb. 20, 1911.

Ellen Sophia,[3] born Aug. 22, 1839; died June 23, 1905; married April 6, 1859, James Alden, who died Dec. 31, 1900. (See Alden Gen.) They had three children.

Gillen David,[3] born March 14, 1843; died May 10, 1910.

Gillen David Atchinson,[3] son of David Ladd,[2] was born March 14, 1843, and died May 10, 1910; married June 6, 1866, Julietta Snow Keith of Granby. Children:

Fred Green,[4] born May 10, 1868.
Almon Scott,[4] born May 1, 1873.
Ada Maria,[4] born April 1, 1876.
Mary Ladd,[4] born Nov. 28, 1877.

Fred Green Atchinson,[4] son of Gillen David,[3] was born May 10, 1868, in Granby; married May 8, 1890, Leila Eliza Bennett, born Nov. 1, 1868, daughter of Adelbert Lathrop and Helen (Spellman) Bennett. (See Bennett Gen.) Children:

Gertrude,[5] born May 16, 1893.
Earle Spellman,[5] born July 9, 1895.
Ralph Keith,[5] born Aug. 6, 1896; died Sept. 12, 1896.
Helen Louise,[5] born June 10, 1898.

Almon Scott Atchinson,[4] son of Gillen David,[3] was born May 1, 1873; married Sept. 27, 1898, Elizabeth Gebhardt of Clinton. Children:

Chester,[5] born Nov. 15, 1899; died Nov. 22, 1899.
Fred Gillen,[5] born Sept. 3, 1902.
Myrtle Celeste[5] and Myron Scott,[5] twins, born Dec. 14, 1904.

Ada Maria Atchinson,[4] daughter of Gillen David,[3] was born April 1, 1876; married July 17, 1907, Alden Pope Marsh of Boston. Child:

Caroline Juliaetta,[5] born July 7, 1908.

Mary Ladd Atchinson,[4] daughter of Gillen David,[3] was born Nov. 28, 1877; married May 1, 1901, Charles Henry Goldthwaite of Granby.

The Joseph Banister Family.

Joseph Banister[1] married Mary Hines. Children: Barzillai,[2] Christopher,[2] Nathan,[2] John,[2] Lemuel,[2] William,[2] Beulah,[2] Mary,[2] Persis.[2]

William Banister,[2] son of Joseph,[1] was born in 1760. He served one month and twelve days as corporal in Captain Barney's company of Hampshire County, at New London, Conn. He enlisted July 21, 1779. Roll was dated at Chesterfield. He married first, Mehitable Brown. Children:

Jotham,[3] born 1782.
Cynthia,[3] lived five years.
Luther.[3]
Nathan.[3]
Cynthia,[3] born Jan. 6, 1791.
William,[3] born March, 1794.
John,[3] born Sept., 1796.
David,[3] born Dec., 1799.

William Banister[2] married a second time and had three sons.

Jotham Banister,[3] son of William,[2] was born in 1782 and died June 15, 1822; married Electa Kingsley, born Sept. 25, 1784, died May 7, 1851. Children:

Mary Alice,[4] born Aug. 26, 1804; died Sept. 12, 1806.
Mary Alice,[4] born June 21, 1806.
Daniel Kingsley,[4] born March 23, 1808.
Abigail Lyman,[4] born Nov. 15, 1809.
Julius,[4] born Oct. 13, 1811.
Eveline,[4] born Aug. 15, 1813.
Nancy Hannum,[4] born Feb. 13, 1815.
Edwin,[4] born June 8, 1817.
Luther,[4] born March 26, 1819.
Jonathan Fitch,[4] born July 13, 1821.

Daniel Kingsley Banister,[4] a Methodist clergyman, son of Jotham,[3] was born in Chesterfield, March 23, 1808, and died June 27, 1886; married June 2, 1836, Harriet Newell Steele, born Feb. 29, 1816, in Barre Vt., died Dec. 12, 1890, daughter of Joel and Jerusha (Higgins) Steele. Children:

Jane Electa,[5] born Dec. 16, 1838; married Nov. 4, 1863, Warren D. Fuller. (See Fuller Gen.)
Edwin Kingsley,[5] born July 26, 1840.
Henry Martin,[5] born May 6, 1843.
Mary Minerva,[5] born Aug. 3, 1848.
George Neander,[5] born Sept. 3, 1850.
Hattie Marshall,[5] born June 11, 1853.
Charles Albert,[5] born Nov. 14, 1855.

The Linus Banister Family.

Linus Banister[1] was born in West Brookfield, Aug. 31, 1789; married Celia Gilbert, born Jan. 31, 1794. Children:
Almira,[2] born May 22, 1828.
John Linus,[2] born July 28, 1830.
Jonas,[2] born in 1833.
Henry,[2] born in 1835.

John Linus Banister,[2] son of Linus,[1] was born in West Brookfield, July 28, 1830, and died Dec. 24, 1908; married May 3, 1859, in Chester, Emmeline T. Fuller, born May 4, 1841, in Ludlow, daughter of Edmund Warren and Almira (Jenks) Fuller. (See Fuller Gen.) Children: Albert,[3] Frank,[3] Edith.[3]

Albert Banister,[3] son of John Linus,[2] was born in Ludlow; married May 13, 1886, Mary Emma Chapin, daughter of Edwin and Henrietta (Fuller) Chapin. (See Fuller Gen.) Children:
Edwin John,[4] born Dec. 23, 1888; died Feb. 4, 1899.
Alberta May,[4] born Sept. 5, 1902.

The Barber Family

Ebenezer Barber,[1] a town officer in 1777, lived, raised his family, and died in Ludlow. Children: Ebenezer,[2] Lewis,[2] David,[2] Abner,[2] John[2] (the last three lived in Vermont), Abigail,[2] who married Zerah Chapin; Anna,[2] who married Zelotes Parsons of Wilbraham; and Tirzah,[2] born July 7, 1776.

Ebenezer Barber,[2] son of Ebenezer,[1] married first, July 29, 1784, Lovicy Bartlett of Wilbraham. They had one daughter, Lovicy.[3] He married second, Rebecca ———. Children: Ira,[3] Joel,[3] Warren,[3] Eli,[3] and Hollis.[3]

Ira Barber,[3] son of Ebenezer,[2] had a son, Hollis.[4]

Hollis Barber,[4] son of Ira,[3] married Lucinda Martin Bennett, born Oct. 10, 1822, daughter of Charles and Sarah (Young) Bennett. (See Bennett Gen.) Children: Oren Hollis,[5] Abby Ann,[5] Loretta Jane,[5] Emma Lucinda,[5] Carrie M.,[5] Bertha Belle.[5]

Loretta Jane Barber,[5] daughter of Hollis,[4] married Austin A. Adams. Children:
Sybil Loretta,[6] born July 22, 1871.
Hollis Alden,[6] married Fannie J. Moore. Children: Arthur,[7] died young; Esther Frances.[7]

Emma Lucinda Barber,[5] daughter of Hollis,[4] married G. Lee Smith. Children:
Ginevra May,[6] married Waldo S. Belmar.
Ruby Lee,[6] married Homer J. Strope. Children: Winifred Elizabeth,[7] Margaret Lee,[7] Thelma Irene.[7]

The Thomas Bartlett Family.

Thomas Bartlett[1] was born in Plymouth, Mass., in 1741, and died Sept. 17, 1808; married in 1765, Elizabeth Bartlett, born in 1747, died in 1779, daughter of Sylvanus Bartlett of Plymouth. Children:
Thomas,[2] born May 19, 1771.
Daniel,[2] and four daughters.

Thomas Bartlett,[2] son of Thomas,[1] was born in Plymouth, May 19, 1771. He went to Sutton, Vt., in 1787, and later broke land for a farm at Burke; attended Dartmouth College, but did not graduate on account of ill health. In 1800 he was elected town clerk of Burke, and in 1805 elected the first representative from the town to the Legislature of Vermont, serving two years. He married May 8, 1806, Anna Little, born in South Kingston, R. I., Sept. 18, 1785, daughter of William and Phœbe (Marchant) Little. Thomas Bartlett and his wife both died in Lyndon, Vt. Children:
Thomas,[3] born June 18, 1808; died in 1852.
Mary Ann,[3] born July 11, 1813.
Alfred Henry,[3] born August 9, 1816; died in 1852.

Alfred Henry Bartlett,[3] son of Thomas,[2] was born Aug. 9, 1816, in Burke, Vt., and died in 1852 at Danville, Vt. He was captain of a company of militia, and high sheriff of Caledonia County, Vt. He married April 14, 1839, Anna Hepsibeth Joy, born Sept. 14, 1817, died in West Burke, Vt., a daughter of Joseph and Olly (Benson) Joy. Children:

Frances,[4] born Jan. 2, 1840.
Henry,[4] born Feb. 6, 1841.
Mary,[4] born May 5, 1843.
Charles,[4] born July 18, 1845.
Clara Ann,[4] born June 25, 1849.
Alfred H.,[4] born April 29, 1851.

Alfred H. Bartlett,[4] son of Alfred Henry,[3] was born April 29, 1851, in Danville, Vt. He was town clerk and treasurer of Ludlow. He married Feb. 24, 1883, Nellie L. Joy, born in Sutton, Vt., May 28, 1862, daughter of David and Laura (Beckwith) Joy. Children:

Ruth Marian,[5] born Feb. 28, 1884.
Katharine,[5] born July 8, 1888.
Grace Laura,[5] born Jan. 13, 1893.

The Eleazer Bartlett Family.

Andrew E. C. Bartlett,[2] son of Eleazer,[1] was born in Belchertown, Feb. 16, 1849, and died Aug. 31, 1901; married Dec. 9, 1869, Alice A. Cleaveland, born Feb. 19, 1853, daughter of Cyrus and Eleanor (Plumley) Cleaveland. (See Cleaveland Gen.) Children:

Herbert A.,[3] born June 19, 1876.
Lewis G.,[3] born May 1, 1882.

Lewis G. Bartlett,[3] son of Andrew E. C.,[2] was born May 1, 1882; married July 17, 1907, Marjorie H. Green. Child:

Miriam Cleaveland,[4] born Jan. 9, 1910.

The Beebe Family.

"Bebi" was one of a series of fifty-eight kings existing about 3000 B.C., to whom Rameses II. is represented as paying homage. Book 21 of Livy's History of Rome relates how one Quintus

Beebius was sent as ambassador to Hannibal in the year of Rome 534.

The name appears twice among the Royal Guard of William the Conqueror.

The name Joh. Beby appears among the records of Northamptonshire, England, as Master of St. Leonard's Hospital, Feb. 10, 1403.

The Bebarini family is found in early Italian history. One was a personal friend of Galileo. They were the discoverers of the famous Portland vase.

The church register of St. Andrews in the village of Broughton, England, verifies the names of John Beebe and his children, who emigrated to this country about 1650, as stated in his will on file in Hartford, Conn. Probably ninety-nine per cent. of the Beebes in this country descended from the three sons of John of Broughton. They landed in Boston, made their way to New London, Conn., branching in all directions from there.

Individuals of the name were prominent in King Philip's War, many of them were "minute men" in 1776, and became soldiers and officers in the Revolution, as the pension rolls show fourteen spellings of the name.

In the Revolutionary records for the state of Massachusetts, the following names of men from Ludlow are found, viz.: Ammon Beebe, Christopher Beebe, Ezekiel Beebe, Gideon Beebe, Samuel Beebe, Samuel Beebe, Jr., and Solomon Beebe. Samuel Beebe, Jr., enlisted when fourteen years of age, and on that account failed to pass muster under Colonel Woodbridge, but later he went as a waiter to Colonel Mason at Springfield and soon went into actual service.

John Beebe,[1] who emigrated to America in the spring of 1650, died on shipboard. Children:

John,[2] born Nov. 4, 1628. He was very prominent in the early wars in the colonies. He married in 1660, Abigail Yorke, born about 1668, died March 9, 1725, daughter of James Yorke. Children: John,[3] Benjamin,[3] and Rebecca.[3]

Rebecca,[2] born Aug. 11, 1630; married John Ruscoe.

Thomas,[2] born June 23, 1633. He was prominent in King Philip's War. He married before 1663, Millicent Addis, daughter of William Addis. Children: Thomas,[3] Rebecca,[3] Hannah,[3] Millicent.[3]

Samuel,[2] born June 23, 1633; died 1712.

Nathaniel,[2] born Jan. 23, 1635; died 1728.

Mary,[2] baptized March 15, 1637.

Hannah,[2] baptized June 23, 1640.

James,[2] born in 1641. He was one of the early settlers of Hadley, and prominent in early politics. He married first, Agnes Boltwood, daughter of Robert Boltwood; second, Sarah, daughter of Thomas Benedict. He died April 22, 1728. They had 10 children.

Samuel Beebe,[2] son of John,[1] was born June 23, 1633; died in 1712; married first, Agnes Keeney; second, Mary Keeney, daughters of William Keeney. Children:

Samuel,[3] born about 1660; died June 10, 1716; married Elizabeth Rogers.

Susannah,[3] born about 1663; died 1680; married Aaron Fountain.

William,[3] born about 1665; died 1750; married Ruth Rogers.

Agnes,[3] born about 1667; died Dec. 3, 1685; married John Daniels.

Nathaniel,[3] born about 1670; died July 2, 1697; married Elizabeth Wheeler.

Ann,[3] born about 1672; married April 23, 1700, Thomas Crocker.

Jonathan,[3] born about 1674; died Oct. 12, 1761.

Mary,[3] born about 1678; died before 1712; married April 8, 1702, Richard Tozer.

Thomas,[3] born about 1682; married Dec. 20, 1707, Anna Hobson.

Jonathan Beebe,[3] son of Samuel,[2] was born in 1674 and died Oct. 12, 1761; married first, Bridget Brockway; second, Elizabeth Staples. Children:

Jonathan,[4] born between 1693 and 1695; married first, Hannah Coley; second, Lydia Spencer; third, Remember Nye.

William,[4] born about 1700; died Jan. 29, 1788; married first, Phœbe ——; second, Eleanor ——.

Joshua,[4] born about 1713; married Hannah Brockway.

Caleb,[4] born about 1717; married Phœbe Buckingham.

Joshua Beebe,[4] son of Jonathan,[3] was born in 1713 and died in 1797; married in Oct., 1733, Hannah Brockway. Children:

Brockway,[5] born in 1734; died Feb. 13, 1815; married Phœbe Dutton.

Joshua,[5] born in 1736; moved to Pennsylvania.

GENEALOGIES

Gideon,[5] born in 1738; married Betty Sherwood.

Damaris,[5] married Jeremiah Dutton. (See Dutton Gen.)

Gideon Beebe,[5] son of Joshua,[4] was born in East Haddam in 1738. He settled in Ludlow about 1768. He served in the Revolutionary War. He married May 10, 1768, Betty Sherwood, daughter of John and Hannah (Morehouse) Sherwood. They had one son, Sherwood.[6] (See Sherwood Gen.)

Sherwood Beebe,[6] son of Gideon,[5] was born in Ludlow, Nov. 16, 1768. He held various town offices, a selectman six years; a member of the State Legislature in 1811. He married first, Lucinda Damon, daughter of Peter and Lydia (Putnam) Damon. (See Damon Gen.) Children:

Amanda,[7] born July 25, 1796; died Sept. 24, 1878; married Stillman Alden. (See Alden Gen.)

Sylvia,[7] married David Bissell. They had one daughter, Sylvia,[8] who married first, F. J. Putnam (see Putnam Gen.); second, Elijah Munsell.

Ruby,[7] who married Ambrose Allen, an early settler of Warren.

Emmeline,[7] born Aug. 19, 1804; died Dec. 26, 1864; married Eber Stebbins. Children:

George Sherwood,[8] born Jan. 9, 1828.

Solomon Bliss,[8] born June 18, 1830; died June 8, 1910.

Lucy Maria,[8] born May 10, 1832; died June 9, 1889.

Damon,[7] died in infancy.

Minerva,[7] died in infancy.

Dura,[7] died in infancy.

Sherwood Beebe[6] married second, Bernis Hubbard, daughter of Elisha and Mary Hubbard. (See Hubbard Gen.) Children:

William Hubbard,[7] born March 6, 1811; died in Fond du Lac, Wis.

Selina,[7] married John Weeks; died Jan. 18, 1889.

Selucia,[7] married William Morrill.

Robert,[7] born in 1817; died Oct. 5, 1835.

Andrew,[7] married Charlotte Lougee. Children: George Andrew,[8] Lucilla,[8] Charlotte Luret[8] (married Alfred A. Warriner), William Edwin[8] (had one son, William[9]).

Edwin,[7] a "forty-niner," married Margaretta Maria Wentworth Thompson. Children: Clara,[8] Cecil,[8] Otis.[8]

William Hubbard Beebe,[7] son of Sherwood,[6] was born March 6, 1811, and died ——— —, ———. He was one of the pioneers of southern Wisconsin. He married Rebekah Olds, born Dec. 25, 1814, died June 14, 1878, daughter of Nathan and Hannah (Wright) Olds. (See Olds Gen.) Children:

Ellen Rebekah,[8] born March 7, 1836, one of the pioneers in the study of medicine in the West.
Emeline Ruby,[8] born Sept. 24, 1838; died Dec. 4, 1883.
Robert William,[8] born June 13, 1841.
Nathan Sherwood,[8] born March 29, 1844.
Edwin Hubbard,[8] born July 3, 1846, one of the pioneers of Nebraska; died Nov. 24, 1871.
Andrew Hiram,[8] born Feb. 5, 1852.
Evanore Olds,[8] born April 12, 1858, in Fond du Lac, Wis.

Emeline Ruby Beebe,[8] daughter of William Hubbard,[7] was born Sept. 24, 1838, and died Dec. 4, 1883; married March 12, 1868, Melvin Roblee. Children:

Lenore Malinda,[9] born Feb. 18, 1869.
Andrew Melvin,[9] born April 25, 1872; married Dec. 27, 1898, Amy Lowell.
Edwin Thomas,[9] born Aug. 25, 1874; married July 1, 1903, Bertie Shortt.
Emelyn Beebe,[9] born April 23, 1876.
Carleton Olds,[9] born Sept. 27, 1880.

Robert William Beebe,[8] son of William Hubbard,[7] was born June 13, 1841; a Civil War veteran and Minnesota pioneer; married first, Jennie Jones; second, Netty Rogers. Children: William Edwin,[9] Florence,[9] Blanche.[9]

Nathan Sherwood Beebe,[8] son of William Hubbard,[7] was born March 29, 1844; married Elizabeth Baxter. Children: Henry,[9] Wilfred Eugene.[9]

Andrew Hiram Beebe,[8] son of William Hubbard,[7] was born Feb. 5, 1852; married Feb. 11, 1888, Anna Wolfram. Children: Edwin,[9] Albert,[9] Lester,[9] Evanore Olds.[9]

THE BENNETT FAMILY.

The Ludlow Bennetts are descended from **Peter Bennett**[1] of Bristol, England, through his son, **John Bennett,**[2] born 1642.

John came to Jamestown, Va., in 1665, but soon went to Beverly, Mass., where he married in 1671, Deborah Grover. They removed to Middleboro, where he died in 1718.

Joseph Bennett,[3] son of John,[2] was born in Middleboro about 1679. He married Joanna Perry. Children:
Mary,[4] born Nov. 5, 1708.
John,[4] born July, 1711.
Joanna,[4] born Feb. 19, 1714.
Timothy,[4] born Sept. 13, 1717.
Arthur,[4] born Sept. 7, 1720.
Joseph,[4] born Oct. 18, 1721.

John Bennett,[4] son of Joseph,[3] was born July, 1711; married April 8, 1736, Deborah Reynolds. He removed from Middleboro to Cumberland, R. I., and later lived in Coventry and Smithfield, R. I. Children: Robert,[5] Ezra,[5] Timothy,[5] Hosea,[5] Charles,[5] Sally,[5] Deborah,[5] Elizabeth,[5] Joseph.[5]

Charles Bennett,[5] son of John,[4] was born 1752 and died Dec. 20, 1834; married May 21, 1775, Anne, daughter of Amos and Marcy Sprague, born at Smithfield, R. I., Jan. 31, 1755, died Feb. 16, 1847. They came to Ludlow before 1807, and settled in the "Cherry Valley" district, near the present Springfield Reservoir. Both are buried in the old burying ground near the First Congregational Church in Ludlow Center. Children: Reynolds,[6] Marcy,[6] Shadrach,[6] George,[6] Charles,[6] Anna,[6] John.[6]

Charles Bennett,[6] son of Charles,[5] was born in Smithfield, R. I., Sept. 14, 1783, and came to Ludlow in 1813, where he died Sept. 4, 1859. He married first, Jan. 26, 1809, Sarah Young. Children:
Laura Ann,[7] born Oct. 15, 1809; died May 7, 1893.
Emily,[7] born Dec. 7, 1812.
Seth Jenks,[7] born March 31, 1815; died July 1, 1887.
Hannah Carey,[7] born June 13, 1817; died Jan. 27, 1894.
Sarah Young,[7] born Feb. 21, 1821.
Charles Sprague,[7] born Feb. 21, 1821; died Feb. 11, 1897.
Lucinda Martin,[7] born Oct. 10, 1822; married Hollis Barber. (See Barber Gen.)
   Charles Bennett[6] married second, Lovina Curtis, born 1805, died June 18, 1889. Children:

Horace A.,[7] born 1838; died Sept. 28, 1839.
Mary Ardelia,[7] born July 6, 1840.
Minerva Jane,[7] born Feb. 23, 1842.
Warren Jerome,[7] died June 26, 1876.
Homer Augustus,[7] born Jan., 1848.
Horace Horatio,[7] born Jan., 1848; died Aug. 18, 1848.

Laura Ann Bennett,[7] daughter of Charles,[6] was born Oct. 15, 1809, and died May 7, 1893; married Jefferson Bennett. Children:
Laura Lovinia,[8] born Aug. 20, 1830; died Nov. 20, 1899.
Nancy Ann,[8] born May 31, 1832.
Lyman Jefferson,[8] born Jan. 10, 1835; died in Civil War, Nov. 4, 1862.
Alonzo Jackson,[8] born March 4, 1837; married Amelia Sikes; one child.
Alanson Joseph,[8] born in 1840; died in 1842.
Louisa Amelia,[8] born in 1843; died in 1844.
Lewis Judson,[8] born April 22, 1846; married Carrie A. Cornish.
Nelia Ada,[8] born March 19, 1848; died Nov. 4, 1910.
Lora Ella Maria,[8] born Oct. 15, 1851; married Frank W. Hawley, who died Oct. 28, 1883.
Sallie Eva,[8] born May 31, 1854.

Laura Lovinia Bennett,[8] daughter of Laura Ann,[7] was born Aug. 20, 1830, and died Nov. 20, 1899; married first, Gilbert Howard. Children: Franklin Gilbert,[9] Clara Lovinia,[9] Frederick Bennett,[9] and Lonza Erwin.[9] She married second, Henry Tufts. One child: Bert Howard,[9] who married Carrie Goodale. They had one son: Hermon R.[10]

Clara Lovinia Howard,[9] daughter of Laura Lovinia Bennett,[8] married Moses Woodward. Children:
Winfred,[10] who married Kate Smith. Children: Harold,[11] Chester,[11] Richard.[11]
Lena,[10] who married Myron Collins. Children: Carleton,[11] Gertrude,[11] Edna.[11]

Lonza Erwin Howard,[9] son of Laura Lovinia Bennett,[8] married Cora B. Keep. Children: Ida May,[10] Edna.[10]

Nancy Ann Bennett,[8] daughter of Laura Ann,[7] was born May 31, 1832; married first, William Bennett (Bell). Children:

GENEALOGIES 357

Hannah Welcome,[9] Shadrach Jefferson,[9] Luna Rockwood.[9] She married second, Daniel W. Smith.

Nelia Ada Bennett,[8] daughter of Laura Ann,[7] was born March 19, 1848, and died Nov. 4, 1910; married Frank H. Clark.
An adopted child:
Nettie Jackson,[9] born Oct. 1, 1876; married Charles E. Bliss. Children:
Stanley Clark,[10] born Feb. 19, 1904.
Marion,[10] born Aug. 6, 1906.
Milton Eugene,[10] born Aug. 28, 1908.

Sallie Eva Bennett,[8] daughter of Laura Ann,[7] was born May 31, 1854; married William N. Graves. Children: Maude Adelia,[9] Charles Elmer,[9] Bessie Myrtle,[9] Frederic Clifton,[9] Robert Francis.[9]

Emily Bennett,[7] daughter of Charles,[6] was born Dec. 7, 1812; married Reuben Green. Children:
Emily Elvira,[8] born April 2, 1829; died July 21, 1830.
George Henry Bartlett,[8] an adopted son.

Seth Jenks Bennett,[7] son of Charles,[6] was born March 31, 1815, and died July 1, 1887; married Susan Larned. Children:
Flavilla Eugenia Janet,[8] born Feb. 4, 1840; died May 4, 1904.
Wesley Jenks,[8] born Aug. 6, 1850; died Sept. 25, 1851.

Flavilla Eugenia Janet Bennett,[8] daughter of Seth Jenks,[7] was born Feb. 4, 1840, and died May 4, 1904; married Charles Sumner Knight. Children:
Herbert,[9] born June 24, 1868; died Oct. 1, 1868.
Susan,[9] died young.
Jewell Bennett,[9] born May 26, 1871.
Ruby Flavilla,[9] born March 11, 1874.
Pearl Charles Ward,[9] born June 15, 1876.
Jasper Merrill,[9] born April 18, 1879.
Garnet Susan Mary,[9] born April 21, 1881.

Jewell Bennett Knight,[9] son of Flavilla Bennett,[8] was born May 26, 1871; married Martha Grover. Children:
Charles Elmer,[10] born Feb. 22, 1903, in Rahuri, India.
Martha Grover,[10] born April 4, 1906, in Kirkee, India.

Jasper Merrill Knight,[9] son of Flavilla Bennett,[8] was born April 18, 1879; married Bertha Davis. Child:
Jasper Merrill,[10] born in 1905.

Garnet Susan Mary Knight,[9] daughter of Flavilla Bennett,[8] was born April 21, 1881; married Walter O. Terry. Children:
Aileen Bertha,[10] born May 19, 1905.
Natalie,[10] born Oct. 27, 1908.

Hannah Carey Bennett,[7] daughter of Charles,[6] was born June 13, 1817, and died Jan. 26, 1895; married in 1838, Enoch Gilbert Shaw. Child:
Fernando Gilbert,[8] born Dec. 13, 1841.

Fernando Gilbert Shaw,[8] son of Hannah Carey Bennett,[7] was born Dec. 13, 1841; married in 1868, Viola Thompson, born 1845, daughter of Asa and Ruth Thompson. Children:
Harriet Belle,[9] born Sept. 10, 1868.
Cora Evangeline,[9] born Sept. 29, 1870.
Harold Fernando,[9] born in Oct., 1872; died Nov. 22, 1896.
Clarence Irving,[9] born in Jan., 1874.
Nettie Lenore,[9] born in Jan., 1878.
Mary Hannah,[9] born April 24, 1880.
Roy Gilbert,[9] born in Nov., 1882.
Robert Thompson,[9] born May 29, 1884.
Roland Merrill,[9] born July 1, 1890.

Harriet Belle Shaw,[9] daughter of Fernando Gilbert,[8] was born Sept. 10, 1868; married in 1884, Lewis H. Dickinson, born 1861, son of Mary and Eastman Dickinson of Amherst. Children:
Leon Lewis,[10] born June 19, 1885.
Earle Eastman,[10] born July 24, 1893.

Leon Lewis Dickinson,[10] son of Harriet Belle Shaw,[9] was born June 19, 1885; married in Oct., 1909, Eva Goddard, daughter of Lillie and Peter Goddard. Child:
Leon Lewis,[11] born Oct. 11, 1910.

Sarah Young Bennett,[7] daughter of Charles,[6] was born Feb. 21, 1821. She married first, Richard D. Bartlett. Children:

Alonzo.[8]
George Henry,[8] born Dec. 15, 1845, was adopted by Emily and Reuben Green. He married Nancy Sanford, who died July 31, 1911. Children:
Iva Louise,[9] born May 17, 1870; married Lurin White. Child:
Carleton Eugene,[10] born July 7, 1894.
Carleton DeWitt,[9] born Oct. 21, 1871; died Jan. 11, 1892.
Susan Dwight,[9] born March 19, 1873; died Nov. 10, 1874.
Sarah Sanford,[9] born July 14, 1875; died in 1910; married Addison D. Moore.
Harriet Sophia,[9] born May 22, 1878; died Jan. 23, 1903; married Edwin F. Shumway. Child:
Richard Bartlett,[10] born Dec. 30, 1902; died March 23, 1903.
Elsa Rachel,[9] born May 11, 1880; died Dec. 2, 1893.
Clayton Reuben,[9] born July 18, 1882; married Pearl Burchmore. Child:
Ralph Bartlett,[10] born May 5, 1908.
George Henry,[9] born Aug. 22, 1884.

Charles Sprague Bennett,[7] son of Charles,[6] was born Feb. 21, 1821, and died Feb. 11, 1897; married Nov. 2, 1842, Anne Angeline Buell, born Jan. 26, 1822, died Dec. 14, 1904, daughter of Chauncey and Ann (Lathrop) Buell. (See Buell Gen.) Children:
Adelbert Lathrop,[8] born Aug. 31, 1844.
Lansing Charles,[8] born July 26, 1846; died Aug. 25, 1848.
Francis Oliver,[8] born Jan. 13, 1849; died Feb. 10, 1849.
Francelia Orvilla,[8] born Jan. 13, 1849; died Oct. 21, 1907; married Rev. Charles H. Vinton.
Clarence Nelson,[8] born Aug. 30, 1851; died Feb. 12, 1864.
Charles Buell,[8] born Oct. 15, 1853.
Anne Susette,[8] born April 9, 1856.
Franklin Green,[8] born July 25, 1858.
Merton Raymond,[8] born May 10, 1864.

Adelbert Lathrop Bennett,[8] son of Charles Sprague,[7] was born Aug. 31, 1844; married Helen E. Spellman. Children:
Leila Eliza,[9] born Nov. 1, 1868; married Fred Green Atchinson. (See Atchinson Gen.)
Grace Angeline,[9] born June 8, 1874; married Charles Bowles. Child:
Harland Bennett,[10] born Nov. 29, 1910.

Burtis Adelbert,[9] born April 13, 1879; died April 21, 1902; married Anna I. Yenney.

Charles Buell Bennett,[8] son of Charles Sprague,[7] was born Oct. 15, 1853; married first, Lillian T. Sargent. Child:
Bertha Lillian,[9] born July 22, 1876; died Feb. 28, 1880.
    Charles Buell Bennett[8] married second, Emma J. Green. Children:
George Green,[9] born Oct. 5, 1879.
Archer Clarence,[9] born June 2, 1881; married Clara Witham.
Addie Florence,[9] born June 2, 1881.
Charles Ernest,[9] born Dec. 31, 1882.

George Green Bennett,[9] son of Charles Buell,[8] was born Oct. 5, 1879; married Julena Eliza Burr, daughter of Frederick Lyman and Fannie E. (Fuller) Burr. (See Burr Gen.) Children:
Mildred Burr,[10] born July 31, 1905.
Frederick Charles,[10] born Nov. 28, 1906.
Dorothy Elizabeth,[10] born Aug. 6, 1908.

Anne Susette Bennett,[8] daughter of Charles Sprague,[7] was born April 9, 1856; married Charles F. Fuller. Children:
Nellie Augusta,[9] born Nov. 19, 1878.
Raymond Charles,[9] born June 14, 1887; married Sylvia M. Claflin. Child:
    Dorothy Anne,[10] born May 5, 1911.
Clifford Bennett,[9] born Dec. 6, 1895; died March 19, 1896.

Franklin Green Bennett,[8] son of Charles Sprague,[7] was born July 25, 1858; married first, Ida M. Groves, born June 5, 1856, died in 1907. Children:
Nina May,[9] born March 29, 1882; married Walter R. Sawin. Children:
    Myrtle Vivian,[10] born March 25, 1908.
    Kenneth Bennett,[10] born March, 1910.
Florence Lillian,[9] born Sept. 20, 1889.
    Franklin Green Bennett[8] married second, Ada L. Stone.

Merton Raymond Bennett,[8] son of Charles Sprague,[7] was born May 10, 1864; married Alice E. Webster. Children:
Howard Webster,[9] born Oct. 23, 1890.
Myron Lathrop,[9] born July 14, 1892.
Ralph Dudley,[9] born March 7, 1894.

Mary Ardelia Bennett,[7] daughter of Charles,[6] was born July 6, 1840. She married first, Daniel H. Gilman. Child:
Elmer Augustus,[8] born in 1861; married Fannie J. Beatty. Child:
Elsie Ardelia,[9] born in 1883; married Charles A. Dunham.
Mary Ardelia Bennett[7] married second, John Henry Cooper. Child:
Maude Lovina,[8] born March 23, 1882.

Minerva Jane Bennett,[7] daughter of Charles,[6] was born Feb. 23, 1842; married Alonzo S. Bond. Children:
Charles Zephaniah,[8] born June, 1864; married Mrs. Mary Petgen. Child:
Charles Z.,[9] born Aug. 16, 1911.
Lulu.[8]

Warren Jerome Bennett,[7] son of Charles,[6] served in the Civil War in both the infantry and cavalry. He died June 26, 1876; married Louise Lewis. Children:
Alonzo Jerome,[8] born April 29, 1872.
Myrtle Cathryn,[8] born Feb. 10, 1876; married Charles Moore.

Homer Augustus Bennett,[7] son of Charles,[6] was born in Jan., 1848; married first, Rebecca J. Warner. Children:
Washington Homer,[8] born Jan. 10, 1871; married Olive M. Carson. Children:
Norris Jeanette,[9] born Oct. 18, 1895.
Fred C.,[9] born Aug. 24, 1897.
Charles Englehart,[8] born Sept. 16, 1885.
Homer Augustus Bennett[7] married second, Frances Eva Ritter. Child:
Homer Niles,[8] born in 1890.

The Brewer Family.

Daniel Brewer[1] was born in England in 1605. He had six children.

Daniel Brewer,[2] son of Daniel,[1] was born in England in 1624. He married Hannah Morrill of Roxbury, Mass. They had three children.

Daniel Brewer,[3] a clergyman, son of Daniel,[2] was born in 1668. He married Catherine Chauncey. They had eight children.

Isaac Brewer,[4] son of Rev. Daniel,[3] was born in Springfield, Mass., in 1713, and died in 1788. He married first, in 1736, Mary Bliss, who died in 1759. They settled in Wilbraham. Children: Mary,[5] Eunice,[5] Katherine,[5] Isaac,[5] William,[5] Charles,[5] O. S.,[5] Gaius.[5]

Isaac Brewer,[5] son of Isaac,[4] was born Aug. 17, 1742, and died July 21, 1788. He came to Ludlow about 1772 and settled on the Lawrence place. He married, Dec. 17, 1762, Sybil Miller, born in 1747, died in 1834, daughter of Joseph and Catherine (Ferry) Miller. (See Miller Gen.) (Isaac,[5] when he died, left ten children, the twelfth child being born after his death. The widow held the farm, paying off the large amount of debts and giving her son Pliny a collegiate education. All the Brewers now in town are descendants of the son Chauncey.) Children:

Isaac,[6] died in infancy.
Daniel,[6] died at the age of 19; served against the Shays Rebellion.
Pliny,[6] married Lois Stebbins of Springfield and settled in Norwich, Conn.
Catherine,[6] married Walter Stebbins of Springfield.
Betsey,[6] married Jerre Snow of Springfield.
Chauncey,[6] born in 1776; died in 1845.
Polly,[6] married Joshua Fuller. (See Fuller Gen.)
Isaac,[6] died young.
Abigail,[6] married John Smith of South Hadley.
Isaac,[6] married Catherine Fox of Brooklyn, N. Y.
Lyman,[6] married Harriet Tyler of Norwich, Conn.
Clarissa,[6] married Zenas Lawrence of Ludlow.

Chauncey Brewer,[6] son of Isaac,[5] was born in 1776 and died in 1845; married Asenath Mandaville, born in 1784, died in 1868. Children:

Mary,[7] born 1803; married George Waid.
Daniel,[7] born 1805; died 1884.
James,[7] born 1808; died 1885.
Isaac,[7] born 1810; died 1897; married first, Angeline Clark; second, Catharine Dempsey.

Sybil,[7] born 1812; died 1873.
Lyman,[7] born 1814; died 1871.
Catharine,[7] born 1817; married Robert Barton; died 1903.
John M.,[7] born 1820; married Abbie Cottrell; died 1889.
Pliny,[7] born 1822; married Ellen Whittemore; died 1903.

Daniel Brewer,[7] son of Chauncey,[6] was born in 1805 and died in 1884. He married Sarah K. Miller, born 1807, died 1871, daughter of Moses and Lucy (Jones) Miller. (See Miller Gen.) Children:

Harriet Sarah,[8] born 1831.
Mary Jane,[8] born Dec. 31, 1832; married March 29, 1854, Benjamin F. Burr. (See Burr Gen.)
Melissa P.,[8] born 1835; married in 1860, Marvin Henry King. (See King Gen.)
Amarilla C.,[8] born 1837; died 1893.
Daniel W.,[8] born 1839; died 1839.
Angenette D.,[8] born 1840.
John D.,[8] born 1843; died 1906.
Lucy Jones,[8] born 1846; married Arthur D. King. (See King Gen.)

Harriet Sarah Brewer,[8] daughter of Daniel,[7] was born in 1831; married in 1855, Coleman M. Walker, born in 1831, died 1909. Children: A son who died young,[9] Jennie B.,[9] Edward C.,[9] Sarah M.[9]

Angenette D. Brewer,[8] daughter of Daniel,[7] was born in 1840; married John Coash in 1858. He served in the Civil War and died in Libby Prison. Children: Hattie,[9] Louis.[9]

John Daniel Brewer,[8] son of Daniel,[7] was born in 1843 and died in 1906. He married Lillian Seymour, born 1850, died 1908. Children: Sadie A.,[9] Charles H.,[9] Abbie C.[9] (born 1874; died 1909), Allen S.,[9] Earl J.[9]

THE BROWNING FAMILY.
(Von Brünig, De Bruni.)

Nathaniel Browning,[1] the founder of the family in New England, was born in London, England, about 1618. His mother, Elizabeth Browning, was born about 1599; she was married about 1615. There were two children: Samuel, born in 1615, and Nathaniel, who came to America in 1640 and landed in Boston, then proceeded to Portsmouth, R. I. The first mention of Nathaniel in Rhode Island was in 1645, when he purchased a house and lands. He married about 1650, Sarah Freeborn, daughter of William Freeborn of Portsmouth. In 1654, Nathaniel was made a freeman. They had two children:

William,[2] born about 1651.

Jane,[2] born about 1655. She married James Sweet and they had eight children.

William Browning,[2] son of Nathaniel,[1] was born about 1651; married in 1687, Rebecca Wilbur, daughter of Samuel and Hannah (Porter) Wilbur. They had five children.

William Browning,[3] son of William,[2] was born at North Kingston, R. I., July 29, 1693, and died Feb. 11, 1733. His first wife was Mary Freelove and they had one child. He married second, August 5, 1728, Mary Wilkinson of Westerly, R. I. They had seven children.

John Browning,[4] son of William,[3] was born July 26, 1733, at South Kingston, R. I., and died in Charlestown, R. I., June 19, 1770. He married Jan. 1, 1754, Ann Browning, daughter of John and Ann (Hazard) Browning. They had five children.

John Browning,[5] son of John,[4] was born at Charlestown, R. I., Jan. 1, 1761, and died in 1797. He enlisted as a private, July 27, 1777, and served 34 days with General Stark in the expedition against Bennington, Vt. He married Mary Clarke in 1784. They had four children.

Ephraim Browning,[5] son of John,[4] was born Jan. 16, 1763, at Charlestown, R. I. He married first, Eunice Browning; second, Rebecca Clark, daughter of Judge Gideon Clark, on March 1, 1787, by whom he had eight children. He removed from Rhode Island to Colrain, Mass., and bought a farm in the east part of that town, where Horace Browning now lives. He conducted an inn in Greenfield for a time, but returned to Colrain and died there April 13, 1819. His widow died Dec. 6, 1830.

John Clark Browning,[6] son of Ephraim,[5] was born in Colrain, Sept. 20, 1801. He married Nov. 7, 1830, Joanna Peck, daughter of Abraham Peck. They had eight children. In 1838 he moved to Leyden, in 1845 to Chicopee, and in 1869 to Ludlow Center, where he died March 8, 1876. His widow died Nov. 1, 1898. Children:

Louisa,[7] born Sept. 16, 1831; married —— Chandler. They had one son, Wilson Browning Chandler.[8]

Fidelia,[7] born Nov. 25, 1833; died Aug. 10, 1858.

Elizabeth,[7] born June 4, 1836; married first, a Mr. Megrath; second, a Mr. Needham.

Joanna,[7] born Jan. 3, 1839; died Sept. 15, 1841.

Arabella,[7] born Nov. 17, 1840; died April 21, 1868.

Ansel W.,[7] born Oct. 10, 1843; died Sept. 1, 1895.

Latham C.,[7] born March 4, 1846; died July 11, 1874.

Charles S.,[7] born July 7, 1854; married Hannah C. Crowninshield, born June 1, 1859, daughter of Caleb and Lucy (Lyon) Crowninshield. (See Crowninshield Gen.)

The Buell Family.

The Buell family of Ludlow was descended from William Buell (or Bewell) of Chesterton, Huntingdonshire, England, who came to New England about 1630 and settled at Dorchester, Mass., but removed a few years later to Windsor, Conn., where the family took a prominent part in the early history of the town.

Chauncey Buell,[1] the first of the Ludlow Buells, was born March 1, 1793, at Somers, Conn., coming to Ludlow about 1820, where he died Sept. 12, 1853; married April 24, 1821, at Longmeadow, Anne Lathrop, born Dec. 24, 1794, at East Windsor, Conn., died Feb. 17, 1886. Children:

Anne Angeline,[2] born Jan. 26, 1822; died Dec. 14, 1904; married Nov. 2, 1842, Charles Sprague Bennett. (See Bennett Gen.)

Chauncey Lyman,[2] born March 29, 1824; married Jan. 23, 1853, Mary A. Chandler, who died Dec. 16, 1896.

Cordelia S.,[2] born March 27, 1827; died July 24, 1894; married Dec. 2, 1848, Henry Kendall.

Miriam C.,[2] born June 24, 1829; died Sept. 19, 1911.

Amanda F.,[2] born April 24, 1832.

Lucina M.,[2] born Feb. 1, 1836; married Feb. 3, 1857, John Dunbar.

Miriam C. Buell,[2] daughter of Chauncey,[1] was born June 24, 1829, and died Sept. 19, 1911; married Dec. 2, 1848, Austin F. Newell. Children:

Celia A.,[3] born March 19, 1853.
Leslie A.,[3] born Nov. 29, 1854; married July 9, 1902, Minnie A. Pepper.
Estella M.,[3] born Dec. 21, 1857.
Thankful A.,[3] born Nov. 1, 1863; died Feb. 5, 1894; married William Potter.
Winifred E.,[3] born July 27, 1871.

Celia A. Newell,[3] daughter of Miriam C. Buell,[2] was born March 19, 1853; married March 3, 1875, Hiram S. Ranney. Children:

Howard A.,[4] born May 27, 1880.
Clayton N.,[4] born Oct. 7, 1894.

Estella M. Newell,[3] daughter of Miriam C. Buell,[2] was born Dec. 21, 1857; married Oct. 19, 1886, Asaph S. Barstow. Children:

Harold D.,[4] born Jan. 2, 1888.
Miriam A.,[4] born June 16, 1890.
Florence,[4] born Sept. 17, 1892.

Winifred E. Newell,[3] daughter of Miriam C. Buell,[2] was born July 27, 1871; married Oct. 19, 1896, Walter Shaw. Children:

Everett Walter,[4] born Aug. 20, 1897.
Arthur Newell,[4] born Oct. 15, 1899.
Doris Evelyn,[4] born July 11, 1904.
Leslie Rupert,[4] born Feb. 12, 1910.

The Burley Family.

John Burley,[1] the founder of this family in America, was born in England.

Samuel Burley,[2] son of John,[1] was born Sept. 22, 1745.

Abner Burley,[3] son of Samuel,[2] was born April 2, 1776, and died Feb. 14, 1859; married first, May 5, 1805, Louisa Cleveland, who died March 20, 1824. Children:

Abner C.,[4] born June 11, 1807.
Benjamin A.,[4] born Jan. 13, 1811.

Louisa A.,[4] born Feb. 15, 1815.
Abner Burley[3] married second, Feb. 1, 1826, Deborah Hawse. She died June 3, 1869. Children:
Joseph,[4] born Jan. 11, 1827.
Elizabeth,[4] born June 23, 1829.
Jacob,[4] born April 26, 1834.

Jacob Burley,[4] son of Abner,[3] was born April 26, 1834, in Monson, and died April 13, 1908, in Ludlow. He was a soldier in Company G, 46th Regiment, Mass. Volunteers, and fought in the Civil War. He married Feb. 14, 1858, in Monson, Harriet M. Mitchell, born July 16, 1840, in Ware, daughter of Warner and Phœbe (Priest) Mitchell. Children:
Adin M.,[5] born Dec. 13, 1858.
Aimee J.,[5] born July 15, 1862; died Aug. 10, 1864.
Jesse L.,[5] born Jan. 26, 1866; died April 18, 1867.
Mary E.,[5] born May 5, 1867.
Joseph O.,[5] born July 26, 1882.

The Burr Family.

In 1630, three brothers, Jehu, Benjamin, and Rev. Jonathan Burr, came from England in Winthrop's fleet.

Benjamin Burr[1] settled in Roxbury, Mass. He was the ancestor from whom the Burrs in Ludlow descended. He came from Roxbury in 1635, and was one of the founders of Hartford, Conn. He was married and had four children.

Samuel Burr,[2] son of Benjamin,[1] married Mary Bazey(?). They had six children.

Jonathan Burr,[3] son of Samuel,[2] married Abigail Hubbard. They had six children.

Jonathan Burr,[4] son of Jonathan,[3] married Elizabeth Belding. They had three children.

Jonathan Burr,[5] son of Jonathan,[4] was born in 1740 and died in 1807; married in 1763, Priscilla Freeman, born 1745, died 1830. They came from East Windsor, or Ellington, Conn., to Ludlow about 1771. They settled east of

Warren D. Fuller's sawmill on a road formerly extending by the mill. He bought the mill privilege and equipments, and it was called the Burr mill. They were buried in the First Church Cemetery. Children:

Noadiah,[6] born 1764; died 1817. He was a Revolutionary soldier. He removed to New York.

Timothy,[6] born 1767; died 1859; married Hannah Gorham. He removed to New York state. Children: Billy Graham,[7] born 1790; Hannah,[7] born 1792; Betsey,[7] born 1794; Charles,[7] born 1797; Halsey,[7] Hart,[7] Barton,[7] Almira.[7]

Jonathan,[6] born 1769; married Mindwell Chapin. They had three children. They were both buried in the First Church Cemetery. Children: Ashbel,[7] born 1799; Estes,[7] born 1801; Polly,[7] born 1803.

Freeman,[6] born 1771; died 1861; married Mary Goodell in 1798, Removed to New York state. Children: Matilda,[7] Maria,[7] Solomon,[7] Freeman,[7] Columbus,[7] Elmina,[7] Julena.[7]

Ansel,[6] born 1773; died 1843. He moved to New York state. Children: Emily,[7] Anna,[7] Ansel,[7] Eli.[7]

Ashbel,[6] born 1776; died 1861.

Sally,[6] born 1779; died 1863; married Roswell Tarbox. They lived in Granby. They had eight sons.

Mary, or Polly,[6] born 1782; married Simon Smith of East Lyme, Conn. They had five children.

Eli,[6] born 1784; married Cynthia Burchard.

Elizabeth, or Betsey,[6] born 1787; married Ezra Bennett of Chicopee Falls. They had ten children.

Ashbel Burr,[6] son of Jonathan,[5] was born 1776 and died 1861; married in 1803 Clarissa Sikes, born in 1782, died in 1848, daughter of John Sikes. (See Sikes Gen.) They are buried in the Center Cemetery. Children:

Lyman,[7] born 1805; died 1880.
Abigail,[7] born 1808.

Lyman Burr,[7] son of Ashbel,[6] was born in 1805 and died in 1880; married in 1828, Harriet Stebbins, born 1804 in Brattleboro, Vt., died 1895, daughter of Edward and Anne (Taylor) Stebbins. Children:

Harriet Eliza,[8] born 1829; died 1843.
Benjamin Franklin,[8] born July 6, 1831.

Martha Julena,[8] born 1836; died 1879; married Charles C. Goldsmith of Milford, Mass. No children.
Mary Hall,[8] born 1839; died 1841.

Abigail Burr,[7] daughter of Ashbel,[6] was born in 1808 and died in Sacramento, Cal., in 1874. She married P. Watson Burnett in 1829. They buried two children in Thorndike, Mass. In 1849 they went to California, their remaining six children going with them. All died and were buried in California.

Benjamin Franklin Burr,[8] son of Lyman,[7] was born July 6, 1831; married March 29, 1854, Mary Jane Brewer, born Dec. 31, 1832, daughter of Daniel and Sarah K. (Miller) Brewer. (See Brewer Gen.) Children:

A daughter,[9] born July 7, 1856; died July 7, 1856.
Frederick Lyman,[9] born Feb. 9, 1862.

Frederick Lyman Burr,[9] son of Benjamin F.,[8] was born Feb. 9, 1862; married Feb. 13, 1881, Fannie Eliza Fuller, born Feb. 22, 1860, daughter of Edmund and Eliza (Lyon) Fuller. (See Fuller Gen.) Children:

Julena Eliza,[10] born Sept. 28, 1881; married George Green Bennett. (See Bennett Gen.)
Frank Rood,[10] born Dec. 10, 1882.
Benjamin Frederick,[10] born March 31, 1891.
Ralph Brewer,[10] born Dec. 29, 1897.

Frank Rood Burr,[10] son of Frederick Lyman,[9] was born Dec. 10, 1882; married in 1909, Minnie H. Adolphson, born Nov. 11, 1883.

The Cady Family.

Abner Cady[1] came from Stafford, Conn. He had two sons, Amasa[2] and Abner.[2]

Amasa Cady,[2] son of Abner,[1] married Lovina Allen. Children:
Mary,[3] who married Benjamin Deland; no children.
Caroline,[3] who married John Burbank; one son.[4]
Marcus,[3] who was unmarried.
Jane,[3] married Frederick N. Leonard; one son,[4] one daughter.[4]
Jackson Cady,[3] born Oct. 29, 1823.

Jackson Cady,[3] son of Amasa,[2] was born Oct. 29, 1823; married in 1851, Lucy Caroline Sikes, born in 1831, daughter of Benjamin and Lucy (Brainard) Sikes. (See Sikes Gen.) Child:

Herbert J.,[4] born in 1855; died Aug. 8, 1856.

Abner Cady,[2] son of Abner,[1] was born in 1795 and died May 16, 1847; married Dimmis Dutton, born in 1799, died Oct. 3, 1847, daughter of Oliver and Judith (Hubbard) Dutton. (See Dutton Gen.) Child:

Zachariah,[3] died at the age of 16 years.

The Carver Family.

Robert Carver[1] was the Pilgrim progenitor of the Carver family of Granby. He was born in England about 1594; bought land in Marshfield, Mass., in 1638; was in the train band in 1643, and a freeman in 1644. He married Christian ———. He died in 1680, outliving his wife 22 years. If a well authenticated tradition is correct, he was a brother of John Carver, the first governor of Plymouth Colony. (See New England Historical and Genealogical Register, vol. 26, page 333.) From him the descent is as follows:

John Carver,[2] son of Robert,[1] was born in England in 1637 or 1638; lived in Duxbury, Mass.; married Nov. 4, 1658, Millicent Ford, daughter of William and Anna Ford. He died June 23, 1679.

David Carver,[3] son of John,[2] was probably born in Weymouth, Mass.; removed to Canterbury, Conn., in 1718; died there Sept. 14, 1727. The settlement of his estate is found in the Windham Probate Records. He married first, Ruth ———. They had two children, Ruth[4] and Samuel.[4]

Samuel Carver,[4] son of David,[3] was born in Weymouth, Mass., Nov. 4, 1704; died in Bolton, Conn., May 17, 1780. He removed, first, with his father to Canterbury, Conn., and to Bolton about 1735. The settlement of his estate is found in the Hartford Probate Records. He married Esther Church, born Nov. 2, 1710, daughter of Samuel and Elizabeth Church of Hartford. They had a son, David.[5]

GENEALOGIES

David Carver,[5] son of Samuel,[4] was probably born in Canterbury, Conn., tradition says in 1729. He bought land in Hebron, Dec. 27, 1750. With his three youngest sons he moved to Granby in 1794, where he died in 1805. He married in 1749, Amy Filer. Children:

Amy,[6] born 1751; married David Strong of Hebron; had six children.
David,[6] born 1753; had ten children; died 1813.
John,[6] born 1756; died 1784; childless.
Joseph,[6] born 1759; a Revolutionary soldier and died an English prisoner.
Aldrick,[6] born July 4, 1761; married Sept. 12, 1782, Asenath Tarbox; died 1828; had twelve children.
Jonathan,[6] born in Hebron, Conn., Nov. 1, 1763; died in Granby, Aug. 3, 1823.
Warren,[6] born in 1766; died June 29, 1841.
Aaron,[6] born Oct. 12, 1769; died in 1805.

Jonathan Carver,[6] son of David,[5] was born in Hebron, Conn., Nov. 1, 1763, and died in Granby, Aug. 3, 1823; married Elizabeth Horsford, born Nov. 13, 1768, died Sept. 14, 1837. Children:

Lewis H.,[7] born Jan. 8, 1794; died March 3, 1855.
Augustus,[7] born March 2, 1796; died May 10, 1880.
Amy,[7] born Oct. 8, 1798; died Dec. 4, 1855.
Mary,[7] born Feb. 15, 1802; died May 27, 1837.
Derrick O.,[7] born Oct. 27, 1804; died Nov. 29, 1850.
David,[7] born Dec. 23, 1807; died April 20, 1810.

Warren Carver,[6] son of David,[5] was born in 1766 and died in Granby, June 29, 1841; married first, Sally Stiles of Hebron and had one child, William[7]; married second, Eliza Phelps of Hebron and had two children, Reuben[7] and David.[7]

Aaron Carver,[6] son of David,[5] was born Oct. 12, 1769, and died in 1805; married Mrs. Jerusha (Kendall) Lyon, born Feb. 23, 1773, died Jan. 20, 1853, daughter of James and Jerusha (Beebe) Kendall, and widow of Gad Lyon. (See Kendall and Lyon Gens.)

Derrick Obadiah Carver,[7] son of Jonathan,[6] was born in Granby, Oct. 27, 1804; died Nov. 29, 1850, in Brattleboro, Vt.;

married Clarissa Ingalls, born Dec. 26, 1803, died March 3, 1885, daughter of Samuel and Nancy Ingalls. Children:

Mary E.,[8] born Feb. 22, 1839, in Granby; died Oct. 16, 1883.
Augustus Everett,[8] born July 27, 1840, in Granby.
Henry Ingalls,[8] born Dec. 27, 1841.

Henry Ingalls Carver,[8] son of Derrick Obadiah,[7] was born Dec. 27, 1841; married Ellen Martha Kendall, born Aug. 4, 1845, daughter of James W. and Martha (Loomer) Kendall. (See Kendall Gen.) Children:

Laura Etta,[9] born Aug. 17, 1871; married Howard M. White. (See White Gen.)
Elmer Henry,[9] born Oct. 15, 1873.
Lizzie Adelma,[9] born April 12, 1881.
Florence Ellen,[9] born July 8, 1886.
Leroy Loomer,[9] born Oct. 12, 1887; died Sept. 24, 1888.

Elmer Henry Carver,[9] son of Henry Ingalls,[8] was born Oct. 15, 1873; married June 4, 1896, Elizabeth May Anderson of West Boylston. Children:

Lucy Ellen,[10] born March 31, 1897.
Henry Emerson,[10] born Sept. 30, 1899.
Ralph Anderson,[10] born Dec. 26, 1902.
Wells Elmer,[10] born July 31, 1905.

Lizzie Adelma Carver,[9] daughter of Henry Ingalls,[8] was born April 12, 1881; married Sept. 20, 1905, John Emerson Anderson of Worcester. Children:

John Carver,[10] born Jan. 3, 1907.
Martha Alice,[10] born Sept. 10, 1909.

The Chapin Family.

Deacon Samuel Chapin,[1] the progenitor of this family in the United States, came to Springfield in 1642. He died Nov. 11, 1675. He married Cisily ——, who died Feb. 8, 1683. Children: Japhet,[2] Henry,[2] Catherine,[2] David,[2] Josiah,[2] Sarah,[2] Hannah.[2] The dates of birth are mostly unknown.

Japhet Chapin,[2] son of Deacon Samuel,[1] was born in 1642 and died Feb. 20, 1712; married first, July 22, 1664, Abilenah

Cooley, who died Nov. 17, 1710; married second, May 31, 1711, Dorothy Root. He probably resided at Milford, Conn. In the fight at Turners Falls, May 18, 1676, he took an active part. Children:

Samuel,[3] born July 4, 1665; died Oct. 19, 1729.
Sarah,[3] born March 16, 1668; married March 24, 1690, Nathaniel Munn.
Thomas,[3] born May 10, 1671; died Aug. 27, 1755.
John,[3] born May 14, 1674; died June 1, 1759.
Ebenezer,[3] born June 26, 1677; died Dec. 13, 1772.
Hannah,[3] born June 21, 1679; died July 7, 1679.
Hannah,[3] born July 18, 1680; died July 7, 1767.
David,[3] born Nov. 16, 1682; died July 7, 1772.
Jonathan,[3] born Feb. 20, 1685; died March 1, 1686.
Jonathan,[3] born Sept. 23, 1688; died Feb. 23, 1761.

Thomas Chapin,[3] son of Japhet,[2] was born May 10, 1671, and died Aug. 27, 1755. He married Sarah Wright, born in 1672, died July 26, 1770. Children:

Thomas,[4] born Jan. 2, 1694; died in 1781.
Japhet,[4] born March 16, 1697; died Feb. 8, 1786.
Abel,[4] born Jan. 28, 1700; died May 3, 1772.
Shem,[4] born Feb. 23, 1702.
Sarah,[4] born Feb. 18, 1708; married May 17, 1753, Luke Parsons.
Nathaniel,[4] born Aug. 9, 1711; died in 1745.
Bathsheba,[4] born Dec. 19, 1713; married first, April 2, 1745, Jacob Hitchcock; married second, Dr. Lamberton Cooper.
Jabez,[4] born April 3, 1716; died April 20, 1716.
Deborah,[4] born Oct. 31, 1719; married April 30, 1746, Eleazer Frary.
Martha,[4] born Dec. 5, 1724; died July 8, 1801; married Oct. 20, 1740, Samuel Wells.
Esther,[4] born Dec. 5, 1724; died Sept. 2, 1790; married first, Oct. 22, 1747, Noah Cook; married second, Deacon Nathaniel Horton.

Hannah Chapin,[3] daughter of Japhet,[2] was born July 18, 1680, and died July 7, 1767; married Dec. 3, 1703, John Sheldon of Deerfield. About three months after her marriage she was taken captive by the Indians and marched to Canada. Two years later she was redeemed and returned home.

Abel Chapin,[4] son of Thomas,[3] was born Jan. 28, 1700, and died May 3, 1772; married Jan. 9, 1720, Hannah Hitchcock, daughter of Luther and Elizabeth Hitchcock. She died April 12, 1778. Children:

Hannah,[5] born July 22, 1729; died in Dec., 1741.
Abiah,[5] born Sept. 3, 1731; married Samuel Smith.
Abel,[5] born April 18, 1734; died in Dec., 1741.
Jemima,[5] born Dec. 12, 1735; died Nov. 1, 1804; married Capt. Ephraim Chapin.
Elizabeth,[5] born Dec. 27, 1737; died in Dec., 1741.
Moses,[5] born Feb. 25, 1739; died May 19, 1771.

Moses Chapin,[5] son of Abel,[4] was born Feb. 25, 1739, and died May 19, 1771. He was taken prisoner at Lake George, January, 1757. He was a fine Latin scholar, and his Latin books still exist, besides his surveying instruments and a copy of "Love's Surveying," printed in London in 1760. He married Bethia Chapin, born in 1740, died Nov. 10, 1784, daughter of Phineas and Bethia Chapin. Their marriage was published Dec. 17, 1761. Children:

Moses,[6] born July 11, 1762; died Dec. 30, 1824.
Hadassah,[6] died Aug. 3, 1808.
Ashbel,[6] born Aug. 21, 1765; died July 21, 1840.
Editha,[6] born Aug. 27, 1767; died young.
Rufus,[6] born Sept. 3, 1770; died Aug. 13, 1777.

Ashbel Chapin,[6] son of Moses,[5] was born Aug. 21, 1765, in Chicopee, and died July 21, 1840. He was a farmer and captain of a military company. In his later years he was a cripple and confined to the house. He married Eleanor Van Horn, born in 1765, died Nov. 22, 1833, daughter of Abraham Van Horn. Children:

Orythia,[7] born Oct., 1794; died April 22, 1855.
Alvin,[7] born March 11, 1796; died Sept. 6, 1874.
Louisa,[7] born Aug., 1797; died March 11, 1850.
Ashbel,[7] born July, 1799; died June 18, 1801.
Titus,[7] born May, 1801.
Lysander,[7] born Jan. 5, 1804.

Alvin Chapin,[7] son of Ashbel,[6] was born in Chicopee, March 11, 1796, and died in Ludlow, Sept. 6, 1874. He married

May 7, 1829, Eunice Parsons, born Sept. 3, 1805, died Dec. 16, 1853, daughter of Luke and Esther (Jones) Parsons of West Springfield. Children:

Ashbel Parsons,[8] born July 11, 1830; died Oct. 31, 1888.
Julia Maria,[8] born July 4, 1832.
Andrew Jackson,[8] born Oct. 30, 1835; died Sept. 30, 1907.
Lester Van Horn,[8] born Feb. 25, 1840; died Sept. 28, 1870.

Ashbel Parsons Chapin,[8] son of Alvin,[7] was born in Chicopee, July 11, 1830, and died in Ludlow, Oct. 31, 1888. He married Susan A. Fuller, born Nov. 5, 1838, died March 16, 1908, daughter of Edmund W. and Almira (Jenks) Fuller. (See Fuller Gen.) Mr. and Mrs. Chapin were influential in securing the post office for Ludlow Center, and Mrs. Chapin became the first postmistress, an office she held for many years. Children:

Frederick,[9] born March 12, 1855; died Nov. 8, 1860.
Frankie Clifford,[9] born Nov. 14, 1861; died Jan. 14, 1862.
Louis Wilfred,[9] born Sept. 19, 1872.

Louis Wilfred Chapin,[9] son of Ashbel Parsons,[8] was born Sept. 19, 1872, in Ludlow. He is a teacher of the piano. He married June 21, 1900, Ada Elizabeth Alden, born April 22, 1869, daughter of Charles Wesley and Lura S. (Chapin) Alden. (See Alden Gen.)

Andrew Jackson Chapin,[8] son of Alvin,[7] was born Oct. 30, 1835; died Sept. 30, 1907. He married Anna C. Riese, daughter of Fred and Emilia Riese. Children: Emilia,[9] Anna,[9] Alvin Riese,[9] Florence C.,[9] Mabel,[9] Frank Chapin,[9] an adopted son.[9]

Shem Chapin,[4] son of Thomas,[3] was born Feb. 23, 1702; lived and died in Ludlow. He married Mrs. Anna Clark of Uxbridge, a widow. Their banns were published Dec. 4, 1752. She died in Hadley, aged 101 years and 8 months. Children:

Esther,[5] born June 17, 1754.
Job,[5] born Sept. 19, 1758.
Joel,[5] born Jan. 13, 1761.

Job Chapin,[5] son of Shem,[4] was born Sept. 19, 1758. He married Abiah Gilligan of Ludlow. Children:

Azuba,[6] who married Deacon Colton of Ludlow. They had three or four children.

Sybel,[6] who married first, a Mr. Fox. They had one child. She married second, Deacon Root of Greenwich. They had no children.

Aaron.[6]

Joel Chapin,[5] a clergyman, son of Shem,[4] was born Jan. 13, 1761. He died in Bainbridge, N. Y., in 1845. His marriage to Eunice Lucretia, daughter of Deacon Edward Chapin of Chicopee, was published Nov. 10, 1789. They had three children. He was a soldier in the Revolution; then a graduate of Dartmouth College in 1791. He settled as a minister in the Susquehanna valley.

The Chapman Family.

David Chapman[1] was born and died in Springfield. His wife was Sarah Howe. Children: Earl,[2] Albert,[2] Charles.[2]

Charles Chapman,[2] a merchant, son of David,[1] was born in Springfield, March 5, 1824, and died July 10, 1876. He married in Nov., 1845, Sarah Whittemore Popkins, born May 22, 1826, died Nov. 28, 1898, daughter of Stephen and Beulah (Bates) Popkins. Children:

Charles Albert,[3] born April 26, 1848.
Sarah Howe,[3] born July 3, 1852; died Dec. 5, 1871.
John Benjamin,[3] born July 16, 1855; died Dec. 6, 1909.
Martha Popkins,[3] born Feb. 28, 1858.
Edward Earle,[3] born Feb. 13, 1862.
Amelia Hopkins,[3] born Sept. 11, 1866.

Edward Earle Chapman,[3] a farmer and musician, son of Charles,[2] was born in Springfield, Feb. 13, 1862; a member of the school committee nine years; since 1890, member of quartet of Third Congregational Church in Chicopee, most of the time director. He married in Wilbraham, Dec. 6, 1883, Charlotte Elizabeth Corbin, born July 9, 1862, daughter of Charles A. and Lovisa (Lawson) Corbin. Children:

Charles Earle,[4] born Sept. 11, 1886; married Sept. 29, 1909, Mabel Cheney Johnson, daughter of A. Lincoln and Levia (Emmons) Johnson. (See Johnson Gen.)

Myron Edward,[4] born June 9, 1890; married March 29, 1911, Jeannette Florence Jones.
Isabelle Louise,[4] born Aug. 8, 1892.

THE HUGH CLARK FAMILY.

Hugh Clark[1] was born about 1613. He is first mentioned in the town records of Watertown in 1641, when the birth of his eldest son is recorded. He lived there about 20 years. His wife's name was Elizabeth. Children:

John,[2] born Oct. 13, 1641.
Uriah,[2] born June 5, 1644; admitted as a freeman, May 5, 1685.
Elizabeth,[2] born Jan. 31, 1648.

John Clark,[2] son of Hugh,[1] was born Oct. 13, 1641; received from his father in 1681, 67 acres of land in Newton, then called New Cambridge. He removed thither from Roxbury in the same year. This land was situated in Newton Center near the present site of the Newton Theological Seminary.

John Clark,[3] son of John,[2] was born in 1680. He married for his second wife, Elizabeth Norman of Boston. They had several children.

Isaac Clark,[4] the fifth child of John,[3] was born Oct. 19, 1707, and died June 22, 1730. He was selectman of Newton. He married Ann Peirce of Dorchester, who died in 1748.

John Clark,[5] son of Isaac,[4] was born July 21, 1730. He lived in Framingham and later in Hopkinton, where he died in 1783. He married Aug. 7, 1749, Experience Wilson of Newton, daughter of Samuel and Experience (Trowbridge) Wilson.

John Clark,[6] eldest son of Captain John,[5] was born June 7, 1750; married Elizabeth Norcross, daughter of Joseph and Hannah (Shepherd) Norcross of Weston.

Martha Clark,[6] daughter of Captain John,[5] married Sept. 16, 1790, Aaron Rice Clark of Barre.

The George Clark Family.

George Clark[1] came to Rutland in 1765. He was a soldier of the Revolution. He kept his final settlements after the war until they sold for $500, then he opened a store. He married in Sept., 1765, Elizabeth Rice, born in 1745, daughter of Quartermaster or Captain Aaron and Elizabeth (Bullard) Rice. (See Rice Gen.) Children: Patty,[2] Sally,[2] and Aaron Rice.[2]

Aaron Rice Clark,[2] son of George,[1] married first, Sept. 16, 1790, Martha Clark, daughter of John and Experience (Wilson) Clark. (See Hugh Clark Gen.) Children:

William,[3] who married Elizabeth Root, daughter of Timothy and Dorothy (Shumway) Root. (See Root Gen.)
Elijah.[3]
Charles.[3]
Sophia.[3]
George,[3] born in Rutland, May 27, 1792.
Moses,[3] born Jan. 24, 1803; died March 24, 1872.
    Aaron Rice Clark[2] married second, Jerusha Andrews.

George Clark,[3] son of Aaron Rice,[2] was born May 27, 1792, and died Oct. 9, 1876; married Oct. 5, 1817, Cynthia Root, born Oct. 30, 1801, died Aug. 9, 1875, daughter of Timothy and Dorothy (Shumway) Root. (See Root Gen.) Children:

Caroline,[4] born April 10, 1819; died Nov. 16, 1839.
Franklin,[4] born Jan. 24, 1821; died Dec. 26, 1896.
John,[4] born Jan. 29, 1827; died May 8, 1890.
George Root,[4] born Oct. 6, 1834; died May 5, 1893.
Maria Cynthia,[4] born Aug. 29, 1841.

George Root Clark,[4] son of George,[3] was born Oct. 6, 1834, and died May 5, 1893; married Oct. 2, 1867, Pamelia Jones, born Feb. 5, 1838, daughter of Simeon and Mary (Chapin) Jones. (See Jones Gen.) Children:

Martha Gray,[5] born April 8, 1869.
Alice Maude,[5] born July 25, 1870.
Mary Eliza,[5] born Nov. 5, 1875.

Alice Maude Clark,[5] daughter of George Root,[4] was born July 25, 1870; married June 3, 1896, Everett Dwight Francis. Children:

Helen,[6] born May 10, 1897.
Dwight Clark,[6] born April 30, 1899.

Moses Clark,[3] son of Aaron Rice,[2] was born Jan. 24, 1803, and died March 24, 1872; married Oct. 7, 1824, Lovey Adams. Children: Caroline,[4] Mary,[4] Moses.[4]

The William Clark Family.

Noah Clark[1] was born in Northampton, Mass., in 1719, and died about 1790. He married Rachel Phelps, daughter of Samuel Phelps of Northampton, and later removed to Granby. Children:

Rachel,[2] born Dec. 14, 1745.
Gad,[2] born Feb. 17, 1747.
Ancaziah,[2] born Nov. 26, 1748.
Rufus,[2] born Feb. 22, 1751.
Eunice,[2] born April 27, 1753.
Rhoda,[2] born Aug. 28, 1755.
Esther,[2] born Aug. 28, 1757.
Kezia,[2] born May 21, 1759.
Noah,[2] born April 27, 1762.

Noah Clark,[2] son of Noah,[1] was born April 27, 1762; moved to Ludlow soon after 1808, and settled on the farm now owned by George N. Hubbard. He married Mary Butterfield of Granby or Springfield. Children:

Ruth,[3] born April 21, 1786; married Amos Ferry of Granby.
Sylvester,[3] born June 5, 1788.
Nancy,[3] born June 2, 1793.
Joel,[3] born April 19, 1796.
Alva,[3] born Nov. 16, 1800; died in 1811.
Joshua,[3] born Jan. 16, 1808; died 1889.
Mary,[3] birth date unknown; married a Mr. Tower of Hadley.

Joel Clark,[3] son of Noah,[2] was born April 19, 1796; married Jerusha Pease. Children:

Sarah Orcutt,[4] born Aug. 1, 1826; died May 21, 1898; married first, John Clark; married later, a Mr. Keeney.
William Pease,[4] born July 22, 1830; died Feb. 28, 1910.
Jane A.,[4] born Aug. 26, 1832; died April 25, 1907; married Luman Bartlett.

William Pease Clark,[4] son of Joel,[3] was born July 22, 1830, and died Feb. 28, 1910. He is perhaps the best known of this branch of the family, as he lived in Ludlow almost continuously for 70 years. He married May 21, 1851, Lydia Ann Edson of Wilbraham, who died Dec. 3, 1889. Children:

William Merrick,[5] born Sept. 1, 1853. He went West when 16 years old, first to Michigan, where he engaged in railroading, then to the Black Hills in Dakota, finally settling in Idaho.

Lydia Ann,[5] born March 1, 1857; died Jan. 12, 1860.

Edwin Edson,[5] born March 21, 1862; married in Ludlow and lived there for many years, but in 1890 moved to Meadows, Idaho.

Clifford Pease,[5] born Feb. 13, 1872.

Clifford Pease Clark,[5] son of William Pease,[4] was born Feb. 13, 1872; married Sept. 7, 1898, Louise Jane Earle. Child:

Carita Louise,[6] born Feb. 16, 1900.

Joshua Clark,[3] son of Noah,[2] was born Jan. 16, 1808, and died in 1889; married first, Abigail Rumrill; married second, Lucy A. Aldrich. Children: Frederick[4] and Eugene.[4] He married third, Charlotte M. Lyon, born Aug. 5, 1842, daughter of Solon and Hannah (White) Lyon. (See Lyon Gen.) Child: Alva L.[4]

Alva L. Clark,[4] son of Joshua,[3] was born May 23, 1878; married Sept. 24, 1903, Alice M. Page, born April 19, 1876. Child:

Bertha C.,[5] born Sept. 18, 1905.

The Cleaveland Family.

David Cleaveland[1] was born in Canterbury, Conn., June 12, 1776, and died in Ludlow, Sept. 18, 1838; married March 1, 1793, Aurilla Brown, born Aug. 27, 1774, died April 4, 1809, in Shutesbury. Children:

David,[2] born June, 1799.
Cyrus,[2] born April 3, 1800.
Hiram,[2] born Aug. 17, 1801.
Aurilla,[2] born Dec. 3, 1803.
Almira,[2] born Oct. 17, 1806.

Cyrus Cleaveland,[2] son of David,[1] was born in Palmer, April 3, 1800, and died at Ludlow, April 23, 1856; married in Wilbraham, Feb. 6, 1826, Eleanor Plumley, born April 25, 1808, died Feb. 19, 1900, daughter of Isaac and Tamson (Barrows) Plumley of Wilbraham. Children:
Eleanor L.,[3] born Dec. 23, 1828.
Tamson A.,[3] born Oct. 15, 1832.
Sally M.,[3] born Aug. 17, 1836.
Cyrus N.,[3] born June 14, 1840.
Cyrus C. W.,[3] born Dec. 31, 1845.
Alice A.,[3] born Feb. 19, 1853, in Ludlow; married Dec. 9, 1869, Andrew E. C. Bartlett of Belchertown. (See Bartlett Gen.)

The Timothy Clough Family.

Timothy Clough[1] was the first of the name in Ludlow. Children:
Uriah,[2] born 1757; died 1832.
Jonathan.[2]

Uriah Clough,[2] son of Timothy,[1] was born in 1757 and died in 1832; married Polly Orcutt, born 1759, died 1837. Children:
Huldah,[3] born 1780; married a Mr. Moffit.
Uriah,[3] born 1783; died 1784.
Uriah,[3] born 1785.
Mordecai,[3] born 1787; died 1831.
Gaius,[3] born 1789.
Mary,[3] born 1791.
Lydia,[3] born 1793; married Seymour Talmage.
Joseph,[3] born 1797; died 1834.
Seth,[3] born 1799.

Mordecai Clough,[3] son of Uriah,[2] was born in 1787 and died in 1831; married Lucy Case. Children:
Mordecai,[4] born 1813.
Roselle,[4] born 1815.
Sarah,[4] born 1818.
Mary Ann,[4] born 1820.
Ambrose,[4] born 1822; died April 2, 1889.
Uriah,[4] born 1824.

Ambrose Clough,[4] son of Mordecai,[3] was born in 1822 and died April 2, 1889; married Nov. 24, 1843, Theodocia Parsons, who died Aug. 21, 1907, daughter of Zenas Parsons. Children:

Franklin F.,[5] born Feb. 27, 1850; died Jan. 1, 1871.
Lizzie C.,[5] born March 11, 1856; died Sept. 14, 1861.

Jonathan Clough,[2] son of Timothy,[1] had two sons, Dan[3] and Timothy.[3]

Dan Clough,[3] son of Jonathan,[2] had three children:
Desire,[4] born 1800.
Jonathan,[4] born 1802; died 1803.
Abner,[4] born 1805.

Timothy Clough,[3] son of Jonathan,[2] married Lucy ———. Children:
Abigail,[4] born 1792.
Susa,[4] born 1794.
Hannah,[4] born 1797.
Olive,[4] born 1801.
Candace,[4] born 1801.
Timothy,[4] born 1804.
Jonathan,[4] born 1806.
Daniel,[4] born 1808; died 1810.
Daniel,[4] born 1811.

The John Clough Family.

John Clough[1] married first, Sarah ———; married second, Lovisa ———. Children:
Sarah,[2] born 1796.
Kezia,[2] born 1798.
Charlotte,[2] born 1800.
Clarissa,[2] born 1802.
Lovisa,[2] born 1804.
Sophronia,[2] born 1805.
Nancy,[2] born 1811.
Ann J.,[2] born 1814.
John,[2] born 1816.
Mary,[2] born 1818.

The Cooley Family.

Sumner Cooley[1] married in 1829, Caroline Munger, born May 20, 1811, daughter of Stillman and Susannah (Lane) Munger. (See Munger Gen.) Children:

GENEALOGIES 383

Calvin S.,[2] born 1831; died 1879.
Ariel,[2] born 1833.
William,[2] born 1839.

Calvin S. Cooley,[2] son of Sumner,[1] was born in 1831 and died in 1879. He married in 1852, Harriet Robbins, born 1836. Children:
Delia V.,[3] born 1854; died 1854.
Lucy M.,[3] born 1855; married Charles A. White. (See White Gen.)
Merrick H.,[3] born 1857.
George E.,[3] born 1859.
Carrie B.,[3] born 1867.
Edward S.,[3] born 1870; died 1893.
Gracie E.,[3] born 1875; died 1877.
Amy,[3] born 1878.

Merrick H. Cooley,[3] son of Calvin S.,[2] was born in 1857; married in 1884, Isabella E. Alden, born May 19, 1859, daughter of Orsamus and Eliza Ann (Lemmon) Alden. (See Alden Gen.)

George E. Cooley,[3] son of Calvin S.,[2] was born in 1859; married in 1882, Annie A. Jagger, who died in 1902. Children:
Ernest W.,[4] born 1884.
Edna M.,[4] born 1887; married in 1905, E. Leonard McChesney. They have one son, Herbert L.,[5] born 1907.

Carrie B. Cooley,[3] daughter of Calvin S.,[2] was born in 1867; married in 1888, Vila A. Shaw. Children:
Edward,[4] born 1891; died 1893.
Ethel L.,[4] born 1895.
Clarence,[4] born 1897.
Marion E.,[4] born 1909.

Amy Cooley,[3] daughter of Calvin S.,[2] was born in 1878; married in 1898, Mahlon Foskit. Children:
Edward,[4] born 1903; died 1903.
Eda H.,[4] born 1906.
George L.,[4] born 1909.

The Crowninshield Family.

Caleb Crowninshield[1] was born in Chesterfield, N. H., Aug. 10, 1828. He came to Ludlow and married Feb. 12, 1849, Lucy Lyon, born April 4, 1827, died June 19, 1887, daughter of Solon and Hannah (White) Lyon. (See Lyon Gen.) On Sept. 5, 1861, Mr. Crowninshield enlisted in the U. S. Army for three years as a member of the 27th Regiment, Mass. Volunteers. He was discharged Dec. 22, 1863, but re-enlisted, was captured, and taken to Andersonville prison, where he died Sept. 15, 1864. Children:

Emma Eliza,[2] born April 15, 1850; married E. T. Wood.
Charles C.,[2] born Dec. 7, 1851; married Lucy Snay.
Viola J.,[2] born Jan. 9, 1854; died Oct. 29, 1855.
George H.,[2] born Aug. 27, 1856; married Elsie Davis.
Hannah C.,[2] born June 1, 1859; married C. S. Browning. (See Browning Gen.)
Harriet A.,[2] born March 14, 1861; died Sept. 29, 1861.
Hattie E.,[2] born Nov. 1, 1864; married Rufus Lane.

The Damon Family.

The Damon family is an old English family dating back to the thirteenth century. Originally of French descent, some authorities claiming that the founder of the family went to England with William the Conqueror. A coat-of-arms bearing the motto, "Pro rege, pro lege, pro grege," would indicate that they were a family of standing. The name is variously spelled Damon, Demond, Daming, Damond, Daymon, and many others. There were three families of the early settlers of this name, the Reading, the Wayland, and the Scituate. **Deacon John**[1] founded the Reading; **Thomas**,[1] the Wayland; and **John**,[1] the Scituate family. The family in Ludlow are descendants of Thomas[1] of Wayland. His name first appears on the records of Reading in 1681. It is believed that he left the north of England about 1650, and went to Stoneham, not far from the home where his son Thomas[2] afterwards lived in South Reading.

Thomas Damon[1] was born Jan. 31, 1659, and died Oct. 20, 1723; married May 16, 1683, Lucy Ann Emerson, daughter of Rev. Josiah Emerson. Children: Lucy Ann,[2] Joseph,[2] Ebenezer,[2] Thomas,[2] Elizabeth,[2] John,[2] Hannah,[2] Mehitable,[2] Mary,[2] Abigail.[2]

John Damon,[2] son of Thomas,[1] was born May 10, 1709; went to Brookfield, and in 1745 bought land in Warren. He was a private in the same company with his son Peter. He married —— Gleason. Children: Peter,[3] John,[3] Jude.[3]

Peter Damon,[3] son of John,[2] was born in Warren in 1740 and died Nov. 27, 1818. He went from Warren to Ludlow and his three youngest children were born there. In 1794, Peter Damon's land in Ludlow was joined to Granby and taxed for school purposes. His house stood partly in Granby and partly in Ludlow, and until recently was owned by Alonzo C. Warner. In 1816, Mr. Damon gave the property in Granby to his son Eli. Peter Damon was corporal in Capt. Josiah Putnam's company and Col. Jedediah Foster's regiment, which marched to Roxbury, April 21, 1775, in response to the alarm from Lexington. Peter Damon married Aug. 9, 1766, Lydia Putnam, born in 1744, died May 28, 1809, daughter of Capt. Josiah Putnam and niece of Gen. Israel Putnam. Children:

Lucinda,[4] born Nov. 25, 1767; married Sherwood Beebe. (See Beebe Gen.)
Lydia Putnam,[4] born July 10, 1769.
Asa,[4] born April 21, 1771; died Aug., 1849.
Pattie,[4] born Jan. 30, 1773.
Henry,[4] born May 6, 1775; died March 9, 1851.
Sally,[4] born 1777, in Ludlow.
Roxy,[4] born 1779, in Ludlow.
Eli,[4] born 1783, in Ludlow; died in Aug., 1826.

Lydia Putnam Damon,[4] daughter of Peter,[3] was born July 10, 1769, in Warren; married Orlando Chapin. Children:
Orlando.[5]
Horatio.[5]
Lyman,[5] married first, Amelia Simms West; married second, Helen Simms West.
Philo,[5] married Laura Ferry.

Asa Damon,[4] son of Peter,[3] was born in Warren, April 21, 1771, and died Aug., 1849; married Catherine Wright, born in 1773, died May 24, 1848. Child:
Eliza Damon,[5] born 1806; died March 12, 1833; married in 1827, Nason Fifield. (See Fifield Gen.)

Henry Damon,[4] son of Peter,[3] was born May 6, 1775, in Warren, and died March 9, 1851; married Ruby Winchester, born in 1794, died in 1864. Children:

Dexter,[5] born March 4, 1813; died Sept. 29, 1884. (See Biography.)

Austin,[5] whose children were Charles,[6] George,[6] Herbert,[6] and Ruby.[6]

Alden P.,[5] born 1821; died 1882. Children: James,[6] Dell,[6] Maud,[6] Etta,[6] Henry.[6]

Andrew,[5] whose children were:
Lucinda,[6] born 1827; died 1859.
Lowell,[6] born 1831; died 1883.
Lovira,[6] married Dr. Purrington.
Elmira.[6]

Dexter Damon,[5] son of Henry,[4] was born March 4, 1813, and died Sept. 29, 1884; married Nov. 26, 1846, Harriet Matilda Frank, in Kirtland, Ohio. Children:

Henry Dexter,[6] born Nov. 7, 1847.
James Frank,[6] born Feb. 24, 1849.
Libbie Matilda,[6] born March 21, 1855.
Byron Winchester,[6] born July 18, 1859.

Henry Dexter Damon,[6] son of Dexter,[5] was born Nov. 7, 1847; married Nov. 21, 1871, Luella Brown Arnold, whose parents were natives of Rhode Island. Children: two daughters.

James Frank Damon,[6] son of Dexter,[5] was born Feb. 24, 1849; married Jan. 11, 1871, Mary Louise Kellogg. No children.

Libbie Matilda Damon,[6] daughter of Dexter,[5] was born March 21, 1855; married Oct. 18, 1877, Arnold C. Saunders, who died in Jan., 1908. Children: two sons and one daughter.

Byron Winchester Damon,[6] son of Dexter,[5] was born July 18, 1859; married in 1889, Dorothy Enbank. No children.

Sally Damon,[4] daughter of Peter,[3] was born in Ludlow in 1777; married Josiah Simms. Children: Lydia Putnam,[5] Sarah,[5] Jane,[5] Louise,[5] Duane,[5] Edward,[5] and Julia,[5] who married William Haughton.

Lydia Putnam Simms,[5] daughter of Sally,[4] married John West.
Children:
Helen,[6] married first, Aaron Smith; child, Sarah West[7]; married second, Lyman Chapin.
Amelia,[6] married Lyman Chapin.

Eli Damon,[4] son of Peter,[3] was born in Ludlow in 1783 and died in Aug., 1826; married Bathsheba Fletcher in 1813.
Children:
Lucy Damon,[5] born 1817; married Freeman M. Brown.
Laura,[5] born 1819; died 1905.
Edwin Putnam,[5] born 1822; died 1910; married Amelia Colburn.
Sarah,[5] born 1824; died 1868; married William Webber. Child: Ellen M. Webber.[6]

Jude Damon,[3] son of John,[2] was born in 1744 or 1745 and died Jan. 15, 1820; married Nov. 16, 1768, Ruth Putnam, born 1744-5, died 1820, daughter of Capt. Josiah Putnam.
Children:
Anna,[4] born March 23, 177–.
Isaac,[4] born May 1, 177–.
Archelas,[4] born Dec. 29, 177–.
Pearses,[4] born Oct. 1, 1776.
Daniel,[4] born March 18, 1779.
Thomas,[4] born June 1, 1781; died 1864.
John,[4] died March 27, 1823.
Perley.[4]
Polly.[4]

Thomas Damon,[4] son of Jude,[3] was born June 1, 1781, and died in 1864. He became a captain. He married Abigail Lincoln, born 1785, died Jan. 10, 1866. Children:
Pardon,[5] born Dec. 26, 1805.
George,[5] born Sept. 26, 1807.
Eliza,[5] born June 24, 1809.
Thomas,[5] born June 16, 1811.
William,[5] born Nov. 9, 1813.
Cassandra,[5] born June 6, 1818.
John,[5] born May 28, 1822.
Morgan,[5] born July 29, 1828.

George Damon,[5] son of Captain Thomas,[4] was born Sept. 26, 1807, and died April 3, 1860; married Sept. 1, 1831,

Mary Tyler, born Nov. 3, 1811, died Oct. 11, 1864.
Children:

Henry,[6] born March 26, 1834.
Harrison,[6] born Feb. 18, 1837; married June 12, 1865, Emeline M. Greene.
Mary,[6] born Feb. 20, 1839.
William,[6] born Aug. 7, 1841.
Isaac,[6] born July 14, 1843.
Frances,[6] born April 4, 1845.
Edward,[6] born Aug. 2, 1847.
John,[6] born June 4, 1850.
Charles,[6] born Sept. 7, 1852.
Martha,[6] born June 4, 1856.

The Davenport Family.

Paul Davenport.[1] Children: Daniel,[2] Alice,[2] Levi.[2]

Daniel Davenport,[2] son of Paul,[1] was born in Colrain in 1799 and died in 1889; married Martha Barnes. Children: David,[3] Tertius,[3] Thomas,[3] Orrin,[3] Eron,[3] Alonzo,[3] Hiram,[3] Emily,[3] Caroline,[3] Lucinda.[3]

Hiram Davenport,[3] son of Daniel,[2] was born June 11, 1839, in Colrain; married first, April 12, 1865, Maria Wealthy Pease, born March 4, 1841, daughter of Gaius and Wealthy (Wolcott) Pease. Children:

Alice Maria,[4] born Nov. 4, 1874, in Springfield.
Edwin Augustus,[4] born Oct. 13, 1882, in Ludlow.
   Hiram Davenport's[3] second wife was Hannah Dickinson.

The Davis Family.

Job Davis[1] was born in Somers, Conn., in 1759 and died May 9, 1807, in Rochester, N. Y. He was a Revolutionary soldier. He married Sarah Johnson, born 1769, died 1844. Children:

Chauncey Davis,[2] born Jan. 23, 1796; died April 6, 1854.
Sally,[2] born Feb. 14, 1798.
Submit,[2] born April 8, 1800.
Guy,[2] born Jan. 6, 1802.
Uriel,[2] born Aug. 27, 1805.
Job,[2] born March 5, 1807.

Chauncey Davis,[2] son of Job,[1] was born in Somers, Conn., Jan. 23, 1796, and died in Ludlow, April 6, 1854; married in 1824, Janett Melross, born in Willington, Conn., in 1804, died Oct. 12, 1888, daughter of William and Cynthia (Sanger) Melross. Children:

Sarah,[3] born Oct. 8, 1837; married —— Pease.
Hattie,[3] born 1839; married —— Clark.
John R.,[3] a soldier, 1861-1865, in Company K, 27 Mass. Regiment, died April 17, 1867.
Wilbur F.,[3] a soldier, 1861-1865, in Company K, 27th Mass. Regiment, died March 3, 1906.
Martha,[3] born July 4, 1844; married —— Sanderson.

The Day Family.

Robert Day[1] came from Ipswich, England, to Boston on the bark "Elizabeth" in 1634, when three years of age. He went first to Cambridge. In 1639 he was a resident of Hartford, Conn., being one of its first settlers.

Zechariah Day,[7] a descendant in the seventh generation from Robert Day,[1] was born in East Haddam, Conn., Sept. 4, 1800, and died Dec. 6, 1889. He came to Ludlow in 1834. In 1804 his father and grandfather, with their families, came up the river, while their stock was driven overland. On account of ill health, he lived in the South from 1825 to 1827 or 1828, when he came to Ludlow to live. He married May 7, 1834, Caroline C. Cargill, born Feb. 16, 1803, died May 7, 1887. Children:

Lucy Ann,[8] born April 8, 1835.
Benjamin Cargill,[8] born Sept. 11, 1836; died Jan. 18, 1838.
Charles Finney,[8] born July 17, 1838; died Nov. 3, 1838.
An infant son,[8] born Aug. 30, 1840; died Sept. 15, 1840.
John Q. A.,[8] born Nov. 7, 1842; died Aug. 21, 1843.

Lucy Ann Day,[8] daughter of Zechariah,[7] was born April 8, 1835; married in 1855, Joseph S. Perry of Worcester, born Nov. 3, 1828, died June 19, 1902. Child:

Lucy D.,[9] born 1865; died 1888; married in 1884, Frank C. Green, son of Rev. Jonathan Green, missionary to the Hawaiian Islands. They had two sons.

The Dutton Family.

Jeremiah Dutton[1] came from East Haddam, Conn., about 1776; married Damaris Beebe, daughter of Joshua and Hannah (Brockway) Beebe. (See Beebe Gen.) Children:

Sally,[2] married a Mr. Maxwell.
Betsey,[2] married a Mr. Van Horn.
Charlotte,[2] married a Mr. Eaton.
Oliver,[2] married Judith Hubbard.
Calvin.[2]
Cone.[2]

Oliver Dutton,[2] son of Jeremiah,[1] was born in 1760 and died in 1843; married Judith Hubbard. Children:

Lois,[3] born 1784; died 1844.
Lorin,[3] born 1792; died 1866.
Dimmis,[3] born 1799; died Oct. 3, 1847; married Abner Cady. (See Cady Gen.)
Asenath,[3] born 1802; died 1803.
Hubbard,[3] born 1806; died in March, 1883.

Hubbard Dutton,[3] son of Oliver,[2] was born in 1806 and died in March, 1883; married Adeline Smith, born 1812, died in May, 1883. Children:

Caroline,[4] born in April, 1835; died May 8, 1904; married Charles Sikes, born 1833, died Sept. 13, 1900.
Eliza,[4] born 1837 or 1838; died 1880; married Philo W. B. Alden. They had one son and four daughters.

The Estey Family.

Jacob Estey[1] died Dec. 4, 1845; married Lucy Williams of Roxbury. Children: Polly,[2] Lucy,[2] Jacob,[2] Joseph W.,[2] Lemuel,[2] Jeremiah,[2] Abigail,[2] Edward Payson.[2]

Joseph Williams Estey,[2] son of Jacob,[1] was born in Roxbury, March 16, 1790, and died Nov. 16, 1854; married Jan. 27, 1820, in Ludlow, Lucinda Stebbins of Brattleboro, Vt., who died Dec. 20, 1886. Children:

Joseph Williams,[3] born Jan. 14, 1821; died Oct. 24, 1843.
Edward Stebbins,[3] born Oct. 9, 1822; died July 10, 1900.
Samuel Bradlee,[3] born Oct. 4, 1824; died Oct. 31, 1888.
Eleazer Williams,[3] born Dec. 19, 1826; died May 20, 1906.

GENEALOGIES

Jacob Lemuel,[3] born Sept. 27, 1828; died Oct. 15, 1864.
Lucinda Rebecca,[3] born June 19, 1831.
Elizabeth Bradlee,[3] born Feb. 15, 1834; died March 10, 1840.
Catherine Abigail,[3] born Aug. 19, 1836; died April 29, 1864.
Alva Sikes,[3] born Dec. 18, 1839; died Sept. 22, 1865.

Edward Stebbins Estey,[3] son of Joseph Williams,[2] was born in Greenwich, Oct. 9, 1822, and died July 10, 1900. He served three years in the Civil War in Company G, 2d Heavy Artillery. He was constable and member of the school committee in Ludlow. He married Jan., 1847, in North Dana, Cordelia Augusta Morgan of West Springfield, who was born July 18, 1821, and died Aug. 6, 1893, daughter of Joseph Warren and Emma (Wolcott) Morgan. Children:

Emma Cordelia,[4] born Sept. 6, 1849; died Nov. 10, 1849.
Joseph Williams,[4] born Sept. 11, 1850.
Caleb Bradlee,[4] born Nov. 30, 1853.
Clara Ellen,[4] born Nov. 14, 1855.

Caleb Bradlee Estey,[4] son of Edward Stebbins,[3] was born in Greenwich, Nov. 30, 1853. He attended school in the Salem Academy about four years. He served as constable and special police for Ludlow. He married in Sterling, May 13, 1885, Izzora Elnora Stockwell, born Feb. 22, 1856, in Fitchburg, died Aug. 7, 1891, daughter of Calvin Lincoln and Maria (Wheeler) Stockwell. Children:

Bertha Maria,[5] born Aug. 29, 1887.
Mabelle Izzora,[5] born July 28, 1891.

THE FERRY FAMILY.

Clifford William Ferry[1] was born in Granby, Aug. 7, 1857. He has served the town as a member of the school committee and as assessor. He married April 2, 1879, in Granby, Anne Hayes Smith, born in Granby, Nov. 7, 1854, died Sept. 17, 1899, daughter of George and Julia (Ayers) Smith. Children.

William George,[2] born March 6, 1880.
Douglas Mills,[2] born March 16, 1882.
Rutherford Hayes,[2] born May 25, 1885.

Rutherford Hayes Ferry,[2] son of Clifford William,[1] was born in Granby, May 25, 1885. He was graduated from the Granby high school. He married June 23, 1910, in Ludlow, Sadie Agnes Tilley, born Sept. 1, 1886, daughter of Clarence and Mary (Chamberlain) Tilley. (See Tilley Gen.)

The Fifield Family.

The Fifield family was among the early settlers of Gilmantown, now Belmont, N. H. Some of the family received grants of land there and were soldiers in the Revolutionary War.

Benjamin Fifield[1] was born in 1774 and died in 1859; married Abigail Bachelor, who died in 1860. Children:

Nason,[2] born 1801.
Benjamin,[2] born 1803.
Ira,[2] born 1812; died 1893; moved from Gloucester to Ohio, thence to Canada.

Nason Fifield,[2] son of Benjamin,[1] was born in 1801 and died in 1859. He came to Ludlow, May 30, 1824. He married in 1827, Eliza Damon, born 1806, died March 12, 1833, daughter of Asa and Catherine (Wright) Damon. (See Damon Gen.) Children:

Adeline F.,[3] born July 4, 1829; married Stephen D. Pierce of Saugus.
Julia L.,[3] born April 7, 1831; married John W. Morgan of Brimfield.
Eliza D.,[3] born Feb. 28, 1833; married G. Yagla of Beloit, Wis.

Benjamin Fifield,[2] son of Benjamin,[1] was born in 1803 and died Aug. 12, 1879; married Theodate ———. Child:

Mary Jane,[3] married John Wardwell of Concord, N. H.

Ira Fifield,[2] son of Benjamin,[1] was born in 1812 and died in 1893; married Mary Billings. Children:

Mary Jane,[3] born 1839; died 1909; married Robert Bolton.
Benjamin,[3] born 1840; died 1896; married Marcia ———, in Canada.
Eugene,[3] born 1847; died 1895; married Lucy Bolton.

THE FISHER FAMILY.

Salem Fisher[1] married Amanda Barrett. Children:
E. Newton,[2] born Dec. 29, 1844.
Susan M.,[2] born Jan. 22, 1848; died Dec. 20, 1904; married May 1, 1873, A. E. Fuller. (See Fuller Gen.)

E. Newton Fisher,[2] son of Salem,[1] was born Dec. 29, 1844, in Belchertown. He married Oct. 26, 1869, Sarah Eliza Sikes, born in Ludlow, Oct. 26, 1848, daughter of Reuben and Eliza Ann (Keyes) Sikes. (See Sikes and Keyes Gens.) Children:
Alva Newton,[3] born Aug. 20, 1870; married Sept. 22, 1898, Grace Johnson of East Providence, R. I.
Ella Maria,[3] born Aug. 3, 1872.
Willis Sikes,[3] born Sept. 12, 1877.
Walter M.,[3] born Sept. 12, 1877; died Sept. 12, 1877.

Ella Maria Fisher,[3] daughter of E. Newton,[2] was born Aug. 3, 1872; married April 25, 1899, John O. Mosely, Jr., of West Springfield. Children:
John Ogden,[4] born April 27, 1900.
Esther,[4] born Aug. 18, 1901.

Willis Sikes Fisher,[3] son of E. Newton,[2] was born Sept. 12, 1877; married June 26, 1907, Lillian Clark of Springfield. Children:
Walter Clark,[4] born April 23, 1908.
Kenneth Sikes,[4] born Aug. 18, 1909.

THE FROST FAMILY.

Selah Frost[1] was born in 1784 and died in 1853; married in 1812, Anna Butler, born 1789, died 1854. Children:
Maria,[2] born 1814.
William,[2] born 1815.
Ephraim,[2] born 1817.
Samuel,[2] born 1819.
Margaret,[2] born 1822.
Mary,[2] born 1824.
Augustus,[2] born 1826.
Orrin,[2] born 1828.
Abigail,[2] born 1830.

Roxanna,[2] born 1832.

Harriet R.,[2] born 1834; married April 25, 1852, Lovinski White. (See White Gen.)

THE FULLER FAMILY.

Edward Fuller,[1] the founder of the family in Ludlow, was the son of Robert Fuller, and was baptized Sept. 4, 1575, in the parish of Redenhall, County of Norfolk, England. He came with his wife and son Samuel to Plymouth on the "Mayflower." His name appears in a compact which was drawn up in the cabin of the ship just previous to the landing at Cape Cod in Nov., 1620. He and his wife died in Plymouth in 1621. His son was Samuel.[2]

Samuel Fuller,[2] son of Edward,[1] was born in England in 1612. He grew up under the care of his uncle, Dr. Samuel Fuller, and lived in Barnstable. He married Jane Lathrop, daughter of Rev. John Lathrop of Scituate, the ceremony having been performed by Miles Standish, magistrate, "on ye fourthe daye of ye weeke, April 8, 1635." Samuel Fuller joined the church of Scituate, Nov. 7, 1636, by letter of dismission from the church of Plymouth. Children:

Hannah.[3]
Samuel,[3] born Feb. 11, 1637.
Elizabeth.[3]
Sarah,[3] born 1641.
Mary,[3] born 1644.
Thomas,[3] born 1651.
Sarah,[3] born 1654.
John,[3] born 1656.

Samuel Fuller,[3] son of Samuel,[2] was born Feb. 11, 1637; married Anna Matthew. Children:

Barnabas,[4] born 1659.
Joseph,[4] born 1661.
Matthew,[4] born 1664.
Benjamin,[4] born 1665.
Desire,[4] born 1667.
Sarah,[4] born 1669.

Matthew Fuller,[4] son of Samuel,[3] was born in Barnstable in 1664, and moved to Colchester, where he died in 1744; mar-

ried Patience Young, born 1670, died 1746, daughter of George and Hannah Young. Children:
Anna,[5] born 1693; married Isaac Putnam. (See Putnam Gen.)
Jonathan,[5] born 1696.
Content,[5] born 1698.
Jean,[5] born 1704.
David,[5] born 1706.
Young,[5] born 1708.
Cornelius,[5] born 1710.
Hannah,[5] born 1712.

Young Fuller,[5] son of Matthew,[4] was born in Barnstable in 1708; moved to Ludlow from Ellington, Conn., with his oldest son, Joshua, in 1767; died June 17, 1796. He married Jerusha Beebe, daughter of Jonathan and Bridget Beebe. Children:
Joshua,[6] born Sept. 9, 1731.
David,[6] born 1733.
Caleb,[6] born 1735.
Jerusha,[6] born July 30, 1737.
Lydia,[6] baptized Dec. 13, 1741.
Anne,[6] baptized March 15, 1747.

Joshua Fuller,[6] son of Young,[5] was born Sept. 9, 1731, in Colchester, Conn., and died in Monson, Oct. 6, 1810. He came to Ludlow in 1767. He married in Jan., 1753, Mercy Lathrop, born Oct. 1, 1736, died Jan. 15, 1827, daughter of Solomon and Susannah Lathrop. Children:
Elisha,[7] born April 8, 1754; died May 15, 1850.
Solomon Lathrop,[7] born Dec. 4, 1756.
Ezekiel,[7] born July 23, 1758; died Oct. 16, 1838.
Sarah,[7] born Dec. 28, 1762.
Lydia,[7] born May 11, 1765.
Benjamin,[7] born July 23, 1767.
Jonathan Beebe,[7] born Sept. 28, 1769.
Mariana,[7] born Nov. 19, 1773.
Olive,[7] born Feb. 13, 1777.

Elisha Fuller,[7] son of Joshua,[6] was born in Ellington, Conn., April 8, 1754, and died May 15, 1850. He served in a Hampshire County (Mass.) regiment at Ticonderoga in 1776-1777. He represented Ludlow in the General Court in 1808. He married first, Dec. 21, 1774, at Chatham-

Portland, Conn., Rebecca Waterman, who was born July 21, 1754, and died Aug. 19, 1796, daughter of Isaac and Mercy (Hall) Waterman. Children:

John,[8] born April 30, 1775.
Isaac,[8] born Oct. 30, 1776.
Joshua,[8] born April 4, 1778.
Susanna,[8] born April 21, 1780; died April 30, 1805; married Perley Munger. (See Munger Gen.)
Ely,[8] born Nov. 12, 1782.
Joel,[8] born Sept. 11, 1786.
Infant,[8] born March 17, 1788.
Asenath,[8] born June 16, 1789; died 1828; married Asahel Rood. (See Rood Gen.)
Samuel,[8] born March 25, 1791.
Martha,[8] born Oct. 30, 1793.
Waterman,[8] born Aug. 7, 1796.

Elisha Fuller[7] married second, in 1797, Sarah Cleveland, who died July 18, 1862, 87 years old. Children:

Henry S.,[8] born Dec. 11, 1798.
Rebecca,[8] born Jan. 16, 1803.
Zerah,[8] born Sept. 29, 1804.

John Fuller,[8] son of Elisha,[7] was born in Ludlow, April 30, 1775; married first, Bathsheba Colton, born Nov. 11, 1783. Children:

Walter,[9] born March 24, 1806.
Norman C.,[9] born March 24, 1808.
Edmund W.,[9] born Feb. 13, 1811.
Orra,[9] born May 13, 1813; married Justin Lombard. (See Lombard Gen.)

John Fuller[8] married second, June 10, 1815, Theodocia Capen. Children:

Lodesia,[9] born March 26, 1816.
Purchase,[9] born Nov. 3, 1817.
Marcia A.,[9] born Aug. 24, 1823; married David Kinsley Paine. (See Paine Gen.)

Edmund Warren Fuller,[9] son of John,[8] was born Feb. 13, 1811. He served the town two years as selectman; married Aug. 28, 1833, Almira Jenks, born Dec. 7, 1805, daughter of Shepherd Jenks. Children:

Warren Dwight,[10] born July 21, 1834.
Mary Ellen,[10] born Sept. 16, 1835.

George Albert,[10] born Dec. 27, 1836.
Susan Almira,[10] born Nov. 5, 1838; died March 16, 1908; married Ashbel Parsons Chapin. (See Chapin Gen.)
Martha Madelia,[10] born Nov. 27, 1839.
Emmeline Theodocia,[10] born May 4, 1841; married May 3, 1859, John L. Banister. (See Banister Gen.)
Sabra Jane,[10] born April 22, 1843.
William Albert,[10] born March 11, 1847.

Warren Dwight Fuller,[10] son of Edmund Warren,[9] was born July 21, 1834; served the town three years on the school committee, eleven years as town clerk, and one year as representative; married Nov. 4, 1863, Jane Electa Banister, born Dec. 16, 1838, daughter of Daniel K. and Harriet (Steele) Banister. (See Banister Gen.) Children:

Daniel Edmund,[11] born Jan. 5, 1865; died in Aug., 1865.
Herbert Emerson,[11] born July 18, 1867.
John Wilson,[11] born Jan. 29, 1871.

Herbert Emerson Fuller,[11] son of Warren Dwight,[10] was born July 18, 1867; married Cora May Downie. Child:
Pauline Downie,[12] born Sept. 20, 1899.

John Wilson Fuller,[11] son of Warren Dwight,[10] was born Jan. 29, 1871; married Elizabeth Dempsey. Child:
Dorothy,[12] born Feb. 16, 1900.

Henry Seymour Fuller,[8] son of Elisha,[7] was born in Ludlow, Dec. 11, 1798, and died March 15, 1886. He married in Ludlow, April 3, 1820, Esther Miller, born March 26, 1800, died Feb. 16, 1831, daughter of George and Esther (Cleveland) Miller. Children:
Esther Augusta,[9] born May 20, 1822.
Sarah M.,[9] born July 9, 1827.

Henry Seymour Fuller[8] married second, Oct. 27, 1831, Mary Needham Alden, born Sept. 13, 1811, died March 31, 1877, daughter of Josiah and Olive (Brown) Alden. She was a descendant from John Alden in the seventh generation. (See Alden Gen.) Children:
Mary N.,[9] born Aug. 1, 1832.
Henrietta S.,[9] born Dec. 15, 1833; married Edwin Chapin. Child:

Mary Emma Chapin,[10] who married Albert Banister. (See Banister Gen.)
Olivet B.,[9] born May 1, 1835.
Henry S.,[9] born Feb. 5, 1837.
Edward E.,[9] born May 25, 1839.
Emma A.,[9] born June 1, 1841.
Henry S.,[9] born Aug. 27, 1843.
Francis S.,[9] born April 27, 1846.
Fannie V. A.,[9] born Oct. 17, 1848.
Lillian E.,[9] born Sept. 22, 1850.
Hattie B.,[9] born Feb. 16, 1854.

Edward Everett Fuller,[9] son of Henry Seymour,[8] was born May 25, 1839, in Ludlow. He served eleven months in the Union army in the Civil War; represented the town in the Legislature in 1893; has occupied the offices of assessor, selectman, cemetery commissioner, and library trustee. On Nov. 20, 1861, he married in Wilbraham, Diantha Jane Prentice, born Dec. 8, 1839, in Millbury, daughter of James and Diantha (Joslyn) Prentice. Children:

Emma Jane,[10] born Sept. 16, 1864; married Feb. 2, 1888, Alfred Tuck Jones. (See Jones Gen.)
Etta Elizabeth,[10] born June 28, 1873; died March 10, 1874.
George Everett,[10] born Aug. 25, 1875.
Laura Gertrude,[10] born May 27, 1877.
Henrietta Evangeline,[10] born Dec. 1, 1882.

Ezekiel Fuller,[7] son of Joshua,[6] was born July 23, 1758, in Ellington, Conn. He was a Revolutionary soldier and enlisted for three years in the Continental army, serving in Captain Oliver's company, Colonel Greaton's regiment. He also served as a minuteman and as sergeant. He was placed on the pension rolls May 27, 1819. He died in Ludlow, Oct. 16, 1838. He married Mary Bartlett of Granby. She was born in 1762 and died May 26, 1852. Children:

Marania,[8] born Oct. 12, 1782.
Elijah,[8] born Aug. 26, 1784; died July 22, 1841.
Rachel,[8] born Oct. 17, 1786.
Polly,[8] born March 11, 1789.
Mercy,[8] born May 2, 1791.
Ezekiel,[8] born Feb. 25, 1794; died Sept. 5, 1877.

Lyman,[8] born Oct. 25, 1796.

Franklin,[8] born Oct. 3, 1799; married Joan Miller, daughter of Sylvester and Charlotte Little Miller. (See Miller Gen.)

Elijah Fuller,[8] son of Ezekiel,[7] was born in Ludlow, Aug. 26, 1784, and died July 22, 1841. He married first, Nov. 12, 1806, Polly Miller, born 1784, died March 11, 1824, daughter of Leonard and Mary (Sikes) Miller. (See Miller and Sikes Gens.) Children:

Mary S.,[9] born Jan. 29, 1808; died Nov. 11, 1882; married Jan. 30, 1830, Elisha A. Fuller, who died April 12, 1876.

Electa,[9] born Dec. 14, 1809; died Sept. 15, 1870; married Oct. 28, 1830, Daniel L. Atchinson.

Catherine,[9] born Feb. 19, 1812; died Jan. 26, 1849; married Carlo Kendall. (See Kendall Gen.)

Gilbert E.,[9] born Jan. 4, 1818; died July 24, 1874.

Harriet A.,[9] born Jan. 19, 1820; died Jan. 11, 1907; married May 25, 1843, David Tenney.

Gilbert Elijah Fuller,[9] son of Elijah,[8] was born Jan. 4, 1818, in Ludlow, and died July 24, 1874. He was fourth lieutenant of Company B, 10th Regiment of Light Infantry, in the Sixth Brigade and Third Division of the Massachusetts Militia; selectman of Ludlow for six years. He married first, April 24, 1841, in Ludlow, Eliza Ann Fuller, born June 28, 1818, died Sept. 1, 1846, daughter of Lyman and Parma (Barton) Fuller. Child:

Elijah G.,[10] born July 27, 1843; died Feb. 12, 1844.

Gilbert Elijah Fuller[9] married second, May 5, 1847, in Somers, Conn., Harriet Meacham, born July 19, 1822, died Jan. 15, 1900, daughter of Lyman and Naomia (Bliss) Meacham. Children:

Harriet E.,[10] born Nov. 23, 1848; married first, Sept. 16, 1869, William Albert Fuller, who died Aug. 9, 1888; married second, June, 1900, Arthur Wheelock.

Warren Gilbert,[10] born April 17, 1851.

Frederick Henry,[10] born June 10, 1855; died Feb. 14, 1857.

Sarah Amelia,[10] born Sept. 4, 1858; married first, Dec. 27, 1879, Stuart Dermot, died 1885; married second, April 25, 1889, Arthur O. Shepardson.

Warren Gilbert Fuller,[10] son of Gilbert Elijah,[9] was born April 17, 1851; married Dec. 24, 1872, Estella Maria Baggs, born

May 17, 1853, daughter of Amasa and Ann (Alexander) Baggs. Children:

Flora Ann,[11] born Nov. 11, 1874; died Sept., 1908; married Nov., 1893, Henry C. Walker. (See Walker Gen.)

Warren Meacham,[11] born Feb. 9, 1886.

Warren Meacham Fuller,[11] son of Warren Gilbert,[10] was born Feb. 9, 1886, and married Sept. 27, 1910, Alice Ella Munsell, born Feb. 24, 1884, daughter of Frank and Lizzie (Fuller) Munsell.

Ezekiel Fuller,[8] son of Ezekiel,[7] was born in Ludlow, Feb. 25, 1794, and died Sept. 5, 1877; married March 2, 1815, Lucy Rood, born Dec. 10, 1794, died March 27, 1878, daughter of Elias and Anna Rood. (See Rood Gen.) Children:

Elias Albert,[9] born March 17, 1816.
Edmund,[9] born May 22, 1818; died June 9, 1901.
Davenport Lambert,[9] born Feb. 28, 1823; died Nov. 17, 1897.
Henry Caleb,[9] born March 1, 1831; died Jan. 23, 1895.

Elias Albert Fuller,[9] son of Ezekiel,[8] was born March 17, 1816, in Ludlow, and died Feb. 5, 1886; married Nov. 24, 1838, Violate Miller, born May 16, 1815, died Sept. 22, 1892, daughter of Sylvester and Charlotte (Little) Miller. Children:

Lucy Ann,[10] born Dec. 4, 1839; died Nov. 15, 1911; married William H. Pease. They had three daughters.

Albert E.,[10] born March 6, 1852.

Albert E. Fuller,[10] son of Elias Albert,[9] was born March 6, 1852, in Ludlow; married first, in Belchertown, May 1, 1873, Susan M. Fisher, born Jan. 22, 1848, died Dec. 20, 1904, daughter of Salem and Amanda (Barrett) Fisher. (See Fisher Gen.) Children:

Edith A.,[11] born March 29, 1875.
Maude V.,[11] born April 9, 1877.
Frank A.,[11] born Dec. 20, 1878; died June 3, 1879.
George C. A.,[11] born July 27, 1883.
Ada B.,[11] born Sept. 18, 1886.

Albert E. Fuller[10] married second, Jan. 26, 1910, Harriette A. Bliss, born April 29, 1858.

George Clarence Albert Fuller,[11] son of Albert E.,[10] was born in Ludlow, July 27, 1883; married May 16, 1906, in Ludlow, Carrie J. Munsing, born April 19, 1883, daughter of Henry and Lillian (Brewer) Munsing. (See Munsing Gen.) Child:
Albert Henry,[12] born Aug. 22, 1908.

Edmund Fuller,[9] son of Ezekiel,[8] was born in Ludlow, May 22, 1818, and died June 9, 1901; married at Ludlow, April 27, 1843, Eliza Ann Lyon, born April 24, 1821, died July 7, 1893, daughter of David and Fannie (Wright) Lyon. (See Lyon Gen.) Children:
David Lyon,[10] born May 14, 1851.
Fannie Eliza,[10] born Feb. 22, 1860; married Feb. 13, 1881, Frederick Lyman Burr. (See Burr Gen.)

David Lyon Fuller,[10] son of Edmund,[9] was born in Ludlow, May 14, 1851; married first, Emma L. Baggs, born at Belchertown, Jan. 13, 1850, died Oct. 24, 1890, in Indian Orchard, daughter of Amasa and Ann (Alexander) Baggs. They had one daughter:
Mabel Louise Fuller,[11] born in Ludlow, Oct. 22, 1872.
David Lyon Fuller[10] married second, June 15, 1892, Clara E. Copeland, daughter of Oliver and Rebecca (Fulmer) Copeland.

Davenport Lambert Fuller,[9] son of Ezekiel,[8] was born in Ludlow, Feb. 28, 1823, and died in Indian Orchard, Nov. 17, 1897. He was graduated from the Ludlow schools and was a member of the Ludlow Militia. He married first, April 3, 1844, Susannah P. McClintic, born March 4, 1823, died Jan. 8, 1865. Children:
Frank Davenport,[10] born Jan. 14, 1849.
Ida Ellen,[10] born Jan. 5, 1852.
Davenport Lambert Fuller[9] married second, Nov. 14, 1865, Melina N. Charles, born March 11, 1836, daughter of Henry and Nancy (Parsons) Charles. Child:
Henry Charles,[10] born June 20, 1869; died Dec. 24, 1885.

Frank Davenport Fuller,[10] son of Davenport Lambert,[9] was born Jan. 14, 1849, in Ludlow. He was graduated from the Ludlow schools and Wilbraham Academy. He married May 10, 1876, in North Wilbraham, Mary E. Green, born

May 10, 1852, daughter of Job and Abbie E. (Mann) Green.

Henry Caleb Fuller,[9] son of Ezekiel,[8] was born March 1, 1831, in Ludlow, and died Jan. 23, 1895, in Springfield; married first, Martha M. Pease, who died July 6, 1864; married second, Mrs. Abbie R. Carroll, daughter of Aaron Howe, who died Dec. 18, 1909.

THE GATES FAMILY.

Ephraim Gates[1] was born June 25, 1750, in Palmer. He married May 21, 1789, Mary Hill, born May 13, 1765. Children: John,[2] Samuel,[2] Ephraim,[2] Rebekah,[2] Patience.[2]

John Gates,[2] son of Ephraim,[1] was born Sept. 17, 1789, in Palmer, and died Aug. 15, 1855. He married Dec. 4, 1814, Dorothy Root, born Jan. 3, 1790, in Ludlow, died Nov. 20, 1858, daughter of Timothy and Dorothy (Shumway) Root. Children:

George C.,[3] born Feb. 14, 1816.
Ann M.,[3] born May 1, 1818.
Sarah J.,[3] born Aug. 15, 1824.
Cynthia J.,[3] born Oct. 20, 1826.
John R.,[3] born Aug. 25, 1829.

John R. Gates,[3] son of John,[2] was born Aug. 25, 1829, in Ludlow, and died Feb. 6, 1896; married April 12, 1855, in Holyoke, Lucy A. Hill, born March 10, 1835, in Belchertown, died March 6, 1897, daughter of James and Mary (Arnold) Hill. Children:

George H.,[4] born Dec. 8, 1858.
Charles A.,[4] born Oct. 31, 1862.

George H. Gates,[4] son of John R.,[3] was born in Ludlow, Dec. 8, 1858; married May 4, 1887, in Ludlow Center, Katherine M. Pomeroy, born in South Amherst, Dec. 28, 1865, daughter of Edward P. and Katherine (Van Steenburgh) Pomeroy. Children:

John Edward,[5] born Oct. 20, 1888.
Georgia Mable,[5] born April 21, 1890.
Raymond Charles,[5] born Aug. 4, 1893.

Katherine Pomeroy,[5] born Feb. 21, 1895.
Dorothy Root,[5] born March 31, 1898.
Herbert George,[5] born Nov. 26, 1903.

THE GOVE FAMILY.

Charles Gove[1] was born March 26, 1790, in Ludlow, and died April 8, 1868; married Oct. 22, 1818, Rhoda Stearns, born July 19, 1794, died Feb. 7, 1876. Children:

Charles Otis,[2] born July 5, 1819; died May 11, 1851.
Eleanor,[2] born Aug. 20, 1820; died Feb. 7, 1866.
Almira Bemis,[2] born March 4, 1822; died Dec. 18, 1896.
Rhoda Maria,[2] born April 20, 1823; died Dec. 29, 1849.
Mary Elizabeth,[2] born May 14, 1825; died Aug. 31, 1847.
Abigail Sophia,[2] born Aug. 5, 1827; died Jan. 28, 1863.
Austin Cyrus,[2] born Feb. 17, 1829; died Feb. 28, 1908.
Sarah Jane,[2] born Nov. 29, 1830; died April 17, 1867.
Joseph Edward,[2] born Sept. 29, 1831; died July 8, 1832.
Sophronia Elvira,[2] born Aug. 29, 1832; died Nov. 1, 1832.
Sophronia Elvira,[2] born Sept. 17, 1833; died Nov. 4, 1833.
George Henry,[2] born Aug. 10, 1835; died June 4, 1842.

Austin Cyrus Gove,[2] son of Charles,[1] was born in Lexington, Feb. 17, 1829, and died Feb. 28, 1908. He was graduated at Wesleyan Academy; was orderly sergeant, Company I, 46th Regiment, Mass. Volunteers, and registrar of voters for 20 years. He married in Ludlow, Aug. 15, 1849, Caroline A. Andrus, born in Northbridge, Feb. 8, 1830, died at Granby in Aug., 1904, daughter of Jonathan and Lucina (Parsons) Andrus. Children:

Carrie Maria,[3] born March 11, 1850.
Charles Otis,[3] born June 13, 1853.
Albert Austin,[3] born June 22, 1866.

Albert Austin Gove,[3] son of Austin Cyrus,[2] was born June 22, 1866, in Ludlow. He was a member of the school board for 10 years. He married in Ludlow, Jan. 21, 1891, Ada Alice Spence, born June 6, 1868, in St. John, N. B., daughter of Magnus A. and Mary (Urquhart) Spence. Children:

Eva Lillian,[4] born Nov. 10, 1891.
Charles Magnus,[4] born Jan. 2, 1894.
Otis Nelson,[4] born June 11, 1897.

The Hannum Family.

Aaron Hannum,[3] son of **William**[2] of Northampton, Mass., and great grandson of **William**,[1] who came from England in 1630, was born in Northampton in 1722; married Rachel Smith, born 1726, died 1811, daughter of John and Elizabeth (Hovey) Smith, who were married in 1709. Her father was prominent in the early history of Belchertown and his name was the first among the members of the Congregational Church there. He died in 1776. Children:

Caleb,[4] born 1750.
Rachel.[4]
Sarah.[4]
Mary,[4] born March 16, 1764.
Silas,[4] born Oct. 3, 1768.

Silas Hannum,[4] son of Aaron,[3] was born Oct. 3, 1768, in Belchertown, and died Dec. 7, 1846, in Williamsburg, where he had lived most of his life. He married first, Sept. 15, 1793, Lucinda Warren, born Sept. 5, 1775, in Williamsburg, died April 10, 1810, daughter of Mather and Esther (Hart) Warren. Children:

Melinda,[5] born July 1, 1794.
Spencer,[5] born Sept. 3, 1798.
John,[5] born Nov. 24, 1805.
Silas,[5] born May 4, 1808.

Silas Hannum[4] married second, Esther Harwood Potter. They had three daughters.

John Hannum,[5] son of Silas,[4] was born in Hatfield, Nov. 24, 1805, and died Dec. 9, 1853; married first, Eliza Fairfield. Children:

John Wesley,[6] born Jan. 1, 1837.
Silas,[6] born July 28, 1839.
Leroy Sunderland,[6] born Dec. 15, 1842.
Henry Francis,[6] born April 15, 1844.

John Hannum[5] married second, in Montgomery, Nov. 25, 1847, Eunice Squier, born July 16, 1813, died April 24, 1898, daughter of Lathrop and Betsey (Leffingwell) Squier. Children:

Charles Spencer,[6] born April 14, 1849.
William Lathrop,[6] born July 31, 1850.
James Wilson,[6] born Sept. 24, 1851; died Dec. 9, 1911.

GENEALOGIES 405

James Wilson Hannum,[6] son of John,[5] was born in Williamsburg, Sept. 24, 1851, and died Dec. 9, 1911. He was graduated from the College of Physicians and Surgeons, Columbia University, N. Y.; has served on the school committee and as medical inspector of schools. He married Nov. 17, 1886, in Ludlow, Maria Louise Miller, born Nov. 24, 1866, daughter of Wilbur F. and Julia Maria (Runnels) Miller. (See Miller Gen.) Children:

Alice Louise,[7] born Dec. 30, 1887.
John Squier,[7] born May 1, 1890.
William Porter,[7] born Dec. 16, 1900.

THE HARRIS FAMILY.

Nathan Harris[1] married Mercy Green.

Nathan Alonzo Harris,[2] son of Nathan,[1] was born in Wilbraham, July 7, 1814, and died Dec. 30, 1887. He married April 19, 1837, Marcia Ann Daniels, born Sept. 22, 1820, in Ludlow, daughter of Asa and Sally (Blodgett) Daniels. Children:

Philo Alonzo,[3] born Nov. 5, 1840; died July 24, 1876.
Elliott Dadman,[3] born Aug. 15, 1843.
Sarah Arethusa,[3] born April 7, 1846.
Almira Eliza,[3] born Nov. 25, 18—.
Henry W. B.,[3] born Feb. 9, 1857; died Oct. 4, 1857.
Belle,[3] born Sept. 15, 1862.

Elliott Dadman Harris,[3] son of Nathan Alonzo,[2] was born Aug. 15, 1843; married first, Jan. 1, 1868, Lucy Mariah White, born Aug. 27, 1844, died Oct. 20, 1881, daughter of Samuel and Angeline (Keyes) White. (See White Gen.) Children:

Samuel Myrton,[4] born March 29, 1869.
Leon Lamont,[4] born Oct. 16, 1870.
Lillian Genevra,[4] born Aug. 7, 1876; died Sept. 22, 1877.
James Garfield, born Sept. 20, 1881.

Elliott Dadman Harris[3] married second, Aug. 10, 1882, Jeanette Amy Woolson, born Feb. 6, 1860, daughter of Daniel Putnam and Frances (St. John) Woolson. Children:

Elliott Raymond,[4] born Oct. 27, 1883.
Amy,[4] born Jan. 12, 1886.

Earl Woolson,[4] born June 24, 1887.
Neal Eliphalet,[4] born June 10, 1898.

The Hobson Family.

Joshua Hobson[1] was born and lived in Huddersfield, England.

John Hobson,[2] son of Joshua,[1] was born Sept. 18, 1804, in Huddersfield, and died Aug. 12, 1883; married Mary A. Hudson, who was born in Huddersfield, June 24, 1805. Children: John,[3] George,[3] Hobson,[3] Sarah,[3] Henry,[3] Martha,[3] William,[3] Edwin,[3] Joshua,[3] Henry,[3] Elizabeth,[3] Mary,[3] Hannah.[3]

John Hobson,[3] son of John,[2] was born Sept. 11, 1825, in Huddersfield, and died Dec. 10, 1903, in Ludlow. He was a member of the 46th Regiment, Mass. Volunteers. He was constable for several years. He married first, in Wilbraham, Sept. 1, 1852, Mary Lewis; married second, March 14, 1869, Celia E. Robbins, born July 21, 1833, died Sept. 12, 1908, daughter of Amos and Elizabeth (Hoar) Robbins. Children:
Carrie.[4]
Alfred John,[4] born in Palmer, Nov. 26, 1857.

The Hubbard Family.

The Hubbards came to America in 1630. Elisha and John Hubbard, Jr., came to Ludlow about 1740 and settled near the Center.

Elisha Hubbard[1] died at the age of 72. He married Mary ———. Children: Russell,[2] Titus,[2] Luther,[2] Lowell,[2] Judah,[2] Anstis,[2] Calvin[2] (left Ludlow), and Bernis,[2] who married Sherwood Beebe. (See Beebe Gen.)

John Hubbard, Jr.,[1] brother of Elisha,[1] married Anna ———. Children:
Rachel,[2] born 1762.
John,[2] born 1764.
Asa,[2] born 1769.
Anna,[2] born 1770.
Ira,[2] born 1772.
Martha,[2] born 1774.
Charles,[2] born 1777.
Ethan,[2] born 1779.

Russell Hubbard,[2] son of Elisha,[1] born in 1769, and died in 1814; married Olive Rood, daughter of Zephaniah Rood. (See Rood Gen.) Children: Lovina,[3] Warren,[3] Asahel,[3] Harvey,[3] Ann,[3] Dan[3] (born 1802), Jemima,[3] and Susan,[3] who married Elijah Caswell, one of the pioneer physicians.

Dan Hubbard,[3] son of Russell,[2] was born in Monson in 1802; served as selectman of Ludlow; married in 1830, Alvina Brainard of Haddam Neck, Conn., born 1810, died 1894. Children:

Emeline C.,[4] born 1832; died 1903.
Henry A.,[4] born 1836; died Feb. 12, 1862; married in 1861, Amnie Booth, born July 22, 1838, died Jan. 6, 1903, daughter of George and Harriet (Miller) Booth. (See Miller Gen.) (See Biography.)
William H.,[4] born 1840; died 1909.

Emeline C. Hubbard,[4] daughter of Dan,[3] was born in 1832 and died in 1903; married Warren Lee Collins in 1854. Children:

Emma S.,[5] born 1856.
Lizzie C.,[5] born 1858; married in 1889, Fred A. Warren.
Grace M.,[5] born 1868; died 1872.

Emma S. Collins,[5] daughter of Emeline C. Hubbard,[4] was born in 1856; married in 1881, DeWitt Mowry. Children:

Grace Eloise,[6] born 1882; married in 1907, Ernest Thompson.
Ethel Leigh,[6] born 1884.
Harold Hubbard,[6] born 1886; died 1906.

Titus Hubbard,[2] son of Elisha,[1] was born in Ludlow, April 12, 1771, and died in Ludlow, Dec. 9, 1837; married Aug. 30, 1796, Phœbe Padelford of Taunton, born March 6, 1771, died Sept. 21, 1850. Children:

Harry,[3] born June 6, 1797.
Calvin,[3] born Aug. 17, 1798.
Lowell,[3] born Oct. 5, 1801.
Elisha,[3] born Sept. 1, 1804.
Israel N.,[3] born July 1, 1808.
A son,[3] born April 21, 1812.
John Padelford,[3] born Aug. 15, 1813.
Lovina,[3] born July 22, 1818.

Israel Newton Hubbard,[3] son of Titus,[2] was born July 1, 1808, in Ludlow, and died Nov. 18, 1864; married in Stafford, Conn., Nov. 29, 1832, Dorothy Benham Hudson, born in Stafford, April 9, 1808, died Dec. 4, 1898, daughter of Daniel and Roxanna (Wood) Hudson. Children:

A daughter,[4] who died in infancy.
Truman N.,[4] born July 22, 1837.
Daniel Hudson,[4] born July 25, 1842; died in July, 1900.

Truman Newton Hubbard,[4] son of Israel Newton,[3] was born July 22, 1837, and died in 1911 at Ludlow Center; married in Belchertown, Nov. 19, 1860, Mary Jane Draper, born in Belchertown, Feb. 23, 1839, daughter of Arnold and Marcia (Moore) Draper. Children:

Hattie Jane,[5] born Aug. 26, 1861; died May 12, 1862.
Ellen Winifred,[5] born Oct. 28, 1863; died March 6, 1878.
George Newton,[5] born July 30, 1866.
Clarence Edgar,[5] born Dec. 17, 1871.
Ida May,[5] born May 21, 1880.

John Padelford Hubbard,[3] son of Titus,[2] was born Aug. 15, 1813, and died Feb. 21, 1881. He was a major in the state militia; served the town as representative, trial justice, clerk, and town treasurer. He married in Ware, April 14, 1835, Harriet Maria Parsons, born Jan. 1, 18—, died March 31, 1867, daughter of Benjamin and Betsey Cornelia (Shepard) Parsons. Children:

Jane Elizabeth,[4] born Oct. 12, 1836.
Lorinda Phœbe,[4] born Dec. 11, 1837.
Martha Parsons,[4] born Dec. 18, 1839.
John Wilson,[4] born July 18, 1849.

John Wilson Hubbard,[4] son of John Padelford,[3] was born July 18, 1849. He has served the town as selectman 14 years, as tax collector five years, and the county 17 years as deputy sheriff. He has served as sexton over 30 years. He married Adelaide Frances Mann. One child: Eugene Howry.[5]

Eugene Howry Hubbard,[5] son of John Wilson,[4] married first, Jennie Carlton Keyes. Children: Ruth,[6] John Padelford,[6] Adelaide Carlton.[6] He married second, Rachel Banks. One child: Jack Woodburn.[6]

THE JOHNSON FAMILY.

Ebenezer Johnson,[1] the ancestor of this branch, was a farmer and lived in West Stafford, Conn.

Cyril Johnson,[2] son of Ebenezer,[1] was a farmer, also, in West Stafford, Conn.; married Clarissa McKinney. Children: William,[3] Mary,[3] Clarissa,[3] Cyril,[3] Henrietta,[3] Orpha,[3] Joy,[3] Edwin,[3] Lucius.[3]

Edwin Johnson,[3] son of Cyril,[2] was born in West Stafford, Conn., Jan. 10, 1843, and died in Hartford, Conn., Oct. 14, 1910; married in Stafford Springs, Conn., Feb. 1, 1863, A. Martha Cheney, born April 8, 1839, in Enfield, died July 19, 1895, daughter of Asa and Sophronia (Randall) Cheney. Children:

A. Lincoln,[4] born Sept. 1, 1864.
Cyril S.,[4] born Oct. 5, 1868.

A. Lincoln Johnson,[4] son of Edwin,[3] was born in Stafford Springs, Conn., Sept. 1, 1864; married in Enfield, Mass., Jan. 1, 1888, Levia J. Emmons, born Jan. 19, 1864, in Hardwick, daughter of Edward and Caroline (Towne) Emmons. Children:

Mabel C.,[5] born Nov. 22, 1888; married Sept. 29, 1909, Charles Earle Chapman. (See Chapman Gen.)
Edith L.,[5] born Oct. 24, 1892.
Gladys M.,[5] born June 27, 1897.

THE JONES FAMILY.

Thomas Jones[1] came from Wales.

Benjamin Jones,[2] son of Thomas,[1] was an early settler in Enfield, Conn., and a first settler of Somers, Conn., in 1706. He died in 1718. He had six sons:

Thomas,[3] married Mary Meacham in 1708.
Ebenezer,[3] married Priscilla Smith in 1713.
Eleazer,[3] married Mehitable Grey in 1719.
Benjamin,[3] born 1710.
Levi,[3] born 1716.
A son,[5] name unknown.

Benjamin Jones,[3] son of Benjamin,[2] was born in 1710. One son: Stephen.[4]

Stephen Jones,[4] son of Benjamin,[3] was born in Somers, Conn., June 27, 1750, and died in Ludlow, Jan. 2, 1828. He was a captain in the Revolution. He married Dec. 22, 1779, Lucy Cooley. They came to Ludlow in 1799, bringing six children. She died in Ludlow, July 15, 1808. Children:

Stephen,[5] born Feb. 12, 1781; died May 12, 1852.
Levi,[5] born May 9, 1782; died July 22, 1783.
Phœbe,[5] born June 19, 1786; died Dec. 20, 1857.
Lucy,[5] born May 15, 1787; died Feb. 14, 1845; married Moses Miller. (See Miller Gen.)
Levi,[5] born Jan. 6, 1789; died Oct. 3, 1831.
Pamelia,[5] born April 22, 1793; died Jan. 10, 1828; married Daniel Miller. (See Miller Gen.)
Simeon,[5] born Sept. 10, 1799.

Stephen Jones[4] married second, Sept. 27, 1811, Mrs. Mary Chapin of Springfield. She died July 26, 1841.

Simeon Jones,[5] son of Stephen,[4] was born in Ludlow, Sept. 10, 1799, and died Feb. 6, 1867; married Nov. 8, 1821, Mary Chapin, born Aug. 31, 1801, died Feb. 27, 1881, daughter of Captain Israel and Mary (Boothe) Chapin (his father's second wife). Children:

Hannah,[6] born Oct. 13, 1822; died Sept. 27, 1855; married Sept. 25, 1851, Quartus Sikes. (See Sikes Gen.)
Delia,[6] born June 22, 1824; died April 17, 1855.
David Chapin,[6] born Sept. 3, 1826; died March 10, 1905.
Henry Simeon,[6] born Oct. 31, 1828; died Jan. 12, 1898.
Daniel,[6] born Jan. 4, 1831; died June 10, 1832.
Daniel,[6] born July 17, 1833; died Jan. 24, 1859.
Mary Eliza,[6] born July 5, 1835; died July 24, 1893.
Pamelia,[6] born Feb. 5, 1838; married Oct. 2, 1867, George Root Clark. (See Clark Gen.)
A daughter,[6] born June 3, 1841; died June 4, 1841.
Sarah A.,[6] born Feb. 26, 1843; died Aug. 3, 1858.
Irene Tuck,[6] born March 10, 1845.
Charles P.,[6] born July 8, 1848; died Dec. 22, 1848.

David Chapin Jones,[6] son of Simeon,[5] was born Sept. 3, 1826, and died March 10, 1905; married May 7, 1848, Harriet A. Miller. Children:

Frederic David,[7] born Dec. 1, 1850; died Nov. 15, 1851.
Willie Merritt,[7] born July 1, 1854; died July 27, 1859.
Alfred Tuck,[7] born Oct. 21, 1859.

Alfred Tuck Jones,[7] son of David Chapin,[6] was born Oct. 21, 1859; married Feb. 22, 1888, Emma J. Fuller, born Sept. 16, 1864, daughter of Edward Everett and Diantha Jane (Prentice) Fuller. (See Fuller Gen.) Children:
Emma Pauline,[8] born July 27, 1889.
Etta Laura,[8] born July 2, 1892.
Katherine,[8] born March 25, 1894.
Myron Fuller,[8] born May 18, 1902; died Dec. 14, 1902.

Henry Simeon Jones,[6] son of Simeon,[5] was born Oct. 31, 1828, and died Jan. 12, 1898; married Oct. 28, 1852, Sarah Elizabeth Parsons, daughter of Elisha Taylor and Hannah Danforth (Charles) Parsons. (See Parsons Gen.) Children:
Charles Parsons,[7] born Sept. 14, 1856.
Robert Henry,[7] born Feb. 2, 1863; died Aug. 5, 1894; married Sept. 14, 1887, Alice Ruth Miller, born Oct. 21, 1861, died March 24, 1908, daughter of Francis and Almira (Smith) Miller. (See Miller Gen.)
Clinton Howell,[7] born Feb. 11, 1871; died Jan. 2, 1875.

Charles Parsons Jones,[7] son of Henry Simeon,[6] was born Sept. 14, 1856; married Nov. 24, 1880, Josephine E. Fuller, born Oct. 20, 1857, daughter of Lathrop and Joanna (Wood) Fuller. Children:
Lillian Maude,[8] born March 3, 1882.
Arthur Merrick,[8] born May 22, 1884.
Wilfred Fuller,[8] born Sept. 20, 1887.
Marion Elizabeth,[8] born Aug. 10, 1891.
Henry Charles,[8] born Jan. 5, 1895.

Lillian Maude Jones,[8] daughter of Charles Parsons,[7] was born March 3, 1882; married Oct. 22, 1908, Ernest Leroy Blish. Children:
Stanford Charles,[9] born Dec. 17, 1909.
Virginia, born Nov. 11, 1911.

The Keefe Family.

Frank Keefe[1] came from Limerick, Ireland, and was the progenitor of the family in Ludlow.

John Keefe,[2] son of Frank,[1] was born in Limerick, Ireland, in 1825, and died Jan. 24, 1882; married in 1848, Mary

Speight, born in Limerick, Ireland, in 1827, died in 1907, daughter of John and Catherine (Nile) Speight. Children:

Catherine,[3] born Feb. 20, 1849.
Julia,[3] born Nov. 6, 1850.
Frank Alvin,[3] born Feb. 22, 1852.
Amos John,[3] born July 23, 1856.
Rebecca,[3] born May 29, 1860.
Mary Jane,[3] born March 21, 1864.

Amos John Keefe,[3] son of John,[2] was born July 23, 1856, in Ludlow; married Aug. 18, 1892, in Springfield, Cora Ellen Richards, born Aug. 18, 1864, in Lincolnville, Me., daughter of Philander and Priscilla (Mansfield) Richards. Child:

John Amos,[4] born May 13, 1893.

The Kendall Family.

Ensign James Kendall[1] died March 9, 1820, aged 74 years; married Jerusha Beebe, who died Oct. 24, 1836, aged 90 years. (See Beebe Gen.) Children:

Chapman,[2] whose children were Daniel,[3] Mosely,[3] Mary,[3] and Sophia.[3]
Reuel,[2] whose children were John,[3] James,[3] Wealthy,[3] Hannah,[3] Horace,[3] and Filer.[3]
James,[2] whose children were Levi,[3] Reuben,[3] James,[3] Sally,[3] and Onelia.[3]
Selah,[2] whose children were J. Munroe,[3] William,[3] Eunice,[3] Vienna,[3] and Lucy.[3]
Jerusha,[2] born Feb. 23, 1773; died Jan. 20, 1853; married first, March 13, 1794, Gad Lyon; married second, Aaron Carver. (See Lyon and Carver Gens.)
Amos,[2] born 1786; died June 19, 1836.
Via,[2] died when young.
Sally,[2] married Moses Rood. (See Rood Gen.)

Amos Kendall,[2] son of Ensign James,[1] was born in 1786 and died June 19, 1836; married Sila Miller, born 1785, died Sept. 18, 1859, daughter of Leonard and Sarah (Kellogg) Miller. (See Miller Gen.) Children: Carlo M.,[3] Caroline,[3] Eliza,[3] Salome,[3] James W.,[3] Henry Burt,[3] William W.,[3] Horace,[3] Jerusha,[3] and Delia.[3]

GENEALOGIES

James W. Kendall,[3] son of Amos,[2] was born Nov. 10, 1817, and died March 13, 1879; married Martha Loomer of South Hadley. Children:
James Osmyn,[4] born March 3, 1843; died April 23, 1892.
Ellen M.,[4] born Aug. 4, 1845; married Henry I. Carver. (See Carver Gen.)
Laura,[4] born July 7, 1848; died Aug. 29, 1871.
Wells Loomer,[4] born May 25, 1850; died Jan. 10, 1875.
Lizzie,[4] born March 19, 1855; died Nov. 6, 1898.

James Osmyn Kendall,[4] son of James W.,[3] was born March 3, 1843, and died April 23, 1892; married Alice Montague of Belchertown. They had an adopted child:
Mabel E.,[5] who married Harold Barton of Belchertown. Children:
Alice Ruth,[6] born May 30, 1896.
Clifton A.,[6] born Oct. 2, 1897.
Gordon Kendall.[6]
Donald Eugene,[6] born Oct. 18, 1909.

Laura Kendall,[4] daughter of James W.,[3] was born July 7, 1848, and died Aug. 29, 1891; married Frank Smith of Granby. Child: Clarence Kendall.[5]

Clarence Kendall Smith,[5] son of Laura Kendall,[4] married Ida Holman of Chicopee Falls. Children:
Lester H.,[6] born May 23, 1893.
Ralph L.,[6] born Dec. 21, 1897.

The Keyes Family.

Willis Keyes[1] was born in Wilbraham in 1798 and died in Feb., 1874; married Chloe Frost, born 1799, died Feb. 18, 1851. Children:
Samuel F.,[2] born Feb. 8, 1820; died Jan. 21, 1864.
Angeline,[2] born 1822.
Eliza Ann,[2] born 1827; died Feb. 23, 1884; married Jan. 13, 1848, Reuben Sikes. (See Sikes Gen.)
William.[2]

Samuel F. Keyes,[2] son of Willis,[1] was born Feb. 8, 1820, and died Jan. 21, 1864; married Jan. 20, 1842, Thankful M. Taylor, born Nov. 6, 1820, died March 9, 1905, daughter of Chester and Eunice (Strong) Taylor. Children:

Leroy S.,[3] born April 1, 1843.
Henry W.,[3] born June 5, 1845.
Elvin V.,[3] born April 2, 1847.
Laura A.,[3] born Oct. 28, 1849.
Julia E.,[3] born Feb. 7, 1853; married William C. Walker. (See Walker Gen.)
Emma S.,[3] born July 1, 1856.
Myron H.,[3] born July 4, 1858.
Eddie S.,[3] born May 27, 1862.

Henry W. Keyes,[3] son of Samuel F.,[2] was born June 5, 1845. He served 28 months in the Third Rhode Island Cavalry during the Civil War, and was a member of the Springfield fire department for 32 years. He married Dec. 25, 1869, Jessie J. Leslie, born Nov. 9, 1848, died Sept. 22, 1889, daughter of James and Mary (Ross) Leslie. Children:

Emma G.,[4] born Aug. 26, 1871.
Cora B.,[4] born Aug. 26, 1873.
Henry S.,[4] born Oct. 2, 1875.

The King Family.

James King,[1] the founder of the King family in Suffield, Conn., was born in Devonshire, England. He came to Suffield and died there in 1722.

Marvin King,[7] a descendant of James[1] in the seventh generation, was born in Somers, Conn., Jan. 20, 1807, and died Jan. 5, 1902. He moved to Ludlow about 1831. He married first, Eunice Brown Alden, born Dec. 23, 1813, died April 22, 1876, daughter of Josiah and Olive (Brown) Alden. (See Alden Gen.) They had 12 children, all born in Ludlow:

Mary Madelia,[8] born Feb. 4, 1834; died Jan. 15, 1874.
Marvin Henry,[8] born April 5, 1835; died Dec. 26, 1907.
Ann Frances,[8] born Feb. 28, 1837; died March 14, 1897.
Samuel Alden,[8] born Dec. 15, 1838; died Nov. 4, 1900.
Julia Isadora,[8] born March 22, 1841; married Jan. 9, 1892, Forrester Prouty.
Arthur Delano,[8] born May 13, 1843.

Homer Washington,[8] born Dec. 8, 1844; died Sept. 5, 1845.
Homer Rising,[8] born June 4, 1846; died Nov. 29, 1911.
Olive Eugenia,[8] born May 14, 1848; died Oct. 28, 1908; married May 12, 1867, Charles Woolley.
Frank Emmett,[8] born May 26, 1850; died Oct. 1, 1852.
Frederick Augustus,[8] born Nov. 17, 1852.
Leila Imogene,[8] born Dec. 23, 1854; married Jan. 3, 1876, Edward Payson Miller. (See Miller Gen.)

Mary Madelia King,[8] daughter of Marvin,[7] was born Feb. 4, 1834, and died Jan. 15, 1874; married Nov. 26, 1852, Justus B. Alden. He served in the navy during the Civil War. (See Alden Gen.) Children:
Edward C.,[9] born in Ludlow.
Elmer E.,[9] born in Ludlow.

Marvin Henry King,[8] son of Marvin,[7] was born April 5, 1835, and died Dec. 26, 1907; married in Jan., 1860, Melissa Pamelia Brewer, born Feb. 17, 1835, daughter of Daniel and Sarah K. Brewer. (See Brewer Gen.) Children: Alford Archie,[9] Samuel Marvin,[9] Mary Mabelle.[9]

Ann Frances King,[8] daughter of Marvin,[7] was born Feb. 28, 1837, and died March 14, 1897; married April 7, 1863, Charles Henry Knapp. He served in the Civil War. Child: Charles Albert.[9]

Samuel Alden King,[8] son of Marvin,[7] was born Dec. 15, 1838, and died Nov. 4, 1900. He was wounded seven times during his service in the Civil War. He married in Dec., 1870, Emma A. Boynton. Children: Edith Emma,[9] Archie Alden,[9] Walter Raymond.[9]

Arthur Delano King,[8] son of Marvin,[7] was born May 13, 1843. He served in the Civil War, returning without a wound. He married Nov. 23, 1870, Lucy Jones Brewer, daughter of Daniel and Sarah K. Brewer. (See Brewer Gen.) Child: Howard Arthur.[9]

Howard Arthur King,[9] son of Arthur Delano,[8] was born Sept. 16, 1871, in Wilbraham; married June 10, 1896, Edith Amelia Fuller, born March 29, 1875, daughter of Albert E. and Susan (Fisher) Fuller. (See Fuller Gen.) Children:
Clifton Fuller,[10] born Aug. 10, 1902.
Vera Margarita,[10] born Sept. 24, 1906.

416   HISTORY OF LUDLOW

Homer Rising King,[8] son of Marvin,[7] was born June 4, 1846, and died Nov. 29, 1911. He served throughout the Civil War and was wounded twice. He married Dec. 2, 1869, Hattie Louisa Ward. Child: Mabelle Lena.[9]

THE LOMBARD FAMILY.

The Lombards came to America in the seventeenth century, settling in Springfield and later in the northern part of Ludlow, called Cherry Valley.

Jonathan Lombard,[1] the first member of the family in Ludlow, was born in 1761, and served in the War for Independence. He married Asenath Olds, born Sept. 23, 1764, daughter of Jonathan and Hannah (Jones) Olds. (See Olds Gen.) Children:

Jonathan,[2] born Dec. 19, 1786; died Sept. 30, 1869.
Asenath.[2]
Cynthia,[2] married Samuel Bennett.
Justin,[2] born 1818.

Jonathan Lombard,[2] son of Jonathan,[1] was born Dec. 19, 1786, and died Sept. 30, 1869; married Dec. 29, 1814, Lydia Daniels, born Dec. 15, 1788, died Feb. 6, 1876, daughter of Justin Daniels. Children:

Sophia,[3] born Aug. 10, 1815.
Eli,[3] born March 2, 1817.
Charles,[3] born Aug. 19, 1820.
Quartus,[3] born Feb. 11, 1824.
Carlos,[3] born Dec. 28, 1825; died Oct. 10, 1889.
Martha M.,[3] born Sept. 3, 1829.

Carlos Lombard,[3] son of Jonathan,[2] was born Dec. 28, 1825, and died Oct. 10, 1889; married Jan. 18, 1854, Maria Louisa Barton, born Oct. 31, 1833, died June 5, 1893, daughter of William Barton of Belchertown. Children:

Olive Maria,[4] born May 31, 1856; married March 23, 1898, Fred Carlton Adams.
Emma Louise,[4] born July 10, 1858.
Erwin Milton,[4] born Aug. 31, 1863.

Justin Lombard,[2] son of Jonathan,[1] was born in 1818; married Orra Fuller, born May 13, 1813, daughter of John and

GENEALOGIES

Bathsheba (Colton) Fuller. (See Fuller Gen.) Child: Dexter Lombard.[3]

Dexter Lombard,[3] son of Justin,[2] was a member of the 37th Mass. Regiment; married Mary Trimm, daughter of Charles Trimm. Children: Ida May,[4] Flora Bella,[4] Josephine Maud,[4] Lester Albert,[4] Lonia Granby,[4] George Edward,[4] Charles,[4] Frank.[4]

George Edward Lombard,[4] son of Dexter,[3] was born in Ludlow, March 20, 1868; married July 1, 1908, Olive Edith Bryant, born in Wilbraham, Sept. 12, 1886, daughter of Albro and Emma (Cummings) Bryant.

The Lyon Family.

Deacon David Lyon,[1] born 1735, came from Woodstock, Conn., in 1776. He is said to have been the first deacon of the Congregational Church, after the town was set off from Springfield. **Dr. Philip Lyon,**[1] born in 1762, died July 25, 1802, is supposed to have been David's brother. David married Eunice Stebbins in 1764. Children:

Eunice,[2] born 1766; died 1804; married James Sheldon.
Gad,[2] born Feb. 28, 1769; died Dec. 26, 1815.
Nathaniel,[2] born Jan. 24, 1772; died Feb. 11, 1839.
Stephen,[2] born 1775; died Dec. 23, 1837.

Gad Lyon,[2] son of Deacon David,[1] was born Feb. 28, 1769, and died Dec. 26, 1815. He is the first chorister mentioned in the history of the First Church; was a representative to the General Court for three years. He married, March 13, 1794, Jerusha Kendall, born Feb. 23, 1773, died Jan. 20, 1853, daughter of Ensign James and Jerusha (Beebe) Kendall. (See Kendall Gen.) Children:

David,[3] born Jan. 15, 1795; died June 17, 1853.
Dexter,[3] born Oct. 3, 1796.
Homer,[3] born Dec. 12, 1798; died Dec. 14, 1798.
Homer,[3] born Jan. 13, 1800; married Maria Taylor.
Helena,[3] born Jan. 10, 1803; died April 28, 1829.

David Lyon,[3] son of Gad,[2] was born Jan. 15, 1795, and died June 17, 1853. He was appointed drum major of the First Regiment, First Brigade and Fourth Division of the

Massachusetts Militia, Sept. 14, 1826. His drum is now in the possession of Ralph Burr, his great grandson. He married March 6, 1817, Fannie Wright, born Aug. 22, 1794, died May 28, 1879. Children:

Eliza Ann,[4] born Aug. 28, 1818; died May 1, 1819.

Eliza Ann,[4] born April 24, 1821; died July 7, 1893; married Edmund Fuller. (See Fuller Gen.)

Nathaniel Lyon,[2] son of Deacon David,[1] was born Jan. 24, 1772, and died Feb. 11, 1839; married Dec. 31, 1804, Hannah Kendall, born Dec. 5, 1776, died June 17, 1811. Children:

Norman,[3] born Feb. 3, 1806; died Nov. 28, 1808.

A son,[3] born Aug. 5, 1808; died Aug. 5, 1808.

Nathaniel[2] married second, May 8, 1814, Sophia Root, born Dec. 20, 1786, died Jan. 9, 1840, daughter of Timothy and Dorothy (Shumway) Root. (See Root Gen.) Children:

Hannah,[3] born Feb. 25, 1815; died May 8, 1856; married Urbane Carver.

Sophia,[3] born March 11, 1817; married George Taylor.

Norman,[3] born Dec. 12, 1818; died March 10, 1870.

Olive,[3] born Jan. 28, 1821; died Nov., 1839.

Albert,[3] born Aug. 8, 1825; died April 11, 1858.

David,[3] born Sept. 21, 1827; married Jane Slate.

Norman Lyon,[3] son of Nathaniel,[2] was born Dec. 12, 1818, and died March 10, 1870. He was an assessor for the town. He married Lydia W. Cooley, born Aug. 21, 1821, died Sept. 19, 1891, daughter of Calvin and Chloe (Bliss) Cooley. Children:

Henry N.,[4] born April 5, 1844; died Oct. 9, 1894.

Lucien N.,[4] born March 30, 1846.

Albert B.,[4] born Feb. 25, 1865.

Lucien Nathaniel Lyon,[4] son of Norman,[3] was born in Ludlow, March 30, 1846; a real estate agent, and lives in Chicopee Falls (1911); was an assessor one year in Ludlow. He married April 25, 1877, Matilda Martha Munsing, born in Brooklyn, N. Y., June 25, 1853, daughter of Michael and Elizabeth Ann (Swan) Munsing. (See Munsing Gen.) Children: Georgia E.,[5] Irving R.[5]

Stephen Lyon,[2] son of Deacon David,[1] was born in 1775 and died
   Dec. 23, 1837; married Jan. 22, 1799, Patience Wright.
   Children:
Lucy,[3] born Nov. 22, 1800; married a Mr. Cleveland.
Solon,[3] born Aug. 22, 1802; died 1873.
Eunice,[3] born June 8, 1804; married a Mr. Hilliard.
Ruth,[3] born June 10, 1806; died Sept. 3, 1858.
Esther,[3] born Sept. 26, 1808; married a Mr. Barrett.
Ephraim,[3] born Jan. 21, 1811.
Gad,[3] born April 21, 1813; died Dec. 9, 1849.
Mary,[3] born July 13, 1815.
Dexter,[3] born May 10, 1817.
Sarah,[3] born April 24, 1819; married a Mr. Swart.
Josiah,[3] born Aug. 3, 1820; died May 11, 1822.
Caroline,[3] born April 23, 1823; died Jan. 5, 1859.

Solon Lyon,[3] son of Stephen,[2] was born Aug. 22, 1802, and died
   in 1873; married Hannah White of South Hadley, born
   July 17, 1803. Children:
Josiah,[4] born Aug. 23, 1825.
Lucy,[4] born April 4, 1827; died June 19, 1887; married Caleb
   Crowninshield. (See Crowninshield Gen.)
Ruth,[4] born March 8, 1829.
Solon,[4] born Oct. 21, 1830.
Ruth,[4] born Feb. 2, 1833.
Christian,[4] born Oct. 11, 1835.
Ebenezer,[4] born June 16, 1838.
Orange W.,[4] born June 5, 1840.
Charlotte M.,[4] born Aug. 5, 1842; married Joshua Clark. (See
   Clark Gen.)
Caroline M.,[4] born Sept. 5, 1846.

The Miller Family.

Their ancestry in this country is traced back to the period of King Philip's War. **Thomas Miller** was killed by the Indians, in the defense of Springfield, Oct. 6, 1675. **Solomon Miller,** grandson of Thomas, died Aug. 20, 1760, aged 30 years.

Captain Joseph Miller,[1] the progenitor of the Miller family in
   Ludlow, was born in 1698 and died April 5, 1760; married Mary ——. Child: Joseph Miller.[2]

Joseph Miller,[2] son of Captain Joseph,[1] was born in May, 1724,
   and died April 8, 1803; married Catherine Ferry. Children:

Sybil,[3] born 1747; died 1834; married in 1767, Isaac Brewer. (See Brewer Gen.)
Aaron John,[3] born Jan. 11, 1750; died Nov. 4, 1838.
Leonard,[3] born 1752; died 1820 or 1828.
Martha,[3] married Levi Bliss.
Moses,[3] died young.
Joseph,[3] born Sept. 1, 1756; died April 1, 1829.
Catherine,[3] died young.
George,[3] born 1759; died 1829.
Catherine,[3] born 1764; died 1852; married Benjamin Sikes. (See Sikes Gen.)
Polly,[3] born 1766; died 1855; married Moses Wood.
Margaret,[3] born 1768; died 1820.

Aaron John Miller,[3] son of Joseph,[2] a physician and surgeon in the Revolutionary War, was born Jan. 11, 1750, and died Nov. 4, 1838; married Esther Burr. Children:
Betsey Elizabeth,[4] born Feb. 3, 1782; died Sept. 24, 1872; married Asa Larned.
Asenath,[4] born June 3, 1784; died Aug. 4, 1850.
Aaron John,[4] born April 22, 1787; died Jan. 12, 1866; married Theodosia Parsons.
Gordon Bliss,[4] born Sept. 7, 1789; died July 3, 1874.
William Abelard,[4] born July 30, 1797; married Nancy Burr.
Mary Eloise,[4] born 1799; died 1842; married Harvey Moody.

Leonard Miller,[3] son of Joseph,[2] was born in 1752 and died in 1820 or 1828; married first, Mary Sikes (see Sikes Gen.); married second, Sarah Kellogg, born 1754, died 1838. Children:
Moses,[4] born 1778; died 1855.
Catherine,[4] born 1780; died 1854; married Jonathan Dan.
Orris,[4] born 1781; died 1863; married Willard Munsell.
Ithamar,[4] born 1783; married Rachel Akers. Children: Charles L.,[5] born 1808, died Jan. 3, ——; Albert,[5] Harriet,[5] Eliza,[5] Henry.[5]
Polly,[4] born 1784; died 1824; married Elijah Fuller. (See Fuller Gen.)
Sila,[4] born 1785; died 1859; married Amos Kendall. (See Kendall Gen.)
Joseph,[4] born 1787; died 1871; married Martha Walker, born April 4, 1786, died Sept. 17, 1847, daughter of James and Rebecca (Warner) Walker. (See Walker Gen.)

GENEALOGIES

Leonard,[4] born 1788; died young.
Susan,[4] born 1790; died 1872; married Amos Putnam. (See Putnam Gen.)

Moses Miller,[4] son of Leonard,[3] was born in 1778 and died in 1855; married first, Lucy Jones, born May 15, 1787, died Feb. 14, 1845; married second, Mrs. Sally Fuller, born 1792, died 1877. Children:

Lucy Cooley,[5] born 1804; died 1876; married Elea Walker. (See Walker Gen.)
Lorenzo,[5] born 1805; died 1805.
Sarah Kellogg,[5] born 1807; died 1871; married Daniel Brewer. (See Brewer Gen.)
Moses Horatio,[5] born 1809; died 1858; married Sophronia Collins.
Mary Sikes,[5] born 1811; died 1811.
Mary Sikes,[5] born 1813; died 1880; married Ebenezer Bartlett.
Stephen Jones,[5] born Aug. 22, 1815; died Feb. 27, 1895.
Tabitha Delia,[5] born 1817; died 1878; married Dexter Taylor.
Delina,[5] born 1820; died 1860; married first, James Sikes; married second, Harvey Moody.
Charlotte,[5] born 1822; died 1832.
Leonard,[5] born 1823; died 1894.
Lorenzo W.,[5] born 1827; died 1894; married Helen Rice. He served in the Civil War and was honorably discharged.

Stephen Jones Miller,[5] son of Moses,[4] was born in Ludlow, Aug. 22, 1815, and died Feb. 27, 1895; married May 1, 1844, Mary W. Walker, born March 12, 1811, died Dec. 11, 1894. Children:

Oliver B.,[6] born May 7, 1845.
Edward Payson,[6] born 1850.

Oliver B. Miller,[6] son of Stephen Jones,[5] was born in Ludlow, May 7, 1845; married May 7, 1879, Martha Louise Nelson, born in New Haven, Conn., in 1856, daughter of James and Mary (Connor) Nelson. Children:

Nina Belle,[7] born March 29, 1880.
Oliver Walker,[7] born March 14, 1886.

Edward Payson Miller,[6] son of Stephen Jones,[5] was born in 1850; married in 1877, Leila Imogene King, born 1854, daughter of Marvin and Eunice (Alden) King. (See King Gen.) Children:

Inez Alfaretta,[7] born 1877; died 1892.
Raymond Edward,[7] born 1879.
Mary Catherine,[7] born 1883.
Robert King,[7] born 1886.
Leila Alden,[7] born 1891.

Raymond Edward Miller,[7] son of Edward Payson,[6] was born in 1879; married in 1906, Josephine Eunice White, born Feb. 3, 1883, daughter of James M. and Lillian (Pike) White. (See White Gen.) Children:

Donald Raymond,[8] born 1907.
Earl Kennard,[8] born 1910.

Mary Catherine Miller,[7] daughter of Edward Payson,[6] was born in 1883; married in 1902, Fred Labroad, born 1882. Children:

Inez Marilla,[8] born 1903.
Edward Louis,[8] born 1904.
Ralph Gladyn,[8] born 1906.
Josephine Leila,[8] born 1909.

Robert King Miller,[7] son of Edward Payson,[6] was born in 1886; married in 1909, Amy Sweatland, born 1893. Child:

Ruth Elizabeth,[8] born 1910.

Leonard Miller,[5] son of Moses,[4] was born in 1823 and died in 1894; married in 1855, Mary R. Walker. Children:

William A.,[6] born 1858; died 1896.
Lizzie M.,[6] born 1860; died 1862.
Mary D.,[6] born 1862.
James O.,[6] born 1867; died 1868.
Lillie J.,[6] born 1869.
Herbert L.,[6] born 1871; died 1905.

William A. Miller,[6] son of Leonard,[5] was born in 1858 and died April 26, 1896; married in 1884, Eva E. Severance. Children:

Mary W.,[7] born March 31, 1886.
Arthur L.,[7] born July 28, 1890.
Edith R.,[7] born March 6, 1892.
Elizabeth T.,[7] born Dec. 14, 1893.

GENEALOGIES

Mary D. Miller,[6] daughter of Leonard,[5] was born in 1862; married in 1882, Alva S. Smith of Connecticut. Children:
William T.,[7] born 1883.
Bertha R.,[7] born 1886; married in 1906, George Clark.
Bessie P.,[7] born 1888.
Hattie E.,[7] born 1890.
Bernice E.,[7] born 1905.

Herbert L. Miller,[6] son of Leonard,[5] was born in 1871; married first, in 1895, Bernice S. Nash, born July 27, 1873, died June 20, 1905, daughter of Francis Austin and Imogene H. (Simonds) Nash (see Nash Gen.); married second, in 1906, Katherine Lyman. Child:
Wells L.,[7] born 1909.

George Miller,[3] son of Joseph,[2] was born in 1759 and died in 1829; married first, Esther Cleveland; married second, Eunice Parsons; married third, Mary Lyman. Children:
Seth,[4] born 1790; left town.
Dolly,[4] born 1792; died 1856; married Abner Beebe.
Zebina,[4] born 1794; died 1867; married Polly Miller, daughter of Joseph[3] and Mary (Wilder) Miller. (See Joseph Miller[3] Gen.)
Almira,[4] born 1796; died 1859; married Asahel Bartlett.
Esther,[4] born 1797; died 1798.
Esther,[4] born March 26, 1800; died Feb. 16, 1831; married Henry S. Fuller. (See Fuller Gen.)
George,[4] born 1801; married Mary Ann Burgess.
Lyman,[4] born 1804; died 1867; married Hannah Stocking.
Edwin,[4] born 1807; died 1807.
Edwin,[4] born 1817.

Joseph Miller,[3] son of Joseph,[2] was born Sept. 1, 1756, and died April 1, 1829; married Mary Wilder, born 1757, died 1845. Children:
A son,[4] killed by a cart, which ran over him.
Sylvester,[4] born Dec. 27, 1783; died Jan. 16, 1881.
Joanna,[4] born Sept. 5, 1785; burnt in a barn, 1787.
Joseph,[4] born Nov. 28, 1787; died 1877.
Daniel,[4] born Oct. 30, 1789; died May 21, 1870.
Charlotte,[4] born Nov. 14, 1791; died 1839; married Zenas Parsons.
John,[4] born Oct. 26, 1793; died May 7, 1881.

Maria,[4] born May 7, 1796; married Gordon B. Wood.
Polly,[4] born March 23, 1798; married Zebina Miller.[4] (See George Miller[3] Gen.)

Sylvester Miller,[4] son of Joseph,[3] was born Dec. 27, 1783, and died Jan. 16, 1881; married Charlotte Little. Children: Joan,[5] who married Franklin Fuller (see Fuller Gen.), Jerre,[5] Sylvester,[5] Violate.[5]

Violate Miller,[5] daughter of Sylvester,[4] was born May 16, 1815, and died Sept. 22, 1892; married Elias A. Fuller. (See Fuller Gen.)

Joseph Miller,[4] son of Joseph,[3] was born Nov. 28, 1787, and died in 1877; married first, Julia Bissell; married second, Electa Button, who died in 1876. Children:

Horace,[5] who became a physician.
Elihu,[5] died young.
Joseph,[5] died in 1836.
All removed to Ithaca, N. Y.

Daniel Miller,[4] son of Joseph,[3] was born Oct. 30, 1789, and died May 21, 1870; married first, Pamelia Jones, born April 22, 1793, died Jan. 10, 1828, daughter of Stephen and Lucy (Cooley) Jones. (See Jones Gen.) Children:

Almerin D.,[5] born Jan. 21, 1813; died Oct. 4, 1885.
Simeon,[5] born March 20, 1815; died March 29, 1898.
Harriet,[5] born June 22, 1818; died Jan. 18, 1891.
Samuel Newell,[5] born July 16, 1820; died Jan. 30, 1909.
Francis,[5] born April 16, 1823; died Feb. 19, 1890.

Daniel Miller[4] married second, Mrs. Lucy (Carr) Smith, who died April 11, 1859. Children:

Calvin,[5] born Jan. 4, 1830.
Josiah Smith,[5] born Jan. 7, 1833; died March 10, 1885.
Joseph,[5] born Sept. 19, 1836; died July 25, 1864, in Andersonville prison.
Edward,[5] born Aug. 31, 1838.

Almerin Daniel Miller,[5] son of Daniel,[4] was born Jan. 21, 1813, and died Oct. 4, 1885; married first, May 7, 1835, Asenath M. Smith, born 1815, died Feb. 4, 1860. Children:

An infant.[6]
Pamelia Jones,[6] born March 25, 1837; died Aug. 8, 1867; mar-

ried Oct. 18, 1859, Seth Morris Coe, born Dec. 17, 1832, died April 6, 1896.
Harriet Atwood,[6] born June 26, 1839; died Oct. 9, 1845.
Mary Smith,[6] born Aug. 14, 1843; died Jan. 25, 1845.
William Howland,[6] born April 23, 1845; died Feb. 3, 1846.
Joseph Condit,[6] born June 2, 1847; married May 21, 1874, Emily Childs Howe.
William Howland,[6] born Sept. 1, 1849; married Sept. 23, 1886, Gertrude Lincoln Meserve, born March 18, 1861, died July 21, 1899.
Mary Jane,[6] born Aug. 19, ——; died Oct. 10, ——.
Almerin Daniel Miller[5] married second, Aug. 29, 1860, Martha Lane, born Aug. 13, 1837, died June 21, 1883. Children:
Harriet Brown,[6] born Jan. 13, 1862; died Sept. 5, 1878.
Bessie,[6] died July 1, 1869.

Simeon Miller,[5] son of Daniel,[4] was born March 20, 1815, and died March 29, 1898; married first, Sept. 11, 1849, Charlotte Amelia Ewing, died Oct. 29, 1851; married second, Jan. 3, 1860, Lucretia White Lamb, born July 26, 1830, died March 17, 1882, daughter of Ezra and Lucretia (White) Lamb. Children:
Harriet Lamb,[6] born Dec. 28, 1860; died Oct. 24, 1861.
Daniel Edward,[6] born Aug. 12, 1862; married Oct. 17, 1900, Mary Eldred Ball.
Mary Elizabeth,[6] born May 8, 1864; died Nov. 23, 1864.
Simeon Bradford,[6] born Sept. 18, 1865; died Dec. 20, 1871.
Gilbert Spencer,[6] born May 19, 1867.
Samuel Osgood,[6] born Oct. 12, 1868.

Gilbert Spencer Miller,[6] son of Simeon,[5] was born May 19, 1867; married Nov. 6, 1905, Aurelia Beane, born Aug. 31, 1877, daughter of John and Christine Beane. Child:
Edward Osgood,[7] born Sept. 19, 1909.

Samuel Osgood Miller,[6] son of Simeon,[5] was born Oct. 12, 1868; married Dec. 22, 1898, Pauline Bencker, born Oct. 12, 1872, daughter of Albert and Louise Bencker. Child:
Louise White,[7] born Sept. 26, 1899.

Harriet Miller,[5] daughter of Daniel,[4] was born June 22, 1818, and died Jan. 18, 1891; married Sept. 7, 1837, George Booth, born Jan. 11, 1812, died July 9, 1865. Children:

Amnie,[6] born July 22, 1838; died Jan. 6, 1903; married Oct. 19, 1861, Henry A. Hubbard, born 1836, died Feb. 12, 1862. (See Hubbard Gen.)

Edwin,[6] born April 20, 1843; died Nov. 28, 1881; married May 28, 1872, Lucy Evaline Root.

Hattie Marie,[6] born Sept. 24, 1858; died April 19, 1859.

Samuel N. Miller,[5] son of Daniel,[4] was born July 16, 1820, and died Jan. 30, 1909; married Nov. 30, 1843, Nancy Fales Cook, born Jan. 10, 1822, died Aug. 8, 1911. Children:

Infant,[6] born May 25, 1845; died May 26, 1845.

Mary Jane,[6] born Aug. 11, 1846; died Sept. 26, 1850.

Henry Lewis,[6] born Feb. 20, 1848; married Sept. 3, 1873, Wanda Wunsch.

George Booth,[6] born Jan. 17, 1850; married Sept. 2, 1874, Florence Stoddard.

Elliott,[6] born Nov. 12, 1851; married Dec. 24, 1874, Abby L. Burnett.

Harriet,[6] born June 19, 1853; married Feb. 28, 1877, Charles Adelbert Judd.

Lucy Asenath,[6] born July 9, 1855.

Eliza Smith,[6] born May 3, 1857; married July 30, 1873, Frederick Clifford Babson.

Francis Miller,[5] son of Daniel,[4] was born April 16, 1823, and died Feb. 19, 1890; married May 20, 1852, Almira Marilla Smith, born June 28, 1827, died June 28, 1895. Children:

Lilla Ida,[6] born Sept. 21, 1856.

Alice Ruth,[6] born Oct. 21, 1861; died March 24, 1908; married Sept. 14, 1887, Robert Henry Jones, born Feb. 2, 1863, died Aug. 5, 1894. (See Jones Gen.)

Wilford Lincoln,[6] born Nov. 5, 1866; died March 14, 1867.

Calvin Miller,[5] son of Daniel,[4] was born Jan. 4, 1830; married Sept. 22, 1857, Frances A. Johnson, born Jan. 22, 1831, died Dec. 13, 1892. Children:

Helen,[6] died at the age of three months and eleven days.

Helen A.,[6] born Jan. 23, 1861; died 1868.

Louie A.,[6] born 1864; married Dec. 27, 1882, A. S. Bowles.

Josiah S. Miller,[5] son of Daniel,[4] was born Jan. 7, 1833, and died March 10, 1885; married Jan. 14, 1863, Jane Ann Miller, born March 11, 1830, daughter of John and Lucinda (Barton) Miller. (See John Miller[4] Gen.) Child:

Charles H.,[6] born June 18, 1864.

Charles H. Miller,[6] son of Josiah S.,[5] was born June 18, 1864; married Jan. 17, 1895, Harriet Elizabeth Stearns, born 1867. Children:

Edith,[7] born Nov. 22, 1895.
John S.,[7] born Aug. 6, 1897.

Edward Miller,[5] son of Daniel,[4] was born Aug. 31, 1838; married Sept. 10, 1867, H. Augusta Shedd, who died Nov. 9, 1904.

COL. JOHN MILLER AND FAMILY

John Miller,[4] son of Joseph,[3] was born in Ludlow, Oct. 26, 1793, died May 7, 1881. He was a colonel in the First Mass. Militia, and held various town offices. He married Oct. 26, 1815, Lucinda Barton, born March 26, 1795, died May 30, 1885, daughter of Ezekiel and Lucinda Barton. Children:

Julia,[5] born Aug. 8, 1816; married Estus Franklin Smith. (See Smith Gen.)
William B.,[5] born July 25, 1818; died April 14, 1883.
Rosannah,[5] born July 16, 1820.

Infant son,[5] born and died July 17, 1822.
Electa,[5] born Sept. 25, 1823; died May 16, 1900; married a Mr. Stone.
Minerva,[5] born Aug. 28, 1825; died Dec. 10, 1905; married Asel H. Bartlett.
John W.,[5] born March 27, 1827; died July 13, 1865; married Dec. 4, 1856, Marietta Porter Burt.
Jane A.,[5] born March 11, 1830; married Josiah Smith Miller. (See Daniel Miller[4] Gen.)
Almira,[5] born July 4, 1832; died Aug. 1, 1908.
Walter S.,[5] born Oct. 2, 1834.
Ellen M.,[5] born Dec. 13, 1836.
Wilbur F.,[5] born March 20, 1840.

William B. Miller,[5] a physician, son of John,[4] was born July 25, 1818, and died April 14, 1883; married Nov. 27, 1847, Diana Atwood, born July 4, 1816, died April 19, 1911. Children:

William Lee,[6] born Aug. 22, 1848; died Dec. 27, 1878.
John Oscar,[6] born Sept. 8, 1851; died March 3, 1858.

William Lee Miller,[6] son of Dr. William B.,[5] was born Aug. 22, 1848, and died Dec. 27, 1878; married Etta Foss, born Jan. 20, 1850, daughter of Merrill M. and Betsey J. Foss. Children:

William Foss,[7] born June 18, 1875.
Winifred Louise,[7] born April 3, 1878.
Wellington Lee,[7] born May 1, 1879; died Sept. 3, 1879.

William Foss Miller,[7] son of William Lee,[6] was born in Westboro, June 18, 1875; married Marguerite M. Foote, born Aug. 28, 1875, daughter of Mitchell J. and Delia (Fay) Foote. Children:

Donna Maria,[8] born July 1, 1904; died Oct. 8, 1904.
William Barton,[8] born Aug. 22, 1905.

Walter S. Miller,[5] son of John,[4] was born Oct. 2, 1834; married first, Caroline Alden, born 1835, died 1869, daughter of Josiah and Clarissa (Willey) Alden. (See Alden Gen.) Children:

Walter Leslie,[6] born Aug. 18, 1860.
Fred Alden,[6] born Feb. 26, 1864.

Walter S. Miller[5] married second, Aug. 15, 1894, Jane Clark.

Walter Leslie Miller,[6] son of Walter S.,[5] was born Aug. 18, 1860; married first, Jan. 26, 1880, Lilly E. Wyant, born March 1, 1861, died June 27, 1885, daughter of Harvey and Charlotte Wyant. Children:

Carrie J.,[7] born Dec. 14, 1881.
Walter Scott,[7] born Feb. 12, 1883; died June 25, 1890.
William L.,[7] born Jan. 24, 1884; died June 25, 1884.
Alfred B.,[7] born June 14, 1885.

Walter Leslie Miller[6] married second, Jan. 15, 1889, Bertha J. Cargill, born Dec. 27, 1868, daughter of William A. and Merinda Cargill. Children:

Leslie C.,[7] born Nov. 9, 1890.
Marjorie A.,[7] born Feb. 14, 1894.

Fred Alden Miller,[6] son of Walter S.,[5] was born Feb. 26, 1864; married Aug. 15, 1888, Mary C. Thayer, born April 30, 1867, died Oct. 10, 1904, daughter of David and Emma Thayer. Children:

Kenneth T.,[7] born June 2, 1889.
Beatrice L.,[7] born May 7, 1892.
Gladys,[7] born Sept. 21, 1895.

Wilbur F. Miller,[5] son of John,[4] was born in Ludlow, March 20, 1840; married March 20, 1862, Julia Maria Runnels, born April 9, 1842, in Canada, daughter of John and Almira (Butterfield) Runnels. Children:

John Wesley,[6] born Sept. 15, 1864; died Dec. 5, 1865.
Maria Louise,[6] born Nov. 24, 1866; married Nov. 17, 1886, Dr. James Wilson Hannum. (See Hannum Gen.)

The Munger Family.

Joseph Munger[1] was born in Hampton, Conn., in July, 1719, and died in Paris, N. Y., in 1805. An old record found at Springfield shows him to have been a resident of Ludlow in 1754. He married in 1747, Jemima Lyon. She and her infant son died in Oct., 1754. He joined the expedition to Crown Point, and then returned to Brimfield, where he married Naomi Needham in 1756, daughter of Capt. Anthony Needham. In 1783 he returned to Ludlow. In 1794 he leased his mill privilege, and in 1796 removed to Oneida County, N. Y., with his son Reuben. Children: Nathan,[2] Joseph,[2] Reuben,[2] and Perley.[2]

Nathan Munger,[2] son of Joseph,[1] was born in 1759, in South Brimfield, and died in Copenhagen, N. Y., in 1813. He became a Revolutionary soldier at 17 years of age. He located in Ludlow about 1782 and lived there till 1792, when he moved to "Chicopee Parish," a part of Springfield. About 1800 he went to Oneida County, N. Y., thence to Lewis County, where he was one of the original settlers of Copenhagen. He married Louisa Bishop of South Brimfield. Children:

Betsey,[3] born 1783.
Polly,[3] born 1785.
Sylvester,[3] born 1787.
Roswell,[3] born 1788.
Elijah,[3] born 1791.

Joseph Munger,[2] son of Joseph,[1] was born in South Brimfield in 1760 and died in Paris, N. Y., in 1823. He was a Revolutionary soldier at the age of 17. He was a licensed innholder in Ludlow in 1800, 1801, and 1802. He married Hannah Fisk, daughter of Capt. Asa Fisk of "Fisk Hill," South Brimfield. They had 15 children. Asa,[3] their first child, was born in Granby, and the next two in South Brimfield. The 12 born in Ludlow were:

Ariel,[3] born 1782.
Olive,[3] born 1784.
Stephen,[3] born 1786.
Perley,[3] born 1788; moved to Rochester, N. Y.
Sylvester,[3] born 1790.
Sally,[3] born 1793.
Philena,[3] born 1794.
Annis,[3] born 1795.
Joseph,[3] born 1797.
Alanson,[3] born 1801.
Lyman[3] and Linas,[3] twins, born 1802.

Asa Munger,[3] son of Joseph,[2] moved from Ludlow to Herkimer, N. Y., thence to Auburn, N. Y., where he died.

Alanson Munger,[3] son of Joseph,[2] was born in 1801. He removed to New York state and became master of chancery and a judge in Madison County; later removed to Oswego; then to Tioga County, where he held the offices of judge, district attorney, and surrogate.

Reuben Munger,[2] son of Joseph,[1] was born in 1769 and died in 1848. He removed to Paris, N. Y., in 1796, being one of its early settlers. He married in 1788, Lorinda Chapin, born 1770, died 1852. Children born in Ludlow:

Naomi,[3] born June 15, 1790.
Joseph,[3] born April 17, 1792.
Jemima,[3] born March 15, 1794.
Jeremiah Chapin,[3] born July 20, 1795.

Perley Munger,[2] son of Joseph,[1] was born Nov. 11, 1775, and died in Chautauqua County, N. Y. He was one of the first physicians in Ludlow. He served as surgeon at Sacket Harbor in the War of 1812. He married Susanna Fuller, born April 21, 1780, died April 30, 1805, daughter of Elisha and Rebecca (Waterman) Fuller. (See Fuller Gen.) Children:

Susan,[3] born in Ludlow.
Ely Fuller,[3] born in Ludlow; died in Hanover, N. Y., Sept. 25, 1801.
Polly,[3] born in Ludlow.

The Stillman Munger Family.

Stillman Munger,[1] son of Joseph and Huldah (Squier) Munger, was born in South Brimfield, Jan. 26, 1783, and died May 22, 1860; married March 12, 1805, Susannah Lane, born May 22, 1784, died Dec. 31, 1861, daughter of Robert Lane. Children:

Hiram,[2] born Sept. 27, 1806.
Alfred Squier,[2] born May 30, 1809.
Caroline,[2] born May 20, 1811; married in 1829, Sumner Cooley. (See Cooley Gen.)
Susan,[2] born Sept. 14, 1813.
Sophronia,[2] born June 17, 1816.
William,[2] born Jan. 14, 1819.
Charles E.,[2] born July 27, 1820.
Austin,[2] born Oct. 31, 1822.
Huldah Alvira[2] and Miriam Almira,[2] twins, born Sept. 3, 1825.
Lucy Maria,[2] born Aug. 4, 1830.

The Munsing Family.

Michael Munsing[1] was born April 29, 1821, in Germany. He was a member of Company D, 37th Regiment, Mass. Volunteers. He married in New York City, Dec. 21, 1843, Elizabeth Ann Swan, born in Germany, Sept. 29, 1823. Children:

Elizabeth Ann,[2] born Sept. 29, 1844.
Caroline Mary,[2] born Jan. 7, 1847.
Jacob,[2] born June 9, 1850.
Matilda Martha,[2] born June 25, 1853; married April 25, 1877, Lucien N. Lyon. (See Lyon Gen.)
Henry Adam,[2] born April 16, 1856.
George Daniel,[2] born March 8, 1858.
Franklin Benjamin,[2] born June 8, 1860.
Charles Ellsworth,[2] born Jan. 9, 1863.

Henry Adam Munsing,[2] son of Michael,[1] was born in Ludlow, April 16, 1856; married May 20, 1882, Lillian Ida Brewer, born May 18, 1860, in Brodhead, Wis., daughter of Solomon B. and Almira Jane (Olds) Brewer. (See Brewer Gen.) Children:

Carrie Jane,[3] born April 19, 1883; married May 16, 1906, G. C. A. Fuller. (See Fuller Gen.)
Robert Henry,[3] born April 23, 1884.
Ruby Lillian,[3] born March 3, 1889.

The Nash Family.

Thomas Nash,[1] the first ancestor in this country, lived in New Haven, Conn., and died May 12, 1658. He was admitted to the General Court of New Haven, Sept. 1, 1640. He married Margery Baker of Hertsfordshire, England, who died Feb. 11, 1665, daughter of Nicholas Baker. Children: Mary,[2] John,[2] Sarah,[2] Joseph,[2] Timothy[2] (born 1626).

Timothy Nash,[2] son of Thomas,[1] was born in 1626, in Leyden, Holland, and died March 13, 1699. He lived in Hadley, Mass., and represented the town at the General Court from 1690 to 1695. He married Rebekah Stone, daughter of Rev. Samuel Stone of Hartford, Conn. She died in April, 1709. Children:

Rebekah,[3] born March 12, 1657.

Samuel,[3] born Feb. 3, 1659.
Thomas,[3] born 1661.
Joseph,[3] born Jan. 27, 1663.
Timothy,[3] born 1665.
John,[3] born Aug. 21, 1667.
Samuel,[3] born June 17, 1669.
Hope,[3] born Nov. 26, 1670.
Ebenezer,[3] born Oct. 25, 1673.
Daniel,[3] born 1676.
Ephraim,[3] born 1682.
Mary.[3]

Ephraim Nash,[3] son of Timothy,[2] was born in Hadley in 1682 and died Nov. 9, 1759. He served as an ensign. He married Joanna Smith, born in South Hadley in 1686, daughter of Deacon John Smith. Children:
Timothy,[4] born Jan. 26, 1707.
Ephraim,[4] born Jan. 16, 1710.
Aaron,[4] born Feb. 23, 1712.
Joanna,[4] born July 4, 1715.
Joanna,[4] born Aug. 28, 1716.
Martin,[4] born Jan. 19, 1718.
Eleazer,[4] born Feb. 10, 1720.
Elisha,[4] born Oct. 8, 1729.

Elisha Nash,[4] son of Ephraim,[3] was born in Granby, Oct. 8, 1729; married Lois Frost, who died in Nov., 1820. Children:
Samuel,[5] born Feb. 1, 1760.
Rebecca,[5] born Nov. 7, 1762.
Lois,[5] born Jan. 15, 1765.
Elisha,[5] born Sept. 11, 1766.
Justin,[5] born April 25, 1768.
Adonijah,[5] born March 1, 1770.
Dorcas,[5] born Feb. 18, 1772.
Simeon,[5] born Sept. 8, 1776.

Elisha Nash,[5] son of Elisha,[4] was born Sept. 11, 1766, in Granby; married Elizabeth Ludlen or Ludoen of Williamsburg. She died Nov. 24, 1830. Children:
Albin,[6] born Aug. 20, 1793.
Elisha,[6] born Oct. 2, 1796.
Lois,[6] born Sept. 11, 1798.
Lewis,[6] born Feb. 7, 1801.

Betsey L.,[6] born Feb. 28, 1803.
Sally.[6]
Joseph,[6] born Sept. 2, 1806.
Dorcas,[6] born June 12, 1809.

Lewis Nash,[6] son of Elisha,[5] was born in Derby, Vt., Feb. 7, 1801, and died in Feb., 1871; married first, Jan. 10, 1826, in Guilford, Vt., Maria Elwell, born Nov. 15, 1804, in Shaftsbury, Vt., and died Sept. 25, 1845. Children:

Henry,[7] born Aug. 26, 1826.
Lucinda E.,[7] born April 16, 1828.
Harriet A.,[7] born Jan. 6, 1829.
Albin,[7] born Sept. 10, 1831.
Charles W.,[7] born March 5, 1833.
Louisa M.,[7] born May 21, 1835.
Mary J.,[7] born March 15, 1837.
James L.,[7] born June 30, 1839.
Frances A.,[7] born June 13, 1841.
Betsey A.,[7] born April 26, 1843.

Lewis Nash[6] married second, May 10, 1848, Cynthia Bennett; and third, Sept. 5, 1857, Susan Eaton. Child:

Willy T.,[7] born July 23, 1858.

Charles W. Nash,[7] son of Lewis,[6] was born in Ludlow, March 5, 1833. He was a volunteer in the infantry and served from 1862 to 1865 in the Civil War as a member of Company D, 37th Mass. Regiment. He married in Ludlow, May 10, 1855, Clarissa Ann Smith, born July 20, 1837, died April 29, 1906, daughter of Martin and Abigail (Abbey) Smith. (See Smith Gen.) Children:

Idella C.,[8] born April 20, 1856.
Franklin W.,[8] born July 1, 1860.
Loella M.,[8] born Feb. 9, 1863.
Charles Oliver E.,[8] born July 1, 1865.
Levi L.,[8] born Dec. 30, 1871.
Edna S.,[8] born Feb. 14, 1876.
Bertha L.,[8] born July 22, 1880.

Franklin W. Nash,[8] son of Charles W.,[7] was born in Ludlow, July 1, 1860; married July 3, 1884, Agnes Lavery, born March 10, 1860, in Waterbury, Conn., daughter of James and Elizabeth (Campbell) Lavery. Children:

Robert F.,[9] born April 29, 1885.
Elizabeth C.,[9] born Sept. 5, 1886.

A daughter,[9] born March 16, 1889.
Clara I.,[9] born Aug. 2, 1893.
Gladys L.,[9] born Jan. 12, 1896.
Mildred L.,[9] born April 30, 1902.

The Joel Nash Family.

Joel Nash,[5] son of Timothy Nash,[4] Esq., of Ellington, Conn., was born June 19, 1731, in Longmeadow. He eventually removed to Ludlow and died there Dec. 19, 1797. He married first, June 11, 1754, Zerviah Ladd, born March 29, 1730, died Sept. 28, 1768. Children:

Joel,[6] born May 5, 1755; settled in Copenhagen, N. Y.
Elizabeth,[6] born March 11, 1757; married Samuel Frost.
Eleazer,[6] born Nov. 28, 1759; died Aug. 18, 1777. He joined the Revolutionary forces at Fort Montgomery, N. Y., where he died.
Stephen,[6] born April 13, 1762; died Oct. 22, 1776.
Timothy,[6] born March 19, 1764; died July 25, 1847.

Joel Nash[5] married second, March 30, 1769, Sarah Paulk, born Jan. 31, 1735, died in 1816 or 1817. Children:

Aaron,[6] born Oct. 12, 1770; died Oct. 8, 1776.
Samuel,[6] born May 1, 1774; died young.
Abner,[6] born Aug. 29, 1776; died young.

Timothy Nash,[6] son of Joel,[5] was born March 19, 1764, and died in Ludlow, July 25, 1847. He was noted for his singing, and served the town as selectman. He married March 4, 1790, Catherine Keyes, born June 9, 1770, died Dec. 11, 1832. Children:

Julius,[7] born March 15, 1791; settled in Ludlow; died in Wilbraham.
Francis,[7] born Sept. 23, 1795; died Dec. 15, 1850.
Asahel,[7] born Aug. 16, 1801; died May 6, 1872.

Asahel Nash,[7] son of Timothy,[6] was born in Ludlow, Aug. 16, 1801, and died May 6, 1872; married March 31, 1835, Samantha Robinson, born in Springfield, May 24, 1805, died Dec. 2, 1870, daughter of Lewis and Rebecca (Bartlett) Robinson. Children:

Timothy S.,[8] born March 15, 1836; died Sept. 18, 1842.
Romana A.,[8] born July 27, 1837; died May 22, 1897.
Caroline A.,[8] born Dec. 22, 1838.

Francis Austin,[8] born March 4, 1843; died Jan. 3, 1903.
Georgiana S.,[8] born Oct. 20, 1845; died Oct. 15, 1879.

Caroline A. Nash,[8] daughter of Asahel,[7] was born in Ludlow, Dec. 22, 1838; married Nov. 22, 1859, Monroe Keith, born in Granby, March 28, 1835. Adopted child:

Alice Bertha,[9] born May 10, 1871; died Aug. 21, 1894; married James Leroy Simonds.

Francis Austin Nash,[8] son of Asahel,[7] was born in Ludlow, March 4, 1843, and died Jan. 3, 1903; married Imogene H. Simonds of Longmeadow, daughter of Orville Simonds. Children:

Florence S.,[9] born March 31, 1870; married in 1895, Henry S. Moody.
Raymond A. P.,[9] born May 9, 1872.
Bernice S.,[9] born July 27, 1873; died June 20, 1905; married in 1895, Herbert L. Miller. (See Miller Gen.)
George S.,[9] born 1881.

Raymond A. P. Nash,[9] son of Francis Austin,[8] was born May 9, 1872; married Clara Sprague of Providence, R. I. Children:

Charles R.,[10] born 1897; died 1900.
Harold A.,[10] born 1902.

George S. Nash,[9] son of Francis Austin,[8] was born in 1881; married in 1901, Genevieve M. Dow. Children:

Mildred,[10] born 1903.
Richard,[10] born 1907.

The Olds Family.

The American branch of this family is traced from:

William Wold or **Old,** of Staunton, England (1522), married Elizabeth Ryton.
Richard Old, of Sherborne, County of Dorset, England, married Agnes Courtney; died in 1566.
Bartholomew Old, of Sherborne, England, married Margaret Churchill, a great aunt of the grand Duke of Marlborough; died in 1594.
William Old, of Sherborne, England, born in 1592, married Elizabeth Greensmith.

John Olde, born in 1615, in Sherborne, England, died at Hillfield in 1682; married —— Gatherest.

Robert or **Robard** (**Ould**) **Old,**[1] the founder of the Olds family in America, was born in 1645 and died Jan. 16, 1727 or 1728. "Dr. Robert Old" came to America in 1669 and settled at Windsor, Conn. He was one of the first five proprietors of Suffield, Conn. He married first, in 1669, Susannah Hanford. She died Jan. 6, 1688. Children:

Robert,[2] born Oct. 9, 1670.
Jonathan,[2] born Dec. 24, 1672; died Dec. 19, 1696.
Mindwell,[2] born Feb. 4, 1674; the first white child born in Suffield, Conn.
Hanford,[2] born March 24, 1677; died March 13, 1765.
William,[2] born Feb. 7, 1679; died Aug. 24, 1680.
William,[2] born Aug. 23, 1680; died Sept. 21, 1749.
Ebenezer,[2] born Dec. 23, 1682; died Dec. 30, 1688.
Susannah,[2] born Oct. 31, 1683.

Robert Old[1] married second, April 1, 1689, Dorothy Granger, born Feb. 17, 1665. Children:

John,[2] born Jan. 11, 1691.
Ebenezer,[2] born Jan. 23, 1692 or 1693.
Jonathan,[2] died Dec. 19, 1696.
Josiah,[2] born March 4, 1695; died Dec. 28, 1712.
Jonathan,[2] born June 8, 1698.
Nathan,[2] born March 2, 1702.
Joseph,[2] born Feb. 3, 1704.

Robert[2] and Jonathan[2] had lands allotted them in Springfield, west of the river, in 1720.

Robert Olds,[2] son of Robert,[1] was born Oct. 9, 1670; married Jan. 28, 1697, Elizabeth Lamb. Children:

Jonathan,[3] born Nov. 30, 1697.
Elizabeth,[3] born March 19, 1699.
Robert,[3] born June 6, 1701.
Daniel,[3] born July 19, 1703.
Benoni,[3] born Feb. 28, 1706.
Merci,[3] born Nov. 29, 1707.
A child,[3] born Aug. 18, 1710.
Joshua,[3] born Oct. 3, 1715.

Jonathan Olds,[3] son of Robert,[2] was born in Springfield, Nov. 30, 1697; married Feb. 18, 1720, Martha Wright. Children:

Martha,[4] born Dec. 12, 1720; died Dec. 12, 1720.

Martha,[4] born April 1, 1722.
Lurana,[4] born April 28, 1724.
Jonathan,[4] born Oct. 19, 1726.
Zebulon,[4] born Aug. 13, 1728; died 1730.
Comfort,[4] born Jan. 1, 1730 or 1731.
Luci,[4] born June 23, 1733.

Jonathan Olds,[4] son of Jonathan,[3] was born Oct. 19, 1726, and died in 1779 or 1780; married Aug. 15, 1749, Hannah Jones. Children:

Hannah,[5] born Nov. 20, 1750; died 1775; married a Winslow, a pioneer in New York.
Jonathan,[5] born Feb. 10, 1753, in Brimfield; died Aug. 22, 1775.
Justun,[5] born Aug. 16, 1754; died April 26, 1819.
Samuel,[5] born Dec. 6, 1756, in Ware; died 1854.
Enoch,[5] born Oct. 3, 1759.
Lurana,[5] born Jan. 10, 1762; died Nov. 3, 1853.
Asenath,[5] born Sept. 23, 1764; married Jonathan Lombard. (See Lombard Gen.)
Tirzah,[5] born May 11, 1767; died April 13, 1839. She was the heroine of the ballad, "Nick and Tarzy."
David,[5] born March 3, 1771; died Sept. 23, 1810; married Sally Thornton.

Justun Olds,[5] son of Jonathan,[4] was born Aug. 16, 1754, and died April 26, 1819. He was the first permanent settler in Monson. He married June 3, 1775, Mehetable Hixon. Children:

Jonathan,[6] born Nov. 1, 1780; died July 6, 1842.
Mehetable,[6] born Sept. 13, 1782.
Susanna,[6] born Aug. 9, 1785.
Cate,[6] born Sept. 30, 1790.
Amanda,[6] born Feb. 14, 1800; died 1855.
Nearly all their descendants left Massachusetts.

Samuel Olds,[5] son of Jonathan,[4] was born Dec. 6, 1756, and died about 1854; married Anny Daniels. Children:

Ruth,[6] born July 27, 1779; died May 5, 1855.
Anna,[6] married Aaron Wright.
Reuben,[6] born 1786; died Nov. 21, 1862.
Nathan,[6] born Sept. 12, 1791; died Aug. 8, 1864.
Polly,[6] married Ransom Cook. They were pioneers of Ohio.

Sally,⁶ married Bluet Button.
Hannah,⁶ married David Daniels.

Ruth Olds,⁶ daughter of Samuel,⁵ was born July 27, 1779, and died May 5, 1855; married May 5, 1795, George Moors. Children:
Mehetable,⁷ born May 29, 1797; died May 25, 1831; married Rev. Ephraim Scott.
Electa,⁷ born June 22, 1799; died Aug. 5, 1826; married Jonathan Waid.
Orlando,⁷ born March 14, 1801; died July 31, 1839.
Asenath,⁷ born May 31, 1803; died Nov. 27, 1847; married Saul Wade.
George,⁷ born May 3, 1805; died Oct. 17, 1820.
Lydia,⁷ born May 13, 1807; died July 9, 1841; married a Mr. Alden.
Phœbe,⁷ born March 15, 1809; died in Feb., 1830.
Ruth Elizabeth,⁷ born July 17, 1811; died Feb. 13, 1845; married Rudolphus Converse.
Orpha Katherine,⁷ born Nov. 30, 1813; died May 2, 1896; married Edwin Lombard Tupper.
Julia A.,⁷ born Feb. 27, 1817; died Dec. 21, 1818.
James G.,⁷ born Jan. 7, 1820; died Dec. 24, 1888.
Juliaett,⁷ born May 9, 1822; died July 18, 1869; married Adin Whitney.

Reuben Olds,⁶ son of Samuel,⁵ was born in 1786 and died Nov. 21, 1862; married first, Polly Hayden, who died July 20, 1831. Children: Mary,⁷ David,⁷ and Caroline,⁷ who married a Mr. Fuller of Ludlow, and their children were Austin,⁸ Charles,⁸ Josephine,⁸ who married Marshall Wright, and Ellen,⁸ who married Hiram Danks. Reuben Olds⁶ married second, Charlotte Parsons, who died leaving a son, Elijah Caswell.⁷ He married third, Polly Brown, who died March 23, 1857, leaving a son, John.⁷ He married fourth, Betsy Eaton.

Nathan Olds,⁶ son of Samuel,⁵ was born Sept. 12, 1791, and died in Holyoke, Aug. 8, 1864; married Hannah Wright, born May 15, 1792, died Oct. 1, 1881. Children:
Rebekah,⁷ born Dec. 25, 1814; died June 14, 1878; married William Hubbard Beebe. (See Beebe Gen.)
Hannah,⁷ born March 19, 1816; married Alanson Poole. Children:

Burlin M.,[8] married Ida Gray.
Caroline,[8] married Auburn P. Capen.
Orra,[7] born Nov. 11, 1817; died Aug. 12, 1818.
Ruby,[7] born Nov. 9, 1819; married Joseph N. Hendrick.
Ora,[7] born March 27, 1821; married Hiram Danks.
Enoch,[7] born April 22, 1822; died Jan. 26, 1899; married Rachel Barnes. Children:
Edwin.[8]
Charles Sumner,[8] married Carrie White.
Anna,[7] born June 7, 1825; died Oct. 28, 1906; married in Nov., 1846, Marcus Daniels.
Maria,[7] born June 3, 1829; died Oct. 3, 1852.
Jonathan,[7] born Aug. 13, 1832.

Jonathan Olds,[7] son of Nathan,[6] was born Aug. 13, 1832; married Sarah Wyman. Children:
Hiram Eugene,[8] born Nov. 4, 1855; died 1909; married Hattie Furrow.
Anson Jonathan,[8] born Oct. 31, 1863; married in Aug., 1896, Sarah Fenton.
Lena Maria,[8] born Aug. 12, 1875; married Oct. 8, 1895, Charles Herbert Calkins. Child:
Thyra Vivyan,[9] born July 15, 1906.

Hannah Olds,[6] daughter of Samuel,[5] married David Daniels. Children:
Laura,[7] married Mitchel Goris.
Marcia,[7] married Nathan A. Harris. (See Harris Gen.)

Enoch Olds,[5] son of Jonathan,[4] was born Oct. 3, 1759; married first, Patty Wright; married second, Eunice Hatch. Children:
David,[6] married Sally Thornton.
Azubah,[6] married Lois Hogerny.
Aaron.[6]
Cyrus,[6] married Kesiah Holbrook.
Two other children[6] died young.

Aaron Olds,[6] son of Enoch,[5] married first, Melinda Taylor; married second, Laura Skinner. Children:
Eunice,[7] married Joseph Wilder.
Emily.[7]
Mary,[7] married Byron Nichols.

Leonard,[7] married Phœbe Jane Hadley.
James Monroe,[7] married Katie Ryan.
David.[7]

David Olds,[7] son of Aaron,[6] married Mary Underwood. Child: Minnie Etta,[8] born April 12, 1864; married Sept. 21, 1886, Alfred Kinsley Paine, born Oct. 14, 1855. (See Paine Gen.)

Lurana Olds,[5] daughter of Jonathan,[4] was born Jan. 10, 1762, and died Nov. 3, 1853; married Asa Daniels. Children:
Asa,[6] married Azubah Cowles.
Lydia,[6] born Dec. 15, 1788; died Feb. 6, 1876; married Jonathan Lombard. (See Lombard Gen.)
David,[6] married Hannah Olds.
Roxana,[6] married Francis Morgan.
Justin.[6]

Justin Daniels,[6] son of Lurana Olds,[5] married Prudence Shaw, born Sept. 14, 1794. Children:
Lodica,[7] born May 26, 1821; married May 9, 1839, Ariel C. Keith.
Marcus,[7] born Jan. 12, 1824; married in Nov., 1846, Anna Olds.

THE PAINE FAMILY.

David Paine[1] was born in Braintree in 1737 and died in 1807. He was a soldier in the Revolutionary War. He married Abigail ——, born 1748, died 1834. Children: Lemuel,[2] Jonathan.[2]

Jonathan Paine,[2] son of David,[1] was born in Ludlow, Jan. 5, 1784, and died April 23, 1872; married Sally Hayden, born Aug. 4, 1791, died Nov. 28, 1867, daughter of Moses Hayden. Children:
Caroline,[3] born March 16, 1813.
Louisa,[3] born March 2, 1815; married Charles Alden. (See Alden Gen.)
David Kinsley,[3] born May 2, 1817.
Chester,[3] born March 15, 1819.
Albert,[3] born Sept. 27, 1821.
Elvira,[3] born May 26, 1823.
Sally E.,[3] born Aug. 19, 1827.
Harriet N.,[3] born Sept. 29, 1830.
Caroline,[3] born July 15, 1833.

David Kinsley Paine,[3] son of Jonathan,[2] was born in Ludlow, May 2, 1817, and died Dec. 16, 1886. He served the town as assessor, juror, and highway surveyor. He married May 1, 1841, Marcia Asenath Fuller, born Aug. 24, 1823, died April 15, 1906, daughter of John and Theodosia (Capen) Fuller. (See Fuller Gen.) Children:

Henry Albert,[4] born April 1, 1846.
Alice Augusta,[4] born Dec. 12, 1850; married Alfred S. Putnam. (See Putnam Gen.)
Herbert Newton,[4] born Oct. 12, 1852.
Alfred Kinsley,[4] born Oct. 14, 1855.
Arabell Theodosia,[4] born Dec. 5, 1861.

Alfred Kinsley Paine,[4] son of David Kinsley,[3] was born in Ludlow, Oct. 14, 1855. He served the town as juror and fire warden. He married, Sept. 21, 1886, Minnie Etta Olds, born April 12, 1864, in Pelham, daughter of David M. and Mary M. (Underwood) Olds. (See Olds Gen.) Children:

Ralph David,[5] born Dec. 17, 1888.
Ernest Norman,[5] born June 29, 1891.
Lora Marcia,[5] born July 27, 1893.
Herman Chester,[5] born June 11, 1895.
Olive Jessie,[5] born May 10, 1897.
Walter Erwin,[5] born Sept. 28, 1899.
Alice Sylvia,[5] born Oct. 10, 1901.
Milton Kinsley,[5] born June 22, 1904.
Morris Stanley,[5] born Feb. 7, 1909.

The Parsons Family.

Elisha Taylor Parsons,[2] son of Elisha[1] and Louisa (Gleason) Parsons of Enfield, Conn., was born April 1, 1805, and died March 12, 1895. He was educated in the schools of Hartford and Suffield, Conn. He taught school several terms and came to Ludlow as a teacher; married and settled in the western part of the town. He served the town as assessor, moderator of town meetings, and two terms in the Legislature. He was deacon in the Congregational Church for about 50 years. He married April 29, 1829, Hannah Danforth Charles, born June 27, 1807, died Jan. 27, 1874, daughter of Danforth and Independence (Booth) Charles. Children:

Sarah Elizabeth,[3] born March 21, 1830; married Oct. 28, 1852, Henry S. Jones. (See Jones Gen.)
Nancy Maria,[3] born Jan. 20, 1832; died June 6, 1845.
Charles Danforth,[3] born July 24, 1834; died Aug. 21, 1834.
Infant daughter,[3] born and died Dec. 6, 1837.
Henrietta Danforth,[3] born Nov. 24, 1840.
Julia Taylor,[3] born July 2, 1843.

Henrietta Danforth Parsons,[3] daughter of Elisha Taylor,[2] was born Nov. 24, 1840; married May 9, 1869, William C. Howell. Children:
Elizabeth Maria,[4] born Feb. 17, 1872.
Robert Parsons,[4] born Sept. 28, 1873.

Julia Taylor Parsons,[3] daughter of Elisha Taylor,[2] was born July 2, 1843; married Sept. 3, 1872, Sumner H. Bodfish. He died May 17, 1894.

THE PERHAM FAMILY.

John Perham[1] was born in Dracut. He married Sarah Moore, who was born on the journey to America.

John Perham,[2] son of John,[1] was born in Manchester, N. H., Feb. 20, 1771, and died Jan. 5, 1858; married Eunice Richardson, born April 9, 1773, in Litchfield, N. H., died April 1, 1855, daughter of Josiah Richardson. They had eight children, three of whom died of spotted fever when young.

Franklin Perham,[3] son of John,[2] was born in Acworth, N. H., Aug. 20, 1807, and died April 10, 1890; married in Londonderry, N. H., in Feb., 1837, Margaret Dickey, born May 5, 1813, died June 17, 1895, daughter of John and Margaret (Woodburn) Dickey. They had eight children, four of whom grew up.

Leavitt Perham,[4] son of Franklin,[3] was born in Acworth, N. H., Nov. 11, 1848. He was postmaster in Ludlow Center for 19 years. He married Dec. 25, 1884, Laura Ellen Stoughton, born April 19, 1850, in Weathersfield, Vt., daughter of John P. and Laura (Hull) Stoughton. (See Stoughton Gen.) Child:
John Franklin,[5] born Oct. 12, 1888.

The Pike Family.

Jonas Pike[1] was born in Sturbridge, March 14, 1815, and died in 1886. He was a stage driver from Springfield to Westfield and to Palmer. He married March 7, 1838, Eunice Prince, born Aug. 15, 1818, died 1895. Children:

Jane A.,[2] born Aug. 29, 1840.
Richard,[2] born Aug. 28, 1841.
Richard,[2] born Jan. 14, 1843.
Mary A.,[2] born Sept. 3, 1844.
Olive S.,[2] born May 17, 1846.
Lillian Elvira,[2] born Sept. 26, 1848; married Jan. 3, 1870, James M. White. (See White Gen.)
Areoline E.,[2] born March 1, 1851.
Flory E.,[2] born Sept. 10, 1856.

The Potter Family.

Edward T. Potter,[2] son of Josiah[1] and Olive (Ackerman) Potter, was born Sept. 26, 1842, in Southbridge. He moved from Palmer to Ludlow in 1888. At the first call for volunteers for the Civil War, he enlisted and served throughout, for three years as a member of the Tenth Mass. Regiment, Company E, later in the 37th, Company K, and 20th Regiment, Company K. He married first, in May, 1866, Mary A. Seaver of Palmer, born June 9, 1836, died April 13, 1884, daughter of John and Adelaide (Flint) Seaver; married second, May 20, 1885, Isabel Henrietta Searle of Southampton, daughter of Stephen E. and Henrietta (Bliss) Searle. Children:

Carl Howard,[3] born 1887.
Hazle Belle,[3] born 1890.
George Raymond,[3] born 1893.
Helen Augusta,[3] born 1896.

The Putnam Family.

The name Putnam was originally Puttenham(?). The family is of Welsh descent.

Nicholas Putnam[1] was the first one recorded.

John Putnam[2] was the son of Nicholas.[1]

George Putnam[2] was the son of Nicholas.[1]

John Putnam,[3] the son of George,[2] was born in 1560.

GENEALOGIES

John Putnam,[4] son of John,[3] was born in 1583. He came to America in 1634 from Berne, Buckinghamshire, England, with three sons, Thomas,[5] Nathaniel,[5] and John.[5] They settled in Danvers, formerly a part of Salem.

Thomas Putnam,[5] son of John,[4] lived in Salem. He had two sons and four daughters. His two sons were Thomas[6] and Edward.[6]

Thomas Putnam,[6] son of Thomas,[5] had a son Joseph,[7] who was the father of Gen. Israel Putnam,[8] senior major general of the armies of the United States of America, born Jan. 7, 1718, died May 19, 1790.

Edward Putnam,[6] son of Thomas,[5] was born July 5, 1654; married a Miss Hale. They had seven sons and three daughters.

Isaac Putnam,[7] youngest son of Edward,[6] was born March 19, 1698; married Anna Fuller, born 1693, daughter of Matthew and Patience (Young) Fuller. (See Fuller Gen.) They had six sons and four daughters.

Nathan Putnam,[8] third son of Isaac,[7] was born Oct. 24, 1730; married Betsey Buffington of Salem. They had eight sons and seven daughters.

Abner Putnam,[9] the fifth son of Nathan,[8] was born in Sutton, March 17, 1765; married Abigail Waters of Sutton, who died Feb. 16, 1856. He came to Ludlow in 1796 and built a shop for the business of scythemaking on the bank of the Chicopee River. After the first bridge was built across the river, the village was called for a number of years "Put's Bridge." He died Oct. 23, 1831. Three sons came with him to Ludlow:

James,[10] born 1787.
Nathan[10] and Amos,[10] twins, born Oct. 8, 1788.

James Putnam,[10] son of Abner,[9] was born in 1787; married Marcia Cox. Children: John Cox,[11] Betsey Buffington.[11]

John C. Putnam,[11] son of James,[10] married Julia Buxton. Children:

Ellen A.,[12] married Joseph W. Hayden.
John C.,[12] died in infancy.

Nathan Putnam,[10] son of Abner,[9] married Polly Look. Children; Abner,[11] Mary,[11] Waters,[11] James.[11]

Amos Putnam,[10] son of Abner,[9] was born Oct. 8, 1788, and died Jan. 30, 1871; married April 6, 1810, Susan Miller, born 1790, died 1872, daughter of Leonard and Mary (Sikes) Miller. (See Miller Gen.) Children:

Abigail Waters,[11] born May 16, 1811; died June 6, 1886; married David Ladd Atchinson. (See Atchinson Gen.)
Amos Hurley,[11] born Jan. 20, 1814; died Feb. 25, 1884; married Sarah Warner.
Leonard Miller,[11] born Aug. 19, 1815; died Oct. 12, 1884; married Lucy Smith.
Susan Alosia,[11] born June 28, 1817; died Nov. 1, 1901; married Avery Green.
Zadoc Porter,[11] born May 8, 1819; died April 21, 1882; married Lucia Chapin.
Flavius Josephus,[11] born Nov. 11, 1821.
Sarah Ann,[11] born June 4, 1824; died Oct. 2, 1887; married Gordon M. Fisk. (See Biography.)
Adeline Eliza,[11] born July 19, 1830; died Oct. 11, 1902; married Lyman S. Hills.

Flavius Josephus Putnam,[11] son of Amos,[10] was born in Ludlow, Nov. 11, 1821; served in the Civil War and died in Andersonville prison in Aug., 1864; married in April, 1845, Sylvia Bissell, died June, 1877, daughter of David and Sylvia (Beebe) Bissell. (See Beebe Gen.) Children:

Alfred S.,[12] born March 28, 1846.
Ella J.,[12] born May 19, 1850.
Lucy A.,[12] born Aug. 31, 1852.
Edwin A.,[12] born Jan. 21, 1859.

Alfred S. Putnam,[12] son of Flavius Josephus,[11] was born March 28, 1846, in Ludlow; married Nov. 29, 1871, Alice A. Paine, born Dec. 12, 1850, died Aug. 16, 1905, daughter of David K. and Marcia A. (Fuller) Paine. (See Paine and Fuller Gens.) Children:

Harry F.,[13] born March 7, 1873.
Robert H.,[13] born Dec. 2, 1875.
Addie B.,[13] born Oct. 15, 1877.
Rufus E.,[13] born May 6, 1880.
Marian,[13] born Jan. 10, 1886.

THE RAY FAMILY.

David Ray[1] married Sarah Jenks. Children:
Knight,[2] born 1789.
William,[2] born 1791.
Preston,[2] died Dec., 1867.

William Ray,[2] son of David,[1] was born in Cumberland, R. I., in 1791. He was an assessor 12 years and a selectman two years. He married Mehitable Cook, born 1795, died 1859. Children:
Samuel C.,[3] born June 25, 1815; died Jan. 29, 1896; married Emily A. Saunders.
William,[3] born May 24, 1821; died March 22, 1875; married Jane Ferry.
Albert,[3] born June 25, 1824; died April 19, 1862; married Fanny Cutler.
John,[3] born Nov. 25, 1834; died May 29, 1891.

John Ray,[3] son of William,[2] was born in Ludlow, Nov. 25, 1834, and died May 29, 1891. He was a selectman for several years. He married Dec. 24, 1855, in Ludlow, Achsah M. Driggs, born in Fulton, N. Y., Jan. 24, 1827, died Feb. 6, 1903, daughter of Hiram and Betsey (Hollady) Driggs. Children:
Harriet F.,[4] born Nov. 15, 1856.
Kate A.,[4] born Feb. 20, 1858; married A. G. Mixer.
Mabel C.,[4] born July 22, 1860.
Fannie R.,[4] born Dec. 12, 1861; married C. E. Pease.
Mary L.,[4] born April 19, 1863; married G. H. Pease.

THE RICE FAMILY.

John Rice[3] was born about 1647 and died Sept. 6, 1719. He resided in Sudbury (now Wayland) on part of the homestead of his grandfather, **Edmund Rice.**[1] It was not far from the "spring" near the residence of his brother, Deacon Edmund Rice.[3] He married Nov. 27, 1674, Tabitha Stone, born 1655, daughter of John and Anna Stone. They had a large family of children.

Aaron Rice,[4] the eleventh child of John,[3] lived in Rutland and was a corporal in Samuel Wright's company. He was in service from April 12 to Nov. 10, 1724. His name appears on the military rolls every year till the time of his death, in 1755, at Crown Point. He was called Quartermaster Rice. He married first, Aug. 29, 1726, Hannah Wright, who died April 23, 1741. Children: Beulah,[5] Mary,[5] Anna,[5] Susanna,[5] Adonijah,[5] Isaac.[5] He married second, April 14, 1743, Elizabeth Bullard of Rutland, the widow of Benjamin Bullard. Children: Elizabeth,[5] born about 1745, married Sept., 1765, George Clark (see Clark Gen.); Aaron,[5] Tamar.[5]

The Rood Family.

The name Rood has been spelled in several ways,—Rhood, Roode, Rude, Rhodes, Roude, and Rood. In an English directory of the year 1830, both Rude and Rood are found.

The story of the first Rood settler is as follows: Mr. Mariner Rood, who was a French sea captain and owned his vessel, was cast ashore in a storm on the Arabian coast and taken prisoner. His crew escaped with the ship and left him to his fate. When out of sight of land, the ship was becalmed. On the following day when all preparations for binding him to the stake had been made, he was led towards the scene. At an unguarded moment he broke away and dived into the water, swimming beneath the surface till safe from his captors, and towards the spot where he thought the ship might be. That night the cabin boy dreamed that his captain was swimming towards them. He told his dream to the mate in charge, who would not believe him. The boy returned to his berth and dreamed that his captain was near. He then asked the mate for a glass, through which he saw an object moving in the water. A boat was lowered and the captain rescued. The vessel finally landed at Stonington, Conn., where it was sold and its owner settled. Another tradition claims that Rhode Island was first called Rood Island, perhaps from the fact that this ship landed first at some point on Rhode Island. It is a fact that this island bore the name Rood Island as late as 1639, according to John Hall's Diary. After that it was called Rhoad and finally Rhode Island.

Ten years later, in 1649, **Thomas Rood**,[1] the first Rood whose record is traceable, settled in Norwich, Conn., with his wife Sarah and nine children. He died in March, 1668, and his wife in 1672. Their children, Sarah,[2] Thomas,[2] Micah,[2] John,[2] Samuel,[2] and George,[2] are named in the list of inhabitants of the town of Norwich and Preston.

Micah Rood,[2] son of Thomas,[1] obtained some notoriety on account of a peculiar variety of apple which grew upon the farm inherited from his father, Thomas. This fruit was large, had a silvery skin and very white pulp, which during Micah Rood's day developed red spots like drops of blood. These apples, called "Mike apples," are still cultivated, and bear the red markings. Micah Rood died in December, 1728.

John Rood,[2] son of Thomas,[1] married Mary Ede. Children: Zachariah,[3] Jacob,[3] Mary,[3] John,[3] Joseph.[3]

Zachariah Rood,[3] son of John,[2] was born July 1, 1690 (according to the Preston records), and died Feb. 10, 1795, aged 105 years. He married Dorothy Downing "Nov. ye 21st, 1727." Children:
Zachariah,[4] born Sept. 21, 1728.
James,[4] born May 10, 1730.
Elizabeth,[4] born Feb. 4, 1731.
Zephaniah,[4] born Jan. 20, 1733.
Moses[4]; Dorothy[4]; Lydia[4]; Jason,[4] born in 1744.

Zephaniah Rood,[4] fourth child of Zachariah,[3] was born Jan. 20, 1733, and died April 1, 1813. He married June 6, 1765, Olive Phelps, born July 8, 1742, and died Nov. 24, 1818, daughter of Asahel and Annie (Pinney) Phelps. They removed from Hebron, Conn., to Ludlow between 1783 and 1785. Children:
Oliver,[5] born March 28, 1766; died Dec. 4, 1766.
Zephaniah,[5] born Sept. 15, 1767; died Dec. 5, 1805.
Olive,[5] born Jan. 4, 1769; died March 17, 1814.
Elias,[5] born Dec. 6, 1770; died Sept. 28, 1847.
Dorothy, or Dolly,[5] born Nov. 26, 1771; died in December, 1771.
Moses,[5] born July 6, 1773; died Sept. 17, 1852.
Oliver,[5] born Nov. 6, 1775.
Dorothy,[5] born Dec. 31, 1777.
Asahel,[5] born July 10, 1780; died March 26, 1853.
Joseph,[5] born July 9, 1783; died May 31, 1806.

Elias Rood,[5] son of Zephaniah,[4] was born Dec. 6, 1770, and died Sept. 28, 1847; married Anna Hancock, daughter of John Hancock, president of the Continental Congress which drafted the Declaration of Independence. Elias settled in Feeding Hills. Children:
Lucy,[6] born Dec. 10, 1794; died March 28, 1878; married March 2, 1815, Ezekiel Fuller. (See Fuller Gen.)
Francis,[6] born Sept. 22, 1796, died Sept. 4, 1798.
Davenport,[6] born July 25, 1798; died Sept. 20, 1861.

Phoebe,⁶ born April 2, 1800; died Sept. 5, 1856.
Francis,⁶ born April 15, 1802; died Nov. 26, 1865.
Mary,⁶ born April 15, 1802; died July 17, 1880.
Hannah,⁶ born Feb. 15, 1804; died Feb. 15, 1870.
Nancy,⁶ born Nov. 11, 1805; died Feb. 22, 1898.
Solomon,⁶ born April 9, 1808; died July 3, 1875.
Lemuel,⁶ born Aug. 8, 1910; died June 28, 1811.
Lemuel,⁶ born Oct. 25, 1812; died Nov. 8, 1865.

Moses Rood,⁵ son of Zephaniah,⁴ was born July 6, 1773, and died Sept. 17, 1852; married Oct. 31, 1799, Sally Kendall, born 1781 and died 1866, daughter of Ensign James and Jerusha (Beebe) Kendall. (See Kendall Gen.) Child:

Hannah,⁶ born March 2, 1802.

Hannah Rood,⁶ daughter of Moses,⁵ was born March 2, 1802, and died June 5, 1873; married Dec. 14, 1826, Roger M. Chandler, born in 1798, died in 1876. Children:

Mary A.,⁷ born April 27, 1831, died Dec. 16, 1896; married Jan. 31, 1853, Chauncey L. Buell, born in 1824. (See Buell Gen.)
Frances,⁷ born April 17, 1839.

Frances Chandler,⁷ daughter of Hannah Rood,⁶ was born April 17, 1839; married Feb. 29, 1860, Oscar B. Sikes, born in 1826, died in 1908. (See Sikes Gen.) Children:

Evelyn,⁸ born April 8, 1861; died Sept. 26, 1872.
Herbert O.,⁸ born July 26, 1865.
Eugene A.,⁸ born May 9, 1869.

Eugene A. Sikes,⁸ son of Frances Chandler,⁷ was born May 9, 1869; married Aug. 1, 1894, Dora Hunt, born in 1870. Children:

Clarence E.,⁹ born Jan. 5, 1897.
Gertrude D.,⁹ born Oct. 31, 1900.
Howard A.,⁹ born Aug. 29, 1902.
Philip E.,⁹ born July 13, 1904.
Edgar B.,⁹ born June 17, 1909.

Asahel Rood,⁵ son of Zephaniah,⁴ was born July 10, 1780, and died March 26, 1853; married Asenath Fuller, born June 16, 1789, died in 1828, daughter of Elisha and Rebecca (Waterman) Fuller. (See Fuller Gen.) Children:

Asahel Orlean,⁶ born May 5, 1811; died Dec. 5, 1887.
J. Dexter,⁶ born Feb. 21, 1815; died May 12, 1889.

Horace,⁶ born Nov. 22, 1818; died Jan. 1, 1893.
Erasmus,⁶ born Sept 10, 1822; died in 1896.
Ely,⁶ born July 7, 1828; died in 1906.

Asahel Orlean Rood,⁶ son of Asahel,⁵ was born May 5, 1811, and died Dec. 5, 1887; married May 31, 1845, Julia A. Barnes, born Oct 18, 1818, died Dec. 21, 1906. He saw the meteor of Nov. 14, 1833, fall like snow for about an hour. Child: Clara Lucinda,⁷ born June 30, 1855.

Clara Lucinda Rood,⁷ daughter of Asahel Orlean,⁶ was born June 30, 1855; married June 1, 1875, G. Wallace Andrews, born June 1, 1854. Children:
Benjamin Rood,⁸ born Oct. 20, 1876; married Nov. 10, 1897, Emma May Hart.
Cora Maud,⁸ married in 1901, James A. McGill. Child:
Olive Francis,⁹ born Aug. 14, 1906.

J. Dexter Rood,⁶ son of Asahel,⁵ was born Feb. 21, 1815, and died May 12, 1889; married Clarissa A. Walker, born Jan. 13, 1819, died June 19, 1905, daughter of Joel and Huldah (Willey) Walker. (See Walker Gen.) Child: Charles Dexter.⁷

Charles Dexter Rood,⁷ son of J. Dexter,⁶ married first Anna S. Marble, one child; married second Caroline Abbe. Children:
Madaline,⁸ Gladys,⁸ Dexter.⁸

Gladys Rood,⁸ daughter of Charles Dexter,⁷ married December, 1908, William M. Williams. Child:
Charles Rood,⁹ born Dec. 5, 1911.

Horace Rood,⁶ son of Asahel,⁵ was born Nov. 22, 1818, and died Jan. 1, 1893; married Aug. 2, 1843, Nancy Louden. They removed to Illinois. Children:
Florence Asenath,⁷ died when five years old.
Clarence E.,⁷ born May 9, 1853; married Evadene T. Halloway.
Horace Edgar,⁷ born Nov. 21, 1855.
Maude,⁷ born in 1858; died Oct. 6, 1875.

Horace Edgar Rood,⁷ son of Horace,⁶ was born Nov. 21, 1855; married Aug. 30, 1888, Josephine Norton. Children:
Dorothy Norton,⁸ born July 30, 1892.
Rudyard Kipling,⁸ Horace Fuller.⁸

Erasmus Rood,[6] son of Asahel,[5] was born Sept. 10, 1822, and died in 1896; married Samantha Billings. They removed to Illinois. Children: Eugene,[7] Flora.[7]

Ely Rood,[6] son of Asahel,[5] was born July 7, 1828, and died in 1906; married in 1850, Sarah Chapman. Children:
Asenath,[7] born in 1851.
Harriet Idella,[7] born in 1853.
Fred Kirk,[7] born in 1856; married in 1887, Tirzah B. Atwood.
Nettie Maria,[7] born in 1859.
Alma Luella,[7] born in 1861; married January, 1878, Everett Kendall.
Lottie Frances,[7] born in 1867; died January, 1887.

Asenath Rood,[7] daughter of Ely,[6] was born in 1851; married first, Albert Hayden, in 1870. Children:
Infant.[8]
Nettie Orpha,[8] born in 1876; married first, in 1895, Samuel More Scott. Children:
  Rena Orpha,[9] born in 1897.
  Ralph Hayden,[9] born in 1900.
  Walter Louis,[9] born in 1904.
  Stanley Avery,[9] born in 1907.
Mrs. Asenath Rood Hayden married second, Henry Fuller.

Harriet Idella Rood,[7] daughter of Ely,[6] was born in 1853; married May 25, 1872, Robert Rust. Children:
Geneva Adelaide,[8] born Dec. 25, 1874.
Alma Eliza,[8] born Oct. 12, 1875.
Harriet Luella,[8] born June 6, 1877.
Robert Ely,[8] born May 28, 1881.
Fred Samuel,[8] born April 11, 1882.
Lotta Maria,[8] born Oct. 13, 1884.

Nettie Maria Rood,[7] daughter of Ely,[6] was born in 1859; married Jan. 1, 1884, Edward J. Fuller. Children:
Leona Elizabeth,[8] born in 1885; died in 1893.
Harry Edward,[8] born in 1886; died in 1887.
Philip Ely,[8] born in 1889.

Joseph Rood,[5] son of Zephaniah,[4] was born July 9, 1783, and died May 31, 1806; married Jan. 7, 1805, Paulina Wood, died Oct. 2, 1853. Children:
Joseph,[6] born Sept. 23, 1805, died Jan. 13, 1871. He served in the Mexican War and the Civil War.
Paulina,[6] born Nov. 23, 1806, died Oct. 2, 1846.

ASAHEL ORLEAN ROOD

HORACE ROOD

ERASMUS ROOD

ELY ROOD

SONS OF ASAHEL ROOD

Paulina Rood,[6] daughter of Joseph,[5] was born Nov. 23, 1806, and died Oct. 2, 1846; married Simeon Pease, who died Sept. 16, 1866. Children:

Merrick,[7] who died in the West.
Mary Ann,[7] married George Philips.
Eliza J.,[7] married Lyman Nelson.
Henry,[7] served in the Second Regiment, Mass. Vol., and died in Portsmouth, N. C., Jan. 28, 1863, aged 23 years.
Lyman.[7]
Sarah,[7] married Francis Simonds. Child:
Flora,[8] born Sept. 16, 1854; married Charles S. Goodell.

THE ROOT FAMILY.

Thomas Roote[1] was born in Badby, England, Jan. 16, 1605, and came to Hartford, Conn., where he lived for about 15 years. Then he moved to Northampton, where he died July 17, 1694. He was a farmer and weaver of cloth. His wife's name is unknown. Children: Joseph,[2] Thomas,[2] John,[2] Jonathan,[2] Hezekiah,[2] Jacob,[2] Sarah.[2]

Joseph Roote[2] (later Root), son of Thomas,[1] was born in Hartford, Conn., in 1640, and died April 19, 1711; married first, Dec. 30, 1660, Hannah Haynes, who died Jan. 28, 1691. Children:

Hannah,[3] born July 9, 1662.
Joseph,[3] born Jan. 15, 1664.
Thomas,[3] born April 13, 1667.
John,[3] born Sept. 11, 1669.
Sarah,[3] born March 4, 1671; died in infancy.
Sarah,[3] born March 4, 1672.
Hope,[3] born Sept. 25, 1675.
Hezekiah,[3] born Jan. 1, 1677; died 1766.

Joseph Roote[2] married second, Mary, daughter of William Holton and widow of David Burt.

Hezekiah Root,[3] son of Joseph,[2] was born in Northampton, Jan. 1, 1677, and died in 1766; married March 23, 1713, Martha Bridgman, died June 4, 1766, daughter of John and Mary (Sheldon) Bridgman. Children:

Hezekiah,[4] born Jan. 29, 1714.
Dorothy,[4] born Oct. 7, 1715.
Simeon,[4] born April 20, 1718.
Martha.[4]

Jemima,[4] born April 1, 1722.
Hannah.[4]
Miriam.[4]

Hezekiah Root,[4] son of Hezekiah,[3] was born in Northampton, Jan. 29, 1714; married a widow, Mary (Bridgman) King. Children: Elisha,[5] Hezekiah,[5] Miriam,[5] Rhoda.[5]

Elisha Root,[5] son of Hezekiah,[4] was born in Belchertown, Sept. 23, 1744, and died June 10, 1817; married in 1766, Mary Cowles, born Sept. 23, 1742, died 1822. Children:
Darius,[6] born Nov. 2, 1767.
Remembrance,[6] born Dec. 6, 1770.
Electa,[6] born Jan. 23, 1772.
Esther,[6] born Sept. 18, 1779.

Darius Root,[6] son of Elisha,[5] was born in Belchertown, Nov. 2, 1767, and died Feb. 8, 1847; married first, March 21, 1799, Dorcas Sikes, born April 13, 1774, died Jan., 1826. Children: Delia,[7] Eliza,[7] Hezekiah,[7] Maria,[7] Eunice Smith,[7] Elisha King,[7] Julia,[7] Emeline,[7] Franklin.[7] He married second, Dec. 2, 1828, Martha Green. They had no children.

Hezekiah Root,[7] son of Darius,[6] was born in Ludlow, Feb. 6, 1803, and died Aug. 16, 1881. He represented the town from 1862 to 1865. He married first, Sally Weatherbee. They had no children. He married second, Maria Jenks, died Nov. 16, 1891, daughter of Benjamin Jenks of Smithfield, R. I. Children: Josephine,[8] George E.,[8] Ellen Eliza,[8] William,[8] Charles Benjamin Jenks.[8]

Charles Benjamin Jenks Root,[8] son of Hezekiah,[7] was born in Ludlow, in March, 1846, and died Sept. 29, 1901; married first, Ann Eliza Atchinson, born Jan. 19, 1846, died July 24, 1879. One son, Charles Arthur.[9] Charles Benjamin Jenks[8] married second, in 1882, Genevra McLean of Ludlow.

Charles Arthur Root,[9] son of Charles Benjamin Jenks,[8] was born Sept. 11, 1874, in Ludlow; a member of the school board of Uxbridge for seven years; married Oct. 12, 1898, Jane Frances Wheelock, born Sept. 24, 1872, daughter of

Charles Edwin and Jane Frances (Sprague) Wheelock. Children:

Dorothy Emogene,[10] born July 15, 1899.
Deborah,[10] born Oct. 27, 1903.
Charles Arthur,[10] born April 6, 1907.

The Timothy Root Family.

Timothy Root[5] was born in Somers, Conn., in 1749 and died Nov. 22, 1822; married first, Sarah Bartlett, who died in 1785. They removed to Ludlow about 1770. Dec. 2, 1822, his real estate was valued at $2,675 and personal property at $369, large for the times. Children:

Timothy,[6] died in infancy.
William,[6] married Eunice Sheldon and settled in Granby.
Sally,[6] died in Ludlow, unmarried, at the age of 86.
Nancy,[6] married William Snow and settled in Granby.
Flavia,[6] married Gaius Taylor and settled in South Hadley.
Amy.[6]
Pliny,[6] married Ruth Cleaveland of Palmer; removed to Steuben County, N. Y., and then to Jackson, Mich.

Timothy Root[5] married second, Dorothy Shumway. Children:

Sophia,[6] married Nathaniel Lyon and settled in Ludlow. (See Lyon Gen.)
Amos,[6] married Mary A. Graves of Richmond, Va., and settled there; served in the War of 1812.
Dorothy,[6] married John Gates of Ludlow. (See Gates Gen.)
Mary or Polly,[6] married Gaius Clough; lived in Franklin, N. Y., and Chicopee. (See Clough Gen.)
Parmelia,[6] married first, Otis Horr of Ludlow; married second, Warren Squires.
Elizabeth,[6] married William Clark, son of Aaron Rice Clark. (See Clark Gen.)
Cynthia,[6] born Oct. 30, 1801; died Aug. 9, 1875; married Oct. 5, 1817, George Clark. (See Clark Gen.)

The Sikes Family.

Benjamin Sikes[1] was of Scotch descent. He died Aug. 2, 1781, at the age of 77. Children: Benjamin,[2] Abner,[2] John,[2] and four daughters.[2]

Benjamin Sikes,[2] son of Benjamin,[1] lived where Danforth W. Sikes now lives. Children: Benjamin,[3] Jonathan,[3] Silas,[3] Ithamar,[3] Polly,[3] Margaret,[3] Lucy,[3] Tabitha,[3] Sally,[3] Dolly.[3]

Benjamin Sikes,[3] son of Benjamin,[2] was born in 1762 and died in 1850; married Catherine Miller, born 1764, died 1852, daughter of Joseph and Catherine (Ferry) Miller. (See Miller Gen.) Children:

Catherine,[4] born 1788; married a Mr. Whittlesey; had three children.
Amanda,[4] born 1790.
Theodore,[4] born 1792; died May 1, 1879; married Anna Stebbins; one son, Theodore.[5]
Lucy,[4] born 1794; married William Brainard.
Polly,[4] born 1797; married Daniel Fisk; one son, Quartus E.[5]
Benjamin,[4] born 1799.
Adeline,[4] born 1803; married Spencer Talmadge.
Margaret,[4] born 1805; married Chester Sikes, son of Jonathan.[3]
Otis,[4] born 1807; married Fidelia Sanderson; three children.
Quartus,[4] born Feb. 4, 1810; died March 10, 1879.

Amanda Sikes,[4] daughter of Benjamin,[3] was born in 1790; married first, Henry Baggs. Children: John,[5] Amasa,[5] Benjamin,[5] Angeline[5] (married Pliny Pease), Theodore,[5] William.[5] She married second, Noah Clark. Child: Mary,[5] who married David C. Fisk.

Benjamin Sikes,[4] son of Benjamin,[3] was born in 1799; married first, Lucy Brainard. Children:

Oscar,[5] born 1826; died in 1908; married Frances Chandler; had three children. (See Rood Gen.)
Otis,[5] born 1828.
Edgar,[5] born 1830; married Sarah Cooper. Children: Edgar C.,[6] Minnie.[6]
Lucy Caroline,[5] born 1831; married Jackson Cady. (See Cady Gen.)
Nancy,[5] born 1835; married Austin Miller; two children, Hattie[6] and Fred Austin.[6]

Benjamin Sikes[4] married second, Harty Works. Children:

Danforth W.,[5] born 1837; married Amanda Jones; no children.
Festus Eugene,[5] born 1844; married Lucy Boodry; two children:

Alice L.,[6] married Joseph Gardner; one child, Ruth.[7]
Walter S.,[6] unmarried.
Benjamin Sikes[4] married third, Cornelia Barrett.

Adeline Sikes,[4] daughter of Benjamin,[3] was born in 1803; married Spencer Talmadge. Children:
William,[5] married Maria ——; had one child, Estella.[6]
Nathaniel,[5] married —— ——; had one child.
Margaret,[5] unmarried.

Quartus Sikes,[4] son of Benjamin,[3] was born in Ludlow, Feb. 4, 1810, and died March 10, 1879; married first, in 1832, Sophronia Hubbard, born April 12, 1812, died March 3, 1848, daughter of Joseph and Miriam (Brown) Hubbard. He married second, Sept. 25, 1851, Hannah Jones, born Oct. 13, 1822, died Sept. 27, 1855, daughter of Simeon and Mary (Chapin) Jones. (See Jones Gen.) Children:
Frank,[5] born Oct. 17, 1852.
A daughter,[5] born Sept. 20, 1855; died Oct. 11, 1855.
Quartus Sikes[4] married third, Nov. 19, 1856, Sophia A. Porter, born April 18, 1824, daughter of Jonathan and Electa (Allis) Porter. They had one daughter:
Delia E.,[5] born Oct. 20, 1858. She lives in Amherst.

Frank Sikes,[5] son of Quartus,[4] was born Oct. 17, 1852; married June 11, 1880, Clara A. Dickinson, born Jan. 16, 1856, daughter of Pomeroy and Amelia (Sanderson) Dickinson of Conway. Children:
Jessamine Amelia,[6] born April 12, 1881; married July 3, 1906, Harry S. Cobb. Child:
Harrison Sikes,[7] born March 24, 1908.
Clara Pauline,[6] born Feb. 25, 1884.
Margaret Frances,[6] born July 5, 1886.

Jonathan Sikes,[3] son of Benjamin,[2] was born in 1765; married Mary Montague. Children:
Chester,[4] born 1789; married Margaret,[4] daughter of Benjamin[3] and Catherine (Miller) Sikes.
Vila,[4] born 1792.
Silas,[4] born 1794.
Alva,[4] born March 19, 1796; died Aug. 6, 1852.

Increase,⁴ born 1798.
Sally,⁴ born 1800.
Mary,⁴ born 1802; married Orrin Walker. (See Walker Gen.)
Oren,⁴ born 1805.
Infant daughter,⁴ born 1807.
Reuben,⁴ born 1808.
Jonathan,⁴ born 1811.
Cyrene,⁴ born 1814.
Infant daughter,⁴ born 1816.

Alva Sikes,⁴ son of Jonathan,³ was born March 19, 1796, and died Aug. 6, 1852; married Oct. 14, 1819, Emilia Walker, born March 6, 1800, died Nov. 8 1885. Children:
Harriet E.,⁵ born Feb. 1, 1822.
Reuben,⁵ born April 25, 1824; died July 22, 1901.
Elijah,⁵ born July 5, 1827; died Jan. 12, 1832.

Harriet E. Sikes,⁵ daughter of Alva,⁴ was born Feb. 1, 1822; married Oshea Walker. Children: Henry M.,⁶ Emilie Sikes.⁶

Reuben Sikes,⁵ son of Alva,⁴ was born April 25, 1824, and died July 22, 1901; married first, Jan. 13, 1848, Ann Eliza Keyes, born March 28, 1826, died Feb. 23, 1884, daughter of Willis and Chloe (Frost) Keyes. (See Keyes Gen.) Children:
Sarah E.,⁶ born Oct. 26, 1848; married Oct. 26, 1869, E. Newton Fisher. (See Fisher Gen.)
Maria L.,⁶ born March 2, 1854; married April 26, 1876, Sanford L. Briggs.
Alva,⁶ born March 10, 1856.
Willis K.,⁶ born April 18, 1859; died April 19, 1876.
Martha B.,⁶ born Aug. 13, 1866.
Reuben Sikes⁵ married second, July 9, 1885, Juliette Walker, born May 12, 1833, daughter of Orrin and Mary (Sikes) Walker. (See Walker Gen.)

Alva Sikes,⁶ son of Reuben,⁵ was born March 10, 1856; married Dec. 3, 1885, Emma Frances Thompson, born Nov. 23, 1856, died Nov. 29, 1905, daughter of Amory and Mary Ann (Pellette) Thompson. Children:
Anna Thompson,⁷ born June 5, 1887.
Blanche Emilie,⁷ born Nov. 9, 1893; died Jan. 31, 1894.

Martha B. Sikes,[6] daughter of Reuben,[5] was born Aug. 13, 1866; married Nov. 30, 1882, G. Lincoln Smith. Children:
Clarence Lincoln,[7] born Jan. 20, 1884.
Harold Sikes,[7] born March 8, 1890; died May 7, 1890.
Herbert Stanley,[7] born Dec. 21, 1891.

Abner Sikes,[2] son of Benjamin.[1] Children: Abner,[3] Increase,[3] Pliny,[3] Mercy,[3] Experience,[3] Lois.[3]

Increase Sikes,[3] son of Abner,[2] was born about 1760. Children:
Abner,[4] born 1805.
Lusina,[4] born 1807.
Pamelia,[4] born 1809.
Sophia,[4] born 1812.
William,[4] born 1814.
Sophia,[4] born 1816.
Wealthy,[4] born 1820.

Pliny Sikes,[3] son of Abner.[2] Children:
Zenas,[4] born 1791.
Orrin,[4] born 1792.
Arua,[4] born 1795.
Lucinda,[4] born 1796.

John Sikes,[2] son of Benjamin,[1] was born in 1748 and died in 1807. Children:
Anna,[3] born 1772; died 1776.
Calvin,[3] born 1779.
Anna,[3] born 1781.
Clarissa,[3] born 1782; died 1848; married in 1803, Ashbel Burr. (See Burr Gen.)
John,[3] born 1784.
Sarah,[3] born 1786.
Azuba,[3] born 1788.
Elihu,[3] born 1790.
Hannah,[3] born 1792.
Electa,[3] born 1794.

Calvin Sikes,[3] son of John,[2] was born in 1779. Children:
Calvin,[4] born 1805.
Edward,[4] born 1808.
Joshua,[4] born 1811.
Nancy,[4] born 1813.

John,[3] son of John,[2] was born in 1784. Children:
Sarah,[4] born 1808.
Caroline,[4] born 1810.
Joseph,[4] born 1812.
Tryphenia,[4] born 1813.
Clarissa,[4] born 1821.
Nancy,[4] born 1825.
Harriet,[4] born 1829.

The Martin Smith Family.

Martin Smith[1] lived in East Windsor, Conn., in 1806 and in Ludlow in 1811; died in 1814. The birth record of a Martin Smith, born in East Windsor, Conn., bears the date Aug. 3, 1759. He married Jemima Chapin, born Feb. 19, 1762, died in the latter part of 1816 or in Jan., 1817, daughter of Captain Ephraim and Jemima (Chapin) Chapin. (See Chapin Gen.) They had one son and several daughters.

Martin Smith,[2] son of Martin,[1] married Abigail Abbey. They had one daughter, Clarissa Ann,[3] born July 20, 1837, died April 29, 1906, who married Charles W. Nash. (See Nash Gen.)

The John Smith Family.

John Smith,[1] a farmer, lived in Granby and died Jan. 10, 1873; married June 11, 1846.

Estus Franklin Smith,[2] son of John,[1] was born in Granby; married Julia Miller of Ludlow, born Aug. 8, 1816, daughter of John and Lucinda (Barton) Miller. (See Miller Gen.) Children:
Emma L.,[3] born June 29, 1847.
John F.,[3] born July 26, 1849.
Charles M.,[3] born July 23, 1852.

The Stoughton Family.

The Stoughtons are descended from an ancient family in the time of King Stephen, Godwinde Stocton, who were seated in Stoughton, County Surrey, England. In the reign of Edward III. they had royal license to empark there 150 acres of land. A large and ancient mansion called Stoughton Place was situated on a delightful eminence near the middle of the manor. In the church of Stoke, at the east end of the north aisle, is Stoughton Chapel, where are many ancient monuments of the families, with quaint and interesting inscriptions. The Stoughtons in the United States are descended from:—

Thomas Stoughton,[1] who came from England in 1630 and settled at Dorchester. His wife was Mary Wadsworth.

Thomas Stoughton,[2] son of Thomas,[1] moved to Windsor, Conn. His wife was Mary Elsworth.

John Stoughton,[3] son of Thomas,[2] married Elizabeth Bissel.

Nathaniel Stoughton,[4] son of John,[3] married Martha Elsworth.

Nathaniel Stoughton[5] was born in East Windsor, Conn. He removed to Weathersfield, Vt., in Feb., 1781, and was one of the original settlers. He filled many offices of trust in the town and was elected several times representative to the General Assembly. He was the only justice of the peace for many years, marrying meantime 53 couples. He married Abigail Potwine, daughter of the Rev. Thomas Potwine, ordained first pastor of the North Church and Society of East Windsor, Conn., May 1, 1754. Children:

Abigail.[6]
Nathaniel.[6]
Lydia,[6] married a Mr. Tolles.
A child,[6] name unknown.
Sarah,[6] married a Mr. Weatherbee.
John.[6]
Daniel.[6]
Alice,[6] married a Mr. Williams.
Richard.[6]
William.[6]

John Stoughton,[6] son of Nathaniel,[5] was born in Weathersfield, Vt.; married Betsey Watson of East Windsor, Conn. Children: John Potwine,[7] Elizabeth.[7]

John Potwine Stoughton,[7] son of John,[6] was born in Weathersfield, Vt., and died May 20, 1903; married Laura Hull, born in East Windsor, Conn., Oct. 5, 1820, died June 26,

1900, daughter of George and Ruth (Watson) Hull. Children:

A daughter,[8] born July 24, 1848; married J. G. McKeen.
Laura Ellen,[8] born April 19, 1850; married Leavitt Perham. (See Perham Gen.)
Mary E.,[8] born Jan. 14, 1853.
A daughter,[8] born Aug. 9, 1854; married L. A. McKeen.
George J.,[8] born Feb. 1, 1857.
Ormate T.,[8] born Dec. 3, 1859.
Joseph G.,[8] born May 12, 1862.
Olin W.,[8] born Jan. 21, 1866.

Olin Watson Stoughton,[8] son of John Potwine,[7] was born Jan. 21, 1866, in Weathersfield, Vt.; married in South Reading, Vt., Nov. 28, 1889, Emma Jane Vittum, daughter of Asahel and Harriet (Cram) Vittum. They have no children.

The Streeter Family.

Paul Streeter[1] was born in Cumberland, R. I., Nov. 9, 1778, and died Nov. 6, 1857; married Jan. 1, 1800, Anna Dresser, born Dec. 13, 1784, died March 7, 1859. Children:

Lucretia,[2] born 1802.
Luther,[2] born March 27, 1804; died 1908.
Noyes,[2] born March 10, 1806; died 1886.
Philander Hurlbert,[2] born May 9, 1808; died 1861.
Benjamin Arnold,[2] born July 14, 1810; died 1864.
Lucinda,[2] born April 17, 1813; died 1847.
July Ann,[2] born Sept. 23, 1814; died 1862.
Mary Louisa,[2] born Sept. 23, 1816; died 1854.
Jerusha,[2] born Dec. 30, 1819; died Nov. 6, 1899.
James Paul,[2] born Feb. 8, 1821; died Nov. 9, 1898.
Nancy Belinda,[2] born May 30, 1823; died April 9, 1844.
Hannah Erminda,[2] born May 20, 1825; died Jan. 18, 1840.

James Paul Streeter,[2] son of Paul,[1] was born in Vernon, Vt., Feb. 8, 1821, and died Nov. 9, 1898; married Nov. 26, 1840, in Wilbraham, Minerva Loomis Langdon, born Sept. 8, 1820, daughter of Walter and Sophia (Badger) Langdon. Children:

Erluna Sophia,[3] born Nov. 3, 1846.
Merrill Eugene,[3] born Aug. 2, 1850.

Elbridge James,[3] born Jan. 5, 1853.
Frank Raymond,[3] born Aug. 19, 1858.

Elbridge James Streeter,[3] son of James Paul,[2] was born Jan. 5, 1853, in Wilbraham. He was graduated from Wilbraham Academy. He married March 26, 1874, Jane Dolly Pelkey, born May 5, 1846, in Pittsford, Vt., daughter of Edward and Elizabeth (Wesson) Pelkey. Children:
Edward James,[4] born Dec. 20, 1874.
Charles William,[4] born July 9, 1880.
Cora Emogene,[4] born April 6, 1882.

Edward James Streeter,[4] son of Elbridge James,[3] was born Dec. 20, 1874; married Mrs. Agnes (Casey) Chamberlin. Children:
Howard Francis,[5] born Oct. 12, 1902.
James Paul,[5] born Nov. 5, 1904.
Vera May,[5] born May 28, 1907.
Elmer John,[5] born July 17, 1909.
Charles Edward,[5] born Oct. 14, 1911.

Charles William Streeter,[4] son of Elbridge James,[3] was born July 9, 1880; married Aug. 21, 1907, Ida May Hubbard, born May 21, 1880, daughter of Truman and Jane (Draper) Hubbard. (See Hubbard Gen.)

Cora Emogene Streeter,[4] daughter of Elbridge James,[3] was born April 6, 1882; married Oct. 2, 1907, Lemont Harding Cassidy, born Aug. 27, 1886. Children:
Alton Bertram,[5] born Sept. 24, 1908.
Carlton Douglas,[5] born March 13, 1910.
Elbridge Floyd,[5] born Sept. 4, 1911.

The Talmage Family.

Persis Talmage[1] was born in Ludlow, Nov. 9, 1790, and died in West Stafford, Conn., Sept. 20, 1849. She married Nov. 25, 1813, Philip Orcutt of Stafford, Conn., born about 1790, died Oct. 8, 1844. He was postmaster and hotel keeper at West Stafford. Children:
A child,[2] died in infancy.
Fidelia,[2] died Jan., 1894; married Alanson Hawley. Children: Elizabeth,[3] Persis Elizabeth[3] (married Rev. J. D. Fenn), Mary A.,[3] Charles,[3] Edward,[3] Frederick Alanson.[3]

Seymour Talmage,[1] brother of Persis,[1] married Lydia Clough, daughter of Uriah and Polly (Orcutt) Clough. (See Clough Gen.) Children: Francis,[2] Anstice,[2] Amelia,[2] Nathaniel.[2]

The Tilley Family.

Porter Tilley[1] was born in Ludlow; married Asenath B. ——. Children: Franklin P.,[2] Albert J.,[2] Orrin E.[2]

Franklin P. Tilley,[2] son of Porter,[1] was born in Granby, March 6, 1825; married Susan E. Barnes. Child: Otis E.[3]

Otis E. Tilley,[3] son of Franklin P.,[2] was born in Ludlow, Aug. 25, 1857; married in South Hadley, Nov. 27, 1879, Amy J. Bennett, born in South Hadley, daughter of William and Eliza (Tilley) Bennett. No children.

The Towne Family.

Benjamin Towne[1] was born and died in Plainfield; married Martha Hitchcock, born in Brimfield.

Benjamin Towne,[2] son of Benjamin,[1] was born in Plainfield, April 18, 1778.

Marquis de Lafayette Towne,[3] son of Benjamin,[2] was born in Plainfield, Sept. 25, 1832, and died in Ludlow, July 13, 1895; married first, Emma Stafford, born 1842, died 1866, daughter of James and Roxanna (Gladden) Stafford. They had one son, Frank A.,[4] born Aug. 29, 1861. He married second, Oct. 1, 1868, Franceneh A. Morse, born in Belchertown, July 21, 1839.

Frank A. Towne,[4] son of Marquis de Lafayette,[3] was born Aug. 29, 1861, in Green River, Vt. He has served as selectman of Ludlow.

The Tucker Family.

Ephraim Tucker[1] was born, probably, in Norwich, Conn. He later removed to Lexington, Ill., where he died. He married Mary Coit. Children: Ephraim,[2] Cynthia,[2] William Coit,[2] Caroline,[2] Samuel,[2] Mary.[2]

William Coit Tucker,[2] son of Ephraim,[1] was born in Norwich, Conn., Feb. 11, 1818, and died Dec. 3, 1901; married May 8, 1851, Laura Almira Moore, born June 10, 1826, in Montgomery, died Sept. 18, 1893, daughter of Abner and Lora (King) Moore. Children:
Myron William,[3] born Feb. 11, 1854.
Oscar Dwight,[3] born Jan. 7, 1858.
Elmer Moore,[3] born Jan. 3, 1861.

Oscar Dwight Tucker,[3] son of William Coit,[2] was born in Montgomery, Jan. 7, 1858; married Feb. 19, 1885, Ella Maria Sheldon, born July 29, 1861, in Southampton, daughter of Mahlon C. and Evelyn A. (Morse) Sheldon. Children:
Orland William,[4] born Oct. 24, 1888.
Evelyn May,[4] born Feb. 25, 1896.
Laura Julia,[4] born Feb. 11, 1898.

The Walker Family.

James Walker[1] was born in Belchertown, March 5, 1758, and died Nov. 7, 1853. He was a cook in the Revolutionary War. He married Jan. 24, 1783, Rebekah Warner, born Nov. 15, 1760, died April 17, 1839. Children:
William,[2] born March 29, 1784.
Martha,[2] born April 4, 1786; died Sept. 17, 1847.
Clarissa,[2] born Nov. 15, 1787.
Bina,[2] born Nov. 17, 1789.
James M.,[2] born Nov. 25, 1791; died May 4, 1814.
Elea,[2] born Sept. 5, 1793; died March 11, 1797.
Joel,[2] born July 11, 1795; died Aug. 24, 1829.
Elea,[2] born June 25, 1797; died Aug. 10, 1848.
Orrin,[2] born May 30, 1799; died April 4, 1885.

Joel Walker,[2] son of James,[1] was born July 11, 1795, and died Aug. 24, 1829; married Huldah Willey, who died about 1859. Children:
Clarissa A.,[3] born Jan. 13, 1819; died June 19, 1905; married J. Dexter Rood. (See Rood Gen.)
William C.,[3] born July 2, 1821; died Nov. 22, 1892.

William C. Walker,[3] son of Joel,[2] was born July 2, 1821, in Springfield, and died Nov. 22, 1892; married Dec. 17, 1846, Jane

A. Miller, born Dec. 26, 1824, died Nov. 13, 1892, daughter of Zebina and Polly Miller. (See Miller Gen.) Children:

William C.,[4] born March 19, 1850.
Zebina M.,[4] born Oct. 16, 1854; died Jan. 15, 1860.
Charles O.,[4] born Feb. 27, 1859.

William C. Walker,[4] son of William C.,[3] was born March 19, 1850; married Jan. 26, 1871, in Ludlow, Julia E. Keyes, born Feb. 7, 1853, daughter of Samuel F. and Thankful (Taylor) Keyes. (See Keyes Gen.) Children:

Isabell K.,[5] born March 4, 1872.
Henry C.,[5] born May 26, 1874.

Isabell K. Walker,[5] daughter of William C.,[4] was born March 4, 1872; married June 19, 1897, James T. Campbell of Warren. Child:

Kennard C.,[6] born March 9, 1901.

Henry C. Walker,[5] son of William C.,[4] was born May 26, 1874; married Flora A. Fuller, born Nov. 11, 1874, died Sept., 1908, daughter of Warren Gilbert and Estella (Baggs) Fuller. (See Fuller Gen.) Children:

William Warren,[6] born Jan. 20, 1894.
Gilbert Fuller,[6] born Nov. 17, 1895; died July 9, 1900.
Crawford Henry,[6] born Jan. 4, 1902.

Charles O. Walker,[4] son of William C.,[3] was born in Granby, Feb. 27, 1859; married Dec. 18, 1880, Ellen M. Morse, born in Belchertown, Sept. 8, 1858, daughter of Jason and Lydia E. (Sibley) Morse. Children:

Theda S.,[5] born April 2, 1884; married Oct. 30, 1907, Charles M. Heidel.
Alice L.,[5] born Nov. 23, 1887; married Oct. 21, 1911, Wendell A. Hodgkins.
Elinor M.,[5] born Oct. 25, 1894.

Orrin Walker,[2] son of James,[1] was born May 30, 1799, and died April 4, 1885; married Mary Sikes, born 1802, daughter of Jonathan and Mary (Montague) Sikes. Child:

Juliet,[3] born May 12, 1833; married July 9, 1885, Reuben Sikes. (See Sikes Gen.)

The Warner Family.

Alonzo Warner[1] was born July 3, 1796, and died Dec. 19, 1884; married Ann Cutler, born Aug. 8, 1797, died April 6, 1879, daughter of Asa and Mary (Combs) Cutler. Children:

Alonzo Cutler,[2] born May 5, 1828; died July 20, 1899.
Mary Ann,[2] born Oct. 22, 1829; died Nov. 7, 1832.
Stephen Montague,[2] born Sept. 23, 1831; died April 14, 1896.
Mary Ann,[2] born July 15, 1833; died Sept. 24, 1904.
Susan Ellis,[2] born June 22, 1835.
Pamelia B.,[2] born Nov. 11, 1837; died Jan. 26, 1864.
Elmina S.,[2] born June 1, 1840; died Jan. 17, 1897.

Alonzo Cutler Warner,[2] son of Alonzo,[1] was born May 5, 1828, and died July 20, 1899; married Margaret Smith Towne, born Oct. 7, 1840, died Jan. 31, 1902, daughter of Israel and Hannah Towne. Children:

Arthur Towne,[3] born April 21, 1872.
Walter Stephen,[3] born Nov. 3, 1874; died Nov. 2, 1891.
Anna Cutler,[3] born Sept. 28, 1882.

Arthur Towne Warner,[3] son of Alonzo Cutler,[2] was born April 21, 1872, in Granby; married Jan. 3, 1901, in Granby, Carrie L. Taylor, born Oct. 13, 1878, daughter of Sylvester H. and Caroline (Boynton) Taylor. They have no children.

The White Family.

Montgomery White[1] was born in 1789 and died in 1874; married in 1812, Roxanna Howard, born 1789, died 1872. Children:

Tamerson,[2] born 1814; died 1885.
Samuel,[2] born 1818; died 1875.
Austin.[2]
James.[2]
Eunice.[2]
Lovinski,[2] born Sept. 22, 1831.
Elihu,[2] born 1834; died 1910.

Samuel White,[2] son of Montgomery,[1] was born in 1818 and died in 1875. He served the town as selectman. He married Angeline Keyes, born 1822, daughter of Willis and Chloe (Frost) Keyes. (See Keyes Gen.) Children:

Lucy M.,³ born Aug. 27, 1844; died Oct. 20, 1881; married Elliot D. Harris. (See Harris Gen.)
James M.,³ born Aug. 23, 1848.

James M. White,³ son of Samuel,² was born in Ludlow, Aug. 23, 1848. He has served the town as selectman. He married Lillian Eliza Pike, born Sept. 26, 1848, daughter of Jonas and Eunice (Prince) Pike. (See Pike Gen.) Children:

Howard Montgomery,⁴ born Dec. 12, 1873.
R. Samuel,⁴ born Feb. 5, 1879.
Josephine Eunice,⁴ born Feb. 3, 1883; married Raymond E. Miller. (See Miller Gen.)

Howard Montgomery White,⁴ son of James M.,³ was born Dec. 12, 1873; married Sept. 12, 1894, Laura Etta Carver, born Aug. 17, 1871, daughter of Henry I. and Ellen (Kendall) Carver. (See Carver Gen.) Children:

Ethel May,⁵ born March 6, 1896; died March 6, 1896.
Harold Samuel,⁵ born April 17, 1898.
Lillian Ellen,⁵ born June 23, 1899.

R. Samuel White,⁴ son of James M.,³ was born Feb. 5, 1879; married a daughter of Levi Frost.

Lovinski White,² son of Montgomery,¹ was born Sept. 22, 1831. He was a private in the Civil War. He married April 25, 1852, Harriet R. Frost, born Sept. 28, 1834, daughter of Selah and Anna (Butler) Frost. (See Frost Gen.) Children:

Charles A.,³ born Feb. 7, 1853.
Herbert E.,³ born 1857; died 1910.
Eliot,³ born 1860; died 1876.
Percy L.,³ born 1863.
Hattie,³ born 1866; died 1869.
Clarence,³ born 1871; died 1872.
Edith,³ born March 1, 1874; died 1899.
Sadie,³ born April 7, 1876.

Charles A. White,³ son of Lovinski,² was born Feb. 7, 1853. He was past commander of Camp No. 68, Mass. Sons of Veterans. He served without a commission from 1888 to 1891, and with one from 1891 to 1898. He married Dec. 25, 1876, Lucy M. Cooley, born Oct. 29, 1855, daughter of Calvin

C. A. White, Camp 68, Div. Mass. S. V., U. S. A.

GENEALOGIES 473

and Harriet L. (Robbins) Cooley. (See Cooley Gen.) Children:

Alice G.,[4] born Dec. 19, 1877.
Clara V.,[4] born Nov. 8, 1881; married in 1910, Charles Moore.
Emily A.,[4] born Sept. 17, 1888.

Alice G. White,[4] daughter of Charles A.,[3] was born Dec. 19, 1877; married in 1902, Frederick Parsons, born 1878. Children:

Emily,[5] born 1905.
Eloise,[5] born 1911.

Herbert E. White,[3] son of Lovinski,[2] was born in 1857 and died in 1910; married Ida M. Severance. Children:

Vernon,[4] born 1883.
Gladys,[4] born 1889.
Addie,[4] born 1891.
Victor,[4] born 1897.

Percy L. White,[3] son of Lovinski,[2] was born in 1863; married in 1888, Clara Ellsworth. Children:

Leroy,[4] born 1888.
Earl,[4] born 1889.

Sadie White,[3] daughter of Lovinski,[2] was born April 7, 1876; married in 1896, Arthur Frost. Children:

Ethel,[4] born 1897.
Blanch,[4] born 1899.
Dorothy,[4] born 1901.
Lewis,[4] born 1903.
Loma,[4] born 1905.

THE WILLEY FAMILY.

Gates Willey[1] came from Haddam, Conn., to Ludlow. He served the town as selectman, assessor, and town clerk. He was chorister of the first church built in Ludlow. He died at the age of 84. He married in 1814, Jerusha Parsons, who died at the age of 97 years and six months, daughter of Ezra and Anne (Fuller) Parsons. Children: Clarissa,[2] who married Nov. 27, 1827, Josiah Alden (see Alden Gen.); Jerusha,[2] Parsons,[2] Sabrina,[2] Madison,[2] Betsey,[2] Eliza,[2] Harriet.[2]

IV

FARMS OF LUDLOW

Following is a list of the homesteads of the town, in their order, on the different roads and crossroads. The names of present owners are given, also those of former owners, beginning with the earliest known, and any items of interest regarding them which we have been able to collect.

EAST FROM THE CENTER—BELCHERTOWN ROAD

1 Owned by Mrs. Ashbel P. Chapin. Former owners: Ely Fuller, Jerusha Fuller (his widow), Caroline (Fuller) Warner (their daughter); Isaac Plumley, Ashbel P. Chapin. The house was probably built by Ely Fuller, and was used by him as a hotel, which after his death was kept by his widow. Formerly piazzas, above and below, extended across the south side, and there was a wing running toward the east, the upper story being a hall and the lower a store.

2 Owned by Mrs. Charlotte M. Clark. Former owners: Henry S. Fuller, Cyrus Moody, Hiram Aldrich, Mrs. Woolley, Mrs. Borthwick. Hiram Aldrich had a shoemaker's shop.

3 Owned by Eugene Clark. Former owners: Joshua Clark, Eugene and Fred Clark. The old house was torn down and the present structure built by Eugene Clark.

4 Owned by Eugene Clark. Former owners: Zachariah Day, William Baggs, (his heirs) Mrs. Harriet Baggs and Mrs. Hattie (Baggs) Taylor. Zachariah Day built the present house and barn about 1850.

5 Morrill place. House in field near Warren D. Fuller's sawmill. Former owners: Silas Moody, Edward Morrill. House was built by Silas Moody.

6 About a mile from Center. Present owner, Mrs. Solon Lyon, widow. Former owners: Lewis Nash, Jonas Pike (Chauncey Davis lived there), Miss Mary Lyon, Mrs. Julia King. Unoccupied.

7 About a mile from Center. Owned by Mrs. Solon Lyon, widow. Former owners: Austin Dutton, Mrs. Austin Dutton (his widow).

8 Owned by —— Stebbins. Former owners: Theodore Sikes, Francis Wilson, William Wait, Lemuel D. Wait, Elisha H. Dutton, William Dutton, Henry A. Munsing, Eugene Patenaude. William Dutton remodeled the buildings.

9 On opposite side of road and near Lovinski White's. Owned by Alvah Clark. Former owners: Justus B. Alden, afterward his heirs.

10 Near Springfield Waterworks. Owned by Lovinski White. Former owners: Amasa Cady, Alfred Sprout and Jeremiah Dutton, Arthur D. King.

11 Near Springfield Reservoir. Owned by Rudolph Hennaman. Former owners: Marvin King, Arthur King. Marvin King tore down the old house in 1858 or 1859 and purchased and moved upon the site a house formerly belonging to Solomon Towne, which still stands. He also remodeled the barn.

12 Near Springfield Reservoir. Owned by Danforth Work Sikes, Jr. Inherited from Benjamin Sikes, Jr. Former owners: Abner Sikes, Benjamin Sikes, Benjamin Sikes, Jr. The present house is the third built; the first was built ten to fifteen rods from the road, the second on present site. This place has been the home of four generations of the Sikes family.

13 Owned by Edward T. Potter; purchased by him in 1887. Former owners: Mr. Kimball (father of Rufus), Rufus Kimball, Silas Billings. The present house and barn were built by Silas Billings about 1869. Rufus Kimball buried his wife, two children, and his mother from this place in 1848, all his family within one month. He was the first to leave by bequest a sum of money for yearly care of his burial lot in Ludlow Center Cemetery. He also bequeathed a sum of money, the income to be used for the worthy poor.

14 Situated in eastern part of Ludlow. Owned by Newell W. Alden. Purchased in 1865. Former owners: Increase Sikes, Jessie Brainard, Azel Alden. The house and barn were built in 1851 by Azel Alden, who was one of the three large landowners.

MARVIN KING
Born January 20, 1807
Photograph taken on 93d birthday

South from Center—Wilbraham Road

1 Owned by Mrs. Andrew J. Chapin. Purchased by Andrew J. Chapin in 1861. Former owners: Zera Fuller, Henry S. Fuller, Otis Fuller, Lucius Simonds, David C. Jones, James Miller, Andrew J. Chapin. The house was burned during the ownership of D. C. Jones; present house was built in 1867 by Andrew J. Chapin.

2 Opposite old M. E. Church. Owned by Charles M. Foster, who purchased it in October, 1901. Former owners: Andrew J. Chapin, Willis F. Grant. House was formerly the Methodist parsonage and was built in 1890. It was removed to its present site and remodeled in 1902 by Mr. Foster. He also built the barn and other buildings.

3 Situated south of the old Methodist Church. Owned by Charles M. Foster, who purchased it February 1, 1911. Former owners: Joshua Fuller, John Dorman, Frederick G. Riese, Warren D. Fuller, Warren D. Fuller's heirs. House was built about 1810, and is supposed to have been in its earlier years a tavern and dance house.

4 Situated a little south of the old Fuller tavern. Owned by William Ellison. Former owners: Dr. Francis Percival, Dea. Stephen Jones, Simeon Jones. Since Mr. Ellison purchased the place the barn has been burned.

5 Owned by William E. Birge. Former owners: Stephen Jones, Stephen Cooley Jones, Mrs. Ida White. The house was burned while Stephen C. Jones was the owner and he built the one now standing.

6 Owned by Franklin H. Ellison. Former owners: —— Pasco, Abner Cady, Chauncey Buell, Chauncey L. Buell, William H. Hubbard. Chauncey L. Buell built the barn now standing, also tore down the old house and built a new one, which was burned and has never been replaced.

7 Owned by Arick Anderson. Former owners: George Carver, Mrs. Wilmer Converse, Frank Kendall.

8 About a mile from Center. Owned by Mrs. Herbert E. White. Former owners: John Fuller, Purchase Dwight Fuller, Charles Fuller. Purchase Dwight Fuller used to play the fife when the militia met to drill. He took down the original house and built the front as it now stands and Mrs. Herbert E. White built the large L and for years cared for State wards, teaching them in a schoolroom which she had fitted for the purpose.

9 Near Albert C. Wilson's place, on the opposite side of the road, is a cellar hole where formerly were a house and barn owned by Edmund W. Fuller, then by his son, Warren D. Fuller, during whose ownership they were burned and have not been rebuilt. The land is now owned by Albert C. Wilson.

10 About a mile and a half from Center. Owned by Albert C. Wilson. Former owners: Edmund W. Fuller, who built the house between 1850 and 1860; Mrs. Tamason Pratt, who bought the place soon after the Civil War; F. N. Pratt (her son); Albert C. Wilson, who purchased the place in 1889.

11 Owned by Mrs. Alice (Cleaveland) Bartlett. Former owners: Cyrus Cleaveland, who died in 1856; his widow, who died in 1900. The old house was built by Cyrus Cleaveland in 1835, the new house, also a new barn, by the sons of Mrs. Bartlett, in 1903.

12 Owned by Mrs. Mary Dempsey; purchased in 1860. The house was built in 1884.

13 Owned by William Thayer. Former owners: Edward Jencks, then his widow. The present house was built by William Thayer.

14 About a mile and a half from Center. Southern part of farm borders on road to Ludlow Village and on road to Three Rivers. Owned by Charles H. Calkins. Former owners: Willard Munsell, Aaron Davis, Martin J. Davis. A part of the house as it now stands was built by Willard Munsell early in 1800.

15 Next house north of George Green place. Owned by William Savage. Former owners: Anson Davis and Frederick A. Davis.

16 Owned by William Savage. House supposed to have been built and occupied a few years by Martin Davis.

17 The Plumley place. Owned by Homer M. Bartlett; purchased in 1908. Former owners: Joseph Pease and others, Elijah Plumley, George D. Green. Elijah Plumley thoroughly remodeled the present house and built the barn.

18 Saul Wade homestead. Owned by Homer M. Bartlett. A cellar hole near this place marks the site of the former home of Moses Wood.

19 Owned by Charles Wood. Former owners: James Sheldon, George Miller, Zebina Miller, Isaac Plumley, 1st, Mrs. Lucy (Plumley) Keith, Alexander Whitney. The buildings were remodeled by Mrs. Lucy (Plumley) Keith.

20 North of Collins Station. Owned by Richard Trombly. Former owners: Isaac Brewer, Edwin Brewer. House and barn were built by Isaac Brewer about 1840.

21 About a mile north of Collins Station. Owned by Patrick Logan. Former owners: Ithamar Miller, Daniel Miller, Daniel Brewer, David C. Jones. The house was built by Daniel Brewer about 1850.

22 North of Collins Station. Owned by Jo Casperzack. Former owners: Chauncey Brewer, George Underwood, Patrick Sullivan. The first house was built by Chauncey Brewer.

23 Near Collins Station. Owned by Walter W. Eaton. Former owners: Capt. Isaac Brewer, Lillian Brewer (his daughter), Homer M. Bartlett, Patrick Sullivan. Captain Brewer was a sea captain. The house was built about 1831.

24 Owned by Alfred T. Jones. The house was built by Mr. Jones.

25 Near Collins Station. Owned by Frank Netupsky. Former owners: Horatio Miller, Philo Miller, David C. Jones. House was built by Horatio Miller about 1830. David C. Jones built a barn which was burned and he replaced it by that now standing.

26 Owned by James Butler. Former owners: Edward E. Fuller, Mrs. Elizabeth Wade. The house was built by Edward E. Fuller.

27 Near Collins Station. Owned by Caleb B. Estey. Former owners: Moses Miller, Leonard Miller, Mary Miller, and William Miller. The house was burned during ownership of Leonard Miller and he built the house and barn now standing.

28 Near Collins Station. Owned by Herbert L. Miller. House was built by him.

29 A little north of Collins Station. Owned by Alfred T. Jones. Former owners: Elea Walker, Coleman M. Walker, Mrs. Harriet Jones. The former house and the barn were built by Elea Walker, the present house by Alfred T. Jones.

30 A little north of Collins Station. Owned by Alfred T. Jones. House was built by him.

31 Near Collins Station. Owned by A. Dexter Tufts. The former house was burned and the present house was built by Mr. Tufts in 1879.

32 Near Collins Station. Owned by Patrick Eagan. Former owner, Wilmer Converse, who built the house.

33 Near Collins Station. Reuben Sikes estate. Reuben Sikes built the house and barn in 1886.

34 Near Collins Station. Owned by Howard A. King. House was built by him.

35 Near Collins Station. Owned by Arthur D. King, who purchased it in 1873. Former owners: Aaron Colton, Jonathan Button, Elihu Collins, Roderick Collins, Charles S. Bennett, Henry Phelps, David C. Jones. The L was one of the first houses built in town. The present building was a tavern and was a stopping place for the stages on the Northampton line. The bar is said to have been in the northeast corner and a hall in the east end of the house, on the second floor.

36 Near Collins Station. Owned by Collins Paper Company. Former owners: Joseph Miller, Leonard Miller, Dea. Joseph Miller, James L. Miller, Mrs. Elihu J. Sikes, Frank Sikes, the widow of Frank Sikes. The barn was burned when Mrs. Elihu Sikes was the owner and was rebuilt by her. She also remodeled the house.

North from Center—Old Granby Road

1 At Center. Owned by heirs of Warren D. Fuller; purchased by him April, 1866. Former owners: Elisha Fuller, son of Joshua Fuller; Henry S. Fuller, son of Elisha Fuller, 1st; Lucien Cooley. It is not known when the house was built, but it is supposed to be over a hundred years old. In Elisha Fuller's day it had no porch or bay windows, but there was an extension of the same width as the main part where the L is now with an entrance into it. The main part had a door in place of the first window. On the second floor was a ballroom extending the length of the house with painted frieze, the first and only one seen in those parts at that time. Continuing on beyond the front was a variety store which made an entertaining exhibit at the auction about 1850.

2 At Center. Owned by Louis F. Freitag; purchased by him January, 1898. Former owner, Louis W. Chapin.

HOME OF MRS. WARREN D. FULLER, LUDLOW CENTER
Formerly Elisha Fuller House

3 At Center. Known as the Richard Collins place. Owned by Frederick Fedette. Former owners: Sylvester Clark, Richard Collins, Richard Collins' heirs, John Duteau.

4 About one fourth mile from Center. Owned by George H. Parsons, by whom it was inherited in 1904. Former owners: Samuel Parsons, 1st; Samuel Parsons, 2d; The front part of the house was built by Samuel Parsons, 1st.

5 Owned by Daniel Tewhrane, by whom it was purchased in 1911. Former owners: Rodolphus Clark, Miss Mary Lyon, John Browning,

George H. Sprague. The house was probably built about a hundred years ago. Mr. Sprague remodeled the buildings in 1890.

6 Owned by Leonard S. Lyon, who inherited it from his father about 1908. Former owner, Josiah Lyon.

7 Owned by Leonard S. Lyon, who inherited it in 1908. Former owner, Josiah Lyon.

8 Owned by Albert Mastoo, by whom it was purchased in 1902. Former owners: Horace Gates, Ephraim Gates, Hollis Barber, Fred

ELISHA FULLER HOUSE AT LUDLOW CENTER

Dubrava. The buildings were erected by Horace Gates and have been remodeled by Mr. Mastoo.

9 Owned by Albert Mastoo, by whom it was purchased in 1895. Former owners: Stillman Alden, Ephraim Gates, Albert Warner, Anna Warner. House was built about a hundred years ago by Stillman Alden. Now unoccupied.

10 About a mile from Center. Owned by George E. Lombard. Former owners: Thomas Shean, Angeline Miller, Samuel Parsons, Mrs. Edwin Blair. The house was built by Mr. Shean. Mr. Lombard has remodeled the buildings.

11 Owned by Quartus E. Fisk, who inherited it. Former owners: Lieut. John Sikes, Wealthy Sikes, David Fisk, Polly Fisk (his widow). On this place were the glass works.

12 Owned by Elbridge J. Streeter, by whom it was purchased in 1886. Former owners: Benjamin Sikes, William Pease, Walter Pease, Albert Fuller, John L. Mann, George Page. The former house was probably built in 1774, since that date was on the chimney, and was burned October 16, 1886. The present house was built by Mr. Streeter in 1887. It was the ancestral home of Benjamin Sikes; his son, Lieut. John Sikes, lived with him.

13 A little north of Elbridge J. Streeter's home, on the east side of the road, is a cellar hole marking the site where a house and barn were burned and never rebuilt. It was formerly owned by David Lyon. Elbridge J. Streeter is the present owner of the place.

14 Owned by Mrs. Homer M. Bartlett. Former owners: Homer Lyon, Horace Lyon. The house and barn were built about 1850 by Homer Lyon. They were burned several years since and have not been rebuilt.

15 A cellar hole marks the spot where once stood a red house formerly owned by Frank Clark, later by Matthew Galligan. The barn also has been removed.

16 Near Granby line. Owned by Charles A. White, who purchased it in 1879. Former owners: James Sheldon, Lucien Cooley, John Clark, Lucien Lyon, Calvin Cooley. Mr. White built a new house in 1887 and a new barn in 1910.

17 Owned by Mrs. Emeline T. Banister, who inherited it in 1908. Former owners: Frank Clark, John Coon, James O. Kendall, John L. Banister. House was built in 1866 by John Coon. John L. Banister was a blacksmith and built the shop.

18 About half a mile from Granby line. Owned by Michael T. Kane, who purchased it about 1904. Former owners: David Lyon in 1795, Nathaniel Lyon, Norman Lyon, Lucien N. Lyon. House was built about 1800. Norman Lyon remodeled the house in 1855 and built a new barn in 1859. The buildings were burned about 1906, during Mr. Kane's ownership, and have not been rebuilt. An Indian is said to have been buried on the farm.

19 Owned by Katherine M. Gates. Former owners: Timothy Root, John Gates, Sr., John Gates, Jr. Mr. Root built a house that used to stand in the garden just south of present house.

20 Owned by Kastantinas Pranaitis, who purchased it in 1893. Former owners: Ezra White, George Clark, George R. Clark, Amelia J. Clark. George Clark built the house and barn, the former in 1859.

West from First Church at Center to Granby Road

1 Owned by Charles Tetreault, who purchased it in 1910. Former owners: Increase Sikes, Samuel Parsons, Reuben Sikes, Henry S. Fuller, Charles S. Bennett, Austin F. Newell, Henry A. Munsing. Increase

Sikes used to build plows and wagons and had a blacksmith and a woodworking shop; he also built the first hearse owned by the town. The present house was built by some of the later owners, perhaps Henry S. Fuller or Austin F. Newell. The barn has been remodeled.

2 Owned by Philip Suprenant, who purchased it in 1910. Former owner, Homer Tetreault. The house was built in 1908.

3 About three fourths of a mile west of First Church. Known as the Burr place. Owned by Camille Gokey, who purchased it in 1910.

THE B. F. BURR HOMESTEAD, LUDLOW CENTER

Former owners: Joshua Fuller, who sold it to Henry Starkey in 1823; Waterman Fuller purchased it in 1830, Ashbel and Lyman Burr in 1843. Lyman Burr inherited it from his father, Ashbel Burr, in 1861, and Benjamin F. Burr from his father, Lyman Burr, in 1880. Henry A. Munsing bought it of B. F. Burr in 1905, and sold it to Clarence Fuller. The upright part of the house was remodeled, a new L and wing added, and a new barn built by Lyman Burr in 1860.

CROSS ROAD FROM OLD GRANBY ROAD TO LUDLOW CENTER ROAD

1 About a mile west from First Church. Owned by Richard M. Taft, who purchased it in 1907. Former owners: Pliny Pease, Albert Fuller, William Baggs, Henry A. Swan (a cigar manufacturer), Oren B. Todd, Adelbert L. Bennett and Charles B. Bennett, William Cooley,

—— Bement, —— Haywood, Henry A. Munsing. House was built about 1830.

2 About three quarters of a mile northwest of Center. Owned by Henry A. Munsing, who purchased it in 1891. Former owners: Alpheus Rice (a manufacturer of scythe snaths), Orange Rice, Michael Munsing (a tailor, also a soldier in the Civil War). Henry A. Munsing remodeled the house in 1905 and built a new barn and sheds in 1906. The barn was struck by lightning July, 1911, and burned.

3 About a mile northwest from Center. Owned by Alfred J. Hobson, who inherited it in 1908. Former owners: Doctor Wood, Mrs.

HOME OF HENRY A. MUNSING

Polly Rood, Joseph Rood, Town of Ludlow, Matthew Galligan, Mrs. Sarah Swart, Mrs. Adeline Trask, John Hobson. This is quite a historic place and has been the home of many people. It was once owned by Dr. Wood, who practiced in the town at the close of the 18th century; he gave it to his daughter, Mrs. Paulina Rood, who was a skillful and obliging nurse and was "Aunt Polly" to the whole town. Once upon a time the house was burned to the ground and the neighbors went into the woods, cut and prepared the timber, and rebuilt the house. An L has been built and other improvements made by the last two or three owners.

The Rood Homestead. Charles D. Rood, Owner

4 One mile northwest of Center. Owned by Truman N. Hubbard, who purchased it in 1865. Former owners: Sarah Goodell, William Clark (father of Gilbert Clark), Martin Smith. The house was built about 1870. The former house, or part of it, was the old glass works that used to be on the premises now owned by Quartus E. Fisk.

5 About a mile northwest of Center. Owned by George N. Hubbard. Former owners: Seneca Wood, Newton Hubbard, Daniel H. Hubbard. The house was burned in 1908 or 1909 and has not been rebuilt.

6 Near junction with Old Granby Road. Owned by Gilbert S. Atchinson, who purchased it in 1872. Former owners: Joel Clark, Noah Clark, Benjamin Baggs. Benjamin Baggs built the barn and hanged himself there.

GRANBY ROAD—WEST AND NORTH OF THE BURR PLACE

1 Opposite schoolhouse. Owned by Charles Shaw, by whom it was purchased in 1909. Former owners: Calvin Hubbard, Henry Swan, Alva Noble, Edmund Fuller, John W. Hubbard, John P. Hubbard, Mrs. Caroline E. Hubbard (his widow). The house was burned when John W. Hubbard owned it and the present house was built by him.

2 The Rood Homestead. Asahel Rood purchased this farm of Selah Kendall, Nov. 12, 1816. In 1853 it was sold to Reuben Sikes, whose young daughter, seeing a snake run under the barn, procured a match to set fire to some straw there, and thus kill the snake. The barn was totally destroyed. Mr. Sikes built another of white oak with enormous stone underpinnings. Albert Fuller was the next owner, and in turn sold it to his brother Edmund Fuller from whom Charles D. Rood, the present owner, purchased it. Extensive alterations have been made upon the buildings. On this farm are two noted springs of excellent water. One situated on the top of a high hill has furnished water for more than a century and in 1912 supplies three dairy farms and two others. This spring was mentioned in Asahel Rood's deed, the water being reserved to the use of Moses Rood (brother of Asahel) and James Kendall. The second spring has a temperature of 45° in the hottest weather.

3 Known as the Josiah Alden place. Cellar hole is a little north of Charles D. Rood's place. Place is owned by Charles D. Rood. Former owners: Josiah Alden (who built the house), Edmund Fuller. The house was burned when Edmund Fuller owned it and has not been rebuilt.

4 Known as the Roger M. Chandler place. Owned by John Knight. Former owners: Moses Rood, Roger M. Chandler, Adelbert L. Bennett.

5 Owned by George N. Hubbard. Former owners: Elam Wright,

Joel Clark, Noah Clark, George Smith, Charles S. Bennett, Franklin Bennett, Henry Granger. Elam Wright used it as a tavern.

6 Opposite cross road. Owned by Merton R. Bennett. Former owners: Stillman Alden, A. S. Putnam, a Mr. Whitcher (a few days only), F. G. and M. R. Bennett. M. R. Bennett purchased the entire interest in the place in November, 1906. How long the house has been built is not known, but it is supposed to be more than seventy-five years. Stillman Alden built both house and barn. Both have

THE MOSES ROOD PLACE
Later owned by Adelbert L. Bennett

been remodeled. Stillman Alden was a cooper by trade and won a prize in competition for making the best hogshead, having taken it to Boston on an ox sled. His hogshead did not leak on first trial, but those of all his competitors did. Some of his tools are still in existence.

7 Fuller Street. Owned by Mrs. Hiram Davenport, who purchased it in September, 1879. Former owners: Sherwood Beebe, Ezekiel Fuller, Fuller brothers. Mr. Beebe kept a tavern here when he owned it. Ezekiel Fuller tore down the old house and built the one now standing.

8 Fuller Street—beyond cross road to Granby road. Owned by Charles W. Nash, by whom it was purchased May 12, 1883. Former owners: Flavius Putnam, Mendal Latham, Davenport L. Fuller, David Fuller, William Pease.

9 Fuller Street. Owned by Franklin W. Nash, who purchased it October 8, 1900. Former owners: Davenport L. Fuller, Warren Hubbard, Elijah Munsell, E. Newton Fisher, Charles Syriac, George Streeter.

THE FRANKLIN NASH HOUSE

Who built the original house is not known, but it was enlarged about one half and the old part remodeled by Davenport L. Fuller.

FULLER STREET—SOUTH AND WEST TO HOME OF AMOS KEEFE ON HOLYOKE ROAD

1 Formerly known as the Ruel Kendall farm. Owned by Mrs. Mary G. Severence, who purchased it in 1874. Former owners: Ruel Kendall, M. Clough, Timothy Seymour, Albert Fuller, Sr. The house has been remodeled and enlarged by Mrs. Severence.

2 Fuller Street. Owned by Chauncey L. Buell. Former owners: Albert Fuller, Mrs. Lucy A. (Fuller) Pease. The house and barn were built by Albert Fuller.

3 Fuller Street above Harris Pond Road. Owned by Adrian G. Hatch, who purchased it in 1911. Former owners: Rev. Ebenezer B. Wright, Rev. Chester Bridgman, Lucius Simonds, Albert Fuller, Albert E. Fuller, Henry A. Munsing. Albert Fuller remodeled the house and built the barn.

4 Fuller Street. Owned by James Leroy Simonds, who came into possession by bequest of his grandfather, Lucius Simonds. Former owners: Josiah Hitchcock and his son, Abner (among the earliest settlers), Simeon Pease, heirs of Simeon Pease, Lucius Simonds. The present house and barn were built by Lucius Simonds.

HOME OF CHARLES S. BENNETT

5 Fuller Street. Owned by Mrs. Warren G. Fuller, by whom it was purchased in 1899. Former owners: Ezekiel Fuller, Lyman Fuller, Lathrop Fuller, Andrew Beebe. Mr. Beebe thoroughly repaired the house while he owned it.

6 Fuller Street. Owned by Hart Webster. Former owners: Franklin Fuller, Ambrose Clough, Mrs. Ambrose Clough (widow), William Miller, Louis Coté, John Blanchard. The house was burned while Mr. Blanchard was owner and he built the house now standing. The barn was thoroughly remodeled by Mr. Clough.

7 Fuller Street. Owned by Charles B. Bennett, who purchased it in 1875. Former owners: Elijah Fuller, Gilbert Fuller. The house was built about a hundred years ago.

8 Fuller Street. Owned by Charles B. Bennett. Former owners: Gates Willey, Mrs. Jerusha Willey, Daniel Green. It is thought Gates Willey built the house and barn. He formerly lived and his children were born where Charles Fairbanks now lives. He worked at the mill now owned by Albert Banister.

9 A little east of Harris Mill, so-called. Known as the Selah Kendall place. Present owner not known. Former owners: Selah Kendall, James Monroe Kendall, Mrs. Lucy (Kendall) McLean, James Kirk McLean, J. Leroy Simonds, Ensign Morse. James Monroe Kendall built a fine barn, which was burned, and he built the one now standing. Later the original house was burned and the present house was built.

10 Off Holyoke Road, near Harris Mill. Owned by John Purchase. Former owners: Eliphal Booth, George Booth, Frederick F. Fairbanks. The house is old and Mr. Purchase is making thorough repairs (1911).

11 Harris Mill—Holyoke Road. Present owners: John Purchase, of house, barn, and land; John Height, of water privilege and mill. Former owners: Tyrus Pratt was probably first owner. The mill in 1805 was called "The Continental Mill." John B. Paulk succeeded Pratt; it then passed to Napoleon B. Paulk, who sold it about 1857 to Nathan A. Harris. It passed to Philo A. Harris about 1861, and at his death without issue to the heirs of Nathan A. Harris. The Harris heirs sold the house and land to Charles O. Churchill, who conveyed same to John Purchase. The house and barn were built by Nathan A. Harris about 1858 or 1859.

12 Holyoke Road, a little north of Harris Mill. Owned by Mrs. Mowry and Mrs. Warren, who inherited it. Former owners: Ezekiel Barton, Dan Hubbard, Mrs. Emeline Collins and William H. Hubbard (Dan Hubbard's heirs), then to their heirs, Mrs. Mowry and Mrs. Warren. Ezekiel Barton built the house about 1786 and used it as a tavern. The barn was then on the opposite side of the road. When Dan Hubbard was owner he built the present barn. Dan Hubbard was the father of Capt. Henry A. Hubbard, who enlisted a company in the Civil War.

13 Holyoke Road. Owned by Mrs. Charles F. Fairbanks, who purchased it in 1874. Former owners: John Paulk, Dan Hubbard. Mrs. Fairbanks remodeled the house and barn.

14 Holyoke Road. Known as the Austin F. Nash place, opposite Amos Keefe's. Owned by George Codare, who purchased it about 1893. Former owners: Julius Nash, Asahel Nash, Austin F. Nash. The former house was fitted up and used for a select school while Asahel Nash owned it. In 1888, Austin F. Nash, while owner, tore down the old house and built the house and barn now standing.

15 Holyoke Road. Owned by Amos J. Keefe, by whom it was purchased in 1910. Former owners: Timothy Nash, Asahel Nash, William Pease, John Keefe, Keefe brothers. Asahel Nash thoroughly remodeled the former house in 1857. This house was burned while the Keefe brothers owned it. Amos Keefe built the present house and barn in 1903.

16 Holyoke Road, at Moody Corners. Owned by Amos Keefe, who purchased it in 1892. Former owners: John Moody, Cyril A. Southworth, Keefe brothers. John Moody was a carpenter and had a shop on the southeast corner, on the opposite side of the highway from the house, where he used to make coffins. Mr. Keefe has repaired the house where Mr. Moody lived.

HOME OF EDWARD EARLE CHAPMAN

LUDLOW CITY ROAD. NORTH FROM AMOS KEEFE'S TO LUDLOW CITY AND CROSS ROAD FROM GRANBY ROAD

1 Ludlow City Road beyond Holyoke Road. Owned by Mrs. Wallace Dostal, who purchased it in 1910. Former owners: Ebenezer Barber, David Atchinson, Gillen D. Atchinson. David Atchinson built the barn, Gillen D. Atchinson the present house.

2 Ludlow City Road, north of Holyoke Road. Known as the Elisha T. Parsons place. Owned by Michael Dubinski. Former owners: —— Stacey, Lewis Barber, Elisha T. Parsons, Lucius Simonds, J. Leroy Simonds, George N. Hubbard. Mr. Parsons built the house and barn.

3 Ludlow City Road near corner of cross road. Known as the old Chapin farm. Owned by Edward Earle Chapman, who purchased it in

April, 1886. Former owners: Abel Chapin, Jacob Newell, Austin Newell, Henry Phelps, James M. White. The barn was burned in 1891, and the present barn built in 1893. The old house was burned in September, 1899. It was one of the oldest houses in town. No one seems to know when it was built, but it was probably at least one hundred and fifty years old. It is said there never was a death in the house. There is an old cellar hole on the hill, also a well near the old road, which was perhaps the site of the oldest house on the farm. The house now standing was designed and built by the present owner in 1899. It is said that Abel Chapin, the first owner of the farm, could travel on his own land from this farm to the Connecticut River.

HENRY DAMON HOUSE AT LUDLOW CITY
Now Owned by Clarence Tilley

4 Ludlow City Road. Owned by Howard M. White, who purchased it in 1895. Former owners: Austin Newell, William Walker, James White, Edward Clark, James White. Former house was built about 1851. This house was torn down and a new one built near the site in 1911.

5 Ludlow City Road. Owned by James M. White, who inherited it in 1875. Former owners: Noah Bowker, Elias Frost, Samuel White. Mr. Frost built the house in 1827. Samuel White built a barn 75 feet in length and James M. White has added 75 feet, making 150 feet. He has also added a horse barn and sheds, also remodeled the original house. Samuel White was killed by a boar, May 17, 1875.

6 Ludlow City Road, near Ludlow City. Owned by R. Samuel White, to whom it was deeded in 1899 by his father, James M. White, of whose farm it had been a part. The house was built in the summer of 1900 by R. Samuel White.

7 At Ludlow City. Owned by Mrs. Wallace Dostal. Former owners: Amos Lazell, James W. Kendall, Luman Bartlett, Elisha Dutton, Lowell Damon, Frank Kendall. Mrs. Dostal has remodeled the house and barn.

8 Granby Road, at Ludlow City. Owned by Clarence Jerome Tilley, who purchased it in October, 1891. Former owners: Henry Damon, Alden Damon, Mrs. Alden Damon.

9 Granby Road, at Ludlow City. Owned by Rutherford Hayes Ferry, who purchased it May 5, 1910. Former owners: P. Jewett,

HOME OF RUTHERFORD H. FERRY, LUDLOW CITY

Samuel Dickinson, Samuel White, William P. Clark, Hugh Kane. The former house was built in 1876. This was torn down and the present one erected by William P. Clark. The barn was burned when Mr. Clark was the owner and he built the one now standing. August 28, 1907, during the time Mr. Kane owned the place, his son, Hugh J. Kane, was murdered while driving home from Holyoke in his milk cart.

10 Ludlow City. Owned by Henry I. Carver, by whom it was purchased in 1866. Former owners: Edmond Damon, who sold to Joseph Munger in 1783; Munger leased to David Carver in 1794 for 900 years; in 1803 David, Jonathan, and Aaron Carver, and John Filer leased to Joel Eastman; in 1807 Joel Eastman leased to Joseph Eastman; in 1820 Joseph Eastman conveyed to Hezekiah Fisk, he to Barton and Marsh, they to Josiah Simms, and he, in 1836, to Jefferson Alden, he to Rufus Kimball, he to Damon, and Alden Damon to present owner. Henry I. Carver built the house now standing in 1880.

11 Ludlow City. Owned by Arthur T. Warner. Former owner, Hezekiah Fisk. He used to have a mill on the opposite side of the pond from H. I. Carver's, where he manufactured woolen cloth and carded wool. He was father of Gordon M. Fisk, founder of the *Palmer Journal*.

12 Cross road from Granby Road, Ludlow City. Asa Damon place. A house formerly stood between the Fisk house and Arthur T. Warner's at the end of the road leading to Otis Tilley's, where Asa Damon lived.

HOME OF HENRY I. CARVER, LUDLOW CITY

It was torn down several years ago. A cider mill, now torn away, stood about half way between Arthur T. Warner's and Otis Tilley's.

13 On Granby line, Ludlow City. Owned by Arthur T. Warner, who inherited it from Alonzo C. Warner, July 20, 1899. Former owners: Eleazar Owen, who sold to Amos Kendall, deed being dated February 20, 1835; Elisha T. Parsons, administrator of Amos Kendall's estate, sold to William E. Montague, deed being dated March 27, 1838; William E. Montague sold to Alonzo Warner, September 4, 1838; Alonzo C. Warner inherited it from Alonzo Warner, December 19, 1884. The present house was built in 1887 by Alonzo C. Warner, who also built the barn now standing. The town line passes through the house.

14 Cross road from Granby Road at Ludlow City. Owned by Oscar D. Tucker, by whom it was purchased in November, 1892. Former owners: James W. Kendall, James Osmyn Kendall, Alice Kendall (his widow). The first house was built about 1852 and was burned in October, 1896. The present house was built in the spring of 1897 by Mr. Tucker.

15 Northwest corner of Ludlow, on cross road from Granby Road. Owned by Otis E. Tilley, who purchased it in 1883. Former owners:

HOME OF ARTHUR T. WARNER, LUDLOW CITY

Eli Dickinson of Granby, who sold to Erastus Dickinson; Erastus Dickinson to Gordon B. Miller (1821); Gordon B. Miller to Ashbel Burr (1833); Ashbel Burr to Napoleon B. Paulk (1842); Napoleon B. Paulk to Franklin P. Tilley; Franklin P. Tilley to Otis E. Tilley (1883). The old house was burned some time after 1842. The Paulks fashioned a dwelling by moving several buildings together, which stood till the present house was built by Otis E. Tilley in 1899.

16 Northwest corner of Ludlow, on cross road from Granby Road. Owned by Charles H. Farr, who purchased it in 1909. Former owners: Napoleon B. Paulk, who sold to Franklin P. Tilley, Franklin Tilley's heirs. House was built about 1858. When Mr. Tilley bought the land there were no buildings on it and he erected those now standing.

17 Northwest corner of Ludlow, near Chicopee line, cross road from Granby Road. Owned by heirs of Herman P. Jensen. Former owners: Original owner was Porter Tilley; Franklin P. Tilley bought out heirs of Porter Tilley and later sold to James H. Farr; Farr sold to William P. Clark in 1889, and Mr. Clark to Mr. Jensen in 1893. Present house was built by Franklin P. Tilley about 1879, who built it for John B. Caswell, who lived in it about five years.

SOUTH FROM JOHN W. HUBBARD'S TO MARGARET O'NEIL'S

1 Cross road to Granby Road, one mile west of Center, near schoolhouse. Owned by John W. Hubbard, by whom it was purchased in February, 1879. Former owners: Elisha Hubbard, Titus Hubbard, John P. Hubbard. House was built in 1851.

2 Cross road to Granby Road. Owned by Joseph Suprenant. Former owners: Dr. Elijah Caswell, Mrs. Susan Caswell (his widow), Philo H. Miller, Michael Bresnehan, Albert Lyon, Charles D. Rood, Isaac Smith. House was probably built about 1830 by Dr. Caswell. He also built the barn.

3 Cross road to Granby Road. Owned by Isaac Smith. Former owners: ——— Gilligan, Ebenezer Blood, Hollis Barber, George A. Birnie, Reuben H. Chapin. Betweeen 1850 and 1860, when Mr. Blood owned the place, the gambrel roof of the house was changed to its present form.

4 Belchertown Road, about one mile from Ludlow Village. Present owner, Caroline A. Converse, who purchased it in 1880. Former owners: ———Clough, Charles Converse (bought in 1807), Rodolphus Converse. House was built in 1808. Rodolphus Converse built an L to the house in 1834. Miss Converse built the barn in 1900.

5 One mile south of Center, Reservoir Road. Owned by William M. Ashwell, who purchased it May 1, 1908. Former owners: Henry Charles, Edmund Charles, Melina N. Charles (now Fuller), Mr. Lee, Welcome M. Dunlap, Henry Dunlap, William Ellison, Mr. Young, Stephen Duquette. House was built by Henry Charles in 1841. The barn was burned when Welcome Dunlap was the owner, and he built the present barn in 1897.

6 Belchertown Road, about a mile north of the village. Owned by A. Lincoln Johnson, by whom it was purchased in 1893. Former owners: Spencer Talmadge, Margaret Talmadge. The house was built about 1826. Mr. Johnson remodeled the house and barn in 1896.

7 Belchertown Road, about one mile north of the village. Owned by Joseph Goodnow. Former owners: James Chapin, Henry M. Chapin, Labelle brothers. Henry M. Chapin built the house. North of the brook, where the orchard now is, there was once an Indian camp. Some of the land was obtained by the Chapins from the Indians and there was no deed of it.

8 Belchertown Road, near Chapin Pond. Owned by Mrs. E. Newton Fisher; purchased by her in 1886. Former owners: Dea. Oliver Dutton, Hubbard Dutton, heirs of Hubbard Dutton, Mrs. Caroline (Dutton) Sikes. Original house was torn down and the present one built by Hubbard Dutton about 1860. The barn was burned about 1885 and that now standing was built by Mrs. Fisher. Dea. Oliver Dutton was a soldier in the Revolution and the cartridge box he carried during the war is now in the Historical Room of the Hubbard Memorial Library.

9 Belchertown Road, near Chapin Pond. Owned by Margaret O'Neil, who purchased it in 1897. Former owners: Alexander McLean, Mrs. McLean (his widow), James Haviland, John O'Neil. Mrs. O'Neil remodeled the house and barn in 1900.

West and South from Center

1 Ludlow Center. Owned by Michael T. Kane, who purchased it in 1911. Former owners: Mrs. Norman Lyon, Mrs. Elisha Dutton, Fred Taylor, Henry A. Munsing, Jasper Knight. The house and barn were built by Mrs. Norman Lyon about 1866.

2 Ludlow Center. Owned by Olin W. Stoughton, who purchased it in 1906. Former owners: Increase Sikes built the house and barn and lived there several years. George Booth then bought it, and after his death it was inherited by his daughter, Mrs. Amnie (Booth) Hubbard, and, at her decease, willed to her nephews and niece, Charles E. Booth, George R. Booth and Hattie E. Booth. The house was built by Increase Sikes, probably between 1845 and 1850.

3 Ludlow Center opposite First Church. Owned by Mrs. Laura E. Perham, who came into possession by will January, 1892. Former owners: Theodore Sikes, Dr. Washington B. Alden, Lucius Simonds (who sold it in 1864), Elizur Hayes (who sold it in 1871), Gordon Pinney (who willed it to Mrs. Perham). Mrs. Perham has had the post office in this house for nineteen years (1911). House was built by Theodore Sikes nearly a hundred years ago.

4 Ludlow Center, south of First Church. Owned by James Robbins, who purchased it in 1909. Former owners: Rev. J. W. Tuck, Rev. C. L. Cushman, Rev. Chester Bridgman, Henry Swan, Hollis Barber, Ludlow Cassidy, William D. Ellison. Former house was built in 1844 or 1845, and was burned in 1846, during Mr. Tuck's ownership, and rebuilt soon after.

5 Ludlow Center. Owned by Charles P. Jones. Former owner, Henry S. Jones. The house and the former barn were built by Henry

S. Jones in 1852. In July, 1880, the barn was struck by lightning and burned. H. S. Jones then erected a much larger barn with a silo attached, the first silo built in town and the second in the state. In 1884 another house was built across the road, which was enlarged in 1887.

WEST FROM PLUMLEY'S CORNER

1 Three Rivers Road, one mile east of Ludlow Village. Owned by Adelbert L. Bennett, who purchased it in 1904. Former owners: Edwin Chapin, Mrs. Hattie J. Roberts. House was built in 1848.

2 Three Rivers Road, nearly one mile from Ludlow Village. Owned by Edward E. Fuller, who inherited it from his father, Henry S. Fuller, in 1885. House was built by H. S. Fuller about 1840. When Mr. Fuller bought his farm it was covered largely with heavy pine timber. Since E. E. Fuller came in possession he has built a new L and remodeled the upright part of the house, and has built a new barn and other buildings.

3 Three Rivers Road, near Ludlow Village. Owned by Henry S. Fuller, who came into possession August 18, 1875. Part of the land was purchased from F. F. McLean, the remainder was a part of the estate of the late Henry S. Fuller, Sr. The house was built in the fall of 1875 by present owner. The timber for the first church, now known as the "old town house,'" came from the section of the farm which borders on the east side of Wood pond. A part of the trees fell on thin ice on the edge of the pond, where they broke through and sank and may still be seen under water.

4 Three Rivers Road. Owned by Oliver B. Miller, who built the house and barn. The house was burned several years ago and has not been rebuilt.

5 Three Rivers Road. Owned by Edward P. Miller, who purchased it in 1894. Former owner, Herbert E. Miller.

6 Three Rivers Road. Owned by Ludlow Manufacturing Associates. Former owners: Stephen Miller purchased it in 1844. —— Chapman, —— Ray, Stephen J. Miller, Herbert E. Miller. House was built in 1858 by S. J. Miller, who also built a barn. The Ludlow Manufacturing Associates have moved a barn from another place to this and made other alterations.

7 Three Rivers Road, east of Ludlow Village. Owned by Frank N. Moore. Former owners: William Ray, John Ray. House was built about 1820. William Ray used to forge bayonets for the United States Armory during the Civil War in the old shop which used to stand nearly opposite the house.

8 East Street, on road to Three Rivers. Owned by Mrs. Etta M. McLean, who inherited it in 1896. Former owners: Lockland McLean, Francis F. McLean, James K. McLean. Francis F. McLean

thoroughly remodeled or built the present house and remodeled the barn in 1879.

9 East Street, known as the Eli Smith place. Present owner not known. Former owners: Col. John Miller, then Eli M. Smith. It has been altered and at present is used in part as a store.

10 East Street in Ludlow Village. Owned by Frank Warren. Former owners: James Bugbee, Mrs. Storrs Stebbins (his daughter), Myron Hayden, William Pease, Mrs. Lucy A. Pease.

Plumley's Corner to Alden Brothers'

1 Three Rivers Road east of Plumley's corner. Owned by Louis and William Pero, who purchased it in 1905. Former owners: Elijah Plumley, Edward Lawrence, Mitchell Pero. Mitchell Pero built the present house and barn.

2 Three Rivers Road, east of Plumley's corner. Owned by Joseph LaBroad. Former owners: George Miller, Oscar Wood. Mr. Wood built part of the house. Mr. LaBroad remodeled it and built an addition.

3 Three Rivers Road, on north side opposite Joseph LaBroad's. Owned by Dwight Blackmer. Mr. Blackmer built the house and barn.

4 Three Rivers Road. A little east of Dwight Blackmer's, on the south side of the highway, and back a little from it, is a cellar hole where once stood a house and barn. This was known as the Joseph Miller place. He was one of the early settlers of the town.

5 Eastern part of town, near Red Bridge. Owned by —— Day, by whom it was purchased in 1910. Former owners: Sylvester Miller, Franklin Bramble, Mr. Bramble's heirs, Albert Blodgett, Frank Rindge. The original house was burned in 1886. Mr. Bramble built the present house and barn.

6 Eastern part of town, opposite the Day place. Owned by John Davis. House built by a Mr. Pike.

7 Eastern part of the town, near Red Bridge. Owned by Mrs. Julia D. Bramble (wife of William Bramble), who purchased it in 1904. Former owners: Lyman Shearer, Susan Shearer, George D. Shearer. Lyman Shearer built the house. Mrs. Bramble remodeled the house and built the barn.

8 Eastern part of town, a little north of Red Bridge. Owned by Mrs. Edwin Wade. Former owner: Edwin Wade.

9 Eastern part of town, near Red Bridge. Owned by Mrs. William Whitney. Former owners: Hiram Wade, Adin Whitney.

10 On cross road from Three Rivers Road, near Blackmer's, to Mrs. William Whitney's. Owned by Charles Rich. Former owners: Pliny Wade, Daniel Fogerty. Pliny Wade built the house and barn.

11 Eastern part of town, near Mrs. William Whitney's. Owned by William Blackmer. Former owner, Alanson Poole.

FARMS OF LUDLOW

12 Eastern part of town, on cross road from Danforth W. Sikes, south to Red Bridge. Owned by Charles Parker. Former owners: Carlos O. Moore, Prentiss B. Moore, Elexis Wade, John Smith.

13 Eastern part of town, near Red Bridge. Owned by Charles Parker. Former owners: Dwight Daniels, Adin Whitney, William Whitney, Mrs. William Whitney.

14 Near the Reservoir. Owned by A. G. Hiersche, who purchased it in 1891. Former owners: Asa Daniels, Lucius Simonds, Mr. Bramble, Mr. Butterworth. The house has been standing nearly a hundred years. This place was once entirely covered by forests. It is now a fine dairy farm and is known as "Pleasant View Dairy Farm."

15 Red Bridge district, near Belchertown line. Owned by Alfred K. Paine, who purchased it in 1908. Former owners: David Paine, Jonathan Paine, Lemuel and David K. Paine. House was built in 1843. An elm tree stands near it which was planted by Lemuel Paine in 1797. The pond of the Ludlow Manufacturing Associates at Red Bridge sets back a little on the farm.

16 Southeastern part of town, near Belchertown line. Owned by Herbert N. Paine, who purchased it in April, 1874. Former owners: David Paine (a Revolutionary soldier), Jonathan Paine, Chester Paine. The present house was built in 1896. The old homestead was burned in 1895. It was built by David Paine in or about 1812. About 1820 it was struck by lightning and extensive repairs were needed. The farm has been in the Paine family about a hundred years.

17 Eastern part of town, near Mrs. William Whitney's and schoolhouse. Owned by Jacob Burley. Former owners: Jonathan Wade, Edwin Wade. The house was built by Jonathan Wade.

18 Eastern part of town, on Belchertown Road. Owned by Marshall Wright. Former owners: Goss Wright, Pliny Wright. House has been torn down.

19 Eastern part of town, on Belchertown Road. Owned by Samuel A. Thomas. Former owners: Marshall Wright, —— Beaudry, Charles Simonds. Marshall Wright built the house, Charles Simonds the barn.

20 Eastern part of the town, on Belchertown Road. Owned by Jonathan Olds. Former owners: Blanchard brothers, Marcus Daniels, Orlando Moore, Carlos Moore, Elexis Wade. While Mr. Wade owned the farm the house was burned and he built the one now standing.

21 Eastern part of town, on Belchertown Road, north of Elexis Wade place. Owned by Gordon Wood. Former owner, Alexander Whitney.

22 Eastern part of town, on Belchertown Road. Owned by Lorin Wood's heirs. Former owners: Reuben Olds, Lorin Wood.

23 Eastern part of town, on Belchertown Road. Owned by Joseph Benway, Sr. Former owner, Carlos Moore. House was burned and has been rebuilt.

24 Eastern part of town, north, on Belchertown Road. Owned by Michael Nelligan. Former owners: Alexander Whitney, Zuri Whitney.

25 Eastern part of town, north, on Belchertown Road. Alden Brothers' sawmill. They built a house and barn a little north of the mill. The house was burned and has not been rebuilt.

26 Eastern part of town, Belchertown Road, north of Alden Brothers' mill. Owned by Orlando Moore. Former owners: Edward Stewart, Edwin Stewart.

27 Eastern part of town, on Belchertown Road. Owned by Charles W. Alden. Former owner, Charles Alden, who used to manufacture forks.

28 Belchertown Road, east of Broad Brook. John Alden place. Former owner, Darius Olds. House is not occupied or used. An old Alden homestead.

29 Eastern part of town, on Belchertown Road. Owned by Charles Whitney. Former owners: Dexter Capen, Quartus Sikes, Otis Sikes, Zuri Whitney. This house was formerly a hotel.

30 Eastern part of town, still north on Belchertown Road. Owned by Richard Reynolds. Former owners: Henry Graves, Austin Lyman Graves, Mr. West of F. M. West Box Company of Springfield. A. Lyman Graves had a shingle mill and a gristmill on the place.

31 Eastern part of town near Belchertown line. Owned by Caroline Alden. Former owner, Benjamin Alden.

32 Eastern part of town, near Belchertown line. Owned by Alden brothers. Former owners: Josiah Alden, Orsamus Alden, Orsamus Alden's heirs. The house now standing was built by Orsamus Alden.

From Amos Keefe's to Eaton's Mills (now Banister's), to Jackson Cady's, to Owen Clifford's; then North to Amos Nichols's, to W. F. Miller's in Ludlow Village

1 Western part of town, southwest of Amos Keefe's. Known as the David Eaton place. Present owner's name is not known. Former owners: David Eaton, Nelson McGregory, William McGregory.

2 Western part, on road to Eaton's mills. Present owner's name is unknown. Former owners: Curtis Frost, who built the house; Samuel Omrod.

3 Top of the hill, east of Eaton's mills. Owned by Jo Dupal. Former owner: Noah Frost.

4 Western part of town, off Ludlow City Road. Owned by Albert Banister, who purchased it in 1888. Former owners: —— West, Jacob S. Eaton, Mrs. H. K. Wight. The old Eaton mill used to card wool fleeces into rolls, and made a cloth called satinet. There were also a sawmill and a gristmill. The gristmill is still operated by Mr. Banister. He also carries on a dairy farm and has a milk route. Main part of house was built about a hundred years ago. Mr. Banister has remodeled the house and barn.

5 Southwestern corner of town, Chicopee Falls Road, near Ludlow City Road. Owned by Jackson Cady, who inherited it from his father, Amasa Cady, in 1848. Former owners: Samuel Frost, Amasa Cady. House was built in 1851 by Jackson Cady. This farm is a part of the original Amasa Cady farm. Jackson Cady built his present house in 1851 and the barn about 1866. His barn was struck by lightning in July, 1911, and burned.

6 Southwestern part of town, Chicopee Falls Road. Owned by Otis Sikes, who purchased it in 1893. Was formerly a part of the Amasa Cady farm, and included the old farm buildings of Amasa Cady. Former owners: Samuel Frost, Amasa Cady, Mrs. Mary Deland and Mrs. Jane Leonard (daughters and heirs of Amasa Cady). The house was built by Amasa Cady in 1826. He also built a house on the north side of the road in 1839, which was struck by lightning in 1879, but was not destroyed. A balsam tree standing near was struck at the same time, and cut off about three feet from the ground, a piece about five feet long, like a whip stock, being taken from the tree and driven through a window. Mr. Sikes has the piece as a relic. A few years later the house caught fire and was burned. An old house where Amasa Cady lived for a time is still standing on the farm, and is owned by Otis Sikes.

7 Southwestern part of the town, Chicopee Falls Road. Owned by Mr. and Mrs. William C. Walker, who purchased it in 1905. Former owners: —— Bullard; he sold it in 1845 to Samuel Frost Keyes, who died in 1864. It remained in possession of his widow until her death in 1905. The main part of the house was built about 1800, the L in 1859.

8 On Holyoke Road, a little north of the Village. Owned by Owen Clifford. Former owners: Warren Hubbard, Sr., Warren Hubbard, Jr., —— Stebbins.

9 A little south of Harris Mill, Holyoke Road, corner of cross road. Owned by Daniel Nichols. Former owners: —— Pratt, Lemuel Bennett, David Atchinson, Horace Tarbox, Mrs. Margaret Tarbox. Horace Tarbox was drowned while trying to cross Harris Pond on the ice.

10 A little north of Ludlow Village on the Fuller Street Road. Owned by Ann (Bliss) Gasner. Former owner, Edmund Bliss. Mr. Bliss built the house on the east side of the Holyoke Road near Owen Clifford's and afterwards removed it to its present location.

11 At Ludlow Village. Owned by Frank A. Towne, who inherited it. Former owners: —— Washburn, Marquis DeL. Towne. The house and barn were built by Mr. Washburn.

12 At Ludlow Village. Owned by Mrs. Francenah Towne. Former owners: Rev. Chester L. Cushman, Lemuel H. Brigham, Marquis

DeL. Towne. Rev. C. L. Cushman built the house and barn in 1878, and Mr. Towne remodeled them.

13 North Street, Ludlow Village. Owned by Charles M. Smith, who purchased it in 1875. Former owners: Thyla Batholic, Col. John Miller. House was built in 1877. Charles Smith bought the place of John Miller in 1875, tore down the buildings, built the present house in 1877 and the barn in 1888.

14 Ludlow Village. Owned by Wilbur F. Miller, who purchased it in 1873. Former owners: Orrin Andrus, Col. John Miller. House was built about 1825. Colonel Miller built the present front in 1846, the work being done by Eli M. Smith. Colonel Miller also built the barn, the boards used being purchased at the mill in North Blandford for $2.50 per thousand. The barn was burned in 1909. Since W. F. Miller bought the farm of sixty acres there have been one hundred and thirty houses built upon it.

FARMS DESTROYED IN BUILDING SPRINGFIELD RESERVOIR

NORTH AND EAST OF CENTER

Going from the First Church north, we come to an old bridle road leading past the house of Leonard Lyon and up through to Turkey Hill in Belchertown. About half a mile beyond Mr. Lyon's place was what was known as the Calkins place, where used to be a house and sawmill. The mill was burned and never rebuilt. At that time a family by the name of Kimball lived in the house; later Harvey Macomber lived there. The Springfield Water Works diverted the water to their reservoir and the house is gone. It was said that Mr. Calkins believed in eating little and often, and that a pewter milkpan full was all he wanted at one sitting. There was a peach orchard on the place known to be forty years old and still bearing, having escaped the "yellows."

There was another farm, mostly woodland, with buildings, two or three miles farther north. Solon Lyon lived there a few years, and it was known as the Lyon place. Mr. Lyon used to say the only sound he could hear was the crowing of roosters.

Still farther up in the woods lived Jacob Story and his wife, colored people. They made baskets and exchanged them for pork, Indian meal, and other provisions. Mrs. Story did washings and other household tasks for the townspeople.

SIKES STREET—BELCHERTOWN ROAD FROM LUDLOW CENTER.

Before the City of Springfield made its reservoir, the old road to Belchertown extended from the gatehouse through land now covered by water and leading into the new road which was built a little south of where Deacon Alva Sikes lived. The cellar hole where the house stood may still be seen. This was the first house after leaving the gatehouse—the last owner being Reuben Sikes. The former owners were: Jonathan Sikes, then Alva Sikes, who inherited the property from Jonathan and built the barn.

The next house north was owned by Silas Sikes, brother of Alva. There is no other owner known. Near this point, where the old road turned to the right into the reservoir, we come to the site of another house, now covered by water, which was owned by Ashbel Burr and his son, Lyman. It was the birthplace of Benjamin F. Burr. This place was sold to Edmund Sikes in 1833.

A little farther north on the old road and on the east side, now covered by water, was the site of a house owned by Chester Sikes, another brother of Alva; probably never owned by any one outside his family. Farther north, on the west side of the old road, but not covered by water, was a house owned and probably built by Estes Burr, and afterward owned by Lovinski White. Still north, on the west side of the road, stood a gambrel-roofed house, last owned by Adelbert L. Bennett. The former owners were: Jonathan Burr (brother of Ashbel Burr and father of Estes Burr), Seth J. Bennett, and Gilbert Clark.

A little farther along we come into the old road; at a little distance north we turn from the main road to the west, go about thirty rods and come to a house last owned by Gilbert Clark. The former owners were: Welcome Bennett, by whom the house was built, and Charles S. Bennett.

Then westerly by private road about two thirds of a mile, we come to a house built and owned by Carlos Lombard, which was inherited by his daughter, now Mrs. Fred C. Adams. Near by was another house owned by Jonathan Lombard, father of Carlos Lombard.

Coming back to the old road and going north, we find a house last owned by Robert Landers. The former owners were: Charles Bennett, Seth J. Bennett, Fred Sheldon and A. D. Moore, and Charles Clark. Farther north on the west side of the road, was the site of a house owned by Jefferson Bennett, later by Laura A. Bennett. Then farther north, near the Belchertown line, is a house formerly owned by Justin Lombard and Asenath Lombard, later by Dennis Lombard, son of Justin. Since the reservoir was built the City of Springfield has bought most of the places and the buildings have been removed.

PART III

THE CENTENNIAL

PROSPECTIVE—ACTUAL—AFTERPAST

COMMITTEE ON THE CENTENNIAL.

Upper row—Alfred Noon,   Benjamin Franklin Burr,   Francis Fisk McLean.
Center—Ambrose Clough.
Lower row—John Padelford Hubbard,   Chester Lemuel Cushman,   George Root Clark.

COMMITTEE ON THE CENTENNIAL

AMBROSE CLOUGH,
    JOHN PADELFORD HUBBARD,
        GEORGE ROOT CLARK,
            BENJAMIN FRANKLIN BURR,
                CHESTER LEMUEL CUSHMAN,
                    ALFRED NOON,
                        FRANCIS FISK McLEAN.

SUB-COMMITTEE OF PUBLICATION

AMBROSE CLOUGH,	BENJAMIN F. BURR,
GEORGE R. CLARK,	ALFRED NOON.

THE CENTENNIAL

PROSPECTIVE

THE annals of the Bay State had for years declared that in the year 1774 the towns of West Springfield, Ludlow, Leverett, West Stockbridge, and Barre, Mass., and Edgecomb and New Gloucester, Me., then of Massachusetts, had been granted their distinctive title to separate existence. This fact had from time to time attracted the attention of the denizens of Ludlow, and awakened some comment upon the question of a celebration when the century should have rounded itself. The commemorative exercises at the sister town of Wilbraham in 1863 of course attracted more or less attention in this adjoining place. But there appears to have been no agitation of any account until about 1870, when Mr Ambrose Clough, a connoisseur in local history, called the attention of some of his fellow-citizens to the fact that the town was approaching its hundredth birthday, and should not allow the occasion to pass without giving its children an invitation home again. By his efforts was the celebration of the Ludlow centennial given an impetus, and but for him the event would very likely have passed unnoticed. Others were evidently much interested in this historical fact and heartily seconded the efforts of the gentleman named. Indeed, the approaching milestone in the race of life seemed to throw its shadow in advance in the vision of many a citizen, particularly the elderly ones of the town. Nothing was done, however, until the spring of the year 1874, when the selectmen received the following petition:

TO THE HONORABLE THE BOARD OF SELECTMEN OF THE TOWN OF
    LUDLOW:

We, the undersigned, inhabitants and legal voters in the town of Ludlow, petition your honorable body to insert an article in your warrant, to see if the town will take any measures to celebrate the Centennial of the town; also to appropriate money for the same, and to pass all necessary votes.

Ludlow, February 25th, 1874.

(Signed) Ambrose Clough,*
B. F. Burr,[1]
J. P. Hubbard,*
Albert Fuller,*
Gilbert E. Fuller.*

As a result of this petition the article desired appeared in the warrant for the Spring meeting of the town. Its insertion seems to have awakened a little feeling, but not in any way marked, as the citizens very unanimously voted to observe a day of festivities. The following makes evident the result of the agitation so far:

Original meeting, March 9th.

Voted that the town celebrate its Centennial.

Voted to choose a committee of seven to carry out the design of the town, and that this committee report at the adjourned meeting. Ambrose Clough* was chosen chairman of the committee, and the other members are John P. Hubbard,* George R. Clark*, B. F. Burr, Rev. C. L. Cushman,* Rev. Alfred Noon and F. F. McLean.*

Voted to appropriate two hundred and fifty dollars for the same.

Adjourned meeting, April 6th.

Voted to appropriate one hundred and fifty dollars in addition to that appropriated at the March meeting, for the Centennial Celebration.

Let no one think the work of this committee was a sinecure.

The first meeting was held at the house of the chairman on the evening of March 16th, but adjourned, with little result, to the house of Major Hubbard on the 23d. On that evening Mr. B. F. Burr, the ready writer of the town's records, was chosen secretary. From that date the committee met fortnightly, and then weekly, at the town house, until after the Centennial.

In the preliminary arrangements for the celebration of course many things were planned which could not be consummated. The first choice of the committee for the literary orator was Rev. J. W. Dadmun of Winthrop, once pastor of the M. E. Church, but home duties prevented

---

[1] Only signer of the petition in the town warrant now living (1912).
An asterisk (*) appended to a name denotes deceased.

his coming. The next vote on this matter was one of invitation to Rev. Prof. G. Prentice of Middletown, Conn., also a former pastor of the church just named. At first the gentleman was inclined to accept, but finally found his labors at the university of such a character as to interfere with the plan of coming here. The third choice rested upon Prof. Lorenzo White of New Salem, a former resident of the town for a score of years, who could not find it in his heart to refuse the request of his old town. The excellence of the address will be marked by every reader.

Not so long a delay was experienced in securing the services of the historical orator. The first request was to Rev. Mr. Austin of Connecticut, the last minister employed as pastor by the town of Ludlow. Poor health prevented his acceptance, and the choice then was Rev. J. W. Tuck of Jewett City, Conn., for sixteen years pastor of the Congregational Church, whose able address, spoken to the audience at the Centennial, disseminated through the region by the enterprise of the press, and now placed in an enduring form, has become a constituent element in the historic annals of the town.

The following scheme shows concisely the doings of the general committee, as finally revised, in the selection of sub-committees:

On Collation.—District No. 1. Andrew E. C. Bartlett,* Amnie Hubbard.*
  2. John W. Hubbard, Addie F. Hubbard.
  3. Gillen D. Atchinson,* Estelle Newell.
  4. F. F. McLean,* Ellen Root.*
  5. D. C. Jones,* Henrietta Chapin.*
  6. William P. Clark,* Angeline White.*
  7. Charles S. Bennett,* Maria Sikes.
  8. Elliot O. Alden, Florence Graves.*
  9. Alanson Pool,* Carrie R. Waid.*
 10. Lucien Lyon, Alice Kendall.

On Invitation.—Rev. C. L. Cushman,* George R. Clark.*

On Music.—Davenport L. Fuller,* Alfred S. Putnam, Wilbur F. Miller, Henry S. Jones,* Edward E. Fuller.

On Finance.—Samuel White,* Edward E. Fuller, John Ray,* Austin F. Nash,* David C. Jones,* Silas Billings,* Reuben Sikes.*

On Programme.—Rev. C. L. Cushman,* L. H. Brigham,* Edmund E. Charles,* Rev. Alfred Noon, Ambrose Clough,* C. A. Southworth.*

On Sentiments.—John P. Hubbard,* C. L. Buell, Jackson Cady, L. H. Brigham,* Gilbert Pillsbury.*

On Printing.—Rev. C. L. Cushman,* George R. Clark,* B. F. Burr, Rev. Alfred Noon.

On Facts, Portraits, etc.—George R. Clark,* Ambrose Clough,* C. L. Buell, John Hobson, Jr.*

On Decorations.—Eliza Jones,* Genevra B. McLean, Ella Jones, Susan Fuller,* Lucy E. Booth, Anna S. Bennett, Belle L. Kendall,* Nellie Buffington,* Jennie Green,* Lily T. Sargent,* Mrs. N. B. Paulk.*

On Arrangements and Receptions.—C. L. Buell, D. L. Fuller,* Silas Billings,* Reuben Sikes,* Austin C. Gove,* Lyman Burr,* Adin Whitney,* Lucius Simonds,* David K. Paine,* Charles Sikes,* Oliver B. Miller, Albert Fuller,* F. F. Fairbanks.*

President of the Day.—Rev. Alfred Noon.

Vice-Presidents.—Elisha T. Parsons,* Rev. D. K. Banister,* Sylvester Miller,* Hezekiah Root,* Theodore Sikes,* George Clark,* Ezekiel Fuller,* Artemas H. Whitney,* John Miller,* Sylvester Clark,* Jonathan Waid,* Stillman Alden,* Zachariah Day,* Spencer Talmadge,* Aaron Davis,* Franklin Fuller,* Jacob S. Eaton,* Daniel Brewer,* Elijah Plumley,* Marvin King,* Henry Fuller,* Hubbard Dutton,* R. M. Chandler,* Josiah Alden,* Orsamus Alden,* Lyman Burr,* Gordon Pinney.*

Marshal.—J. P. Hubbard.*

Assistant Marshals.—Wilbur F. Miller, John W. Hubbard, James O. Kendall,* Lucius Simonds,* Austin F. Nash.*

The collation committee organized with F. F. McLean for chairman. They voted to invite the town to furnish bread and butter, cake, doughnuts, cheese, cold meats, tea and coffee. The following result of a canvass of the various districts for eatables may be of interest to the committee arranging for the next centennial:

Biscuits, buttered..........3,807   Cake, loaves...............400
Doughnuts................2,165   Tarts.....................750

Besides, there were purchased for distribution:

    27 lbs. of dried beef,   200 lbs. of tongues,
    150 lbs. of ham,   15 lbs. of bologna,
    ½ bbl. of pickles,   10 lbs. of tea,
    15 lbs. of coffee,   204 lbs. of cheese,
    190 lbs. of crackers,   100 lbs. of sugar.

Upon Reuben Sikes fittingly devolved the duties of chief waiter, while his assistants were legion.

The committee on invitations sent out a large number of letters and circulars, besides specially inviting certain dignitaries, as the correspondence read after the collation will show.

The committee on music worked hard and successfully. One and two rehearsals a week gave after a while great proficiency to the singers. D. L. Fuller was chosen leader, and A. S. Putnam organist, while the Armory Band of Springfield was selected to furnish music of its kind.

The committee on printing at first issued five hundred notes of invitation, on postal cards, reading thus:

Centennial at Ludlow

The old town invites all her children and children's children, former residents, and friends, to celebrate her hundredth birthday on the 17th day of June next.

This is to invite most cordially, you and yours, to be present and participate in the festivities of the occasion.

Come one, come all, for one joyous reunion.

The number being inadequate, two hundred more were obtained, all too few, as the sequel showed. They further issued schedules of committees, in two editions, of which over two hundred were distributed. Ten thousand programs provided under their auspices were very soon taken up on the opening of the exercises.

The committee on facts made little demonstration, but were very busy and very useful, as many of the notes in this volume may testify.

The committee on decorations arranged very tastefully the tables in the display tent, with flowers and evergreens, while they showed rare taste in elegantly festooning the tents, besides in an emblematic banner, bearing the legend, "Welcome to our Centennial," and the two dates 1774 and 1874, the one in sere and yellow leaf of age, the other in brilliant foliage of the day.

Next, however, to the Centennial committee in careful plannings and extensive labors, came the committee on arrangements and reception. The only instructions of note given them were to arrange for a free collation and find sitting accommodations for fifteen hundred persons, while upon them devolved the task of providing a place, securing crockery, arranging the details of the day's accommodations, and a myriad of little duties which could not be anticipated and yet must be performed. Two circular tents, one a hundred and one sixty feet in diameter, were placed upon the green near the town house, and the old pews to a considerable extent were removed from that ancient edifice, much to the joy of voters. The area thus obtained was devoted to the purposes of the celebration.

The town house was the general depository of food and crockery, the smaller tent contained tables for display of a moiety of the good things so freely furnished, while the larger canvass covered a network of plank seats and an ample platform for musicians and dignitaries. Six thousand three hundred and seventy pieces of crockery, a load for seven horses, were obtained from the mother city, all of which was requisite. Arrangements were also made for the conveyance of passengers from the depots.

At last the arrangements were pronounced complete, and the day of days for Ludlow began to dawn. Alas for human plans! Could Heaven frown upon such efforts? No ball had been arranged for the finale of the exercises or as their initial. All had been performed with the strictest decorum, and yet the daybreak exhibited humid skies and rain drenched ground. The committee arose with anxiety, and one and another looked eagerly for the signs of fair weather. "How do you feel?" said one of the committee to the indefatigable chairman. "First-rate," was the cheering reply, and the others caught its spirit. Down came the rain in genial showers, until an hour or two before the time for the exercises to begin, when Pluvius had satiated himself, and the rain ceased. Meanwhile the crowds began to start from their homes, and about the hour for the opening of the exercises every barn, shed, and shelter for a team within a radius of two miles had long been filled. At last the appointed time arrived, and all were prepared to enjoy the Centennial Actual.

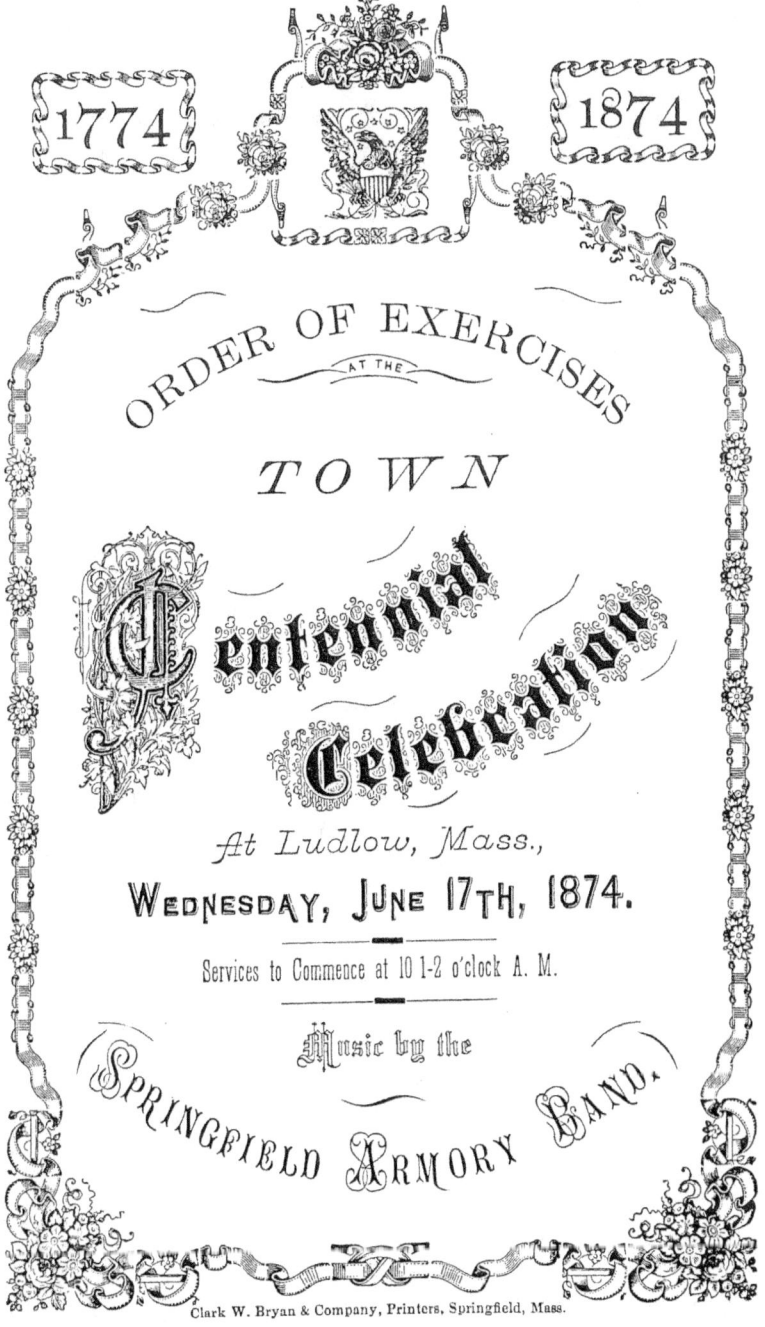

ORDER OF EXERCISES
AT THE
TOWN
Centennial Celebration

At Ludlow, Mass.,
WEDNESDAY, JUNE 17TH, 1874.

Services to Commence at 10 1-2 o'clock A. M.

Music by the
SPRINGFIELD ARMORY BAND.

Order of Exercises.

1.—Music by the Band.

2.—Singing.

3.—Prayer.

      REV. D. K. BANISTER, OF LUDLOW.

4.—Reading of Scripture.

      REV. SIMEON MILLER, OF SPRINGFIELD.

5.—Original Centennial Hymn.

> God of our Fathers, now to Thee
>   We lift our hearts with glad acclaim,
> Rejoicing in that liberty
>   Vouchsafed to them who love Thy name.
>
> The generations live and die,.
>   The earth itself is growing old,
> But Thou, O Lord! art ever nigh,
>   Thou dost the sands of ages hold.
>
> We recognize Thy loving hand,
>   Whose gentle guidings have been felt
> By sires and sons throughout the land,
>   While under care divine they dwelt.
>
> Receive our praise, Messiah King,
>   While here we count thy mercies o'er;
> Accept the offering we bring,
>   And make us thine forevermore.

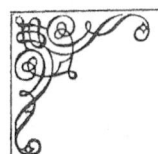

6.—Greeting.

    REV. C. L. CUSHMAN, OF LUDLOW.

7.—Music by the Band.

8.—Literary Address, with Response to Greeting.

    REV. L. WHITE, OF NEW SALEM.

9.—Singing.

10.—Historical Address.

    REV. J. W. TUCK, OF JEWETT CITY, CT.

11.—Music by the Band.

12.—Prayer.

13.—Doxology.

14 —Benediction.

Old Folks' Concert

IN THE

CONGREGATIONAL CHURCH,

ON THE

Evening of June 17th.

PROGRAMME.

PART FIRST.

1.—Anthem for Easter.
2.—a. "Sherburne." b. "Northfield." c. "Rainbow."
3.—Piano and Cornet Duet.
    MR. WILSON and MR. SOUTHLAND.
4.—Duett, "In the Starlight."
5.—a. "China." b. "Greenwich."
6.—Song, selected.
    MISS GENEVRA McLEAN.
7.—Male Quartette.
8.—Cornet Solo.
    MR. SOUTHLAND.
9.—"Invitation."

PART SECOND.

1.—Piano and Cornet Duett.
    MR. WILSON and MR. SOUTHLAND.
2.—a. "Montgomery." b. "Bridgewater." c. "Turner."
3.—Song, Chalet Horn.
    MISS GENEVRA McLEAN.
4.—"David's Lamentation."
5.—Mixed Quartette.
6.—Cornet Solo.
    MR. SOUTHLAND.
7.—a. "Majesty." b. "New Jerusalem."
8.—"Coronation," in which all are invited to join.

All hail the power of Jesus' name!	O, that with yonder sacred throng,
Let angels prostrate fall;	We at his feet may fall;
Bring forth the royal diadem,	We'll join the everlasting song,
And crown him Lord of all.	And crown him Lord of all.

The Concert will commence at 7 1-2 o'clock.

W. F. MILLER, Conductor.

THE CENTENNIAL

ACTUAL

The speakers were assigned their places; the musicians took the seats prepared for them; the marshals occupied their posts of duty; the audience quietly sought accommodations in and about the vast tent, now all too small; the Bohemians were already writing up the exercises in advance. Upon honorary seats near the speaker's desk were ranged the old and elderly men of the town: Sylvester Miller,[1] over ninety, the oldest of all; Col. John Miller,[1] Sylvester Clark, Theodore Sikes, Esq., George Clark, Orsamus Alden, Rev. D. K. Banister, Ezekiel Fuller, Harry Fuller, Jonathan Waid, Dea. Elisha T. Parsons, Franklin Fuller, Lyman Burr, Elijah Plumley, Marvin King, Artemas Whitney, Stillman Alden, Hezekiah Root, Hubbard Dutton and others, while near them were invited guests: Elijah Blake, Chester W. Chapin, J. A. Rumrill, Mayor Stebbins, Aldermen Holt and Fuller, Dea. Roderick Burt and others of Springfield, and others still from towns nearer or more remote. Austin Chapman came from Ellington, Conn., while Joseph Miller, over eighty years of age, who had traveled more than four hundred miles to attend the gathering, arrived at four in the afternoon. Goodly numbers had on previous days arrived at the homes of their friends, taking the very favorable opportunity presented for a visit to the old landmarks. Some had been born here; some had here chosen the companions of their youth, perhaps remembering at this anniversary the "publishment" by crier or posted notice; some had seen their loved ones laid away in graves now marked by mossy monuments, or more recently had visited the old town to attend funereal service. How sad and yet how interesting the greetings of these old friends! Surely all this painstaking was more than recompensed by the gladness of reunion or the tenderness of reminiscence. The programme, which has been elegantly reproduced on the previous pages, was then handed around.

A fine selection played by the band sent a thrill of inspiration through

---
[1] One of the four brothers whose pictures are shown on page 293.

the audience, after which the exercises were formally opened, and the grand choir sang with a will "Strike the Cymbal" and "Home, Sweet Home." Rev. Daniel K. Banister, formerly a pastor in the town, next led the congregation in a fervent and earnest prayer. Rev. Simeon Miller, a native of Ludlow, read selections from the Scripture appropriate to the occasion.[2] The next exercise consisted of the singing of the Centennial hymn, composed for the occasion by the Rev. Alfred Noon, pastor of the Methodist Church, and the compiler of the town history. The grand strains in the old tune "Devotion" rang out like a chorus at the Peace Jubilee, as the whole audience united voice and heart in praise. Rev. C. L. Cushman, then pastor of the Congregational Church, next delivered the following address of welcome:

REV. MR. CUSHMAN'S ADDRESS OF WELCOME

Mr. President, Ladies and Gentlemen: It has been said by some one that there is a class of rather solitary people, who, having reached a certain age, never more grow old. Perpetual youth is what they crave. But we, sir, are proud of our age. The old mother is, to-day, a centenarian, and yet she greets her children in the beauty and freshness of a youthful maiden. We call you to note her youthful appearance. Standing at the opening of a second century, she never looked so fair, so unwrinkled, so youthful as now.

Despite the prevalent indifference to genealogy and to ancestry which so far influenced the early settlers that they neglected to preserve and transmit to us connected and reliable memorials of themselves, it was somehow discovered that the town was reaching its one-hundredth birthday. With a quite marked unanimity of feeling it was thought that the event must not pass without a public recognition in the shape of a family gathering of sons and daughters from far and near. The objects were the gathering into a connected form for preservation our hitherto fragmentary history, the renewal of old friendships, the awakening of a family pride in all hearts, the cultivation of becoming reverence for the past, and the bringing of all who were born here into an acquaintance with the place of their nativity. It is a matter of regret that in New England there has prevailed so great indifference to the men and to the things of the past. No people have so great reason to value their descent as the native-born citizens of our land. Yet, as a fact, no people on earth concern themselves so little about their ancestry, or, after the first degree, feel so little interest in consanguinity. In reply to the question whether such a one is a relative, the negative is given, simply because he is only a second

---

[2] The selections were Psa. 80: 1, 90: 1-6, 78: 1-7.

cousin. If you ask one who was his grandfather he may be able to tell you, but if you ask where *he* came from you will quite likely be answered in some such dubious and traditionary form as the following: "I have heard my father say that his father came from the East or from the South," etc. This ignorance is, of course, the result of indifference. Let us rejoice that this indifference is beginning to be corrected.

We have projected this celebration, to-day, to help in breaking up this indifference. We do not claim that the 17th of June was the exact natal day, but near enough to it to warrant its use as such. We have, however, chosen it largely because there is no month like June, at least till golden-sheaved October comes. Nature is the universal attraction. It has been well said the flowering time of the year is its fresh and virginal period, and surely there is none so enchanting. June is surely a gift out of the heavens. Birds and flowers, beautiful expressions of God's thoughts, make life charming. So, then, the mother has shown her good sense in inviting home her children when she herself is clad in almost celestial beauty.

We are here, to-day, as one family, brought together by this natal occasion, to visit the old family homestead. Let us feel like children, unbend and give way to the impulses of the hour.

Requested as I am to speak words of greeting in the name of my fellow-citizens and of the committee of arrangements, it gives me pleasure to reflect that if we have never been noted for great men and great things, we have at least taken care of ourselves and kept out of prison. Scarcely a name has been on the convict roll. The retirement of the town has been fitted to foster simplicity of feeling and of character. It has been a definition of a wise and pure life to live according to nature. Such a mode of living is well-nigh impossible in the crowded life of cities and large towns. The formalities, the spirit of caste and clique, the tyranny of opinion, make it hard for a man to be true to nature and true to himself. The soul becomes artificial without knowing it, ceases to think its own thoughts and forsakes truth for the voice of the ruling caste. In such cases and places, politeness is wont to be a rule committed to memory and not a prompting of nature. An external standard seizes a man and molds him into a thing of show and quite likely of falsehoods. Some one has somewhere said that simplicity and honesty are the gold of character, but surely how hard are they to keep, and how rare to find. Now these traits have always been nourished and perfected in this rural retreat, away from much of the gloss and falsehood which are wont to abound in the largest communities.

So, then, we congratulate ourselves that we have grown and sent out to other communities the best material, the very bone and sinew of which they are made. As such we welcome you home to-day, to view the rock whence ye were hewn. We are proud of you for the most part. Nobly did our town respond to the country's call, and many of her sons sleep beneath the Southern sky. Nobly has she always done her part. Nobly does she sustain the institutions of religion. In fact she has ever been true to high-toned principle.

The old town is much changed. Even her "woods and templed hills" fail to remain intact. Her fine farmhouses tell of thrift and comfort, if not of wealth and luxury. We promise more in the future. We are here, to-day, to assert anew our right to be, to take a new lease of life, to push ourselves nearer to the front in the family of towns. Before we surrender the trust by you committed to us, we propose to transmit it to posterity greatly enlarged. Everything betokens that the Ludlow of the future will not be the Ludlow of the past. Henceforth we are to be connected with our city friends by iron bands; and, ladies and gentlemen, we shall be the head, while, by their own decree, they will be one of our dependencies. Or, for the moment, waiving that point, if we shall prove true to the confidence reposed in us, and if—if—our prevalent drouths shall not prove too much for us, we shall be the source and fountain. We propose to carry this uncoveted honor with becoming dignity and grace, and conspicuously to wear the sparkling jewel so long as our rocks and hills shall endure.

My friends, this is a birthday party, and it is a solemn and impressive thought that we shall never see the like again. All of our names will be checked on the roll of living men before another. A gentleman was lately overheard declaring that he would have nothing to do with another centennial! We appreciate his sentiments. The next we shall keep on the eternal plains. We are then treading on sacred ground. Age is everywhere entitled to reverence and honor. The town never seemed so sacred as now. Reverence, faith, entire good will, become the hour.

In the name and in behalf of my fellow-townsmen, I bid you welcome. We are glad to see you. Your presence does us good. We are glad you have not forgotten or lost your love for the old homestead. We should have been recreant to real fraternal feeling if we did not invite you home and make ready our best for you. Whether the fatted calf is or is not made ready, I will not say, but I assure you there has been no stint in this getting ready. This is a hearty welcome. With most cordial affection we greet you; glad to take by the hand many of you who have long been known to us as personal friends, we greet those most kindly, who, on returning, find themselves strangers in the land of their birth. We hail with gladness our gray-haired and venerable men who occupy a well-deserved prominence. A hoary head is surely a crown of glory if it be found in the way of righteousness. We know it was with unwonted pleasure that these, our venerable fathers, saw this movement set on foot. We rejoice in your presence here, to-day. Welcome! welcome! honored sires, fathers and mothers, brothers and sisters. Kindred, all, we bid you welcome home. We have come to talk of olden times. We have come to honor the dead, and to carry away with us, if we may, some benefit from such filial homage, for ourselves and for our children. How unwonted our emotions! We welcome you to the home of your earlier years, to the altars of your God, and to the graves of your kindred. Let us to-day press around the time-worn graves of our dead. Let the first sentiments of the heart prevail. Let friendship be renewed.

Welcoming one another to these assemblies on earth, and hailing this occasion for the expression of confidence and love; coming together by the will of God, may you with us be refreshed, and our thoughts run forward to that day when all the servants of Christ, coming from the east and from the west, from the north and from the south, shall meet together at the harvest home in the end of the world. So it is that our hopes of heaven enter into the welcome we once more give you. Modest old town, may she more than ever be the love and delight of her sons and daughters!

A Literary Address, with reply to the Greeting, occupied the next half hour. Prof. Lorenzo White[3], then of New Salem, later principal of Vermont Methodist Seminary and Female College, opened his oration with a few pleasant words not in the manuscript, saying that although not a native of the town he had come within its limits when a boy of four, and received all his early training in its society and schools. Then followed the Address, as follows:

ADVANTAGES OF LIFE IN A COUNTRY TOWN

THE address of welcome to which we have just listened may seem to one who has come to see what we are doing to-day as nothing more than a formality in the carrying out of a prearranged programme. Doubtless your words of greeting have been spoken according to a prescribed order of exercises in the celebration of your Centennial. But in this you have only conformed to a higher law to which we owe allegiance at all times. The order of the day obeys the spirit of the day. To us, who are here in response to your invitation, these words are full of meaning. They come to us freighted with pleasant memories—memories, in the case of many of us, fragrant with the loves and joys of childhood. We are glad to be here, and to feel that we are at home with you. Our esteemed friend who has so well spoken your greetings to us returning wanderers, skilled though he be in the use of words as a fine art, could not, if he would, cheat us with fine phrases. We have heard his voice with gladness because it harmonizes with all the other voices about us. He has but rendered into graceful English the greetings wherewith these hills and valleys and

---

[3] Deceased.

brooks with which we were once so delightfully familiar had already welcomed us—the same old hills and vales over which and through which we so often roamed in childhood, and the same loved brooks where we fished and bathed and frolicked, and in which we built reservoirs that always served their purpose well, and did no harm. Smiles and looks of welcome, too, we receive on every hand from old schoolmates and playfellows—the same boys with whom we always had good times, and the same girls whom we boys used to think the fairest and best. They do not look just as they used to, and we are not sorry, for they point us with pride to their daughters, who are as fair as ever they were, and who wonderfully bear their likeness, while they themselves have just changed in the order of a happy development. They seem only to have been born into a freer and larger and grander life. They have just outgrown the bloom of girlhood, and have put on the riper, richer charms of womanhood, and most of them of wifehood and motherhood. And we boys, as we feel ourselves to-day—if we have been true to the charter of virtue—love them as much as we loved them when they were girls, with the love that every true man has a right to cherish towards every true woman with whose acquaintance he is blessed.

Even the children of to-day, many of them, do not seem strangers to us. Their telltale faces show their ancestry. They are so like the faces of their fathers and mothers, and grandfathers and grandmothers, that I often know them as soon as I see them, and the children quickly know those who know them. These rushing hours speedily make us old friends with them. But we find yet other friends here who pleasantly remind us of the good days of yore. These grand old trees which stood here when the old men of to-day were boys, trees which even the greedy axe has not dared to destroy, wave their greeting to us in the morning breeze, and from their wide-spreading branches, clad in richest foliage, come the greetings of the birds, caroled in their sweetest songs, while all about us, too, even the wayside and hillside flowers, looking up to us lovingly, claim us as their friends and bid us welcome. And well they may. Though these birds and flowers are not just the same that we used to know and love, they are so marvelously like them that they must be the children undegenerate of the very old birds and flowers of our childhood through a line of I know not how many generations. The mother bird has, from year to year, taught her offspring the same sweet songs, and the mother-plant with unerring care has transmitted to the baby-plant the same exquisite taste and skill in displaying its charms and diffusing its fragrance.

It was a happy thought or hit with you to select the charming month of June, when Nature has just arrayed herself anew in her most beautiful attire, as the time of year for holding these exercises; for these blessed children of nature have a right to join with us in the celebration of our

Centennial. They were old citizens here long before the first visit of our ancestors to this continent. They welcomed our fathers here a hundred years ago with the same melodies, the same gorgeous display of their charms, the same wealth of fragrance, with which they welcome us to-day.

I cannot help remarking here that the fashions of Nature do not change, except only as culture develops them more perfectly, and combines them more skillfully, and I am sure none of us would have them change otherwise. Ought we to imitate Nature in this respect, think you, and to hand down the same fashions from generation to generation? Not certainly till human taste shall be so cultivated as to give us fashions true to Nature, and even then there will be room for new combinations in infinite variety. Is it not just here that Nature suggests to us the true solution of the fashion problem? But this only in parenthesis.

On this very year of our Centennial, Iceland celebrates her millennial. Who shall say that the robins, the bluebirds, the violets, the roses, the daisies and their numerous kindred of other names, and along with them the trees as well—the maple, the elm, the pine, and the oak—have not this same year a good right to celebrate the millennial of their occupancy of these loved retreats? Pioneers and teachers they were to our fathers, and they are to us; prophets, too, are they of a better time coming, if we will learn from them their lessons of taste and purity, and sweetness and strength. A millennium they foretell just as glorious as we will make it. Divine sovereignty in the case is the assurance of God's blessing upon our honest and well-directed efforts.

Considerable are the improvements even in this country town which a hundred years have wrought. Providence has, through the fidelity, the hardship, and the wisdom of our fathers, committed to us the trust of these cultivated lands, these pleasant homes, these churches and schools—in a word, *the advantages, such as they are, of life in a country town.* What have we to do to transmit these blessings to those who shall come after us, and to multiply them so as to make the future what it should be? is the question, then, which the occasion gives us with such emphasis that I need offer no apology for making it the starting-point of a few suggestions.

The inspirations of the glad Centennial day awaken, I doubt not, a desire among the people of the town to act each a good part in his day, and may well culminate in an ambition satisfied with nothing less than the best things—a steadily-increasing prosperity for your goodly town, and the brightest and happiest future for the generations coming.

Indulge me, will you not? in saying *we* to-day as much as I have a mind to, for I have always loved to think of myself as one of you, and in this I know I am not alone among those who are counted as guests here to-day. While we have found homes in other places, our hearts are not bounded by the limits of our new homes. We do not have to give you up to make room for new friends. In coming here we are like married daughters, who, returning each Thanksgiving day to their father's with their new recruits of young life, always speak of *going home*.

The first Centenary of the town of Ludlow to-day becomes historic, and we are all anticipating with much pleasure the address which shall more fully make it our own by unfolding to us its records and its lessons. It is in the light of the present as well as of the past that on this day we look forward. And our path is a plain one. If we would make the future bright and prosperous, such as shall give us a claim on the gratitude of those who may follow us, then we have simply to be true to this goodly inheritance received from our fathers.

But to be true to this sacred trust, to make the most of our advantages, we must shun the perils which experience has taught us our liability to meet.

It is wise, then, that we pause just here for a moment amidst the rejoicings of our Centennial Jubilee, and face the dangers against which even the comparative security of country life is not always proof.

It would be out of place here to rehearse the catalogue of sins which are everywhere the peril of careless lives. I must take for granted that those whom I have the honor to address to-day, are chaste, temperate, upright, industrious, and frugal. If any of them are not so, they ought to be, and by all means they had better be. But life, even on this higher plane, where crime is rare, has its failures. Indeed, every plane of life, till you rise to Heaven itself, has its evils to be avoided, and the higher you go in the scale of being, the more deplorable is the ruin which these threaten.

Hence, it now and then comes to pass in the country, that just at the point where intelligent industry with frugality has won thrift and competency, and has thus reached the plane of the highest financial independence that mortals ever can attain, there begins to spring up in the family an ambition for city style. I am warranted, if I mistake not, in taking for granted that the good sense and good blood of the thrifty farmers of Ludlow are generally a guaranty against this evil. This foolish ambition, however, is singularly blinding to its victims, and a word of caution even to the wise may not be out of place.

It need not be urged that attempts at imitation are generally failures, and that the actors besides are very likely to cut awkward figures. It is said that the young men of Byron's time who thought to imitate his genius, only got so far as to make themselves ludicrous by mimicking his limping gait and more limping morals. So it commonly happens that would-be imitations in the country of city life turn out to be only apings, and that, too, not of that which is worth copying, but of the weaknesses and vices of the city—the shoddy parade and slavish subserviency to position and power of those who have not learned to wear the honors of city life with good grace.

But this evil is sure in due time to cure itself. Fifth Avenue style in a farmer's home never fails to show itself, sooner or later, to be as absurd as would be the attempt to devote our New England lands to the raising of tropical fruits. We have all seen enough of this mistake to understand its results. It means heavy and steadily-increasing debts, irredeemable mortgages, bad dreams, haunted rooms, forfeited credit, seedy garments, an aspect of decay within and without, a general unhingement of manhood and womanhood, and then bankruptcy, or else that which is worse—an old age oppressed with intolerable burdens.

The failures of country life are chiefly traceable to causes working nearer the other extreme of society. Not in the excesses of taste and style lurks the demon that oftenest plays first tyrant and then destroyer in homes of industry. As the foremost or parent evil among upright and energetic farmers, I incline to place the tendency of both men and women to become working machines, appendages, the one sex to the soil and the other to the house. I do not refer now specially to the overwork so common that breaks down the constitution and shortens life; for even in the country dissipation doubtless slays more than work does, and when overwork brings premature death, that is not the great evil in the case. But your mere workers may be philosophers enough to adjust the daily demand on their strength to the daily supply, and so drag out the full measure of their days, though whether they do or not is of comparatively small account. The abominable thing is, that man should be degraded to the rank of the instruments which he wields. The curse lies in the debasing not in the shortening of life.

The first result of this all work and no play is to make Jack a dull boy, and next a dull man, if he lives to be one, who, because he is more a machine than a man, drops naturally into the old ruts of his fathers, is incapable of accepting improvements, but plods blindly on, absurdly seeking to perpetuate ideas and customs which the world has outgrown, mistakes narrowness for independence, stupidity for constancy, penuriousness for economy, shows but slight appreciation of the beautiful, pays his church dues as a kind of future life insurance demand, regards money expended for books and pictures as wasted, and the education of his children as useless, save only as the outfit of a drudge like himself. Call this an extreme case, if you please. I mean it as such. But remember that sins invariably lead to extremes.

Extremes are not always reached in a day. But let a man only consent to be a mere working machine, and to make his wife and children the same, or no matter if the wife leads in the case, and in due time this very extreme will be gained, if not in his day, then in his children's.

But let him not flatter himself that he is becoming rich. Such a man is not a possessor at all. The farm or the shop, from first to last, owns him, and works him as its slave. If we would escape these results, then we must shun the sin which leads to them.

Our fathers were hard workers, it is true, and we cannot say that they were always wise; but it is the evidences which we see to-day of the subordination in a good degree of work to the higher purposes of life, that inspires for them our respect and gratitude. They not only made for themselves homes of comfort, and caused their lands to yield for them the supplies demanded for physical life, but they also early founded churches and schools, and cheerfully sustained them from their scanty and hard-earned means. Not least among the legacies which they have left to us is their own example of self-sacrifice in behalf of their children. They did their part well, and thus made it our duty to show that the oft-repeated claim of New England farmers, "we build schoolhouses and raise men," is no idle boast.

To be true to the fathers, our first duty is to be men. Use, then, the good things of life, and let them not use you.

Be a free man, not a slave. Make your homestead not your workshop, nor your prison, nor your world, all which terms in this connection mean about the same thing; but make it what home should be, as beautiful as your means will permit; at all events, make it within doors and without so bright and cheerful, and so warm and radiant with love, as to charm the faculties of your children into joyous and healthful exercise. And you may be assured the work will not suffer as the result. Make work a delight, a fine art; infuse into it the play element; give brain and heart their natural right of dominion over muscle, and we can do a third more work, and do it better, with only the weariness that makes rest sweet and dreams pleasant. And then, too, home, in its industrial character, will become what heaven designed it to be, a gymnasium for the free and happy development and training of mind and body.

There can be no doubt that the right of every man under our free government to sell his property when he pleases, even though it be the old homestead of his fathers, is a wise provision. Though the exercise of this right greatly modifies our local attachments, making them less a clinging to the soil, this is on the whole a great advantage. Fostered by our educational agencies, its tendency is to the cultivation of a nobler style of patriotism, a love that rises above mere matter and place, and cares rather for institutions and principles and life.

By frequent transfers of real estate it has actually come to pass that comparatively few occupy the houses and lands of their fathers. But if you live where the ancestors of your neighbor lived, somebody else lives on the old homestead of your fathers, and plucks the fruit from orchards which they planted, and mows the green fields which their skillful hands first brought under culture. These changes, then, in the ownership of real estate, are but the interchange of trusts committed to us by our fathers, and it is all the same though the boundary line of towns comes between. Our obligation is none the less to enter into the labors of those who have lived and wrought before us.

He who has planted a tree, and by careful culture has made it fair and thrifty and fruitful, has a claim upon those who come after him that they shall take care of it, and, when it dies, plant another in its stead; and so, in general, of whatever improvements he has made during his occupancy. With peculiar emphasis is this true of all that contributes to make our homes beautiful. He whose industry and good taste have made his buildings and grounds a paradise, is a benefactor of the entire community, and of every pilgrim passer-by; and no man can with money purchase the moral right to lay them waste, or neglect them. Money may buy these goodly acres, but the beauty that covers them is the common heritage of all who have minds and hearts to enjoy it. To heathenize grounds that our fathers have Christianized is treason. However, then, the improvements of a century have come into our hands; whether by direct inheritance or by purchase, they are a trust to be kept faithfully, and transmitted to those who may follow us.

The advantages of life in the country, just as in the city, are, for the greater part, what we make them. But take our good country homes as we find them, or as they find us, and they will, I believe, all things considered, bear comparison with the best which the city affords. But it is what the country affords, more or less, that is ours, and the main chance with us is the faithful improvement of what we have.

Success is everywhere achieved by making the most of our own resources. If you please, it is the one talent of a country town, and not the five talents of the city, upon the improvement of which success is here conditioned. But perhaps our one talent may yield us as much substantial good as five talents in the city. It will, if we make the better investment, and take better care of the increase.

There are many things in which it were folly for the country to attempt to compete with the city.

The worshipers of mammon, the devotees of fashion, and all the giddy, fluttering throngs to whom a whirl of excitement is the daily or nightly necessity of life, may gain their ends and end their useless lives more readily in the city. Wealth, fashion, noise, with all their train of ambitions and vexations, find here in but inferior degree either their motives or their means. Some of the advantages of culture, too, it must be admitted, are generally more easily accessible in the city than in the country. The machinery of the city can turn out professional characters as well as sharpers of all kinds with much the greater facility.

But the country can do without many of these. It is not polished instruments of any kind that is the world's great want. Professional training is well; but it is never the great essential. Look out for the man, and you will risk little to let the professor take care of himself. The grand aim of life everywhere should be the development and cultivation of manhood.

Now the first requisite to this is home and neighborhood. And in both these respects the country has the advantage over the city. One can scarcely know what the word neighborhood means till he has lived in the country. The word home has generally, too, in the country a breadth and depth of meaning which is rarely possible in the city. In the city, it means, additional to the family itself, for the greater part a hired house, or part of a house, a temporary abode, often little more than a business headquarters, with but slight local attachments. But in the country, home generally means possession as well as occupancy. Often it means the old homestead, endeared by a thousand tender associations. And it means not only house, but also gardens, lawns, fields, trees, fruit and flowers, flocks and herds. In its fullest realization it is a place where two lives united in one were planted in youth, from which, fertilized by a pure love, other young lives have in due time sprung up around them. Be not afraid of this word planted. Man has not so grown out of relation to other forms of life in the kingdoms of nature, that he can, without a great loss to himself, be tossed hither and thither, with no local attachments, all places being alike to him; and he never will at least in the present life. He need not indeed be attached to the soil like a tree which cannot be moved without endangering its life. But as the very means of insuring for him that vigor and strength of manhood which can withstand the trials of any clime, and make his life everywhere fruitful, his heart must have rootlets that take a strong and permanent hold upon home associations, and become intertwined inseparably with the happiness and prosperity of the people among whom were passed his early days. I do not say that a country birthplace and early home must always be more to him than any other place. It may or may not be the dearest of all places. It ought not to be in the case of those who afterwards have permanent homes in other places where families grow up around them. It must, however, be to them what no other place ever can be, the lovely dreamland of infancy, the charming fairyland of childhood, and a little later, a kind of borderland paradise, in which youth blossoms into young manhood and womanhood. Far from confining his life within narrow limits, these lifelong attachments to an early home become a condition upon which his life may ever after more freely and widely and securely expand itself. He whose infant life is thus planted in the soil of a good home, and whose life, thrice blessed with the culture of home, the school, and the church, all working in harmony, and inviting his faculties into free and happy exercise, is prepared in due time, as he could not be otherwise, to reach out his life in vigorous runners that shall take root, and make his life fruitful in places far remote.

If the raising of men be your chief aim, men whose lives shall be a blessing, whether they have their mission in your quiet town, or are called to other fields of duty, you have, then, no occasion to envy the dwellers in cities. And we need not fear to extend this comparison of advantages with our city neighbors. If their larger material wealth can build more elegant houses and furnish them more sumptuously than you, you can surround your homes with attractions in the form of lawns and flowers and trees, which may well excite their envy. If they can build finer schoolhouses than you, see that you have as good teachers, and you can build men as well as they. If they worship in costlier temples of granite and marble than your means can afford, you may offer as acceptable worship in your modest and not less tasteful churches. Nor need your prayers and praises be restricted to these temples made with hands. They may go up daily,

> From that cathedral, boundless as our wonder,
> Whose quenchless lamps the sun and moon supply,
> Whose choir the wind and waves, whose organ thunder,
> Whose dome the sky.

If the libraries of the city are not easy of access to you, yours are the more inspiring volumes of nature, spreading out for you on every hand their eloquent pages. If you can but rarely visit the galleries of art found in the city, nature's grand museum, filled with the work of the Divine artist, is open to you freely at all times, open to all who have eyes to see. If you may not so often in the country hear words of wisdom from the silver-tongued orator, or music from the great masters, for those who have ears to hear your wooded hills and vales are vocal with richer melodies.

To make the most of our advantages, however, requires us not to be proud of them and satisfied with them, but steadily to increase them. To this end your fruitful soil is an unfailing source of supply. You do not expect to find here buried mines of gold. But even more wondrous is the wealth that slumbers in these lands. They scarcely need your bidding to yield with each returning summer in infinite variety their boundless profusion of grasses, flowers, foliage, and fruits. And this it is in your power to increase almost without limit. Where now the earth sends up the thistle, you can cause it to send up the bearded grain. Where weeds have full possession of the soil, it will presently reward your care with the luscious strawberry, or with flowers fragrant and beautiful. Where the ground is cumbered with thorns, we find it ready under the hand of culture to grow the apple, the pear, the peach, the cherry, the grape, and the plum.

But plant not always in hope of speedy returns. Plant for generations and centuries. By all means plant trees; multiply your groves, that shall be more to coming generations than to yourselves. Neglected fields wait only your planting and culture, to produce thrifty and fruitful orchards for you and the generation after you. The grounds that front your dwelling are waiting only for you to put in the tiny seed or tender sapling, to bless the next Centenary with the thrifty maple, the graceful ash, the evergreen pine, the stately elm, and the giant oak.

Carry the same spirit of improvement with you everywhere. Leave all good things that come into your hands—buildings, grounds, fences, roads—better than you found them. At the same time clear away that which is not good. Above all, make your schools and churches the best and best sustained, the most truly liberal as well as earnest, and keep them always abreast with the times in every real improvement. When the city gets the start of you in a good cause learn from it, and so make it your tributary. From the exhaustless fountains of your highlands you are to supply Springfield with living water. Draw upon her in return from whatever fountains of health she may have for you. No people can afford to live within themselves. A breeding in and in policy is always one of degeneracy. If we draw only from the fountains of our own life we shall presently find that the currents of life run low and languidly. Therefore constantly seek fresh currents of life from abroad. Welcome all new ideas and new things which are good. So may you steadily add to all your resources of power, multiply the advantages of life, reflect honor upon your worthy ancestors, and transmit the goodly heritage received from them, not only unimpaired, but with a generous increase to those who live after you. Above all, may you hope to raise up for the future a generation of men worthy of the name. And this cannot fail to carry with it prosperity in everything good. To your lasting honor may these results appear when a hundred years hence a happy and intelligent people shall gather here to celebrate the second Centennial Jubilee of Ludlow, perhaps under the shadow of the very trees of your planting.

After the choir had again sung, Rev. J. W. Tuck, of Jewett City, Conn., gave the Historical Address, in these words:

HISTORICAL ADDRESS

THOUGH I cannot claim the honor of my nativity with you, citizens of Ludlow, yet I am not a foreigner or stranger here. These fields and forests, so green to-day, are more familiar than those on which I first opened my eyes; these venerable oaks around seem as much

J. Webster Tuck

Historian of Centennial

like old friends as those others under which I sat in childhood; and in many of these open countenances I read the checkered history of a majority of your families, as well as much of my own for sixteen of the best years of my life. A few rods from this place of our gathering, six of my children were born, and the precious dust of half that same family now sleeps in yonder cemetery, side by side with dear departed ones of your own stricken households.

The invitation, therefore, of your honorable Committee of Arrangements to address you at this memorable period of your history, I regard as a call to come home again, to revisit the scenes of former years, to review the pleasant memories of the past, to shake friendly hands, and gather up inspiration from a new brief communion to go on in life's journey with Christian courage, that we may finish our course with joy.

But personal and particular reminiscences belong chiefly to the speakers that will follow me; and while I may indulge in some that have fallen especially under my observation, yet the broader though less luminous field of your local history has been marked out for my survey in this Centennial Anniversary of your town. I am aware of the more than ordinary difficulties of my undertaking, difficulties growing out of the comparative meagerness of your early district records, and also because of a lack of startling incident and adventure, such as may be found in the central, populous places whose history covers a much longer period,—but which can never obtain with a younger and scattered population, devoting themselves exclusively to the quiet pursuits of agriculture. While, therefore, Ludlow cannot boast of many great and astonishing things,—of bloody battle-fields, of Indian burnings and massacres, of giving presidents, senators, and governors to the country,—yet, if it be not assuming too much, in the words of another,— "She can, so far, claim the merit of never having done anything that she or her mother town need be ashamed of." We will take this as no faint praise. Though it be true, as publicly preannounced of this celebration, that this town has not a great deal of history all to herself, may it not be added, neither has she the failing of coveting and contending for that in her chief places, which is as sounding brass and a tinkling cymbal, and from which much claiming to be history frequently comes? No, her ambition is of a higher type; her preference for the more useful, the practical, the permanent. Hence of her sons it may be said, they are industrious, virtuous, sturdy yeomen; and her daughters, they are fit to be the wives and mothers of husbands and children that are "known in the gates, and who sit among the elders of the land."

With so much that is apologetic, and congratulating you, fellow-citizens, friends, and former townsmen, for the auspicious circumstances of this day, and the pleasing unanimity with which you enter on this Centennial, forgetful of political and denominational preferences, I now waive for the present all other things, and give precedence to a brief narrative of the good old dame that has just rounded out her first hundred years, and yet is none the worse for wear, nay, is more vigorous and comely, and even Christian than ever. May we not, then, those of us who are adopted children, as well as you who were to the manner born, like the loyal subjects of gracious sovereigns, say now with united voices, Live, O mother! Live forever! Live on, firm in principle, fair in countenance, of a truly healthy growth, and holding honorable place with a friendly sisterhood of towns around!

NAME

"What's in a name?" is sometimes asked. Enough, perhaps, to claim a moment's thought as we pass along. The name first on our lips to-day, and inscribed on the banner floating highest in the breeze above this assembled multitude, though not euphonious, as some have said, yet is not unpleasant to the ear, and, we doubt not, is of honorable origin. While we have no certain clue to its history, yet it seems to me the most plausible theory among several is, that its derivation may be traced to a prominent English republican living previous to and during the protectorate of Oliver Cromwell—Edmund Ludlow, a member of Parliament and a popular leader of the people in those stormy times, against the encroachments of the crown. Though he was one of the king's judges, yet he was, even then, a thorough, consistent republican, and afterward an earnest supporter of the bill for the abolition of the House of Peers. It is not unreasonable to suppose that his name, associated as it was with genuine republicanism like that of John Hampden, his contemporary,—a name afterwards given to designate your county,—should, for like reasons, have been previously joined to one of its towns.*

SETTLEMENT

The first settlement with specific date in this part of Springfield, called Stony Hill, was made in 1751 by Capt. Joseph Miller, who came from West Springfield, and pitched his tent on the banks of the Chicopee River, near where Elihu J. Sikes now lives, whose wife is a direct descendant of his of the fifth generation. But there were already several families here, supposed to have been on the ground a year or two; those of Aaron Colton, James Sheldon, Shem Chapin, and Benjamin Sikes. Ebenezer Barber came in 1756, locating himself on the place now owned by David L. Atchinson, and Jonathan Lombard followed in 1757. In 1767, Joshua Fuller, whose descendants are numerous, moved into the place, and settled on what is known as the Dorman farm [now owned

---

*See page 52.

by Charles M. Foster], near the Methodist chapel. James Kendall came in 1769, from Ashfield. Most of these names, together with those of Jones and Burr, representing families still living here, are found in the earliest records of Springfield.* Their present numbers, and the places of honor and usefulness they have filled through so many generations, evince the extraordinary vitality and vigor of the stock from which they sprang.

SLOW PROGRESS

For more than a score of years after the arrival of the pioneer settlers in the eastern, or Stony Hill, district of Springfield, the increase of the population, owing to a variety of circumstances, was very gradual. Persons coming from a distance, seeking new homes in this part of the State, preferred planting themselves in the villages, and remaining there, on account of their greater safety, and also that they might the better enjoy the advantages of religion, of education, and social life. With reluctance they went out to take up new lands at a distance; and only the most venturesome, and such as had but small possessions at home, would do it. It is no disparagement of the early inhabitants of this locality, to say they were poor in this world's goods, and adventurers here, seeking to better their scanty fortunes. Their hardships, therefore, were many and great.

ORGANIZATION AND STRUGGLES

At the end of the first quarter of a century, or in the year 1774, the population of the place having reached two or three hundred, measures were taken and perfected for the organizing of a new town, which was denominated in the act of incorporation separating it from Springfield, the district of Ludlow. It was thought the measure would give a new impetus to the prosperity of the place by adding largely to its numbers, and furnishing the people with superior advantages of every kind. But the expectation was not one to be realized then, since the date marks a period in our country's history, distinguished for the beginning of hostilities between the home government of Great Britain and her American colonies. Just previous to this the tea had been destroyed in Boston harbor, in consequence of which Parliament had passed an act interdicting commercial intercourse with that port, and prohibiting the landing and shipping of any goods. This oppressive bill was followed by the passage of others more odious still, and a general state of alarm prevailed throughout Massachusetts and all the colonies. In a twelvemonth afterwards, the war of the Revolution opened in the fight on Lexington Green, followed by the famous battle of Bunker Hill, on the 17th of June, 1775. The news of these battles arrived in this part of the State two

---

*See pp. 36-41.

days after their occurrence, though neither telegraphs nor railroads were then known, and immediately several companies of men, well armed and equipped, were dispatched on their long and toilsome march to the seaboard. Others were organized as minutemen, and constantly drilled, preparatory to being called into the service.

I speak of these things here, not to impart information, but as suggestive of those dark and troublous times a hundred years ago, and as accounting for the slow growth of the new settlements in this part of the State, and particularly outside the larger towns. Men do not go forth into the wilderness in large numbers, nor engage extensively in agricultural pursuits, when the trumpet of war is sending its echoes through the land, and the young and brave are summoned to the battle-field. Drawn from their homes, then, they dwell in camps and sicken in hospitals, or fall in the deadly strife.

EARLY TOWN MEETINGS

The first town meeting in Ludlow was held almost immediately after its organization, at the dwelling-house of Abner Hitchcock, where Lucius Simonds now lives, and at the second meeting a few weeks after, a committee was chosen to secure the services of a minister for the people. This seems to have been the universal practice of the fathers of New England, as soon as they could count up forty or fifty families within a reasonable distance, to provide themselves with the ordinances of religion, and enter into church relations with one another. Even before that, when they might not number more than a score of persons, they would initiate measures looking to their spiritual necessities.

You can find at the City Hall in Springfield, in the first book of records, an ancient document signed by only eight persons, the first little band of immigrants that arrived on the banks of the Connecticut River in the spring of 1636, written thus:

> Wee intend, by God's grace, as soon as we can, with all convenient speede, to procure some Godly and faithful minister, with whom we purpose to join in church covenant, to walk in all the ways of Christ.

Like the Pilgrims on landing at Plymouth, their first thought was a recognition of the hand that had led them, and a humble, public confession of the Mighty God, whom they loved and feared.

At another town meeting, held in less than three months from the first, a committee was chosen to find the center of the town, that they might build a meeting-house thereon. It was in their heart to build a house for the Lord at that time; but nine years intervened before the work was accomplished. The delay is easily accounted for, in the breaking out of the Revolutionary war, the calling into the army of their available young men, and taxing their small pecuniary resources to the utmost to furnish equipments, ammunition, and rations. What prevented their increase in numbers also laid an embargo on their religious prosperity;* so that the very first tax levied, which was £20, lawful money, instead of being appropriated to their wants as a community, had to be diverted to the exigencies of the public peril. But it was done cheerfully. The patriotism of the people in this western part of the State was not a whit behind that of their brethren in the eastern counties, and all were ready to make the greatest sacrifices for the common safety. Stockings and shoes had to be made in the different families for the soldiers, since these articles could not be bought in one place as now, and blankets in many instances were taken from the beds then in use. Tax followed tax and requisition followed requisition for seven long years, reducing their means of support until nothing seemed left them but a depreciated paper currency. The worthlessness of this, though it was nearly all they had, some votes on the records made at that time will show. I quote as examples:

Voted to raise the sum of $11,500 to buy grain to pay the three and six months' soldiers, in addition to their stated wages; also, to raise $32,000 to purchase beef for the state.

The price of wheat then was $30 per bushel, rye $23, Indian corn $15, a day's work $20, and other things in proportion. Another vote I transcribe, viz: "That we pay Sergeant John Johnson and Sergeant Ezekiel Fuller, Samuel Scranton and Samuel Warriner, Jr., £12 silver money for services in the army; also, £6 to Joseph Hitchcock for the same." This was near the close of the struggle for independence, in 1781, and yet I doubt if much more specie can be found in town to-day.

Thus it appears that the infant district of Ludlow, containing only about two hundred inhabitants, was actively engaged in the great Revolutionary conflict, and doing what it could. One seventh of its whole population was mustered into the service, and stands enrolled in the army of Independence. Their names are worthy of record, and may properly be read in your hearing, since they are the inheritance of so many in this assembly. Including those already called, there are:—†

Ichabod Barker,	Solomon Cooley,
Ezekiel Beebe,	Edward Cotton, ||
Cæsar Begory (colored),	Oliver Dutton,
Noadiah Burr,	Ezekiel Fuller,
Reuben Burt,	Lothrop Fuller,
Joel Chapin,	Jabez Goodale,
Charles Chooley,‡	Joseph Hitchcock,
Aaron Colton,§	Joseph Jennings,

*See page 70. †See page 69. ‡ Cooley ? § ? \|\| Colton ?

John Johnson,
David Lombard,
Jonathan Lombard,
Dr. Aaron J. Miller,
George Miller,
Joseph Miller, Jr.,
Leonard Miller,

David Paine,
Tyrus Pratt,
Samuel Scranton,
Thomas Temple,
Moses Wilder,
Cyprian Wright;

twenty-nine in number. There is no record of any tories here, and their number was small in this part of the State; and yet there were a few in the larger places. It is not twenty years since an aged widow lady lived in Springfield, who received an annual pension from the British government for war services rendered the mother country, by her husband, nearly eighty years before. She had, at that time, been paid an aggregate of $10,000 in the course of her long life.

FIRST MEETING-HOUSE*

The war being ended, and peace and prosperity having come once more, the people, as might be expected, turned their attention again especially to the erection of their long-desired sanctuary. Accordingly, in town meeting it was "voted that Dea. Nathan Smith of Granby, Dea. David Nash of South Hadley, and Dea. John Hitchcock of Wilbraham be a committee to set the stake for a meeting-house." At a subsequent meeting their doings were accepted and £200 assessed for building purposes. Then the work went forward as fast as they were able to collect and prepare the material. At length the foundations were laid, and almost a forest of heavy hewn timber covered the ground.

Again turning to the records we read:

October 23, 1783.—Town-meeting at the stake. Voted that the building committee procure a sufficient quantity of rum for raising the meeting-house frame.

This was the only business done at the meeting, so far as the record goes, and no doubt was the passing of the Rubicon, the taking of the last desperate step toward a successful end. A house-raising in those days was an eventful occurrence,—especially if a public building,— calling together whole communities, the men and boys to lift the heavy timbers by broadsides, and the women and girls as joyful witnesses, and also to prepare food and spread the tables for the unusual feast. It was a great day to the people of this town, ninety-one years ago, when the gigantic frame of that now ancient and forsaken sanctuary, standing hard by, was lifted on to its foundations. Indeed, two days were con-

---

* See page 128.

sumed before the last timber went into its place and the last trunnel was driven home, though scores of strong-armed men came in from the towns around, cheerfully contributing their efficient aid and joining in the work from the rising of the morning till the stars appeared. At length it stood erect, complete, immovable.

Then, at a given signal from the master workman, believe me, there was a tossing of hats and bonnets such as you never saw, and a shout so loud and long that it

> Shook the depths of the desert gloom, . . .
> And the sounding aisles of the dim woods rang.

Where the rum came in or went out, or what the young folks did that night, till the "small hours" of the morning, I leave to your conjectures. Strange as it may seem, some of the witnesses to that raising still survive; but they tell no tales, only they whisper at times with bated breath. Do any doubt? Look at those aged oaks. They were then in their prime, and swung out leafy bowers all over this pleasant green; and now, though they are old and less comely than in their youth, they are still loved and cherished, as all tried and time-long friends should be. There is a tradition that when that ancient frame comes down, they, too, will bow their heads and fall. Long may it stand, therefore, let us pray, to befriend and bless this beautiful grove, and tell the old, old story of the past; though we would not object to its being clad in a more comely covering, and looking down upon us, children, with a more cheery, improved face. Built by the hands of the fathers, who gave the chief materials from their forests, and devoted now to secular purposes, let it stand, rejuvenated, as we hope it soon may be, to signalize their worthy deeds and join the generations, old and new, in one.

On account of the poverty of those fathers, it remained unfinished within for several years; and there were those living a short time since, who could remember when its only pulpit was a carpenter's bench, and its pews rough planks, stretched from one block to another. But afterward, as the people were prospered, these rude forms gave place to the improvements of a later day. A real pulpit was built; and how wonderful it was, perched like an eagle's nest far up some dizzy height; and then the deacons' seat a little lower down in front, where grave men sat, 'tis said, to watch the flock, and wake the congregation nodding and, withal, to keep the boys and girls from sparking. As there were no means for warming churches then, each family took to meeting with them their little boxlike stove for the women's feet, while the men sat and kicked their frozen cowhides to force away the winter's cold.

Prayer meetings, at that day, were seldom known. They would have been an intrusion on the dignity of the dominie, whose sole prerogative it was, publicly to pray as well as preach.

THE FIRST CHURCH AND ITS PASTOR

At the formation of the church here, which was in 1789, it was presented with a heavy communion service from the mother town, on which was inscribed, "Springfield 1st Church, 1742," and which was continued in use more than a hundred years, or until 1846, when it gave place to other and more valuable furniture, the bequest of Abner Cady, the former still being preserved as a remembrance and relic of the past.

The Rev. Antipas Steward, the first pastor, was ordained November 27, 1793. He was a native of Marlboro, a graduate of Harvard University and afterward tutor, and distinguished for scholarship. He could read Hebrew, it was said, nearly as readily as English. The town paid him an annual salary of $200 and thirty cords of wood. He was dismissed in 1803 and removed to Belchertown, where he died in 1814, aged 80 years. I have heard it said by those who remembered and knew him well, that he was truly a man of "ye ancient time," finely clad in blouse and breeches, knee-buckles and white-topped boots, gracefully corrugated over long, white hose, and, surmounting all as most prominent, the professional cocked hat, significant of authority and command. At his ordination he invited the Rev. Mr. Howard of Springfield to preach the sermon from the text* "Let a man so account of us as . . . stewards of the mysteries of God;" and near the close of his ten years' pastorate, having been not a little troubled by the complaints of his people, he sent again to his friend, Mr. Howard, to come and preach his farewell discourse, choosing for the text, Revelation 2:13—"I know thy works, and where thou dwellest, even where Satan's seat is, . . . wherein Antipas was my faithful martyr, who was slain among you, where Satan dwelleth." This last request, however, was not granted the retiring pastor.

Dr. Lathrop relates the following anecdote of this eccentric divine: At a ministers' meeting at one time, some one stated his belief that all the wicked hated God. Mr. Steward denied this, and inquired how it was that they should desire to go into his presence if they hated him, and quoted the parable of the virgins, Matthew 25:11—"Afterwards came also the other virgins saying, 'Lord, Lord, open unto us.'" The reply was that parables do not go on all fours. To this Mr. Steward answered, "They go, at least, on two legs, and if your interpretation is right, they cannot go at all; for you cut off all the legs."

The little church, having at first but fifteen members, being now much reduced, and the people somewhat divided, no other minister was settled for sixteen years. Then the Rev. Ebenezer B. Wright, a graduate of Williams College, was ordained December 8, 1819. During this interim of sixteen years, the pulpit was supplied by preachers of

---

*See page 145.

Eng'd by B.D. Hall & Sons, 62 Fulton St. N.Y.

Truly Yours
C. W. Chapin

THE CENTENNIAL   549

The sixth and last church edifice erected in town is the fine, commodious house of worship, built in 1859, standing prominently before us on this common, and long to remain, as we humbly trust, the loved place of Christian assembly.

LUDLOW VILLAGE (JENKSVILLE).

Passing now to physical and material conditions,—the Chicopee River, coming down from the east, forms the southern boundary of the town, and in its course of three or four miles presents several excellent mill privileges, the largest of which are at the falls of Wallamanumps and Indian Orchard. At the former place the water descends along a narrow, rocky channel 42 feet, in a distance of a hundred rods; and at the latter—less than a mile distant—there is a fall of 63 feet from the top of the dam to still water below. The manufacturing business at the former place was nearly the first started in the country.* In the year 1812, Benjamin Jencks, then of Smithfield, R. I., made a journey of survey, passing through Connecticut and Massachusetts into New York to certain waterfalls on the Genesee River, called by the Indians, Gaskosaga, where he spent several days examining and considering the advantages for manufacturing purposes. He was offered the whole of that place, with its splendid water power, for the same sum that the Chicopee River privilege and its surroundings could be bought. He gave preference to the latter, built his dam, started his mill, and Wallamanumps became Jenksville. Sometime afterwards, a certain Marylander, probably a transplanted Yankee, bought Gaskosaga, on the distant Genesee, and it was transformed into Rochester,—the city of Rochester, with its sixty thousand inhabitants [1910 census, 218,149].

The natural scenery along the Chicopee before the swift-running waters were arrested and thrown back upon the rapids, and before the dark woods, skirting the banks of the beautiful river, were cut away, was very fine, and the sites of the present villages were places of considerable resort for pleasure. There once were the favorite hunting grounds and homes of the aborigines, and the relics of their savage warfare and rude agriculture abound to this day, in all the neighborhood.

A little while since, an intelligent townsman of yours, who is versed in Indian lore, and has an aptness for the study of nature, said to me: "On every farm in Ludlow, and especially along the margins of the rivers and ponds, may be found numerous sharp and irregular fragments of stone,—porphyry, quartz, chalcedony and sandstone,— the chippings thrown off by the Indians in fabricating their implements for warfare and the chase and for their domestic use." Thousands

---
* See page 217.

of arrowheads of various sizes, hatchets, chisels, gouges, mortars, and pestles have been picked up within a few years; and I was shown a large spearhead, lately found, of great value as a curiosity, and also a remarkable gravestone, wrought somewhat into the human form, about three feet in height, which once, doubtless, marked the burial of some distinguished chief. Said the gentleman to whom I have referred: "If every farmer would keep an eye on what he turns up with his plow, especially on new lands, and collect the curious-shaped stones lying here and there on the banks of brooks and ponds, and thrown carelessly into old walls and stone heaps, he might soon have a small but valuable museum of his own."

Just below the falls at Jenksville, the river in its tortuous course forms a little peninsula of a few acres of land, formerly densely wooded, and elevated about eighty feet above the water, the extremity of which has long been known by the name of "Indian Leap." The story,* which perhaps is only legendary, is that a party of Indians, being surprised in this secluded spot, and finding no other way of escaping their enemies, sprang over the precipice in fearless desperation, and all of them, save one, perished in the seething waters and among the rocks below. In this place, on the high bank of the river, is supposed to have been the encampment of 600 of King Philip's warriors, the night after they had burned Springfield in 1675, since those who went in pursuit of them the next day found here 24 camp fires and some of their plunder left behind. The new railroad bridge now takes a leap from this celebrated point across the chasm, bearing safely every day scores of passengers as they go and come on business or pleasure.

No less than five bridges span the Chicopee River, connecting Ludlow with the adjoining towns, the oldest of which is at Jenksville, having been built fifty-four years, and apparently as firm and enduring now as ever. Although this is the shortest of the five, and its completion now would have but little significance, yet then it was regarded as an event of extraordinary public importance; so much so as to be celebrated with an eclat not unlike this centennial day.† Accordingly, on the 1st of January, 1823, large numbers assembled to listen to a statement of what had been done; also to hear a sermon suited to the occasion, and join in public praise and thanksgiving to Almighty God for the success of their enterprise. I suppose there is scarcely a person here but has crossed over that friendly bridge, time and again. Please to remember, the next time you enter its dingy arch, that, fifty-four years ago, it was solemnly dedicated,—I use the words of the preacher, Mr. McLean, —"dedicated to the protection of Almighty God and the use of men."

---

*See page 20.
† See page 97.

THE FATHERS

The fathers of New England were a religious people; nor were they often guilty of withholding an acknowledgment of their indebtedness to the Father of Mercies for his protecting care. They believed in a divine providence, and were not ashamed to confess the same, both publicly and privately, in things great and small. They were also a brave, hardy, indomitable people, who dared to contend for their rights; who knew how to fight the devil, as well as how to fear God. Poor in this world's goods, yet they were not complainers; for princely fortunes they knew would be theirs in the world to come. Godliness was the great gain they coveted most; and having food and raiment, they were content therewith. Strong in purpose, uncompromising in principle, and the firm friends of civil and religious freedom, we love to honor them as such, though we may not always imitate their noble virtues.

They were but a handful, comparatively—few and feeble and far separated from one another—yet they could build and endow churches and colleges, scrupulously maintain religious and charitable institutions, and render a cheerful, stated worship to the God they served. Many of the present generation complain, if called to hear a brace of sermons of twenty minutes each on the Sabbath. Strong men cannot digest more than one, they say. But the fathers of a century ago could listen to preaching for two hours, and a prayer of one hour; and, after a short intermission, go the same round again without extraordinary fatigue. It is said they had no prayer meetings then; and how could they, scattered, as they were, many miles apart, without roads or bridges, or any of the conveniences of travel now in vogue? They had no Sunday schools, it is said; but they had; and their schools around the family hearthstone, with the Bible and catechism for textbooks, and father and mother as teachers, were more efficient for good than many a modern, flourishing, fancy school. While thus extolling them—commending their patriotism, their piety, their strong faith, their usually unselfish acts—I would do no injustice to the present age. Though the fathers have gone and the heroic age in which they lived, yet their spirit has not fled. If proof were needed of our patriotism, I would refer to the recent great uprising in defense of our liberties, when imperiled by the slavery rebellion. Then it can be shown also that the hope our pious fathers had of Christianizing the heathen has not died out, but has been gathering inspiration to the present time. In the work of missions, our zeal and success have exceeded theirs. We have mapped out the whole world as the field to be worked, and sent out men to possess it all for the Master. Also our religious, our educational, and benevolent institutions are in advance of anything in the past.

BOYS IN BLUE

It is in place here, in my brief narrative of historical events of this town, that I should refer to some things it did in our national contest, twelve years ago. With a population of only twelve hundred souls, it enlisted one hundred and twenty recruits for the war, or one for every ten persons. I know of no town that did better; and yet the proportion in the Revolutionary conflict was not much greater.* Fathers and mothers here gave up their sons, and wives their husbands, feeling in their bleeding hearts and fearing they might never see them again; yet consenting to the painful sacrifice for God and their country's sake. Those fears and feelings, on the part of many, were the genuine forebodings of what actually followed. The names of sixteen, who went out from these pleasant, quiet homes, and never came back alive, having perished in the terrible strife, are now written on yonder soldiers' monument, erected to commemorate the bravery of their deeds and their martyr-like deaths. I knew many of them well, and from an intimacy with some, esteemed them highly for their moral worth and manly virtues. May I pronounce their names, though it bring a pang of grief to the hearts of some present, on whose fond memories their patient faces are doubtless daguerreotyped forever?

Capt. H. A. Hubbard,	D. Pratt,
Robert Parsons,	W. W. Washburne,
Flavius J. Putnam,	John Coash,
E. F. Brooks,	A. O. Pott,
C. Crowningshield,	L. Bennett,
E. Lyon,	D. D. Currier,
H. M. Pease,	H. W. Aldrich,
A. Chapman,	C. McFarland.

Of the first of these, who was the commander of the Ludlow company, I may be permitted to say, I knew him from his boyhood,—from his first lessons in the district school till he entered college, and thence to the study of the profession of law, and until he left his law books to take the sword. The last time I saw him, he stood in a central position, with the 27th Regiment drawn up to witness the presentation of his sword, by the hands of his pastor. Soon after, he embarked in the Burnside expedition, and before landing was taken sick, and breathed his last on shipboard, in the calm waters of Pamlico Sound, just as his men, flushed with victory, were returning to proclaim the brilliant successes of the battle of Roanoke. He heard their shouts in his last moments, and in the midst of their triumphs, his soul went up to his Saviour. How our hearts bled at hearing of his death, and again, when he was brought home, folded in his country's flag, and then

---

* See page 74.

laid tenderly away in a peaceful grave! The assembled crowds here, the martial array, the solemn music, and the sharp discharges of musketry at his burial, will never be forgotten.*

All these men whose names have been called died young, some on the field of battle, some in hospitals, and more still in the infamous rebel prison at Andersonville. But they lived not in vain. They actually achieved for themselves, in their short lives, a reputation to which but few comparatively attain. Until that granite shaft crumbles in dust their memories will survive, and their manly virtues be rehearsed.

> Sleep, sleep, ye brave who sink to rest
> With all your country's wishes blest.

LABOR AND ITS REWARDS

Thus far in my address have I confined myself chiefly to the past; to so much of the history of the century now ending as relates to this little rural town, and could be conveniently brought within the narrow limits of an hour. Not being a prophet, I will make no attempt to forecast your future, farther than to say that, judging from the quiet annals we have reviewed, you may well hope hereafter to make steady progress—not, perhaps, larger in population nor in the factitious wealth and consequent distinction of cities, but in the increase of your fields and gardens,—the enriching and beautifying of your homes, and what is better still, in giving expansion and efficacy to your religious and educational institutions.

The discounting banks from which your dividends are mostly to come, are those which God and nature have given you,—the gentle slopes of these hills and the fertile intervals of the living streams that flow around your farms. There you will find gold purer than in the mines of the mountains, and silver that is more satisfying. In these fruitful fields of yours the work of your hands will not fail of a rich reward. Be sure the time has gone by, or is swiftly passing, when men of intelligence indulge a prejudice against manual labor as being degrading. The union of hard work with self-respect and mental culture may be seen all over our land; and he that would turn away from the plow and drop from his hands the axe and spade, that he may be a gentleman of leisure, a starched and perfumed creature, should be written down a slothful servant and sent to school to the insignificant ant as a teacher wise enough for him. The measuring off of calico and crinoline, the weighing of sugar and tea, or speculating on 'change in State and Wall streets, bring no enlargement of mind or consciousness of power,—do not make a robust body, nor particularly favor a healthful state of morals. All human growth of highest value, all upward and heavenward progress, come from struggling with difficulties,

---

* See biographical sketch, page 288.

—come from conflict, come from labor, from hard work. The kingdom of heaven, both here and hereafter, suffereth violence. Strive to enter in. No weak and puny effort will lift one to the skies. Toil is a necessity; earnest, persevering labor is indispensable, both to our living worthily and usefully here, and happily hereafter. Alas for the man—the parasite—that does nothing to increase the real wealth of the world, or add to the general sum of happiness. Every righteous verdict is, "Cast ye the unprofitable servant into outer darkness."

I know that the people of this town indorse these sentiments, both in their belief and practice; and I only desire to give emphasis to them and venture the prediction of their ultimate, universal acceptance.

HOPEFUL OUTLOOK

Looking now over broader fields,—to the hopeful mind there are bright prospects and encouraging omens of better days, notwithstanding the dark clouds that float at times over the vision, and carry despondency to timid souls. It cannot be that society is only sliding backward, and hurrying swiftly to the bad. I prefer to think, and with reason as well as in the light of revelation, that this old world of ours, ceaselessly swinging in its orbit, is making progress in the right direction; and that the present age, especially, into which all the past is pouring wisdom, may be justly characterized, for rapid growth, for large developments, for the diffusion of just sentiments, for the practice of a broader philanthropy and a higher morality. True, the evidence is not in credit mobiliers, in salary grabs, in frequent briberies and embezzlements, and numerous first-class frauds; but it is in the fact of their ready exposure, and the denunciation of such deeds, coming from all parties, and the solemn protests of every secular as well as religious journal in the land against them. These frequent criminal acts which make us blush for human kind, are no more numerous now that at any preceding period, other things being equal. But they are in the daylight now; they cannot be covered up as formerly; a thousand voices that used to be silent cry out against them, and load down the winds with just complaints of the wrong. Every man, however obscure, thinks for himself, reads his daily paper, reasons on politics and religion, sees through the disguises and envelopments of pretended rank and equipage and renown, and measures others, of both high and low degree, by some just standard. The men of high repute never trembled as they do now for their sins done in secret. They are seen of men, and held to account, even by those whom they feign to despise.

Are there back-settings and counter-currents in the onflowing tide of good; or, at times, an apparent increase of immorality and evil? It has always been so. It is God's prerogative to evolve good from evil. The night precedes the day. The sharp drouths of last summer with a scanty harvest following, and our cold, backward spring, were prophetic of this beautiful summer, and an unusually fruitful autumn to come. The 17th of June on Bunker Hill was seemingly a disastrous day to the friends of popular institutions; and so were the 18th and 21st of July of Bull Run memory; but they hastened on brighter days than the sun had ever seen, and loosened chains, soon to fall off from both minds and bodies of long-suffering races, crushed to earth.

We are now a free people. Slaves cannot breathe here. Every man, white or black, may carve out his own fortune, may acquire property, may compete for office and honors, yea, even the highest in the land, irrespective of his birth or blood. Has there not been progress, then, in our civil polity? In no other period of our history could slavery be abolished, but the present.

In morals and religion, also, there are the same marked and encouraging changes. Never has the religious element in our churches been so active and aggressive; never before was it clothed with sufficient power to carry forward the grand temperance reformation with such marvelous success until this year. Almost every State and County and Town is reached by this reform. God grant it so much success that soon, like slavery, it may be among the things of the past. I am glad to learn that even your old mother town is adopting the wise, safe practice of drinking pure, cold water; and that she may never want for it, asks of her fair daughter the privilege of constructing an unfailing reservoir between the rocky ramparts of your Mount Mineachogue and Facing Hills.

Taking the progress of the past as a measure, with so much already done, and the prospects ever brightening, what will not another century do? Who says the world does not move? It does, and the possibilities of the future, imagination fails to reach. The people that will live in 1974, on these hills and plains, and in these valleys, shall see the wilderness become as fruitful fields, the fields pleasant gardens, and quietness and assurance be theirs forever. While we do not expect to be present at the Bi-centennial they will celebrate, we send them happy greetings across the intervening space of the century to come.

A bow of promise spans the future. Better days than ever are dawning upon our country and the world; when all men's good shall be the rule of each,—

> And universal peace
> Lie like a shaft of light across the land,
> And like a lane of beams athwart the sea,
> Through all the circle of the golden years.

Following the hour of earnest and appreciative attention, the closing prayer was made by Rev. E. N. Pomeroy, pastor of the upper

Congregational Church in West Springfield, and the benediction was pronounced by Rev. D. R. Austin.

Scarcely had the exercises closed when a terrific shower, whose thunderings had for some moments been muttering in the clouds, broke with torrents upon the assembly. All who could took care of themselves inside the tents, while some hundreds hurried into the adjoining church, kindly opened on the occasion. The town house, horse-sheds, barns, and houses in the vicinity were overrun with refugees for a few moments, until the fury of the storm was expended.

It had been arranged to station the band outside the tent and have played a few stirring airs, to draw the people out, and then to form a procession, march to the music of a dirge to the cemetery, visit the graves of friends and then return to the tent in time to reseat, and receive what the army of waiters might have to offer. But,

> The best laid schemes o' mice an' men
> Gang aft agley.

and so it was proved in this case. A dilemma was presented, but Ludlow wit was not yet exhausted. Happy are they who, when their own plans fail, can adapt themselves to circumstances. The pleasant voice of the marshal was soon heard calling for the withdrawal of two hundred from the rear of the auditorium tent to the galleries of the town house, with which request the desired number soon complied, and the work of distribution of food commenced and continued for nearly an hour, the company meanwhile gathering together in knots and visiting to their hearts' content. At last the keen appetite of the crowd was satiated, and they were ready for the after-dinner exercises.

The first toast, "The Governor of the Commonwealth," elicited the following letter:

COMMONWEALTH OF MASSACHUSETTS.

EXECUTIVE DEPARTMENT,
Boston, 11th June, 1874.

Dear Sir:—I should be happy to accept your invitation to the Ludlow Centennial Celebration if I were not already engaged for the day on which it occurs. Therefore I must ask you to excuse me, and make my regrets to your committee.

Very truly yours, Thomas Talbot.

B. F. Burr, Esq., Secretary.

The second toast, announced by Major Hubbard, toastmaster, "The land we love," received a response from Rev. D. R. Austin, who gave the necessary eulogy to the country, and then related personal reminiscences of his ministry in the town.

"The Historian of the Day," called up Rev. Mr. Tuck, who spoke very pleasantly, gently touching up as he went along those newspapers which had forestalled him in making public the gist of his address.

"Home again," drew out Professor White, whose remarks we are happy to give in the speaker's own language:

Surrounded by those who but a little while ago were boys and girls with me, and are now developed into men and women filling with honor their places in society, I feel that I should be false to the best promptings of our hearts, if I should neglect to refer to the faithful teachers whose careful investments in our young life have been so productive of good to us. To mention the names of Theodocia Howard, afterward the mother of one who has been an esteemed pastor in the town, and of George Booth, so long a pillar in the church and a citizen whom his townsmen delighted to honor, cannot, I am sure, fail to awaken in many hearts feelings of warm affection and high respect. Many others, of earlier or later times, equally worthy, are remembered doubtless with like affection by those whose lives have been enriched by their labors.

But I need make no apology in mentioning as worthy of peculiar honor the name of one young lady teacher of our time, who served us for a series of years with singleness of aim, and with remarkable energy and success. My old schoolmates here to-day will anticipate me in giving the name of Mary B. Newell, now Mrs. E. B. Scott, of Brant, Calumet County, Wis. In my recollections of our teachers, it is but justice to say, that Miss Newell has ever occupied the central place. Nor does she lose this position when I enlarge the group by adding the honored and titled names of the teachers of my subsequent years. It must have been as early as 1830, when in the vigor and bloom of her young womanhood she was first introduced to us as our teacher. In despite of a strictness at which even those days sometimes demurred, she has always been nearest my ideal of a good teacher. No escape was there from sharp work in her school. If she could not instill wisdom into us by gentle means, none better than she knew how to whip it into her pupils, and there were, I think, few among us who did not, sooner or later, test the quality of the birch as plied by her hand, with moderation where that would do, but unsparingly if the case required it.

But whipping by no means describes her usual method. With the instinct of a cultivated Christian young lady, and with rare skill, she found the nobler side of her pupils and awakened in them conscience and a love for their tasks, and then, by an enthusiasm that made her the very embodiment of life, she inspired as well as instructed her pupils, and so in a good degree made the daily work of that old schoolhouse a fine art.

Nor was this all. The pupils of Mary Newell will never forget with what persevering endeavor she taught them to think. With a patience and tact that no dullness on our part could thwart, she made us underderstand the distinction between the questions, *What? How?* and *Why?* and so led our little minds in the path of a true analysis, and contributed to our development more than could any amount of mere learning and saying lessons. Is it a wonder, then, that neither scores of years, nor the rivers, mountains, and plains of a continent that for most of that time have intervened, have removed her from the place she had gained in our hearts? For one I can say that a feeling of grateful respect for her, and a desire to do her honor, placing her in this regard next in my heart to a mother, have been among the inspirations of my life.

Miss Newell, many years ago, removed to the West, where she continued to labor as a teacher till at past the age of sixty she was happily married. At her visit among us a few years since, with her husband, we, the boys and girls of her early days, were proud to find that single life had left no blight upon our dear old teacher. Loving and loved all the way by succeeding generations of young life, neither time nor occasion had she to try the experience of the "anxious and aimless." Fresh and fair, and in heart as young as ever, she furnished a practical refutation of the whim of writers of fiction, that only in wifehood and motherhood can the charms of womanhood be preserved and find their fairest development.

The next toast was, "A name revered, Ebenezer B. Wright," to whose memory Rev. Simeon Miller gave a deserved testimonial.

"Our honored relic, the Old Meeting-house," brought to the front Hon. Edwin Booth, of Philadelphia, a native of the town, who had been desired to preface his remarks by reading a poem handed in anonymously, which was as follows:

> In good old times of which we read,
> Before the thought of gain and greed
> Had blunted all our finer feeling,
> Had set our better judgment reeling,
> There lived a very worthy dame,
> And Springfield they had called her name.
> In fashion then (now 'twould be rare)
> Her frequent offspring claimed her care.

When they had strength and courage shown
To manage matters of their own,
She gave to each a plot of ground
With woods enough to fence it round,
And bade them wise as serpents be,
For deadly foes they soon might see,
Whose craft and cruelty combined
To make them dreaded by mankind.
In those old times of which I write,
Were hearts like oak, and arms of might.
The treacherous foe, subdued at last,
Their watchings and their terror past,
The people quiet tilled the ground,
While plenteous peace their efforts crowned.
Thus of the mother, good and mild;
My theme shall be her youngest child
But one,—Ludlow (you've heard her name,
With others, told on rolls of fame),
Who took her time in seventy-four
But annals show not at what hour.
Her dowry gained was rather damp,
Consisting of a cedar swamp;
Such as it was she took with grace,
And went to work to gain a place
For self in records then kept well;
How well she did those rolls must tell,
Though rather green in gentler art,
Yet claimed to have a clever start
In farmer's skill and district schools,
In which well taught are simpler rules;
(But higher rank from out of town,
For some at Westfield seek renown,
And some at Wilbraham gather lore,
To lay, 'chance, at a farmer's door.)
She's managed well from year to year
To fill the larder, held so dear;
Always was bread on pantry shelves,
And needing ones might help themselves.
Mayhap the pork would all give out,
But then she'd catch the speckled trout;
Turkeys and pigeons from the wood,
Served up in shape, were very good;
Ofttimes a deer, in forest found,
Was easy game with gun and hound.
She struggled on bravely, through trial and ill,

And proved the old saw of a way and a will;
She fixed up her kitchen so tidy and clean,
Nor thought she nor cared she for better, I ween;
For weightier matters had filled up her head,
And her sons into many a confab were led,
On shearing the sheep and carding the wool,
On weaving the cloth already to pull;
"Young Zeke must have pants and Dan a new coat,
And father's old waistcoat is nearly worn out,
Poor Jerry must wait yet a year, perhaps two,
Though his best Sunday breeches are just about through;"
So with making and planning each hour would well fill,
Each helping his brother with hearty good-will.
But the years sped away, and the factories soon
Into garrets consigned wheel and clumsy hand-loom.
Thus relieved, the good housewife could turn her attention
To parlors and carpets of modern invention,
Each article extra she joined to her wares
Increased much her labors, her trials, her cares;
She sought all in vain to deliver her house
From the speck of a fly or the tooth of a mouse;
Till she sighed to return to those primitive times
When luxurious indulgences counted as crimes.
But changes will come and she must keep pace,
Or own up as beat in fashion's wild chase.
The change most dear to farmer's heart
Is that to chaise from clumsy cart.
He drives to town from his plantation,
And thinks he makes a great sensation.
The horse the same, though seeming faster,—
Do people think he is an Astor?
His produce waits, but now's no time;
Is not his turnout quite sublime?
With nothing gained, and something spent,
His chaise shown off, he rests content.
We have the nicest water, we have the purest air,
Our homes may not be splendid, but they are very fair.
  If our water were not wholesome,
   Or our springs were less abundant,
  Madame S. would not be tempted
   To infringe the tenth commandment.
  But she seems to be forgetful
   That her name was once derived
  From the bounteous springs of water
   Found when Pynchon first arrived.

So she comes to Ludlow, panting,
   Seizes now her flowing streams,
While the townsmen stand astounded
   Like a man in troubled dreams.
Till the plan is all completed,
   And the work is well begun;
But we now are ever hearing
   "What by Ludlow can be done?"
Shall we tax the thing in toto,
   Shall we tax the thing in part?
There's a way to do it rightly,
   But at what point shall we start?
Springfield's citizens are saying
   That we find ourselves too late;
That we should have given our veto
   At the very earliest date.
Now the city-full is chuckling
   Over fortune's quiet smiles,
Thinking she shall soon have water
   Brought through pipes so many miles.
Seems to me she soon will laugh from
   T'other corner of her mouth,
When the streamlets' onward moving
   Shall be stopped in time of drouth;
For those brooks, so pure and limpid,
   Are not always found to flow.
Some completely dry in summer,
   Some are often very low;
So, ye city damsels, hasten,
   Washing up your costly laces;
Whence will come the needed torrents
   For the cleansing of your faces?
We may all be croaking plowmen,
   Hardly worth a thought or care,
But, O denizens of Springfield,
   Hear us, when we cry "Beware!"

Mr. Booth then spoke on the theme assigned, alluding to the peculiarities of the church service when he was a boy, relating several incidents, much to the delight of the audience, and pleading for the preservation of the time-honored structure.

"Our Aged Mother, the City of Springfield," was answered by Mayor J. M. Stebbins of that place, who resented the epithet applied, claiming that the City was never so young or thriving as to-day, and bearing the best of wishes to the town, complimenting the citizens upon the sturdy worth of the denizens of Ludlow.

A sentiment from a citizen, "Springfield in 1774, Ludlow in 1874: 'She that watereth shall be watered also herself,'" pleasantly introduced the next toast—

"Our Mother, boasting of riches and independence, must yet ask a drink of water from her child." This sentiment had been assigned to Hon. A. D. Briggs, of the Springfield Board of Water Commissioners, from whom the following letter was now read:—

Springfield, June 15, 1874.

J. P. Hubbard, Esq., Chairman:

My dear Sir:—Your favor inviting me to respond to a "sentiment" at your Centennial Celebration on the seventeenth is at hand, for which I thank you, and regret that an engagement at Boston on that day obliges me to decline, but have done a better thing by you in securing as my substitute, Charles O. Chapin, Esq., the Chairman of our Board of Water Commissioners, who promises to be present and respond to the sentiment referred to in your letter.

It was said by one of the greatest men who ever lived that "he was born one hundred years old, and always grew younger and younger, until after fourscore years he died an impetuous boy!" For this occasion I propose as a sentiment: "Ludlow—May she upon this, the one hundredth anniversary of her existence as a town, experience a new birth; and not only during fourscore years, but forever, continue to grow younger and younger, ever recollecting that the true greatness of a town consists, not in its breadth of territory, or the number or wealth of its people, but in its successful efforts to elevate and ennoble humanity."

Mr. Chapin, being introduced, said, very neatly:—

The graceful allusion to the intimate relationship of Springfield and Ludlow, that of parent and child, the tenderest of all ties, brings to mind the interesting and touching story of that dutiful and, of course, beautiful daughter, who, when her venerable father was in danger of famishing, bared her bosom to his aged lips and proffered him that sustenance without which he would have perished. There can be but one fault in this comparison, one variation from this parallelism, and that would arise from my inability to answer some carping critic or, possibly, some practical councilman from my own city, who may rise in his seat and confound me with the question, "How much did the old gentleman pay for this privilege?" History gives us no light on this point. But for the benefit of the alderman and the common councilman of the future, I would state that every item in the history of this transaction is recorded, and every dollar of expenditure is properly vouched for. And here let me say that I fear very many of the good people of Ludlow regard themselves as sinned against by the citizens of Springfield in general, by the Water Commissioners, all and singular, who are sinners above all their fellows, and by the chairman of the board, who must be the very chief of sinners. What audacity, what temerity must we possess to stand up before this orthodox community with such a characterization, such a stigma upon us! Why, sir, I should expect to see trooping in upon us from yonder quiet inclosure the outraged spirits of the "forefathers of the hamlet" to scourge us from this gathering of their children. We are no such men; we represent no such people. There is a charitable old adage which maintains that the devil is not so black as he has been painted. I trust we shall not prove so bad as you may have feared. I know there have been some misunderstandings, some differences of opinion, but time and a better acquaintance will soften all prejudice, make clear all misunderstandings, and help us to dwell together in peace and unity, and in the exercises of neighborly offices and good fellowship. To that end I will give as a sentiment: "Ludlow and Springfield—Bound and cemented together as they soon will be, may there be no break in the bonds, and may the record of all differences be writ only in water."

The final toast—"The Men Who Drugged Us"—was answered by Dr. William B. Miller of Springfield, a native of the town, who spoke concerning its physicians, and closed with a suggestion that Springfield should give Ludlow an invitation to return into the family again, to which a stentorian voice responded, "Pay your debts first," which the Doctor acknowledged as apropos.

A number of letters of invitation to the centennial exercises were read.

FROM HON. H. L. DAWES,
CONGRESSMAN REPRESENTING THE TOWN.

I am very much obliged to the Committee of the Town of Ludlow for the kind invitation to participate in their approaching Centennial Celebration. I regret that official engagements will prevent my taking part in those interesting exercises. A hundred years in the life of the town cannot but be full of interest and instruction, and I should, had it been possible, have found great pleasure in not only taking part in your Centennial but visiting your people.

FROM HON. GEORGE M. STEARNS,
DISTRICT ATTORNEY.

I received your invitation to be present at the interesting celebration of your Town's Centennial, and should be greatly pleased to participate with you in the ceremonies of the occasion. But my close attention is required at the present term of court, and I shall be compelled to forego the pleasure.

FROM HON. N. T. LEONARD,
OF WESTFIELD.

The state of my health will prevent my complying with your kind invitation to mingle with the citizens of your town in their approaching Centennial Celebration. A residence in the county now wanting but a few days of half a century has afforded me opportunities of making the acquaintance of many of the citizens of Ludlow, and the recollections connected therewith are mainly pleasant.

FROM HON. HENRY FULLER,
SENATOR OF THE DISTRICT.

I most sincerely regret your kind invitation to be present at your Centennial Celebration did not reach me till the 16th, as I should have been most happy to have joined with you and your fellow-townsmen on the occasion.

FROM HON. GEORGE D. ROBINSON,
OF CHICOPEE, THE TOWN'S REPRESENTATIVE TO THE GENERAL COURT.

Accept my thanks for your invitation in behalf of your Town Committee to be present at your Centennial Celebration on the seventeenth instant. I regret to say it will be next to impossible for me to attend. As your representative in Boston, I find that the Legislature will demand my attendance there later than the day named. With best wishes for a happy and successful union of old friends and renewal of old associations, I am yours, &c.

FROM COL. HARVEY CHAPIN,
OF SPRINGFIELD.

Your invitation to be present on the occasion of the Centennial Celebration, on the 17th, has been duly received. I appreciate fully the cordial and kindly feeling which prompts this token of respect to one who was on familiar terms with the men of Ludlow sixty years ago, many of whom are now dead and gone. I should be pleased to make one of your number at this coming celebration, but my weight of years must be my excuse for declining this and similar festivities which would otherwise be most agreeable.

THE CENTENNIAL 565

Letters of regret were also received from Judge Morris, and from W. M. Pomeroy, of the Springfield Union. Jerry Miller, of Beloit, Wis., a former citizen, wrote a long letter containing interesting reminiscences of the town and its people. Letters were also received by the committee from former ministers in the town. Rev. Isaac Jennison, over eighty years of age, the first regular pastor of the Methodist Society, and architect and builder of its original edifice as well, wrote thus:—

I feel disposed to inform the dear friends of Ludlow that I have not forgotten those pleasant days and years I spent while at Wilbraham and Ludlow. The years 1825 and 1826 were employed in superintending the building of the old Academy at Wilbraham and the little Church at Ludlow. What good times we had in the revival at Ludlow when the Fullers, Millers, Aldens and many others were converted! Dr. Wilbur Fisk and myself came over to aid in that good work. Most of them have gone to their reward in heaven. It would afford me much real enjoyment to meet any and all who remain—to be with you on Wednesday of next week, and review the past and exhort you all to cleave to the Lord.

Revs. Philo Hawkes, pastor of the M. E. Church in 1836, J. W. Dadmun, in 1842, George Prentice, in 1859, and Thomas Marcy, presiding elder, 1854-1857, also sent expressions of regret.

The reading of these letters closed the formal exercises of the day, and the congregation was dismissed. But knots of older and newer acquaintances were gathered about the premises until nearly or quite time for the curfew bells.

At an early evening hour the seats of the spacious Congregational Church were all well filled for the concert. A stage had been built across the west end of the room, on which the singers were seated. At about the appointed time Wilbur F. Miller, conductor, gave the signal and the exercises commenced with the anthem. The program was followed throughout the evening, with added pieces. Everything went off in accord with the spirit of the day and to universal satisfaction. Many a dollar concert ticket has been sold to parties who have received for it an entertainment much inferior to this, the gift of the singers to the people of the town. The thanks of the people were more than due to all who participated, and not less to Messrs. J. Gilbert Wilson, pianist, and G. H. Southland, cornetist, of Springfield, and Mrs. Alvin Barton, of Knoxville, Tenn., than to the earnest and gifted singers of our town.

A not unpleasant episode enlivened the recess between parts. A hint had been given Hon. H. L. Dawes, a few days before, that the standing application for a post office at Ludlow Center might find an opportunity for a favorable reply at this time. Mr. Dawes acted at once, and, having secured from the department the desired favor, forwarded directly the requisite papers, which reached Ludlow Center on the afternoon of the Centennial day. An announcement of the fact in the evening was the episode to which reference is made. And every one wondered why the institution had not before been established.

THE CENTENNIAL

AFTERPAST

There were many Ludlow people, who, from their aching limbs and wearied frames, the next morning seemed to realize that the town was upon its second century. Yet bright and early came the helpers to aid in clearing away the outward vestiges of the unique celebration. So faithfully did the parties interested labor, that in two days a stranger would have failed to discover signs of the gathering anywhere about the green. The committee met once or twice to look over accounts and pass resolutions of thanks, and then all was seemingly as before.

And yet not entirely so. The old town seemed to have dreamed a dream, and awoke to new life. The testimonials and encomiums coming from all sources seemed at the same time to encourage and incite the citizens to activity and awaken the feeling of corporate pride. The comments of the press, subjoined, awakened much interest in the town and out of it.

OPINIONS OF THE PRESS

FROM THE SPRINGFIELD REPUBLICAN

Ludlow's history is that of a staunch puritanic town, while her traditions, though they seldom reach out into the great world beyond her own borders, are yet replete with the deeds of good men and true, and rich beyond most towns hereabouts in the striking individualities which they preserve. The sentiment and flavor of the anniversary this week were rich indeed. Few towns there are in the State that have kept so purely and quaintly the New England spirit of twenty-five and even fifty years ago, and none in this immediate region, certainly, have so completely ignored and kept at bay the restive railroad spirit of these latter days.

Alternating sunshine and rain were vouchsafed to Ludlow for her Centennial day, but she had resolved to celebrate the occasion with unction, and so she did, in spite of wind and beating rain. The event as it culminated was a notable one in various ways.

FROM THE SPRINGFIELD UNION

In spite of a drizzling rain this morning, sufficient to dampen the enthusiasm of any less sturdy community, this has been a proud day for old Ludlow. It is quite safe to say that no such ingathering of her sons and daughters had been seen since the town began its corporate existence one hundred years ago. Like children assembling under the old family roof-tree for the annual Thanksgiving festival, they have assembled to celebrate this centennial day of thanksgiving and praise. The figure is not inapt, for in a rural town like this everybody knows everybody else, and the community, with few distractions of any sort, becomes homogeneous to an extent impossible in a city, or even in a bustling village, until its population is, in a notable degree, as one family.

The dinner was one of many manifestations of the splendid, open-hearted hospitality which characterized the whole proceedings, and is indeed characteristic of the people of the whole town. Although the appetites of the multitude had a very keen edge from long waiting, the supplies were so abundant that if anybody went away hungry it was his own fault. It was an absolutely democratic gathering. Every man, woman, and child in the town was freely invited, and was for the day a guest equally with those from abroad.

The whole celebration, from beginning to end, was a success. All who had a share in the large amount of work necessarily involved in such an undertaking, are entitled to credit and commendation. The celebration was, as the Declaration of Independence asserted the government ought to be, "*by* the people and *for* the people."

FROM THE PALMER JOURNAL

Next Wednesday the people of Ludlow will hold their Centennial Anniversary, and it will be a red-letter day for that town. They will have no heroic deeds to recount, no remarkable deeds to glory over, for the town was always a quiet, unostentatious little republic, its inhabitants rugged as its hills and as firm in integrity and principle as the foundation upon which they stand. It has never been celebrated for anything besides the longevity of its citizens, and one or two Indian legends. If it has not excelled in brilliant geniuses or celebrated persons, it has neither given birth to any great rascals or criminals. Ludlow is a quiet, cosy, hospitable little town—a good place to commence life in, to emigrate from, and to return to, at least once in a hundred years.

. . . .

Lowering skies and drenching showers were not in the programme prepared by the committee of arrangements, but they were provided for by two large tents, pitched in the grove just across the road from the Congregational Church, where more than two thousand persons gathered to join the interesting ceremonies of the occasion, Wednesday. There was a general turn-out among the people of the town, and many came from abroad.

FROM THE NEW ENGLAND HOMESTEAD

The One Hundredth Anniversary of the settlement of Ludlow was celebrated on Wednesday of this week. The attendance was very large; probably not less than two thousand persons were crowded in and about the mammoth tent which was provided for the meeting. The 17th of June was not claimed as the exact anniversary day of the town's settlement, but the month was chosen for the celebration because it was the most favorable season of the year to call together the sons and daughters of the town. The arrangements for this celebration were very complete; the entire company were sumptuously fed by the ladies of the town. It is rare to find a more enterprising community of farmers than those of Ludlow, and they have reason to feel proud of their ancestry, the record of the town, and the manner in which the Centennial was observed.

FROM THE TOLLAND (CONN.) PRESS

(*From a letter written by Austin Chapman, of Ellington, Conn.*)

On this notable day the old sanctuary was loaded down with crockery and eatables of every description, smiling with plenty for the hungry and thirsty, as a covert from the storms which caused many to seek protection under its sheltering roof, through a long and dripping shower. The tubs and pails were well filled with the pure water from the Mineachoag Mountain, with the addition of a little ice. The whole thing passed off silently and agreeably, with a general satisfaction to all.

The following financial exhibit shows just how much was taken from the town's treasury to defray Centennial expenses:—

FINANCIAL REPORT

Expenses Committee on Arrangements,	$163 52
Expenses Committee on Collation,	141 42
Expenses Committee on Music,	97 50
Expenses Committee on Printing,	37 00
Expenses Committee on Programme,	70 00
Total,	$509 44

To the credit of all concerned be it said that no individual charged a cent for services rendered in making all these arrangements.

So universal was the approbation given to the celebration that but trifling opposition was made in the fall meeting, November 3d, to the action thus recorded, which action was taken upon a motion made by C. L. Buell, one of the staunchest friends of the enterprise, one, moreover, who would gladly have served on the general committee had health allowed:

Voted that the town cause to be printed five hundred copies of the history of its One Hundredth Anniversary and other historical facts, and that each family living in the town at the time receive a copy gratis.

Voted that the Centennial Committee be the committee to carry out the doings of this meeting.

Voted to appropriate three hundred dollars to defray expenses of the same.

INDEX

A

	PAGE
Ackley, Samuel	128
Acres, Henry	71
Act, General	58
Incorporation	48
Action of Town on Centennial	514
Ainsworth, Benjamin	71
Alabama and Kearsarge	77
Alden Brothers' Mill	209, 210, 502
Alden District	41, 235
Alden Family	337
Alden, Arthur Orvilla	342
Azel	337, 339, 476
Benjamin	342, 502
Caroline	502
Charles	68, 253, 281, 340, 502
Charles Ely	341
Charles W	68, 101, 340, 502
Clarence Elma	342
David	343
Dexter	344
Edward M	343
Edward S	343
Eliza Ann	345
Eliza Dutton	170
Ellen	344
Elliot O	515
Flora Delia	341
George H	344
Harriet	338
James	339
Jefferson	215, 323, 343, 494
Jennie	344
John	93, 337
John B	64, 86, 341
Josiah	337, 338, 339, 487, 502, 516
Justus B	339, 340, 476
Louise	345
Lovinia	338
Lucinda	345
Lucius D	344
Marcenia M	342
Mary	343
Mary Elizabeth	345
Newell W	339, 476
Orsamus	341, 502, 516, 523
Philo W. B	76
Preston	76
Priscilla	93, 94, 337
Sarah Elizabeth	344
Stillman	129, 338, 481, 488, 516, 523
Dr. Washington B., 64, 68, 124, 168, 169, 253, 334, 340, 498	
Winifred Mary	344
Zenas	340
Alden Sash and Blind Shop	208
Alden's Brook	281
Aldrich, Dr. G. H	124
Aldrich, Hiram W	76, 78, 475, 552
Allen, Edgar Olcott	344
Rev. E. P	159, 160
Wilson	76
Alvord, Rev. F	159
America, Troublous Times	47
Anderson, Arick	477
Dennis	76
Andersonville Prison Life	77
Ludlow Soldiers	78
Animals, Wild	41
Annibal, John, Murder	321, 322
Anniversary, Hundredth	159
Ante-Ludlow	19
Antiques	116
Antisel, Perez	36
Aqueduct, Springfield	99, 100
Arminian tenets	179
Armory, Indian	19
Arnold, Samuel	64, 67
Ashton, Geo	76
Ashwell, William M	123, 497
Mrs. William M	166
Assembly, General	48
Assessors	51, 67, 253
First	51
Atchinson Family	345
Atchinson, Ada Maria	346
Almon Scott	346
David L	345, 492, 503, 540
Fred Green	346
Gilbert S	34, 121, 123, 487
Gillen D., ix, 10, 37, 41, 64, 116, 123, 173, 174, 273, 346, 492, 515	
Mary Celeste	170, 346
Mary Ladd	346
Athletic Field	231
Atkins, J. W	157
Austin, Rev. David R., 155, 156, 160, 163, 253, 515, 556, 557	

B

Baggs, Benjamin	485
Mrs. Harriet	168
William	483
Bagley, James	76
Baker, Leonard	76
Ballad, "Nick and Tarzy"	330
Oakley	326
Banister (Joseph) Family	347
Banister (Linus) Family	348
Banister, Albert	210, 348, 491, 502
Rev. Daniel K., 74, 85, 185, 189, 347, 516, 520, 523, 524	
Mrs. Emeline T	348, 482
John L	101, 348, 482
Joseph	347
Jotham	347

INDEX

Banister, Linus..................348
   William........................347
Bank, Ludlow Savings..107–111, 266, 284
   Auditors.......................111
   Committee, Investment..........108
   Deposits.......................107
   Incorporation..................107
   Incorporators..................107
   Presidents.....................107
   Trustees.......................107
Baptists..................139, 147, 155
Barber Family....................348
Barber, Ebenezer........37, 348, 492, 540
   Emma Lucinda..................349
   Hollis..........349, 481, 497, 498
   Ira............................349
   Lewis..................61, 305, 492
   Loretta Jane...................349
Barber's History.................220
Bardwell, Oramel..............143, 147
Barker, Ichabod..................543
   Noah............................41
Barr, Rev. Preston..........197, 198
Bartlett (Eleazer) Family........350
Bartlett (Thomas) Family.........349
Bartlett, Alfred H....64, 65, 103, 121, 350
   Mrs. Alice C...................478
   Andrew E. C...............350, 515
   Homer M........................478
   Mrs. Homer M...................482
   Jonathan.........64, 67, 128, 137, 172
   Lewis G........................350
   Luman..........................494
   Thomas.........................349
Barton, Ezekiel.............107, 491
   Henry......................214, 215
Bear Swamp........................50
Bears.........................41, 57
Beaven, Right Rev. Thomas D.....205
Beebe Family.....................350
Beebe, Andrew Hiram..........354, 490
   Emeline Ruby...................354
   Evanore Olds.............ix, 10, 354
   Ezekiel........................543
   Gideon.................57, 64, 67, 353
   John...........................351
   Jonathan.......................352
   Joshua.........................352
   Nathan Sherwood................354
   Robert William.................354
   Samuel.........................352
   Sherwood.......64, 67, 68, 69, 353, 488
   William Hubbard...........334, 354
Beckwith, D. N...............104, 107
Begory, Caesar...................543
Bennett Family...................354
Bennett, Adelbert L., 101, 143, 359, 483,
                    487, 499, 505
   Anne Susette...............360, 516
   Charles.................68, 355, 505
   Charles B., 68, 122, 123, 252, 253, 322,
               360, 483, 490, 491
Bennett, Charles S., 68, 101, 359, 479, 482,
                    488, 505, 515
   Emily..........................357
   Flavilla Eugenia Janet.........357
   Franklin G......68, 122, 123, 360, 488
   George Green...................360
   Hannah Carey...................358
   Homer Augustus.................361
   Jefferson......................505
   John......................354, 355
   Joseph.........................355
   Laura Ann......................356
   Laura Lovinia..................356
   Lemuel................76, 503, 552
   Lyman...........................76
   Mary Ardelia...................361
   Merton R..................360, 488
   Minerva Jane...................361
   Nancy Ann......................356
   Nelia Ada......................357
   Peter..........................354
   Sallie Eva.....................357
   Sarah Young....................358
   Seth J............67, 68, 357, 505
   Walter.....................121, 203
   Warren D........................76
   Warren Jerome..................361
   Welcome........................505
Benway, Joseph, Sr...............501
Bequests.........................170
Bier, Purchase....................83
Billings, Mrs. Martha.............86
   Silas...................101, 515, 516
Biographies......................265
Birge, William E.................477
Birnie, Alexander C........65, 67, 266
   Mrs. Alexander C., ix, 10, 116, 249, 253
   George A., 64, 104, 107, 108, 110, 111,
       113, 117, 203, 204, 253, 265, 497
Blackmer, Dwight.............236, 500
   William........................500
Blair, Mrs. Edwin................481
Blake, Elijah....................523
Blanchard, John..................490
Blish, Lillian Jones.........169, 170
Bliss, Abel.......................36
   Edmund................64, 107, 503
   Moses......................50, 64
   Oliver..........................36
Blizzard, Great...................63
Blodgett, Albert.................500
Blood, Ebenezer..................497
Bly, Albert.................198, 203
Booth, A. E......................204
   Charles E......................498
   Hon. Edwin, 20, 28, 171, 173, 266, 558,
                        561
   Eliphal............131, 174, 266, 491
   George, 64, 68, 173, 253, 491, 498, 557
   George R.......................498
   Hattie....................247, 498
Boston Flax Mills......225, 226, 287, 288

INDEX 573

	PAGE
Boston Tea Party	69, 123
Bottles, Glass	116, 208
Boundaries, Ludlow	43, 48, 60
Springfield	31
Bounties	70
Bowdoin, James	61
Bowers, Rev. John	157
Bowker Noah	51, 493
Boys in Blue	552
Brainard, Rev. David	288
William	68
Bramble, Franklin	67, 500
Mrs. Julia D	500
William	500
Brewer Family	361
Brewer, Amy	92
Angenette D	363
Chauncey	91, 92, 270, 296, 362, 478
Daniel	86, 361, 362, 363, 478, 516
Edwin	173, 478
Eunice	92
Isaac, Jr	362
Isaac, Sr., 38, 42, 51, 67, 129, 161, 321,	362, 478
Harriet Sarah	363
John Daniel	363
Lillian	478
Luke	328
Lyman	76
Nathaniel	92
Bridge, Collins Depot	97
Cooley	96
Indian Leap	99
Jenksville	97, 228
Put's	95, 96, 97
Red, 97, 99, 228, 229, 230, 257, 500, 501	
Wallamanumps	96
Bridges	93
Appropriation	98
Building Conditions	96
Covered	97
First	95
Iron	97, 98
Toll	96
Bridgman, Rev. Chester, 136, 159, 160,	490, 498
J. C	172
Brigham, Lemuel Hawley, 111, 118, 222,	225, 268, 269, 316, 503, 515
Brigham Lodge	118, 121, 269, 284
Briggs, Hon. A. D	102, 562
Brines, John H	76
Brook, Alden's	281
Broad, 36, 43, 93, 100, 101, 208, 209, 210,	502
Chapin	43
Higher	43, 50, 60, 98, 100, 101, 207, 210
Jabish	100
Stony	43, 213, 214
Brooks, Edward F	75, 76, 552
Browning Family	363
Browning, Charles S	65, 111

	PAGE
Browning, Ephraim	364
John	364, 480
John Clark	365
Nathaniel	363
William	364
Buck Swamp	44
Buckingham, Rev. Mr	159
Buckley, James	76
Bucklin, Joseph	69, 104, 217
Samuel S	64
Buell Family	365
Buell, Chauncey	365, 477
Chauncey L., 64, 67, 74, 122, 123, 169,	171, 174, 253, 255, 365, 477, 489, 515, 516, 570
Miriam C	366
Bugbee, James	500
Joseph A	76
Bullard, David	214
Bungalow, F. L. Burr's	29, 30
Burdon, Rev. Henry F	197, 198
Burley Family	366
Burley, Abner	366
Jacob	367, 501
John	366
Samuel	366
Burr Family	367
Burr, Abigail	369
Ashbel, 64, 67, 163, 172, 368, 483, 496,	505
Benjamin	367
Benjamin F., ix, 10, 38, 64, 67, 69, 85, 86,	97, 115, 121, 131, 168, 169, 170, 172, 173, 217, 236, 270, 271, 369, 483, 505, 510, 511, 514, 516, 556
Estes	505
Frank Rood	369
Frederick L	29, 67, 121, 270, 369
Mrs. F. L	168
Harriet E	85, 171
Jonathan	38, 59, 64, 67, 95, 367, 505
Lyman, 85, 169, 170, 171, 216, 217, 270,	368, 483, 505, 516, 523
Noadiah	543
Samuel	367
Burr, Jonathan & Company	207
Burr, Lyman, Industry	216
Burroughs, Stephen	38, 128, 137, 138
Burt, Enoch	145
Henry	35
Jonathan, Jr	32
Reuben	59, 543
Burying Ground Hill	208, 321
Butler, James	479
Butterfield, Rev. Claude A	197, 198
Button, Jonathan	479

C

Cadets	80, 81, 83
Cady Family	369
Cady, Abner	116, 171, 253, 369, 370, 477, 546

574 INDEX

Cady, Amasa............369, 476, 503
  Jackson, 64, 67, 68, 86, 99, 370, 503, 515
  Mrs. Jackson...................83, 335
Calkins, Charles H..................478
  Rufus...........................207
Calkins Chairs.................207, 208
Call, Isaiah.........................70
Camels..............................96
Capen, Dexter.....................502
Carver Family.....................370
Carver, Aaron.........212, 213, 371, 494
  Austin..........................237
  David..........211, 212, 370, 371, 494
  Derrick O.......................371
  Elmer H....166, 173, 216, 252, 253, 372
  George..........................477
  Henry Ingalls, ix, 10, 214, 215, 216, 276,
                             372, 494, 495
  John............................370
  Jonathan............212, 214, 371, 494
  Lizzie A........................372
  Robert..........................370
  Samuel..........................370
  Warren..........................371
  William.........................213
Carver, H. I., Company.........44, 216
Caswell, Dr. Elijah......64, 68, 124, 497
  John B..........................497
  Mrs. Susan......................497
Caughmanyputs..................28, 29
Causey, Rev. L. P.................189
Causeway, Cedar Swamp............95
Canada, Little....................102
Casperzack, Jo....................478
Cedar Swamp, 35, 44, 58, 59, 60, 95, 128
Cemeteries.........................83
  Bequests.........................86
  Commissioners....................86
  Donors of Gifts..................86
  Epitaphs......................87–90
  Gifts............................86
  Perpetual Care...................86
Cemetery, Center...........85, 87, 155
  East, or "Ould Burying Ground," 36,
                           84, 87, 95, 333
  First, or Sikes..............83, 87
  Deed............................83
  Fuller........................84, 87
  Island Pond, or Village.......85, 86
Centennial, The...............507–570
  Accommodations.............517, 518
  Actual..........................523
  Action of Town..................514
  Address, Literary...............527
    Historical....................536
    Welcome.......................524
  Appropriation...................514
  Collation.............516, 517, 518
  Committees..........511, 515, 516
  Concert.........................522
  Decorations.....................517
  Financial Report................569

Centennial, Fund...................171
  History of Town.................570
  Hymn............................520
  Invitations.....................517
  Letters...........562, 563, 564, 565
  Officers of Day.................516
  Orator, Historical..............515
    Literary......................515
  Order of Exercises.......519, 520, 521
  Petition to Town................513
  Poem............................558
  Prospective.....................513
  Press Opinions..........567, 568, 569
  Sub-committees..................511
Center of District.................128
Center of Town.....................55
Center Cemetery............85, 87, 155
Chamberlain, Capt. George..........83
Chandler, R. M...............487, 516
Chapin Brook.......................43
Chapin Family.....................372
Chapin, Abel...............273, 374, 493
  Alvin...........................374
  Andrew J...................375, 477
  Mrs. Andrew J..............180, 477
  Ashbel..........................374
  Ashbel P..................99, 375, 475
  Charles O..................102, 562
  Hon. Chester W.............270, 523
  Rev. Daniel E...................198
  Edwin...........................499
  Rev. Ephraim..........67, 248, 273
  Erastus.........................273
  Hannah..........................373
  Col. Harvey.....................564
  Henry M.........................497
  James........................76, 497
  Japhet.......................32, 372
  Job.............................375
  Rev. Joel...........249, 275, 376, 543
  Louis W....................375, 480
  Mrs. Mary........................89
  Merrick..........................89
  Moses...........................374
  Moses A.........................145
  Nathaniel.......64, 68, 177, 186, 253
  Oliver..........41, 49, 51, 67, 128, 161
  Pelatiah....................137, 160
  Pliny...........................213
  Reuben H.....................89, 497
  Deacon Samuel..............273, 372
  Shem.........36, 37, 41, 275, 375, 540
  Stephen.........................213
  Submit...........................89
  Sumner...........................68
  Mrs. Susan A................105, 257
  Thomas..........................373
Chapin Pond........................86
Chapman Family...................376
Chapman, Augustus............76, 552
  Austin..............221, 523, 569
  Charles.........................376

INDEX

Chapman, Charles E............174, 376
  David........................376
  Edward Earle...122, 123, 167, 169, 253, 376, 492
  Rev. George E..................198
Charles II........................31
Charles, Edmund E....170, 174, 497, 515
  Mrs. Emma L..................170
  Henry..................64, 67, 497
  Melina W......................497
Charter, Massachusetts Annulment....31
  Petition......................48
Chase, George R..................122
Cherry Valley........37, 41, 94, 100, 236
Chicabee River..............42, 48, 50
Chicopee River, 36, 43, 44, 45, 57, 95, 97, 98, 99, 305, 540, 549, 550
Chicuepe River............19, 29, 38, 41
Children's Sunday..............137, 166
Chooley, Charles..................543
Church, Congregational, 44, 95, 116, 148, 156, 157, 165, 167, 179, 305, 321, 547, 548
  First or Town........44, 85, 127-174
  Methodist, 85, 128, 165, 175-187, 208, 282, 292, 300, 514, 547
  St Andrew's........200, 201, 203, 204
  St. Jean Baptiste..........204, 205
  Union..............189-203, 284, 548
Churchill, Charles O..............491
Circuit Preachers..................178
Citizenship........................61
Civil War..............73, 76, 77, 552
Clapp, W. A......................185
Clark (George) Family..............378
Clark (Hugh) Family...............377
Clark (William) Family............379
Clark, Aaron Rice..................378
  Alice Maud............160, 249, 378
  Alvah L....................380, 476
  Amelia J..................ix, 10, 482
  Charles.......................505
  Clifford Pease.............249, 380
  Edward........................493
  Eugene....................151, 475
  Frank.........................482
  George......321, 322, 378, 482, 516, 523
  George Root...67, 173, 174, 253, 378, 482, 510, 511, 514, 515, 516
  Gilbert....................487, 505
  Hugh..........................377
  Isaac..........................377
  Joel....................379, 487, 488
  John......................377, 482
  Joshua....................380, 475
  Martha........................377
  Moses.....................172, 379
  Mrs. Moses....................172
  Noah....64, 132, 163, 217, 379, 487, 488
  Noah, Jr..................237, 379
  Rodolphus....................480

Clark, Elder Seth..................139
  Sylvester..............480, 516, 523
  William P....31, 380, 487, 494, 497, 515
Cleaveland Family.................380
Cleaveland, Cyrus.............381, 478
  David.........................380
Clerk, First Town..................50
Clough (John) Family..............382
Clough (Timothy) Family..........381
Clough, Ambrose, 57, 67, 275, 381, 490, 510, 511, 513, 514, 515
  Dan...........................382
  Gaius..........................71
  John..........................382
  Jonathan.........59, 64, 161, 172, 382
  Mordecai..............71, 275, 381
  Theodocia P................86, 170
  Timothy...............59, 381, 382
  Uriah..........147, 177, 178, 186, 381
Club, "Know Nothing"............107
  Ludlow Burns Social..........123
  Farmers......................121
  Social and Debating...........123
  Women's......................123
  Young People's Farmers........122
Coash, John................76, 78, 552
Coats, Apportionment..............69
Codare, George...................491
Coffins and Caskets, Manufacture....216
Coleman, Deacon Seth.............145
Collins, Albert....................78
  Emma S......................407
  Elihu.....................68, 479
  Richard......................480
  Roderick..................67, 479
Collins Depot..........45, 78, 95, 99
Collins Manufacturing Co.............36
Collins Paper Co..................479
Colton, Aaron, 36, 51, 59, 60, 67, 145, 146, 479, 540, 543
  Aaron, Jr......................59
  Captain........................71
Columbus Day....................255
Colwell, Walter S.................108
Committees, Antiques and Relics....116
  Centennial........510, 511, 515, 516
  Ministerial....................147
  Prudential...............236, 239
  School..................252, 253
  Town History..............ix, 10
Commons, The.....................31
  Committee of Allotment........35
  Inward....................58, 210
  Individual Shares..............211
  Outward........32, 33, 35, 51, 210
    Extent....................35
    First Division..............32
    Second....................33
  Proprietors..............32, 33, 34
Communion Services, 116, 118, 171, 172, 546
Cone, Rev. Mr....................159

INDEX

Congregational Church, 44, 84, 95, 116, 148, 156, 157, 165, 167, 179, 305, 321, 547, 548
    Deacons 172
    Second..........................548
    Society.........................164
Congregationalists..........147, 151, 194
Congress, Provincial...............55, 69
Constables, First......................51
Convention, Constitutional.......55, 292
    Early..............................55
    Delegates..........................55
Converse, Caroline A................497
    Charles..........................497
    Rodolphus.......................497
    Wilmer..........................479
Cook, David.........................212
Cooley Bridge,........................96
Cooley Family......................382
Cooley, Amy........................383
    Captain Ariel....................97
    Calvin S.................76, 383, 482
    Carrie B.........................383
    George E........................383
    Jacob..........................41, 51
    Lucien.................68, 107, 479, 482
    Merrick H.......................383
    Solomon.........................543
    Sumner..........................382
    William.........................483
Coon, John..........................482
Cormack, Alexander................198
Corwin, Adelbert....................105
Coté, Louis..........................490
Cotton, Edward......................543
    Gideon...........................71
Councils, Ecclesiastical 141, 145, 146, 156, 192
Court, Ludlow, History..............111
"Cow Pasture".......................51
Coyle, Rev. J. P................194, 198
Cramond, Hugh M.............121, 123
Crocker, Rev. H. E........194, 198, 253
Crowell, Joshua......................148
Crowninshield Family................384
Crowninshield, Caleb.76, 78, 185, 384, 552
Currier, Daniel D................76, 552
Cushing, Thomas.....................50
Cushman, Rev. Chester L., 159, 160, 173, 194, 198, 253, 498, 503, 504, 510, 511, 514, 515, 516, 521, 524
Curtis, Rev. J. S...........160, 166, 167
    Rev. Mr.........................162

D

Dadmun, Rev. J. W....185, 253, 514, 565
Dakin, Rev. W. T...................203
Dam, Cherry Valley.................101
    Ludlow..........................102
    Red Bridge......................229
Damon Family.......................384
Damon, Alden..................215, 494
Damon, Asa....................385, 495
    Byron Winchester...............386
    Hon. Dexter................276, 386
    Edmond...............128, 211, 494
    Eli..............................387
    George..........................387
    Henry.................276, 386, 494
    Henry Dexter...................386
    James Frank....................386
    John........................384, 385
    Jude............................387
    Libbie Matilda..................386
    Lowell..........................494
    Lydia Putnam..................385
    Peter...................67, 236, 385
    Sally...........................386
    Thomas....................384, 387
Daniels, Asa..............281, 334, 501
    David......................139, 236
    Dwight.........................501
    Justin..........................441
    Lurana Olds....................334
    Marcus.........................501
    Nicholas...........85, 90, 329, 330
    W. H......................193, 198
Davenport Family...................388
Davenport, Edwin A................174
    Daniel..........................388
    Hiram............32, 41, 70, 291, 388
    Mrs. Hiram....................488
    Rev. Mr........................137
    Paul............................388
Davis Family........................388
Davis, Aaron..............67, 68, 478, 516
    Anson..........................478
    Chauncey..................389, 475
    Rev. Emerson..................157
    Job.............................388
    John...........................500
    Martin J.......................478
    Rev. Samuel.........182, 189, 190
Dawes, Hon. H. L.............563, 566
Day Family.........................389
Day, Rev. Edward..............197, 198
    John Q..........................85
    Lucy Ann.......................389
    Robert..........................389
    Zachariah............85, 389, 475, 516
Deacons, Congregational............172
    of Union Church................198
Deane, George H....................222
Deed, Copy of Old...................91
    Kendall and Munger.........211, 212
Deer.................................57
Deer Reeves......................36, 51
De Forest, Rev. J. A............194, 198
Dempsey, Mrs. Mary................478
Desrochers, Rev. M. A.........204, 205
Dickey, Rev. Myron P., 159, 160, 173, 174
Dickinson, Eli.......................212
    Erastus.........................496
    Henry...........................323

INDEX

	PAGE
Dickinson, Leon Lewis	358
Samuel	494
Distillery	208, 213
District, Center	128
Petition	42
District, Alden	41, 235
Center	235
Cherry Valley	236
Lyon	236
Miller Corner	235, 236
Shoestring	69
Wallamanumps	236
West Middle	236
Districts, First Named	48
Privileges of Towns	58
Representative	68
School	236
Abolishment	243, 254
Location	236
Number of	236
Set off	235, 236
Supervision	246, 257
"Doctor Foggus"	323, 324
Dodge, Chester	87
Dorman, John	67, 477
Dorman Place	38, 105, 128, 322, 540
Dostal, Mrs. Wallace	492, 494
Dow, Lorenzo	323
Downing, Capt. Nathaniel	35
Drawing, First Taught	256
Dubinski, Michael	492
Dunlap, Henry	497
Welcome M	497
Dupal, Jo	502
Duteau, John	480
Dutton Family	390
Dutton, Austin	169, 475
Elisha	475, 494
Hubbard, 168, 169, 170, 324, 390, 498, 516, 523	
Jeremiah	64, 67, 68, 168, 390, 476
Oliver, 55, 64, 68, 116, 163, 164, 168, 172, 390, 498, 543	
William	475
Dwellings, Frame	54
Log	54

E

Eagan, Patrick	479
Eames, Rev. Henry	178
East Cemetery	36, 84, 87, 95, 333
Eastman, Joel	212, 494
Joseph	213, 494
Eaton, Calvin	107
David	502
Elijah C	68, 253
Jacob S	67, 68, 69, 209, 502, 516
Walter W	478
William T	121
Eaton's Mills	97, 178, 210, 502
Educational Interests	235–262
Electric Lights	103

	PAGE
Elevations	43
Ellis, Dr. Simpson	64, 68, 123
Ellison, William	477, 497
Franklin H	477
Elphinstone, George, Sr., 121, 123, 198, 203	
Ely, Rev. Alford	157
Epitaphs	87–90
Estey Family	390
Estey, Caleb Bradlee	123, 391, 479
Edward Stebbins	391
Jacob	390
Joseph Williams	390
Evangelists	151, 163, 177, 178
Evangels, Flying	178

F

Facing Hills	29, 30, 36, 43, 208, 555
Legends	28, 30
Factory, First Cotton	44
Fairbanks, Frederick F	491, 516
Charles F	107, 491
Mrs. Charles F	491
Families, Genealogy	337–472
Farming	207
Farms	475–505
Destroyed	504, 505
Farnum, Joel	177, 186
Farr, Charles H	496
James H	497
Fast Day in 1813	148
Fathers, The	551
Feats of Strength	334
Fedette, Frederick	480
Ferry Family	391
Ferry, Aaron	41, 50, 64
Clifford William	391
Rutherford H	31, 392, 494
Field, Athletic	231
Fifield Family	392
Fifield, Benjamin	392
Ira	392
Nason	392
Filer, John	212, 321, 494
Fire	547
First Cemetery	83, 87
First Church, Springfield	58, 116, 156
First District Clerk	50
First or Town Church	127–174
Additions	136
Benevolences	166
Bequests	170
Building, First	44, 62, 129, 130, 131
Site of	129
Second	132, 547
Cost	132
Dedication	132
Fire	132, 547, 548
Third	135
Cost	135
Dedication	135
Hymn	135
Improvements	136, 137

INDEX

First or Town Church, Chapel.......136
    Cost..........................136
    Christian Endeavor Society........173
    Clerks of the Parish..............173
    Covenant, Adoption..............164
    Communion Services..116, 171, 172, 546
    Creed, Adoption.............164, 165
    Deacons......................163, 172
    Early Places for Meeting..........127
    First Meeting House......127, 129, 544
        Committee to Build............128
        Erection......................129
        Location.....................128
        Tablet in.....................131
    Funds.........................164
    Gifts....................136, 171, 172
    Improvements...............129, 130
    Incorporation...................164
    Instruments, Musical.............169
    Leaders of the Singing............168
    Members, Additional.........162, 163
        Early....................161, 546
        Rules.........................164
    Ministers,................137–160, 546
        Committee to Hire.........54, 161
        Salaries......139, 140, 148, 152, 159
    Old Home Sunday................166
        Exercises.....................166
        Invitations....................166
    Ordination, First................141
    Organists......................170
    Organization.................160, 164
    Parsonage.....................136
    Pastor, First Settled..............140
    Pastors, List...................160
    Prayer Meetings.............166, 545
    Recommendation, Letter..........162
    Regulations....................164
    Sabbath School.................174
    Sexton, First...................161
    Societies...................173, 174
    Standing Committee.........163, 164
First Parish....................164, 165
    Dissolution....................165
    Incorporation with Town..........165
Fisher Family.....................393
Fisher, Ella Maria.................393
    E. Newton........123, 170, 393, 489
    Mrs. E. Newton..........55, 170, 498
    Salem.........................393
    Willis Sikes.............167, 169, 393
Fisk, David......................481
    Rev. Franklin........185, 189, 253, 547
    Hon. Gordon M., 20, 21, 135, 276, 290,
        326, 495
    Hannah.......................212
    Hezekiah..........209, 213, 494, 495
    Polly..........................481
    Quartus E.............208, 481, 487
    William Hezekiah............213, 276
    Rev. Wilbur........180, 189, 547, 565
Fisk's Mills......................209

Five-Mile House...................71
Fleming, Rev. William.............185
Flint, Captain....................71
Flood, A.........................97
Fords............................95
Forward, Rev. Justus..........145, 147
Foster, Charles M......38, 208, 477, 541
    Rev. Mr......................189
Francis, Rev. Mr., 136, 159, 160, 166, 173
Fraternal Organizations.........118, 119
Freitag, Louis F..................480
"Friday, the Hermit"..............324
Frost Family.....................393
Frost, Curtis.....................502
    Elias..................67, 68, 493
    Noah.........................502
    Samuel....67, 68, 147, 177, 178, 323, 503
    Selah.........................393
Fuller Cemetery................84, 87
Fuller Family....................394
Fuller, Albert, 64, 68, 155, 170, 400, 482,
        483, 487, 489, 490, 514, 516
    Albert E................67, 400, 490
    Caroline...................169, 475
    Charles.......................477
    Clarence......................483
    Davenport L., 68, 168, 174, 401, 489,
        515, 516, 517
    David.........................489
    David L.................121, 168, 401
    Edmund..................401, 477
    Edmund W.........67, 210, 396, 477
    Edward.......................394
    Edward E., 38, 67, 68, 69, 76, 84, 85, 86,
        97, 108, 121, 398, 479, 499, 515
    Elijah..................67, 68, 399, 491
    Elisha, 59, 64, 69, 84, 91, 107, 164, 208,
        237, 323, 324, 325, 395, 479
    Ely..........64, 68, 69, 106, 169, 475
    Ezekiel, 61, 64, 67, 68, 70, 105, 106, 147,
        398, 400, 488, 490, 516, 523, 543
    Frank Davenport...............401
    Franklin.............490, 516, 523
    George C. A...................401
    Gilbert E........67, 170, 399, 491, 514
    Harriet.......................170
    Henry Caleb..................402
    Henry S., 64, 67, 68, 84, 85, 397, 475,
        477, 479, 482, 483, 499, 516,
        523, 564
    Herbert Emerson...............397
    Jerusha...................329, 475
    John......................396, 477
    John Wilson...................397
    Joshua, 37, 38, 41, 42, 50, 57, 62, 64, 67,
        68, 92, 128, 129, 137, 138, 139, 141,
        161, 163, 322, 325, 395, 477, 479,
        483, 540
    Lathrop...................490, 543
    Lyman....................168, 490
    Matthew......................394
    Otis..........................477

INDEX

	PAGE
Fuller, Purchase Dwight	477
Samuel	394
Solomon L	64, 67
Rev. Stephen	139
Warren D., 64, 69, 207, 208, 253, 397,	477, 479
Warren G	57, 95, 165, 399
Mrs. Warren G	490
Warren M	400
Waterman	67, 483
Young	37, 322, 395
Zera	180, 477
Fuller's Tavern	70, 106
Fulling Mill	208, 212, 213
Funds, Centennial	171
Ministerial	164, 181
School	164

G

Galligan, Matthew	482, 484
Gardiner, Lemuel	71
Gardner, Rev. Austin	193, 198, 253
Charles Alden	345
Henry, Esq	69
Gates Family	402
Gates, Ephraim	402, 481
George	32
George H	402
Horace	76, 481
John	64, 67, 402, 482
John R	402, 482
Katherine M	482
Samuel	71
Genealogies	337–473
Gifts: Abner Cady	116, 171
C. D. Rood	171, 172
Of Organ	170, 171
Glass Works	208, 487
Glover, Emma M	118
Pelatiah	33, 35
Gobeil, Rev. Louis F	205
Godfrey, Rev. A. C	253
Gokey, Camille	483
Goodale, Jabez	543
Goodell, Sarah	487
Goodnow, Joseph	497
Goodwill, Miss Eliza	243
Gove Family	403
Gove, Albert A	203, 252, 253, 403
A. C	64, 403, 516
Charles	403
Rev. Mr	178, 186
Gowan, Charles W	111
Graduates, Higher Institutions	248, 249
High School	247
Graduation, First	256
Graham, Charles	86
Grand Army	83
Veterans	80
Grange, Ludlow	122, 123, 131
Hall	122, 131
Worthy Masters	122, 123

	PAGE
Granger, Henry	488
"Grate Bay Rode"	41, 42
Graves, Austin Lyman	502
Chester	107
Henry	502
Lyman	57
William	171
Great Cove	27
Great River	31, 32
Green, Daniel	491
George D., 67, 68, 69, 108, 117, 121, 478	
Susan A	170
Greenhalge, Gov. Frederic T	63
Greenhalgh, Charles	64
Gridley, Rev. Elijah	145
Grosvenor, Charles F., 64, 67, 69, 86, 108,	111, 121
Grout, Parma	170
Guideboards	95
Gushee, Helen M	245, 258
Walter E	247, 257
Gun Works	220

H

Halford, A. H	121, 198, 203, 253
Hall, Rev. William	192, 198, 548
Hampden County	61
Hampden, John	540
Hannum Family	404
Hannum, Aaron	404
Dr. James Wilson, 107, 108, 117, 124,	203, 243, 253, 278, 279, 405
John	279, 404
Silas	404
William	404
Harrington, Lewis	104
Harris Family	405
Harris, Elliot D	323, 405
Jasper	77
Nathan	281, 405
Nathan Alonzo	281, 282, 405, 491
Philo A	491
Harris Mill	209, 322, 491
Haschal, Mr. David	139, 140, 160
Haschall, Timothy	324
Hatch, Adrian G	155, 490
Haviland, James	104, 253, 266, 282, 498
Hawkes, Philo	185, 189, 565
Haydon, Ashley	107
Hayes, Elizur	498
Rev. Joel	145
Hearse	84
Hearse House	84
Hedding, Rev. Elijah, 147, 148, 149, 151,	160, 178, 179, 186, 547
Height, John	491
Henderson, James, 107, 108, 111, 121, 203,	284, 285
Hennaman, Rudolph	476
Hiersche, A. G	501
Higher Brook, 43, 50, 60, 98, 100, 101, 207,	210

580 INDEX

High School, 244, 245, 246, 247, 255, 256, 257, 258, 259
Highways....93
  Care of....98
  Commissioner....98
  Early....41, 94
  State....98
  Wages Paid....98
Hill, Rev. Charles E....203
  Collins....319
  Poem....319
Hill, Burying Ground....208, 321
  Stallion....54
  Stony, 37, 47, 48, 51, 53, 93, 540, 541
  Turkey....43, 213, 504
Hills, Facing....29, 30, 36, 43, 208, 555
Historical Address....536
  Orator....515, 536
  Room....116, 171, 279, 498
History, Committee, Town,....ix, 10
  Industrial....207–232
  Military....69
  Town, Votes....570
Hitchcock, Abner, 41, 42, 50, 64, 127, 128, 137, 161, 490, 542
  John....32, 128, 544
  Joseph....41, 51, 64, 67, 137, 543
  Josiah....41, 490
Hobson Family....406
Hobson, Alfred J....121, 484
  Henry....76, 77
  John....121, 406, 484
  John, Jr....76, 406, 516
  Joshua....406
Hog Reeves....51
Holdich, Rev. Dr....191
Horse Company, Famous....70
Hospital, Ludlow....117, 119
  Committee....117
  Donor....117
  Patients, Number of....118
  Society....117, 266
Howard, Rev. Bezaleel, 58, 141, 145, 159, 546
  Charles F....68, 121
  Clara Lovinia....356
  John....71
  Lonza Erwin....356
  Theodocia....557
Hubbard Family....406
Hubbard, Mrs. Amnie, 86, 173, 290, 498, 515
  Bernis....239
  Calvin....487
  Mrs. Caroline....487
  Charles T., 112, 222, 224, 225, 226, 287, 288, 316
  Charles W., 107, 116, 117, 224, 226, 227, 284, 287
  Dan....67, 107, 407, 487, 491
  Elisha, 55, 59, 140, 141, 144, 236, 406, 497

Hubbard, Emeline C....407
  Eugene Howry....408
  George N....487, 492
  Captain Henry A., 76, 116, 249, 288, 289, 491, 552
  Israel N....408
  John....41, 64, 137, 161
  John, Jr....51, 64, 67, 406
  John P., 63, 64, 67, 68, 69, 74, 111, 235, 408, 487, 497, 510, 511, 514, 515, 516, 557, 562
  John W., 67, 94, 95, 408, 487, 497, 515, 516
  Newton....487
  Russell....407
  Titus....58, 59, 60, 67, 334, 407, 497
  Truman N....83, 408, 487
  Warren....71, 489, 503
  Warren, Jr....503
  William H....477, 491
Hubbard Memorial, 112, 115, 171, 228, 255, 279, 287, 288, 498
Hutchinson, Governor Thomas..42, 47, 50
  Rev. Sylvester....137, 139, 186

I

Incidents....61, 323
Incorporation, Act....48
Indian Leap....20, 21, 27, 45, 99, 209, 550
  Legend....21, 28
Indian Legends....20, 21, 28, 30, 549, 550
Indian Orchard....19, 45, 97, 100, 204
  Relics....19, 549, 550
Indians....19, 20, 21, 28, 29, 31, 39
  Purchase of Land....30
Industrial History....207–232
  Training....239
Industry, Lyman Burr....216
Inhabitants, Early....19, 36, 37
Inoculation....61
Inventions....220
Inward Commons....58, 210
Irwin, James B....117
Island Pond Cemetery....85, 86
Itinerants, Early....177, 178, 179

J

Jabish Brook....100
Jefferson's Peak....43
Jencks, or Jenks, Benjamin, 44, 97, 104, 107, 131, 190, 217, 549
  Edward C....104, 478
  Washington....217
Jenksville, 44, 94, 95, 107, 124, 190, 192, 219, 222, 549, 550
  Bridge....97, 228, 550
  Growth....220
  Gun Works....220
  In 1868....225
  Methodist Church....177–190
  People....220, 221
  Sundays....221

INDEX

Jenksville Mills 217-232
  Area of Holdings 217
  Capital, Original 217
  Enlargement 220
  First Buildings 217
  First Company 217
    Failure 222
  Manufactures, Early 218
  Operation, First 217
  Patents 220
  Products, Increase 219
    Value 219
  Stone Buildings 218
Jennings, Beriah 41, 51, 90
  Beriah, Jr. 90
  John, 55, 56, 59, 60, 64, 67, 69, 70, 105,
      124, 140, 145, 146, 291, 319
  Joseph 543
Jennison, Rev. Isaac, 180, 181, 187, 189,
      547, 565
Jensen, Herman P., Heirs 497
Jocelyn, Augustus 178, 186
Johns, Rev. Mr. 152
Johnson Family 409
Johnson, A. Lincoln 173, 174, 409, 497
  Cyril 409
  Ebenezer 409
  Edwin 409
  John 543, 544
Jones Family 409
Jones, Alfred T. ..166, 173, 411, 478, 479
  Arthur M. 86, 247
  Miss Asenath 63
  Benjamin 409
  Charles P., 68, 165, 169, 173, 252, 411,
      498
  Mrs. Charles P. 166, 168
  David C., 67, 68, 121, 174, 410, 477, 478,
      479, 515
  Frederick M. 204
  Mrs. Harriet 479
  Henry S., 68, 173, 174, 411, 498, 499, 515
  Irene T. 116, 253
  Joseph 51, 67, 137, 161
  Lillian Maude 247, 411
  Marion E. 167, 169, 170, 247
  Robert H. 174
  Simeon 67, 68, 173, 410, 477
  Stephen, 68, 130, 144, 145, 147, 163, 172,
      410, 411, 477
  Stephen C. 477
  Thomas 32, 409
Joy, David 67, 104, 107
Joy's Hall 62
  Store 95
Justice, First 111

K

Kane, Hugh 494
  Hugh J. 494
  Michael T. 65, 67, 482, 498
Keefe Brothers 492

Keefe Family 411
Keefe, Amos John 412, 491, 492
  Frank 411
  John 411, 492
Keith, Mrs. Lucy Plumley 478
Kendall Family 412
Kendall, Mrs. Alice 496, 515
  Amos 105, 213, 412
  Chapman 322, 412
  Chester 71
  Frank 477, 494
  Jacob 42, 50, 128
  Ensign James, 38, 51, 59, 64, 67, 69, 128,
      129, 140, 141, 144, 161, 412, 487, 541
  James, Jr. 212, 213, 412
    Deed 212
  James Monroe 412, 491
  James O., 169, 170, 173, 174, 253, 413,
      482, 496, 516
  James W. 68, 174, 413, 494, 496
  Laura 413
  Ruel 489
  Selah 71, 334, 412, 487, 499
Keyes Family 413
Keyes, Henry W. 121, 414
  Lemuel 68
  Samuel Frost 413, 503
  Timothy, 67, 129, 140, 144, 145, 146,
      161, 172, 208
  Willis 67, 413
Kimball, Rufus 86, 215, 476, 494
King Family 414
King, Ann Frances 415
  Arthur D., 36, 38, 68, 69, 73, 76, 107,
      186, 252, 415, 476, 479
  Daniel 67
  Frank S. 68, 69, 121
  Homer Rising 76, 107, 416
  Howard A. 415, 479
  James 414
  Marvin 73, 101, 414, 476, 516, 523
  Marvin Henry 415
  Mary Madelia 415
  Samuel 73, 76
  Samuel Alden 415
King Philip 28, 550
King Philip's War 20
King, Trouble of the 47
Kirkham, John B. 156
Knight, Garnet Susan 358
  Jasper 107, 498
  Jasper Merrill 358
  Jewell Bennett 357
  John 487
Knowlton, Dennis 64, 68, 69
  James B. 64
"Know Nothing Club" 107
Kyle, Robert 86, 117, 203

L

LaBroad, Joseph 500
Lambord, Rev. B. F. 178, 190, 198

582 INDEX

Lands, Ministerial and School, 31, 35, 49, 58, 59, 60
  Committee of Sale................59
  Deed...........................60
  Report.......................58, 59
  Sale...........................58
  Settlement.....................58
Latham, Mendal...................489
Lathrop, Rev. Joseph..........141, 145
  Paoli..........................64
Lawrence Place....................38
Lawyers.........................124
Lazell, Amos....................494
Leaders of Singing...............168
Lee, Jesse......................179
  Rev. Mr.......................191
Leonard, Hon. N. T..............564
Library, Hubbard Memorial, 112, 115, 171, 228, 255, 279, 287, 288, 498
  Donor.........................112
  Resolutions...................112
  Volumes.......................112
License..........................63
Lighting........................103
Lincoln, A. W...................172
Literary Address................527
  Orator........................515
"Little Canada".................102
Lock-up..........................62
Logan, Patrick..................478
Lombard Family..................416
Lombard, Asenath................505
  Carlos....................416, 505
  David......................33, 544
  Dennis........................505
  Dexter.....................76, 417
  George Edward.............417, 481
  Jonathan, 37, 51, 67, 416, 505, 540, 544
  Justin....................416, 505
Long, Gov. J. D.................111
Longevity........................93
Lots, Location...................34
Ludlow, Sir Edmund............52, 540
  Roger or Rodger................52
Ludlow, Town of..........58, 98, 100
  Boundaries................43, 48, 60
  Centennial................507-570
  Center, 38, 42, 44, 62, 63, 72, 83, 98, 99, 105, 107, 116, 165, 186, 194, 257
  Center of..................55, 128
    Committee to Locate...........55
  Charter.....................48, 49
  City, 44, 70, 94, 98, 208, 209, 276, 305
  Code of Laws...................52
  Council.......................145
  Dimensions.....................43
  District..................48, 49, 541
    Incorporation............128, 541
    Petition.......................48
  Early Houses...................54
  Elevations.....................43
  Farmers Club..................121

Ludlow, Farms................475-505
  Fire Alarm Boxes..............103
  Fire Department...............102
    Appropriations..............102
    Mill........................102
    Organization................102
    Station.....................102
    Village.....................103
  Glass Works...................208
  Grange....................122, 131
  Hamlets........................44
  Hospital..................117, 118
    Officers....................117
    Society.................117, 266
  Incident of "Floodwood".........72
  Inhabitants, Early..............19
  Location.......................43
  Militia....................72, 106
  Name, Origin...............51, 540
    Theories.....................52
  Natural Features...............43
  Ponds..........................43
  Prosperity....................218
  Reservoir.....................100
  Savings Bank......107-111, 266, 284
    Auditors....................111
    Deposits....................108
    Investment Committee........108
    Officers....................108
  Settlement.................36, 540
  Social and Debating Club......123
  Surface.....................41, 43
  Swamps.........................44
  Topography..................43-45
  Water Power....................45
  Women's Club..................123
  Village, 44, 45, 62, 104, 107, 165, 225, 549
  Villages.......................43
Ludlow, England, Letter..........53
Ludlow Manufacturing Associates, 38, 44, 86, 99, 102, 104, 107, 112, 116, 117, 186, 204, 205, 225, 227, 228, 230, 231, 249, 257, 259, 260, 280, 284, 287, 316
  Camp.........................260
Ludlow Manufacturing Company, 97, 98, 115, 118, 192, 222, 225, 226, 243, 244, 253, 254, 255, 266, 269, 284, 287, 288, 316
Ludlow Mills Company........222, 225
Ludlow Textile School...........260
Ludlows, Other...................51
Lumbard, The First...............57
Lumber, Cost..................56, 61
Lyman, Dr. T. W..............64, 124
  Rev. Timothy........194, 198, 253
Lyon Family.....................417
Lyon, Albert....................497
  David, 67, 123, 140, 168, 172, 237, 334, 417, 482
  Ebenezer............75, 76, 78, 552
  Gad, 60, 64, 67, 69, 88, 142, 168, 325, 417

INDEX

Lyon, Gad, Poem................325
   Homer..............67, 334, 482
   Horace........................482
   Josiah........................481
   Leonard S.....................481
   Lucien N., 32, 68, 173, 174, 237, 418,
                      482, 515
      Paper.........................237
   Miss Mary............38, 54, 475, 480
   Nathaniel................67, 418, 482
   Norman............31, 54, 68, 418, 482
   Mrs. Norman..................498
   Dr. Philip................87, 124, 417
   Solon.........................419
   Mrs. Solon..............38, 54, 475
   Stephen..................237, 419
Lyons, Michael H.............86, 108

M

MacFarland, Charles...........77, 552
McDuffee, Rev. C. B..............167
   Rev. S. V..................159, 160
McGregory, Nelson................502
   William.......................502
McKinstry, Rev. John.............141
McLean, Rev. Alexander, 64, 69, 117, 151,
   160, 179, 180, 181, 186, 498, 547, 550
   "Appeal to the Public".........181
   Mrs. Etta M...................499
   Francis F., 64, 67, 68, 74, 499, 510, 511,
                      514, 515
   James K...............151, 491, 499
   Lockland......................499
   Lucy K........................491
   Rev. Thomas..............197, 198
McLean Mill Privilege.............207
Madison, President................148
Mann, John L................38, 482
Manual Training.............246, 259
Manufactures, Early...........207, 209
Marcy, Rev. Thomas...............565
Marsh, Lewis................214, 215
Martin, Rev. N. H........186, 189, 253
Masonic Hall.............118, 244, 257
Masons, Brigham Lodge of, 118, 121, 269,
                       284
   Charter Members..............121
   Officers.......................121
   Indian Orchard Lodge..........121
   Newton Lodge.................121
"Master Frost"...................178
Master, Singing...................56
Mastoo, Albert...................481
Mayo, Rev. Warren..........159, 160
Meeting, First District.....49, 50, 127
   First Town....................62
   Places........................128
   Quarterly.....................178
   School........................236
Memorial Day.....................83
Merchants.......................107
Methodism..................180, 181

Methodism, Beginnings....177, 180, 181
   at Jenksville..................224
Methodist Church, 85, 128, 165, 168, 175–
   187, 208, 282, 292, 300, 514, 547
   Building, First........38, 116, 180, 182
   Dedication, First..............181
   Edifice, New..................186
   Evangelists...............177, 178
   First Class....................178
   Leader.......................178
   Itinerants...........177, 178, 179
   Parsonage....................185
   Preachers, Circuit.............178
      Itinerant..................186
   Prominent Laymen.............177
   Quarterly Meeting.............178
   Renovation...................185
   Services......................178
Methodist Ears of Corn...........177
Methodist Episcopal Society......181
   Legal Society........164, 179, 181, 182
   Disbandment.................182
Methodists, 132, 147, 155, 179, 180, 191,
                      548
Mexican War.....................73
Military History..................69
Militia, Ludlow...............72, 106
Mill Privileges, 31, 207, 208, 210, 212, 214,
                      276
Mills, Alden's.............209, 210, 502
   Boston Flax........225, 226, 287, 288
   Carver's, H. I......209, 215, 276, 495
   Cider.........................213
   Continental...........208, 282, 491
   Eaton's............97, 178, 210, 502
   Fisk's, Hezekiah...............209
   Fuller's, E. W.................210
   Fulling, First.........208, 212, 213
   Graves's......................210
   Indian Orchard...............209
   Jenksville.................217–232
   Joel Nash's....................57
   Stone....................218, 222
Miller Brothers..............292, 293
Miller Corner, 36, 38, 42, 45, 95, 123,
                   235, 236
Miller Family....................419
Miller, Dr. Aaron J., 64, 68, 69, 123, 276,
             295, 297, 334, 420, 544
   Almerin Daniel................424
   Angeline......................481
   Calvin........................426
   Charles H.....................427
   Hon. Charles L................296
   Daniel...71, 164, 292, 293, 299, 424, 478
   Edward.......................427
   Edward P................421, 499
   Francis.......................426
   Fred Alden...................429
   George.........59, 423, 478, 500, 544
   Gilbert Spencer...............425
   Gordon B..............67, 295, 496

584 INDEX

Miller, Harriet............192, 425
  Herbert E..............173, 499
  Herbert L..............423, 479
  Horatio....................479
  Ithamar................296, 478
  James L....................479
  Jerre, 64, 67, 68, 69, 104, 107, 192, 424, 565
  Joanna.....................87
  Col. John, 64, 67, 68, 72, 73, 91, 180, 189, 191, 243, 292, 293, 300, 323, 427, 500, 504, 516, 523
  Capt. Joseph 1st.36, 38, 42, 64, 419, 540
  Capt. Joseph 2d, 50, 51, 55, 57, 64, 67, 69, 84, 87, 88, 129, 236, 253, 321, 419, 544
  Joseph 3d, 68, 180, 292, 423, 479, 500
  Joseph 4th......292, 293, 423, 424, 523
  Dea. Joseph, 163, 170, 171, 172, 296, 479
  Josiah S...................426
  Leonard, 88, 144, 145, 420, 422, 479, 544
  Lucinda B..............243, 427
  Mary......................479
  Mary Catherine.............422
  Mary D....................423
  Mrs. Mary Wilder........88, 292
  Moses.................421, 479
  Oliver B...........421, 499, 516
  Philo H...............479, 497
  Raymond Edward............422
  Robert King................422
  Samuel N...................426
  Samuel Osgood..............425
  Rev. Simeon, 135, 159, 249, 299, 425, 520, 524, 558
  Solomon....................419
  Stephen....................499
  Stephen J.............421, 499
  Sylvester, 71, 180, 292, 293, 424, 500, 516, 523
  Thomas.................33, 419
  Violate....................424
  Walter L...................429
  Walter S............104, 107, 428
  Wilbur F., 77, 116, 131, 180, 190, 191, 217, 270, 281, 300, 301, 330, 335, 336, 429, 504, 515, 516, 522, 565
  Wilder.....................87
  William A.........334, 422, 479, 490
  Dr. William B., 68, 104, 124, 180, 243, 249, 253, 428, 563
  William Foss...............428
  William Lee................428
  Zebina.....................478
Millerism....................185
Mineachogue, 19, 35, 41, 43, 50, 51, 53, 93, 555
Ministers, Congregational....160
  First Church...............137
  Methodist.............186, 189
  Union Church..............198

Mirick, Rev. Noah..............42
Moderators....................63
  First......................50
Montague, William............495
Monument, Soldiers'......74, 131
Moody, Cyrus.................475
  Rev. Eli..................151
  Irene M...................158
  John..........68, 131, 132, 216, 492
  Silas.....................475
  Sylvester.................217
Moody Corners............44, 492
Moore, Carlos O..............501
  Frank N........111, 252, 253, 499
  Orlando...............501, 502
  Prentiss B................501
Morgan, Ina L................189
Morrill, Edward..............475
  Harley W..................111
Morse, Ensign................491
  Ransom M..................203
Mortality...............151, 162
Munger Family................429
Munger (Stillman) Family.....431
Munger, Alanson.........212, 430
  Asa................212, 213, 430
  Erastus....................71
  Joseph......67, 211, 212, 214, 429, 494
  Deed.....................211
  Joseph, Jr............212, 430
  Nathan...................430
  Perley...................431
  Polly....................212
  Reuben...................431
  Stillman.................431
Munsell, Elijah..............489
  Willard..................478
Munsing Family...............432
Munsing, Henry A., 432, 475, 482, 483, 484, 490, 498
  Michael.............432, 484
Music, First Teacher.........256
Musical Instruments..........169

N

Name of Ludlow, Origin......51, 540
  Theories..................52
Nash Family..................432
Nash (Joel) Family...........435
Nash, Asahel.........435, 491, 492
  Austin F., 67, 68, 71, 86, 121, 436, 491, 515, 516
  Caroline A...............436
  Charles W..........77, 434, 489
  David....................544
  Elisha...................433
  Ephraim..................433
  Franklin W..........434, 489
  George S.................436
  Joel.............64, 67, 435
  Mill......................57
  Julius................71, 491

INDEX

Nash, Lewis............434, 475
  Raymond A. P............436
  Dr. Sylvester......123, 143, 328
  Thomas....................432
  Timothy......64, 67, 145, 432, 435, 491
Navigation Acts..............31
Nelligan, Michael............502
Netupsky, Frank..............478
Newell, Austin F......482, 483, 493
  Celia A....................366
  Estella M..................366
  Jacob......................493
  Mary B.....192, 239, 240, 243, 557, 558
    Reminiscences...........240
  Winifred E.................366
New England Homestead........569
  Telephone and Telegraph Co....103
Nichols, Daniel..............503
Nick and Tarzy........85, 329, 330
Noble, Alva.................487
Noon, Rev. Alfred, 185, 189, 193, 253, 510,
        511, 514, 515, 516, 524
  Rev. John..................198
Norris, Rev. Mr..............178

O

Oakley Ballad................326
Oakley, Elizabeth............326
Office-holders, Original......50
Old, Bartholomew.............436
  Richard....................436
  William....................436
Olde, John...................437
Old Folks Concert............522
Old Home Sunday..............166
Old Tavern House.............112
Olds Family..............436–441
Olds, Aaron..................440
  Anny.......................330
  Darius.....................502
  David M................77, 441
  Enoch......................440
  Hannah.....................440
  Hannah Jones......84, 85, 90, 332, 333
  Jonathan....90, 332, 437, 438, 440, 501
  Justun.....................438
  Lurana.....................441
  Nathan.....................439
  Rebekah....................334
  Reuben................439, 501
  Robert.....................437
  Ruth.......................439
  Samuel..........59, 70, 333, 334, 438
  Thirza..........85, 329, 330, 438
Omrod, Samuel...............502
O'Neil, John.............32, 498
  Margaret...................498
Orcutt, David................178
Organists....................170
Organization, Church.........160
  District....................48
  First Parish...........155, 164

Organization, Petition for Town....42
  and Struggles..............541
Organizations, Fraternal.....118
Osgood, Rev. Samuel......156, 157
Ostrander, Daniel........178, 186
Ould Burying Place.....36, 84, 87, 95, 333
Ould, Robert.................437
Outward Commons.....32, 33, 35, 51, 210
Owen, Eleazer............213, 495

P

Page, George.................482
Paine Family.................441
Paine, Alfred K..........442, 501
  Chester....................501
  David.......90, 139, 321, 441, 501, 544
  David K......34, 68, 321, 442, 501, 516
  Herbert N..................501
  Jedediah...........291, 319, 321, 333
  Jonathan...........321, 441, 501
  Lemuel.....................501
Palmer Journal.........276, 495, 568
Parish, First Congregational.155, 164, 165
  Organization............155, 164
Parker, Charles..............501
  Mrs. Thornton..............118
Parsons Family...............442
Parsons, Adin.................71
  Rev. David...........145, 147
  Elisha Taylor, 37, 64, 67, 68, 69, 159,
    164, 170, 172, 174, 253, 304, 305,
    442, 492, 495, 516, 523
  Ezra....................41, 51
  George H...................480
  Henrietta Danforth.........443
  Julia Taylor........170, 249, 443
  Reuben......................71
  Robert.................77, 552
  Samuel.............480, 481, 482
  S. P........................34
  Theodocia..................276
Patrons of Husbandry, No. 179.....122
Paulk, John..................491
  Napoleon B.............491, 496
Payne, H. Berton..............86
Pease, Asa...............68, 321
  Henry M................77, 552
  Job.................59, 67, 172
  Levi L.................77, 217
  Mrs. Lucy A. Fuller......489, 500
  Pliny......................483
  Simeon, 84, 97, 128, 132, 213, 214, 215,
    324, 490
  Walter.....................482
  William......64, 147, 213, 482, 489, 500
Penmanship...............56, 256
Percival, Dr. Francis.....64, 67, 477
Perham Family................443
Perham, Franklin.............443
  John...................166, 443
  Mrs. Laura E...............498
  Leavitt............105, 173, 443

INDEX

	PAGE
Perkins, Rev. Nathan	162
Pero, Louis	500
Mitchell	500
William	500
Perrin, Noah	181, 189
Perry, James E	77, 78
Petition to Governor Hutchinson	42
For Centennial	513
For District Organization	42, 48
For Road	95
Phelps, Rev. Abner	147
Henry	479
Physicians	123
Pickering, Rev. George	177, 186
Pierce, Zebinus	218
Pike Family	444
Pike, Jonas	444
Pillsbury, Gilbert	253, 515
Mrs. Gilbert	261
Pinney, Gordon	498
Gustavus	208, 213
Place, Alden	502
Caswell	124
Noah Clark	217
Dorman	38, 128
David Eaton	502
Ezekiel Fuller	32, 291
George Green	478
Kellogg	178
Lawrence	38
Mann	38, 95
Eli M. Smith	500
Torrey	41
Loren Wood	54
"Parson Wright"	155
Plumley, Elijah, 36, 67, 335, 478, 500, 516, 523	
Isaac H	86, 107, 475, 478
Plumley's Corner	500
Saw Mills	209
Poem, Centennial	558
Legend of Indian Leap	21
Poland, Mary L	246, 256, 257
Pomeroy, Rev. E. N	555
Titus	334
Pond, Bliss	43
Chapin	43, 228, 498
Eaton	43
Harris	43
Miller	43
Mineachogue	41
Pickerel	43
Second	43
Slobbery	210
Wood	36, 180
Poole, Alanson	64, 500, 515
Population	93, 161
Porter, Dea. Andrew	157
Post, Rev. Stanley	160
Postmasters	104
Post Office	104
First	61, 104

	PAGE
Post Office, Ludlow Center	95, 105, 207
Put's Bridge	61
Potash, Fuller's Establishment	208
Potatoes, Cost	56, 61
Crops	61
Pott, Anthony O	75, 77, 552
Potter Family	444
Potter, Edward T	116, 444, 476
Pound, A	55, 58
Power, Rev. Father	118
Pranaitis, Kastantinas	482
Pratt, Rev. Allen	139
Daniel	75, 77, 78, 552
F. N	478
Mrs. Tamason	477
Tyrus	70, 144, 145, 491, 544
Prayer Meetings	166
Prentice, Rev. Professor George, 515, 565	
Press Notices	567, 568
Prices for Commodities	61
Priest, Zadoc	178, 186
Prison, Andersonville	77, 78
Program, Centennial	519
Proprietors of Commons	32, 33, 34
Provincial Congress	55, 69
Pupils, Enrollment	245
Transportation	244
Purchase, John	491
Putnam Family	444
Putnam, Abner	97, 209, 217, 445
Capt. Abram	217
Alfred S	129, 446, 488, 515, 517
Amos	446
Edward	445
Eli	44, 64, 67, 68, 96
Flavius J	77, 78, 446, 489, 552
George	444
Isaac	445
James	445
John	444, 445
John C	445
Nathan	445, 446
Nicholas	444
Thomas	445
Put's Bridge	44, 61, 95, 96, 97, 190
Pynchon, William	31, 33, 92, 145, 560

Q

Quarterly Meeting	178
Quick, Rev. Abram J	197, 198

R

Railroads, Boston & Albany, 99, 226, 229, 274, 275, 310	
Hampden	99
Springfield & Athol	32, 99, 226
Western Branch	32, 99, 229, 274
Railway, Street, Springfield	99, 100
Ray Family	447
Ray, Daniel	261
David	447
John	67, 447, 499, 515

INDEX

Ray, Samuel C. 170
   William. 64, 67, 68, 447, 499
Rayner, Menzies. 178, 186
Rebellion, Shays's. 55, 70
   Soldiers. 70
Receipt, Revenue. 72
Recommendation, Letter. 162
Records, Elisha Fuller. 237
Recreation Association. 250, 284
   Park. 250
Red Bridge, 97, 99, 228, 229, 230, 257, 500, 501
Red Man. 19, 20, 21, 28, 29, 30
Relics. 19, 27, 57, 116, 549, 550
Reminiscences, Historic. 319
   of a Musical Life. 335
   of Mary Newell. 240, 243
Representatives to General Court. 69
   First. 55
Reservoir, Ludlow. 100, 101
   Commissioners. 102
   Report of. 101
   Springfield. 236, 476
Resolutions. 63, 112, 172
Restoration, The. 31
Revival, First Great. 162
Revivals, Other Great. 162, 163, 182
Revolutionary War, 58, 69, 116, 123, 128, 129, 541
Reynolds, Richard. 502
Rhodes, Maude Fuller. 169
Rice Family. 447
Rice, Aaron. 447
   Alpheus. 484
   Edmund. 447
   John. 447
   Orange. 484
Rich, Charles. 500
Richardson, Edwin. 343
   Edwina. 343
Riding Places. 95
Rindge, Frank. 500
River, Chicabee. 42, 48, 50
   Chicopee, 36, 43, 44, 45, 57, 95, 97, 98, 99, 305, 540, 549, 550
   Chicuepe. 19, 29, 38, 41
Road, Cherry Valley. 94
   Harris Pond. 490
   Old Granby. 487
   Stony Hill. 32
   Three Rivers. 499
Roads, Early. 41, 94
Roaring Thunder. 20, 28, 29
Robb, Colonel. 190
Roberts, Rev. George. 177, 186
Robinson, Gov. George D. 111, 564
Rogers, Rev. C. D. 185, 189
Rood Family. 448
Rood, Asahel, 67, 71, 305, 310, 324, 450, 487
   Asahel O. 451, 453
   Asenath. 452

Rood, Charles D., 171, 172, 190, 305, 307, 310, 451, 487, 497
   Clara Lucinda. 451
   Elias. 449
   Ely. 452, 453
   Erasmus. 452, 453
   Frances Chandler. 450
   Gladys. 451
   Hannah. 450
   Harriet Idella. 452
   Horace. 310, 451, 453
   Horace Edgar. 451
   J. Dexter. 190, 305, 310, 451
   Mrs. J. Dexter. 310
   John. 449
   Joseph. 73, 77, 452, 484
   Micah. 448
   Moses. 450, 487
   Nettie Maria. 452
   Paulina or Polly (Wood). .329, 455, 484
   Thomas. 448
   Zachariah. 449
   Zephaniah. 236, 449
Rood Fund. 171, 259
   Resolutions. 172
Root Family. 455
Root, Amos. 71
   Charles A. 456
   Charles B. J. 456
   Darius. 456
   Elisha. 456
   George E. 64
   Hezekiah, 69, 74, 97, 455, 456, 516, 523
   Mrs. Sarah. 88
   Timothy. 88, 214, 215, 457, 482
   Family of. 457
Roote, Joseph. 455
   Thomas. 455
Rumrill, James A. 523
Rural Free Delivery. 105
   Mail Carriers. 105
Russell, Rev. E. 157

S

St. Andrew's Church. ...200, 201, 203, 204
   Boy Choir. 204
   Building. 204
   Dedication. 204
   Early Efforts. 203
   First Confirmation. 203
   Gifts. 204
   Mission. 203
   Officers. 204
   Organization. 204
   Services. 203
St. Jean Baptiste Church. 204, 205
   Building, Erection. 205
   Dedication. 205
   First Meeting Place. 205
   Formation of Parish. 204
   Gift of Site. 205
   Increase 205

588 INDEX

St. Jean Baptiste Church, Pastor.....205
    Size of Parish....................205
    Value of Property................205
Sampson, Rev. Mr.............178, 186
Sanderson, Rev. Alonzo, 155, 157, 160, 164, 253
    Acceptance, Letter...............156
    Dismissal........................157
Savage, William......................478
Saw Mills......................213, 216
    Jonathan Burr & Co..............207
    Carver's.....................44, 98
    Warren D. Fuller's...............475
    Harris's..........................98
    Plumley's........................209
    Thornton's..................208, 209
Schools, Appropriations........235, 253
    First............................235
    Buildings.......236, 244, 254, 257, 258
        District....................236, 244
        High School....................246
        Ludlow Manufacturing Co.......244
        New............................244
    Census...........................254
    Committee...................252, 253
    Cooking Lessons.............254, 259
    Courses of Study.................244
    Districts, Abolition...............243
        Committees....................236
        Formation......................235
        Supervision...............246, 257
    Enrollment.......................245
    Evening, First...........249, 254, 255
        Enrollment....................250
        First, Opened.................257
    Expenditures, Early,..............237
    Gardens, First...................258
    Grades in........................244
    Grammar Grades.................259
    High...............244, 245, 246, 247
    Industrial Training..........239, 259
    Meetings.........................236
    Non-English Speaking............259
    No. 6, Granby Agreement.........255
    Records, Early...................237
    Reports, Extracts from 253, 254, 255, 260
    Singing...........................56
    Statistics........................259
    Superintendent, First.............256
    Teachers.........................239
    Text-books, Free.................254
    Textile......................260, 261
    Transportation...............244, 258
    Truant Officer, First..............254
    Vacation, Open-air...............250
    Village...........................243
    Wages...........................239
Schoolhouses, Equipment...........238
    Committee to Build..............236
    First Built.......................236
    Location........................236

Schoolhouses, Fuel.................238
    Furnishings......................238
School, Parochial....................258
School Year, Length,.....253, 258, 259
Scott, Rev. Ephraim.................90
    Mahitable........................90
Scranton, John......................139
    Samuel...............67, 128, 543, 544
Scythes, Manufacture...............209
Selden, David......................162
Selectmen................50, 64, 67, 137
Settlement of Ludlow............36, 540
Settlers, Early.......................36
Severance, Mary G.................489
Sewall, Benjamin...............225, 287
Sewall & Day Co................225, 287
Seymour, Timothy.................489
Shattuck, Veranus............71, 73, 323
Shaw, Charles......................487
    Fernando Gilbert................358
    Harriet Belle....................358
Shays's Rebellion................55, 70
Shean, Thomas.....................481
Shearer, George D.................500
    Lyman..........................500
    Sarah...........................500
Sheldon, Isaac.................237, 334
    James.............36, 67, 478, 482, 540
    James, Jr........................68
Shelter Rock........................41
Shingle Swamp......................50
Sikes Cemetery.............44, 83, 87
Sikes Family........................457
Sikes, Abner, 38, 50, 64, 89, 128, 137, 161, 461, 476
    Adeline.........................459
    Alva, 64, 67, 68, 69, 172, 192, 253, 312, 313, 460, 505
    Amanda.........................458
    Mrs. Anna....................83, 89
    Benjamin, 36, 38, 57, 59, 60, 64, 67, 68, 72, 83, 89, 90, 101, 163, 164, 172, 192, 313, 335, 457, 458, 476, 482, 540
    Benjamin, Jr.................67, 476
    Calvin.......................68, 461
    Caroline.............168, 170, 498
    Charles.................77, 168, 516
    Chester........67, 132, 168, 170, 505
    Mrs. Cyrena.....................88
    Danforth W., ix., 10, 83, 86, 95, 335, 476, 501
    Edmund,................169, 170, 505
    Edward..........................83
    Elihu J......................36, 479, 540
    Eugene A.......................450
    Mrs. Frances Chandler...........117
    Frank........................36, 479
    Frank E......................123, 174
    Hannah..........................89
    Harriet E.......................460
    Increase, 64, 67, 69, 85, 131, 461, 476, 482, 498

INDEX 589

Sikes, James S 168, 170
  Lieut. John, 38, 51, 67, 83, 88, 129, 140,
    141, 161, 461, 462, 481, 482
  Jonathan ..67, 68, 88, 174, 313, 459, 505
  Mrs. Margaret 101
  Martha B 461
  Mrs. Mary 89
  Otis 83, 335, 502, 503
  Pamelia 170
  Pliny 64, 67, 146, 461
  Quartus 459, 502
  Reuben, 44, 67, 68, 69, 89, 101, 236, 313,
    335, 460, 479, 482, 487, 505, 515, 516
  Sarah 89
  Theodore, 64, 67, 68, 69, 132, 164, 173,
    253, 313, 475, 498, 516, 523
  Timothy 161
  Wealthy 481
  William 169, 170
Simms, Josiah 214, 215, 494
  Lydia Putnam 387
Simonds, Charles 77, 501
  J. Leroy 128, 490, 491, 492
  Lucius, 41, 94, 477, 490, 492, 501, 516, 542
  Lucy 41
Singers, Appropriation 56
Singing Master 56
  School 56
Slater, Samuel 217, 220
Slave, Female 37
Smallpox 61
Smith (John) Family 463
Smith (Martin) Family 462
Smith, Charles M 504
  Clarence Kendall 413
  Eli M 64, 67, 68, 69, 104, 107, 504
  Estus F 462
  George 488
  Rev. Hugh W 204
  Isaac 497
  John 462
  Mrs. Julia (Miller) 240
  Rev. Lemuel 178, 186
  Martin 71, 462, 487
  Nathan 544
  Silas 145
  Stephen H 217
  Stukely 218
Snell, Rev. Mr 140
Soldiers, Civil War 76, 77, 552
  Revolutionary 69, 543
  War of 1812 .... 70, 71
Soldiers' Monument 74, 131
Southworth, C. A 492, 515
Sprague, Daniel 67, 68
  George H ...... ix, 10, 166, 173, 174, 481
Springfield, 20, 36, 41, 42, 43, 47, 48, 49, 50,
    71, 97, 98, 99, 100, 141,
    143, 228
  First Church 156, 165, 171, 546
  First Parish 58
Springfield Gas Light Co 103

Springfield Manufacturing Co., 130, 182,
    218, 310
  Charter 218
  Cloth Manufactured 218
  Failure 192, 222
  Machinery, First 218
  Mill, Second 219
Springfield, Original Boundaries 31
Springfield Republican 567
Springfield Reservoir 236, 476
Springfield Union 565, 568
Springfield Waterworks 143, 476
Spry, Christopher 186
Squires, Ezekiel 41, 49, 51
Stacy, Ira 68
Stahl, Lillian 343
Stake, The 128, 544
Starkey, Henry 483
Stearns, Hon. G. M 563
Stebbins, Annie 118
  John Bliss 204
  M. Louise 118
  Mayor J. M 561
  Nathaniel 169
  Solomon Bliss 104, 314
Stevens, John E., 97, 107, 118, 197, 198,
    203, 205, 224, 226, 227, 266, 284, 316
  Sidney 224, 227, 287
Stevens Memorial 231, 232
Steward, Rev. Antipas, 107, 124, 140, 141,
    142, 143, 144, 145, 146, 147, 152,
    160, 161, 162, 546
  Dismissal 143, 144, 145
  Dissatisfaction 143, 144, 145
Stewart, Edward 502
  Edwin 502
Stone, Rev. William 140
Stony Brook 43, 213, 214
Stony Hill ...37, 47, 48, 51, 53, 93, 540, 541
Stony Hill Road 32
Storekeepers 107
Stores 107
Storrs, Rev. R. S 141
Stoughton Family 462
Stoughton, John 463
  John P 463
  Nathaniel 463
  Olin W 464, 498
  Thomas 463
Street Railway 99
Streeter Family 464
Streeter, Charles W 174, 465
  Cora E 465
  Edward J 465
  Elbridge J., 36, 38, 86, 95, 123, 165, 173,
    465, 482
  George 489
  George L 77, 121
  James P 464
  Paul 464
Strength, Feats 334
Sturgis, F. W 107

INDEX

Sullivan, Patrick................478
Suprenant, Joseph...............497
  Philip......................483
Surface of Ludlow............41, 43
Swamps, Bear....................50
  Buck........................44
  Cedar........35, 44, 58, 59, 60, 95, 128
  Fuller.......................44
  Shingle.....................50
  Torrey......................44
Swan, Henry............483, 487, 498
Swart, Mrs. Sarah.............86, 484

T

Tablet, First Church............131
Taft, Richard M................483
Talbot, Governor...............556
Talcott, Mrs. James............172
Talmadge, Margaret.............497
  Spencer................497, 516
Talmage Family.................465
Talmage, Persis................465
  Seymour...................466
Tar Business....................36
  Kilns.....................208
Tarbox, Horace.................503
  Margaret..................503
  Solomon...................212
Taverns........................105
  "The Ark".................105
  Ely Fuller's........72, 105, 107
  Jenksville................107
  Old Fuller............70, 106
Taxes, Collection...............57
  Notices....................57
  Old Bills................56, 57
Taylor, Fred...................498
  Joshua....................186
Teacher, Wages.................239
Teaching, Long Service.........243
Telephones....................103
Temperance.....................63
Temple, Thomas................544
Tetreault, Charles.............482
  Homer.....................483
Tewhrane, Daniel...............480
Thayer, William................478
Thomas, Samuel A..............501
  Rev. William A......197, 198
Thornton's Mill............208, 209
Thunderstorm, Noted............62
Thurber, Rev. Laban...........147
Tilley Family..................466
Tilley, Clarence J........276, 494
  Franklin P....174, 466, 496, 497
  Otis E.............466, 495, 496
  Porter................466, 497
Times, Troublous................47
Tithing Men..................42, 51
Toasts.........................556
Tolland Circuit................177
Tolland County Press...........569

Tomb............................85
Topography...................43–45
Torrey Swamp....................44
Town, Annals................47–92
  Bounds.....................60
  Center..................55, 128
  Church................127–174
  Clerks.....................64
  Development...........93–124
  History...................570
  Meetings...................62
    Moderators..............63
  Officers, 1911.............67
  Early...............51, 56, 62
  Records....................62
Town House, Agitation, New.....62
  First......................62
Town Meeting, at Stake.....128, 544
  First..................62, 127
Town Meetings, Early Places, 62, 127, 542
  Village....................62
Town Unity.....................42
Towne Family..................466
Towne, Benjamin...............466
  Mrs. Francenah...........503
  Frank A......65, 67, 107, 121, 466, 503
  Marquis de L........107, 466, 503, 504
  Solomon...................476
Training, Industrial..........239
  Manual...............246, 259
Trask, Mrs. Adeline...........484
Treasurer, First...............51
Treichler, Dr. A. J...........124
Trial Justice, First..........111
Trombly, Richard..............478
Tuck, Rev. J. W., 85, 86, 132, 135, 145,
  157, 158, 159, 160, 217, 253, 498,
  521, 537, 557
Tucker Family.................466
Tucker, Ephraim...............466
  Oscar D..............467, 496
  Rev. Mr..............178, 186
  William Coit.............467
Tufts, A. Dexter..............479
Turkey Hill............43, 213, 504

U

Underwood, Rev. Almon.........163
  George....................478
Union Church......187, 189–203, 284, 548
  Adoption of Covenant......193
  Beginnings...............189
  Conference Preachers.....193
  Council..................192
  Deacons..................198
  Dedication...............191
  Early Members............192
  Erection, First Building.191
  First Minister...........190
  Growth...................197
  Membership, 1911.........198
  Ministers................198

INDEX

	PAGE
Union Church, Name	193
Organization	192
Rededication	197
Renovation	194, 197
Reorganization	193
Revivals	190

V

Village Cemetery	85, 86
Villages in Ludlow	44
Jenksville	44
Ludlow Center	44
City	44
Village	44, 45
Miller Corner	45
Moody Corner	44
Vinton, Rt. Rev. Dr. Alexander	203, 204
Votes, Anti-Masonic	61
Historical	542, 543
Number Cast	61
Voter, First Woman	63

W

Wade, Edwin	500, 501
Mrs. Edwin	500
Elexis	501
Mrs. Elizabeth	479
Hiram	500
Pliny	500
Jonathan	501
Wages	61
Waid, Jonathan	516, 523
Wait, Mrs. Angelia F	170
Waite, Aaron	189
Walker Family	467
Walker, Coleman M	479
Elea	479
Henry C	468
Isabell K	468
James	467
Joel	467
Jonas	145
Charles O	468
Orrin	468
Oshea	173
William	493
William C	105, 467, 468, 503
Mrs. William C	503
Wallace, Cranmore N	224, 225, 227, 287
Wallamanumps, Bridge	95
Falls, 19, 45, 70, 94, 95, 96, 208, 209, 549
War, Civil	73
Aid for Families	74
Appropriations	73
Bounties paid	73, 74
Monument	74
Soldiers, Ludlow	73, 76, 77
Mexican	73
of 1812	70, 148
Souvenirs	72
"Old Horse Company"	70
Soldiers	71

	PAGE
War, Revolutionary	58, 69, 128, 542
Bounties	70
Funds	70
Incidents	332
Soldiers	543
Wardens, First	50
Warner Family	469
Warner, Albert	481
Alonzo	469, 495
Alonzo C	469, 495, 496
Anna	481
Arthur T	469, 495
Emma A	117
Rev. Moses	145
Zechariah	41, 49
Zechariah, Jr	41, 49
Warnings Out of Town	55, 56
Warrant, A	50
Warren, Frank	500
Mrs	491
Warriner, Isaac	51
Israel	41, 51, 64, 67, 129, 140, 236
Samuel, Jr	543
Washburn, Elijah	214
Thomas	214
Willie or William	77, 78, 552
Water Commissioners	101
Water-power	45
Webster, Hart	490
Welcome, Address	524
Wesleyan Praying Band	185
Western Railroad	229, 274
Whipple, Deacon Joseph	157
White Family	469
White, Alice G	473
Mrs. Angeline	136, 170, 171, 515
Charles A	470, 471, 482
Ezra	482
Herbert E	112, 473
Mrs. Herbert E	477
Howard M	470, 493
James	323, 493
James M	36, 41, 67, 470, 493
Prof. Lorenzo	515, 521, 527, 557
Lovinski	77, 95, 470, 476, 505
Montgomery	469
Percy L	473
R. Samuel	470, 493, 494
Sadie	473
Samuel, 36, 41, 67, 74, 170, 322, 469, 493, 494, 515
Whitney Adin, 64, 68, 253, 500, 501, 516
Alexander	36, 86, 478, 501, 502
Artemas H	64, 67, 69, 516, 523
Charles	502
William	501
Mrs. William	500, 501
Zuri	502
Wilbraham Academy	289
Wilcox, Mr	170
Wilder, Moses, 67, 129, 144, 145, 146, 161, 544

INDEX

	PAGE
Wilder, Minor M.	86
Wilkinson, George	217
Willard, Rev. Joseph	141
Willcott, Philip	237
Willey Family	473
Willey, Benajah	38, 42, 50, 64, 67
Gates	67, 68, 168, 322, 473, 491
Mrs. Jerusha	491
Joel	38, 51
Williams, Rev. N.	141
Wilson, Albert C.	477, 478
John	162
Sabrina	162
"Winding Wave"	261, 262, 305
Witt, Harry	213
Wold, William	436
Wolves	41, 57
Wood, Charles	478
Charles F.	71
Dr.	123, 484
Gordon	501
Gordon B.	71
Harvey	71
Loren	54, 77, 501
Moses	59, 478
Oscar	500
Dr. Robert	124, 253
Seneca	329, 487
Woodchucks	63
Wood & Merritt	222
Wood Pond	36
Woodward, Rev. Aaron	140, 160
Wooing, A	38
Worthington, John	49, 50
Wright, Abel	33, 59, 147
Abel, Jr.	59
Asa	132
Cyprian	87, 544
Rev. Ebenezer B.	85, 152, 153, 155, 156, 160, 162, 163, 174, 181, 253, 490, 546, 558
Letter	152
Elam	67, 106, 487, 488
Goss	501
Lucy	87
Pliny	501
Marshall	501
Solomon	291, 319, 321, 333
Stephen	59
Timothy	59
Wright Murder	322

Y

Yankee Scheme	31
Young People's Society of Christian Endeavor	173

www.ingramcontent.com/pod-product-compliance
Lightning Source LLC
Chambersburg PA
CBHW070004010526
44117CB00011B/1426